DOCUMENTS FROM THE AFRICAN PAST

DOCUMENTS
FROM THE
AFRICAN PAST

Edited by
ROBERT O. COLLINS

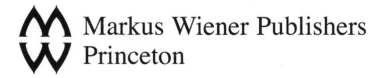 Markus Wiener Publishers
Princeton

For information write to:
Markus Wiener Publishers, 231 Nassau Street, Princeton, NJ 08542
www.markuswiener.com

Book design by Cheryl Mirkin, CMF Graphic Design
Cover design by Maria Madonna Davidoff

Library of Congress Cataloging-in-Publication Data

Documents from the African Past/Robert O. Collins, ed.
 Includes bibliographical references.
 ISBN-13: 978-1-55876-289-3
 ISBN-10: 1-55876-289-2
 1. Africa—History—Sources.
 I. Collins, Robert O. II. Collins, Robert O., 1933–
DT1.D55 2001
960—dc21   2001045551

Markus Wiener Publishers books are printed in
the United States of America on acid-free paper,
and meet the guidelines for permanence and durability
of the Committee on Production Guidelines for
Book Longevity of the Council on Library Resources

CONTENTS

Preface

During my career I have been continually frustrated in my search for a single volume of documents from the African past for college and university students. Monographs and textbooks have failed to provide firsthand accounts upon which the historians of Africa still depend for much of their knowledge of the African past. Without these primary sources the instructor cannot demonstrate to the student the rich history of Africa. Indeed, the documents included in this single volume are but a fragment of the immense volume of archival and published literature about Africa through the centuries.

This selection of documents is that of an historian seeking to give a portrait of the history of a great continent and its peoples. I have been guided by two principles. First, I have sought to embrace the full time span of documentary records pertaining to sub-Saharan Africa by presenting them in chronological order through two millennia. Second, I have sought to cover the vast geographical sweep of sub-Saharan Africa. To achieve these two very ambitious objectives in a single and modest volume has required an eclectic, if not random, selection that betrays my own personal inclinations and interests. I have sought to choose documents that describe Africans and not just the individuals who came to look, to trade, or to rule. I have selected passages from less known accounts and descriptions as well as the more standard authorities. I have tried, where possible, to obtain passages of sufficient length to make them meaningful for the inquiring student. I have prepared brief introductions to guide the beginner and to refresh the memory of the more experienced.

In the last half century the search for the African past has been a demonstrable triumph of international scholarship with new information, interpretations, and ideology. All these, however, rest on the foundation of primary sources that cannot be changed or rewritten. In the exciting discovery of the history of Africa and its peoples, the background and interests that the reader, student, and scholar bring to their encounters with the sources will generate fresh insights; and that, after all, is what history is all about.

Robert O. Collins
Professor of History, Emeritus
University of California, Santa Barbara

1. ANONYMOUS

PERIPLUS OF THE ERYTHRAEAN SEA. First Century C.E.

Probably written about 100 C.E. at Alexandria, The Periplus of the Erythraean Sea *was a merchant's guide to the Red Sea and Indian Ocean ports. It is generally accepted as the earliest firsthand account of the East African coast to have survived to the present.*

From Tabai after 400 stades sailing is a promontory towards which the current runs, and the market-town of Opone. . . . It produces cinnamon, both the *aroma* and *moto* varieties, as well as the better sort of slaves, which are brought to Egypt in increasing numbers, and much tortoise-shell of better quality than elsewhere.

Voyages from Egypt to all these further market-towns are made in the month of July, that is *Epiphi.* The ships are usually fitted out in the inner [Red Sea] ports of Ariake and Barugaza; and they bring the further market-towns the products of these places: wheat, rice, ghee, sesame oil, cotton cloth (both the *monache* and the *sagmatogene*), girdles, and honey from the reed called *sakchari.* Some make voyages directly to these market-towns, others exchange cargo as they go. The country has no sovereign but each market-town is ruled by its own chief.

After Opone the coast veers more towards the south. First there are the Small and Great Bluffs of Azania and rivers for anchorages for six days' journey southwestwards. Then come the Little and the Great Beach for another six days' journey, and after that in order the Courses of Azania, first that called Sarapion, the next Nikon, and then several rivers and other anchorages one after the other, separately a halt and a day's journey, in all seven, as far as the Pyralaae Islands and the island called Diorux [the Channel].

Beyond this, slightly south of southwest after a voyage of two days and nights along the Ausanitic coast, is the island of Menouthesias some 300 stades from the land. It is flat and wooded. There are many rivers in it, and many kinds of birds and the mountain tortoise. There are no wild animals at all except the crocodile, but they never attack men. In this place there are small sewn boats and dug-outs, which they use for fishing and for catching tortoise. In this island they fish in a peculiar way with wicker baskets, which they fasten across where the tide goes out.

Two days' sail beyond the island lies the last mainland market-town of Azania, which is called Rhapta, a name derived from the small sewn boats. Here there is much ivory and tortoise-shell.

Men of the greatest stature, who are pirates, inhabit the whole coast and at each place have set up chiefs. The Chief of the Ma'afir is the suzerain, according to an ancient right which subordinates it to the kingdom which has become the first in Arabia. The people of Mouza hold it in tribute under his sovereignty and send there

From "The Periplus of the Erythraean Sea," in G. S. P. Freeman-Grenville, *The East African Coast, Select Documents from the First to the Earlier Nineteenth Century*, (Oxford: Clarendon Press, 1962), pp. 1–2. Reprinted by permission of the Clarendon Press, Oxford.

small ships, mostly with Arab captains and crews who trade and intermarry with the mainlanders of all the places and know their language.

Into these market-towns are imported the lances made especially for them at Mouza, hatchets, swords, awls, and many kinds of small glass vessels; and at some places wine and not a little wheat, not for trade but to gain the goodwill of the barbarians. Much ivory is taken away from these places, but it is inferior in quality to that of Adulis, and also rhinoceros horn and tortoise-shell, different from that of India, and a little coconut oil.

And these, I think, are the last of the market-towns of Azania on the mainland lying to the right of Berenice; for after all these places the ocean curves westward and runs along the regions of Ethiopia, Libya, and Africa, stretching out from the south and mingling with the western sea.

---

2. COSMAS INDICOPLEUSTES

TRADE IN ETHIOPIA. 547.

The Christian Topography of Cosmas Indicopleustes was written in 547 A.D., when the Mediterranean world was just entering the Middle Ages. Cosmas attempted to establish that the world is flat by citing Greek authors and the Scriptures. Cosmas himself did visit Ethiopia, and his work is one of the few accounts that describe a barren period in East African history.

If one measures in a straight cord line the stages which make up the length of the earth from Tzinitza to the west, he will find that there are somewhere about four hundred stages, each thirty miles in length. The measurement is to be made in this way: from Tzinitza to the borders of Persia, between which are included all Iouvia,[1] India, and the country of the Bactrians, there are about one hundred and fifty stages at least; the whole country of the Persians has eighty stations; and from Nisibis to Seleucia[2] there are thirteen stages; and from Seleucia to Rome and the Gauls and Iberia, whose inhabitants are now called Spaniards, onward to Gadeira, which lies out towards the ocean, there are more than one hundred and fifty stages; thus making altogether the number of stages to be four hundred, more or less. With regard to breadth: from the hyperborean[3] regions to Byzantium there are not more than fifty

From Cosmas Indicopleustes, *The Christian Topography of Cosmas, an Egyptian Monk*. trans. and edited by J. W. McCrindle (London: Hakluyt Society, 1897), pp. 49–54.

1. This would mean the country of the Huns.
2. Nisibis, the capital of Mygdoniia, was, after the time of Lucullus, considered the chief bulwark of the Roman Power in the East. It was an ancient, large, and populous city, and was for long the great northern emporium of the commerce of the East and West. It was situated about two days' journey from the head waters of the Tigris in the midst of a pleasant and fertile plain at the foot of Mount Masius.
3. Far northern regions (ed.).

stages. For we can form a conjecture as to the extent of the uninhabited and the inhabited parts of those northern regions from the Caspian Sea, which is a gulf of the ocean. From Byzantium, again, to Alexandria there are fifty stages, and from Alexandria to the Cataracts thirty stages, from the Cataracts to Axomis, thirty stages;[4] from Axomis to the projecting part of Ethiopia, which is the frankincense country called Barbaria, lying along the ocean, and not near but at a great distance from the land of Sasu which is the remotest part of Ethiopia, fifty stages more or less; so that we may reckon the whole number of stages at two hundred more or less; and thus we see that even here the divine scripture speaks the truth in representing the length of the earth to be double its breadth; *For thou shalt make the table in length two cubits and in breadth one cubit*, a pattern, as it were, of the earth.

The region which produces frankincense is situated at the projecting parts of Ethiopia, and lies inland, but is washed by the ocean on the other side. Hence the inhabitants of Barbaria, being near at hand, go up into the interior and, engaging in traffic with the natives, bring back from them many kinds of spices, frankincense, cassia,[5] calamus,[6] and many other articles of merchandise, which they afterwards send by sea to Adule, to the country of the Homerites, to further India, and to Persia. This very fact you will find mentioned in the Book of Kings, where it is recorded that the Queen of Sheba, that is, of the Homerite country, whom afterwards our Lord in the Gospels calls the Queen of the South, brought to Solomon spices from this very Barbaria, which lay near Sheba on the other side of the sea, together with bars of ebony, and apes and gold from Ethiopia which, though separated from Sheba by the Arabian Gulf, lay in its vicinity. We can see again from the words of the Lord that he calls these places the ends of the earth, saying: *The Queen of the South shall rise up in judgment with this generation and shall condemn it, for she came from the ends of the earth to hear the wisdom of Solomon*—Matt. xii, 42. For the Homerites are not far distant from Barbaria, as the sea which lies between them can be crossed in a couple of days, and then beyond Barbaria is the ocean, which is there called Zingion. The country known as that of Sasu is itself near the ocean, just as the ocean is near the frankincense country, in which there are many gold mines. The King of the Axomites accordingly, every other year, through the governor of Agau,[7] sends thither special agents to bargain for the gold, and these are accompanied by many other traders—upwards, say, of five hundred—bound on the same errand as

4. Axomis (Auxume in Ptolemy) is the modern Axum, the capital of Tigre. In the early centuries our era it was a powerful State, possessing nearly the whole of Abyssinia, a portion of the south-west Red Sea coast and north-western Arabia. It was distant from its seaport, Adule, which was situated near Annesley Bay, about 120 miles, or an eight days' caravan journey. It was the chief centre of the trade with the interior of Africa. The Greek language was understood and spoken, both by the court and the numerous foreigners who had either settled in it or who resorted to it for trading purposes. . . . Christianity was introduced into Axum in the fourth century by Oedisius and Frumentius, the latter of whom was afterwards appointed its first bishop. Sasu, which is next mentioned, is near the coast, and only 5° to the north of the equator.

5. A kind of cinnamon (ed.).

6. Reed used as a pen (ed.).

7. The Agau people is the native race spread over the Abyssinian plateau both to east and west of Lake Tana. . . .

themselves. They take along with them to the mining district oxen, lumps of salt, and iron, and when they reach its neighborhood they make a halt at a certain spot and form an encampment, which they fence round with a great hedge of thorns. Within this they live, and having slaughtered the oxen, cut them in pieces, and lay the pieces on the top of the thorns, along with the lumps of salt and the iron. Then come the natives bringing gold in nuggets like peas, called *tancharas*, and lay one or two or more of these upon what pleases them, the pieces of flesh or the salt or the iron, and then they retire to some distance off. Then the owner of the meat approaches, and if he is satisfied he takes the gold away, and upon seeing this its owner comes and takes the flesh or the salt or the iron. If, however, he is not satisfied, he leaves the gold, when the native seeing that he has not taken it, comes and either puts down more gold, or takes up what he had laid down, and goes away. Such is the mode in which business is transacted with the people of that country, because their language is different and interpreters are hardly to be found. The time they stay in that country is five days more or less, according as the natives more or less readily coming forward buy up all their wares. On the journey homeward they all agree to travel well-armed, since some of the tribes through whose country they must pass might threaten to attack them from a desire to rob them of their gold. The space of six months is taken up with this trading expedition, including both the going and the returning. In going they march very slowly, chiefly because of the cattle, but in returning they quicken their pace lest on the way they should be overtaken by winter and its rains. For the sources of the river Nile lie somewhere in these parts, and in winter, on account of the heavy rains, the numerous rivers which they generate obstruct the path of the traveller. The people there have their winter at the time we have our summer. It begins in the month Epiphi of the Egyptians and continues till Thoth,[8] and during the three months the rain falls in torrents, and makes a multitude of rivers all of which flow into the Nile.

The facts which I have just recorded fell partly under my own observation and partly were told me by traders who had been to those parts.

---

8. From July to September.

3. TUAN CH'ÊNG-SHIH

CHINA'S DISCOVERY OF AFRICA. 863.

Although China long had contacts with the world beyond her frontiers, intercourse with the countries beyond Asia was encouraged during the Tang Dynasty (618–907 C.E.) by a long period of peace and the cosmopolitan outlook of China's rulers. The selection below is from the Yu-yang-tsa-tsu, a general book of knowledge, written by the Chinese scholar Tuan Ch'êng-shih (d. 863 C.E.).

It is, however, in the T'ang period that the first definite information appears in Chinese sources on the countries beyond India, and what is to the point here, on Africa. There is a curious work, written by the scholar Tuan Ch'êng-shih, who died in A.D. 863, called the *Yu-yang-tsa-tsu*. This book was published in the *Chin-tai-pi-shu* by Mao Chin (1598–1657). The antiquity of the text is guaranteed by the *Hsin T'ang-shu*, by Ou-yang Hsiu, completed in 1060, which has an abridged extract of it. From the chapter in which a number of exotic plants are described, it is clear that part of his information is derived from priests of *Fu-lin*, that is Tach'in or the Roman Orient and Magadha in India. Hirth has called attention to this text; in his translation, however, there are a few curious errors which make a new translation necessary.

The text runs: "The country of Po-pa-li is in the southwestern sea. (The people) do not eat any of the five grains but eat only meat. They often stick a needle into the veins of cattle and draw blood which they drink raw, mixed with milk. They wear no clothes except that they cover (the parts) below their loins with sheep-skins. Their women are clean and of proper behaviour. The inhabitants themselves kidnap them, and if they sell them to foreign merchants, they fetch several times their price. The country produces only ivory and ambergris.[1] If Persian merchants wish to go into the country, they collect around them several thousand men and present them with strips of cloth. All, whether old or young draw blood and swear an oath, and then only do they trade their products. From olden times on they were not subject to any foreign country. In fighting they use elephants' tusks and ribs and the horns of wild buffaloes as lances and they wear cuirasses[2] and bows and arrows. They have twenty myriads of foot soldiers. The Arabs make frequent raids upon them."

What is this country? Hirth first identified it with Berbera, on the Somali coast. This identification is confirmed by an important notice in a work about which we shall have to say a little more presently. It is the *Chu-fan-chih*, written by Chao Ju-kua, a Commissioner of foreign trade at Ch'üian-chou in Fukien province. It was

From J. J. L. Duyvendak, *China's Discovery of Africa* (London: Arthur Probsthain 1949), pp. 12–15, 22–24. Reprinted by permission.

1. A substance used in perfumes (ed.).
2. A piece of close-fitting armor for protecting the breast and back; it was originally made of leather (ed.).

completed in 1226. About one-third of its contents is drawn from an earlier work, the *Lingwai-tai-ta*, written by Chou Ch'ü-fei in 1178. This book has a note on a country called Pi-pa-lo which runs as follows:

"The country of Pi-pa-lo has four chou (departmental cities) and for the rest (the people) are all settled in villages which each try to gain the supremacy over the others by violence. They serve Heaven and do not serve the Buddha (presumably meaning that they are Mohammedans). The country produces many camels and sheep and they have camels' meat and milk as well as baked cakes as their regular food. The country produces dragon's saliva (ambergris), big elephants' tusks, and big rhinoceros horns. Some elephants' tusks weigh more than 100 catty[3] and some rhinoceros horns more than 10 catty. There is also much putchuk, liquid storax gum, myrrh, and tortoise-shell which is extremely thick, and which (people from) other countries all come to buy. 'Among the products there is further the so-called camel-crane (i.e. the ostrich, called by the Persians *ushturmurgh* and by the Arabs *teir-al-djamal*, both meaning "camel-bird"), whose body to the crown is 6 or 7 feet high. It has wings and can fly, but not to any height.' Among quadrupeds there is the so-called *tsu-la* (giraffe), striped like a camel and in size like an ox. It is yellow in colour. Its front legs are 5 feet high and its hind legs are only 3 feet. Its head is high up and is turned upwards. Its skin is an inch thick. There is also a mule with red, black, and white stripes wound as girdles around the body. Both (these kinds) are animals of the mountain wilds. They are occasional variations of the camel. The inhabitants are fond of hunting and from time to time they catch them with poisoned arrows."

The *Hsin T'ang-shu*; as I said, reproduces part of the notice on Berbera of the *Yu-yang-tsa-tsu*. It also has a short entry on another African territory, which so far as I am aware has not been noticed in this connection, viz. on Ma-lin, that is Melinda. The text says: "South-west from Fu-lin (that is the country of the Roman Orient of which 'Ch'ih-san, Alexandria, is indicated as the western border), after one traverses the desert for two thousand miles is a country called Ma-lin. It is the old P'o-sa. Its people are black and their nature is fierce. The land is pestilentious and has no herbs, no trees, and no cereals. They feed the horses on dried fish; the people eat *hu-mang*; the hu-mang is the Persian date. They are not ashamed of debauching the wives of their fathers or chiefs, they are (in this respect) the worst of the barbarians. They call this: to seek out the proper master and subject. In the seventh moon they rest completely (i.e. Ramadan). They (then) do not send out nor receive (any merchandise) in trade and they sit drinking all night long."

There is a short note on Ts'eng-po, identified with Zanguebar, which is not particularly interesting, and one on K'unlun Ts'eng-ch'i which deserves our attention. It is in the section dealing with countries on the sea.

"K'un-lun Ts'eng-ch'i is in the southwestern sea. It is adjacent to a large island in the sea. There are regularly great p'êng birds. When they fly they obscure the sun for a short time. There are wild camels, and if the p'êng birds meet them, they swal-

---

3. A unit of weight used in China that is generally equal to 1 1/3 pounds avoirdupois (ed.).

low them up. If one finds a feather of the p'êng bird, by cutting the quill, one can make a water-jar of it.

The products of the country are big elephants' tusks and rhinoceros' horns.

In the west "there is an island in the sea on which there are many savages. Their bodies are black as lacquer and they have frizzled hair. They are enticed by (offers of) food and then captured and sold as slaves to the Arabic countries, where they fetch a very high price. They are employed as gate-keepers, and it is said that they have no longing for their kinsfolk."

There can be little doubt that the island mentioned is Madagascar. The p'êng bird is the legendary rukh, and perhaps it was the presence of the now extinct dodo which is at the origin of the story that it was found there. Marco Polo says that it can swallow an elephant. Yule explains the story of the quills as the fronds of the raphia palm; Ferrand identifies it with the use made of the *langana* (Malgash), a big bamboo, about 15 centimeters in diameter and 2 meters long, in which the knots have been perforated with the exception of the one at the end, so as to turn it into a water vessel. These *langana* are particularly used by the coast tribes of Madagascar.

The capturing of slaves brings up an interesting question. Chou Ch'ü-fei inserts another sentence: "thousands of them are sold as foreign slaves."

It is certain that some of these slaves came to China. Foreign slaves were designated by various names. K'un-lun-nu, K'un-lun slaves is one of them. The word *k'un-lun* has had an interesting history. Used early on as the name of the fabulous mountains in the West, the home of Hsi-wang-mu, the word originally seems to mean the round vault of the sky, in which as it were, these gigantic Tibetan mountains seem to lose themselves. Etymologically, it is certainly connected with the binom *hun-lun*, "chaos." The K'un-lun mountains are also identified with the Anavatapta mountain and the Surmeru in India, well known in Buddhist literature. Now the Chinese have applied the term *k'un-lun* to the peoples, mostly of the Malay race, whom they found at the ends of the earth. At first chiefly confined to the races of the South-West, later, as the geographic knowledge of the Chinese expanded, the same term was applied to the native races of the countries around the Indian Ocean, including the Negroes.

We also find Seng-chih-nu, slaves from Seng-chih, which undoubtedly is the same as Ts'eng-ch'i, as transcription of Zanggi, the general Arabic word for Negroes. In the name of the country K'un-lun Ts'engch'i (k'i), we may therefore recognize the country of the blacks, Zanzibar, prefixed by the appellation K'un-lun, a curious, though perhaps accidental, reminder of the Malay origin of the inhabitants of Madagascar.

Slaves are further called: *kuei-nu*, "devil-slaves," *yeh-jen*, "wild men," *hei-hsiao-ssü*, "black servants," *fan hsiao-ssü*, "barbarian servants," or *fan-nu*, "barbarian slaves." These names may sometimes have designated Malay slaves in general, but often they undoubtedly refer to Negro-slaves. We hear about them quite early: the priest Tao-an is called K'un-lun-tzü, "the K'un-lun," or the Ch'i-tao-jen, "the lacquered monk," because he was so dark in spite of his being a northern Chinese. The later consort of Emperor Chien-wen of the Chin dynasty was nicknamed "K'un-lun" by the courtiers, because she was tall and of a dark colour. The *P'ing-chou-k'o-t'an* writes: "In Kuang-chou most of the wealthy people keep devil-slaves. They are very strong and can lift (weights of) several hundred catties. Their language and tastes are unintelligible. Their nature is simple and they do not run away. They are also called 'wild men.' Their colour is black as ink, their lips are red and their teeth white, their hair is curly and yellow. There are males and females (*N.B.*: the term for animals is used). They live in the mountains (or islands) beyond the seas. They eat raw things. If, in captivity, they are fed on cooked food, after several days they get diarrhoea. This is called 'changing the bowels.' For this reason they sometimes fall ill and die; if they do not die one can keep them, and after having been kept a long time they begin to understand people's language, although they themselves cannot speak it. There is one kind of wild men near the sea who can enter the water without blinking their eyes. They are called K'un-lun slaves."

That the slave-trade, whether of Negroes or other tribes of the Indian Ocean was pretty extensive also appears from a notice in the *Ling-wai-tai-ta*: "The people Of Chan-ch'eng (Champa) buy male and female slaves; and the ships carry human beings as cargo." Chao Jukua adds that a boy was priced at 3 taels of gold or the equivalent in aromatic wood. Slaves were also used on board ships for mending a leaky ship from the outside under water.

There is a strange pathos in the thought of these melancholy, silent, black slaves, who were supposed to have no longing for their home, in medieval China, used as doorkeepers.

---

4. IBN BATTUTA

THE EAST AFRICAN COAST. 1331.

The celebrated Muslim traveler Ibn Battuta (1304–1368/9) traversed nearly the whole of the Muslim world and beyond during his many years of wandering. Born in Tangiers, he made the first of his four pilgrimages to Mecca when he was twenty-one; thereafter, his passion was to "travel throughout the earth," never twice by the same road. His second journey took him through southern Iraq and southwest Persia, then to Tabriz and northwestern Mesopotamia. He subsequently traveled along the Red Sea, down the East African coast, and returned via the Persian Gulf. His fourth journey took him to Constantinople and from there to India, where he arrived in September 1333. He resided in India for several years in the service of the Sultan, traveling to China on the latter's behalf in 1342. Ibn Battuta then returned to the West, visiting Andalusia and the western Sudan. The account of this intelligent and perceptive observer provides an invaluable picture of the East African coast in 1331.

From *The Travels of Ibn Battuta*, A.D. 1325–1354, trans. and edited by H. A. R. Gibb (New York: Cambridge University Press, 1962), vol. II, pp. 373–382. Reprinted by permission of Cambridge University Press on behalf of The Hakluyt Society. In this selection inserts bracketed into the text are those of H. A. R. Gibb.

I travelled from the city of Adan by sea for four days and arrived at the city of Zaila, the city of the Barbara[1] who are a people of the negroes[2] Shafites in rite. Their country is a desert extending for two months' journey, beginning at Zaila and ending at Maqdashaw. Their cattle are camels, and they also have sheep which are famed for their fat. The inhabitants of Zaila are black in colour, and the majority of them are Rafidis.[3] It is a large city with a great bazaar, but it is in the dirtiest, most disagreeable, and most stinking town in the world. The reason for its stench is the quantity of its fish and the blood of the camels that they slaughter in the streets. When we arrived there we chose to spend the night at sea in spite of its extreme roughness, rather than pass a night in the town, because of its filth.

We sailed on from there for fifteen nights and came to Maqdashaw, which is a town of enormous size.[4] Its inhabitants are merchants possessed of vast resources; they own large numbers of camels, of which they slaughter hundreds every day [for food], and also have quantities of sheep. In this place are manufactured the woven fabrics called after it, which are unequalled and exported from it to Egypt and elsewhere. It is the custom of the people of this town that, when a vessel reaches the anchorage, the *sumbuqs*, which are small boats, come out to it. In each *sumbuq* there are a number of young men of the town, each one of whom brings a covered platter containing food and presents it to one of the merchants on the ship saying "This is my guest," and each of the others does the same. The merchant, on disembarking, goes only to the house of his host among the young men, except those of them who have made frequent journeys to the town and have gained some acquaintance with its inhabitants; these lodge where they please. When he takes up residence with his host, the latter sells his goods for him and buys for him; and if anyone buys anything from him at too low a price or sells to him in the absence of his host, that sale is held invalid by them. This practice is a profitable one for them.

When the young men came on board the vessel in which I was, one of them came up to me. My companions said to him "This man is not a merchant, but a doctor of the law," whereupon he called out to his friends and said to them "This is the guest of the qadi." There was among them one of the qadi's men, who informed him of this, and he came down to the beach with a number of students and sent one of them to me. I then disembarked with my companions and saluted him and his party. He said to me "In the name of God, let us go to salute the Shaikh." "And who is the Shaikh?" I said, and he answered, "The Sultan," for it is their custom to call the sultan "the Shaikh." Then I said to him "When I am lodged, I shall go to him," but he said to me, "It is the custom that whenever there comes a jurist or a sharif or a man

---

1. Zaila, on a sandy spit on the Somali coast due south of Aden, was included at this time in the Ethiopian kingdom of Awfat or Ifat. . . . . By the term *Barbara* the Arabic geographers apparently mean the Hamitic tribes who are neither Abyssinian (*Habash*) nor negroes (*Zinj*), and more especially the Somalis, although Ibn Battuta here includes them among the negroes.

2. Arabic Zinj or Zanj, a term ultimately derived from Persian or Sanskrit. Probably in the language of the seamen of the Persian Gulf.

3. i.e., Shiites, probably of the Zaidi sect.

4. Mogadishu was founded in the tenth century as a trading colony by Arabs from the Persian Gulf, the principal group being from al-Hasa. . . .

of religion, he must first see the sultan before taking a lodging." So I went with him to the sultan, as they asked.

Account of the Sultan of Magdashaw.[5] The sultan of Maqdashaw is, as we have mentioned, called only by the title of "the Shaikh." His name is Abu Bakr, son of the shaikh Omar; he is by origin of the Barbara and he speaks in Maqdishi, but knows the Arabic language. One of his customs is that, when a vessel arrives, the sultan's *sumbuq* goes out to it, and enquiries are made as to the ship, whence it has come, who is its owner and its *rubban* (that is, its captain), what is its cargo, and who has come on it of merchants and others. When all of this information has been collected, it is presented to the sultan, and if there are any persons [of such quality] that the sultan should assign a lodging to him as his guest, he does so.

When I arrived with the qadi I have mentioned, who was called Ibn al-Burhan, an Egyptian by origin, at the sultan's residence, one of the serving-boys came out and saluted the qadi, who said to him "Take word to the intendant's office and inform the Shaikh that this man has come from the land of al-Hijaz." So he took the message, then returned bringing a plate on which were some leaves of betel and areca nuts. He gave me ten leaves along with a few of the nuts, the same to the qadi, and what was left on the plate to my companions and the qadi's students. He brought also a jug of rose-water of Damascus, which he poured over me and over the qadi [i.e. over our hands], and said "Our master commands that he be lodged in the students' house," this being a building equipped for the entertainment of students of religion. The qadi took me by the hand and we went to this house, which is in the vicinity of the Shaikh's residence, and furnished with carpets and all necessary appointments. Later on [the serving boy] brought food from the Shaikh's residence. With him came one of his viziers, who was responsible for [the care of] the guests, and who said "Our master greets you and says to you that you are heartily welcome." He then set down the food and we ate. Their food is rice cooked with ghee, which they put into a large wooden platter, and on top of this they set platters of *kushan.*[6] This is the seasoning made of chickens, fleshmeat, fish, and vegetables. They cook unripe bananas in fresh milk and put this in one dish, and in another dish they put curdled milk, on which they place pieces of pickled lemon, bunches of pickled pepper steeped in vinegar and salted, green ginger, and mangoes. These resemble apples, but have a stone; when ripe they are exceedingly sweet and are eaten like [other] fruit, but before ripening they are acid like lemons, and they pickle them in vinegar. When they take a mouthful of rice, they eat some of these salted and vinegar conserves after it. A single person of the people of Maqdashaw eats as much as a whole company of us would eat, as a matter of habit, and they are corpulent and fat in the extreme.

5. The various Arab tribes occupied different quarters in Mogadishu (hence presumably its expansion), but recognized the supremacy of the tribe of Muqri, who called themselves Qahtanis, i.e. south-Arabians, and furnished the qadi of the city. The sultanate seems to have emerged only towards the end of the thirteenth century, and the most noted of its sultans was this Abu Bakr b. Fakhr al-Din.

6. *Kushan* is probably a term of the Persian Gulf seamen for seasonings of meat and vegetables resembling curries, served with rice. The origin may be related to Persian *gushtan*, glossed as "meats and fruit pulps."

After we had eaten, the qadi took leave of us. We stayed there three days, food being brought to us three times a day, following their custom. On the fourth day, which was a Friday, the qadi and students and one of the Shaikh's viziers came to me, bringing a set of robes; these [official] robes of theirs consist of a silk wrapper which one ties round his waist in place of drawers (for they have no acquaintance with these), a tunic of Egyptian linen with an embroidered border, a furred mantle of Jerusalem stuff, and an Egyptian turban with an embroidered edge. They also brought robes for my companions suitable to their position. We went to the congregational mosque and made our prayers behind the *maqsura*.[7]

When the Shaikh came out of the door of the *maqsura* I saluted him along with the qadi; he said a word of greeting, spoke in their tongue with the qadi, and then said in Arabic "You are heartily welcome, and you have honoured our land and given us pleasure." He went out to the court of the mosque and stood by the grave of his father, who is buried there, then recited some verses from the Quran and said a prayer. After this the viziers, amirs, and officers of the troops came up and saluted him. Their manner of salutation is the same as the custom of the people of al-Yaman; one puts his forefinger to the ground, then raises it to his head and says "May God prolong thy majesty." The Shaikh then went out of the gate of the mosque, put on his sandals, ordered the qadi to put on his sandals and me to do likewise, and set out on foot for his residence, which is close to the mosque. All the [rest of the] people walked barefoot. Over his head were carried four canopies of coloured silk, with the figure of a bird in gold on top of each canopy.[8] His garments on that day were a large green mantle of Jerusalem stuff, with fine robes of Egyptian stuffs with their appendages underneath it, and he was girt with a waist-wrapper of silk and turbaned with a large turban. In front of him were sounded drums and trumpets and fifes, and before and behind him were the commanders of the troops, while the qadi, the doctors of the law, and the sharifs walked alongside him. He entered his audience-hall in this disposition, and the viziers, amirs, and officers of the troops sat down in a gallery there. For the qadi there was spread a rug, on which no one may sit but he, and beside him were the jurists and sharifs. They remained there until the hour of the afternoon prayer, and after they had prayed it, the whole body of troops came and stood in rows in order of their ranks. Thereafter the drums, fifes, trumpets, and flutes are sounded; while they play no person moves or stirs from his place, and anyone who is walking stands still, moving neither backwards nor forwards. When the playing of the drum-band comes to an end, they salute with their fingers as we have described and withdraw. This is a custom of theirs on every Friday.

On the Saturday, the population comes to the Shaikh's gate and they sit in porticoes outside his residence. The qadi, jurists, sharifs, men of religion, shaikhs, and

7. The enclosure in the congregational mosque reserved for the ruler.

8. Ibn Battuta does not call these by the name of the ceremonial parasol, jitr, the use of which had been apparently introduced by the Fatimid caliphs of Egypt and spread to all parts of the Muslim world. But apart from the fact of the four "canopies" (*qibab*), it is difficult to see how these differed from the parasols, especially as the latter too were often surmounted by the figure of a bird.

those who have made the Pilgrimage go in to the second audience-hall, where they sit on platforms prepared for that purpose. The qadi will be on a platform by himself, and each class of persons on the platform proper to them, which is shared by no others. The Shaikh then takes his seat in his hall and sends for the qadi, who sits down on his left; thereafter the jurists enter, and the principal men amongst them sit down in front of the Shaikh, while the remainder salute and withdraw. Next the sharifs come in, their principal men sit down in front of him, and the remainder salute and withdraw. If they are guests, they sit on the Shaikh's right. Next the shaikhs and pilgrims come in, and their principal men sit, and the rest salute and withdraw. Then come the viziers, then the amirs, then the officers of the troops, group after group, and they salute and withdraw. Food is brought in; the qadi and sharifs and all those who are sitting in the hall eat in the presence of the Shaikh, and he eats with them. If he wishes to honour one of his principal amirs, he sends for him, and the latter eats with them. The rest of the people eat in the dining-hall, and the order of eating is the same as their order of entry into the Shaikh's presence. The Shaikh then goes into his residence, and the qadi, with the viziers, the private secretary, and four of the principal amirs, sits for deciding cases among the population and petitioners. Every case that is concerned with the rulings of the Divine Law is decided by the qadi, and all cases other than those are decided by the members of the council, that is to say, the viziers and amirs. If any case calls for consultation of the sultan, they write to him about it, and he sends out the reply to them immediately on the reverse of the document as determined by his judgment. And this too is their fixed custom.

I then sailed from the city of Maqdashaw, making for the country of the Sawahil [Coastlands], with the object of visiting the city of Kulwa in the land of the Zinj people. We came to the island of Mambasa, a large island two days' journey by sea from the Sawahil country.[9] It has no mainland territory, and its trees are the banana, the lemon, and the citron. Its people have a fruit which they call *jammun*, resembling an olive and with a stone like its stone. The inhabitants of this island sow no grain, and it has to be transported to them from the Sawahil. Their food consists mostly of bananas and fish. They are Shafiites in rite, pious, honourable, and upright, and their mosques are of wood, admirably constructed. At each of the gates of the mosques there are one or two wells (their wells have a depth of one or two cubits), and they draw up water from them in a wooden vessel, into which has been fixed a thin stick of the length of one cubit. The ground round the well and the mosque is paved; anyone who intends to go into the mosque washes his feet before entering, and at its gate there is a piece of thick matting on which he rubs his feet. If one intends to make an ablution, he holds the vessel between his thighs, pours [water] on his hands and performs the ritual washings. All the people walk with bare feet.

---

9. *Sahil*, literally "coastland," meant in maritime usage a port serving as an entrepôt for the goods of its hinterland. . . . Mombasa is separated from the mainland only by a narrow strait, but Ibn Battuta apparently means that it is two days sailing time from the "Coastlands" properly so called, i.e. the trading ports to the southward.

We stayed one night in this island and sailed on to the city of Kulwa, a large city on the seacoast,[10] most of whose inhabitants are Zinj, jet-black in colour. They have tattoo marks on their faces, just as [there are] on the faces of the *Limis* of Janawa.[11] I was told by a merchant that the city of Sufala[12] lies at a distance of half a month's journey from the city of Kulwa, and that between Sufala and Yufi, in the country of the *Limis*, is a month's journey; from Yufi gold dust is brought to Sufala.[13] The city of Kulwa is one of the finest and most substantially built towns; all the buildings are of wood, and the houses are roofed with *dis* reeds. The rains there are frequent. Its people engage in *jihad*, because they are on a common mainland with the heathen Zinj people and contiguous to them, and they are for the most part religious and upright, and Shafiites in rite.

Account of the Sultan of Kulwa. Its sultan at the period of my entry into it was Abul-Muzaffar Hasan, who was called also by the appellation of Abul-Mawahib, on account of the multitude of his gifts and acts of generosity. He used to engage frequently in expeditions to the land of the Zinj people, raiding them and taking booty, and he would set aside the fifth part of it to devote to the objects prescribed for it in the Book of God Most High. He used to deposit the portion for the relatives [of the Prophet] in a separate treasury; whenever he was visited by sharifs he would pay it out to them, and the sharifs used to come to visit him from al-Iraq and al-Hijaz and other countries. I saw at his court a number of the sharifs of al-Hijaz, amongst them Muhammad b. Jammaz, Mansur b. Lubaida b. Abu Numayy, and Muhammad b. Shumaila b. Abu Numayy, and at Maqdashaw I met Tabl b. Kubaish b. Jammaz, who was intending to go to him. This sultan is a man of great humility; he sits with poor brethren, and eats with them, and greatly respects men of religion and noble descent.

An anecdote illustrating his generosity. I was present with him on a Friday, when he had come out [of the mosque] after the prayer and was proceeding to his residence. He was accosted by a poor brother, a Yamanite, who said to him "O Abul-Mawahib;" he replied "At your service, O faqir—what do you want?" The man said, "Give me those robes that you are wearing." He said "Certainly I shall give you them." The man said "Now," and he said "Yes, now," went back to the mosque and into the khatib's chamber, where he dressed in other garments, and having taken off those robes he called to the poor brother "Come in and take them." So the faqir came in, took them, made a bundle of them in a kerchief, placed them on his head and went off. The population were loud in their gratitude to the sultan for the humil-

---

10. Kilwa (Kulwa is not otherwise attested), Quiloa of the Portuguese chronicles, now Kilwa Kisiwani in Tanganyika (8°57' S., 39°34'E.), 340 miles south of Mombasa. . . .

11. *Limi* is a variant form of *Lamlam*, applied by the Arab geographers to the (supposedly cannibal) tribes of the interior. Janawa was the name given to the country of the pagan tribes south of the Muslim lands in West Africa, which passed into Portuguese and thence into English as Guinea.

12. Sofala, at 20°10'S., 34°42'E., was the southernmost trading station of the Arabs in Africa, founded by colonists from Mogadishu.

13. Yufi is the kingdom of Nupe in West Africa. This confusion between the gold dust of the Niger and the mined gold ore of Sofala and the assumption of a connection between them are probably due to some misunderstanding on Ibn Battuta's part.

ity and generosity that he had displayed, and his son, who was his designated heir, took the clothing from the poor brother and gave him ten slaves in exchange. When the sultan learned of the gratitude expressed by the people to him for that action, he too ordered the faqir to be given ten head of slaves and two loads of ivory, for most of their gifts consist of ivory and it is seldom that they give gold. When this worthy and open-handed sultan died (God have mercy on him), he was succeeded by his brother Daud, who was of the opposite line of conduct. When a petitioner came to him he would say to him "He who gave is dead, and left nothing behind to be given." Visitors would stay at his court for many months, and finally he would make them some small gift, so that at last solicitors gave up coming to his gate.

5. IBN BATTUTA

MALI. 1352.

AUDIENCES OF THE SULTAN OF MALI

Sometimes the sultan [of Mali] holds meetings in the place where he has his audiences. There is a dais in that place, situated under a tree, with three big steps called *penpi*. The dais is covered with silk and embellished with cushions, and above it is placed a parasol that looks like a silken dome. On the top of the parasol is a golden bird as big as a sparrow hawk. The sultan goes out by a well-used door in a corner of the castle. He holds his bow in his hand and wears his quiver on his back. On his head he wears a gold hat that is held in place by a band, also of gold. The ends of the hat are tapered like knives longer than a hand's span. Most often he is dressed in a red velvet tunic, made of either European cloth called *mothanfas* or deep pile cloth.

The singers come out in front of the sultan, and they hold *kanakir* (instruments whose name in the singular is doubtless *konbara*, which means lark) of gold and silver. Behind him are about 300 armed slaves. The sovereign walks patiently, advancing very slowly. When he arrives at the penpi, he stops and looks at those who are there. Then he slowly goes up onto the dais as the priest mounts his pulpit. As soon as the sultan is seated, drums are beaten, a horn is sounded, and trumpets blare.

What I Found to Be Praiseworthy About the Conduct of the Negroes in Contrast to What I Found to Be Bad

Among the good qualities of this people, we must cite the following:

1. The small number of acts of injustice that take place there [in Mali], for of all people, the Negroes abhor it [injustice] the most. Their sultan never pardons anyone

From Ibn Battuta, *Ibn Batoutah*, trans. from the Arabic by C. Defremery and B. R. Sanguinétti (Paris, 1863), vol. IV, pp. 405–407, 421–424, 440–442. Trans. from the French by Nell Elizabeth Painter and Robert O. Collins.

guilty of injustice.

2. The general and complete security that is enjoyed in the country. The traveler, just as the sedentary man, has nothing to fear of brigands, thieves, or plunderers.

3. The blacks do not confiscate the goods of white men who die in their country, even when these men possess immense treasures. On the contrary, the blacks deposit the goods with a man respected among the whites, until the individuals to whom the goods rightfully belong present themselves and take possession of them.

4. The Negroes say their prayers correctly; they say them assiduously in the meetings of the faithful and strike their children if they fail these obligations. On Friday, whoever does not arrive at the mosque early finds no place to pray because the temple becomes so crowded. The blacks have a habit of sending their slaves to the mosque to spread out the mats they use during prayers in the places to which each slave has a right, to wait for their master's arrival. These mats are made from a tree that resembles the palm but that bears no fruit.

5. The Negroes wear handsome white clothes every Friday. If, by chance, one of them possesses only one shirt or a worn-out tunic, he at least washes and cleans it and wears it to the public prayers.

6. They are very zealous in their attempt to learn the holy *Quran* by heart. In the event that their children are negligent in this respect, fetters are placed on the children's feet and are left until the children can recite the *Quran* from memory. On a holiday I went to see the judge, and seeing his children in chains, I asked him, "Aren't you going to let them go?" He answered, "I won't let them go until they know the *Quran* by heart." Another day I passed a young Negro with a handsome face who was wearing superb and carrying a heavy chain around his feet. I asked the person who was with me, "What did that boy do? Did he murder someone?" The young Negro heard my question and began to laugh. My colleague told me, "He has been chained up only to force him to commit the *Quran* to memory."

Some of the blameworthy actions of these people are:

1. The female servants and slaves, as well as little girls, appear before men completely naked. I observed this practice a great deal during the month of Ramadan [the ninth month and time of fasting in the Muslim year], for the usual custom among the Negroes is for the Commanders to break the fast in the sultan's palace and for each of them to be served by female slaves who are entirely nude and who bring the food to the number of twenty or more.

2. All the women who come into the sovereign's house are nude and wear no veils over their faces; the sultan's daughters also go naked. On the twenty-seventh night of the month of Ramadan, I saw about a hundred female slaves come out with the food for the sultan's palace, and they were nude. Two of the sovereign's daughters, who had been gifted with very large chests, accompanied the slaves and had no covering whatsoever.

3. The blacks throw dust and ashes on their heads to show that they are educated and as a sign of respect.

4. Negroes practice a sort of buffoonery when the poets recite their verses to the sultan, as described elsewhere.

5. Finally, a good number of the Negroes eat vultures, dogs, and asses.

THE COPPER MINE

The copper mine is situated outside Takedda. Slaves of both sexes dig into the soil and take the ore to the city to smelt it in the houses. As soon as the red copper has been obtained, it is made into bars one and one-half handspans long—some thin, some thick. Four hundred of the thick bars equal a ducat of gold; six or seven hundred of the thin bars are also worth a ducat of gold. These bars serve as a means of exchange, in place of coin. With the thin bars, meat and firewood are bought; with the thick bars, male and female slaves, millet, butter, and wheat can be bought.

The copper of Takedda. is exported to the city Couber [Gobir], situated in the land of the pagan Negroes. Copper is also exported to Zaghai [Dyakha-western Masina] and to the land of Bernon [Bornu], which is forty days distant from Takedda and is inhabited by Muslims. ldris, king of the Muslims, never shows himself before the people and never speaks to them unless he is behind a curtain. Beautiful slaves, eunuchs, and cloth dyed with saffron are brought from Bernon to many different countries. . . .

6. ANTONIUS MALFANTE

TAWAT AND THE WESTERN SUDAN TRADE. 1447.

No details are known about the author of the following letter, written from Tawat (Tuat) in 1447 by Antonius Malfante and addressed to Giovanni Mariono in Genoa. Tawat was centrally located in the Sahara and was an important oasis on the road from Aïr, over which passed trade from the Hausa city-states of northern Nigeria.

After we had come from the sea, that is from Hono [Honein], we journeyed on horseback, always southwards, for about twelve days. For seven days we encountered no dwelling—nothing but sandy plains; we proceeded as though at sea, guided by the sun during the day, at night by the stars. At the end of the seventh day, we arrived at a *ksour* [Tabelbert], where dwelt very poor people who supported themselves on water and a little sandy ground. They sow little, living upon the numerous date palms. At this *ksour* [oasis, ed.] we had come into Tueto [Tawat, a group of oases]. In this place there are eighteen quarters, enclosed within one wall, and ruled by an oligarchy. Each ruler of a quarter protects his followers, whether they be in the right or no. The quarters closely adjoin each other and are jealous of their privileges. Everyone arriving here places himself under the protection of one of these rulers, who will protect him to the death: thus merchants enjoy very great security, much greater, in my opinion, than in kingdoms such as Thernmicenno [Tlemcen]

From *The Voyages of Cadamosto and Other Documents on Western Africa in the Second Half of the Fifteenth Century,* trans. from the Italian and edited by G. R. Crone (New York: Cambridge University Press, 1937), pp. 85–90. Reprinted by permission of Cambridge University Press on behalf of The Hakluyt Society. In this selection the place names in brackets have been supplied by G. R. Crone.

and Thunisie [Tunis].

Though I am a Christian, no one ever addressed an insulting word to me. They said they had never seen a Christian before. It is true that on my first arrival they were scornful of me, because they all wished to see me, saying with wonder "This Christian has a countenance like ours"—for they believed that Christians had disguised faces. Their curiosity was soon satisfied, and now I can go alone anywhere, with no one to say an evil word to me.

There are many Jews, who lead a good life here, for they are under the protection of the several rulers, each of whom defends his own clients. Thus they enjoy very secure social standing. Trade is in their hands, and many of them are to be trusted with the greatest confidence.

This locality is a mart of the country of the Moors, to which merchants come to sell their goods: gold is carried hither, and bought by those who come up from the coast. This place is De Amamento [Tamentiti], and there are many rich men here. The generality, however, are very poor, for they do not sow, nor do they harvest anything, save the dates upon which they subsist. They eat no meat but that of castrated camels, which are scarce and very dear.

It is true that the Arabs with whom I came from the coast brought with them corn and barley which they sell throughout the year at "f. saracen, la nostra mina."[1]

It never rains here: if it did, the houses, being built of salt in the place of reeds, would be destroyed.[2] It is scarcely ever cold here: in summer the heat is extreme, wherefore they are almost all blacks. The children of both sexes go naked up to the age of fifteen. These people observe the religion and law of Muhammad. In the vicinity there are 150 to 200 *ksour*.

In the lands of the blacks, as well as here, dwell the Philistines [the Tuareg], who live, like the Arabs, in tents. They are without number, and hold sway over the land of Gazola[3] from the borders of Egypt to the shores of the Ocean, as far as Massa and Safi, and over all the neighbouring towns of the blacks. They are fair, strong in body and very handsome in appearance. They ride without stirrups, with simple spurs. They are governed by kings, whose heirs are the sons of their sisters—for such is their law. They keep their mouths and noses covered. I have seen many of them here, and have asked them through an interpreter why they cover their mouths and noses thus. They replied: "We have inherited this custom from our ancestors." They are sworn enemies of the Jews, who do not dare to pass hither. Their faith is that of the Blacks. Their sustenance is milk and flesh, no corn or barley, but much rice. Their sheep, cattle, and camels are without number. One breed of camel, white as

---

1. A *Saracen* was the Arab coin known as the *dinar*; *Mina* was a measure equalling approximately half a bushel. The "f." perhaps stands for "six."

2. De la Roncière suggests that this is not a description of Tamentit but of Taghaza, where the houses were all built of rock salt.

3. Gazola (the *Gazula* of Idrisi) appears on many portolan charts, sometimes applied to a town, sometimes to a region. On the Pizigani chart of 1373 there is a cape, probably Cape Nun, called "Caput finis Gozole." It has been derived from the Berber people, the Guezulah, a branch of which inhabited the Sus; as used by Malfante it appears to be applied to the same area as "Sarra," or Sahara, of other contemporary writers.

snow, can cover in one day a distance which would take a horseman four days to travel. Great warriors, these people are continually at war amongst themselves.

The states which are under their rule border upon the land of the Blacks. I shall speak of those known to men here, and which have inhabitants of the faith of Muhammad. In all, the great majority are Blacks, but there are a small number of whites [i.e. tawny Moors].

First, Tbegida,[4] which comprises one province and three *ksour*; Checoli,[5] which is as large.

Chuchiam,[6] Thambet [Timbuktu], Geni [Djenné], and Meli [Mali], said to have nine towns:

Thora [unidentified], Oden [Wadan], Dendi,[7] Sagoto [unidentified], Bofon [unidentified], Igdem [unidentified], Bembo,[8] all these are great cities, capitals of extensive lands and towns under their rule.

These adhere to the law of Muhammad.

To the south of these are innumerable great cities and territories, the inhabitants of which are all blacks and idolators, continually at war with each other in defence of their law and faith of their idols. Some worship the sun, others the moon, the seven planets, fire, or water; others a mirror which reflects their faces, which they take to be the images of gods; others groves of trees, the seats of a spirit to whom they make sacrifice;[9] others again, statues of wood and stone, with which, they say, they commune by incantations. They relate here extraordinary things of this people.

The lord in whose protection I am, here, who is the greatest in this land, having a fortune of more than 100,000 *doubles* [a billon coin], brother of the most important merchant in Thambet, and a man worthy of credence, relates that he lived for thirty years in that town, and, as he says, for fourteen years in the land of the Blacks. Every day he tells me wonderful things of these peoples. He says that these lands and peoples extend endlessly to the south: they all go naked, save for a small loincloth to cover their privates. They have an abundance of flesh, milk, and rice, but no corn or barley.

Through these lands flows a very large river[10] which at certain times of the year inundates all these lands. This river passes by the gates of Tambet, and flows through Egypt; and is that which passes by Carium.[11] There are many boats on it, by which they carry on trade. It would be possible, they say, to descend to Egypt by this river, were it not that at a certain spot it falls 300 cubits over a rock,[12] on account

4. Takedda, five days' march west-south-west of Agadez.
5. Possible Es Suk (Tadmekka), north of Takedda at the head of the Tilemsi valley.
6. Probably Gao.
7. Dendi, probably the original home of the Songhai.
8. Possibly Bamba, a town on the Middle Niger.
9. Cf. Seligmann. "The Bambara have been little affected by Islam and retain their animistic beliefs and ancestor worship. Each village has its presiding spirit (*dasiri*) or divine ancestor, usually resident in a tree at which sacrifices are made and prayers offered by the *dugutigi* on all important occasions."
10. The Niger. It is to be noted that Malfante correctly implies that it flows eastwards, of which there was no certain knowledge till the end of the eighteenth century.
11. Cairo. On the confusion between the Niger and the Nile.
12. This appears reminiscent of the cataracts of the Nile.

of which boats cannot go or return. This river flows at about twenty days' journey on horseback from here.

These people have trees which produce an edible butter,[13] of which there is an abundance here. I have seen them bearing it hither: it is as wonderful an unguent as the butter of sheep. The slaves which the blacks take in their internecine wars are sold at a very low price, the maximum being two *doubles* a head. These peoples, who cover the land in multitudes, are in carnal acts like the beasts; the father has knowledge of his daughter, the son of his sister. They breed greatly, for a woman bears up to five at a birth. Nor can it be doubted that they are eaters of human flesh, for many people have gone hence into their country. Neither there nor here are there ever epidemics.

When the blacks catch sight of a white man from a distance, they take to flight as though from a monster, believing him to be a phantom. They are unlettered, and without books. They are great magicians, evoking by incense diabolical spirits, with whom, they say, they perform marvels.

"It is not long since I was in Cuchia [Gao], distant fifty days' journey from here, where there are Moors," my patron said to me. "A heathen king, with five hundred thousand men, came from the south to lay siege to the city of Vallo. Upon the hill within the city were fifty Moors, almost all blacks. They saw that they were by day surrounded by a human river, by night by a girdle of flames and looked upon themselves as already defeated and enslaved. But their king, who was in the city, was a great magician and necromancer; he concluded with the besieger a pact by which each was to produce by incantation a black goat. The two goats would engage in battle, and the master of that which was beaten, was likewise to consider himself defeated. The besieger emerged victorious from the contest, and, taking the town, did not allow one soul to escape, but put the entire population to the sword. He found much treasure there. The town to-day is almost completely deserted save for a poverty-stricken few who have come to dwell there."

Of such were the stories which I heard daily in plenty. The wares for which there is a demand here are many: but the principal articles are copper, and salt in slabs, bars, and cakes. The copper of Romania [the Byzantine Empire], which is obtained through Alexandria, is always in great demand throughout the land of the Blacks. I frequently enquired what they did with it, but no one could give me a definite answer. I believe it is that there are so many peoples that there is almost nothing but is of use to them.

The Egyptian merchants come to trade in the land of the Blacks with half a million head of cattle and camels—a figure which is not fantastic in this region.

The place where I am is good for trade, as the Egyptians and other merchants come hither from the land of the Blacks bringing gold, which they exchange for copper and other goods. Thus everything sells well; until there is nothing left for sale. The people here will neither sell nor buy unless at a profit of one hundred per cent. For this reason, I have lost, Laus Deol, on the goods I brought here, two thousand *doubles*.

13. The Karité tree, the most characteristic of the Savannah. The butter is obtained from the kernel.

From what I can understand, these people neighbour on India.[14] Indian merchants come hither, and converse through interpreters. These Indians are Christians, adorers of the cross. It is said that in the land of the Blacks there are forty dialects, so that they are unable to understand each other.

I often enquired where the gold was found and collected; my patron always replied "I was fourteen years in the land of the Blacks, and I have never heard nor seen anyone who could reply from definite knowledge. That is my experience, as to how it is found and collected. What appears plain is that it comes from a distant land, and, as I believe, from a definite zone." He also said that he had been in places where silver was as valuable as gold.

This land is twenty-eight days' journey from Cambacies,[15] and is the city with the best market. It is twenty-five days from Tunis, from Tripoli in Barbary twenty days, from Trimicen [Tlemcen] thirty days, from Fecia [Fez] twenty days, from Zaffi [Safi], Zamor [Azamorl] and Messa twenty days on horseback. I finish for the present; elsewhere and at another time, God willing, I will recount much more to you orally. I am always at your orders in Christ.

Your ANTONIUS MALFANT

14. Probably Abyssinia, the kingdom of Prester John, which was regarded in the Middle Ages as one of the Three Indias.
15. Probably Ghadames.

7. GOMES EANNES DE AZURARA

THE DISCOVERY OF GUINEA. 1435.

Gomes Eannes de Azurara was the Royal Chronicler of Portugal during the time that Prince Henry the Navigator inaugurated the systematic exploration of the coast of West Africa. Although the dates of his birth and death remain unknown, Azurara was probably born in the province of Minho at the beginning of the fifteenth century. He appears to have obtained a post in the Royal Library during the brief reign of Dom Duarte (1433–1438), or shortly thereafter, as assistant to Royal Chronicler Ferndo Lopez, whom he later succeeded. In 1453 he completed the Chronica de Guine, which describes the Portuguese discoveries along the West African coast and which remains one of the earliest records of European activity in West Africa.

So the Infant, moved by these reasons, which you have already heard, began to make ready his ships and his people, as the needs of the case required; but this much you may learn, that although he sent out many times, not only ordinary men, but

From Gomes Eannes de Azurara, *The Chronicle of the Discovery and Conquest of Guinea*, trans. from the Portuguese by C. Raymond Beazley and Edgar Prestage (London: Hakluyt Society, 1896), vol. I, pp. 30–34, 39–43. Reprinted by permission of Cambridge University Press on behalf of The Hakluyt Society.

such as by their experience in great deeds of war were of foremost name in the profession of arms, yet there was not one who dared to pass that Cape of Bojador and learn about the land beyond it, as the Infant wished.[1] And to say the truth this was not from cowardice or want of good will, but from the novelty of the thing and the wide-spread and ancient rumour about this Cape, that had been cherished by the mariners of Spain from generation to generation. And although this proved to be deceitful, yet since the hazarding of this attempt seemed to threaten the last evil of all, there was great doubt as to who would be the first to risk his life in such a venture. How are we, men said, to pass the bounds that our fathers set up, or what profit can result to the Infant from the perdition of our souls as well as of our bodies — for of a truth by daring any further we shall become wilful murderers of ourselves? Have there not been in Spain other princes and lords as covetous perchance of this honour as the Infant? For certainly it cannot be presumed that among so many noble men who did such great and lofty deeds for the glory of their memory, there had not been one to dare this deed. But being satisfied of the peril, and seeing no hope of honour or profit, they left off the attempt. For, said the mariners, this much is clear, that beyond this Cape there is no race of men nor place of inhabitants: nor is the land less sandy than the deserts of Libya, where there is no water, no tree, no green herb and the sea so shallow that a whole league from land it is only a fathom deep, while the currents are so terrible that no ship having once passed the Cape, will ever be able to return.

Therefore our forefathers never attempted to pass it: and of a surety their knowledge of the lands beyond was not a little dark, as they knew not how to set them down on the charts, by which man controls all the seas that can be navigated. Now what sort of a ship's captain would he be who, with such doubts placed before him by those to whom he might reasonably yield credence and authority, and with such certain prospect of death before his eyes, could venture the trial of such a bold feat as that? O thou Virgin Themis, saith our Author, who among the nine Muses of Mount Parnassus didst possess the especial right of searching out the secrets of Apollo's cave, I doubt whether thy fears were as great at putting thy feet on that sacred table where the divine revelations afflicted thee little less than death, as the terrors of these mariners of ours, threatened not only by fear but by its shadow, whose great deceit was the cause of very great expenses. For during twelve years the Infant continued steadily at this labour of his, ordering out his ships every year to those parts, not without great loss of revenue, and never finding any who dared to make that passage. Yet they did not return wholly without honour, for as an atonement for their failure to carry out more fully their Lord's wishes, some made descents upon the coasts of Granada and others voyaged along the Levant Seas, where they took great booty of the Infidels, with which they returned to the Kingdom very honourably.

---

1. Infant is the title of any legitimate son of a king of Spain or Portugal except the eldest. This reference is to the Infant Prince Henry (1394–1460), commonly known as "the Navigator," the third son of King João (or John) of Portugal. Cape Bojador is located at 26°15' North latitude at the western end of the Atlas Mountains of Morocco (ed.).

Now the Infant always received home again with great patience those whom he had sent out, as Captains of his ships, in search of that land, never upbraiding them with their failure, but with gracious countenance listening to the story of the events of their voyage, giving them such rewards as he was wont to give to those who served him well, and then either sending them back to search again or despatching other picked men of his Household, with their ships well furnished, making more urgent his charge to them, with promise of greater guerdons, if they added anything to the voyage that those before them had made, all to the intent that he might arrive at some comprehension of that difficulty. And at last, after twelve years, the Infant armed a "barcha" [bark or boat] and gave it to Gil Eannes, one of his squires, whom he afterwards knighted and cared for right nobly. And he followed the course that others had taken; but touched by the self-same terror, he only went as far as the Canary Islands, where he took some captives and returned to the Kingdom. Now this was in the year of Jesus Christ 1433, and in the next year the Infant made ready the same vessel, and calling Gil Eannes apart, charged him earnestly to strain every nerve to pass that Cape, and even if he could do nothing else on that voyage, yet he should consider that to be enough. "You cannot find," said the Infant, "a peril so great that the hope of reward will not be greater, and in truth I wonder much at the notion you have all taken on so uncertain a matter—for even if these things that are reported had any authority, however small, I would not blame you, but you tell me only the opinions of four mariners, who come but from the Flanders trade or from some other ports that are very commonly sailed to, and know nothing of the needle or sailing-chart. Go forth, then, and heed none of their words, but make your voyage straightway, inasmuch as with the grace of God you cannot but gain from this journey honour and profit." The Infant was a man of very great authority, so that his admonitions, mild though they were, had much effect on the serious-minded. And so it appeared by the deed of this man, for he, after these words, resolved not to return to the presence of his Lord without assured tidings of that for which he was sent. And as he purposed, so he performed—for in that voyage he doubled the Cape, despising all danger, and found the lands beyond quite contrary to what he, like others, had expected. And although the matter was a small one in itself, yet on account of its daring it was reckoned great—for if the first man who reached the Cape had passed it, there would not have been so much praise and thanks bestowed on him; but even as the danger of the affair put all others into the greater fear, so the accomplishing of it brought the greater honour to this man. But whether or no the success of Gil Eannes gained for him any genuine glory may be perceived by the words that the Infant spoke to him before his starting; and his experience on his return was very clear on this point, for he was exceeding well received, not without a profitable increase of honour and possessions. And then it was he related to the Infant how the whole matter had gone, telling him how he had ordered the boat to be put out and had gone in to the shore without finding either people or signs of habitation. And since, my lord, said Gil Eannes, I thought that I ought to bring some token of the land since I was on it, I gathered these herbs which I here present to your grace; the which we in this country call Roses of Saint Mary. Then, after he had finished giving an account of his voyage to that part, the Infant caused a "barinel"[2] to be made ready, in which he sent out Affonso Gonçalvez Baldaya, his cupbearer, and Gil Eannes as well with his "barcha," ordering him to return there with his companion. And so in fact they did, passing fifty leagues beyond the Cape, where they found the land without dwellings, but shewing footmarks of men and camels. And then, either because they were so ordered, or from necessity, they returned with this intelligence, without doing aught else worth recording.

I think I can now take some sort of pleasure in the narrating of this history, because I find something wherewith to satisfy the desire of our Prince; the which desire was so much the greater as the matters for which he had toiled so long were now more within his view. And so in this chapter I wish to present some novelty in his toilsome seed-time of preparation.

Now it was so that in this year 1441, when the affairs of this realm were somewhat more settled though not fully quieted, that the Infant armed a little ship, of the which he made captain one Antam Gonçalvez, his chamberlain, and a very young man; and the end of that voyage was none other, according to my Lord's commandment, but to ship a cargo of the skins and oil of those seawolves of which we have spoken in previous chapters. But it cannot be doubted that the Infant gave him the same charge that he gave to others, but as the age of this captain was weaker, and his authority but slight, so the Prince's orders were less stringent, and in consequence his hopes of result less confident.

But when he had accomplished his voyage, as far as concerned the chief part of his orders, Antam Gonçalvez called to him Affonso Goterres, another groom of the chamber, who was with him, and all the others that were in the ship, being one and twenty in all, and spoke to them in this wise: "Friends and brethren! We have already got our cargo, as you perceive, by the which the chief part of our ordinance is accomplished, and we may well turn back, if we wish not to toil beyond that which was principally commanded of us; but I would know from all whether it seemeth to you well that we should attempt something further, that he who sent us here may have some example of our good wills; for I think it would be shameful if we went back into his presence just as we are, having done such small service. And in truth I think we ought to labour the more strenuously to achieve something like this as it was the less laid upon us as a charge by the Infant our lord. O How fair a thing it would be if we, who have come to this land for a cargo of such petty merchandise, were to meet with the good luck to bring the first captives before the face of our Prince. And now I will tell you of my thoughts that I may receive your advice thereon. I would fain go myself this next night with nine men of you (those who are most ready for the business), and prove a part of this land along the river, to see if I find any inhabitants; for I think we of right ought to meet with some, since 'tis certain there are people here, who traffic with camels and other animals that bear their freights. Now the traffic of these men must chiefly be to the seaboard; and since they have as yet no knowledge of us, their gathering cannot be too large for us to try their strength; and, if God grant us to encounter them, the very least part of our

2. A barinel is a small vessel, characteristic of the type that sailed the Mediterranean (ed.).

victory will be the capture of one of them, with the which the Infant will feel no small content, getting knowledge by that means of what kind are the other dwellers of this land. And as to our reward, you can estimate what it will be by the great expenses and toil he has undertaken in years past, only for this end." "See what you do," replied the others, "for since you are our captain we needs must obey your orders, not as Antam Gonçalvez but as our lord; for you must understand that we who are here, of the Household of the Infant our lord, have both the will and desire to serve him, even to the laying down of our lives in the event of the last danger. But we think your purpose to be good, if only you will introduce no other novelty to increase the peril, which would be little to the service of our lord." And finally they determined to do his bidding, and follow him as far as they could make their way. And as soon as it was night Antam Gonçalvez chose nine men who seemed to him most fitted for the undertaking, and made his voyage with them as he had before determined. And when they were about a league distant from the sea they came on a path which they kept, thinking some man or woman might come by there whom they could capture; but it happened otherwise; so Antam Gonçalvez asked the others to consent to go forward and follow out his purpose; for, as they had already come so far, it would not do to return to the ship in vain like that. And the others being content they departed thence, and, journeying through that inner land for the space of three leagues, they found the footmarks of men and youths, the number of whom, according to their estimate, would be from forty to fifty, and these led the opposite way from where our men were going. The heat was very intense, and so by reason of this and of the toil they had undergone in watching by night and travelling thus on foot, and also because of the want of water, of which there was none, Antam Gonçalvez perceived their weariness that it was already very great, as he could easily judge from his own sufferings. So he said, "My friends, there is nothing more to do here; our toil is great, while the profit to arise from following up this path meseemeth small, for these men are travelling to the place whence we have come, and our best course would be to turn back towards them, and perchance, on their return, some will separate themselves, or, may be, we shall come up with them when they are laid down to rest, and then, if we attack them lustily, peradventure they will flee, and, if they flee, someone there will be less swift, whom we can lay hold of according to our intent; or may be our luck will be even better, and we shall find fourteen or fifteen of them, of whom we shall make a more profitable booty." Now this advice was not such as to give rise to any wavering in the will of those men, for each desired that very thing. And, returning towards the sea, when they had gone a short part of the way, they saw a naked man following a camel, with two assegais in his hand, and as our men pursued him there was not one who felt aught of his great fatigue. But though he was only one, and saw the others that they were many; yet he had a mind to prove those arms of his right worthily and began to defend himself as best he could, shewing a bolder front than his strength warranted. But Affonso Goterres wounded him with a javelin, and this put the Moor in such fear that he threw down his arms like a beaten thing. And after they had captured him, to their no small delight, and had gone on further, they espied, on the top of a hill, the company whose tracks they were following; and their captive pertained to the number of these. And they failed not to reach them through any lack of will, but the sun was now low, and they wearied, so they determined to return to their ship, considering that such enterprise might bring greater injury than profit. And, as they were going on their way, they saw a black Mooress come along (who was slave of those on the hill), and though some of our men were in favour of letting her pass to avoid a fresh skirmish, to which the enemy did not invite them—for, since they were in sight and their number more than doubled ours, they could not be of such faint hearts as to allow a chattel of theirs to be thus carried off:—despite this, Antam Gonçalvez bade them go at her; for if (he said) they scorned that encounter, it might make their foes pluck up courage against them. And now you see how the word of a captain prevaileth among men used to obey; for, following his will, they seized the Mooress. And those on the hill had a mind to come to the rescue, but when they perceived our people ready to receive them, they not only retreated to their former position, but departed elsewhere, turning their backs to their enemies. And so let us here leave Antam Gonçalvez to rest, considering this Chapter as finished, and in the following one we will knight him right honourably.

---

8. RUI DE AGUIAR

KING AFFONSO I. 1516.

Rui de Aguiar, a Portuguese missionary, worked in the Kongo as Vicar-General during the second decade of the sixteenth century. The following description of the greatest King of Kongo, Affonso I (Myemba Nzinga), who ruled from 1506 to about 1545, is contained in a letter from Rui de Aguiar to King Manuel of Portugal Agenuine dated May 25, 1516. A genuine and devout convert to Christianity, Affonso sought to establish Catholicism and to carry out a program of westernization in the Kingdom of Kongo. Only a shrewd and able king could have abandoned the traditional sanctions of divine kingship and introduce new customs to challenge the old without disrupting the kingdom or losing his throne.

This king, Dom Affonso, has nothing else in mind but Our Father and His manifestations. He has presently ordered that every man in all his kingdom pay the tithe,[1] saying that the light must be carried in front and not behind.

In his quality as a Christian, Your Highness will know, it seems to me, that he is not a man but an angel whom God has sent to this kingdom to convert it, according to the things he says and expresses. For I swear that he teaches us, and he knows the prophets and the gospel of Our Lord Jesus Christ and all the lives of the saints and

From Rui de Aguiar to King Manuel of Portugal, May 25, 1516, in Willy Bal, *Le Royaume du Congo aux XVième et Xvième Siècles. Documents d'Histoire* (Kinshasa: Éditions de l'Institute National d'Études Politiques, 1963), pp. 71–72. Trans. by Nell Elizabeth Painter and Robert O. Collins.

1. A tax, usually ten percent, for the support of the church (ed.).

all the things of our sacred mother the church better than we ourselves know them. I swear that such a sight would greatly astonish Your Highness. He says things so well phrased and so true that it seems to me that the Holy Spirit always speaks through him, for he does nothing but study, and many times he falls asleep over his books, and many times he forgets to eat and drink for talking of Our Lord, and he is so absorbed by the things of the Book that he forgets himself, and even when he is going to hold an audience and listen to the people, he speaks of nothing but God and His saints. He studies the sacred gospel, and when the priest finishes saying mass, he begins to preach to the people with great love and charity, asking these people and begging them, for the love of Our Lord, to convert and turn themselves toward God—so much so that his people are taken by amazement and we, even more so, by his virtue and the faith he has in Our Lord. And he does that every day, and he preaches, as I have described to Your Highness.

Your Highness will also know that he is very just and that he greatly punishes those who adore idols and that he burns them with their idols, and that he has, throughout his kingdom, ministers of justice to seize all those of whom it is learned that they possess idols or carry on sacrilege or any other bad actions touching our saintly Catholic faith. And again, throughout his kingdom he has sent many men, natives of the country, Christians, who have schools and teach our saintly faith to the people, and there are also schools for girls where one of his sisters teaches, a woman who is easily sixty years old, and who knows how to read very well and who is learned in her old age. Your Highness would rejoice to see it. There are also other women who know how to read and who go to church every day. These people pray to Our Lord at mass and Your Highness will know in truth that they are making great progress in Christianity and virtue, for they are advancing in the knowledge of the truth; also, may Your Highness always send them things and rejoice in helping them and, for their redemption, as a remedy, send them books, for they need them more than any other things for their redemption.

I am not speaking [here] of the great love and friendship that the King of Congo has for Your Highness. I have heard him say, in fact, that he asked Our Lord not to let him die before having seen Your Highness. I also have heard him say that Your Highness was King of the Congo, and he, King of Portugal. These things he says often to whomever wants to hear them. By that, Your Highness will know that all that I say is very true, and if I write a lie to Your Highness, may God destroy me, body and soul. And may Your Highness remember the very great good that has begun and for that Our Lord will give him the retribution he deserves.

Done today, the twenty-fifth day of the month of May of the year MDXVI.

9. FRANCISCO ALVAREZ

THE LAND OF PRESTER JOHN. 1525.

Father Francisco Alvarez (d. c. 1540) was chaplain to the Portuguese mission that was led by Don Rodrigo de Lima and visited Ethiopia during the years 1520 to 1525. At that time Abyssinia was still known as the land of Prester John, the legendary priest-king whose dominions were thought to be in Ethiopia and whose Christian subjects Portugal was anxious to support against the Muslims of Arabia and the Persian Gulf as part of the continuing Portuguese crusade against Islam.

At a day's journey from this church of Imbra Christo are edifices, the like of which and so many, cannot, as it appears to me, be found in the world, and they are churches entirely excavated in the rock, very well hewn. The names of these churches are these: Emanuel, St. Saviour, St. Mary, Holy Cross, St. George, Golgotha, Bethlehem, Marcoreos, the Martyrs. The principal one is Lalibela. This Lalibela, they say, was a King in this same country for eighty years, and he was King before the one before mentioned who was named Abraham. This King ordered these edifices to be made. He does not lie in the church which bears his name, he lies in the church of Golgotha, which is the church of the fewest buildings here. It is in this manner: all excavated in the stone itself, a hundred and twenty spans in length, and seventy-two spans in width. The ceiling of this church rests on five supports, two on each side, and one in the centre, like fives of dice, and the ceiling or roof is all flat like the floor of the church, the sides also are worked in a fine fashion, also the windows, and the doors with all the tracery, which could be told, so that neither a jeweller in silver, nor a worker of wax in wax, could do more work. The tomb of this King is in the same manner as that of Santiago of Galicia, at Compostella, and it is in this manner: the gallery which goes round the church is like a cloister, and lower than the body of the church, and one goes down from the church to this gallery; there are three windows on each side, that is to say, at that height which the church is higher than the gallery, and as much as the body of the church extends, so much is excavated below, and to as much depth as there is height above the floor of the church. And if one looks through each of these windows which is opposite the sun, one sees the tomb at the right of the high altar. In the centre of the body of the church is the sip of a door like a trap door, it is covered up with a large stone, like an altar stone, fitting very exactly in that door. They say that this is the entrance to the lower chamber, and that no one enters there, nor does it appear that that stone or door can be raised. This stone has a hole in the centre which pierces it through, its size is three palms.[1] All the pilgrims put their hands into this stone (which hardly

From Father Francisco Alvarez, *Narrative of the Portuguese Embassy to Abyssinia During the Years 1520–1527*. Trans. and edited by Lord Stanley of Alderley. (London: Hakluyt Society, 1881), pp. 122–126, 240–245.

1. *Palma*. Measure of four inches.

find room), and say that many miracles are done here. On the left hand side, when one goes from the principal door before the principal chapel, there is a tomb cut in the same rock as the church, which they say is made after the manner of the sepulchre of Christ in Jerusalem. So they hold it in honour and veneration and reverence, as becomes the memory to which it belongs. In the other part of the church are two great images carved in the wall itself, which remain in a manner separated from it. They showed me these things as though I should be amazed at seeing them. One of the images is of St. Peter, the other of St. John: they give them great reverence. This church also possesses a separate chapel, almost a church; this has naves on six supports, that is, three on each side. This is very well constructed, with much elegance: the middle nave is raised and arched, its windows and doorways are well wrought, that is, the principal door, and one side door, for the other gives entrance to the principal church. This chapel is as broad as it is long, that is, fifty-two spans broad, and as many in length. It has another chapel, very high and small, like a pinnacle, with many windows in the same height: these also have as much width as length, that is, twelve spans. This church and its chapels have their altars and canopies, with their supports, made of the rock itself, it also has a very great circuit cut out of the rock. The circuit is on the same level as the church itself, and is all square: all its walls are pierced with holes the size of the mouth of a barrel. All these holes are stopped up with small stones, and they say that they arc tombs, and such they appear to be, because some have been stopped up since a long time, others recently. The entrance of this circuit is below the rock, at a great depth and measure of thirteen spans, all artificially excavated, or worked with the pick-axe, for here there is no digging, because the stone is hard, and for great walls like the Porto in Portugal.

The church of St. Savior stands alone, cut out of a rock; it is very large. Its interior is two hundred spans in length, and a hundred and twenty in width. It has five naves, in each one seven square columns; the large one has four, and the walls of the church have as much. The columns are very well worked, with arches which hang down a span below the vaulted roof. The vaulted roofs are very well worked, and of great height, principally the centre one, which is very high. It is of a handsome height; most of the ends are lower, all in proportion. In the principal height of these naves there is much tracery, such as . . . , or keystones, or roses, which they put on the vaults, on which they make roses and other graceful works. On the sides it has very pretty windows, with much tracery, long and narrow in the middle. Within and without, these are long, like the loopholes of a wall, narrow without and wide within; these are wide both within and without, and narrow in the middle, with arches and tracery. The principal chapel is very high, and the canopy over the altar is very high, with a support at each corner. All this is made from the rock itself. In the other naves they do not deck the chapels and altars with canopies like the high altar in its grandeur. The principal door has at each side many and large buttresses, and the door commences with very large arches, and goes on narrowing with other arches until they reach a small door, which is not more than nine spans high and four and a half wide. The side doors are in this manner, only that they do not commence with so much width, and they end with the width of the principal door. On the outside part of this church are seven buttresses with arches, which are twelve palms distant from the wall of the church, and from buttress to buttress an arch, and above the church, on these arches, a vault constructed in such manner that if it were built of pieces and soft stone it could not be straighter nor better constructed, nor with more work about it. These arches outside may be about the height of two lances. There is not any variation in the whole of this rock in which this church stands; it all looks like one block of marble. The court or cloister which the church has round it is all worked with the same stone. It is sixty palms wide at each end, and in front of the principal church door quite a hundred palms. Above this church, where it should be roofed, there are on each side nine large arches, like cloisters, which descend from the top to the bottom, to the tombs along the sides, as in the other church. The entrance to this church is by a descent through the rock itself, eighty steps cut artificially in the stone, of a width that ten men can go side by side, and of the height of a lance or more. This entrance has four holes above, which give light to the passage above the edges. From this rock to the enclosure of the church is like a field; there are many houses, and they sow barley in it.

On the 4th day of the month of January Prester John sent to tell us to order our tents, both that of the church and our own, to be taken from this place to a distance of about half a league, where they had made a large tank of water, in which they were to be baptized on the day of the Kings, because on that day it is their custom to be baptized every year, as that was the day on which Christ was baptized. We took thither a small tent for resting in and the church tent. The next day, which was the vigil of the day of the Kings, the Prester sent to call us, and we saw the enclosure where the tank was. The enclosure was a fence, and very large, in a plain. He sent to ask us if we intended to be baptized. I replied that it was not our custom to be baptized more than once, when we were little. Some said, principally the ambassador, that we would do what His Highness commanded. When they perceived that, they came back again with another message to me, asking what I said as to being baptized. I answered that I had been already baptized, and should not be so again. They still sent word that if we did not wish to be baptized in their tank, they would send us water to our tent. To this the ambassador replied that it should be as His Highness ordered. The Franks and our people had arranged to give a representation of the Kings, and they sent to tell him of it. A message came that it pleased him, and so they got ready for it, and they made it in the inclosure and plain close to the King's tent, which was pitched close to the tank. They gave the representation, and it was not esteemed, nor hardly looked at, and so it was a cold affair. Now that it was night they told us to go to our tent, which was not far off. In all this night till dawn a great number of priests never ceased chaunting over the said tank, saying that they were blessing the water, and about midnight, a little earlier or later, they began the baptism. They say, and I believe that such is the truth, that the first person baptized is the Prester, and after him the Abima, and after him the Queen, the wife of the Prester. They say that these three persons wear cloths over their nakedness, and that all the others were as their mothers bore them. When it was almost the hour of sunrise, and the baptism in fullest force, the Prester sent to call me to see the said baptism. I went and remained there till the hour of tierce, seeing how they were baptized; they placed me at one end of the tank, with my face towards Prester

John, and they baptize in this manner.

The tank is large, the bottom of it in the earth, and it is cut very straight in the earth, and well squared; it is lined with planks, and over the planks waxed cotton cloth is spread. The water came from a rivulet through a conduit, like those to irrigate gardens, and it fell into the tank through a cane, at the end of which was a bag that was full; because they strain the water which falls into the tank; and it was no longer running when I saw it: the tank was full of blessed water, as they said, and they told me that it contained oil. This tank had five or six steps at one end, and about three fathoms in front of these steps was the dais of Prester John, on which he sat. He had before him a curtain of blue tafetan, with an opening of about a span, by which those who were baptized saw him, because he was with his face to the tank. In the tank stood the old priest, the master of the Prester, who was with me Christmas night, and he was naked as when his mother bore him (and quite dead of cold, because it was a very sharp frost), standing in the water up to his shoulders or thereabouts, for so deep was the tank, that those who were to be baptized entered by the steps, naked, with their backs to the Prester, and when they came out again they showed him their fronts, the women as well as the men. When they came to the said priest, he put his hands on their head, and put it three times under the water, saying in his language: "In name of the Father, of the Son, and of the Holy Spirit," he made the sign of the cross as a blessing, and they went away in peace. (The "I baptize thee," I heard him say it.) If they were little people they did not go down all the steps, and the priest approached them, and dipped them there. They placed me at the other end of the tank, with my face looking to the Prester, so that when he saw the backs, I saw the fronts, and the contrary way when they came out of the tank. After a great number of baptized persons had passed, he sent to call me to be near him; and so near that the Cabeata did not stir to hear what the Prester said, and to speak to the interpreter who was close to me: and he asked me what I thought of that office. I answered him that the things of God's service which were done in good faith and without evil deceit, and in His praise, were good, but such an office as this, there was none in our Church, rather it forbade us baptizing without necessity on that day, because on that day Christ was baptized, so that we should not think of saying of ourselves that we were baptized on the same day as Christ; also the Church does not order this sacrament to be given more than once. Afterwards he asked whether we had it written in books not to be baptized more than once. I replied, Yes, that we had, and that in the Creed, which was made at the Council of Pope Leon, with the three hundred and eighteen bishops, about which at times His Highness had questioned me, it was said: "Confiteor unum baptisma in remissionem peccatorum." Then they said to me that such was the truth, and so it was written in their books; but what were they to do with many who turned Moors and Jews after being Christians and then repented, and with others who did not believe well in baptism, what remedy would they have? I answered: For those who do not rightly believe, teaching and preaching would suffice for them, and if that did not profit, burn them as heretics. And so Christ spoke, and St. Mark wrote it: "Qui crediderit et baptizatus fuerit saivus erit, qui vero non crediderit condemnabitur." And as to those who turned Moors or Jews, and afterwards of their own free will recognised their error, and asked for mercy, the Abima would absolve them, with penances salutary for their souls, if he had powers for this, if not, let them go to the Pope of Rome, in whom are all the powers. And those who did not repent, they might take them and burn them, for such is the use in Frankland and the Church of Rome. To this there came the reply, that all this seemed to him good, but that his grandfather had ordained this baptism by the counsel of great priests, in order that so many souls should not be lost, and that it had been the custom until now; and he asked if the Pope would concede to the Abima to hold these powers, and how much it would cost him, and in how much time could they come. I answered him that the Pope desired nothing except to save souls, and that he would esteem it fortunate to send to him, the Abima, with such powers, and that it would only cost him the expenses of the journey, which would not be much, and also the letters of his powers: and that they could go and come through Portugal in three years: and by the road of Jerusalem, that I did not know it. To this there came no answer except that I might go in peace to say mass. I said it was no longer time for saying mass, that midday was long passed. So I went to dine with our Portuguese and the Franks.

This tank was all closed in and covered over with coloured tent cloths, so well that more could not be said, and so well arranged, with so many oranges and lemons, and boughs suspended and so well disposed, that the boughs, oranges, and lemons appeared to have grown there, and that it was a well ordered garden. The large tent which was over the tank was long and . . . and above covered with red and blue crosses of the fashion of the crosses of the order of Christ. This day, later in the afternoon, Prester John sent to call the ambassador and all his company. The baptism was already ended, and His Highness was still within his curtain where I left him. We entered there, and he at once asked the ambassador what he thought of it. He replied that it was very good, although we had not got such a custom. The water was then running into the tank, and he asked if there were here Portuguese who could swim. At once two jumped into the tank, and swam and dived as much as the tank allowed of. He enjoyed greatly, as he showed by his looks, seeing them swim and dive. After this he desired us to go outside and go to one end of the enclosure or circuit; and here he ordered a banquet to be made for us of bread and wine (according to their custom and the use of the country), and he desired us to raise our church tent and the tent we were lodging in, because he wished to return to his quarters, and that we should go in front of him because he was ordering his horsemen to skirmish in the manner in which they fight with the Moors in the field. So we went in front of him, looking at the said skirmish. They began, but soon there came such heavy rain that it did not allow them to carry out the skirmish which they had begun well.

10. LEO AFRICANUS

THE WESTERN SUDAN IN THE SIXTEENTH CENTURY. 1526.

*Al-Hassan ibn Muhammad al-Wizaz al-Fasi was an Andalusian Moor born in 1493
of wealthy parents. The family was driven from Spain and settled in Fez, from which
Al-Hassan made numerous journeys throughout North Africa and the Western
Sudan as judge, clerk, merchant, and diplomat. In 1518 he was captured by
Christian corsairs off Tunisia, taken to Rome, and baptized Giovanni Lioni, from
which the more popular* Leo Africanus *was derived. His famous* The History and
Description of Africa and the Notable Things Therein Contained, *which he wrote in
Italian, was completed in 1526. The manuscript was published in 1550 in Ramusio's
collection entitled* Voyages and Travels. *An English translation was published in
London in 1600. Al-Hassan's description is the most authoritative one of the
Western Sudan between the writing of Ibn Battuta and the accounts of Heinrich
Barth, the great mid-nineteenth-century Anglo-German explorer of the Bilad al-
Sudan.*

A DESCRIPTION OF THE KINGDOME OF GUALATA [WALATA]

This region in regarde of others is very small: for it containeth onely three great
villages, with certaine granges and fields of dates. From Nun it is distant southward
about three hundred, from Tombuto [Timbuktu] northward fiue hundred, and from
the Ocean sea about two hundred miles. In this region the people of Libya, while
they were lords of the land of Negros, ordained their chiefe princely seate: and then
great store of Barbarie-merchants frequented Gualata: but afterward in the raigne of
the mighty and rich prince *Heli*, the said merchants leauing Gualata, began to resort
vnto Tombuto and Gago, [Gao] which was the occasion that the region of Gualata
grew extreme beggerly. The language of this region is called Sungai, [Songhai] and
the inhabitants are blacke people, and most friendly vnto strangers. In my time this
region was conquered by the king of Tombuto, and the prince thereof fled into the
deserts, whereof the king of Tombuto hauing intelligence, and fearing least the
prince would return with all the people of the deserts, graunted him peace, conditionally that he should pay a great yeerely tribute vnto him, and so the said prince
hath remained tiributarie to the king of Tombuto vntill this present. The people
agree in manners and fashions with the inhabitants of the next desert. Here groweth
some quantitie of Mil-seed, and great store of a round & white kind of pulse, the
like whereof I neuer saw in Europe; but flesh is extreme scarce among them. Both
the men & the women do so couer their heads, that al their countenance is almost
hidden. Here is no forme of a common wealth, nor yet any gouernours or iudges,
but the people lead a most miserable life.

From Leo Africanus, *The History and Description of, Africa and the Notable Things Therein Contained*,
trans. from the Italian by John Pory (1600) and edited by Robert Brown (London, 1896), pp. 821,
823–827, 829–830, 832–834.

OF THE KINGDOME OF MELLI [MALI]

This region extending it selfe almost three hundred miles along the side of a riuer which falleth into Niger, bordereth northward vpon the region last described, southward vpon certaine deserts and drie mountaines, westward vpon huge woods and forrests stretching to the Ocean sea shore, and eastward vpon the territorie of Gago. In this kingdome there is a large and ample village containing to the number of sixe thousand or mo families, and called Melli, whereof the whole kingdome is so named. And here the king hath his place of residence. The region it selfe yeeldeth great abundance of corne, flesh, and cotton. Heere are many artificers and merchants in all places: and yet the king honourably entertaineth all strangers. The inhabitants are rich, and haue plentie of wares. Heere are great store of temples, priests, and professours, which professours read their lectures onely in the temples, bicause they haue no colleges at all. The people of this region excell all other Negros in witte, ciuilitie, and industry; and were the first that embraced the law of Mahumet, [Muhammad] at the same time when the vncle of *Ioseph* the king of Maroco [Yusuf ibn Tashufin] was their prince, and the gouernment remained for a while vnto his posteritie: at length *Izchia* [Askiya Muhammad, 1493–1538] subdued the prince of this region, and made him his tributarie, and so oppressed him with greeuous exactions, that he was scarce able to maintaine his family.

OF THE KINGDOME OF TOMBUTO [TIMBUKTU]

This name was in our times (as some thinke) imposed vpon this kingdome from the name of a certaine towne so called, which (they say) king *Mense Suleiman* [Mansa Sulayman, ed.] founded in the yeere of the Hegeira 610, [1213–1214] and it is situate within twelue miles of a certaine branch of Niger, all the houses whereof are now changed into cottages built of chalke, and couered with thatch. Howbeit there is a most stately temple to be seene, the wals whereof are made of stone and lime; and a princely palace also built by a most excellent workeman of Granada. Here are many shops of artificers, and merchants, and especially of such as weaue linnen and cotton cloth. And hither do the Barbarie merchants bring cloth of Europe. All the women of this region except maid-seruants go with their faces couered, and sell all necessarie victuals. The inhabitants, & especially strangers there residing, are exceeding rich, insomuch, that the king that now [in 1526] is, married both his daughters vnto two rich merchants.

Here are many wels, containing most sweete water; and so often as the riuer Niger ouerfloweth, they conueigh the water thereof by certaine sluces into the towne. Corne, cattle, milke, and butter this region yeeldeth in great abundance: but salt is verie scarce heere; for it is brought hither by land from Tegaza, which is fiue hundred miles distant. When I my selfe was here, I saw one camels loade of salt sold for 80 ducates. The rich king of Tombuto hath many plates and scepters of gold, some whereof weigh 1300. poundes: and he keepes a magnificent and well furnished court. When he trauelleth any whither he rideth vpon a camell, which is lead by some of his noblemen; and so he doth likewise when hee goeth to warfar, and all his souldiers ride vpon horses. Whosoeuer will speake vnto this king must first fall downe before his feete, & then taking vp earth must sprinkle it vpon his owne head & shoulders: which custom is ordinarily obserued by them that neuer saluted the king before, or come as ambassadors from other princes. He hath alwaies three thousand horsemen, and a great number of footmen that shoot poysoned arrowes, attending vpon him. They haue often skirmishes with those that refuse to pay tribute, and so many as they take, they sell vnto the merchants of Tombuto. Here are verie few horses bred, and the merchants and courtiers keepe certaine little nags which they vse to trauell vpon: but their best horses are brought out of Barbarie. And the king so soone as he heareth that any merchants are come to towne with horses, he commandeth a certaine number to be brought before him, and chusing the best horse for himselfe, he payeth a most liberall price for him. He so deadly hateth all Iewes, [Jews] that he will not admit any into his citie: and whatsoeuer Barbarie merchants he vnderstandeth haue any dealings with the Iewes, he presently causeth their goods to be confiscate. Here are great store of doctors, iudges, priests, and other learned men, that are bountifully maintained at the kings cost and charges. And hither are brought diuers manuscripts or written bookes out of Barbarie, which are sold for more money than any other merchandize. The coine of tombuto is of gold without any stampe or superscription: but in matters of smal value they vse certaine shels brought hither out of the kingdome of Persia, fower hundred of which shels are worth a ducate: and six peeces of their golden coine with two third parts weigh an ounce. The inhabitants are people of a gentle and cherefull disposition, and spend a great part of the night in singing and dancing through all the streets of the citie: they keep great store of men and women slaues, and their towne is much in danger of fire: at my second being there halfe the town almost was burnt in fiue howers space. Without the suburbs there are no gardens nor orchards at all.

OF THE TOWNE AND KINGDOME OF GAGO [GAO]

The great towne of Gago being vnwalled also, is distant southward of Tombuto almost fower hundred miles, and enclineth somewhat to the southeast. The houses thereof are but meane, except those wherein the king and his courtiers remaine. Here are exceeding rich merchants: and hither continually resort great store of Negros which buy cloth here brought out of Barbarie and Europe. This towne aboundeth with corne and flesh, but is much destitute of wine, trees, and fruits. Howbeit here is plentie of melons, citrons, and rice: here are many welles also containing most sweete and holesome water. Here is likewise a certaine place where slaues are to be sold, especially vpon such daies as the merchants vse to assemble; and a yoong slaue of fifteene yeeres age is sold for six ducates, and so are children sold also. The king of this region hath a certaine priuate palace wherein he maintaineth a great number of concubines and slaues, which are kept by eunuches: and for the guard of his owne person he keepeth a sufficient troupe of horsemen and footmen. Betweene the first gate of the palace and the inner part thereof, there is a place walled round about wherein the king himselfe decideth all his subiects controuersies: and albeit the king be in this function most diligent, and performeth all things thereto appertayning, yet hath he about him his counsellors & other officers, as namely his secretaries, treasurers, factors, and auditors. It is a woonder to see what plentie of Merchandize is dayly brought hither, and how costly and sumptuous all things be. Horses bought in Europe for ten ducates, are here sold againe for fortie and sometimes for fiftie ducates a piece. There is not any cloth of Europe so course, which will not here be sold for fower ducates an elle: and if it be anything fine they will giue fifteene ducates for an ell: and an ell of the scarlet of Venice or of Turkie-cloath is here worth thirtie ducates. A sword is here valued at three or fower crownes, and so likewise are spurs, bridles, with other like commodities, and spices also are sold at an high rate: but of al other commodities salt is most extremelie deere. The residue of this kingdome containeth nought but villages and hamlets inhabited by husbandmen and shepherds, who in winter couer their bodies with beasts skins; but in sommer they goe all naked saue their priuie members: and sometimes they weare vpon their feet certaine shooes made of camels leather. They are ignorant and rude people, and you shall scarce finde one learned man in the space of an hundred miles. They are continually burthened with grieuous exactions, so that they haue scarce any thing remaining to liue vpon.

OF THE PROUINCE OF CANO [KANO]

The great prouince of Cano stadeth eastward of the riuer Niger almost fiue hundred miles. The greatest part of the inhabitants dwelling in villages are some of them herdsmen and others husbandmen. Heere groweth abundance of corne, of rice, and of cotton. Also here are many deserts and wilde woodie mountaines containing many springs of water. In these woods growe plentie of wilde citrons and limons, which differ not much in taste from the best of all. In the midst of this prouince standeth a towne called by the same name, the walles and houses whereof are built for the most part of a kinde of chalke. The inhabitants are rich merchants and most ciuill people. Their king was in times past of great puissance, and had mighty troupes of horsemen at his command; but he hath since beene constrained to pay tribute vnto the kings of Zegzeg and Casena [Katsina, ed.]. Afterwarde *Ischia* the king of Tombuto faining friendship vnto the two foresaid kings trecherously slew them both. And then he waged warre against the king of Cano, whom after a long siege he tooke, and compelled him to marie one of his daughters, restoring him againe to his kingdome, conditionally that he should pay vnto him the third part of all his tribute: and the said king of Tombuto hath some of his courtiers perpetually residing at Cano for the receit thereof.

OF THE KINGDOME OF BORNO [BORNU]

The large prouince of Borno bordering westward vpon the prouince of Guangara [Wangara] and from thence extending eastward fiue hundred miles, is distant from the fountaine of Niger almost an hundred and fiftie miles, the south part thereof adioining vnto the desert of Set, and the north part vnto that desert which lieth towards Barca. The situation of this kingdome is very vneuen, some part thereof being mountainous, and the residue plaine. Vpon the plaines are sundry villages inhabited by rich merchants, and abounding with corne. The king of this region and all his followers dwell in a certain large village. The mountaines being inhabited by herdesmen and shepherds doe bring foorth mill and other graine altogether vnknowen to vs. The inhabitants in summer goe all naked saue their priuie members which they couer with a peece of leather: but al winter they are clad in skins, and haue beds of skins also. They embrace no religion at all, being neither Christians, Mahumetans, nor Iewes, nor of any other profession, but liuing after a brutish manner, and hauing wiues and children in common: and (as I vnderstood of a certaine merchant that abode a long time among them) they haue no proper names at all, but euery one is nicknamed according to his length, his fatnes, or some other qualitie. They haue a most puissant prince, being lineally descended from the Libyan people called Bardoa. Horsemen he hath in a continuall readiness to the number of three thousand, & an huge number of footmen; for al his subiects are so seruiceable and obedient vnto him, that whensoeuer he commandeth them, they wil arme themselues and follow him whither he pleaseth to conduct them. They paye vnto him none other tribute but the tithes of all their corne: neither hath this king any reuenues to maintaine his estate, but onely such spoiles as he getteth from his next enimes by often inuasions and assaults. He is at perpetuall emnitie with a certaine people inhabiting beyond the desert of Seu; who in times past marching with an huge armie of footemen ouer the said desert, wasted a great part of the kingdome of Borno. Whereupon the king of Borno sent for the merchants of Barbary, and willed them to bring him great store of horses: for in this countrey they vse to exchange horses for slaues, and to giue fifteene, and sometime twentie slaues for one horse. And by this meanes there were abundance of horses brought: howbeit the merchants were constrained to stay for their slaues till the king returned home conquerour with a great number of captiues, and satisfied his creditors for their horses. And oftentimes it falleth out that the merchants must stay three months togither, before the king returneth from the warres, but they are all that while maintained at the kings charges. Sometimes he bringeth not home slaues enough to satisfie the merchants: and otherwhiles they are constrained to awaite there a whole yeere togither; for the king maketh inuasions but euery yeere once, & that at one set and appointed time of the yeere. Yea I my selfe met with sundrie merchants heere, who despairing of the kings paiment, bicause they had trusted him an whole yeere, determined neuer to come thither with horses againe. And yet the king seemeth to be marueilous rich; for his spurres, his bridles, platters, dishes, pots, and other vessels wherein his meate and drinke are brought to the table, are all of pure golde: yea, and the chaines of his dogs and hounds are of golde also. Howbeit this king is extreamely couetous, for he had much rather pay his debts in slaues than in gold. In this kingdome are great multitudes of Negros and of other people, the names of whom (bicause I tarried heere but one moneth) I could not well note.

11. DUARTE BARBOSA

THE EAST COAST OF AFRICA AT THE BEGINNING OF THE SIXTEENTH CENTURY. 1540.

Duarte Barbosa was a Portuguese royal commercial agent whose account of the East African Coast concerns the years 1500 to 151& the beginning of the Portuguese period. He describes the towns of the coast before the major impact of Portuguese control and influence had altered their character and affected their prosperity.

SOFALA

Having passed the Little Vciques, for the Indies, at xviii leagues from them there is a river which is not very large, whereon is a town of the Moors called Sofala, close to which town the King of Portugal has a fort.[1] These Moors established themselves there a long time ago on account of the great trade in gold which they carry on with the Gentiles of the mainland: these speak somewhat of bad Arabic (garabia), and have got a king over them, who is at present subject to the King of Portugal. And the mode of their trade is that they come by sea in small barks which they call zanbucs (sambuk), from the kingdoms of Quiloa, and Mombaza, and Melindi; and they bring much cotton cloth of many colours, and white and blue, and some of silk; and grey, and red, and yellow beads, which come to the said kingdoms in other larger ships from the great kingdom of Cambay [India], which merchandise these Moors buy and collect from other Moors who bring them there, and they pay for them in gold by weight, and for a price which satisfies them; and the said Moors keep them and sell these cloths to the Gentiles of the kingdom of Benamatapa [Munhumutapa] who come there laden with gold, which gold they give in exchange for the before mentioned cloths without weighing, and so much in quantity that these Moors usually gain one hundred for one. They also collect a large quantity of ivory, which is found all round Sofala, which they likewise sell in the great kingdom of Cambay at five or six ducats[2] the hundred weight, and so also some amber, which these Moors of Sofala bring them from the Vciques. They are black men, and men of colour—some speak Arabic, and the rest make use of the language of the Gentiles of the country. They wrap themselves from the waist downwards with cloths of cotton and silk, and they wear other silk cloths above named, such as cloaks and wraps for the head, and some of them wear hoods of scarlet, and of other

From Duarte Barbosa, *A Description of the Coasts of East Africa and Malabar in the Beginning of the Sixteenth Century*, trans. by Henry E. J. Stanley (London: Hakluyt Society, 1866), pp. 4–15, 19–21.

1. Moors are usually defined as dark skinned Muslims from the Iberian Peninsula and the Maghrib, Morocco. Duarte Barbosa obviously applied this appellation to the Muslim Swahili peoples and Arab and Persian merchants of the East African coast (ed.).
2. A ducat was a gold coin of varying value (ed.).

coloured woollen stuffs and camelets, and of other silks. And their victuals are millet, and rice, and meat, and fish. In this river near to the sea there are many sea horses [hippopotamus] which go in the sea, and come out on land at times to feed. These have teeth like small elephants, and it is better ivory than that of the elephant, and whiter and harder, and of greater durability of colour. In the country all round Sofala there are many elephants, which are very large and wild, and the people of the country do not know how to tame them: there are also many lions, ounces, mountain panthers, wild asses, and many other animals. It is a country of plains and mountains, and well watered. The Moors have now recently begun to produce much fine cotton in this country, and they weave it into white stuff because they do not know how to dye it, or because they have not got any colours; and they take the blue or coloured stuffs of Cambay and unravel them, and again weave the threads with their white thread, and in this manner they make coloured stuffs, by means of which they get much gold.

KINGDOM OF BENAMATAPA [MUNHUMUTAPA]

On entering within this country of Sofala, there is the kingdom of Benamatapa, which is very large and peopled by Gentiles, whom the Moors call Cafers. These are brown men, who go bare, but covered from the waist downwards with coloured stuffs, or skins of wild animals; and the persons most in honour among them wear some of the tails of the skin behind them, which go trailing on the ground for state and show, and they make bounds and movements of their bodies, by which they make these tails wag on either side of them. They carry swords in scabbards of wood bound with gold or other metals, and they wear them on the left hand side as we do, in sashes of coloured stuffs, which they make for this purpose with four or five knots, and their tassels hanging down, like gentlemen; and in their hands azagayes, and others carry bows and arrows: it must be mentioned that the bows are of middle size, and the iron points of the arrows are very large and well wrought. They are men of war, and some of them are merchants: their women go naked as long as they are girls, only covering their middles with cotton cloths, and when they are married and have children, they wear other cloths over their breasts.

ZINBAOCH [ZIMBABWE]

Leaving Sofala for the interior of the country, at xv days journey from it, there is a large town of Gentiles, which is called Zinbaoch; and it has houses of wood and straw, in which town the King of Benamatapa frequently dwells, and from there to the city of Benamatapa there are six days journey, and the road goes from Sofala, inland, towards the Cape of Good Hope. And in the said Benamatapa, which is a very large town, the king is used to make his longest residence; and it is thence that the merchants bring to Sofala the gold which they sell to the Moors without weighing it, for coloured stuffs and beads of Cambay, which are much used and valued amongst them; and the people of this city of Benamatapa say that this gold comes from still further off towards the Cape of Good Hope, from another kingdom subject to this king of Benamatapa, who is a great lord, and holds many other kings as his subjects, and many other lands, which extend far inland, both towards the Cape of Good Hope and towards Mozambich. And in this town he is each day served with large presents, which the kings and lords, his subjects, send to him; and when they bring them, they carry them bareheaded through all the city, until they arrive at the palace, from whence the king sees them come from a window, and he orders them to be taken up from there, and the bearers do not see him, but only hear his words; and afterwards, he bids them call the persons who have brought these presents, and he dismisses them. This king constantly takes with him into the field a captain, whom they call Sono, with a great quantity of men-at-arms, and amongst them they bring six thousand women, who also bear arms and fight. With these forces he goes about sub. duing and pacifying whatever kings rise up or desire to revolt. The said king of Benamatapa sends, each year, many honourable persons throughout his kingdoms to all the towns and lordships, to give them new regulations, so that all may do them obeisance, which is in this manner: each one of the envoys comes to a town, and bids the people extinguish all the fires that there are in it; and after they have been put out, all the inhabitants go to this man who has been sent as commissary, to get fresh fire from him in sign of subjection and obedience, and, whoever should not do this is held as a rebel, and the king immediately sends the number of people that are necessary to destroy him, and these pass through all the towns at their expense: their rations are meat, rice, and oil of sesame.

RIVER ZUAMA [ZAMBEZI]

Leaving Sofala for Mozambich, at forty leagues from it, there is a very large river, which is called the Zuama; and it is said that it goes towards Benamatapa, and it extends more than 160 leagues. In the mouth of this river there is a town of the Moors, which has a king, and it is called Mongalo. Much gold comes from Benamatapa to this town of the Moors, by this river, which makes another branch which falls at Angos, where the Moors make use of boats (almadias), which are boats hollowed out from a single trunk, to bring the cloths and other merchandise from Angos, and to transport much gold and ivory.

ANGOY [ANGOCHE]

After passing this river of Zuama, at xi leagues from it, there is a town of the Moors on the sea coast, which is called Angoy, and has a king, and the Moors who live there are all merchants, and deal in gold, ivory, silk, and cotton stuffs, and beads of Cambay, the same as do those of Sofala. And the Moors bring these goods from Quiloa [Kilwa], and Monbaza [Mombasa], and Melynde [Malindi] in small vessels hidden from the Portuguese ships; and they carry from there a great quantity of ivory, and much gold. And in this town of Angos there are plenty of provisions of millet, rice, and some kinds of meat. These men are very brown and copper coloured; they go naked from the waist upwards, and from thence downwards, they wrap themselves with cloths of cotton and silk, and wear other cloths folded after the fashion of cloaks, and some wear caps and others hoods, worked with stuffs and silks; and they speak the language belonging to the country, which is that of the

Pagans, and some of them speak Arabic. These people are sometimes in obedience to the king of Portugal, and at times they throw it off, for they are a long way off from the Portuguese forts.

MOZAMBIQUE ISLAND

Having passed this town of Anguox, on the way to India, there are very near to the land three islands, one of which is inhabited by Moors, and is called Mozambique. It has a very good port, and all the Moors touch there who are sailing to Sofala, Zuama, or Anguox. Amongst these Moors there is a sheriff, who governs them, and does justice. These are of the language and customs of the Moors of Anguox, in which island the King of Portugal now holds a fort, and keeps the said Moors under his orders and government. At this island the Portuguese ships provide themselves with water and wood, fish and other kinds of provisions; and at this place they refit those ships which stand in need of repair. And from this island likewise the Portuguese fort in Sofala draws its supplies, both of Portuguese goods and of the produce of India, on account of the road being longer by the mainland.

Opposite this island there are many very large elephants and wild animals. The country is inhabited by Gentiles, brutish people who go naked and smeared all over with coloured clay, and their natural parts wrapped in a strip of blue cotton stuff, without any other covering; and they have their lips pierced with three holes in each lip, and in these holes they wear bones stuck in, and claws, and small stones, and other little things dangling from them.

ISLAND OF QUILOA [KILWA]

After passing this place and going towards India, there is another island close to the mainland, called Quiloa, in which there is a town of the Moors, built of handsome houses of stone and lime, and very lofty, with their windows like those of the Christians; in the same way it has streets, and these houses have got their terraces, and the wood worked in with the masonry, with plenty of gardens, in which there are many fruit trees and much water. This island has got a king over it, and from hence there is trade with Sofala with ships, which carry much gold, which is dispersed thence through all Arabia Felix, for henceforward all this country is thus named on account of the shore of the sea being peopled with many towns and cities of the Moors; and when the King of Portugal discovered this land, the Moors of Sofala, and Zuama, and Anguox, and Mozambique, were all under obedience to the King of Quiloa, who was a great king amongst them. And there is much gold in this town, because all the ships which go to Sofala touch at this island, both in going and coming back. These people are Moors, of a dusky colour, and some of them are black and some white; they are very well dressed with rich cloths of gold, and silk, and cotton, and the women also go very well dressed out with much gold and silver in chains and bracelets on their arms, and legs, and ears. The speech of these people is Arabic, and they have got books of the Alcoran, and honour greatly their prophet Muhamad. This King, for his great pride, and for not being willing to obey the King of Portugal, had this town taken from him by force, and in it they killed and captured many people, and the King fled from the island, in which the King of Portugal ordered a fortress to be built, and thus he holds under his command and government those who continued to dwell there.

ISLAND OF MOMBAZA [MOMBASA]

Passing Quiloa, and going along the coast of the said Arabia Felix towards India, close to the mainland there is another island, in which there is a city of the Moors, called Mombaza, very large and beautiful, and built of high and handsome houses of stone and whitewash, and with very good streets, in the manner of those of Quiloa. And it also had a king over it. The people are of dusky white, and brown complexions, and likewise the women, who are much adorned with silk and gold stuffs. It is a town of great trade in goods, and has a good port, where there are always many ships, both of those that sail for Sofala and those that come from Cambay and Melinde, and others which sail to the islands of Zanzibar, Manfia, and Penda, which will be spoken of further on. This Mombaza is a country well supplied with plenty of provisions, very fine sheep, which have round tails, and many cows, chickens, and very large goats, much rice and millet, and plenty of oranges, sweet and bitter, and lemons, cedrats, pomegranates, Indian figs, and all sorts of vegetables, and very good water. The inhabitants at times are at war with the people of the continent, and at other times at peace, and trade with them, and obtain much honey and wax, and ivory. This King, for his pride and unwillingness to obey the King of Portugal, lost his city, and the Portuguese took it from him by force, and the King fled, and they killed and made captives many of his people, and the country was ravaged, and much plunder was carried off from it of gold and silver, copper, ivory, rich stuffs of gold and silk, and much other valuable merchandize.

MELINDE [MALINDI]

After passing the city of Mombaza, at no great distance further on along the coast, there is a very handsome town on the mainland on the beach, called Melinde, and it is a town of the Moors, which has a king. And this town has fine houses of stone and whitewash, of several stories, with their windows and terraces, and good streets. The inhabitants are dusky and black, and go naked from the waist upwards, and from that downwards they cover themselves with cloths of cotton and silk, and others wear wraps like cloaks, and handsome caps on their heads. The trade is great which they carry on in cloth, gold, ivory, copper, quicksilver, and much other merchandise, with both Moors and Gentiles of the kingdom of Cambay, who come to their port with ships laden with cloth, which they buy in exchange for gold, ivory, and wax. Both parties find great profit in this. There are plenty of provisions in this town, of rice, millet, and some wheat, which is brought to them from Cambay, and plenty of fruit, for there are many gardens and orchards. There are here many of the large-tailed sheep, and of all other meats as above; there are also oranges, sweet and sour. This King and people have always been very friendly and obedient to the King of Portugal, and the Portuguese have always met with much friendship and good reception amongst them.

ISLAND OF SAN LORENZO

Opposite these places, in the sea above the Cape of the Currents, at a distance of eighty leagues, there is a very large island, which is called San Lorenzo, and which is peopled by Gentiles, and has in it some towns of Moors. This island has many kings both Moors and Gentiles. There is in it much meat, rice, and millet, and plenty of oranges and lemons, and there is much ginger in this country, which they do not make use of, except to eat it almost green. The inhabitants go naked, covering only their middles with cotton cloths. They do not navigate, nor does any one do so for them; they have got canoes for fishing on their coast. They are people of a dark complexion, and have a language of their own. They frequently are at war with one another, and their arms are azagayes, very sharp, with their points very well worked; they throw these in order to wound, and carry several of them in their hands. They are very well built and active men, and have a good method of wrestling. There is amongst them silver of inferior quality. Their principal food is roots, which they sow, and it is called yname,[3] and in the Indies of Spain it is called maize. The country is very beautiful and luxuriant in vegetation, and it has very large rivers. This island is in length from the part of Sofala and Melinde three hundred leagues, and to the mainland there are sixty leagues.

PENDA, MANFIA, AND ZANZIBAR

Between this island of San Lorenzo and the continent, not very far from it, are three islands, which are called one Manfia [Mafia], another Zanzibar, and the other Penda; these are inhabited by Moors; they are very fertile islands, with plenty of provisions, rice, millet, and flesh, and abundant oranges, lemons, and cedrats. All the mountains are full of them; they produce many sugar canes, but do not know how to make sugar. These islands have their kings. The inhabitants trade with the mainland with their provisions and fruits; they have small vessels, very loosely and badly made, without decks, and with single mast; all their planks are sewn together with cords of reed or matting, and the sails are of palm mats. They are very feeble people, with very few and despicable weapons. In these islands they live in great luxury, and abundance; they dress in very good cloths of silk and cotton, which they buy in Mombaza of the merchants from Cambay [India], who reside there. Their wives adorn themselves with many jewels of gold from Sofala, and silver, in chains, ear-rings, bracelets, and ankle rings, and are dressed in silk stuffs: and they have many mosques, and hold the Alcoran [Quran]of Mahomed.

PATE

After passing Melinde, and going towards India, they cross the Gulf (because the coast trends inwards) towards the Red Sea, and on the coast there is a town called Pate, and further on there is another town of the Moors, called Lamon; all these

---

3. Root in the form of a gourd, composed of two bulbs, which grow one above the other. the larger one below the smaller one. It is cut into slices and eaten instead of bread. It throws out very large leaves, without fruit. . . .

trade with the Gentiles of the country, and they are strongly-walled towns of stone and whitewash, because at times they have to fight with the Gentiles, who live in the interior of the country.

BRAVA

Leaving these places, further on along the coast is a town of the Moors, well walled, and built of good houses of stone and whitewash, which is called Brava. It has not got a king; it is governed by its elders, they being honoured and respectable persons. It is a place of trade, which has already been destroyed by the Portuguese, with great slaughter of the inhabitants, of whom many were made captives, and great riches in gold, silver, and other merchandise were taken here, and those who escaped fled into the country, and after the place was destroyed they returned to people it.

KINGDOM OF PRESTER JOHN

Leaving these towns of the Moors and entering into the interior of the country, the great kingdom of Prester John is to be found, whom the Moors of Arabia call Abexi;[4] this kingdom is very large, and peopled with many cities, towns, and villages, with many inhabitants: and it has many kings subject to it and tributary kings. And in their country there are many who live in the fields and mountains, like Beduins: they are black men, very well made: they have many horses, and make use of them, and are good riders, and there are great sportsmen and hunters amongst them. Their provisions are flesh of all kinds, milk, butter, and wheaten bread, and of these things there is a great abundance. Their clothes are of hides because the country is wanting in cloths; and there is a law amongst them by which certain families and ranks of persons may wear cloths, and the rest of the people may wear only hides well dressed and tanned. Amongst them there are men and women who have never drunk water, but only milk, which greatly supports them, and quenches the thirst, on account of its being more healthy and substantial, and there is great abundance of it in the country. These people are Christians of the doctrine of the blessed Saint Bartholomew, as they say; and their baptism is in three kinds, of blood, fire, and water: that is to say, that they circumcise themselves, and mark themselves on the temples and forehead with fire, and also in water, like the Catholic Christians. Many of them are deficient in our true faith, because the country is very large, and whilst in the principal city of Babel Melech, where Prester John resides, they may be Christians, in many other distant parts they live in error and without being taught; so that they are only Christians in name.

BABEL MELECH

In the interior of this country is the great city of Babel Melech, where Prester John holds his residence. The Moors call him the great King of the Habeshys: he is

4. Habeshy, Abyssinian.

Christian, and lord of many extensive countries and numerous people, with whom he makes subject many great kings. He is very rich, and possesses more gold than any other prince. This Prester John holds a very large court, and he keeps many men at arms continually in his pay, whom he takes about with him. He goes out very rarely from his dwelling; many kings and great lords come to visit him. In this city a great feast takes place in the month of August, for which so many kings and nobles come together, and so many people that they are innumerable: and on this day of the feast in August they take an image out of a church, which is believed to be that of Our Lady, or that of St. Bartholomew, which image is of gold and of the size of a man; its eyes are of very large and beautiful rubies of great value, and the whole of it is adorned with many precious stones of much value, and placing it in a great chariot of gold, they carry it in procession with very great veneration and ceremony, and Prester John goes in front of this car in another gold car, very richly dressed in cloth of gold with much jewellery. And they begin to go out thus in the morning, and go in procession through all the city with much music of all sorts of instruments, until the evening, when they go home. And so many people throng to this procession, that in order to arrive at the car of the image many die of being squeezed and suffocated; and those who die in this wise are held as saints and martyrs; and many old men and old women go with a good will to die in this manner.

12. ANDREW BATTELL

THE JAGA. 1568.

Andrew Battell (1565–1614) was an English sailor who was seized from a British privateer operating in South American waters and imprisoned at Luanda by the Portuguese authorities. After numerous adventures, Battell lived with the Jaga for twenty-one months; his account of these mysterious and warlike people is the most authoritative. As is the case of the Funj of the Sudan, the origins of the Jaga are unknown, if they existed at all. In one of the more interesting debates among Africanists, Joseph Miller published an article in 1973 suggesting the Jaga never existed. Later John K. Thornton refuted Miller on this question, declaring that not only had the Jaga existed, but they were just as Battell described them. Miller's

From *The Strange Adventures of Andrew Battell of Leigh in Angola and the Adjoining Regions*, edited by E. G. Ravenstein and reprinted from *Purchas His Pilgrimes* (London: Hakluyt Society, 1901), pp. 19–35. Reprinted by permission of Cambridge University Press on behalf of The Hakluyt Society. Bracketed material in this selection was supplied by E. G. Ravensicin. See Joseph C. Miller, "Requium for the 'Jaga,'" *Cahiers d'Études africaines*, 49 XIII-1, 1973, pp. 131–155. See also John K. Thornton, "A Resurrection for the Jaga," *Cahiers d'Études africaines,* 69–70, XVIII-I-2, 1979, pp. 223–227. Joseph C. Miller, "Thanatopsis," *Cahiers d'Études Africaines*, 69–70, XVIII-1-2, 1979, pp. 229–231. In support for Thornton's findings, see Anne Hilton, "The Jaga Reconsidered," *Journal of African History*, vol. II, no. 2, 1981, pp. 191–102. I am grateful to Joseph Miller for his generous assistance with the continuing sage of the Jaga.

rejoinder, "Thanatopsis," upheld his earlier argument; but later Anne Hilton, in "The Jaga Reconsidered," supported Thornton's "resurrection" of the Jaga. If indeed the Jaga were present in the Kongo in this period they probably had cultural connections with the Luba-Lunda peoples of the interior of Central Africa. In any event, according to Battell, they suddenly appeared in 1568, overran the kingdom of Kongo, and destroyed the capital, San Salvador. Originally, the Jaga were probably small in number, but like the Zulu in the nineteenth century, they rapidly assimilated conquered peoples. Their military superiority was irresistible, and they roamed widely, spreading terror from the Congo River to the Cunene River. A few military units settled and founded states on the Kwango, Cuanza, and Cunene Rivers.

In our second voyage, turning up along the coast, we came to the Morro, or cliff of Benguele,[1] which standeth in twelve degrees of southerly latitude. Here we saw a mighty camp on the south side of the river Cova.[2] And being desirous to know what they were, we went on shore with our boat; and presently there came a troop of five hundred men to the waterside. We asked them who they were. Then they told us that they were the Gagas, or Gindes, that came from Sierra de lion [Serra Leoa],[3] and passed through the city of Congo, and so travelled to the eastward of the great city of Angola, which is called Dongo.[4] The great Gaga, which is their general, came down to the waterside to see us, for he had never seen white men before- He asked wherefore we came. We told him that we came to trade upon the coast. Then he bade us welcome, and called us on shore with our commodities. We loaded our ship with slaves in seven days, and bought them so cheap that many did not cost one real, which were worth in the city [of Loanda] twelve milreis.[5]

AMONG THE JAGAS

Being ready to depart, the great Giaga staid us, and desired our boat to pass his men over the river Cova, for he determined to overrun the realm of Benguele, which was on the north side of the river Cova. So we went with him to his camp, which was very orderly, intrenched with piles of wood; we had houses provided for us that night, and many burthens [loads] of palm-wine, cows, goats and flour.

In the morning, before day, the general did strike his *gongo*, which is an instrument of war that soundeth like a bell, and presently made an oration with a loud voice, that all the camp might hear, that he would destroy the Benguelas, with such courageous and vehement speeches as were not to be looked for among the heathen

1. The Morro, or bluff, of Old Benguella, in lat. 10° 48' S., is a conspicuous headland, presenting a perpendicular cliff towards the sea, its summit being covered with cactus trees. Here Antonio Lopez Peixoto, a nephew of Paulo Dias, in 1587, had built a presidio, which was soon afterwards abandoned.

2. The river Cuvo (Kuvu) enters the sea in 10° 52' S.

3. *Sierra de lion*, or mountains of the lion, is of little help in identifying the origins of the Jaga, because there are many possible mountains of the lion. (ed).

4. Ndongo is the name of the kingdom of Ngola (Angola). Its old capital was at Pungu-a-Ndongo, a remarkable group of rocks, popularly known as Pedras Negras.

5. *Real* and *milreis* were Portuguese monetary units in use before 1911 after which they were superseded by the escudo (ed.).

people. And presently they were all in arms, and marched to the river side, where he had provided *Gingados*.[6] And being ready with our boat and *Gingados*, the general was fain to beat them back because of the credit who should be first. We carried over eighty men at once, and with our muskets we beat the enemy off, and landed, but many of them were slain. By twelve of the clock all the Gagas were over.

Then the general commanded all his drums, *tavales*,[7] *petes*, *pongos* and all his instruments of warlike music to strike up, and gave the onset, which was a bloody day for the Benguelas. These Benguelas presently broke, and turned their backs, and a very great number of them were slain, and were taken captives, man, woman and child. The prince, Hombiang-gymbe, was slain, which was ruler of this country, and more than one hundred of his chief lords, and their heads presented and thrown at the feet of the great Gaga. The men, women and children that were brought in captive alive, and the dead corpses that were brought to be eaten, were strange to behold. For these Gagas are the greatest cannibals and man-eaters that be in the world, for they feed chiefly upon man's flesh [notwithstanding of their] having all the cattle of that country.

They settled themselves in this country and took the spoil of it. We had great trade with these Gagas, five months, and gained greatly by them. These Gagas were not contented to stay in this place of Benguela, although they lacked almost nothing. For they had great store of cattle and wheat, and many other commodities; but they lacked wine, for in these parts there are no palm-trees.

After the five months were expired they marched toward the province of Bambala,[8] to a great lord that is called Calicansamba, whose country is five days up into the land. In these five months' space we made three voyages to the city of San Paul, and coming the fourth time we found them not.

MARCH INTO THE INTERIOR

Being loth to return without trade, we determined to go up into the land after them. So we went fifty on shore, and left our ship riding in the Bay of Benguela to stay for us. And marching two days up into the country we came to a great lord which is called Mofarigosat; and coming to his first town we found it burnt to the ground, for the Gagas had passed and taken the spoil. To this lord we sent a negro which we had bought of the Gagas, and [who] lived with us, and bid him say that he was one of the great Gaga's men, and that he was left to carry us to the camp. This lord bade us welcome for fear of the great Gaga, but he delayed the time, and

6."Gingado," elsewhere spelt "lergado," is evidently a misprint for *Jangada*, a Portuguese word meaning "raft." Such a raft is called *Mbimba*, and is made of the wood of the *bimba*, which is identical with the *Ambaj* of the Nile, and grows abundantly on the swampy banks of the rivers. Battell himself, at a critical point of his career, built himself such a *jangada*.

7. *Tavale*. Mr. Dennet suggests that *tavale* corresponds to the *libala* of Loango, a word derived from the Portuguese *taboa* (table), for the instrument of this name consists of a board supported by two sticks of wood, and kept in its place by wooden pegs driven into the ground. The player beats this board with his two index fingers. A. R. Neves, *Mem. da Epediçao a Cassange*, p. 110, calls *tabalha* a drum, which is beaten to make known the death of a Jaga Cassange.

8. Mbala or Embala merely means town or village. . . .

would not let us pass till the Gaga was gone out of his country. This lord Mofarigosat, seeing that the Gagas were clear of him, began to palter with us, and would not let us go out of his land till we had gone to the wars with him, for he thought himself a mighty man having us with him. For in this place they never saw [a] white man before, nor guns. So we were forced to go with him, and destroyed all his enemies, and returned to his town again. Then we desired him that he would let us depart; but he denied us, without we would promise him to come again, and leave a white man with him in pawn.

LEFT AS AN HOSTAGE

The Portugals and Mulatos being desirous to get away from this place, determined to draw lots who should stay; but many of them would not agree to it. At last they consented together that it were fitter to leave me, because I was an Englishman, than any of themselves. Here I was fain to stay perforce. So they left me a musket, powder and shot, promising this lord, Mofarigosat, that within two months they would come again and bring a hundred men to help him in his wars, and to trade with him. But all was to shift themselves away, for they feared that he would have taken us all captives. Here I remained with this lord till the two months were expired, and was hardly used, because the Portugals came not according to promise.

The chief men of this town would have put me to death, and stripped me naked, and were ready to cut off mine head. But the Lord of the town commanded them to stay longer, thinking that the Portugals would come. And after that I was let loose again, I went from one town to another, shifting for myself within the liberties of the lord. And being in fear of my life among them I ran away, purposing to go to the camp of the Gagas.

HE JOINS THE JAGAS

And having travelled all that night, the next day I came to a great town which was called Cashil, which stood in a mighty overgrown thicket. Here I was carried into the town, to the lord Cashil. And all the town, great and small, came to wonder at me, for in this place there was never any white man seen. Here were some of the great Gaga's men, which I was glad to see, and went with these Gagas to Calicansamba, where the camp was.

This town of the lord Cashil is very great, and is so overgrown with *Olicondie* [baobab][9] trees, cedars and palms, that the streets are darkened with them. In the middle of the town there is an image, which is as big as a man, and standeth twelve

9. The baobab is indifferently called by Battell *alicunde, licondo, elicondi, olicandi, or alicunde,* all of which are corruptions of *nkondo,* by which name the tree is known in Congo. The Portuguese know this characteristic tree of the coast-land and the interior as *imbondeiro* (from *mbondo* in Kimbundu). Its inner bark yields a fibre known as *licomte,* is made into coarse cloth, and is also exported to Europe to be converted into paper. The wood is very light. The pulp of the fruit is refreshing, and was formerly esteemed as a remedy against fever and dysentery. The seeds are eaten. The shell (*macua*) is used to hold water (hence the popular name of Calabash tree). Ficalho distinguishes three species, viz., *Adansonia digitata,* Linn., the fruit of which is longish; *A. Subglobosa,* bearing a bell-shaped fruit; *A. Lageniformis,* yielding a fruit shaped like a cucumber. . . .

feet high; and at the foot of the image there is a circle of elephants' teeth, pitched into the ground. Upon these teeth stand great store of dead men's skulls, which are [were] killed in the wars, and offered to this image. They used to pour palm oil at his feet, and kill goats, and pour their blood at his feet. This image is called Quesango,[10] and the people have great belief in him, and swear by him; and do believe when they are sick that Quesango is offended with them. In many places of this town were little images, and over them great store of elephants' teeth piled.[11]

The streets of this town were paled with palm-canes, very orderly. Their houses were round like a hive, and, within, hanged with fine mats very curiously wrought. On the south-east end of the town was a mokiso [*mukishi*] which had more than three tons of elephants' teeth piled over him.

From this town of Cashil I travelled up into the country with the Gagas two days, and came to Calicansamba, where the great Gaga had his camp, and was welcome to him. Among the cannibal people I determined to live, hoping in God that they would travel so far to the westward that we should see the sea again; and so I might escape by some ship. These Gagas remained four months in this place, with great abundance and plenty of cattle, corn, wine, and oil, and great triumphing, drinking, dancing and banquetting, with man's flesh, which was a heavy spectacle to behold.

At the end of four months they marched towards the *Serras*, or mountains of Cashindcabar, which are mighty high, and have great copper mines, and they took the spoil all the way as they went. From thence they went to the river Longa,[12] and passed it, and settled themselves in the town of Calango,[13] and remained there five or six months. Then we arose and entered into the province of Tondo,[14] and came to the river Gonsa [Coanza],[15] and marched on the south side of the river to a lord that was called Makellacolonge, near to the great city of Dongo. Here we passed over mighty high mountains, and found it very cold.

Having spent sixteen months among these cannibals, they marched to the westward again, and came along the river Gonsa, or Gunza, to a lord that is called Shillambansa,[16] uncle to the King of Angola. We burnt his chief town, which was after their fashion very sumptuously builded. This place is very pleasant and fruitful. Here we found great store of wild peacocks,[17] flying up and down the trees, in as great abundance as other birds. The old lord Shillambansa was buried in the middle of the town, and had a hundred tame peacocks kept upon his grave, which peacocks he gave to his *Mokeso*, and they were called *Angello Mokeso*,[18] that is, the

10. Kizangu, in Kimbundu, means fetish. . . .
11. The so-called fetishes (from *feitiço*, a Portuguese word meaning sorcery) are not idols, but charms and amulets, generally known as *nkissi, nkishi,* or *mukisht.* . . .
12. The river Longa [Lungu] enters the sea in lat. 10° 20' S.
13. A soba Calungo is shown on the most recent maps as residing north of the river Longa.
14. Perhaps we ought to read *Tunda*, the bush, the East. . . .
15. The Gonsa or Gunza (Ngunza) of Battell is undoubtedly the Coanza. A river Ngunza enters the sea at Novo Redondo.
16. *Shila*, nasty; *mbanza*, towns.
17. According to Duarte López, the feathers of peacocks and of ostriches are used as a standard in battle. Hence, peacocks are reared within a fence and reserved for the king.
18. *Njilo* (in Kimbundu), bird; *mukishi*, a charm.

Devil's or Idol's Birds, and were accounted as holy things. He had great store of copper, cloth and many other things laid upon his grave, which is the order of that country.

From this place we marched to the westward, along the river Coanza, and came right against the *Serras* or mountains of Cambambe, or Serras de Prata.[19] . . . Here is the great fall of water, that falleth right down, and maketh a mighty noise that is heard thirty miles. We entered into the province of Casama,[20] and came to one of the greatest Lords, which was called Langere. He obeyed the great Gaga, and carried us to a Lord called Casoch,[21] which was a great warrior, for he had some seven years before overthrown the Portugals camp, and killed eight hundred Portugals and forty-thousand negroes, that were on the Portugals side. This Lord did stoutly withstand the Gagas, and had the first day a mighty battle, but had not the victory that day. So we made a sconce of trees after their fashion, and remained four months in the wars with them. I was so highly esteemed with the great Gaga, because I killed many negroes with my musket, that I had anything that I desired of him. He would also, when they went out to the wars, give charge to his men over me. By this means I have been often carried away in their arms, and saved my life. Here we were within three days' journey of Massangano, before mentioned, where the Portugals have a fort: and I sought means, and got to the Portugals again with merchant negroes that came to the camp to buy slaves.

MILITARY ORGANISATION OF THE JAGAS

There were in the camp of the Gagas twelve captains. The first, called Imbe Calandola, their general, a man of great courage. He warreth all by enchantment, and taketh the Devil's counsel in all his exploits. He is always making of sacrifices[21] to the Devil, and doth know many times what shall happen unto him. He believeth that he shall never die but in the wars. There is no image among them, but he useth certain ceremonies. He hath straight laws to his soldiers: for, those that are faint-hearted, and turn their backs to the enemy, are presently condemned and killed for cowards, and their bodies eaten.[22] He useth every night to make a warlike oration upon an high scaffold, which doth encourage his people.

It is the order of these people, wheresoever they pitch their camp, although they stay but one night in a place, to build their fort, with such wood or trees as the place

19. Cambambe (*Ka*, diminutive; *mbambi*, gazelle), a village on the north bank of the Coanza, below the falls formed by the rivet in forcing its way through the Serra de Prata. Silver, however, has never been found there (at least not in appreciable quantities), nor anywhere else in Angola or Congo. Still we are told that the King of Congo, in 1530, sent the wife of King Manuel two silver bracelets which he had received from one of his chiefs in Matamba, and that among the presents forwarded by Ngola Nbande, the King of Ndongo, to Paulo Dias in 1576, there were several silver bracelets, which the Regent of Portugal, Cardinal Henrique, had converted into a chalice, which he presented to the church at Belem. According to Capello and Ivens, silver ore is plentiful in Matamba, although they never saw any in loco.
20. Battell's Casama is the wide province of Kisama (Quiçama), to the south of the Coanza.
21. This Casoch (a misprint for Caloch) is the Cafuxe (Cafuche) of the Portuguese, who defeated Balthasar de Almeida on April 22, 1594. On August 10, 1603, the Portuguese, led by Manuel Cerveira Pereira, retrieved this disaster.
22. Human victims are still sacrificed by the diviner when consulting departed spirits.

yieldeth: so that the one part of them cutteth down trees and boughs, and the other part carrieth them, and buildeth a round circle with twelve gates.[23] So that every captain keepeth his gate. In the middle of the fort is the general's house, intrenched round about, and he hath many porters to keep the door. They build their houses very close together, and have their bows, arrows and darts standing without their doors; and when they give alarm, they are suddenly all out of the fort. Every company at their doors [gates?] keep very good watch in the night, playing upon their drums and *tavales*.

A RIVER OF GOLD

These Gagas told us of a river that is to the southward of the Bay of Vaccas,[24] that hath great store of gold: and that they gathered up great store of grains of gold upon the sand, which the fresh water driveth down in the time of rain. We found some of this gold in the handles of their hatchets, which they use to engrave with copper; and they called it copper also, and do not esteem it.

PALM WINE

These Gagas delight in no country, but where there is great store of Palmares, or groves of palms. For they delight greatly in the wine and in the fruit of the palm, which serveth to eat and to make oil. And they draw their wine contrary to the Imbondos.[25] These palm-trees are six or seven fathoms high, and have no leaves but in the top: and they have a device to go up to the top of the tree, and lay no hands on it, and they draw the wine in the top of the tree in a bottle.

But these Gagas cut the palm-trees down by the root, which lie ten days before they will give wine. And then they make a square hole in the top and heart of the tree, and take out of the hole every morning a quart, and at night a quart. So that every tree giveth two quarts of wine a day for the space of six and twenty days, and then it drieth up.

JAGA RAIDS

When they settle themselves in any country, they cut down as many palms as will serve them wine for a month: and then as many more, so that in a little time they spoil the country. They stay no longer in a place than it will afford them maintenance. And then in harvest-time they arise, and settle themselves in the fruitfullest place they can find; and do reap their enemy's corn, and take their cattle. For they will not sow, nor plant, nor bring up any cattle, more than they take by wars. When

23. Cavazzi gives a plan of a Jaga camp, or Kilombo. It is formed of a square stockade, having in its centre the quarters of the Commander-in-chief, within a triple hedge of thorns. Between the stockade, which has only a single gate, and the inner enclosure are the quarters of the six principal officers, including the Golambolo (*ngolo*, strength; *mbula*, a blow), or Lieutenant-General, the Tendala, or Commander of the Rear-guard, and the Mani Lumbo (*lumbu*, a stockade), or Engineer-in-chief.

24. Bahia das Vaccas, old name for Benguella Bay. . . .

25. The Imbondos are clearly the Nbundu of Angola, who draw the palm wine from the top, whilst the Jagas cut down the tree.

they come into any country that is strong, which they cannot the first day conquer, then their General buildeth his fort, and remaineth sometimes a month or two quiet. For he saith, it is as great wars to the inhabitants to see him settled in their country, as though he fought with them every day. So that many times the inhabitants come and assault him at his fort: and these Gagas defend themselves and flesh[26] them on for the space of two or three days. And when their General mindeth to give the onset, he will, in the night, put out some one thousand men: which do ambush themselves about a mile from their fort. Then in the morning the great Gaga goeth with all his strength out of the fort, as though he would take their town. The inhabitants coming near the fort to defend their country, being between them, the Gagas give the watchword with their drums, and then the ambushed men rise, so that very few escape. And that day their General overrunneth the country.

DRESS AND ORNAMENTS

The great Gaga Calando[27] hath his hair very long, embroidered with many knots of Banba[28] shells, which are very rich among them, and about his neck a collar of *masoes*,[29] which are also shells, that are found upon that coast, and are sold among them for the worth of twenty shillings a shell: and about his middle he weareth *landes*, which are beads made of the ostrich eggs.[30] He weareth a palmcloth about his middle, as fine as silk. His body is carved and cut with sundry works, and every day anointed with the fat of men. He weareth a piece of copper cross his nose,[31] two inches long, and in his ears also. His body is always painted red and white. He hath twenty or thirty wives, which follow him when he goeth abroad; and one of them carrieth his bows and arrows, and four of them carry his cups of drink after him. And when he drinketh they all kneel down, and clap their hands and sing.[32] Their women wear their hair with high frompes full of bamba [*mbamba*] shells, and are anointed with civet.[33] They pull out four of their teeth, two above and two below, for a bravery. And those that have not their teeth out are loathsome to them, and shall neither eat nor drink with them. They wear great store of beads about their necks, arms and legs; about their middles, silk cloths.

INFANTICIDE

The women are very fruitful, but they enjoy none of their children: for as soon as the woman is delivered of her child, it is presently buried quick [alive], so that

26. "Flesh" in the sense of encourage.
27. Calando should be Calandola.
28. Mbarnba, a whelk or trumpet-shell.
29. Mr. Dennet suggests *msose*, a turritella, popularly known as screw-shell.
30. No ostriches are met with in Angola, and as to beads made of ostrich eggs, I can give no explanation.
31. The practice of wearing such nose ornaments exists to the present day in Lunda, among the Bangala and other tribes.
32. Marginal note by Purchas: "They use this ceremony in Florida."
33. Civet-cats are numerous in this part of Africa.

there is not one child brought up in all this generation.[34] But when they take any town they keep the boys and girls of thirteen or fourteen years of age as their own children. But the men and women they kill and eat. These little boys they train up in the wars, and hang a collar about their necks for a disgrace, which is never taken off till he proveth himself a man, and bring his enemy's head to the General: and then it is taken off and he is a freeman, and is called Gonso or soldier.[35] This maketh them all desperate, and forward to be free, and counted men: and so they do increase. In all this camp there were but twelve natural Gagas that were their captains, and fourteen or fifteen women. For it is more than fifty years since they came from Serra de Lion, which was their native country. But their camp is sixteen thousand strong, and sometimes more.

HUMAN SACRIFICES[36]

When the great Gaga Calandola undertaketh any great enterprise against the inhabitants of any country, he maketh a sacrifice to the Devil, in the morning, before the sun riseth. He sitteth upon a stool, having upon each side of him a man-witch: then he hath forty or fifty women which stand round about him, holding in each hand a zevra [zebra][37] or wild horse's tail, wherewith they do flourish and sing. Behind them are great store of petes, ponges and drums, which always play. In the midst of them is a great fire; upon the fire an earthen pot with white powders, wherewith the menwitches do paint him on the forehead, temples, 'thwart the breast and belly, with long ceremonies and inchanting terms. Thus he continueth till sun is down. Then the witches bring his Casengula,[38] which is a weapon like a hatchet, and put it into his hand, and bid him be strong against his enemies: for his *mokiso* is with him. And presently there is a man-child brought, which forthwith he killeth. Then are four men brought before him; two whereof, as it happeneth, he presently striketh and killeth; the other two he commandeth to be killed without the fort.

Here I was by the men-witches ordered to go away, as I was a Christian, for then the Devil doth appear to them, as they say. And presently he commandeth five cows to be killed within the fort, and five without the fort: and likewise as many goats,

34. I am inclined to believe, from what we learn from Cavazzi and other missionaries, that only those children were killed which were born within the Kilombo. On the other hand, at the Court of the ferocious queen Jinga, we are told by Captain Foller, a Dutchman, that, on two days in 1648, 113 new-born infants born outside the camp were killed.

35. *Ngunza*, according to Cordeira da Matta, means all-powerful; according to Bentley a herald, who speaks on behalf of a chief.

36. Human sacrifices among the Jaga are even now [1900] of frequent occurrence. They are made at the installation of a Jaga, one year after his election (when the sacrifice and its accompanying banquet are intended to conciliate the spirit of Kinguri, the founder of the Dynasty), at his death, on the outbreak of war, etc. The ceremony witnessed by Battell was an act of divination. The soothsayer summons the spirit of Kinguri, who is supposed to foretell the results of any enterprise about to be undertaken. In 1567, the Jaga Ngonga Kahanga, of Shela, having been advised by his soothsayers that he would suffer defeat in a war he was about to enter upon against the Portuguese, declined the arbitration of the sword, and submitted voluntarily. The body of the victim is cooked with the flesh of a cow, a goat, a yellow dog, a cock and a pigeon, and this mess is devoured (ceremoniously) by the Jaga and his *makotas* (councillors).

37. The handle of this switch contains a potent medicine, which protects the owner against death.

38. Casengula, called Kissengula, was perhaps a trombash, for *sanguld* means to kill at a long range.

and as many dogs, and the blood of them is sprinkled in the fire, and their bodies are eaten with great feasting and triumph. And this is used many times by all the other captains of their army.

BURIAL OF THE DEAD

When they bury the dead they make a vault in the ground, and a seat for him to sit.[39] The dead hath his head newly embroidered, his body washed, and anointed with sweet powders. He hath all his best robes put on, and is brought between two men to his grave, and set in seat as though he were alive. He hath two of his wives set with him, with their arms broken, and then they cover over the vault on the top. The inhabitants when they die are buried after the same fashion, and have the most part of their goods buried with them. And every month there is a meeting of the kindred of the dead man, which mourn and sing doleful songs at his grave for the space of three days, and kill many goats, and pour their blood upon his grave, and palm-wine also; and use this ceremony as long as any of their kindred be alive.[40] But those that have no kindred think themselves unhappy men, because they have none to mourn for them when they die. These people are very kind one to another in their health; but in their sickness they do abhor one another, and will shun their company.

39. The Jagas are still buried sitting, and wives are sacrificed. In Ngois, likewise, the dead are occasionally buried in a sitting posture.

40. These feasts are intended to secure the goodwill of the deceased, so that he may not injure the living. Human beings are occasionally sacrificed, in addition to goats and fowls.

13. FILIPPO PIGAFETTA AND DUARTE LÓPEZ

PAULO DIAZ DE NOVAIS IN ANGOLA. 1571.

The kingdom of Ndongo was probably founded at the beginning of the sixteenth century. The king took the title of ngola. From 1519 on, the ngola sought to make contact with the Portuguese. In 1560 four Jesuit priests and a young nobleman, Paul Diaz de Novais, arrived at the capital of Kabasa. Diaz returned to Portugal in 1565 and sought to obtain a commercial monopoly of the silver mines that he believed were in the interior. He obtained a donatario, or land grant, from the Portuguese crown in 1571, allowing him to colonize Angola at his own expense and to receive land and a commercial monopoly. Diaz appeared off the island of Luanda with 400 men in February 1575. He moved into the interior in 1576 and began a long series of campaigns that culminated in a great victory in 1583 and the construction of the Fort of Masangano at the confluence of the Lukala and Cuanza. Diaz died in 1589.

From Filippo Pigafetta and Duarte López, *Description du royaume du congo et des Contrées Environonantes*, 1591, trans. and annotated by Willy Bal (Louvain: Éditions Nauwelaerts, 1963), pp. 39–41, 44. Trans. from the French by Nell Elizabeth Painter and Robert O. Collins. Reprinted by permission.

In the direction of the sea several lords are found who accord themselves the title of king but whose domains are tiny. There are not suitable ports on these coasts. Already many times we have made mention of the kingdom of Angola. That is why it is now time to talk of it in more detail. We have said that in the past a governor of the King of Congo ruled this territory. This governor proclaimed himself king long before the conversion of the king [of Congo] to Christianity. In this way he usurped absolute power in the whole area under his administration, and then in time he conquered other neighboring territories so that he has now become a great and rich prince, hardly less powerful than the King of Congo, to whom he pays or refuses tribute as he pleases.

It came about that King Joao II of Portugal implanted the Christian faith in the Congo and that the king of this land converted [to Christianity]. Since that time the Lord [King] of Angola has always been his friend and, so to speak, his vassal, sending him a present every year. The people trade with each other. With the permission of the King of Congo, the Portuguese traded with the people of Angola at the port of Luanda. Slaves were brought there and were traded for various sorts of merchandise, and all were sent to the island of Sao Tomé. In this way the trade of Luanda was linked with that which was carried on in the island. First the boats landed at São Tomé before going to Luanda. Because the commerce continually increased, they began to send boats from Lisbon expressly for Angola. A governor was sent there [in 1575]; his name was Paulo Diaz de Novais. The trade belonged to him because his ancestors had discovered its beginnings. The King of Portugal, Dom Sebastian, awarded him the right to conquer thirty-three leagues of coast from the mouth of the Cuanza toward the south and in the interior all that he could conquer entirely at his expense for himself and his heirs. Diaz left with many boats and began a prosperous trade in Angola, always directing it from the already-mentioned port of Luanda where the boats were unloaded. Little by little he penetrated into the interior and established himself in a village called Anzelle, one mile from the river Cuanza, for convenience and to get closer to his market in Angola. The traffic increased even more; the Portuguese as well as the Congolese freely brought the merchandise that they wanted to sell or trade to Cabaza, which is situated 150 miles from the sea and where the court of the Lord of Angola is to be found.

The Lord of Angola gave the order to massacre all the merchants and seize their wealth, on the pretext that they came to spy and invade his state. It is believed that in reality the Lord of Angola simply wanted to appropriate their goods, which were considerable, for himself. These people, whose business was trade, were merchants and had nothing to make war. The massacre took place the same year that King Sebastian suffered a defeat from the Berbers [1578].

Seeing this, Paulo Diaz took arms against the King of Angola. He assembled as many Portuguese as he could find in the region. With two canal barges and some other boats that were anchored in the Cuanza, he ascended the river, conquering both banks. By force of arms he subjugated many lords and rendered them vassals and friends.

Seeing that his vassals surrendered to Paulo Diaz, who was continually gaining ground, the King of Angola raised a great army to destroy the Portuguese. Then

Paulo Diaz asked for help from the King of Congo, who sent reinforcements of 60,000 men, led by one of his cousins, Dom Sebastian Manibamba, and a captain with 120 Portuguese soldiers who were in the region and whom he had hired for this campaign.

This army was to join the forces of Paulo Diaz in order to combat the King of Angola. When the army arrived at the river Bengo twelve miles from Luanda, the numerous embarkations caused the army to be late in coming. For this reason and because a good deal of time had been lost in trying to move so many men, the army ascended the river along the bank. Advancing in this way it encountered the troops of the King of Angola, whose mission was to prevent the Congolese penetration of the country. . . .

A few advances were made by each side. From the first battles the Congolese emerged victorious. In the combats that followed, the losses were equal on both sides. Already food had become short. Some men became sick and died. The army of the King of Congo dissolved as the soldiers returned to their homes.

Not being able to join the friendly army, Paulo Diaz marched at that moment. He passed the river and stopped at Lukala because this place, naturally fortified, could permit him to resist the King of Angola. Lukala is situated at the confluence of the Cuanza and the Lukala, 105 miles from the coast. A little upstream from the confluence, the two rivers are separated by just the distance of a shot of a harquebus and thus form a peninsula. At its end, where the two waterways meet there is a hill. Paulo Diaz occupied it and fortified it for more security. The place was not inhabited when he arrived. Now a small congregation of Portugueses has formed there.

From this lake called Lukala, which Paulo Diaz occupied, one can go down the river as far as the sea in small boats. By land there are 105 miles to cover and the way is not dangerous. Nor far from there are the mountains called Cambambe. An infinite quantity of silver is extracted from them.. Diaz is still trying to conquer these mountains because of the numberous silver mines. Thus they apply more force to repulse the Portuguese. Fighting takes place in other areas as well because the Portuguese cross the river and make continual incursions into the territory belonging to the King of Angola.

14. JOÃO DOS SANTOS

THE WAZIMBA. 1590.

"Ethiopia Oriental," by Father João dos Santos, is one of the most complete sources of written information on the peoples living in southeastern Africa in the late sixteenth century—Bantu, Arab, and Portuguese. Dos Santos resided at Sofala and traveled to the interior stations of Sena and Tete between 1586 and 1590, when the marauding Wazimba were sweeping through the region northward out of Central Africa.

Opposite the fort of Sena, on the other side of the river, live some Kaffirs, lords of those lands, good neighbours and friends of the Portuguese, and always most loyal to them.[1] It so happened at the time I was there that the Muzimba Kaffirs, of whom I previously made mention, who eat human flesh, invaded this territory and made war upon one of these friendly Kaffirs, and by force of arms took from him the kraal in which he resided and a great part of his land, besides which they killed and ate a number of his people. The Kaffir, seeing himself thus routed and his power destroyed, proceeded to Sena to lay his trouble before the captain, who was then André de Santiago, and to beg for assistance in driving out of his house the enemy who had taken possession of it. The captain, upon hearing his pitiful request, determined to assist him, both because he was very friendly to us and because he did not wish to have so near to Sena a neighbour as wicked as the Muzimba.

Therefore, having made all necessary preparations for this war, he set out, taking with him a great number of the Portuguese of Sena with their guns and two pieces of heavy cannon from the fort. On arriving at the place where the Muzimbas were, they found them within a strong double palisade of wood, with its ramparts and loopholes for arrows, surrounded by a very deep and wide trench, within which the enemy were most defiant. André de Santiago, seeing that the enterprise was much more formidable than he had anticipated and that he had brought with him but few men to attack so strong an enemy and his fortress, fixed his camp on the bank of a rivulet which ran by the place, and sent a message to the captain of Tete, Pedro Fernandes de Chaves, to come to his assistance with the Portuguese of Tete and as many Kaffir vassals of his fort as he could bring.

Pedro Fernandes de Chaves immediately prepared to go to the assistance of André de Santiago, and assembled more than a hundred men with their guns, Portuguese and half-castes, and the eleven vassal chiefs. They all crossed to the other side of the river and proceeded by land until they were near the place where the Muzimbas had fortified themselves. These had information of their approach, and greatly feared their arrival. For this reason they sent out spies secretly upon the road, that when they approached they might see them, and report concerning the men who were coming. And learning from these spies that the Portuguese were in front of the Kaffirs in palanquins and hammocks and not disposed in order of battle, they sallied out of their fortress by night secretly, without being heard by André de Santiago, and proceeded to conceal themselves in a dense thicket at about half a league's distance, through which the men of Tete would have to pass. When they were thus stationed the Portuguese came up nearly half a league in advance of the Kaffirs of their company, quite unsuspicious of what might befall them in the thicket. Just as they were entering it the Muzimbas fell upon them suddenly with such violence that in a short time they were all killed, not one surviving, and when they

From Friar João dos Santos. "Ethiopia Oriental," in George McCall Theal, *Records of South-Eastern Africa, Collected in Various Libraries and Archive Departments in Europe* (London, 1898), vol. VII, pp. 293–304.

1. Sena is located on the Zambezi River, in Mozambique (ed.).

were dead the Muzimbas cut off their legs and arms, which they carried away on their backs with all the baggage and arms they had brought with them, after which they returned secretly to their fortress. When the chiefs reached the thicket and found all the Portuguese and their captain dead, they immediately turned back from the place and retreated to Tete, where they related the lamentable event that had occurred.

At the time that preparations for this war were being made there was a friar of St. Dominic preaching at Tete, named Nicolau do Rosario, a native of Pedrãgdo, a man who had reached perfection in many virtues. The captain Pedro Fernandes and the Portuguese of Tete begged this friar to accompany them on the expedition, to receive confessions and administer the sacraments to those who required them. To this the father acceded, thinking that in doing so he was serving our Lord and showing friendship to the Portuguese, and therefore he accompanied them. In the ambush he was severely wounded, and seizing him yet alive the Muzimbas carried him away with them to put him to death more cruelly afterwards, which they did upon arriving at their fortress, where they bound him hand and foot to a tree and killed him with their arrows in the most cruel manner. This they did to him rather than to others because he was a priest and head of the Christians, as they called him, laying all the blame for the war upon him and saying that Christians did nothing without the leave and counsel of their cacis. And in this manner the father met his death with great constancy, never ceasing to preach in a loud voice and profess the faith of Christ, as I shall relate more in detail in another place.

These Zimbas, or Muzimbas, do not adore idols or recognise any God, but instead they venerate and honour their king, whom they regard as a divinity, and they say he is the greatest and best in the world. And the said king says of himself that he alone is god of the earth, for which reason if it rains when he does not wish it to do so, or is too hot, he shoots arrows at the sky for not obeying him; and although all these people eat human flesh, the king does not, to seem different from his vassals.

All these Kaffirs as a rule are tall, well proportioned, and very robust. The arms they carry are battle-axes, arrows, assagais, and large shields with which they entirely cover themselves. These shields are made of light wood covered with the skins of wild animals which they kill and eat. They are in the habit of eating the men they kill in war, and drinking out of their skulls, showing themselves in this boastful and ferocious. If any of the Kaffirs of their tribe fall ill or are severely wounded in war, to save themselves the trouble of tending them they kill and eat them. They are addicted to many other brutalities similar to these, which I leave for the sake of brevity.

After the Zimbas had put Father Nicolau to death they rested during the remainder of that sad day, and on the night that followed they celebrated their victory and success, playing upon many cornets and drums, and the next day at dawn they all sallied out of their fortress, the chief clothed in the chasuble that the father had brought with him to say mass, carrying the golden chalice in his left hand and an assagai in his right, all the other Zimbas carrying on their backs the limbs of the Portuguese, with the head of the captain of Tete on the point of a long lance, and beating a drum they had taken from him. In this manner, with loud shouts and cries they came within sight of André de Santiago and all the Portuguese who were with him, and showed them all these things. After this they retired within their fortress, saying that what they had done to the men of Tete who had come to help their enemies, they would do to them, and that it was the flesh of those men that they were about to eat.

André de Santiago, who was waiting for Pedro Fernandes de Chaves with much anxiety, and who knew nothing of what had taken place, was greatly shocked, as also were all the other Portuguese, at this most horrible and pitiful spectacle, for which reason they decided to retreat as soon as night came on. In carrying this decision into execution they were in so great a hurry to reach the other side of the river that they were heard by the Muzimbas, who sallied out of their fortress and falling upon them with great violence killed many of them on the bank of the river. Among the slain was André de Santiago, who died as the valiant man he was, because it being within his power to escape he did not do so, but remained fighting and defending his companions on the bank, where he killed a great number of the Muzimbas before he was killed by them.

Thus these robbers and fierce Muzimbas killed one hundred and thirty Portuguese and half-castes of Tete and Sena and the two captains of these forts. This they accomplished with very little loss on their side, with their usual cunning, as they always took the Portuguese unawares, when they were unable to fight. This took place in the year 1592.

Great sorrow was felt at the death of Father Nicolau, whom all looked upon as a saint, and for all the Portuguese who lost their lives in this most disastrous war, both because some of them were married and left wives and children at these rivers, and because the Zimbas were victorious, more insolent than before, and were within fortifications close to Sena, where with greater audacity they might in the future do much damage to the Portuguese who passed up and down these rivers with their merchandise. For these reasons Dom Pedro de Sousa, captain of Mozambique, determined to chastise these Zimbas, conquer them, and drive them from the vicinity of Sena. To do this he proceeded to the rivers of Cuama from Mozambique in the following year, 1593, accompanied by some soldiers from the said fortress, with whom he reached Sena.

After obtaining information of the condition of the Zimbas, he commanded all the necessary preparations to be made for this war, and assembled nearly two hundred Portuguese and fifteen hundred Kaffirs, with whom he crossed to the other side of the Zambesi and proceeded by land to the fortress of the Zimbas, where he formed a camp at the same place that André de Santiago had formed his. Then he commanded that the various pieces of artillery which he had taken with him for the purpose should be fired against the wall of the fortress, but this had no effect upon it, as it was made of large wood, strengthened within by a strong and wide rampart which the Zimbas had constructed with the earth from the trench.

Dom Pedro, seeing that his artillery had no effect upon the enemy's wall, determined to enter the fortress and take it by assault, and for this purpose he commanded part of the trench to be filled up, which was done with great difficulty and danger to our men, as the Zimbas from the top of the wall wounded and killed some of them with arrows. When this part of the trench was filled up, a number of men crossed over with axes in their hands to the foot of the palisade, which they began to cut down, but the Zimbas from the top of the wall poured so great a quantity of boiling fat and water upon them that nearly all were scalded and badly wounded, especially the naked Kaffirs, so that no one dared go near the palisade, because they were afraid of the boiling fat and through fear of certain iron hooks similar to long harpoons, which the Zimbas thrust through the loopholes in the wall and with which they wounded and caught hold of all who came near and pulled from within with such force that they drew them to the apertures, where they wounded them mortally. For this few the captain commanded all the men to be recalled to the camp to rest, and the remainder of that day was spent in tending the wounded and the scalded.

The following day the captain commanded a quantity of wood and branches of trees to be collected, with which huge wickerwork frames were made, as high as and higher than the enemy's palisade, and he commanded them to be placed in front of the wall and filled with earth that the soldiers might fight on them with their guns and the Zimbas would not dare to appear on the wall or be able to pour boiling fat upon the men cutting down the palisade. When this stratagem of war was almost in readiness, another peaceful or cowardly device was planned in the following manner. The war had lasted two months, for which reason the residents of these rivers, who were there rather by force than of their own free will, being away from their homes and trade, which is their profession, and not war, pretended to have received letters from their wives in Sena relating the danger they were in from a rebel Kaffir who they said was coming with a number of men to rob Sena, knowing that the Portuguese were absent, for which reason they ought immediately to return home. This false information was spread through the camp, and the residents of Sena went to the captain and begged him to abandon the siege of the Zimbas and attend to what was of greater importance as otherwise they would be compelled to return to their homes and leave him.

Dom Pedro, seeing their determination and believing the information said to be given in the letters to be true, abandoned the siege and commanded the men to pass by night to the other side of the river and return to Sena, but this retreat could not be effected with such secrecy as to be unknown to the Zimbas, who sallied out of their fortress with great cries, fell upon the camp, killed some men who were still there, and seized the greater part of the baggage and artillery, that had not been taken away.

With this defeat and disappointment the captain returned to Sena, and thence to Mozambique, without accomplishing what he desired; and the Zimba's position was improved and he became more insolent than before. Nevertheless he offered peace to the Portuguese of Sena, saying that he never wished to be at war with them, and always desired their friendship and commerce, but that the Portuguese had unjustly made war upon him, without his having done them any injury, and that he had killed them in just defence, as he was compelled to do. Peace was conceded to him, I fancy, on account of the benefit that would result from it to the Portuguese of this river. The affairs of the country were in this condition when I left it to proceed to Mozambique.

A Muzimba Kaffir of the tribe of which I spoke in the last chapter, who was lord of a little kraal and had a few vassals, but who was most ambitious of human honour, meditating upon the means by which he might become a great lord and renowned in the world, decided that for this purpose it would be expedient to sally out of his country with an armed force and destroy, rob, and eat every living thing that came in his way. This his diabolical intention he made known to his vassals and other Muzimbas of the same tribe, to whom his design did not appear objectionable, because as they are usually addicted to idleness, robbery, and cannibalism, by it they had an opportunity offered to them of satisfying their cruel and depraved inclination. Their course of action having been decided upon and arranged, they sallied forth from their country and commenced expending their fury upon their neighbours, and they traversed all the kingdoms of Kaffraria, proceeding constantly towards the east.

Through these lands they marched, destroying and plundering all they found, and devouring every living thing, not only men, women, and children, but cattle, dogs, cats, rats, snakes, and lizards, sparing none except Kaffirs who came to them and wished to accompany them on this expedition, whom they admitted into their army. In this manner they assembled more than fifteen thousand warriors, with whom they laid waste all the lands they traversed, so that they appeared to be a cruel scourge and punishment that God chose to send to Kaffraria.

Having reached the island of Kilwa, which is close to the mainland and peopled by Moors, they saw that they could not enter it because of the sea by which it was surrounded. They therefore formed a camp upon the mainland, opposite the island, and besieged it for several months, devouring all the animals and crops that the Moors possessed upon the mainland, so that nothing from it could reach the island.

Meantime a Moor of the said island, moved by greed and ambitious of honour, proceeded secretly one night to the mainland, where the Muzimbas were stationed, by a ford, well known to him, where one could cross at low tide. On reaching the camp, he informed the Kaffirs who met him that he came from the island and wished to speak to the chief captain of the army upon a matter of great importance. Being taken by them and presented to the captain, he said: "Powerful captain, you must know that I am a native of this land and a resident of the island of Kilwa that you are besieging, and I know for certain that very soon you will be lord of it and will punish the people for not recognising you as the great lord that you are, and obeying you as is right. I, knowing this, have come to offer you the obedience that is your due, and further I wish to lead you into the island of Kilwa with all your army, by the ford by which I have come, which is well known to me, upon condition that you will spare the lives of my relatives who are in the place and divide with me the spoils and riches which you seize in the island, and also that you will bestow upon me the lands there that I shall point out to you, as this is of little consequence to you and of great importance to me." The Zimba replied that he was well pleased, and that if he would lead him into the island with all his men, as he said he would do, he promised to perform what he desired.

Upon this all were disposed in order to cross the ford, and the Moor led them to it, going in front to show them the way. Thus they all reached the island after midnight, and seized the Moors who were asleep and unsuspicious of the treachery being enacted or of what was about to happen. The Muzimbas killed the greater number without any resistance, and the remainder they took prisoners and ate gradually while they remained there, so that they killed and ate more than three thousand Moors, men and women, among whom many were very beautiful and delicate; and they plundered the whole town of Kilwa, in which they found great spoils and riches. Of the Moors only those escaped who had time to flee to the thickets on the island, where they remained in hiding until the Muzimbas returned to the mainland, after which they went back to the town, which in former years was a most noble one, the residence of the kings of all that coast, and even at the present time the ruins of the vast and sumptuous mosques and dwelling-houses give proof of its former grandeur.

When the Muzimbas had nothing more to do in the island their captain sent for the Moor who had conducted them to it by the ford, who was yet alive with all his relatives, as the captain had commanded them to be guarded, not wishing any of them to be put to death as the others had been. When they were all assembled before him he turned to the Moor and said: "I do not wish, nor am I satisfied, that a creature as wicked as thou art should live any longer, as thou wert so cruel that for thy own interest thou deliveredst thy country and thy compatriots into the hands of their enemies." And turning to the Kaffirs he said: "Take this wicked man and all his family who are here present and bind them hand and foot and throw them into the sea to be eaten by the fishes, as it is not proper that any one belonging to so wicked a race should live, nor do I wish you to eat them, as their flesh must be poisonous." This command was forthwith carried into execution, a sentence which surely was not that of a barbarian such as this man was, but of a wise man, and which shows with what reason Alexander the Great said that he profited by the treachery of those who delivered cities to him, but that he hated the traitors.

When this war of Kilwa was thus concluded the Muzimba returned to the mainland by the same ford by which he had entered the island when he was guided by the Moor.

After Kilwa was destroyed, the Zimba continued his journey along the coast until he reached that part of the mainland which is opposite the island of Mombasa, where he fixed his camp on the shore and determined to enter the island as he had entered Kilwa, but he could not immediately do so, as at the same time four Turkish galleys from the straits of Mecca, of which I shall give more detailed information later on, had put in there. These Turks defended the entrance of the island against him and fought with him on many occasions, killing a number of men with their artillery fired from two galleys that they had stationed in the passage by which the Zimba wished to enter.

This contest was continued for several days, until it happened that Thomé de Sousa arrived from India with a powerful fleet to oppose these same galleys, and finding them in this strait he fought with them and captured them with all that they carried, taking the Turks who were in them prisoners, and also ravaged the island of

Mombasa. All this was accomplished in sight of the Muzimbas who were on the mainland, who marvelled much to see the wonders performed by the Portuguese, for which reason the Muzimba chief said that the Portuguese were the gods of the sea and he god of the land, and forthwith sent an ambassador to Thomé de Sousa to say that he was a friend of the Portuguese and did not wish to be at war with them, and that as they had completed their work with such honour he also wished to perform his, which had already occupied him a long time, and which was to enter the island and kill and eat every living thing he should find in it. This design he immediately carried into execution with the consent of the Portuguese, and entering the island he searched all the palm groves and thickets in it, where he found many Moors hiding, who had escaped from the town, of whom he killed and ate all he could seize. When this was done Thomé de Sousa with his fleet returned victorious to India, as I shall relate farther on, and the Zimba returned to the mainland and proceeded on his journey, marching with his army towards Melinde.

The king of Melinde was greatly alarmed by the intelligence he received of the approach of the Muzimbas, knowing the ruin they had caused in Kilwa and Mombasa; nevertheless he placed great confidence in the valour of Matheus Mendez de Vasconcellos, who was then captain of this coast, and was at the time in Melinde with only thirty Portuguese soldiers and merchants, who were prepared to defend the town until they died in combat. The Zimbas reached Melinde with great insolence and boastfulness, as men who had never feared any nation, and attacked the town with great fury. Although our soldiers killed many of them with their guns, some of them succeeded in entering at different parts of the wall, which was low, and were already almost masters of a rampart, while a fierce combat was raging on all sides. At this moment more than three thousand Kaffirs called Mosseguejos, friends of the king, came to the succour of Melinde. These Kaffirs, knowing how hard pressed their friend the king of Melinde was by the arrival of the Muzimbas, had come to succour and assist him.

These Mosseguejos are most valiant men, who love war, of whom I shall give more detailed information farther on.

Arriving then at this point of the combat, they attacked the Muzimbas in the rear with such courage and force that in a short time they assisted in defeating and putting them to flight. And as these Muzimbas were strangers and had committed so many barbarities and killed so great a number of people upon the roads and in the countries through which they had passed, the same was done to them in their flight, all that were found being put to death; only the chief and about one hundred men escaped, and these returned the same way they had come, keeping in one body, without again separating, until they were once more in their own country.

Thus was destroyed in the town of Melinde, by the help of the Mosseguejos, the host of Muzimbas that had sallied out of the land which extends along the river of Sena, and reached Melinde, which is a journey of about three hundred leagues, without encountering any resistance or finding any who could meet them in battle, but on the contrary the kraals and lands were abandoned when it was known that this cruel army of cannibals was about to pass through them.

What I have said here concerning the Kaffis who inhabit the interior appears to me sufficient for the present. And as we began by describing the peculiarities of the river of Luabo, we should follow the river Quilimane until we reach the shore of the sea, saying something of its inhabitants.

15. ABD-AL-RAHMAN AL-SADI

SONGHAY AND THE MOROCCAN INVASION. 1591.

Abd-al-Rahman al-Sadi (1569–c. 1655) belonged to a leading family in Timbuktu andwas a notary public in Djenné before being made Imam of Timbuktu. After 1629 he played an influential role in the affairs of the city. His Tarikh al-Sudan describes the origins of the Sonni dynasty of Songhay. The first ruler in this dynasty was Ali Kolon, who probably reigned late in the thirteenth century. The influence of Mali on Songhay fluctuated during succeeding generations until the Songhay empire was established under the fifteenth Sonni, Ali (1464–1492). Ali died mysteriously, and the throne of the Songhay was seized by one of Ali's generals, Muhammad Ture ibn Abu Bakr, a Soninke by origin, who took the title askiya. Ture consolidated Ali's conquests and became the greatest king of Songhay. He was eighty-five years old and blind when deposed in 1528; he died ten years later. The subsequent history of Songhay is marked by a series of fratricidal struggles that lasted until the coming of the Moroccans. In 1590 the Sadid Sultan of Morocco, Ahmad al-Mansur, sent an expeditionary force to the Sudan under Judar Pasha, consisting of 4,000 men. Judar defeated the Songhay army of Askiya Ishaq and occupied Timbuktu, but the Moroccans never were able to impose their control throughout the Sudan, which soon fell into anarchy and disorder.

THE ORIGINS OF THE SONNI

This is the story of the first Sonni, Ali Kolon. Employed in the service of the King of Mali, Ali and his brother, Salman-Nari, lived with this ruler. The two brothers were both sons of Za-Yasi Boi, and the name Salman, which was originally Sulayman, had been deformed by the barbarous language of the people of Mali.

The mother of Ali and the mother of Salman were two full sisters. Omma was the name of the mother of Ali Kolon; Fati was the name of the mother of Salman-Nari. Fati was the favorite wife of the father of the two princes. Despite many pregnancies, she never had any children, and as she no longer hoped to have any, she said to her husband, "Marry my sister Omma—perhaps she will give you the heir that I have not been able to produce."

Za-Yasi Boi followed his wife's counsel. He was not aware of the [Muslim] law

From Abderrahman Ben Abdahah Ben lmran Ben Amir Es-Sadi, *Tarikh es-Soudan*, trans. from the Arabic by O. Houdas (Paris, 1898), vol. II, pp. 9–17, 22–24, 121–123, 215–225, 256–261. Trans. from the French by Nell Elizabeth Painter and Robert O. Collins. Reprinted by permission of Centre Universitaire des Langues Orientales Vivantes.

forbidding the marriage of two sisters to the same husband. God willed that the two wives should become pregnant during the same night and equally that on the same night they each should give birth to a son. The two newborn children were placed on the ground in a dark room. Not until the next day were they washed, for custom dictated that when a child is born during the night, one must wait until the next day to wash him.

The first newborn child to be washed was Ali Kolon, and because of this fact he was considered the elder. The ablution of Salman-Nari followed and he was, for that reason, declared the junior.

When the two children were old enough to enter the service, the Sultan of Mali took them with him. At that time, in fact, these princes were his vassals, and the prevailing custom dictated that the sons of kings were compelled to serve their sovereign. (This custom continues to the present with all the sultans of the Sudan.) Some of these young men went back to their countries after having served for a certain time. On the other hand, some continued to stay with the sovereign until their death.

During the time that the two princes were at the court of the King of Mali, Ali Kolon would leave his residence from time to time to make a fruitful expedition, according to established custom, and would then return to his post. Ali Kolon, a very sensible man who was very intelligent and full of shrewdness and cunning, enlarged his circle of operations each day in order to get closer and closer to Songhay and to become acquainted with all the roads leading there. Then he conceived a plan to flee into this country and thus to make himself independent. Toward this end, he secretly prepared all the arms and provisions that he would need and hid them in places that he knew on the road to Songhay.

When he finished his preparations, Ali Kolon notified his brother and confided his secret designs to him. After having fortified their horses with choice feed so that they would not tire on the way, the two brothers left for Songhay. Upon being advised of their escape, the Sultan of Mali sent some men after the fugitives to kill them. Each time they were closely pressed, the two brothers turned around and fought their pursuers. In these battles, the fugitives always had the advantage, and they successfully regained their country without a single defeat.

When Ali Kolon had become king of the land of Songhay, he called himself Sonni and delivered his subjects from the yoke of the Sultan of Mali. After the death of Ali Kolon, his brother, Salman-Nari, succeeded him. Only during the reign of the great Kharijite tyrant, Sonni Ali, did the limits of the kingdom spread beyond the area of its capital. This prince gathered more troops and expended more energy than did those of his dynasty who had preceded him. He made expeditions and conquered provinces, and his fame spread to the east and to the west, as we will tell later on, if it pleases God. Ali may be considered the last king of his dynasty, for his son Abu Bakr Dao, who ascended the throne after his father's death, ruled only a short time before his power was torn from him by Askiya al-Hajj Muhammad.

THE KING OF MALI, MANSA KANKAN MUSA

Sultan Kankan Musa was the first of the kings of Mali to take over Songhay. A pious and equitable prince, his virtue and courage were unequaled by any other King of Mali. He made the pilgrimage to the Holy Dwelling of God [Mecca] in the early years of the ninth century of the hijra, but God knows the exact date [1324–1325] better than anyone else.

The prince had with him an immense cortege and a considerable force of 60,000 men. Each time he mounted a horse, he was preceded by 500 slaves, each carrying a rod of gold worth 500 mitqals of gold [weighing about 6 pounds].

Kankan Musa set out toward Walata, in Awkar, and arrived at the present site of Tawat. He left a great many of his companions there who had been struck during the journey with a foot disease that they called touat. The locality where they separated and where the sick people established their homes took the name of their disease.

The people of the Orient have related the journey of the prince in their annals; they indicated their surprise at the strength of his empire, but they did not describe Kankan Musa as a liberal and generous man; despite the extent of his empire, for he gave the sum of only 20,000 pieces of gold as alms to the two Holy Cities, whereas Askiya al-Hajj Muhammad set aside 100,000 pieces of gold for the same purpose.

After the departure of Kankan Musa on a pilgrimage, the people of Songhay were subjected to his authority. On his return, the prince passed through Songhay and had a mosque with a mihrab built just outside the city of Kagho [Gao], where he said Friday prayers. This mosque still exists today. In all the places he passed on Fridays, the prince customarily built mosques.

Then Kankan Musa took the road to Timbuktu. He took possession of the city and was the first sovereign to make himself master of it. He installed a representative of his authority there and had a royal palace built, called Madugu, meaning "palace of the king." In this area, still well known because of the palace, butcher shops have since been established. . . .

It has been said that Sultan Kankan Musa built the minaret of the great mosque of Timbuktu and that one of the princes of his dynasty, the Sultan of Mossi, during his reign headed a strong army and made a raid upon the city. Seized with terror, the people of Mali fled, abandoning Timbuktu to its assailants. Then the Sultan of Mossi entered the city and sacked, burned, and ruined it. Having killed all those he could get his hands on, he took away all the wealth he could find and returned to his country.

"Timbuktu has been sacked three times," said the very learned jurist, Ahmad Baba, "the first time by the Sultan of Mossi, the second by Sonni Ali, and the third by Mahmud ibn Zargun Pasha. This last devastation was less terrible than the first two." It is said that more blood was spilled during Sonni Ali's sacking than during the sacking of the Sultan of Mossi.

Toward the end of the domination of the princes of Mali, the Maghcharan Taureg [Saharan nomads] began their incursions against the city of Timbuktu. Headed by their sultan, Akil Akamalul, they ravaged the country on all sides and in every way. The inhabitants suffered great damages from these depredations. However, they did not take up arms to fight the enemy. It is said that a prince who is unable to defend his states is not worthy of allegiance. Thus the people of Mali had to abandon the area and return to their country. Akil took over Timbuktu and remained master there for forty years. . . .

DESCRIPTION OF DJENNÉ

This city is large and prosperous; it is rich and blessed by heaven. God has accorded all his favors to this land as though to do so were a natural and innate thing. The inhabitants of Djenné are benevolent, admirable, and hospitable. Even so, they are inclined by nature to be jealous of those who are successful in this world. If one of them obtains a favor or advantage, the others gather against him in a common feeling of hate, without letting any of this animosity show until that person is struck by bad fortune (May God preserve us from such an end!). Then each one displays by word and deed all the hate he has felt toward the misfortunate one.

Djenné is one of the great markets of the Muslim world. Merchants bringing salt from the mines of Taghaza and those with gold from the mines of Bitu meet there. These two marvelous mines have no equal in the entire universe. Everyone going to Djenné to trade reaps large profits and thus acquires fortunes whose amount can be known only by God. (May he be praised!)

Because of this city, caravans flock to Timbuktu from all the points of the horizon—from the east, west, north, and south. Djenné is situated to the southwest of Timbuktu, behind the two rivers [the Niger and the Bani], on an island formed by the [Bani] river. Sometimes the waters of the [Bani] river overflow (and come together); sometimes they fall back and separate, little by little. The high water comes in the month of August, and the waters go down in February.

In the beginning the city was built in a place called Zoboro; later it was moved to its present location. The ancient city was situated just to the south of the modern one.

Djenné is surrounded by a rampart that at one time contained eleven gates. Three of them have since been closed so that today only eight are left. When a person views the city from a certain distance outside the city, the trees are so numerous that he thinks he sees only a simple forest. However, once inside the city, he doubts that there is even a single tree in the area.

Djenné was founded by pagans in the mid-second century of the hijra of the Prophet. (The best salutations and benedictions be his!) The inhabitants were not converted to Islam until toward the end of the sixth century of the hijra. Sultan Konboro was the first to adopt Islam, and the inhabitants of the city followed his example.

When Konboro decided to enter the bosom of Islam, he gave the order to assemble the 4,200 ulema [Muslim scholars] then within the territory of the city. He abjured paganism in their presence and called upon them to pray that God would accord three things to Djenné: (1) that he who was chased from his country by injustice and misery would come live in Djenné and would find in exchange, by the grace of God, abundance and wealth, so that he would forget his old homeland; (2) that the city would be peopled by foreigners who were superior to its natives; (3) that

God would deprive of their patience all those who came to sell their merchandise, so that they would become bored by staying in the place and would sell their packets at low prices, to the benefit of the inhabitants. Following these prayers the first chapter of the *Quran* was read, and the prayers were answered, as can be verified by seeing the city today.

As soon as he was converted to Islam, the sultan demolished his palace and replaced it with a temple intended for the worship of the almighty God—this is the present grand mosque. Konboro constructed another palace for the lodging of his court, and this palace is adjacent to the mosque on the east side. The territory of Djenné is fertile and populous; numerous markets are held every day of the week. This area allegedly is composed of 7,077 adjacent villages. . . .

ASKIYA MUHAMMAD TURE (1493–1538)

In the third year of the century [of the hijral] Askiya Muhammad returned from his pilgrimage and entered Kagho [Gao] in the last month of that year (July 31, 1497–August 30, 1497).

God favored the reign of Askiya Muhammad. He assured him great conquests and covered him with His bountiful protection. This ruler took over all the lands of the West, and his authority spread to the frontiers of the land of Bonduku as far as Taghaza and its dependencies. Askiya Muhammad subjected all these people by the sword and by force, as will be seen in the narrative of his expeditions. Everywhere God accomplished all that this sovereign desired, so that Askiya Muhammad was obeyed in all his states as loyally as he was in his own palace. There was great abundance everywhere and absolute peace reigned. Praise to Him who favors whom He wishes in the ways that please Him; He possesses the supreme good.

During the year 903 (August 1497—August 1498), Askiya Muhammad undertook an expedition against Naasira, the Sultan of Mossi. He took the blessed Sayyid Mur Salih-Ojaura with him, inviting him to give the necessary blessings so that this expedition would be a veritable holy war in the name of God. Mur did not refuse this order and explained to the prince all the rules relative to holy war. The Prince of the Believers, Askiya Muhammad, then asked the sayyid to be his messenger to the Sultan of Mossi. The sayyid accepted this mission. He went to the land of Mossi and submitted the letter of his master, summoning the sultan to embrace Islam.

The Sultan of Mossi unwittingly declared that he first wanted to consult his ancestors in the other world. Consequently, accompanied by his ministers, he went to the temple of the idol of the land. The sayyid went along in order to see how one went about consulting the dead. First, the customary offerings were made. Then a very old man appeared. At the sight of him everyone lay prostrate, and the sultan announced the object of his journey. Answering in the name of the ancestors, the old man said, "I will never accept such a thing for you. On the contrary, you must fight to the last man until either you or they have fallen."

Then Naasira answered the blessed sayyid. "Return to your master and tell him that between him and us there can never be other than struggles and war." Left alone in the temple with the personage who had showed himself in the form of an old man, the sayyid questioned the man in these terms: "In the name of almighty God, I ask you to say who you are." "I am Iblis" [the devil], answered the pseudo old man, "I am leading them astray so that they will all die as infidels."

Mur returned to Askiya al-Hajj Muhammad and gave him an account of all that had taken place. "Now," he added, "your duty is to fight them." As soon as the sovereign had begun to fight the Mossi, he killed many of their men, devastated their fields, sacked their houses, and took their children prisoner. All those who were taken captive—men and women—were the object of divine benediction. In all the land, no other expedition had the character of a holy war made in the name of God.

THE COMING OF JUDAR PASHA TO THE SUDAN

Judar was short and had blue eyes. Following are the circumstances that led to his coming. A certain Ould-Kirinfil was one of the servants of the Prince of Songhay. His master, the sovereign Askiya Ishaq, son of Prince Askiya Daud, who was son of Prince Askiya al-Hajj Muhammad, was angry with Ould-Kirinfil and had sent him to be interned at Taghaza, which was part of the empire of the kings of Songhay and was administered by them.

Destiny had it that Ould-Kirinfil managed to escape from his confinement and succeeded in reaching the red [clay] city of Marrakech. He had planned to present himself to the sovereign of the land, Sultan Ahmad al-Mansur, but at that moment the sultan was in Fez, where he had gone to punish the sharif of that city. The sultan had the eyes of the insurgents put out, and a good number of them died of this punishment. (We belong to God and we must return to him.) Thus, he had acted with only temporal advantages in view. (May God preserve us from such a fate!)

Ould-Kirinfil stayed in Marrakech, and from there he wrote the Moroccan sovereign a letter informing him of his arrival and giving him news of the land of Songhay, whose inhabitants, he said, were in a deplorable situation because of the baseness of their nature. Thus, he strongly encouraged Ahmad al-Mansur to take over the country and to rescue it from the hands of its masters.

As soon as he had received this letter, the sultan wrote to Prince Askiya Ishaq announcing his intention to return to his land. He said that he was momentarily in Fez, far from his capital, but that if God wished, the askiya could be informed of his intentions by the document attached to the letter. In the document, Ahmad al-Mansur demanded, among other things, that the salt mine of Taghaza be given over to him—a mine that he, more than any other, had the right to possess because due to his efforts, the land had been protected from incursions of the Christian infidels [the Portuguese]. These dispatches were sent by messenger and arrived in the city of Kagho while the sovereign was still in Fez, in the month of Safar of the year 998 of the Prophet's flight (December 10, 1589–January 8, 1590). (The best of salutations and benedictions and benedictions upon him!) I myself saw the original of these documents. Then Ahmad al-Mansur returned to Marrakech. The snow fell so abundantly during the course of the trip that he nearly died. A great number of his people lost hands or feet from the effects of the cold, and they arrived in the capital in a most pitiable condition. (Let us ask God to save us from these trials.)

Not only did Prince Askiya Ishaq not consent to abandon the mine of Taghaza, but he answered in violent and abusive terms and sent javelins and two iron shoes along with his answer. As soon as this message reached him, Ahmad al-Mansur decided to send an army to the Sudan, and the following year—that is to say, the year 999 (November 1590)—he sent out an important army corps against Songhay that included 3,000 men in arms and as many horsemen as foot soldiers, accompanied by a double number of all sorts of followers, several sorts of workers, doctors, and so on.

Judar Pasha was placed in command of this expedition. He had a dozen generals with him: Qaid Mustafa al-Turki, Qaid Mustafa ibn Askar, Qaid Ahmad al-Harusi al-Andalusi, Qaid Ahmad ibn al-Haddad al-Amri (chief of the constabulary), Qaid Ahmad ibn Atiya, Qaid Bu-Chiba al-Amri, Qaid Bu-Gheta al-Amri, Qaid Ammar al-Fata (the renegade), Qaid Ahmad ibn Yusuf (the renegade), Qaid Ali ibn Mustafa (the renegade). The latter was the first Moroccan chief invested with the command of the city of Kagho [Gao] and died at the same time as Mahmud ibn Zargun Pasha when the latter was killed at al-Hadjar. Two lieutenant generals commanded the two wings of the army: Ba-Hasan Ffiru (the renegade, the right wing) and Qasim Waradui al-Andalusi (the renegade, the left wing). Such were the generals and lieutenants who left with Judar.

The Moroccan prince [Ahmad al-Mansur] announced to his generals that the results of divination had shown that the land of Songhay should cease being dominated by the Sudanese and that his army should take over a certain part of their land. Then the army set out toward Songhay.

As soon as he got news of the departure of this army, Prince Askiya Ishaq brought together his generals and the principal people of his kingdom in order to consult them on the measures to be taken and to ask their opinions, but each time a judicious counsel was given, they hastened to reject it. God, in his foreknowledge, had thus decided that the kingdom should disappear and that the dynasty should perish. No one can reject what He has decided or obstruct His decisions. . . .

The Moroccan troops reached the Niger in the neighborhood of the town of Karabara. They stopped there, and Judar gave a great feast to celebrate their safe arrival at the river. The fact that the men arrived safe and sound was a portent that success would crown the efforts of their chief. This event took place on Wednesday, the fourth day of the month of Jumada 11 of the year 999 of the hijra (March 30, 1591), as stated above.

The army did not pass through the city of Arawan but rather passed to the east of it. On the road they encountered the camels of Abdallah ibn Qair al-Mahmudi. Judar took the number of camels he required, and then Abdallah left immediately for Morocco. He went to Marrakech and complained to Ahmad al-Mansur that he had been the victim of injustice. He was the first to announce the arrival of the Moroccan army at the Niger. The first person whom the ruler asked about was Ba-Hasan Friru. "Ba-Hasan," Abdallah answered, "is doing well perhaps." The sovereign asked of Qaid Ahmad ibn al-Haddad al-Amri and of Judar Pasha. Then he wrote Judar, instructing him to pay for the camels he had taken.

The Moroccans then resumed their march. They advanced toward the city of

Kagho and met Askiya Ishaq on the road at a place called Tondibi, near Tonbodi. The Prince of Songhay [Askiya Ishaq] was at the head of 12,500 cavalrymen and 30,000 foot soldiers. The armies did not meet sooner because the people of Songhay could not believe the reports of the expedition and had awaited news of its arrival at the river.

The battle began on Tuesday, the seventeenth day of the month mentioned above (April 12). In the twinkling of an eye, the troops of the askiya were routed. Several notable persons perished in that battle; among the horsemen were the *Fondoko* Bubu Maryama (the former chief of Masina), the *Cha-Farma* Ali-Djauenda, the *Bintra-Farma* Osman Durfan ibn Bukar Kirin-Kirin (the son of Prince Askiya, named Al Hajj-Muhammad). He was very old at the time, and Askiya Ishaq had named him *Binka-Farma* when the Binka-Farma Muhammad Haika had died, as previously mentioned, on the expedition to Nemnatako.

On that day a great many of the foot soldiers died as well. When the army was defeated, the soldiers threw their shields on the ground and squatted on these improvised seats, awaiting the arrival of Judar's troops, who massacred them in this position because they could present no resistance. And that was because they must not flee in the case of a retreat by the regular army. The Moroccan soldiers stripped them of the gold bracelets they had on their arms.

Askiya Ishaq turned his horse's head and galloped away with the rest of his troops. Then he requested the people of Kagho to leave the city and flee to the other side of the Niger in the direction of Gurma. He sent the same recommendation to the inhabitants of Timbuktu, and continuing on his way without passing by Kagho, he arrived at Kurai Gurma in that state, where he camped with the remnants of his troops amid tears and lamentations. The group sorrowfully began to cross the river in boats. In the scuffle that took place, many people fell in the river and perished. Furthermore, such a quantity of wealth was lost that only God knows its value.

The people of Timbuktu could not leave the city and cross the Niger because of the obstacles they met and the difficulties of the situation. Only the Timbuktu *Mondzo*, Yahya-ould-Bordam, and the servants of the askiya who were there left the city and went to camp at Al-Kif-Kindi, a place near Tonga.

Judar Pasha continued with his army as far as Kagho. No one was left in the city except the *khatib*, Mahmud Dararm (who was a very old man at that time), and the students and traders who had not been able to get out and flee. Khatib Mahmud went to the Moroccans and welcomed them, showing them deference and offering them generous hospitality. He had conferences and long meetings with Judar Pasha, during which he was treated with the greatest respect and consideration.

Judar expressed his desire to enter the palace of Askiya Ishaq. Consequently he sent for two witnesses, and when they arrived, he entered the palace with them, but after having resisted acknowledging their lack of wealth, and having examined everything, it seemed to him that the palace was, in fact, rather miserable.

Askiya Ishaq requested the pasha to negotiate with him. The pasha undertook to remit 100,000 pieces of gold and 1,000 slaves to the Moroccan sovereign, Ahmad al-Mansur. In return the pasha was to leave his country and take his army back to Marrakech. Judar replied that he [Askiya Ishaq] was only a docile slave and could not act without orders from the sovereign, his master. Then with the accord of the merchants of his country, he [Judar] wrote [to al-Mansur] in his name and in that of Qaid Ahmad ibn al-Haddad al-Amri, in an attempt to transmit these proposals, having taken care to say that the house of the chief of the ass drivers in Morocco was worth more than the palace of the askiya which he had visited. This letter was carried to its destination by Ali al-Adjimi, who was in charge of communications at that time.

Judar led his troops back to Timbuktu, where he awaited the response of the Sultan of Morocco. Unless I am mistaken, he stayed only seventeen days at Kagho. They arrived at Mosa-Benko on Wednesday, the last day of the month of Jumada II (April 24, 1591). They departed from there on Thursday, the first day of the month of Radjib (April 25). Then they camped for thirty-five days under the walls on the south side of Timbuktu.

The Qadi of Timbuktu, the jurist Abu Hafs-Umar (son of God's saint, the jurist), and Qadi Mahmud sent the Muezzin Yahma, to greet the pasha, but unlike Khatib Mahmud Darami, when the Moroccans had arrived at Kagho, Yahma did not offer the pasha the least hospitality. Judar was extremely annoyed by his reception. Nevertheless he [the pasha] sent all sorts of fruit, dates, and almonds, as well as a great deal of sugar cane. Then he had the qadi put on a coat of scarlet red cloth. Those with any common sense feared that nothing good was presaged by all this, and the facts soon confirmed their apprehensions.

The Moroccans entered the city of Timbuktu on Thursday, May 30, 1591. They covered the city in all directions and realized that the most flourishing quarter was that populated by the people from Gadàmes. Thus they chose it for their casbah, which they began to build after having expelled a certain number of the people of that quarter from their houses.

Then Judar let Hammu ibn Abd al-Haqq al-Diri out of prison and entrusted him with the functions of amir in the name of Sultan Ahmad al-Mansur. Both Rafi and Ahmad Nini-Bir died before his [Hammu ibn Abd al-Haqq al-Diri's] arrival. The pasha had sanctioned a delay of forty days in order for the officer in charge of communications to reach Marrakech and return.

When the Moroccan army arrived in the Sudan, it found one of the countries that God had favored most in wealth and fertility. Peace and security reigned everywhere in all the provinces, thanks to the sovereign—the very successful, the blessed, the Prince of the Believers, Askiya al-Hajj Muhammad ibn Abu Bakr, whose justice and strength spread everywhere, so that his orders, which were effortlessly accomplished in his palace, were executed with equal facility in the farthest corners of the empire-from the frontiers of the land of Dendi to the frontiers of the land of al-Hamdiyya, and from the countries of the land of Bonduku to Taghaza and Tawat, as well as in the dependencies of these countries.

Everything changed at that moment. Danger took the place of security, misery replaced opulence, and trouble, calamity, and violence succeeded tranquillity. People destroyed each other on all sides, in all places, and in all directions. There was rapine and war. Neither life nor goods nor the condition of the inhabitants was spared. General disorder intensified and spread in all directions.

The first to give the signal for this violence was Sanba Lamdu, the Chief of Donko. He ruined the land of Ras al-Ma by taking possession of all the goods, by having a certain number of the inhabitants killed, and by reducing a great number of free men to slavery. His example was followed by the Zaghranians [of Zaghai], who devastated the lands of Bara and Dirma. The territory of Djenné was ransacked in the most horrible fashion by the idolatrous Bambara who, to the East as to the West, in the North as in the South, destroyed all the villages, pillaged the goods, and made concubines of free women and with them had children who were brought up in the religion of the Mages [pagans]. (May God preserve us from such calamities!) All these calamities were executed under the direction of Chaa-Kor of Qasim (the son of the Binka-Farma), Alu Zulail ibn Umar Kamzagho (the paternal cousin of the *Baghena-Fari* and of Bohom, the son of the Fondoko Bubu Maryama, of Masina). . . .

These troubles endlessly continued and increased, whereas from the time that Prince Askiya al-Hajj Muhammad mounted the throne of Songhay, no chief of any region dared attack the sovereigns of the land [Songhay], because God had dispensed so much vigor, audacity, courage, and majesty to their force. Very much to the contrary, the prince went to attack these chiefs in their lands, and most often God accorded him the victory, as has been seen in the recitation of the history of Songhay.

The situation remained thus until the moment when the dynasty of Songhay drew to its end and its empire ceased to exist. At that moment faith was transformed into unbelief. All the things forbidden by God were overtly being practiced. The people drank wine and indulged in sodomy; adultery became so frequent that its practice seemed to have become legal. Without adultery there was no elegance and no glory; this popular feeling existed to such an extent that the children of sultans committed adultery with their sisters.

It is told that this moral corruption first took place at the end of the reign of the sultan, the just, the Prince of the Believers, Askiya al-Hajj Muhammad, and that his son Yusuf-Koi invented this type of debauchery. When the father learned of these practices, he became violently angry and cursed his son, asking God to deprive Yusuf of his virile member before he entered the other world. God answered that wish, and a disease made the young prince lose the organ of his virility. (May heaven preserve us from such a fate!) The malediction spread to the son of Yusuf, Arbinda, the father of the Bana-Kor, Yaqub, for he too lost his virile member toward the end of his life after an attack of the same disease.

Because of these abominations, God took revenge by causing the victorious Moroccan army to attack Songhay. He made the attack come from a very far-off country, and amid terrible suffering, the roots of this people were separated from the trunk and the punishment they underwent was an exemplary one. . . .

The pasha's [Mahmud ibn Zargun Pasha] principal subordinate and most influential councillor at that time was Habib Muhammad Anbabu. The first act, taken after deliberation, was to announce to Timbuktu by public crier that the pasha would search all the houses of the city the next day and that any individual living in a house where arms were found would have only himself to blame for the fate awaiting him if he were found to possess weapons; only the homes of the jurists, children of Sidi Mahmud, would be exempt from the search.

Upon hearing this announcement, the whole population hastened to transport all its wealth to the houses of the jurists for safekeeping. The people thought, in fact, that if the pasha found money in any one of the houses during the search, he would take it unfairly and by violent means. Such was, in fact, the real objective of those [the pasha and his councillor] who had taken this measure.

The search took place the next day and all the houses were thoroughly investigated. After this operation the pasha announced by public crier that in the following days, all the inhabitants would have to meet in the Sankore mosque to pledge allegiance to Sultan Ahmad al-Mansur.

When everyone was assembled in the mosque, the people of Tawat, Fezzan, and Awjila were made to pledge allegiance. That procedure lasted all the first day, which was Monday, the twenty-second day of the sacred month of Muharram, the first month of the year 1002 (October 18, 1593). Then on Tuesday, the twenty-third day of the same month, the people of Walata and Ouadane had their turn.

"Now only the jurists have not yet sworn," said the pasha. "That will be tomorrow in the presence of everyone." The following day, when everyone was assembled in the mosque, the gates were closed and all the spectators were made to go out except the jurists, their friends, and their followers. Pasha Mahmud arrested them all on that day, which was Wednesday, twenty-fourth day of the month of Muharram of the year 1002 (October 20, 1593). Having made them prisoners in this way, the pasha ordered them to be led to the casbah in two groups. One group went to the casbah by crossing through the city, and the other group took a street that circled outside the city on the east side.

The persons who composed the second group were massacred on that day. As they were walking and reached the quarter of Zim-Konda, one of them, a Wankore [a resident of the Sankore quarter] named Andafo, seized the saber of one of the soldiers who was leading the group and struck him. Immediately the soldiers slaughtered fourteen of the prisoners.

Nine of the victims of this massacre belonged to great Sankore families: the very learned jurist Ahmad Muyaj, the pious jurist Muhammad al-Amin (son of the Qadi Muhammad ibn Sidi Mahmud), the jurist al-Mustafa (son of the jurist Masira Anda Umar), Muhammad ibn Ahmad Bir (son of the jurist Sidi Mahmud), Buzu ibn Ahmad Usman, Muhammad al-Mukhtar ibn Muya Akhar, Ahmad Bir ibn Muhammad al-Mukhtar (son of Ahmad, the brother of al-Fa Salha Takuni, who was the last son of the brother of Masira Anda Umar), Muhammad Siri ibn al-Amin (father of Surma), Mahmud Kiraukurik (one of the inhabitants of the Kabir quarter), Yburhum Buyzuli al-Tawati, the shoemaker (one of the men of Koira-Kona), two Wankores, Andafo (who had provoked the catastrophe) and his brother, two hartani [serfs] belonging to the children of Sidi Mahmud, and finally Fadl and Chinun, both tailors.

A single individual of this group escaped the massacre—Muhammad ibn al-Amin Kanu. He was delivered from his bonds by the brother of Qaid Ahmad ibn al-Haddad al-Amri, who took the prisoner on his horse and carried him safe and sound to his house. Learning of this catastrophe, Mahmud Pasha, who was still in the mosque, cried that he had not authorized this massacre and immediately sent orders that such a thing should not be repeated. . . .

The massacre of the prisoners took place near the house of Amraduchu, one of the hartani of the city of Timbuktu, and Amraduchu received the order to bury the bodies in his house. Jurist Ahmad Muyaj, jurist Muhammad al-Amin, and jurist al-Mustafa were buried in the same pit, and the very learned jurist Muhammad Bughyu took care of all the funeral ceremonies. Amraduchu then left Timbuktu in order to travel. He settled in the city of Chiki, where he lived until his death.

When the ascetic Sidi Abd al-Rahman learned of the event, he cried out, "Of all the members of this family, all were killed today with the exception of Muhammad al-Amin!" When he learned of the death of Fadl, he said, "Fadl has died in this affair, but he will have the supreme recompense."

Mahmud Pasha broke into the houses of the jurists and took from them all the money, goods, and furnishings—so much that only God knows the amount, for in addition to the possessions of the jurists, these houses contained the wealth deposited by the people for safekeeping.

The troops of the pasha pillaged all they could find and stripped men and women naked to search them. The troops then abused the women and took them and the men to the casbah, where they were kept as prisoners for six months. Mahmud Pasha wasted all the wealth he had seized and scattered it far and wide. He gave generously to his soldiers but sent nothing to Sultan Ahmad al-Mansur except 100,000 pieces of gold.

16. IMAM AHMAD IBN FARTUWA
IDRIS ALAWMA AND THE KANEM WARS. 1602.

The state of Kanem was probably founded in the ninth century in the region north-east of Lake Chad by black Saharan nomads called Zaghawa. Between the eleventh and thirteenth centuries Islam was introduced and was accompanied by the politi-cal transformation of the chief of Kanem from a nomadic shaykh to a Sudanese king, the mai, with his capital at Njimi. During the reign of Dunama Dabalemi ibn Salma (1221–1259), the authority of the mai was strengthened, but his enthusiasm for Islam alienated the pagan branch of the ruling clan known as the Bulala. There-after, the kings of Kanem sought to crush the pagan Bulala, but in the fourteenth century this struggle intensified and the pagan reaction triumphed. Between 1384 and 1388, the mai abandoned Kanem to the Bulala and took refuge in Bornu, west

From Imam Ahmad ibn Fartuwa, "A History of the First Twelve Years of the Reign of Mai Idris Alooma," in H. R. Palmer, *Mai Idris of Bornu, 1571–1583* (Lagos: Government Printer, 1926), pp. 11–13. The section describing the Fifth Expedition is from Imam Ahmad ibn Fartuwa, "The Kanem Wars," in H. R. Palmer, *Sudanese Memoirs* (Lagos: Government Printer, 1928), vol. I, pp. 48–51, 62–65, 67–69.

of Lake Chad. Victorious, the Bulala established their capital at Gaw, north of Lake Fitri. Meanwhile, the former rulers of Kanem revived under Ali ibn Dunama (1476–1503), who established the kingdom of Bornu with its capital at Ngazargamu. Bornu flourished and reached its golden age during the reign of Idris ibn Ali (1570–1602), known as Idris Alawma. Idris Alawma was a great warrior king. He made the pilgrimage to Mecca, during which he learned the power of firearms and imported Turkish musketeers to consolidate his authority in Bornu. He then launched the Kanem wars against the Bulala. In seven expeditions he defeated the Bulala but was never able to subdue them. In the end he acknowledged the independence of Kanem under its Bulala king and agreed upon a defined frontier between Bornu and Kanem. Ahmad ibn Fartuwa was the principal imam under Idris Alawma. His rich and detailed A History of the First Twelve Years of the Reign of Mai Idris Alooma *and* The Kanem War of Idris Alooma *were first procured by Heinrich Barth in 1853 from the then Wazir of Bornu, al-Hajj Bashir. The selections in this section describe the pilgrimage, the return to Bornu, and the consolidation of the authority of Idris Alawma and are followed by excerpts from his fifth, sixth, and seventh expeditions to Kanem, which culminated in the peace treaty with the Bulala.*

So he made the pilgrimage and visited Tayiba, the Tayiba of the Prophet, the chosen one (upon whom be peace and the blessing of God), the unique, the victorious over the vicissitudes of day and night.

He was enriched by visiting the tomb of the pious Sahabe the chosen, the perfect ones (may the Lord be favourable and beneficent to them), and he bought in the noble city a house and date grove, and settled there some slaves, yearning after a plenteous reward from the Great Master.

Then he prepared to return to the kingdom of Bornu. When he reached the land called Barak he killed all the inhabitants who were warriors. They were strong but after this became weak; they became conquered, where formerly they had been conquerors. Among the benefits which God (Most High) of His bounty and beneficence, generosity, and constancy conferred upon the Sultan was the acquisition of Turkish musketeers and numerous household slaves who became skilled in firing muskets.

Hence the Sultan was able to kill the people of Amsaka with muskets, and there was no need for other weapons, so that God gave him a great victory by reason of his superiority in arms.

Among the most surprising of his acts was the stand he took against obscenity and adultery, so that no such thing took place openly in his time. Formerly the people had been indifferent to such offences, committed openly or secretly by day or night. In fact he was a power among his people and from him came their strength.

So he wiped away the disgrace, and the face of the age was blank with astonishment. He cleared away and reformed as far as he could the known wrong doing.

To God belong the secret sins, and in His hands is direction, and prevention, and prohibition and sanction.

Owing to the Mai's noble precepts all the people had recourse to the sacred Sheria [Quranic law], putting aside worldly intrigue in their disputes and affairs, big or little.

From all we have heard, formerly most of the disputes were settled by the chiefs, not by the "Ulema" [Muslim jurists].

For example, he stopped wrong doing, hatred and treachery, and fighting between Muslims, in the case of the Kuburi and Kayi. They had been fighting bitterly over their respective prestige, but on the Sultan's accession, he sternly forbade them to fight till they became as brothers in God.

Then again there was his leniency in his remarkable expedition to Gamargu and Margi and Kopchi and Mishiga and to the hills of Womdiu.

He also came to the people of the hills of Zajadu and the hills of N'garasa, called N'guma, who had allied themselves with the sons of Sultan Daud and his grandsons and relatives and made raids on the land of Bornu, killing men and enslaving women and children right down to the time of our Sultan (may God ennoble him in both worlds). He scattered their host, and divided them, but of the N'guma he spared all and established them in settlements under his direction as his subjects nor did they resist or become recalcitrant.

The tribe of N'gizim, the people of Mugulum, and the people of Gamazan and others of the N'gizim stock who were neighbours were insolent and rebellious, till our Sultan went out to them with a large host, destroyed their crops, and burnt their houses in the wet season. Thus they felt the pinch of a ruined country, yielded to him obedience, and submitted to his rule.

He introduced units of measure for corn among these people by the power and might of God. The N'gizim who dwelt in the West, known as Binawa, would not desist from enslaving Muslims in their country and doing other evil and base actions. They kept seizing the walled towns of the Yedi as fortresses and places of refuge and hiding, using them as bases treacherously to attack the Muslims by day and night, without ceasing or respite. But when our Sultan ascended the throne, he and his Wazir in chief Kursu took counsel to stem the torrent of their guile and deceit, so that they left off their wickedness, and some followed the Sultan, others the Wazir Kursu, others various leaders who had waged "Holy War" with the Sultan.

To some the Sultan gave orders to settle, and devote their time to agriculture.

Again there is the record of the Sultan's dealings with the So whose home was in the East on the shores of the great lake of Chad. These people, known as Tatala, formerly perpetrated many iniquities and crimes. It is said that they took stores of water in gourds or other receptacles, and then with their weapons and shields, sallied forth to harry the towns of the Muslims, sometimes going two or three days distance on these forays.

But when the time of our Sultan came, he rebuked them with a stern rebuke, and chastised them with divers sorts of chastisement till they became downcast and ashamed. Many of their dwellings became desolate, empty, forlorn and deserted.

Know, my brethren, that in what we have told you, we have failed to tell all. We have but told you a part of the story of the deeds of the early years of our Sultan's reign, with hand and pen. How can that be easy or possible for us, considering his actions covered most of that which is ordained in the Kura'an and Sunna concerning "Holy War" in the path of God, seeking the noble presence of God, and His great reward.

Thus we have cut short the recital of his wars, in this brief compilation. As for his wars on the tribe of Bulala we will—please God—relate the Sultan's dealings with them in a separate work plainly and clearly and accurately, according to the accounts obtained, and following all the descriptions which have been given of the wars which our Sultan brought to an end by the might and power of God.

FIFTH EXPEDITION

So we arrived at Garku by slow stages. When we reached it and halted there, every man with great caution as had been ordered, the people began to cut down the thorn trees to protect the Sultan's camp, every man according to his share, according to the custom of our people which was initiated by our Sultan Hajj Idris (may God ennoble him in the time of his power).

When we halted with his army at any camp whatsoever, he used to order the people to divide up their camping place into sections so that every chief and captain should have his share of it, and should live in it, and make a fence for its enclosure. Thus the circumference of the "zariba" [fenced enclosure] was finished with great speed and rapidity. It comprised a large area, so great that everyone could find his share of dwelling space.

It was in this very town of Garku that fighting broke out at night between us and between our enemies. They rushed upon us unexpectedly though its perimeter was fortified in the same way as other places. In the building of these stockades, which the experienced thought and sound prudence of our Sultan had established, there was great advantage and usefulness. Firstly in that it obviated the need of tying up animals, so that they could be allowed to roam about in the midst of the camp. The horses and other animals also were unable to stray away. Then again it prevented thieves from entering for infamous and evil purposes, for they were frustrated and turned back. Again it prevented any one from leaving the camp on errands of immorality, debauch or other foolishness. Again when the enemy wished to force an entrance upon us either by treachery or open fighting he was obliged to stand up and occupy himself with the defences before he reached us. If we had taken many captives and much booty and put them inside, we could sleep restfully and the night hours were safe: also if the male or female slaves wished to run away from the camp, they were afraid to go out. The advantages of a stockade cannot be numbered.

There was no early warning that the Bulala would make a surprise attack on the Sultan's camp. Their onset only became known after the evening prayer. Some did not know until the night, and some did not even know until the enemy had entered the camp or had come close to it. Had there been a stockade there would not have been fighting and slaughter on this occasion between the Bulala and our Sultan Hajj Idris ibn Ali (may God ennoble him and bless him in his children and descendants for ever and ever by the grace of the Lord of creation, our master Muhammad the chosen, and his house, upon whom be blessing Amen).

The Sultan went to Kanem four times before this journey in which there was fighting between us and them openly night and day. In this fighting he ravaged the three great and famous valleys until they were like vast empty plains: one of them the great town Ikima, the second the stockade of Aghafi and the third the town of Ago.

When the Sultan laid waste these three valleys, there resulted to the inhabitants great misfortune, in that he laid waste the whole country. Then too the people who lived in Kanem were removed to the land of Bornu, including the people who lived at Kulu to the south and were riverain peoples. There did not remain in Kanem any branches of the tribes which went to Bornu. They did not however move to Bornu of their own will or desire, but impressed by the news of the conqueror, and the fear he inspired.

Had it not been for the Tubu, who wished to support Sultan Abdul Jalil and be his subjects, we had only gone to Kanem once.

God knows best the truth about character, and how He richly endowed Sultan Idris, by His grace, and abundant beneficence, and strengthened him, so as to be a terror to his many enemies, and, what time he gained the mastery over the Bulala Sultan, who relied on the Tubu, to go out to battle against them all.

Is it not stated in the account we have heard from our Sheikhs and elders who have gone before us that the Tubu attacked Sultan Dunama ibn Dabale, the son of Sultan Salma, son of Bikuru openly so that a state of war ensued, and lasted between the Tubu and Sultan Dunama for seven years seven months and seven days, raising fires of hate which lasted for all that time?

Thus we have heard from trustworthy sources; but there was no tribe of Bulala in those days.

We heard too from Wunoma Muhammad Al-Saghir ibn Tuguma in his life time, when he was telling us about the early Sultans (he was learned in ancient history) that the number of the horsemen of Sultan Dunama ibn Dabale was 30,000. Thus we heard from him, nor are we ignorant of, nor have we forgotten what he told us, since the day he told us.

But the war of Sultan Dunama ibn Dabale was with the tribe of the Tubu.

Whereas our Sultan fought the Bulala and Tubu and other people of different tribes, whose origin is unknown, and fought them all patiently, relying on God, and going forward trusting Him, till he vanquished them, and put them to flight.

We shall talk of this plainly in what follows, if God wills.

The Bulala, after our Sultan had destroyed all their towns in the land of Kanem, even the town of Ikima and the stockade of Aghafi, wished to build up the old town of Ago and to return to it. They dwelt in it still, as we have heard. Whilst they were sojourning with the intention of settling there, they heard the news of our Sultan Hajj Idris, what time he came to Yisambu in the rainy season on a military expedition and halted in Dalli.

When they heard of his coming, they were afraid with a very great fear, and left the town of Ago; leaving it altogether and not returning to it. The people were amazed and stupefied throughout the villages and towns of Kanem, for they were certain that Sultan Hajj Idris ibn Ali would not cease from coming to Kanem so long as Sultan Abdul Jalil was there as ruler.

They therefore abandoned this town of Ago, and left it empty as the desert so that the troops of our Sultan should not surprise them there. Their women, however, daughters of the royal house, sent to Sultan Abdul Jalil and his army whom they knew were utterly cowed, to say that they did not love them and were bewildered. So the Bulala became even more terrified, and planned to build a stockade at Kiyayaka. In fact they built huts and sheds and found all that they needed as supports for these buildings.

We heard from trustworthy persons who had entered the country of Sultan Abdul Jalil that the towns of Yaki and Makaran and Kurkuriwa were inhabited would never move the from this region. As Poet says:

My master wept when he saw the road behind him, and felt that we should never find Kaisira. I said to him weep not, we will change the seat of power or we will die, and seek help from God.

Thus they built on the borders of this region which was contiguous to the river near the town of Kulu. They built at the town which had the largest perimeter, stockades on all sides but one, i.e., the south. When they had finished building they set about moving the people so that the town should be filled.

Every one they saw in Kanem was sent to their new fortress, except the people of Tatalu, and Afaki near by, or those whose villages were afar off and difficult of access. As for the Tubu they removed them to the town of Kiyayaka mentioned above, as for instance the tribe of Kashards. There were no Tubu tribes in the remotest parts of the land of Kanem which did not come in *en masse* without leaving anyone behind. All who came willingly or unwillingly built grass huts in which they dwelt with their families, until there was gathered together in the above mentioned place a great number of people. God (who is exalted) alone knows the number of them. They took their stores and grain supply as food. Between them and the people of the south there was made a pact of friendship and alliance and concord. Traders in foodstuffs were constant in coming and going between this region and the south to buy and sell. They sold food in exchange for cattle and clothes and other articles.

Trading did not cease between the Bulala and the owners of foodstuffs until the Emir of the Faithful camped at Garku, the Emir Hajj Idris ibn Ali (may God who is exalted ennoble him and bless him in his children and posterity until the end of the ages).

SIXTH EXPEDITION

On Wednesday they set out and at siesta time halted at Wurni; on Thursday about midday they set out and encamped at Labudu which was left on the Friday and a hasty march made to Kasuda; next day they went on to Buluji and spent the night there, while Sunday was spent at Bari. A halt was made at Ruru at noon on Monday, but the Sultan did not remain there longer than was necessary for the two o'clock and afternoon prayers, after which they rode on fast, halting only for the evening prayer at a pool called Kintak. They continued eastwards in the direction of the Kananiyya country [of the Kanuri] in order to reach there by dawn and fare according as God had decreed for them. They travelled on continuously through the night, without halting for exhaustion or fatigue, until between a quarter and a third of the night was over. In this expedition of ours, since we set out from Fakara on the Friday we have mentioned, inclusive of the subsequent eleven days culminating on the Monday, we were not afflicted with exhaustion similar to that which befell us on this night. So greatly were we taxed, that some of us did not know in which direction to turn when praying unless guided by our camels in that direction; while others were unable to find their quarters although fully accustomed to their position. There were still others who, cut off from the main body, could not find their way back again. Such was the condition of some of our men on that night after the Sultan had encamped. It is surely enough to show that the conditions of that journey were a foretaste of hell (as a matter of fact the word Jihad only receives its name on account of the strife and toil entailed in it). This was why our Sultan Al Hajj Idris (may God exalt his rank and abase his detractors and bless his children and issue for ever and ever) in setting out on this forced march on Monday, particularly avoided all drumming and ordered every soldier to take three days rations neither more nor less. He also laid emphasis on the fact that no fit infantry man should remain behind (Rajil is the singular of Rawajil and that is a foot soldier) and that no healthy horse, pack animal or camel should remain with the casualties at the base. He also ordered the various shieldbearers not to follow him but similarly to remain behind at the base. His aim was to concentrate around himself every fit man and beast. He mounted with the forces remaining in his hands, but before setting out appointed his deputy to take charge of the sick and baggage. This was Yuroma Yagha. The Sultan set out at the head of his army encamping at Ruru sometime after noon but only stayed there long enough to celebrate the two prayers, that of two o'clock and the afternoon prayer.

Then the force set out and travelled at a rapid pace so that the exhaustion we have referred to above overtook them. We continued on until we reached Siki (a well known place) or thereabouts, and there we spent the night. At dawn the Sultan divided the troops into three portions for the purpose of raiding, fighting and plunder. His son Kaigama Abdul Jalil, he sent out with his Wazir Idris ibn Harun towards the south against the Kananiyya to proceed as far as Ririkmi and other cities. He sent his son Yarima Idris with the army known as the "Northern Force" which was under the command of Arjinoma and other northern captains, northwards to harass the Kananiyya and penetrate as far as their city Mai and others. They slaughtered a large number of the enemy and took captive many women and children. The Sultan himself had followed the course of the main road with the remaining troops and proceeded as far as Didi and other cities of the Kananiyya.

His troops worked great havoc among the enemy and carried off much property and about a thousand or more of their women and children. The fires of war having died down the Sultan turned his steps towards Ririkmi and there encamped towards evening. His senior captain Kaigama Abdul Jalil and the Wazir Idris ibn Harun had taken up their quarters at Ririkmi before the arrival of the Sultan as they had been detailed to raid it. They had taken a large store of booty. The senior commander Yarima Idris ibn Idris did not return with his army until after nightfall when he arrived with much loot having accounted for large numbers of the enemy.

Sultan Al Hajj Idris ibn Ali was at Ririkmi of good cheer and bright of eye; while discomfiture, rout, slaughter and despoilment fell upon his bellicose enemies who had persisted in hindering the free passage of Muhammadans. The troops were overjoyed and rejoiced at the victory of their Sultan over their rebellious and impious foe. The whole army spent the night at that town without taking any measures of defence; for they felt they had nothing to fear from the enemy, some of whom had been slain, others of whom had fled to a place of refuge and concealment.

Our troops ate their full there of mutton and goats' flesh; their tiredness left them; and they rested and slept the whole night through. When the dawn broke the Sultan gave the signal for departure and mounted, followed by his army, travelling westwards towards Ruru. They went on till the sun was declining and then halted in a place known as Kintak where there was a pond of water. There they stopped for a siesta, and celebrated the two o'clock and afternoon prayers after which they went on to Ruru without any of the captains, commanders or body-guards remaining behind. The complement was complete even including the pack animals and camel drivers. They carried their booty along with them not forcing the pace but proceeding very slowly. When they reached the place on the frontier where our drum was beaten on our first expedition to Kanem on the occasion when we retraced our steps, our Sultan (the Commander of the Faithful Al Hajj Idris whom may God render victorious and whose children and grandchildren be blessed till the sounding of the Trumpet by the grace of the Lord of mankind, the Bringer of Good Tidings, the Eternal, the Seal of the Prophets, the Imam of the Pure, our Lord and Master Muhammad the Pure, and his descendant on whom be the mercy of God) halted, firmly reining in his horse near some tamarisk trees which I know are known far and wide. The people were dismayed at not rejoining the sick who were with the deputy commander Yuroma, but the Sultan was not minded to rejoin them on that day and dismounted under those trees, the tamarisks we mentioned, at the beginning of the book. Upon seeing this, the army bivouacked without delay, unsaddled both camels and horses, and constructed their quarters for the night as best they were able. They spent the night there cheerful and happy and free from fear of theft or attack together with the rich spoil we had taken.

They returned safely without the loss of a single man with the exception of those who were wounded or overcome at the first shock, but our infidel enemy's losses cannot be computed except after long search and investigation. That is because the warriors were killed at the first onset in the field of battle and overthrown, and all those who attempted to withstand our army were at once slain except those who prolonged their life by flight. Our armed patrols were unremitting in searching out fugitives in every place where we encamped, by search and investigation, and they killed our pagan prisoners by order of the Sultan. Not one of them was spared by the guards to remain in anyone's possession. One of the strangest things I have heard about our behaviour was that Kamkama Bamu, one of the Sultan's chief officers, put to death the youths and striplings who were not yet fully adult, in punishment of their evil deeds. Not one survived except him whom God saved. The prisoners were slain there just as their companions had been slain on the field of battle.

He who escaped, escaped; and he who died, died. The only survivors in our hands were the women and children.

After this, the Kananiyya rapidly became extinct. These were the people who only a short time before were puffed up with pride and insolence and considered themselves second to none. According to what I have heard, they were the most numerous tribe in Kanem, and it has been said that if any of their enemies angered them they used to set out with the whole of their people and attack the country of their adversaries without fear of living man, just as our Sultan does to his enemies. This was what emboldened them to deeds of evil and tyranny until they went to the length of openly opposing the armies of our Sultan by attacking and robbing them. They had no organisation of any sort and were led astray by their overweaning pride and insolence, until spoliation, slaughter and destruction fell upon them, as we have described, and the country which our Sultan raided became so much scattered dust. These oppressors were exterminated from the face of the earth. This Tuesday came to them a day of deadly poison. May the dawn of the day be hateful to infidels and evildoers. So we have seen in the book of the creation of the world, what time punishment was inflicted on the people of Sodom because of their disobeying their prophet Lot. The Kananiyya took no heed of the fate of bygone scoffers and profited naught by the lessons of this changing life. As the proverbialist has said: "He who does not learn in the school of the world's experience will not profit by the exhortations of the preacher, preach he never so long." But the Kananiyya of Kanem are people senseless and stupid, ignorant and stubborn, lacking in all qualities of intellect and common sense, and entirely devoid of organisation. Our reason for designating them by these three epithets, i.e., Khurq, Humq, and Jahil, which are distinct in form but close in meaning, is because Khurq is a stronger term than Humq, and Humq is stronger than Jahil; for a senseless man (Akhraq) is one who cannot distinguish between what is beneficial and what is noxious and exhortation is entirely wasted on him, while the stupid man (Ahmaq) is one who will accept no service at all whether it be to his advantage or disadvantage and in this he resembles the senseless man. As regards the ignorant (Jahil) his case is simpler than that of the other two for, if he is adjured, he listens, and after listening, turns away from the advice to his own hurt. It is now time to return to the story of Ruru when we went to the great city called Birni. After encamping at Ruru on Thursday we only remained there three days and the whole of our army recovered from their fatigue and rested from their preparations.

SEVENTH EXPEDITION

We now return to the events which occurred on the seventh journey of the Sultan Al Hajj Idris to Kanem. This great and just king and pious administrator of the lands of Islam and respecter of the rights of all Muhammadans, on setting forth for Kanem on this journey, after the destruction of the rebels, gave orders to his captains, commanders and bodyguard and the remainder of his army to collect rations for the journey without delay. They did so. The Sultan set out from Gambaru in the month of Shawwal and encamped at Zantam; from there he passed on to Ghotuwa, then to

Milu, Lada, Burkumwa, Ghawali, Milti, Bari, Gayawa, Malahe, Dagimsil and Hugulgul, in the neighbourhood of Dilaram, then to Ruru and on to Kasuda.

The Sultan stayed at Kasuda three or four days having previously sent Malagalma Dalatu, chief of Miri, to Sultan Muhammad ibn Abdul Lahi to summon him to Sulu in the Kananiyya country with his people the Bulala. Dalatu left Kasuda on Saturday and was followed on Tuesday by the Sultan who travelled eastwards and halted at Siki Danamna to await the Sultan Muhammad Abdul Lahi. The Bulala Sultan arrived with his army headed by our messenger Malagalma Dalatu on Friday night and encamped in front of our Sultan's house. The troops were ordered to parade outside in full strength. Our Sultan and Sultan Muhammad ibn Abdul Lahi sat together in the same council. Many matters were discussed and the boundary was delimited between Bornu and Kanem, whereby we obtained Kagusti and the whole Siru district. This was made public to all and the commanders on both sides who were present at the proclamation heard it without dismay or opposition. Babaliya also was alloted to Bornu, but our Sultan granted them what remained of Kanem through his affection for Sultan Muhammad ibn Abdul Lahi. But for this he would not have given them an inch of territory in Kanem. I lay emphasis on this, because when our Sultan made his expedition to Kanem, and encamped at Ma'o, it was he who routed Abdul Jalil in three separate actions; firstly, at the town of Kirsila, then at Tusa or Gamira, and lastly at Aghafi. The Sultan remained there some time to await the arrival of his partisans and was joined by many of the troops of Abdul Jalil. Such captains and commanders as gave him their allegiance, he placed under the command of Sultan Muhammad ibn Abdul Lahi, having previously made them swear on the Kura'an that they would obey him and help him to victory. Having pronounced his friendly intentions towards Sultan Muhammad he gave him sway over the remaining territories of Kanem because of his affection for him. It was this affection alone which led him to alienate his territory.

Everyone of the Bulala whom he swore in at Aghafi heard the speech of our Sultan which we have mentioned above and also the captains and commanders of the Bulala. After the settling of the frontiers of Bornu and Kanem the Sultan returned to Bornu.

Let us now resume the account of the treaty between ourselves and the Bulala entered into at Siki. When the conference took place between our Sultan and Sultan Muhammad ibn Abdul Lahi in front of the Sultan's house at Siki, everyone of the Bulala applauded, and sought pardon and swore by God that they would never again oppose our Sultan neither would they oppose their own Sultan Muhammad or his son. This they swore a second time after having sworn it previously to our Sultan.

Sultan Muhammad ibn Abdul Lahi and his people who had come with him then returned on Friday night, the night of the full moon, after obtaining a complete pardon, with their minds at ease after the terror which they had previously felt. We have heard from those who know the facts, that when the Bulala approached our Sultan's dwelling at Siki, they came into his presence invoking the protection of God, and humbly mentioning His name, and in such terror of their lives that they dismounted from their horses. The only one who felt no fear was their Sultan, Muhammad ibn Abdul Lahi in person, for he relied on the affection which our Sultan felt for him.

When they had sworn in at Aghafl heard the speech of our Sultan which we have mentioned above and also the captains and commanders of the Bulala. After the settling of the frontiers of Bornu and Kanem the Sultan returned to Bornu.

Sultan Muhammad ibn Abdul Lahi and his people who had come with him then returned on Friday night, the night of the full moon, after obtaining a complete pardon, with their minds at ease after the terror which they had previously felt. We have heard from those who know the facts, that when the Bulala approached our Sultan's dwelling at Siki, they came into his presence invoking the protection of God, and humbly mentioning His name, and in such terror of their lives that they dismounted from their horses. The only one who felt no fear was their Sultan, Muhammad ibn Abdul Lahi in person, for he relied on the affection which our Sultan felt for him. When they had sworn an oath and received a free pardon from our Sultan, they were overjoyed, and praised God for escaping with their lives. On mounting to take their departure, they offered up thanks to God and returned with their sultan to the place from which they had come.

When Friday dawned, Chiroma Burdima arrived with the remaining commanders and chiefs of the Bulala. They were given audience of our Sultan on Saturday and clapped their hands and sought pardon as their predecessors had done on the previous day.

The Sultan ordered his Wazir Idris ibn Haruna to swear them on the Book of God, and they all took the oath without exception. Our Sultan gave orders that on the following day, a Saturday, every commander and captain was to parade fully equipped, each in a separate position, accompanied by his followers, grooms, and shieldbearers, since he intended to review them one after the other and wished to inspect them without confusion. On the appointed day the whole army in smart array took up their positions one by one in great number without overcrowding, for the Sultan to inspect them. On the Sunday, the Sultan did not inspect the shieldbearers and the Koyam, but did so on the next day. All our commanders and captains rejoiced at our increase of territory and at our eastward journey having come to a conclusion.

17. ALVARE II AND ALVARE III, KINGS OF CONGO

RELATIONS BETWEEN THE KINGDOM OF CONGO AND THE PAPACY. 1613.

After the Jaga attack had been subdued, the kings of Congo, Alvare I (1568–1587), Alvare II (1587–1614), and Alvare III (1614–1622) sought to reassert their authority and to disengage themselves from dependence on the Portuguese. Alvare I had sent Duarte López to Rome in 1583, hoping to enlist Vatican support against Portugal. In 1590, Alvare II allied himself against the Portuguese in Angola and in

1604 sought to make the Congo a papal vassal. The Vatican rejected this proposal but agreed to intercede with the King of Spain on behalf of Congo. The appointment of Monsignor Vivès inaugurated an era of close relations between Rome and San Salvador. Acting on the appeal of Alvare III for support, the Vatican remonstrated with the King of Spain to check the Portuguese who invaded the Congo from Angola.

ALVARO II TO POPE PAUL V
SAN SALVADOR
(CAPITAL OF THE KINGDOM OF CONGO)
27 FEBRUARY 1613

Dom Alvaro II by divine grace, augmenter of confession to the faith of Jesus Christ and defender of that same faith in these lands of Ethiopia, king of the very ancient kingdom of Congo, Angola, Matamba, Ocango, and of the Ambandu, and also of many other kingdoms and sovereignties that are subject to him this side and beyond the marvelous river Zaire. Written from his royal city of San Salvador, the 27th of February 1613.

To the very Holy Father, Pope Paul V, at present head of the Church of God Our Lord.

He expresses the desire that he has to come personally to kiss the feet of His Holiness.

He acknowledges the reception of the letter from His Holiness, received in the year 1611. He thanks him for the title of Majesty, which was given to him in that letter, which was read from the pulpit by a father of Saint Dominic who was here at that time.

He expresses his thanks for the welcome made for Dom Antonio Manuel, his ambassador, who died in Rome.

Dom Antonio Manuel, not being able to be admitted as ambassador and thus unable to kiss the feet of His Holiness, having been taken away by death; the king not being able to come himself, nor send others at short notice, has chosen for his ambassador to Your Holiness Monsignor Jean-Baptiste Vivès, prothonotary of the number of participants and referendary [arbitrator] of the one and the other signature, so that with all the solemnity of ambassadors of kings, he may kiss the feet of His Holiness in his name, swear allegiance and express the joy which he feels about his elevation to the Sovereign Pontry. Monsignor Vivès will be able to take care of the business entrusted to D. Antonio Manuel. . . .

He chooses the Cardinal of Saint Cecilia as protector of his kingdom. If both should die, His Holiness may replace them as he sees fit.

From J. Cuvelier and L. Jadin, *L'Ancien Congo d'après les Archives Romaines (1518–1640)*, (Brussels: Académie Royale des Sciences d'Outre-Mer, 1954), pp. 329–331, 333–335, 348–351. Trans. by Nell Elizabeth Painter and Robert O. Collins. Reprinted by permission. Bracketed material has been supplied by Robert O. Collins.

He has been informed that the Portuguese in this country seek to bring about a division between himself and the King of Spain, so that the latter would be prompted to conquer the kingdom of Congo. For his own part, he has always shown friendship to this king and he has favored his subjects.

He has always treated the churches and priests well and has made sure that the tithes are paid. He has had the tithes collected by his servants in specie because foodstuffs could not be transported due to the size of the kingdom and could not be taken out of the villages. They have agreed on a certain number of measures of Nzimbu, the word that designates their money.

He has not received the brief mentioned in the letter.

He asks that by means of a brief, everyone would be prohibited, on pain of censure, from encroaching on the lands of his kingdom or taking possession of the mines. . . .

He asks for a brief in order to be able to defend himself against the attacks of the bishops. If he is not treated justly, may he notify them by a priest or cleric, because the bishop threatens to interdict him and deprive him of priests. This suggests to him that the Portuguese desire to conquer his kingdom. In the past pontiffs accorded very ample briefs, but these briefs were lost during the wars with the "Giacchi" [Jaga]. . . .

He is very badly treated by the Portuguese and the prelates. He is very ashamed of this. He hides it so that the pagan kings may not be glad of it and because he expects protection from Rome. If his authority is maintained these other kings may be converted.

He suffers many vexations because of the distance from the King of Portugal and because his business is sent to Portugal, where the relatives of the Portuguese who are in the Congo occupy certain offices.

The Christian religion is making no progress because there are no priests. . . . The foreign priests who come to the Congo have no preoccupation other than that of enriching themselves and returning to their countries; they take no interest in gaining souls for heaven. If religious personnel are sent, may they be like the "Mariani" (Monks of Mary), or Carmelites, who came during his father's time. They got very good results because of the example they set, their doctrine, and their charity.

As for the Dominican fathers requested from the King of Portugal, of the four he sent, two died during the course of the trip and the two who arrived at their destination are hardly useful.

They interfere in the foreign affairs of the kingdom and in the plans and duties of the king at their own bidding. May those fathers who will come in the future be ordered to keep to their own duties.

He begs that a brief be accorded the bishop giving him the faculty of dispensing with irregularities of notable persons wanting to be ordained and also the faculty to dispense with the impediment of consanguinity and affinity, with the order that the bishop not make difficulties in according them and not do so according to his own desires, but that he carry out what Your Holiness commands and what the king asks.

At the time of the first vacancy of the episcopal seat, there was much dispute and disorder among the members of the chapter. They abused themselves publicly at mass and in the offices in the presence of the king, imposing conflicting censures. If the situation had not been remedied, it would have become aggravated. The remedy (there was no other means) was to threaten them with expulsion from the kingdom. Then they calmed down.

He begs that remedies be found for other similar cases, for they take excessive liberties. The king asks that the vicar, who at that time did not conduct himself according to law, be sent away and another chosen by means of a brief that he requests and that the new one be of the best group and chosen from among those who are in agreement with him.

ALVARO III TO POPE PAUL V
SAN SALVADOR, 25 OCTOBER 1617

Very Holy Father,

Myself, Dom Alvaro the Third, by divine grace, augmenter of the faith of Jesus Christ and defender of the faith in these lands of Ethiopia, king of the very ancient kingdom of Congo, Angola, Matamba, Ocanga, and of the Ambandu, here and beyond the marvelous river Zaire [Congo], and of many other kingdoms and neighboring sovereignties, . . .

As the very humble and very obedient son of Your Holiness, I kiss his very holy feet in my name and of my royal person as well as in the name of all my kingdoms and states, I give him the allegiance due him as the universal pastor of the flock of Christ. I beg Your Holiness with all possible ardor to accept the above-said allegiance, which I have given and offered by the intermediary of my procurer, Dom Jean-Baptiste Viv6s of Valencia. The prothonotary and referendary [arbitrator] of Your Holiness will remit it, according to the mode and manner which the other Catholic Kings are accustomed to in dealing with the apostolic Holy See. I give him all necessary faculties to pledge allegiance as well as to treat affairs in my name to Your Holiness and to all the Roman pontiffs, his successors. If for any reason he cannot do so, we would like Your Holiness and his successor to have the power to name other procurers in my name and in the name of my kingdoms. In this way the designs of King Dom Alvaro II, my lord and father whom God has, in His glory, taken up again. This is what he had in mind when he sent Dom Antonio Manuel, who died in Rome, to the apostolic Holy See. He entrusted letters to him, affairs to be discussed and commissioned him with an embassy. it is necessary that these projects be developed for the greater service of God and for the greater good of Christianity.

I reconfirm the instructions he gave and the business he negotiated, and I humbly beg Your Holiness to give orders so that old requests and those which more recently have been addressed to the abovenamed procurer, to be submitted by him to Your Holiness, may be examined. All these affairs are contained in instructions that I have sent, signed by my hand, which manifest that my goal is to promote the divine cult for the greater glory of God, the exaltation of His Church, the confusion of barbarians and pagans, and the consolidation of Catholics.

By other routes I have written to Your Holiness, to the Seignior Cardinal, protector of these kingdoms, and to the above-named procurer, my ordinary ambassador resident at that Roman court, Dom Jean-Baptiste Vivès.

In those letters I announced the death of King Alvaro II, my lord and father. I related that after his death, given my young age, the kingdom was put in the possession of Dom Bernard, my uncle, bastard half-brother of the above-named king, with the help of a few important people. But after less than a year, the kingdom, seeing the injustices done to me, scandalized by some disorders indicative of little Christian religion, took up arms against him without my knowing. This was under the command of Dom Antonio da Silva, Grand Duke of Mbamba, a province of the kingdom, and general of the kingdom, to whom the above-named king, my lord and father, before dying, had given over my person, as executor of his will. Dom Bernard was deprived of the kingdom and his life, and I was reestablished in power to the great joy of all, and I was recognized by all the states as their king and their universal lord.

I beg Your Holiness to deign to send many favors and spiritual graces to me and to all my subjects, to deign to let us rejoice in his letters, which will bring us many benefits and much honor, and the courage to resist the barbarous pride of paganism by which, from all sides of our kingdom, we are besieged.

We also beg Your Holiness to deign to receive us forever under the. protection and defense of the apostolic Holy See and to make his Catholic Majesty, King Dom Philippe [of Spain], whom we greatly esteem and honor as our well-loved brother, favorable to us, recognizing the great benefits that I and all these kingdoms and this Christianity owe to his magnificence. These benefits have cost His Majesty great expenditures, which he has not ceased to make in favor of this Christianity whose culture he assures. Even so, we are under the weight of injustice on the part of his captains-general and governors who reside in Angola. They enter the lands belonging to our crown and make themselves masters there, as if it were enemy territory, without receiving any such orders from His Majesty. On the contrary, the king orders them in his instructions, which he gives them, to aid and serve us in all instances. They do not do this, having only their own interests in mind. They commit numerous unjust acts, making alliance with a nation of extremely barbarous men called Gindas and Ingas [Jagas], who live on human flesh.

May Your Holiness deign to find a remedy for this. I beg him to accord me his immediate protection.

May the Lord care for the very holy person of Your Holiness in the measure that his very humble and very obedient son desires. . . .

18. GASPAR BOCARRO

FROM TETE TO KILWA. 1616.

Gaspar Bocarro appears to have been the first European to travel overland from Tete on the Zambezi to Kilwa in 1616 through what is now the southern interior of Tanzania. The account of this journey appears in Extractos da Decada, by Antonio Bocarro, Keeper of the Archives and Chronicler of India at Lisbon from 1631 to 1649. In his official capacity, Bocarro had access to official correspondence from East Africa and India. The Extractos were dedicated to Philip III of Portugal (1621–1640) but were not actually printed by the Royal Academy of Sciences at Lisbon until 1876. Gaspar Bocarro may have been related to Antonio Bocarro. Gaspar performed the journey to ensure the safe passage of African silver to Portugal.

At the time when Diogo Simoës sent the silver to His Majesty by means of the religious of Saint Dominic, who perforce had to pass by the fortress of Moçambique, and to go from thence to India, there were in the rivers of Cuama[1] certain persons dissatisfied with Diogo Simoës, who said openly that the Captain of Moçambique ought to seize the silver and send it on his own orders to His Majesty; and some wrote that this should be done.

When Diogo Simoës heard this, he was very angry. For this reason Gaspar Bocarro, a man of noble birth, brought up in the household of the Marquis of Ferreira, who had spent many years in these rivers, offered to make the journey by land from Tete[2] to the coast of Melinde[3] so he could put Moçambique out of his way, and from the coast pass to Ormuz[4] and from there make his way by land to Spain and deliver the silver, which Diogo Simoës had given to him, to His Majesty: which journey he would make at his own expense, so as to serve the said lord: and he also would lend two thousand cruzados[6] to help to maintain the fort at Chicove[7] for which no provisions had come from India.

Diogo Simoës was pleased, accepted his offer, and received the said money, which Gaspar Bocarro gave him for the maintenance of the fort; then he delivered

---

From Sir John Gray, "A Journey by Land from Tete to Kilwa in 1616," in *Tanganyika Notes and Records*, vol. XXV (1948), pp. 40–45. Reprinted by permission of the Tanzania Society, Dar es Salaam.

1. The name given at this date to the country in the region of the Zambesi delta.
2. A town about 270 miles up the Zambesi, where at this date there was a fort.
3. In contemporary Portuguese letters and chronicles [of] the coast between Cape Delgado and Cape Guardafui [are] usually related to "the coast of Malindi." . . .
4. An island at the entrance to the Persian Gulf, which was at this date in the possession of the Portuguese.
5. Portuguese historians call the period 1580–1640 "the Spanish captivity," it being the period during which their country was ruled by the kings of Spain. At this date Philip III of Portugal (1599–1621) was also Phillip IV of Spain.
6. The cruzado was valued at 400 reis. . . At the beginning of the seventeenth century 400 reis were worth about 5s. 4d.
7. On the banks of Zambesi above Tete.

to him two frasilas[8] of silver ore in one of which there was a small stone of pure silver, which appeared to have been smelted, but was pure in origin: (he also gave him) authenticated papers and credentials, so that he might deliver all to His Majesty. When this had been arranged and concluded, Gaspar Bocarro provided himself with necessaries for his very long and risky journey. Gaspar Bocarro left Tete in March, 1616, taking in his company ten or twelve of his slaves. He crossed to the other side of the River Zambeze and made his way through the lands of Bororo. After two days' journeying he reached the village of Inhampury, where he bought a thousand bracelets of copper wire, which are made by the Cafres of this village, because they have plenty of copper there. These bracelets serve as money for petty expenses on all these roads in Cafraria. Bocarro gave Inhampury a present of some garments and beads, which came to seven cruzados. They left there and slept at Baue, a village of the same Inhampury, where one of his wives lived, to whom he gave another present, which was worth three cruzados. Thence they made their way for three days through thickets and desert land to Danda, a town subject to Muzura, who is the biggest Cafre Lord in all the lands of Bororo. To the governor of this town Bocarro gave cloths and beads, which were worth two cruzados. After this they slept at Bunga, a large village, subject to Muzura, where he gave the governor one cruzado's worth of cloth and beads. Thence Gaspar Bocarro sent Muzura word of his coming and sent ahead of him a present, which the Cafres call "the mouth," consisting of cloth and beads, which were worth five cruzados. On reaching the town, in which he dwelt and which is called Marauy, he went to see Muzura and gave him garments, and beads, and silk cloths, which were worth seventy cruzados. He also gave him his bed which included the hangings, a bolster of damask, and linen sheets, because it was a heavy weight to carry such a bed on the shoulders for such a long journey. Muzura gave Bocarro two tusks of ivory, which were worth eighteen cruzados, and a black woman, and food during the fifteen days that he stayed there (and he also gave) to all his people plenty of millet, rice, hens, capons, cows and figs, and he also gave him three Cafres, who were his subjects and were to act as guides and to guard them safely when passing through his lands.

With these three guides Bocarro left Muzura and slept at Moromba, a town of Muzura. He gave the governor thereof, who was called Inhamocumba, garments and beads, which were worth two cruzados, and he gave Bocarro three more Cafres to accompany him and to be his guides. Near this town of Moromba is the great river Manganja,[9] or lake which looks like a sea, from which flows the river Nhanha,[10] which enters the Zambesi below Sena,[11] where it is called the river of Chiry.[12] From Moromba Gaspar Bocarro set out with this three additional guides, and made his way alongside this river Nhanha, and slept on its shore, and on the fol-

8. The frasila weighed 35–36 English pounds.
9. "Manganja" appears to be a Portuguese corruption of some Bantu word which has "nyanja" (cf. Note 10) as one of its roots. Manganja is clearly identifiable with Lake Nyassa.
10. Apparently the common Bantu word "nyanja" meaning an expanse of water such as a lake.
11. A town about 150 miles up the Zambesi, where at this date the Portuguese had a fort.
12. Sc. the Shire, which flows out of Lake Nyassa and joins the Zambesi a little below Sena.

lowing day crossed over to the other side in vessels belonging to the native Cafres.[13] (Then) he made his way North and slept at the town of Caramboe, a son of Muzura, to whom Bocarro gave garments and beads which were worth seven cruzados. Thence he dined at a village called Mocama and slept at another village called Mogombe, to the governor of which he gave cloths and beads which were worth one cruzado. There he slept on the confines of the lands of Muzura's son.

From here onward begin the lands which are called Manguro, and are subject to Chicoave, who is a friend and quasi-vassal of Muzura, for he is afraid of him. He began to make his way through these lands and slept at the village of Machambe, to whom he gave cloths and beads which were worth two cruzados. From there he slept at the village of Muzunguira, to whom he gave bracelets and beads which were worth one cruzado. From there he slept at the town, in which dwelt Chicoave, the lord of these lands. Before he came to him he gave him in advance for "the mouth" one hundred bracelets, one cloth, and some beads, which were worth seven cruzados. When he spoke with this Cafre, he gave him another present, which was worth seven cruzados, and the Cafre gave him a tusk of ivory, which was worth three cruzados. Muzura sent this Cafre a present so that he might give the road and guides to Bocarro, and he gave him his son, who thenceforward accompanied him together with the other guides of Muzura. Thence he crossed a river called Ruambara, which he crossed in boats. After leaving the town of Chicoave he slept at the village Chipanga and after at the village of Changuessa, to whom he gave a cloth and a bundle of beads. Thence he slept in an uninhabited place and on the following day at the village of Mauano, to whom he gave a cloth and a necklace of beads. Thence slept at a village called Rupapa, the lord of which was Quitenga, to whom he gave three cloths and twenty bracelets. From there he slept in a thicket and on the following day proceeded along the river Rofuma[14] to the village of Muangongo, to whom he gave fifty bracelets, two necklaces of beads, a machira,[15] and a cloth. He ferried Gaspar Bocarro and all his people in his boat to the other bank of the river and accompanied them for three days.

The lord of the lands, which extend from this river Rofuma as far as the salt sea, is Manhanga. Leaving this river Bocarro slept at the house of Darama, to whom he gave six bracelets and a few beads. Thence he slept at the village of Davia, to whom he gave twenty bracelets and a necklace of beads. From there he slept in the town in which dwells Manhanga, the lord of these lands. Before he came to him, Bocarro sent in advance to acquaint him as to his coming, and sent as "the mouth" two hundred bracelets and a machira. When he came to him, he gave him a further six hundred bracelets. Muzura likewise sent this Cafre a hundred bracelets, and a machira, and a black girl, so that he might make the roads through his lands free to Bocarro. He (sc. Manhanga) gave Bocarro a tusk of ivory and sent to Muzura a present of garments, which had come there from the coast of Melinde,[16] because this Cafre is

13. Bocarro evidently made his crossing in the upper reaches of the Shire very close to its exit from Lake Nyassa, but never actually reached that lake.
14. Sc. the Rovuma.
15. "A sort of cloak or upper garment worn by the Cafres."
16. Probably from Kilwa Kisiwani.

obedient to Muzura. Here Muzura's three guides returned, and also the three guides of Inhamocumba, the governor of Moramba, and also Chicoave's son. From here Bocarro travelled onwards with guides, who were given to him by Manhanga and to whom he gave forthwith twenty bracelets. They made their way for seven days through country, which was uninhabited, because it had been destroyed by the Zimbas, who passed that way making war. At the end of seven days they reached the village of Chiponda, brother of Manhanga, to whom he gave fifty bracelets and a machira; and he (sc. Chiponda) gave him a small tusk of ivory; and he also gave him another Cafre to act as his guide and to accompany him on the road from there to the seashore, to whom Bocarro gave twenty bracelets. From there they made their way for four days through desert lands, and at the end of that time came to the village of Ponde, to whom they gave a few beads. Thence they went to the village of Morengue, to whom they gave a machira and a few beads. Thence they travelled through desert land for four days and came to Bucury, a village of Moors,[17] where they slept. The next day they came to the shore of the salt sea at the hour of midday. From there they embarked and passed over to the island of Quiloa,[18] which is opposite to the shore, where were the factor and other Portuguese, who made Bocarro their guest.

The inhabited lands along this road abound in foodstuffs, that is to say, millet, rice, fruits, hens, sheep, cows, and goats, all of which are cheap. Gaspar Bocarro spent fifty-three days on the road and also spent more than one hundred and fifty cruzados in presents and for his own food and for the food which he gave to the people who accompanied him on the road. Though Gaspar Bocarro spent fifty-three days on the road with all his servants, they (sc. the servants) were able to return from Quiloa to Tete, travelling light, in no more than twenty-five days.

At Quiloa Bocarro took ship for his voyage to Ormuz. On reaching Mombaça he heard that the roads in Persia were being obstructed by the Shah, and the land was at war. Therefore he decided to return to Moçambique and thence to the rivers of Cuama, where he arrived safely.

I have written all the details of this journey, the names of the villages and the lands, and their lords, and the expenses incurred by Gaspar Bocarro, because, if any one in time to come wishes to make this journey, the adventurer, who makes it, may know about the road and the expense.

17. Like other Portuguese chroniclers Bocarro used the word Moor (Mouro) to distinguish the coast inhabitant of mixed Arab and African blood from the pure Arab from Asia.

18. Kilwa Kisiwani was at this date ruled by a "Moorish" Sultan, who was independent of the Portuguese, but was on friendly terms with them.

19. FATHER LOBO

PORTUGUESE MISSIONARIES IN ETHIOPIA. 1620.

Father Jeronimo Lobo (1593–1678) left Portugal for Goa, India, in 1622. After residing in India for a year, during which he completed his studies in divinity, he received letters from Ethiopia proclaiming that the Emperor of Ethiopia had been converted to the Church of Rome and desired Roman Catholic missionaries. Father Lobo was among the eight Jesuit priests who were selected to go to Ethiopia and administer to the emperor. At the time, Ethiopia was in constant revolt against the emperor's flirtation with Roman Catholicism. The emperor returned to the Coptic (Egyptian Christian) Church in 1632.

I continued two years at my residence in Tigre [in northern Ethiopia], entirely taken up with the duties of the mission, preaching, confessing, baptising, and enjoyed a longer quiet and repose than I had ever done since I left Portugal. During this time one of our fathers, being always sick, and of a constitution which the air of Abyssinia was very hurtful to, obtained a permission from our superiors to return to the Indies. I was willing to accompany him through part of his way, and went with him over a desert, at no great distance from my residence, where I found many trees loaded with a kind of fruit, called by the natives Anchoy, about the bigness of an apricot, and very yellow, which is much eaten without any ill effect. I therefore made no scruple of gathering and eating it, without knowing that the inhabitants always peeled it, the rind being a violent purgative; so that, eating the fruit and skin together, I fell into such a disorder as almost brought me to my end. The ordinary dose is six of these rinds, and I had devoured twenty.

I removed from thence to Debaroa, fifty-four miles nearer the sea, and crossed in my way the desart of the province of Saraoe. The country is fruitful, pleasant, and populous. There are greater numbers of Moors in these parts than in any other province of Abyssinia; and the Abyssins of this country are not much better than the Moors.

I was at Debaroa when the persecution was first set on foot against the Catholics. Sultan Segued, who had been so great a favourer of us, was grown old, and his spirit and authority decreased with his strength. His son, who was arrived at manhood, being weary of waiting so long for the crown he was to inherit, took occasion to blame his father's conduct, and found some reason for censuring all his actions; he even proceeded so far as to give orders sometimes contrary to the emperor's. He had embraced the Catholic religion, rather through complaisance than conviction or inclination; and many of the Abyssins, who had done the same, waited only for an opportunity of making public profession of the ancient erroneous opinions, and of re-uniting themselves to the [Coptic] church of Alexandria. So artfully can this people dissemble their sentiments, that we had not been able hitherto to distinguish our

From Father Jerome Lobo, *A Voyage to Abyssinia*, trans. by Samuel Johnson (London: A. Bettesworth and C. Hitch, 1735), pp. 125–131.

real from our pretended favourers; but as soon as this prince began to give evident tokens of his hatred, even in the life-time of the emperor, we saw all the courtiers and governors, who had treated us with such a shew of friendship, declare against us, and persecute us as disturbers of the public tranquillity; who had come into Ethiopia with no other intention than to abolish the ancient laws and customs of the country, to sow divisions between father and son, and preach up a revolution.

After having borne all sorts of affronts and ill-treatments, we retired to our house at Fremona, in the midst of our countrymen, who had been settling round about us a long time, imagining we should be more secure there, and that, at least during the life of the emperor, they would not come to extremities, or proceed to open force. I laid some stress upon the kindness which the viceroy of Tigre had shown to us, and in particular to me; but was soon convinced that those hopes had no real foundation, for he was one of the most violent of our persecutors. He seized upon all our lands, and advancing with his troops to Fremona, blocked up the town. The army had not been stationed there long before they committed all sorts of disorders; so that one day a Portuguese, provoked beyond his temper at the insolence of some of them, went out with his four sons, and wounding several of them, forced the rest back to their camp.

We thought we had good reason to apprehend an attack; their troops were increasing, our town was surrounded, and on the point of being forced. Our Portuguese therefore thought, that without staying till the last extremities, they might lawfully repel one violence by another; and sallying out, to the number of fifty, wounded about threescore of the Abyssins, and had put them to the sword, but that they feared it might bring too great an odium upon our cause. The Portuguese were some of them wounded, but happily none died on either side.

Though the times were by no means favourable to us, every one blamed the conduct of the viceroy; and those who did not commend our action, made the necessity we were reduced to of self-defence an excuse for it. The viceroy's principal design was to get my person into his possession, imagining, that if I was once in his power, all the Portuguese would pay him a blind obedience. Having been unsuccessful in his attempt by open force, he made use of the arts of negociation, but with an event not more to his satisfaction. This viceroy being recalled, a son-in-law of the emperor's succeeded, who treated us even worse than his predecessor had done.

When he entered upon his command, he loaded us with kindnesses, giving us so many assurances of his protection, that, while the emperor lived, we thought him one of our friends; but no sooner was our protector dead, than this man pulled off his mask; and quitting all shame, let us see that neither the fear of God nor any other consideration was capable of restraining him, when we were to be distressed. The persecution then becoming general, there was no longer any place of security for us in Abyssinia; where we were looked upon by all as the authors of all the civil commotions; and many councils were held to determine in what manner they should dispose of us. Several were of opinion, that the best way would be to kill us all at once, and affirmed, that no other means were left of re-establishing order and tranquillity in the kingdom.

Others, more prudent, were not for putting us to death with so little consideration; but advised, that we should be banished to one of the isles of the lake of Dambia [Tana], an affliction more severe than death itself. These alledged, in vindication of their opinions, that it was reasonable to expect, if they put us to death, that the viceroy of the Indies would come with fire and sword to demand satisfaction. This argument made so great an impression upon some of them, that they thought no better measures could be taken than to send us back again to the Indies. This proposal, however, was not without its difficulties; for they suspected, that when we should arrive at the Portuguese territories, we would levy an army, return back to Abyssinia, and under pretence of establishing the Catholic religion, revenge all the injuries we had suffered.

While they were thus deliberating upon our fate, we were imploring the succour of the Almighty with fervent and humble supplications, intreating him, in the midst of our sighs and tears that he would not suffer his own cause to miscarry; and that however it might please him to depose of our lives, which we prayed he would assist us to lay down with patience and resignation, worthy of the faith for which we were persecuted, he would not permit our enemies to triumph over the truth.

Thus we passed our days and nights in prayers, in affliction and tears, continually crowded with widows and orphans that subsisted upon our charity, and came to us for bread, when we had not any for ourselves.

While we were in this distress, we received an account that the viceroy of the Indies had fitted out a powerful fleet against the king of Mombaza, who, having thrown off the authority of the Portuguese, had killed the governor of the fortress, and had since committed many acts of cruelty. The same fleet, as we were informed, after the king of Mombaza was reduced, was to burn and ruin Zeila, in revenge of the death of two Portuguese Jesuits who were killed by the king in the year 1604. As Zeila was not far from the frontiers of Abyssinia, they imagined that they already saw the Portuguese invading their country.

The viceroy of Tigre had enquired of me, a few days before, how many men one India ship carried; and being told that the compliment of some was a thousand men, he compared that answer with the report then spread over all the country, that there were eighteen Portuguese vessels on the coast of Adel; and concluded, that they were manned by an army of eighteen thousand men. Then considering what had been achieved by four hundred, under the command of Don Christopher de Gama, he thought Abyssinia already ravaged, or subjected to the king of Portugal. Many declared themselves of his opinion, and the court took its measures with respect to us from these uncertain and ungrounded rumours. Some were so infatuated with their apprehensions, that they undertook to describe the camp of the Portuguese, and affirmed that they had heard the report of their cannons.

All this contributed to exasperate the inhabitants, and reduced us often to the point of being massacred. At length they came to a resolution of giving us up to the Turks, assuring them that we were masters of a vast treasure; in hope, that after they had inflicted all kinds of tortures on us, to make us confess where we had hid our gold, or what we had done with it, they would at length kill us in rage for the disappointment. Nor was this their only view, for they believed that the Turks would, by killing us, kindle such an irreconcilable hatred between themselves and our nation, as would make it necessary for them to keep us out of the Red sea, of which they are entirely masters: so that their determination was as politic as cruel. Some pretend, that the Turks were engaged to put us to death as soon as we were in their power.

20. JAN VAN RIEBEECK AND Z. WAGENAAR

OF THE NATIVE TRIBES OF SOUTH AFRICA. 1652.

The first two governors of the Cape of Good Hope after it was annexed as a trading and revictualing station by the Dutch East India Company in 1652 were Jan van Riebeeck (governor, 1652–1662) and Z. Wagenaar (governor, 1663–1666). Among the documents that they wrote for their successors were the following descriptions of the Khoikhoi (Hottentot) population of the Cape.[1] At this time the Khoikhoi still retained their traditional organization of chiefdoms. This organization was soon disrupted by the alien influence of the Europeans, and the Khoikhoi became a landless population that existed in outlawry or in servitude to white masters. The chiefdoms were incorporated under the law of the Cape and were given some rights and partial protection only in 1828 as the result of missionary agitation on their behalf.

EXTRACTS OF MEMORANDUM LEFT BY COMMANDER J. VAN RIEBEECK, FOR THE INFORMATION AND GUIDANCE OF HIS SUCCESSOR Z. WAGENAAR

May 5. [The first paragraph merely refers to the several instructions and other papers explanatory of the objects in taking possession at the Cape. Then follow the several subjects here omitted, which are denoted by the following marginals, given in italics].

Company's first object attained; in addition to other refreshments. A good prospect of fruit, particularly from the vines; also olives in time. The corn lands turn out much poorer than was supposed. Trade, and the condition of the Cape Tribes.

Coming now to the subject of the trade with these native tribes, the same is now, thanks to God! on a much better footing than ever, through the knowledge which we are gradually acquiring of various races of people in the interior, whose names, with their places of abode and mode of living are thus briefly stated, in order to convey a better idea of their circumstances. We have then, in the first place:

From D. Moodie, *The Record* (Cape Town: A. S. Robertson, 1838), vol. I, pp. 246–251, 290–293.

1. Although these are the first reliable contemporary accounts of the Khoikhoi, others of the same period may be found in Isaac Schapera and B. Farrington (eds.), *The Early Cape Hottentots, 1688–1695* (Cape Town: Van Riebeeck Society, 1933), vol. XIV.

The GORINGHAICONAS,[2] of whom Herry has been usually called the Captain; these are strandloopers, or fishers, who are, exclusive of women and children, not above 18 men in number, supporting themselves, without the least live stock of any description, by fishing from the rocks along the coast, thus furnishing a great accommodation to the Company's people and freemen, and also rendering much assistance to those who keep house, by washing, scouring, fetching firewood, and other domestic work; and some of them placing their little daughters in the service of the married people, where they are clothed in our manner, but they must have a slack rein, and will not be kept strictly, such appears to be contrary to their nature; some of them, however, begin to be tolerably civilized, and the Dutch language is so far implanted among them, old and young, that nothing can any longer be kept secret when mentioned in their presence, and very little in that of the:

GORINGHAIQUAS, whose Chief is named Gogosoa, and who are the Capemans; they are, exclusive of women and children, about 300 men capable of bearing arms, supplied with about enough cattle to provide for their own wants, but as they begin to be somewhat fond of mercantile gains, (coopmanachtige) they are rather increasing their stock, particularly as they have always been knowing enough, upon the approach of strangers from the interior with pretty good cattle, to act as brokers and guides to conduct the strangers to us; exchanging their leanest and worst cattle for the good, and then bringing those strangers to us, and insisting upon it that they have been the means of enticing and fetching them out of the interior, &c. in which manner they well know how to enrich themselves, becoming every day worse and more cunning; these are they who pretend that this Cape land has been theirs from all ages, and who, seeing that we were betaking ourselves to permanent agriculture, made war upon us in the year 1659, on account, according to their statements, of their harsh treatment by some of the free men; but on seeing, contrary to their expectation, that we, though assailed at the weakest, were not to be so easily driven away, and that, meanwhile, the chief or king of the Saldanhars, took the opportunity of that disturbed time, to form an alliance with us-which alliances they had always used every art to prevent, &c. they were induced two years ago to request and to conclude a peace with us, as also did:

The GORACHOUQUAS, or tobacco thieves, so called because they once stole, from the field, the tobacco belonging to some free men, and whose chief is named Choro. You have been in both their camps—they have, besides women and children, 6 or 700 men capable of bearing arms, and are fully 6 times as rich in cattle as the last mentioned tribe, and a few head are sometimes bought from them; but nothing of importance.

They have, since the war before mentioned, generally lived close to the Capemans, and about a day's journey to the N. E. behind the Leopards Hill, not far from, and as it would seem, under the wing of the Saldanhars; but this April both tribes have come back to live at the foot of the Bosheuvel, under our protection, in consequence, as it would seem, of some difference which has arisen between them

2. The Goringhaiconas and other tribes mentioned therein are all Hottentot peoples (ed.).

and the Saldanhars, who are the:

COCHOQUAS, consisting of two divisions, under 2 chiefs, or choquees, (which means kings) the first is named Oedasoa, a quiet man, whose wife—last year deceased—was sister of the interpreter Eva, who is also a niece of Herry, and has from her childhood been brought up in our house, and can speak Dutch almost as well as a Dutch girl, and we thus derive much service from her in translation, although she does lead us a dance now and then . . . and some things must be received from her with caution.

The other chief of the Saldanhars, or Cochoquas, is named Gonnoma, and is often some distance apart from Oedasoa. They have, together, several thousand men, and generally occupy the middle of the country opposite to us, under the African mountains, extending from near False Bay, quite to Saldanha Bay, but not always remaining in one place, and moving about for change of pasture. With which Oedasoa and Gonnoma we appear to have a very firm alliance, and with whom we carry on a good, indeed a constant trade in live stock—chiefly in sheep—but not so many horned cattle that we have ever been able to spare so many as now for the refreshment of the Company's shipping; they have helped however; but we have never procured any stock whatever, deserving of the name, from the:

LITTLE CHARIGURIQUAS, a people about as numerous as the Goringhaiquas, who chiefly reside between Saldanha Bay and midway between Robben and Dassen Island—about 4 or 5 hours' walk from the sea coast, subject to Oedasoa, though they have rebelled against him; they were accustomed to be his stock keepers, but appropriated his cattle to their own use; and therefore they are not recognized by any of the Hottentoos as a people who have a Choeque or Hunque, that is a hereditary king or chief; they seem, however, to be able to take their own part, as it now begins to appear, through the fear which Oedasoa entertains for the:

NAMAQUAS, with whom the great Chariguriquas have sought and formed an alliance; this people have recently been found by us, after long search; they are very rich in cattle, and very tall in stature, almost half giants, dressed in fine prepared skins, as may be seen at full by the notes kept by our travellers, and inserted in our Journal under date the 11th March 1661; where it may also be seen that they are very favorably disposed towards us, and that they seem to be a people who carry on trade with other tribes residing further inland, and through whom the way is now in so far opened, that it is only now that we can properly begin to discover any thing better than cattle. Of these people, to all appearance, more will come to you than you can wish; and thus after 10 years toil we hope that we have opened for you a fortunate road to the North side of this Africa; whither, towards the end of September, another journey must be taken, in order to be enabled to cross the dry country (which at that season will probably be still moist after the rains) to the river upon which there is laid down, in Linschoten's map, a town (vaste plaets) called Vigiti Magna, and where there is a race of people quite different from the Hottentoos, of whom we have been hitherto treating, and to whom we shall also return, namely, to those whom we have found to be the richest, almost all of whom reside to the Eastward, along the East coast of Africa, where they sometimes show themselves in some bays, as we can discover from their own statements.[3] We have only begun to know them well during the last two years, and they are the:

CHAINOUQUAS, whose Choque or King is named Sousoa, with whom we are upon very good, and rather firm terms of friendship, and who have since that time bartered to us a great number of cattle, and a good many sheep also. They are able to supply us abundantly, and on taking leave of us last year promised to come back with a still larger quantity; we sincerely trust that you may, on the Company's account, enjoy the fortunate result, and also that, as we are given to expect by the accounts of all the Hottentoos, you may be soon visited by the:

HEUSAQUAS, from whom a messenger was last year at the fort, with intelligence that his Chief also intended to come to visit the Sourye (that is the Lord of the Land, the name by which I have been generally known,) of the Dutch, with money and cattle, to try to procure, like his friends, the Chainouquas, a share of our merchandize, which will be a most desirable event, as they are very rich in cattle, and have a strong liking for the consumable tobacco, and for certain red beads in the Company's stores, for which the cattle are procured from those people at a very cheap rate. The Hottentoos who live near us, speak in high terms of this tribe, saying that now that Sousoa is gone, they will come with such great herds of cattle, that the merchandize will fall short. This, however, need not be feared, but hoped for, *item*, also for the arrival of the:

HANCUMQUAS, who, according to the hopes held out to us, and from all that we have been able to learn, are the greatest and most powerful of all the race of greasy Hottentoos, living in houses, which like their's, are covered with mats, but of a very large size, and living permanently on the same spot, where they cultivate and dry a certain plant which they call Dacha, this they chew and eat, and consequently become very light-headed, as in India from opium, and this is the reason why they are so eager for the strongest tobacco. The Chiefs of this tribe appear to be Chiefs over all the other Choques or Kings, being entitled Choebaha, which seems to mean Emperor, or at least Upper King, or Lord over all the others.

Those now who reside further than this Chief Lord of the Hottentoos, though of the same race, and much richer in cattle than all those who live on this side of this supreme Chief, are named first, the:

CHAMAQUAS, and next them the OMAQUAS, ATIQUAS, HOUTUNQUAS, and CHAUQUAS, all subsisting like the Hancumquas, besides their countless herds of cattle, by Dacha plantations, living on fixed spots, in large mat huts, dressed in skins like all the Hottentoos, and also equally greasy, &c.

After those, are said to begin, though beyond the river Vigiti Magna, and in an Easterly direction, another race of people, called by all the before mentioned Hottentoos:

CHOBOQUA or COBONA, residing in fixed houses constructed of wood, clay, and other materials, but at the same time maintaining themselves by cattle, and

---

3. Jan van Linschoten (1563–1611), a Dutch traveler, spent nine years in the Portuguese service in the East Indies and wrote a detailed account of the Indian Ocean. His Voyages was an important contribution to sixteenth-century Europe's knowledge of Africa and Asia (ed.).

wearing clothes, whom we conjecture to be the people of Monomotopa, as Eva would often persuade us, and that—as we have also been informed through her interpretation, by the said Sousoa—there is Chory or gold and white gems among those Choboquas, of which he has promised to bring proofs, and also some one of that people. We trust that you may, for the good of the Company, experience the success of this, and procure some further account of the people of whom the messenger from the HEUSAQUAS told us, that they keep lions as tame as we keep dogs, and among whom it is said that the gold and the white gems are to be found. I trust that diligent inquiry will afford us further knowledge upon all these matters, either through their own people coming to us, or through our men, who are sufficiently well disposed to visit them, as the roads have, through the alliances formed with the several tribes of the race of Hottentoos, become so safe that our people have nothing to look for, in any quarter, but the most friendly reception. In consequence of this, had I remained here, we fully intended, as soon as the rains were over, and at the commencement of the dry season, to send out a party of volunteers to try whether we could not find out the said Choboquas, as we last year, as before mentioned, found the long sought Namaquas.

Jealousy of the Saldanhars. But there is no doubt that Oedasoa, who is the greatest among the natives who live near to the Cape, is as jealous upon this matter, as were the Capemans formerly, when we were endeavoring to become better acquainted with him; and equally fearful of failing into less esteem, in proportion to the extent of our discoveries; this may be fully relied upon, as we have already begun to perceive it from Oedasoa's demeanor, but we have endeavored to remove his apprehension by friendly and affable treatment; and this course must of necessity be continued, for, upon any coolness with him, we can see no prospect of profit for the Company, and deem the preservation of friendship the preferable course; although he (just like the Goringhaiquas or Capemans, who long kept us in ignorance of him) has had in view precisely the same object as to the other tribes, in hoodwinking us, and leading us to believe that he was the greatest *heer* of this country.

But now, seeing that we have at length discovered the Namaquas, (a different, and as before observed, a more active race than the Hottentoos) and hearing that we have been well received by them, and that they have promised to come hither, whether he likes it or not—they having, however, first shown their inclination to be reconciled to him, and for that purpose offering to send 2 or 3 with our party to express their disposition for peace, and to settle old disputes with him (for the Namaquas did not dare to attack him here, for fear of our assisting him)—the said Oedasoa allowed himself to be in so far guided by us, that on the 21st March last year he sent 3 of his people to them as commissioners, in company with our party who went thither, and who were to act between the parties as mediators. This endeavour succeeded according to our wishes, and the result has been that they not only now leave each other unmolested on journeys, and in trading with us, but the Saldanhars may carry on a friendly intercourse and traffic with the said Namaquas, who are, as before observed, a different race from these Hottentoos, of much larger stature, clothed in fine well dressed skins without hair and using rushes (ruyge) at night to sleep on. Their own hair, although like that of the Caffers, is worn long, and plaited in an ornamental manner like locks, with many ornaments of copper, iron, and red beads; also, *caurys* and *bougys*, for which they are very eager, as well as for red caps, and for the red cloth of which to make them.

Hopes of Elephants' teeth among the Namaquas, and why. It would seem also that ivory is much more plentiful among them than among the Hottentoos, from the very thick bracelets of that article which they wear, and from the very singular plates of ivory which they wear over a finely dressed skin, worn as an apron. A specimen of each has been sent to our masters in Holland, and 2 such plates are in the office here; it may therefore happen that a trade in ivory and other articles may yet be opened with them, which were much to be desired for the relief of the Company's expenditure at this place.

Whereabouts the Namaquas are to be found by sea. From a calculation of the courses and distances travelled by our land parties, we are led to conjecture that those people reside not far distant from the coast, and near the bay called by Linschoten, *Angra das Voltas*, between the 29th and 30th parallel to the Northward; and had I staid here, I had it in contemplation, upon a favorable opportunity, to send a Cape galiot, or any small vessel that could be spared, to ascertain that point, as well as whether that bay might not be found suitable, in respect of anchorage, water, and other refreshments, for Company's ships to touch at, when occasionally blown to leeward of the Cape by the S. S. E. gales in February and March, when the ships arrive from India, and when those winds are usually most severe; or in the event of ivory or other merchandize being found (which might be too bulky for conveyance by land) to place a trading station there, or otherwise, according to circumstances. I therefore bring the subject under your notice in order that you may, at a fitting opportunity, improve upon the suggestion in as far as you may deem it to be practicable, and serviceable to the Company; but the vessel must first be sent to Madagascar for rice and whatever else our masters have directed, or may hereafter direct to be done there.

Nothing more serviceable to the Company than peace with the Hottentoos. It being, above all things necessary, that you always endeavour to live in constant peace with the Hottentoos—one tribe as well as the other, not only that the roads may be every where safe, to facilitate further discoveries, but also that the tribes above named may always be able to come down without apprehension, with their cattle, for the refreshment of the crews of the Company's ships. To this object—in the first place, a more than usually liberal reception will much contribute, and especially if little squabbles occurring between our people—particularly the ship people—and them, be not too seriously taken up, but rather passed over occasionally, as if in ignorance, especially at first, or otherwise they would become so shy that they would fly inland with all they possess, making the other tribes so shy also, that they would keep away altogether; and you would thus find yourselves in a moment deprived, not only of the daily barter with the Saldanhars, but also of the trade with all the other tribes before named. The best advice, therefore, that I am able to give you in this matter is—that you keep your attention constantly fixed—steadfast as a wall, to this point: to live without any of the slightest estrangement from your neighbours here, the Capernans or Goringhaiquas, and the tobacco thieves or Gora-chouquas, as well as with Oedasoa, the king of the Saldanhars; which may be effect-ed—besides the friendly treatment aforesaid—by keeping so sharp and strict a watch, by mounted and other guards, (already brought so far into order) over the Company's live stock, and that belonging to the freemen, that a fair opportunity of driving them off is never left open to the natives, without exposing their lives to danger. For, should they have even the least chance of success, they could not refrain from the attempt; and on this account a very close watch will be always required here. *Au reste*, that when they sometimes perceive some simple green horn from the ships going to some retired spot and rob him of his tobacco, bread, and brass, or iron buttons from his clothes, is not a matter of such mighty importance, but that it may be easily arranged. The quarrels also, which occur between them and the ship people, more than those who are resident here, and which proceed perhaps to the length of pelting each other with stones, ought not to be too gravely regard-ed, for, our men, who, when playing and wrestling (stoeyende) with them, some-times get a thump a little harder than they will bear, and are thus provoked to abuse them, and call them black stinking dogs, &c.—are themselves in a great measure the cause. For the natives fully understand these, and other Dutch words, and reply, that they are men as well as the Dutch, and so forth—so that I will add that our common people are often found, when out of our presence, to be the first cause of many dis-putes (questien) which are sometimes attended with trouble, in order to restore tran-quillity among these natives; and this may be best accomplished by a show of injus-tice towards our own people, paying the others by a friendly promise of inflicting some kind of punishment on our men on board of their ships.

And although this course appears to many of our people somewhat improper, it is nevertheless most absolutely necessary, in order that we may live in peace and quiet; and I have therefore always pursued this line of conduct, and enforced it upon others; and whatever better course you may be able to adopt, cannot fail to be still more serviceable to the Company; for, in the event of disagreement you will not be able to keep a single Hottentoo here or hereabouts; and therefore friendship, with those who have been herein named, should be kept in mind as one of the principal maxims; in which case the trade will not only continue to flourish more and more, but the roads also will be safe for travelling in every direction, to search for what has not been hitherto found; and, as before observed, the Directors [of the Dutch East India Company] and their Honors at Batavia will be thus best satisfied; for it may be seen from the public and private letters from both quarters, that journeys for the purposes of discovery are not disapproved, but expressly ordered to be prose-cuted with every assiduity; and therefore—so far from dissuading you from contin-uing them at fitting seasons of the monsoon—I would most earnestly recommend their being prosecuted with vigor at the seasons before mentioned.

And to give out any lands beyond the Company's enclosure is, on account of the attendant expense of protecting the freemen, quite unadvisable; even should they be disposed to live out there at their own risk, we have never dared to venture upon it, for they would instantly lose their cattle, and would be robbed of them, even by our best friends—unless indeed any one were mad enough, and rich enough to hazard his own capital—but with the Company's means—upon which all the farmers here have been set up—this would be entirely wrong, and ought never to be thought of; for the Hottentoos, upon seeing the least opportunity, could not abstain from stealing the cattle, as we have, at full length and breadth, explained to the Directors. And for the same reason I would not venture to sell cattle, even for ready money, to any one who was about to farm there, for he would forthwith lose them, and would then be troubling the Company for more.

The slaves here learn nothing but Dutch, and also the Hottentoos, so that no other language is spoken here, and if this can be continued it will be a desirable thing, as it always will keep the Portuguese and others from communicating with these tribes, so that they will be the less able to mislead them, &c. Herry and Doman live chiefly here at the fort, as interpreters or advocates, the first, as it were, for the tobacco thieves, and the other for the Capernans. They get their food and drink from us, and they should continue to be thus supported, to bind them to the Company, and to keep mischief out of their heads; though indeed, now that we are so well supplied with horses, I do not think that they will easily be inclined to undertake any thing against us, so long as good attention is paid to the mounted guard and the outposts.

How the interpreter Eva is retained and treated has been already mentioned, and verbally communicated. She acts chiefly for the Saldanhars, and others who come from a distance.

As I cannot but think that every thing has now been detailed at sufficient length, I do not know what more I can say, than to repeat briefly the most advantageous, and the chief rules to be attended to, for the service of the Company, namely,

1st. That you always endeavour to live, and trade, in peace with these tribes, at the same time and for the same purpose, to penetrate-by parties of volunteers further and further into the interior.

2d. To have constantly in readiness sufficient refreshments for the shipping.

3d. The necessary increase of the stock of cattle and sheep, and also of pigs, &c.

4th. To keep up the cultivation of corn, and as far as practicable to extend it more and more, for the purpose of provisioning this Residency, and that the less food may be required from abroad.

5th. The cultivation of the olive, as urgently recommended by the last letter from the Directors.

And now, trusting that I have sufficiently explained the objects of our Honorable Masters. I shall conclude by recommending you to the merciful protection of the Almighty, and by recommending to you the command and management of affairs here in the manner most serviceable to the Hon. Company. In the Fort the Goede Hope, adij 5th May Ao. 1662. Jan Van Riebeeck

EXTRACTS OF A MEMORANDUM LEFT BY COMMANDER Z. WAGENAAR, BY ORDER OF THE DIRECTORS, FOR THE INFORMATION OF HIS SUCCESSOR, MR. C. VAN QUAELBERGEN, &C.[4]

4. This memorandum is dated September 24, 1666 (ed.).

Respecting these aboriginal inhabitants. And although Mr. van Riebeeck has written very clearly upon every point, and in particular, has given so good a sketch of the disposition, character, and habits of these greasy Africans, commonly called Hottentoos, that I might be well excused from making any allusion to the subject, I shall, nevertheless, take a brief view of these savages, *en passant,* that I may let you know, by way of warning, from what kind among that people, the Company has to look for the greatest advantage in that very essential point, the cattle trade, (without which, there would be very little for us to do here,) and who, on that account, ought to be gratified and well treated in preference to others.

The said Hottentoos then, who usually reside inland within a space of 40 or 50 mylen to the east and north of this African Cape, and are in the habit of wandering from one place to another with their cattle, for the sake of pasture, are, (in so far as they are, for the greater part, known to us,) divided into 9 hordes, or assemblages of families, or rather of villagers, or members of the same kraal: they are named

Goringhaiconas, Goringhaiquas, Gorachouquas, Cochoquas, Charequriquas, Namaquas, Chainouquas, Heusequas, and Hancumquas.

The Cochoquas bring us the greatest number of cattle. Of all these tribes we procure the greatest quantity of live stock, chiefly sheep, from the Cochoquas, they live to the north, towards Saldanha Bay, whence their name of Saldanhars. They consist of two divisions, under separate Choques or Chiefs, Oudasoa and Gonnoma; they were formerly, with the kraals under their authority, so strong, that both together might have mustered three thousand men capable of bearing arms; but they were, some time ago, very much diminished and melted away by a sickness which prevailed among them. The others, who are nearer to us, and are in the habit of bringing their cattle close to us for good pasture, are the Goringhaiquas, or the Capernans, thus called because they at first made pretensions to a right of property in this Cape land; with the Gorachouquas, nicknamed the tobacco thieves; but at present both kraals, exclusive of women and children, can scarcely make out 800 men. The last, namely, the Gorachouquas, are however, much richer in cattle than the first, and bring us for sale, now and then, a lean ox or cow, or a few sheep equally lean; and although such supplies are of little use to us, we receive, notwithstanding, all they offer us, whether it be large or small, young or old, fat or lean.

What is commonly given for their cattle. Neither do we allow them to stand long waiting, but give instantly what they desire in exchange, such as copper in plates, or brass in bars, various kinds of beads, but chiefly a small blood red sort, or tobacco, the first thing they ask for; and when they have received for each cow, calf, or sheep, such a quantity of those articles of merchandize as has been long since brought into train, we give to each of them a dram (pimpeltje) of brandy, and occasionally, to such as bring us many, or very fine fat cattle, a little biscuit or boiled rice besides; and thus dismiss them well satisfied. In this, or in some such manner, it will be necessary to attract these strangers to us, and to keep the trade alive. But to sell them thin square bar iron, as the Cochoquas or Saldanhars would have recently wished, is by no means advisable, as they know how to beat it into *pickysers,* or sharp points for their arrows and assagais, and to harden it very tolerably; so that, should they again come to ask for this iron, you should, upon one pretence or other, decline supplying it.

The Goringhaiconas subsist in a great measure by begging and stealing. Among this ugly Hottentoo race, there is yet another sort called Goringhaiconas, whose chief or captain, named Herry, has been dead for the last three years; these we have daily in our sight and about our ears, within and without the fort, as they possess no cattle whatever, but are strandloopers, living by fishing from the rocks. They were at first, on my arrival, not more than 30 in number, but they have since procured some addition to their numbers from similar rabble out of the interior, and they now constitute a gang, including women and children, of 70, 80, or more. They make shift for themselves by night close by, in little hovels in the sand hills; in the day time, however, you may see some of the sluggards (*luyoerts*) helping to scour, wash, chop wood, fetch water, or herd sheep for our burgers, or boiling a pot of rice for some of the soldiers; but they will never set hand to any work, or put one foot before the other, until you have promised to give them a good quantity of tobacco or food, or drink. Others of the lazy crew, (who are much worse still, and are not to be induced to perform any work whatever,) live by begging, or seek a subsistence by stealing and robbing on the common highways; particularly when they see these frequented by any novices out of ships from Europe.

Bold attempt of these Hottentoos. This was evident enough last year, when some men were ordered to go to the wood to assist in dragging out some timber; for, the corporal of the party being a little way behind with two soldiers who were carrying the provisions, and being attacked by seven or eight of those thieves, scarcely 1/4 of a myl from the fort, stood up bravely in his own defence, not being inclined to part with his bread and cheese so cheaply; at last, however, he was so fearfully assailed from all sides with stones, that he was driven back and compelled to return to the fort with a bleeding pate.

In the same manner, shortly before, those vagabonds broke open a house at Salt River, belonging to a certain poor fisherman, and stole from it 200 guilders in cash, and all his little stock of tobacco, and food, and drink.

And although these, and similar daring acts require that an appropriate punishment should be inflicted upon those who commit them, or at least that this good for nothing gang should be denied a free access to the fort or the burgers' houses in the country, or entirely turned away from us; yet still we could not well dare to do so hitherto, for several reasons, but have winked at it all, and suffered it to pass unnoticed; for our masters in the Fatherland, in their letters from time to time, recommend to us nothing more earnestly than to deal with these men in a kind and peaceful manner; and not be too easily led to apply to them terms of opprobium, still less to kick, push, or ill use them, upon every slight cause of offence, so that they may not acquire any dislike towards us.

This was also the course followed by Mr. van Riebeeck, as you may see in several parts of the memoir left by him.

Who should one day be severely punished. But as, subsequently to his departure, this crew (*gespuys*) have not only (as before stated) increased in number, but have daily become more impudent and daring in the commission of every kind of mischief, we have deemed it as improper, as it is impossible, any longer to put up with such violence, breaches of the peace, and theft; but, ever since that time we have intended to have the first person that we can get hold of, who may be convicted of housebreaking or highway robbery, bound to a whipping post in front of the fort, and there to have his greasy hide so well rubbed down with good rods, that all his mischievous countrymen who might witness the punishment, should be frightened from the commission of the same offence; for to this it must come (would we live in peace and quiet) if we are annoyed by these *rappaille*, particularly because our honorable masters, upon our representations upon the subject, have been pleased to give their full approval and consent, but at the same time it will be much better and safer for us all if they will take a turn of their own accord, or if the greater part of the males could be induced to go away, without violence, than that the proposed punishment, or any kind of banishment should be resorted to. You will however be able to ascertain what may be hereafter the best course in this respect, with the aid of time and good counsel.

A close watch should also be kept on them. Meanwhile it will do no harm to keep a strict eye upon those idlers, while they are allowed to pass freely in and out, particularly now that all our soldiers are daily working upon the ditch of the new castle, and only 10 or 12 sick or lame men are on guard at the gate; for it has been seen already what these dirty creatures have dared to undertake against the Fort. It has been well apprehended and remarked by Commissioner Overtwater, (as you may see by the *memorie* he left here) that the maintenance of peace and concord with these tribes, should be attended by a proper degree of caution.

We also procure many cattle from the Chainouquas. For the last six years we have begun to be acquainted with the tribes who live to the Eastward, named the Chainouquas; and have always lived in perfect friendship with them, as we still do; they are very rich in cattle, for upon two missions which I sent to them in 1663 and 64, the first under fiscal Lacus, and the second under secretary Cretser, we procured 170 fine cattle and 400 sheep; and I would have sent a third party last year, but that we were then without tobacco, the merchandize chiefly in demand; we have however recently sent thither a party of 12 men under Mr. Cretser, and I hope that before my departure he may return with a good herd.

Which excites the jealousy of the Cochoquas. In consequence of Sousoa the chief of the Chainouquas not only inviting us into his country, but sending oxen to carry our provisions and merchandize; and of our availing ourselves of his invitation and assistance, the Saldanhars—and particularly the chief Oudasoa [Oudasoa's proposal]—conceived such a jealousy of them, that he came to the Fort and apprised us that he meant to make war upon Sousoa (who is since dead) as he could no longer suffer him to play the master everywhere; and requesting, not only the aid of some troops, but that we would take charge of 2500 of his cattle during the war, promising to send us, in 3 or 4 days 600 cattle in payment, and an equal number in the event of his getting the victor but after mature consideration, it appeared to us that the proposal would lead to much embarrassment, and perhaps eventually to some dispute, and we civilly declined his offer, allowing him to go away rather dissatisfied. The Directors have fully approved of our conduct in this respect, as may be seen by their letter Oct. 8, 1664, in which they state the desire, that we should not concern ourselves with the mutual disputes or wars of these inland tribes; which will serve as rule for your guidance under similar circumstances. Meanwhile it would appear that Oudasoa still feels much vexed, it is more than 2 years since he has been the Fort.

The Namaquas recently discovered. Of the Namaquas whom we first discovered in 1661, and who are a very *robust* people as also of the tribes bordering on them to the Eastward, and who are all very rich in cattle, I am unable to add any thing to the remarks of Mr. Van Riebeeck, as contained in his memoir, to which I merely refer, and pass on to some thing else.

---

21. GIOVANNI CAVAZZI

QUEEN ANNA NZINGA. 1654.

Father Cavazzi was a Capuchin missionary, originally from Modena, who went to Angola in 1654. He returned to Rome in 1658 and, with Father Alamandini di Bologna, wrote the History of Ethiopia. He returned to Angola in 1670. Queen Anna Nzinga came to the throne of Ndongo in 1623 after having poisoned her brother, the king. Thereafter this able and determined woman began her long struggle against the Portuguese. She allied with the Jaga and induced Portuguese vassal chiefs to rebel. The Portuguese retaliated by proclaiming Aidi Kiluanji the rightful king of Ndongo in 1625. For the next fifteen years, Nzinga and the Portuguese fought indecisively for control of Angola until the Dutch, in their struggle against the combined empires of Portugal and Spain, captured Luanda in August 1641. Allied with the Dutch and the King of Congo, Garcia II Nzinga's armies consistently defeated the Portuguese, destroying their field army in 1648, and besieging the fortress of Massangano. Massangano probably would have fallen had not the Dutch suddenly withdrawn. The Africans could not defend themselves against a strong Portuguese expeditionary force from Brazil under Salvador de Sa. After protracted negotiations Nzinga signed a peace treaty in 1656, by which she lost much territory but retained her independence. Peace prevailed between the Portuguese and Queen Nzinga until her death in 1663.

In 1641 a Dutch fleet composed of twenty-two warships with good land troops appeared in the port of Luanda. The Portuguese defended Luanda so badly that the town was taken, along with a goodly part of the kingdom.

Having learned of these advantageous events, Queen Zingha [Nzinga] thought that the time had arrived for her to revenge herself against the Portuguese. She had always remembered in her heart how they had affronted her by proclaiming Ngola Arij [Aidi Kiluanji] the King of Dongo [Ndongo]. She sent them [the Dutch] ambassadors to congratulate them on their victories and to invite them to join their troops

From Giovanni Antonio Cavazzi, *Relation Historique de l'Ethiopie Occidentale*, trans. by J. B. Labat (Paris, 1732), pp. 80–86. Trans. from the French by Nell Elizabeth Painter and Robert O. Collins.

to hers so as to get rid of their common enemies once and for all. She assured them that she would be happy to have them as neighbors because she knew of their justice and politeness, whereas she could no longer bear the proud and haughty manner of the Portuguese.

The Dutch accepted these propositions with joy; these were offers that they had not expected. The King of Congo [Garcia II] entered the alliance so that the Portuguese found themselves attacked in three different places all at once. They faced them all. They had some advantages, but they were so closely pressed that they lost all the flat country and were besieged in their fortresses of Massangano, Muzzima, Cambamke, and Embacca, as well as in a few little islands in the Cuanza.

Queen Zingha had a few encounters with them that were not favorable to her. This made her think again. She wanted to consult the demon about the outcome of the war she had entered. She did it because of a superstition that is common to the Negroes of that country. They use two cocks, one white and the other black. From the outcome of the combat, they judge whether the whites or the blacks will gain victory. Thus two cocks were prepared, one black and the other white, and they had them fight. They saw wonderful things. The black one always came out on top. Finally on the third day he pulled out all the white one's feathers and killed it.

For those people, the victory absolutely decided the outcome of the war and there were great celebrations. Without waiting any longer they went to attack the fortress of Massangano, but the queen's army was almost completely defeated. The Portuguese took a great many prisoners, and among them were the two sisters of Zingha, Cambo and Fungi, and it was only by luck that she herself escaped a trap that they had set for her.

This defeat did not discourage her but curbed her desire to attack such places and obliged her to decimate the countryside, which the Portuguese had carefully cultivated and which she made a desert.

It is true that she once surprised a few Portuguese troops and defeated them, taking a rather sizable number of prisoners. This made her think that she could surprise a frontier fort that the Portuguese had on the borders of one of her tributary vassals. She attacked it with a vigorous assault, and she was vigorously thrown back, losing part of her army on that occasion, so that comparing her losses with her gains, she found that the losses were infinitely more considerable than the advantages, despite the fact of the information she had of the Portuguese, even in the fortress of Massangano where her sister Fungi was prisoner.

That Princess had been given the freedom of the town out of respect for her birth, and she abused it by winning over a large number of Negro subjects of the Portuguese and other discontented people. By means of presents and promises, she had them agree to seize one of the gates of the fortress and relinquish it to the troops of Zingha, who were to approach on a certain day with a new army that she had assembled. The treason was discovered, Fungi was tried and strangled, and her body was thrown in the river.

Meanwhile the war continued between the Portuguese and the Dutch, but the Dutch, having been defeated on several occasions, were so closely pressed by the victors that at the end they were forced to abandon the country and even the city of

Luanda, which the Portuguese reentered and fortified better than it had been before.

Queen Zingha was deeply upset by the defeat of her allies. She could easily see that she missed the help of Europeans and would be exposed to all the vengeance of the Portuguese with even less hope of resisting, for the King of Congo had also made a settlement with them.

God took advantage of this misfortune to touch her and bring her back to herself. In her heart she had always kept some of the kind sentiments that she had had when she was outwardly a Christian. These good thoughts came to her, and she thought seriously of the crimes she had committed. She cried over them in secret, beginning to show signs of repentance. Here are some events that mastered her conversion.

Her army was in the Province of Onnando, which it sacked. A priest named Dom Augustine Floris was taken and killed by one of the soldiers. This miserable canni-bal, along with a few of his companions, resolved to eat the cadaver, but at the first cut he made to take a piece and eat it, it fell off dead stiff, which destroyed the desire of the others to taste such meat.

The queen was advised of this and was possessed by a very great fear of the judg-ments of God. She published an edict that forbade, under threat of very vigorous punishment, the killing of the priests of the whites. She even ordered that the sacred ornaments of the deceased should be conserved.

Dom Jerome Segueira, a priest in the Portuguese Army, was wounded and was taken in battle. She ordered that he be carefully taken care of and that all that had been taken from him be returned to him. She saw that he was well fed, and when he was cured, she permitted him to come and go at liberty in her camp. When he went out, whether on foot or carried in a hammock by the slaves whom she had given him, those who accompanied him cried out from time to time, "This is how we respect the Ganga, or the Priest of the God of the Catholics."

She did more than that. She permitted the building of a church to which she gave some carpets for decoration, as well as all that had been taken from the priest killed at Onnando. It is true that she never entered the church. She still had political rea-sons for not doing so, but every time she passed by it, she gave signs of the respect that she had for the Sovereign Master of the Universe, to whom it was dedicated.

---

22. MANUEL DE FARIA E SOUSA

THE KINGDOM OF THE MONOMOTAPA. 1666.

At the beginning of the fifteenth century, a group of patrilineal Bantu clans known collectively as the Karanga occupied southwestern Zimbabwe. They were organized under a dominant clan, the Rozvi, which, under the leadership of Mutota, sought to

From Manuel de Faria e Sousa, *Asia Portuguesa* (first published in Lisbon in 1666), trans. and reprinted by George McCall Theal in *Records of South-Eastern Africa, Collected in Various Libraries and Archive Department in Europe* (London, 1898), vol. II, pp. 22–25.

secure control of the whole of Central Africa from the Kalahari Desert to the Indian Ocean, between the Zambezi and the Limpopo Rivers. Known as Mwana Mutapa, "the great plunderer," Mutota swept northward and established the center of the kingdom of the Mwanamutapa in northeastern Zimbabwe. Mutota's son and successor, Matope, continued to expand the empire, but upon his death about 1480, Changa, a Rozvi vassal, took the title of Changamir and asserted his independence in southwestern Zimbabwe. Although the empire of the Mwanamutapa was thus beginning to disintegrate within two generations of its founding, the kingdom continued to exist until the end of the nineteenth century. The Mwanamutapa had, in fact, been dominated by the Portuguese since the beginning of the seventeenth century. Manuel de Faria e Sousa (1590–1649), author of Asia Portuguesa, was regarded as one of the most learned men of his time. His description of the kingdom of the Mwanamutapa in 1569 is based on an account of the expedition of Francisco Barreto. Barreto was sent to avenge the murder of Father Gonçalo da Silveira, who had been killed by the Mwanamutapa at the instigation of Muslim traders at his court. At this time the Mwanamutapa were only beginning to confront the challenge of the Portuguese newcomers.

The empire of Monomotapa from the mouth of Cuama in the east runs two hundred and fifty leagues, is divided by the great river Zambesi, which falls into that of Chiri [Shire], running through the country of Bororo, where are many other large rivers, and on their banks many kings, some absolute, some subjects of Monomotapa. The greatest of the first is Mongas, bordering on Sena and the Zambesi, which falls into the sea between Mozambique and Sofala, to the south-east by four mouths: the first that of Quilimane, 90 leagues from Mozambique, the second Cuama, 25 to the southward, the third Luabo, 5 leagues lower, and the fourth Luaboel, 15 more to the south.[1] Between them are fruitful and large islands, whereof one is sixty leagues in compass. The river is navigable the same number of leagues up to the town of Sena, inhabited by Portuguese, and as many more to Tete, a colony of theirs also. The richest mines are those of Masapa, called Aufur, the Ophir where the queen of Sheba had her riches, when she went to Jerusalem.[2] In these mines has been found a lump of gold worth twelve thousand ducats. It is not only found among stones, but grows up within the bark of several trees to the top where the branches spread.

The mines of Manchica and Butica are not much inferior to these. There are many others not so considerable. There are three fairs or markets, whither our people trade for this gold from the castle of Tete on the river Zambesi, 120 leagues from the sea: the first is Luane, four days' journey up the inland; the second Buento, farther distant; and Masapa the third, yet farther off. This gold was purchased for cloth, glass beads, and other things of no value among us. At Masapa resides a Portuguese officer appointed by the commander of Mozambique, by consent of the emperor of Monomotapa, but upon condition not to go into the country without his leave upon

---

1. Leagues. A unit of measure varying from 2.4 to 4.6 miles (ed.).
2. Some scholars have identified the gold mines of Zimbabwe and the port of Sofala with the Biblical land of Ophir whence came the gold for the Queen of Sheba (ed.).

pain of death. He is judge of the differences that arise there. There are churches of the Dominicans at Masapa, Bocuto, and Luanze.

The original number and time of the reign of the kings is not known; it is believed there were several in the time of the queen of Sheba, and that they were subject to her, for thence she had her gold. In the mountain Afur, near Masapa, are seen the ruins of stately buildings, supposed to be palaces and castles. In process of time the empire was divided into three kingdoms: Quiteve, Sabanda, and Chicanga, this last the most powerful, as possessing the mines of Manchica, Butua, and others. It is believed the blacks of Butua of the kingdom of Chicanga are those that carry the gold to Angola, because it is thought there are but one hundred leagues distance between those two places. This country bears rice and what we call Indian wheat, has abundance of all sorts of cattle, fowl, and gardening. Their chief care is pasturage and tillage. This empire is divided into twenty-five kingdoms, which are Mongas, Baroe, Manica, Boesa, Macingo, Remo, Chique, Chiria, Chidima, Boquiza, Inakanzo, Chiruvia, Condesaca, Daburia, Macurumbe, Mungussi, Anturaza, Chove, Chungue, Diza, Romba, Rassini, Chirao, Mocaranga, and Remo de Beza. There are many lordships that have not the title of kings.

The emperor has a great palace, though of wood; the chief apartments in it are three: one for himself, another for his wife, and a third for his menial servants. It has three doors into a court: one for the queen to go in and out at, another for him and the servants that attend his person and are sons of his noblemen, the third for his cooks, who are two great men and his relations, and the under-cooks who are also men of quality. None of these must be above twenty years of age, for till that age they do not believe they have to do with women, and if any do they are severely punished; after that time they are preferred to great employments. Those within doors are governed by a captain, and those without by another, as formerly in Spain.

The principal officers about the king are Ningomoxa, governor of the kingdoms; Macomoaxa, captain-general; Ambuya, great steward, to him it belongs when the Mazarira, or the king's principal wife, dies, to name another in her stead, but it must be one of the king's sisters or nearest relations; Inhantovo, the head musician, who has many under him, and is a great lord; Nurucao, captain of the vanguard; Bucurumo, which signifies the king's right hand; Magande, the chief conjuror; Netambe, the apothecary that keeps the ointments and utensils for sorcery; Nehono, chief porter. All these offices are executed by lords. There is no delicacy in cookery used; they only eat boiled and roasted; they eat the same as is usual with us, with the addition of mice, which they esteem as good as partridge or rabbit.

The king has many wives, only nine called great queens, which are his sisters or near relations, the others the daughters of nobles. The chiefest is called Mazarira, and mother of the Portuguese, who often present her, because she solicits their business with the king, and he sends no ambassador to them without some servants of hers; the second is Inahanda, that solicits for the Moors; the third Nabuiza, that lives in the same apartment with him; the fourth Navemba; the fifth Nemangore; the sixth Nizingoapangi; the seventh Negangoro; the eighth Nessani; the ninth Necarunda. Each of them lives apart, with as great state as the king, and have several revenues and kingdoms for their expense. As soon as one dies, another succeeds in place and name. They have power to reward and punish, as well as the king. Sometimes he goes to them, sometimes they come to him. There are many women waiting on them, of whom he makes use as he pleases.

The principal people of Monomotapa, and whereof the emperor is, are the Mocaranga, not warlike, nor furnished with any other arms but bows, arrows, and javelins. They have no religion nor idols, but acknowledge one only God, and believe there is a devil, that he is wicked, and they call him Muzuco. They believe their kings go to heaven, and call them Muzimos, and call upon them in time of need, as we on the saints. They speak of things past by tradition, having no knowledge of letters. They give ear to the doctrine of Christianity: the lame and blind they call the king's poor, because maintained by him with great charity, and if they travel the towns they go through are obliged to maintain and furnish them guides from one place to another: a good example for Christians.

Every month has its festival days, and is divided into three weeks, each of ten days; the first day is that of the new moon, and the festivals the fourth and fifth of each week. On these days they put on their best apparel, the king gives public audience to all, holding a truncheon [club] about three quarters of a yard long in each hand, as it were leaning upon it; they who speak to him lie prostrate; this lasts from morning till evening. If he is indisposed Ningomoxa stands in his place; nobody can speak to him or go to court on the eighth day of the new moon, because it is held most unlucky.

On the day the new moon appears, the king with two javelins runs about in his house as if he were fighting, the great men are present at this pastime, and it being ended, a pot full of Indian wheat, boiled whole, is brought, which he scatters about the ground, bidding them eat, because it is the growth of the earth; they know how to flatter, for every one strives to gather most, knowing that pleases him, and they eat it as savourly as if it were the greatest dainty.

Their greatest holy day is the first day of the moon of May, they call it Chuavo. On this day all the great men, which are a great number, resort to court, and there with javelins in their hands run about representing a fight. The sport lasts all day. Then the king withdraws, and is not seen in eight days after, during which time the drums never cease beating. On the last day he orders the nobleman he has the least affection for to be killed; this is in the nature of a sacrifice to his Muzimos or ancestors; this done, the drums cease, and every man goes home. The Mumbos eat man's flesh, whereof there is a public butchery. Let this suffice for the customs of this empire, for it would be endless to relate all.

23. ANTONIO SUAREZ
THE CONVERSION OF THE MONOMOTAPA. 1652.

During the mid-fifteenth century, a vast empire that included most of what is now Zimbabwe and part of Mozambique was created by Mutota and his son and successor Matope. Known to the Portuguese as the Monomotapa, the empire of Mutapa began to disintegrate and finally broke up in the early sixteenth century during the successful revolt of a provincial chief Changa. While Changa established an independent center of power at Zimbabwe in the south, the Mutapa empire in the northeastern part of the country contracted. Here the Mwanamutapa became increasingly dependent upon the Portuguese, whose influence was moving steadily up the Zambezi valley. Father Gonçalo da Silveira baptized the Mwanamutapa in 1560 but was assassinated soon thereafter. To avenge the death of Father da Silveira, the Portuguese sent punitive expeditions against the Mwanamutapa in 1572 and 1574. Although these expeditions failed to establish permanent Portuguese control, Portuguese influence in the seventeenth century reduced the Mwanamutapa to a puppet king. Upon the death of Mavura in 1652, the Mwanamutapa were baptized by Dominican missionaries, as described in the following account.

Dom Dominic Manamotapa, by the grace of God king and lord of Mocharanga, Boessa, Borongha, Quiteve, Monghos, Inhaxamo, &c., make known to all to whom these presents shall come, that during the life of our father and lord the king Philip, we, being prince of these kingdoms, were brought up by the Religious of St. Dominic, to whose care the said king, our father, consigned us in the days of our early youth, and by them we were instructed and catechised and many times persuaded, until we desired to embrace the holy faith of Jesus Christ, and to receive the waters of holy baptism, and though we fervently desired the fulfilment of this our longing, being firmly convinced that this was the true path, in which the fathers walked; nevertheless we deferred the effect of our desire until such time and season as God our Lord should have done us the grace of bringing us to the actual possession of this our kingdom, wishing to imitate in this particular all that was done by the king our father, who being instructed and catechised in the doctrines of the holy faith, by Friar Emanuel Sardigna, of the said order of St. Dominic, would not receive holy baptism until he was in possession of his kingdoms, the Divine Majesty being afterwards pleased to call the said king our father to his holy glory on the 25th of May 1652, immediately the fathers of St. Dominic and the nobles of the kingdom, who were present at court, informed us of his death, and several of these religious, although they were assisting the vicar of the court in person, Friar Ignatius of St. Thomas and others in his company came to us in the place where we resided,

"Authentic testimony of the baptism of the emperor and king Manamotapa, signed by the said emperor, scaled with the royal sea], signed by his secretary and interpreter, and sent to the Father Provincial Friar Dionysio de Lancastro of the Portuguese province of the Order of Preachers." Trans. by Miss A. de Alberti in George McCall Theal, *Records of South-Eastern Africa. Collected in Various Libraries and Archive Departments in Europe* (London, 1898), vol. II, pp. 445–448.

many leagues distant from the court, such being the custom and usage of these kingdoms, and after they had arrived we immediately prepared to depart with all possible haste, fearing some disturbance upon our succession on the part of Caprasine the
tyrant king, who for his oppressions was expelled from the kingdom, and whose turbulent risings have brought forth many evils to these realms, in particular the death
of many of our Portuguese vassals and of several religious, during the space of three
years that the rising lasted. Therefore, before setting forth from the retreat where we
resided, we caused the captain of Dambarare to see that the Portuguese were in
order and readiness for any event which might occur. Afterwards there came Friar
Giovanni de Melo, to whom our father gave our person in charge to instruct and
make learned in letters, which charge the said Father ever fulfilled with the utmost
diligence and zeal, and therefore we hold him in great consideration and esteem,
keeping him next our person in the place of a father, being confident that if in this
our government he assists us with his good counsel and aid we shall govern it with
the same peace and tranquillity with which it was ever governed by the king our
father with the assistance of Friar Emanuel Sardigna. And treating with the said
Friar Giovanni de Melo of grave matters, he did not fail to remind us that the time
was now come to receive holy baptism, in order to procure the assistance of God
our Lord in our government, which is what the said father places above everything.
We were well pleased with his reminder, agreeing in every way with his wish that
we should receive holy baptism, to which end we greatly desired to keep him in our
company as far as the court, but it was not possible to gratify this wish, it being necessary that the said father should go to Dambarare in person to treat of different matters of great importance to our person. He therefore hastened his journey thither, and
on arriving, in a few days he successfully dispatched the business with which we
had charged him, and there also overcame the difficulties which might have
deferred the fulfilment of our desire of receiving holy baptism, and returned directly to this court, in company with the Presentado Friar Salvador of the Rosary, and
arrived at court on the 1st of July of the year aforesaid. We rejoiced greatly at his
coming, great signs of joy being also shown by all the nobles of our court, who were
all ready, owing to the zeal of the said fathers, to receive the waters of holy baptism.
We omitted no occasion of encouraging the holy work of the said fathers, and hearing that some of our nobles showed some reluctance to receive the waters of holy
baptism, we ordered them to be summoned to our presence, and making use of the
doctrine learned from the said fathers, we made them an exhortation by means of
which they were fully convinced and resolved to become Christians. The fathers did
not fail, for many days following, in catechising the said nobles, and their instructions came to an end on the feast of St. Dominic. On this day we issued from our
palace with great pomp, accompanied by all the nobles, the soldiers of the garrison,
and by the aforesaid religious who walked on each side of our person. On arriving
at their church, richly decorated and prepared with great magnificence, we prescribed the order in which the waters of baptism were to be administered, which was
in this manner following: we caused Friar Giovanni de Melo to baptize us and the
queen our consort, Friar Salvador of the Rosary being godfather and bestowing
upon us the name of Dom Dominic, the day being consecrated to that saint, and

upon the queen the name of Dona Louisa. Then we ordered the two chief nobles of our kingdom to be baptized, Inigomaxa receiving the name of Dom John, and Inevinga that of Dom Sebastian, and after these two Inhamapa. was baptized by the name of Dom Ferdinand, and Inhamafunhe our friend by the name of Dom Peter, who five or six months before dreamed that a religious of St. Dominic was baptizing him and making him a Christian, as he himself related to us in the presence of the said fathers. All the above named are nobles of our kingdom, lords of many lands, and nearly related to ourself. This baptism was celebrated with great rejoicing, especially by those of our court, who with musical instruments and festive dances gave incredible signs of joy. The said fathers are continuing their religious and Christian office, by which it is held as certain that in a few days there will be another baptism of other nobles, who are all ready and disposed to receive holy baptism. From all that has been said it cannot be denied that glory and the greatest praise are due to the Order of St. Dominic and the friars thereof, who are ministers in these our realms. We have therefore commanded Antonio Suirez, interpreter and secretary in this our court, faithfully and well to draw up an authentic document with the royal seal, confirmed by which these presents may come to the Superiors of the said Order, that they may certify the same to the Most Serene Majesty of Portugal, our brother, that this kingdom may remain under his protection, and that he may be pleased to command the Superiors of the said fathers to recognise their labours and the great services they have rendered to God, his Majesty, and ourself, in these realms.

Given at our court of Zimbaoe, signed by us and the aforesaid secretary, and sealed with the royal seal, the 14th of August 1652.

MANAMOTAPA, THE KING
ANTONIO SUAREZ
Secretary and interpreter in the faith.

24. JOHN BARBOT

BENIN. 1680.

John Barbot was an employee of English and French trading companies who made at least two voyages to West Africa between 1678 and 1682. He wrote the following account in French in 1682 and translated it into English; much of his material was derived from his journal of a voyage that began at La Rochelle, France, on October 22, 1678. At the time Barbot visited the Guinea Coast, the kingdom of Benin was one of the most powerful and effectively organized states of West Africa and was a center of the slave trade.

From John Barbot, *An Abstract of a Voyage to Congo River, or the Zair, and to Cabinde, in the Year 1700*, in Awnsham and John Churchill, *A Collection of Voyages and Travels* (London: Henry Linton and John Osborn, 1746), vol. V, pp. 367–370.

GOVERNMENT

The government of *Benin* is principally vested in the king, and three chief ministers, call'd great *Veadors*; that is, intendants, or overseers: besides the great marshal of the crown, who is intrusted with the affairs relating to war, as the three others are with the administration of justice, and the management of the revenue; and all four are obliged to take their circuits throughout the several provinces, from time to time, to inspect into the condition of the country, and the administration of the governors and justices in each district, that peace and good order may be kept as much as possible. Those chief ministers of state have under them each his own particular officers and assistants in the discharge of their posts and places. They call the first of the three aforemention'd ministers of state, the *Onegwa*, the second *Ossade*, and the third *Arribon*.

They reside constantly at court, as being the king's privy council, to advise him on all emergencies and affairs of the nation; and any person that wants to apply to the prince, must address himself first to them, and they acquaint the king with the petitioner's business, and return his answer accordingly: but commonly, as in other countries, they will only inform the king with what they please themselves; and so in his name, act very arbitrarily over the subjects. Whence it may well be inferr'd, that the government is intirely in their hands; for it is very seldom they will favour a person so far as to admit him to the king's presence, to represent his own affairs to that prince: and every body knowing their great authority, indeavours on all occasions to gain their favour as much as possible, by large gratifications and presents, in order to succeed in their affairs at court, for which reason their offices and posts are of very great profit to them.

Besides these four chief ministers of state, there are two other inferior ranks about the king: the first is composed of those they call *Reis de Ruas*, signifying in Portuguese, kings of streets, some of whom preside over the commonalty, and others over the slaves; some again over military affairs; others over affairs relating to cattle and the fruits of the earth, &c. there being supervisors or intendants over every thing that can be thought of, in order to keep all things in a due regular way.

From among those *Reis de Ruas* they commonly chuse the governors of provinces and towns; but every one of them is subordinate to, and dependent on the aforemention'd great *Veadors*, as being generally put into those imployments, by their recommendation to the king, who usually presents each of them, when so promoted to the government of provinces, towns or districts, with a string of coral, as an ensign or badge of this office; being there equivalent to an order of knighthood in European courts.

They are obliged to wear that string continually about their necks, without ever daring to put it off on any account whatsoever; and in case they lose it by carelessness, or any other accident, or if stolen from them, they forfeit their heads, and are accordingly executed without remission. And there have been instances of this nature, five men having been put to death for a string of coral so lost, tho' not intrinsically worth two-pence: the officer to whom the chain or string belong'd, because he had suffer'd it to be stolen from him, the thief who own'd he had stolen it, and three more who were privy to it, and did not timely discover it.

This law is so rigidly observ'd, that the officers so intrusted with a string of coral by the king, whensoever they happen to lose it, though it be taken from about their necks by main force, immediately say, *I am a dead man*; and therefore regard no perils though ever so great, if there be hopes of recovering it by force from those who have stolen it. Therefore I advise all sea-faring *Europeans*, trading to those parts, never to meddle with the strings of coral belonging to any such officers, not even in jest; because the *Black* that permits it, is immediately sent for to the king, and by his order close imprison'd, and put to death.

The same punishment is inflicted on any person whatsoever that counterfeits those strings of coral, or has any in his possession, without the king's grant.

That we have here call'd coral, is made of a pale red coctile earth or stone, and very well glazed, much resembling red speckled marble, which the king keeps in his own custody, and no body is allow'd as I have said, to wear it, unless honour'd by the prince with some post of trust in the nation.

The third rank of publick ministers or officers, is that of the *Mercadors*, or merchants; *Fulladors*, or intercessors; the *Veilhos*, or elders, imploy'd by the king in affairs relating to trade: all which are also distinguish'd from the other subjects not in office or post, by the same badge of a coral-string at their neck, given each of them by the king, as a mark of honour.

All the said officers from the highest to the lowest, being men that love money, are easily brib'd: so that a person sentenc'd to death, may purchase his life if he is wealthy in *Boejies*, the money of this country; and only poor people are made examples of justice, as we see is no less practised in *Europe*: yet it being the king's intention, that justice should be distributed without exception of persons, and malefactors rigidly punish'd according to the laws of the realm, the officers take all possible care to conceal from him, that they have been brib'd, for preventing the execution of any person condemn'd.

THE KING'S PREROGATIVE

The king of *Benin* is absolute; his will being a law and a bridle to his subjects, which none of them dare oppose; and, as I have hinted before, the greatest men of the nation, as well as the inferior sort, esteem it an honour to be call'd the king's slave, which title no person dares assume without the king's particular grant; and that he never allows but to those, who, as soon as born, are by their parents presented to him: for which reason, some geographers have thought, that the king of *Benin* was religiously ador'd by all his subjects, as a deity. But that is a mistake, for the qualification of the king's slaves, is but a bare compliment to majesty; since none of the natives of *Benin*, can by the law of the land, be made slaves on any account, as has been observ'd before.

The present king is a young man of an affable behaviour. His mother is still living, to whom he pays very great respect and reverence, and all the people after his example honour her. She lives apart from her son in her own palace out of the city *Oedo*, where she keeps her court, waited on and serv'd by her proper officers, women and maids. The king her son uses to take her advice on many important affairs of state, by the ministry of his statesmen and counsellors: for the king there is not to see his own mother, without danger of an insurrection of the people against him, according to their constitutions. The palace of that dowager is very large and spacious, built much after the manner, and of the same materials as the king's, and those of other great persons.

The king's houshold is compos'd of a great number of officers of sundry sorts, and slaves of both sexes, whose business is to furnish all the several apartments with all manner of necessaries for life and conveniency, as well as the country affords. The men officers being to take care of all that concerns the king's tables and stables; and the women, for that which regards his wives and concubines: which all together makes the concourse of people so great at court, with the strangers resorting continually to it every day about business, that there is always a vast croud running to and fro from one quarter to another. It appears by ancient history, that it was the custom of the eastern nations, to have only women to serve them within doors, as officers in the king's houses. *David* being forced to fly before *Absalom* his son, and to leave Jerusalem his capital, to shelter himself in some of his strong cities beyond Jordan, left ten of his concubines for the guard of his palace.

The king being very charitable, as well as his subjects, has peculiar officers about him, whose chief imployment is, on certain days, to carry a great quantity of provisions, ready dress'd, which the king sends into the town for the use of the poor. Those men make a sort of procession, marching two and two with those provisions in great order, preceded by the head officer, with a long white staff in his hand, like the prime court officers in *England*; and every body is obliged to make way for him, tho' of never so great quality.

Besides this good quality of being charitable, the king might be reckoned just and equitable, as desiring continually his officers to administer justice exactly, and to discharge their duties conscienciously: besides that, he is a great lover of *Europeans*, whom he will have to be well treated and honoured, more especially the *Dutch* nation, as I have before observ'd. But his extortions from such of his subjects as are wealthy, on one unjust pretence or other, which has so much impoverish'd many of them, will not allow him to be look'd upon as very just.

He seldom passes one day, without holding a cabinet council with his chief ministers, for dispatching of the many affairs brought before him, with all possible expedition; besides, the appeals from inferior courts of judicature in all the parts of the kingdom, and audiences to strangers, or concerning the affairs of war, or other emergencies of state.

REVENUE

The king's income is very great, his dominions being so large, and having such a number of governors, and other inferior officers, each of whom is obliged, according to his post, to pay into the king's treasury so many bags of *Boejies*, some more some less, which all together amount to a prodigious sum; and other officers of inferior rank are to pay in their taxes in cattle, chicken, fruits, roots and cloths, or any other things that can be useful to the king's houshold; which is so great a quantity, that it doth not cost the king a penny throughout the year to maintain and subsist his family; so that there is yearly a considerable increase of money in his treasury. Add to all this, the duties and tolls on imported or exported goods, paid in all trading places, to the respective *Veadors* and other officers, which are also partly convey'd to the treasury; and were the collectors thereof just and honest, so as not to defraud the prince of a considerable part, these would amount to an incredible sum.

WARS

This prince is perpetually at war with one nation or other that borders on the northern part of his dominions, and sometimes with another north-west of his kingdom, which are all potent people, but little or not at all known to *Europeans*, over whom he obtains from time to time considerable advantages, subduing large portions of those unknown countries, and raising great contributions, which are partly paid him in jasper, and other valuable goods of the product of those countries. Wherewith, together with his own plentiful revenue, he is able, upon occasion, to maintain an army of an hundred thousand horse and foot; but, for the most part, he doth not keep above thirty thousand men, which renders him more formidable to his neighbours than any other *Guinea* king: nor is there any other throughout all *Guinea*, that has so many vassals and tributary kings under him; as for instance, those of *Istanna, Foreado, Jaboe, Issabo,* and *Oedoba*, from whom he receives considerable yearly tributes, except from him of Issabo, who, though much more potent than all the others, yet pays the least.

ARMY

To speak now something of the soldiery in the king's pay. They generally wear no other clothes but a narrow silk clout about their middle, all the other parts of their body being naked; and are arm'd with pikes, javelins, bows, and poison'd arrows, cutlaces and bucklers or shields; but so slight, and made of small *Bamboos*, that they cannot ward off any thing that is forcible, and so are rather for show than for defence. Some, besides all these weapons, have also a kind of hooked bill, much of the form of those we use in *Europe*, for cutting of small wood whereof bavins and faggots are made, and some others have small poniards.

These soldiers are commonly distributed into companies and bands, each band commanded by its respective officer, with others of lower rank under him: but what is pretty singular there, those officers do not post themselves in the front of their troops, but in the very centre, and generally wear a scymitar hanging at their side, by a leather girdle fasten'd under their arm-pits, instead of a belt, and march with a grave resolute mien, which has something of stateliness.

The king's armies are compos'd of a certain number of those bands, which is greater or smaller, according to circumstances; and they always march like the ancient *Salij*, dancing and skipping into measure and merrily, and yet keep their ranks, being in this particular better disciplin'd than any other *Guinea* nation; however, they are no braver than the *Fida* and *Ardra* men, their neighbours westward, so that nothing but absolute necessity can oblige them to fight: and even then, they had rather suffer the greatest losses than defend themselves. When their flight is prevented, they return upon the enemy, but with so little courage and order, that they soon fling down their arms, either to run the lighter, or to surrender themselves prisoners of war. In short, they have so little conduct, that many of them are asham'd of it; their officers being no braver than the soldiers, every man takes his own course, without any regard to the rest.

The great officers appear very richly habited in the field, every one rather endeavouring to out-do another in that particular, than to surpass him in valour and conduct. Their common garment is a short jacket or frock of scarlet cloth over their fine clothes, and some hang over that an ivory quiver, lin'd with a tyger's [lion or leopard] skin, or a civet-cat's, and a long wide cap on their heads, like the dragoons caps in *France*, with a horse-tail pretty long hanging at the tip of it. Thus equipp'd, they mount their horses, to whose necks they commonly tie a tinkling bell, which rings as the horse moves. Thus they ride, with an air of fierceness, attended by a slave on foot on each side, and follow'd by many others, one carrying the large *Bamboo* shield, another leading the horse, and others playing on their usual musical instruments; that is, drums, horn, flutes; an iron hollow pipe, on which they beat with a wooden stick; and another instrument, the most esteemed among them, being a sort of large dry bladder, well swell'd with air, cover'd with a net, fill'd with peas and brass bells, and hung or tied at the end of a wooden handle, to hold it by.

When return'd home from a warlike expedition, every man delivers back to the king's stores, the quivers and arrows he has left. That store-house, or arsenal, is divided into many chambers; and immediately the priests are set to work to poison new arrows, that there may be always a sufficient stock for the next occasion.

Having observ'd what little courage there is in this nation, we shall not have much to say of their wars; nor is it easy to account for their becoming so formidable among their neighbours to the north and northwest, but by concluding those nations to be as bad soldiers as themselves, and not so populous; for there are other nations south and east of them who value not their power, amongst whom are the pirates of *Usa*, who give them no little disturbance, as has been hinted before.

THE KING APPEARING ABROAD

The king of Benin at a certain time of the year rides out to be seen by his people. That day he rides one of his best horses, which, as has been observ'd, are but ordinary at best, richly equipp'd and habited, follow'd by three or four hundred of his principal ministers and officers of state, some on horseback, and some on foot, arm'd with their shields and javelins, preceded and follow'd by a great number of musicians, playing on all sorts of their instruments, sounding at the same time something rude and pleasant. At the head of this royal procession, are led some tame leopards or tygers in chains, attended by some dwarfs and mutes.

This procession commonly ends with the death of ten or twelve slaves, sacrificed in honour of the king, and paid by the people, who very grosly imagine those wretched victims will in a little time after, return to life again, in remote fertile countries, and there live happily.

There is another royal feast, at a fixed time of the year, call'd the coral-feast, during which the king causes his treasure to be exposed to publick view in the palace, to shew his grandeur.

On that day the king appears in publick again, magnificently dress'd, in the second court or plain of his palace, where he sits under a very fine canopy, incompass'd by all his wives, and a vast croud of his principal ministers and officers of state, all in their richest apparel, who range themselves about him, and soon after begin a procession; at which time the king rising from his place, goes to offer sacrifice to his idols in the open air, and there begins the feast, which is attended with the universal loud acclamations of his subjects. Having spent about a quarter of an hour in that ceremony, he returns to his former place under the canopy, where he stays two hours, to give the people time to perform their devotions to their idols; which done, he goes home in the same manner he came thither, and the remaining part of that day is spent in splendid treating and feasting; the king causing all sorts of provisions and pardon-wine to be distributed among the people; which is also done by every great lord, in imitation of the prince. So that nothing is seen throughout the whole city, but all possible marks of rejoicings and mirth.

The king on that day also uses to distribute men and women slaves among such persons as have done the nation some service, and to confer greater offices on them; but for his jasper-stone and corals, which, with the *Boejies*, make the greatest part of his treasure, he keeps them to himself.

25. WILLIAM BOSMAN

JUSTICE AND WARFARE AT AXIM. 1700.

William Bosman was the chief factor for the Dutch West India Company at Elmina Castle on the coast of the present Republic of Ghana. His A New and Accurate Description of the Coast of Guinea consists of twenty letters written about 1700. Bosman may have borrowed some material from the Amsterdam geographer Olfert Dapper, whose Description of Africa had been published nearly twenty years earlier. Axim was one of the important trading towns on the Gold Coast.

The government of the Negroes is very licentious and irregular, which only proceeds from the small authority of their chief men or Caboceros, and frequent wars are occasioned by their remiss government and absurd customs.

The difference betwixt the administration of the government of monarchies and commonwealths is here very great. Of the former, the power and jurisdiction being vested in a single person, I shall not say much at present; but shall only speak of the republics; amongst which that of Axim and Ante seeming the most like regular, I shall represent them as instances of the rest; though indeed the best of their govern-

From William Bosman, *A New and Accurate Description of the Coast of Guinea*, in John Pinkerton, *A General Collection of the Best and Most Interesting Voyages and Travels in All Parts of the World. Many of Which are Now First Translated into English* (London: Longman, Hurst, Rees, Orme, and Brown, 1808–1814), vol. XVL, pp. 404–405, 411–415.

ments and methods of administration of justice are so confused and perplexed, that they are hardly to be comprehended, much less, then, are they to be expressed with any manner of connexion on paper.

The government of Axim consists of two parts, the first whereof is the body of Caboceros, or chief men; the other the Manceros or young men. All civil or public affairs which commonly occur are under their administration; but what concerns the whole land, and are properly national affairs, as making of peace and war, the raising tributary impositions to be paid to foreign nations (which seldom happens), that falls under the cognisance of both parts or members of the government: and on these occasions the Manceros often manage with a superior hand, especially if the Caboceros are not very rich in gold and slaves, and consequently able by their assistance to bring over the other to their side.

Their distribution of justice is in the following manner:—If one of the Negroes hath any pretension upon another, he doth not go empty-handed, but loaded with presents of gold and brandy (the latter of which is here of a magnetic virtue), and applies himself to the Caboceros; after the delivery of which he states his case to them, desiring they will dispatch his cause with the first opportunity, and oblige his adversary to an ample satisfaction. If they are resolved to favour him highly, a full council is called immediately, or at farthest within two or three days, according as it is most convenient; and after having maturely consulted, judgment is given in his favour, and that frequently as directly opposite to justice as to any other reason than the received bribe.

But on the contrary, instead of favouring, are they incensed against the plaintiff, or have they received a larger bribe from his adversary, the justest cause in the world cannot protect him from judgment against him; or if right appear too plainly on his side, to avoid an ensuing scandal, they will delay and keep off a trial, obliging the injured person, after tedious and vain solicitations, to wait in hopes of finding juster judges hereafter, which perhaps does not happen in the course of his life, and so of consequence the suit devolves upon his heirs as an inheritance; who, whenever an opportunity offers, though thirty years after, know very well how to make use of it; as I myself have several times had such causes come before me, that one would be apt to think it were impossible they should remember so long, considering they want the assistance of reading and writing.

It sometimes falls out that the plaintiff, or perhaps the defendant, finding the cause given against him contrary to reason, is too impatient to wait to have justice done him, but makes use of the first favourable one of seizing such a quantity of gold or goods as is likely to repair his damage, not only from his adversary or debtor, but the first which falls in his way, if at least he does but live in the same city or village; and what he possessed himself of, he will not re-deliver till he receive plenary satisfaction, and is at peace with his adversary, or is obliged to it by force. If he be strong enough to defend himself and his capture, he is sure to keep it, and thereby engage a third person in the suit on account of the seizure of his effects for security, who hath his remedy on the person on whose account he hath suffered this damage; so that hence proceed frequent murders, and sometimes wars are thereby occasioned, but of this more hereafter.

The consultations with the Caboceros in conjunction with the Manceros principally relating to war, we shall at present touch upon.

When they are desirous of entering into a war, on account of ambition, plunder, or to assist other countries already engaged in a war, these two councils consult together: but otherwise the greatest part of their wars are chiefly occasioned by the recovery of debts, and the disputes of some of the chief people among them. I have formerly hinted something on this subject, with promise to proceed farther on it.

The firmest peace of neighbouring nations is frequently broken in the following manner:—One of the leading men in one country hath money owing him from a person in an adjacent country, which is not so speedily paid as he desires; on which he causes as many goods, freemen, or slaves to be seized by violence and rapine in the country where his debtor lives, as will richly pay him: the men so seized he claps in irons, and if not redeemed sells them, in order to raise money for the payment of the debt: if the debtor be an honest man and the debt just, he immediately endeavours by the satisfaction of his creditors to free his country-men: or if their relations are powerful enough they will force him to it: but when the debt is disputable, or the debtor unwilling to pay it, he is sure to represent the creditor amongst his own countrymen as an unjust man, who hath treated him in this manner contrary to all right, and that he is not at all indebted to him: if he so far prevails on his countrymen that they believe him, he endeavours to make some of the other land prisoners by way of reprizal; after which they consequently arm on each side, and watch all opportunities of surprizing each other. They first endeavour to bring the Caboceros over to their party, because they have always some men at their devoir; next the soldiers: and thus from a trifle a war is occasioned betwixt two countries, who before lived in amity, and continues till one of them be subdued; or, if their force be equal, till the principal men are obliged to make peace at the request of the soldiers; which frequently happens, especially about sowing time, when all the warriors desire to return to till the ground; for in serving in the war without pay, and defraying all expences out of their private fortunes, they quickly grow tired; especially if they get no advantage of, and consequently no plunder by the enemy.

When the governors of one country are inclined to make war with those of another, perhaps on account that they make a better figure in their manner of living, or that they are richer; so that these have a mind to some of their effects: then they assemble together, in conjunction with the Manceros, who also give their advice, and being young, and puft up with hopes of plunder, are easily induced by the persuasions of the Caboceros; and the joint resolution is no sooner formed than every one prepares for war; and being got ready, make an irruption into the designed country, without giving the least notice or declaring war, urging much the same reasons with a present European potentate, "It is My royal will and pleasure, and for My glory." And thus they kill and pillage each other. The injured nation, to revenge this perfidious breach of peace, if not powerful enough of itself, hires another to assist it for less than 2,000£ sterling; for which price the best are here to be had, well armed and appointed for an engagement: so that, indeed, war is not here very dear, though at this cheap rate you cannot imagine the armies so formidable that are hired for such trivial wages: but plunder is their chief aim, instead of which they often get good store of blows, which prove all the perquisites to their mentioned wages. These wages they divide amongst the Caboceros and the Manceros; but the former manage the affair so cunningly, that the latter have not above four or five shillings each, or perhaps half that sum; for the leading men are sure to adjust the account so well in favour of themselves, that a mighty residue is not likely to be left to make a future dividend. But as for the plunder, though particularly appropriated to defray the expence of the war in the first place, and the remainder to be divided, yet every man seizes the first part thereof he can lay hold on, without any regard to the public: but if no booty is to be come at, the Manceros, like cats that have wet their feet, make the best of their way home, not being obliged to stay longer than they themselves please. Each is under a particular chieftain in a sort, though he can command only his slaves; a free Negro not owning his authority, or submitting even to their kings, unless compelled by their exorbitant power, without which they live entirely at their own pleasure: but if their leader is disposed to march up first towards the enemy, he may, but will not, be followed by many.

War, as I have twice before told you, is not so expensive as in Europe; our four years war with the Commanyschians (except the damage done to our trade) did not cost us in all six thousand pounds sterling: for which sum we had successively five nations in our pay. But I have formerly treated this subject so largely, that I need not say any more of it at present.

A national offensive war may very well be managed here with four thousand men in the field; but a defensive requires more. Sometimes the number of what they call an army does not amount to more than two thousand. From whence you may infer of what force the monarchies and republics on the coast are, Fantyn [Fanti] and Aquamboe [Akwamu] only excepted; the first of which is able to bring an army of twenty-five thousand men, and the latter a much larger. But the inland potentates, such as Akim, Asiante [Asante] &c. are not to be reckoned amongst these, they being able to overrun a country by their numerous armies; though I cannot inform you any otherwise concerning those people, than what by hints we learn from the Negroes, who are not always to be believed. But as for the monarchies situate near us, I dare affirm, that though each of the two contending armies were composed of five or six several nations, they would not together make twenty-five thousand men; upon which account, joined to their cowardice, very few men are killed in a battle; and that engagement is very warm which leaves one thousand men upon the place; for they are so timorous, that as soon as they see a man fall by them, they run for it, and only think of getting safe home. In the last battle between the Commanyschians and those of Saboe, Acanni, Cabes Terra, and two or three other countries, I do not believe that one hundred men were killed, and yet the Commanyschians drove their enemies out of the field, and obtained a complete victory.

They are very irregular in their engagements, not observing the least shadow of order; but each commander hath his men close together in a sort of crowd, in the midst of which he is generally to be found; so that they attack the enemy man for man, or one heap of men against another; and some of their commanders seeing their brother-officer furiously attacked, and somewhat put to it, choose rather to run with the hare than hold with the hounds, and that frequently before they had struck one stroke, or stood so much as one brush; and their friends whom they left engaged certainly follow them, if in the least pressed, unless so entangled with the enemy that it is not for want of good will if they do not; but if no opportunity offers, though against their will, they get the reputation of good soldiers.

In fight, the Negroes do not stand upright against one another, but run stooping and listening, that the bullets may fly over their heads. Others creep towards the enemy, and, being come close, let fly at them; after which they run away as fast as they can, and, as if the devil were sure of the hindmost, get to their own army as soon as possible, in order to load their arms and fall on again. In short, their ridiculous gestures, stooping, creeping, and crying, make their fight more like monkeys playing together than a battle.

The booty which the commonalty chiefly aim at are the prisoners and ornaments of gold, and Conte de Terra; for some, especially the in-land Negroes, are so simple as to dress themselves in the richest manner possible on these occasions; wherefore they are frequently so loaded with gold and Conte de Terra, that they can scarcely march.

Common prisoners who cannot raise their ransom, are kept or sold for slaves at pleasure: if they take any considerable person, he is very well guarded, and a very high ransom put upon him; but if the person who occasioned the beginning of the war be taken, they will not easily admit him to ransom, though his weight in gold were offered, for fear he should in future form some new design against their repose.

The most potent Negro cannot pretend to be injured from slavery, for if he ever ventures himself in the wars, it may easily become his lot; he is consequently obliged to remain in that state till the sum demanded for his redemption is fully paid, which withal is frequently set so high, that he, his friends, and all his interest, are not sufficient to raise it; on which account, he is forced to a perpetual slavery, and the most contemptible offices. Some amongst them are so barbarous, that finding their hopes of a high ransom frustrated, they pay themselves by cruelly murdering the wretched prisoner.

Wars betwixt two despotical Kings, who have their subjects entirely at their command, are of a long duration, and frequently last several years successively, or till the utter ruin of one of them ends the dispute. They frequently lie a whole year encamped against each other without attempting any thing, a few diverting skirmishes excepted: only against rainy weather they each return home without molesting one another.

Though this is chiefly owing to their priests, without whose suffrage they are not easily induced to attempt a battle; they advise them against it, under pretence that their gods have not yet declared in favour of them; and if they will attempt it notwithstanding, they threaten an ill issue: but if these crafty villains observe that their army is much stronger than the enemies, and the soldiers well inclined to fighting, they always advise to attempt it; though with such a cautious reserve, that if it succeeds contrary to expectation, they never want an excuse to bring themselves off. the commanders or soldiers have done this or that thing, which they ought not to have done; for which reason the whole army is punished. In short, let the event prove how it will, the priest is infallibly innocent, and his character always maintains its own reputation.

I doubt not but I have sufficiently enlarged on their ridiculous wars, if I have not dwelt longer on them then they deserve; wherefore I shall relate the events which happened in my time, and apply myself to the description of their military arms.

The chief of these are musquets or carabins, in the management of which they are wonderfully dextrous. It is not unpleasant to see them exercise their army; they handle their arms so cleverly, discharging them several ways, one sitting, the second creeping, or lying, &c. that it is really to be admired they never hurt one another. Perhaps you wonder how the Negroes come to be furnished with fire-arms, but you will have no reason when you know we sell them incredible quantities, thereby obliging them with a knife to cut our own throats. But we are forced to it; for if we would not, they might be sufficiently stored with that commodity by the English, Danes, and Brandenburghers; and could we all agree together not to sell them any, the English and Zealand interlopers would abundantly furnish them: and since that and gun-powder for some time have been the chief vendible merchandise here, we should have found but an indifferent trade without our share in it. It were, indeed, to be wished that these dangerous commodities had never been brought hither, or at least, that the Negroes might be in a short time brought to be content with somewhat else in their room: but this in all appearance is never likely.

Next their guns, in the second place are their swords, shaped like a sort of chopping-knives, being about two or three hands broad at the extremity, and about one at the handle, and about three or four spans long at most; and a little crooked at the top. These sabres are very strong, but commonly so blunt that several strokes are necessary to cut off a-head: they have a wooden guard, adorned on one side, and sometimes on both, with small globular knobs, covered with a sort of skin, whilst others content themselves with bits of rope singed black with the blood of sheep or other cattle, with the additional ornament of a bunch of horsehair, amongst people of condition thin gold plates are usual: to this weapon belongs a leather-sheath almost open on one side; to which, by way of ornament, a tiger's head, or a large red shell is hung; both which are valuable here. These sabres they wear when they go out at their left hip, hanging in a belt, which is girt about their waists for that end, or stuck in their Paan, which is round about their bodies, and comes betwixt their legs, that they may run the swifter; besides which, they are begirt with a bandalier belt, with about twenty bandaliers. They have a cap on their heads made of a crocodile's skin, adorned on each side with a red shell, and behind with a bunch of horse-hair, and a heavy iron-chain, or something else instead of it, girt round their head. Thus appointed, with their bodies coloured white, our heroes look liker devils than men.

Their other weapons are first a bow and arrow; but these are not much in vogue amongst the Coast Negroes, those of Aquamboe alone excepted, who are so nicely dextrous in shooting, that in harehunting they will lodge their small fine arrows in what part of the hare's body is desired. These arrows have feathers at their head, and are pointed with iron. The Negroes of Awinee usually poison them; but on the Coast that pernicious custom is not practised, nor do they so much as know what poison is.

Next follow the Assagay or Hassagay [assegai, or slender hardwood spear tipped with iron], as some call them, which are of two sorts; the smaller sorts are about a Flemish ell [about 27 inches], or perhaps half an ell longer, and very slender, and these they cast as darts; the second, or larger sort, are about twice as long and large as the former, the upper part pointed with iron like a pike; some of them are covered for the length of one span or two, though in all manner of shapes. The Assagay serves them instead of a sabre, that having their shield in the left hand, they may the more conveniently dart the Assagay with the right, for they have always somebody or other to carry them after them.

Last of all are their shields, which serve only as a defensive covering of the body, and not to the offending any person. I have seen Negroes wonderously dextrous in the management of these shields, which they hold in their left hand, and a sabre in the right; and playing with both, they put their body into very strange postures, and so artificially cover themselves with the shield, that it is impossible to come at them. These shields, which are about four or five foot long, and three broad, are made of osiers; some of which are covered with gold leather, tigers' [lion or leopard] skins, or some other materials; some of them also have at each corner and in the middle broad thin copper-plates fastened on, to ward off the arrows and the light Assagayes, as well as the blows of the sabre, if they are good, though they are not proof against a musquet-ball.

I think these are all the weapons used amongst the Negroes, without I should tell you that some of them also are possessed of a few cannon; it is indeed true, but they use them in a very slovenly manner. The King of Saboe hath a very small number, with which he has been in the field, but he never made use of them. Some of them, after once firing them, have suffered the enemy to take them, as it happened to the Commanyschians; after which, those who took them were ignorant of the use of them; so that these monarchs' cannon only serves to shoot by way of compliment and salutation, of which the Blacks are very fond.

Promises create a debt; and at the beginning of this letter you have my word that it should conclude with the grandeur of their Kings; in pursuance of which, let us see wherein it consists.

The extent of their territories is so small, that some of them have not more land under their jurisdiction than a single captain or bailiff of a village, and bear the same name accordingly amongst the Negroes: for before the arrival of the Europeans in this country, no higher title was known amongst them than that of captain or colonel, with this only difference, that the one was appropriated to a country, but the other to a village. But since their conversation with us, they, or rather we, make a distinction betwixt a king and a captain. The first word by which it was expressed, was Obin or Abin, which signifies captain in our language, but they always understood by it a commander of a country, town, or nation, for our masters of ships generally assume the same title; and by the same appellation would also be applied, without any distinction, to our director-general and chief of forts, if we did not better inform the natives of the difference. Kings are obliged in this country to preserve their power by dint of force; wherefore the richer they are in gold and slaves, the more they are honoured and esteemed; and without those, they have not the least command over their subjects; but on the contrary, would not only be obliged to pray, but pay their underlings to execute their commands. But if the goddess Fortune has endowed them with a rich share of treasure, they are naturally cruel enough to govern their people tyrannically, and punish them so severely in their purses for trivial crimes, that they cannot forget it all the remainder of their lives; and this is done with a seeming colour of justice; for the King, having any thing to charge on another, delivers the matter into the hands of the Caboceros, and submits it to their decision; who, knowing his mind, are sure to aggravate the crime as much as possible, and take care that their judgment be consonant to his royal will and pleasure.

26. WILLIAM SNELGRAVE

THE SLAVES MUTINY. 1730.

William Snelgrave was an English slave trader on the Guinea Coast early in the eighteenth century. His account of the conduct of the slave trade describes events that occurred between 1720 and 1730. During this period the slave trade prospered and slave mutinies on the ships became more common as the trade became dominated by independent traders who were probably more careless in their supervision of the slaves and who carried fewer crew members in relation to the size of their cargoes than did trading company vessels. The mutiny described by Snelgrave took place in 1727 when the author was trading at Ouidah, the principal trading center on what was then called the Slave Coast and is now Benin.

The first Mutiny I saw among the Negroes, happened during my first Voyage, in the Year 1704, It was on board the Eagle Galley of London, commanded by my Father, with whom I was as Purser. We had bought our Negroes in the River of Old Callabar in the Bay of Guinea. At the time of their mutinying we were in that River, having four hundred of them on board, and not above ten white Men who were able to do Service: For several of our Ship's Company were dead, and many more sick; besides, two of our Boats were just then gone with twelve People on Shore to fetch Wood, which lay in sight of the Ship. All these Circumstances put the Negroes on consulting how to mutiny, which they did at four a clock in the Afternoon, just as they went to Supper. But as we had always carefully examined the Mens Irons, both Morning and Evening, none had got them off, which in a great measure contributed to our Preservation. Three white Men stood on the Watch with Cutlaces in their Hands. One of them who was on the Forecastle, a stout fellow, seeing some of the Men Negroes take hold of the chief Mate, in order to throw him over board, he laid

From William Snelgrave, *A New Account of Some Parts of Guinea and the Slave Trade*, in Elizabeth Dorman, *Documents Illustrative of the History of the Slave Trade to America* (Washington, D.C.: Carnegie Institution, 1930), vol. II, pp. 353–361. Reprinted by permission.

on them so heartily with the flat side of his Cutlace, that they soon quitted the Mate, who escaped from them, and run on the Quarter Deck to get Arms. I was then sick with an Ague [malaria], and lying on a Couch in the great Cabbin, the Fit being just come on. However, I no sooner heard the Outcry, That the Slaves were mutinying, but I took two Pistols, and run on the Deck with them; where meeting with my Father and the chief Mate, I delivered a Pistol to each of them. Whereupon they went forward on the Booms, calling to the Negroe Men that were on the Forecastle; but they did not regard their Threats, being busy with the Centry, (who had disengaged the chief Mate) and they would have certainly killed him with his own Cutlace, could they have got it from him; but they could not break the Line wherewith the Handle was fastened to his Wrist. And so, tho' they had seized him, yet they could not make use of his Cutlace. Being thus disappointed, they endeavoured to throw him overboard, but he held so fast by one of them that they could not do it. My Father seeing this stout Man in so much Danger, ventured amongst the Negroes to save him; and fired his Pistol over their Heads, thinking to frighten them. But a lusty Slave struck him with a Billet [a round wooden bar] so hard, that he was almost stunned. The Slave was going to repeat his Blow, when a young lad about seventeen years old, whom we had been kind to, interposed his Arm, and received the Blow, by which his arm-bone was fractured. At the same instant the Mate fired his Pistol, and shot the Negroe that had struck my Father. At the sight of this the Mutiny ceased, and all the Men-Negroes on the Forecastle threw themselves flat on their Faces, crying out for Mercy.

Upon examining into the matter, we found, there were not above twenty Men Slaves concerned in this Mutiny; and the two Ringleaders were missing, having, it seems, jumped overboard as soon as they found their Project defeated, and were drowned. This was all the Loss we suffered on this occasion: For the Negroe that was shot by the Mate, the Surgeon, beyond all Expectation, cured. And I had the good Fortune to lose my Ague, by the fright and hurry I was put into. Moreover, the young Man, who had received the Blow on his Arm to save my Father, was cured by the Surgeon in our Passage to Virginia. At our Arrival in that place we gave him his Freedom; and a worthy Gentleman, one Colonel Carter, took him into his Service, till he became well enough acquainted in the Country to provide for himself.

I have been several Voyages, when there has been no Attempt made by our Negroes to mutiny; which, I believe, was owing chiefly, to their being kindly used, and to my Officers Care in keeping a good Watch. But sometimes we meet with stout stubborn People amongst them, who are never to be made easy; and these are generally some of the Cormantines, a Nation of the Gold Coast. I went in the year 1721, in the Henry of London, a Voyage to that part of the Coast, and bought a good many of these People. We were obliged to secure them very well in Irons, and watch them narrowly: Yet they nevertheless mutinied, tho' they had little prospect of succeeding. I lay at that time near a place called Mumfort on the Gold Coast, having near five hundred Negroes on board, three hundred of which were Men. Our Ship's Company consisted of fifty white People, all in health: And I had very good Officers; so that I was very easy in all respects. . . .

After we had secured these People, I called the Linguists, and ordered them to bid the Men-Negroes between Decks be quiet; (for there was a great noise amongst them.) On their being silent, I asked, "What had induced them to mutiny?" They answered, "I was a great Rogue to buy them, in order to carry them away from their own Country, and that they were resolved to regain their Liberty if possible." I replied, "That they had forfeited their Freedom before I bought them, either by Crimes or by being taken in War, according to the Custom of their Country; and they being now my Property, I was resolved to let them feel my Resentment, if they abused my Kindness: Asking at the same time, Whether they had been ill used by the white Men, or had wanted for any thing the Ship afforded?" To this they replied, "They had nothing to complain of." Then I observed to them, "That if they should gain their Point and escape to the Shore, it would be no Advantage to them, because their Countrymen would catch them, and sell them to other Ships." This served my purpose, and they seemed to be convinced of their Fault, begging, "I would forgive them, and promising for the future to be obedient, and never mutiny again, if I would not punish them this time." This I readily granted, and so they went to sleep. When Daylight came we called the Men Negroes up on Deck, and examining their Irons, found them all secure. So this Affair happily ended, which I was very glad of; for these People are the stoutest and most sensible Negroes on the Coast: Neither are they so weak as to imagine as others do, that we buy them to eat them; being satisfied we carry them to work in our Plantations, as they do in their own Country.

However, a few days after this, we discovered they were plotting again, and preparing to mutiny. For some of the Ringleaders proposed to one of our Linguists, If he could procure them an Ax, they would cut the Cables the Ship rid by in the night; and so on her driving (as they imagined) ashore, they should get out of our hands, and then would become his Servants as long as they lived.

For the better understanding of this I must observe here, that these Linguists are Natives and Freemen of the Country, whom we hire on account of their speaking good English, during the time we remain trading on the Coast; and they are likewise Brokers between us and the black Merchants.

This Linguist was so honest as to acquaint me with what had been proposed to him; and advised me to keep a strict Watch over the Slaves; For tho' he had represented to them the same as I had done on their mutinying before, That they would all be catch'd again, and sold to other Ships, in case they could carry their Point, and get on Shore, yet it had no effect upon them.

This gave me a good deal of Uneasiness. For I knew several Voyages had proved unsuccessful by Mutinies; as they occasioned either the total loss of the Ships and the white Mens Lives; or at least by rendring it absolutely necessary to kill or wound a great number of the Slaves, in order to prevent a total Destruction. Moreover, I knew many of these Cormantine Negroes despised Punishment, and even Death it self. It having often happened at Barbadoes [West Indies] and other Islands, that on their being any ways hardly dealt with, to break them of their Stubbornness in refusing to work, twenty or more have hang'd themselves at a time in a Plantation. However, about a Month after this, a sad Accident happened, that brought our Slaves to be more orderly, and put them in a better Temper: And it was this. On our going from Mumfort to Annamaboe, which is the principal port on the Gold Coast, I met there with another of my Owner's Ships, called the Elizabeth. One Captain Thompson that commanded her was dead; as also his chief Mate: Moreover the Ship had afterwards been taken to Cape Lahoe on the Windward Coast, by Roberts the Pirate, with whom several of the Sailors belonging to her had entered. However, some of the Pirates had hindered the Cargoe's being plundered, and obtained that the Ship should be restored to the second Mate: Telling him, "They did it out of respect to the generous Character his Owner bore, in doing good to poor Sailors."

When I met with this Vessel I had almost disposed of my Ship's Cargoe; and the *Elizabeth* being under my Direction, I acquainted the second Mate, who then commanded her, that I thought it for our Owner's Interest, to take the Slaves from on board him, being about 120, into my Ship; and then go off the Coast; and that I would deliver him at the same time the Remains of my Cargoe, for him to dispose of with his own after I was sailed. This he readily complied with, but told me, "He feared his Ship's Company would mutiny, and oppose my taking the Slaves from him." And indeed, they came at that instant in a Body on the Quarterdeck; where one spoke for the rest, telling me plainly, "they would not allow the Slaves to be taken out by me." I found by this they had lost all respect for their present Commander, who indeed was a weak Man. However, I calmly asked the reason, "Why they offered to oppose my taking the Slaves?" To which they answered, "I had no business with them." On this I desired the Captain to send to his Scrutore, for the Book of Instructions Captain Thompson had received from our Owner; and he read to them, at my request, that Part, in which their former Captain, or his Successor (in case of Death) was to follow my Orders. Hereupon they all cried out, "they should remain a great while longer on the Coast to purchase more Slaves, if I took these from them, which they were resolved to oppose." I answered, "That such of the Ship's Company as desired it, I would receive on board my own; where they should have the same Wages they had at present on board the *Elizabeth*, and I would send some of my own People to supply their Places." This so reasonable an Offer was refused, one of the Men who was the Ship's Cooper telling me, that the Slaves had been on board a long time, and they had great Friendship with them: therefore they would keep them. I asked him, "Whether he had ever been on the Coast of Guinea before?" He replied no. Then I told him, "I supposed he had not by his way of talking, and advised him not to rely on the Friendship of the Slaves, which he might have reason to repent of when too late." And 'tis remarkable this very person was killed by them the next Night, as shall be presently related.

So finding that reasoning with these Men was to no Purpose, I told them, "When I came with my Boats to fetch the Slaves, they should find me as resolute to chastise such of them as should dare to oppose me, as I had been condescending to convince them by arguing calmly." So I took my leave of their Captain, telling him, "I would come the next Morning to finish the Affair."

But that very Night, which was near a month after the Mutiny on board of us at Mumfort, the Moon shining now very bright, as it did then, we heard, about ten a Clock, two or three Musquets fired on board the *Elizabeth*. Upon that I ordered all our Boats to be manned, and having secured every thing in our Ship, to prevent our

Slaves from mutinying, I went my self in our Pinnace, (the other Boats following me) on board the *Elizabeth*. In our way we saw two Negroes swimming from her, but before we could reach them with our Boats, some Sharks rose from the bottom, and tore them in Pieces. We came presently along the side of the Ship, where we found two Men-Negroes holding by a Rope, with their heads just above water; they were afraid, it seems, to swim from the Ship's side, having seen their Companions devoured just before by the Sharks. These two Slaves we took into our Boat, and then went into the Ship, where we found the Negroes very quiet, and all under Deck; but the Ship's Company was on the Quarter-deck, in a great Confusion, saying, "The Cooper, who had been placed centry at the Fore-hatch way, over the Men-Negroes, was, they believed, kill'd by them." I was surprized to hear this, wondring that these cowardly fellows, who had so vigorously opposed my taking the Slaves out, a few hours before, had not Courage enough to venture forward, to save their Ship-mate; but had secured themselves by shutting the Quarter-deck door, where they all stood with Arms in their Hands. So I went to the fore-part of the Ship with some of my People, and there we found the Cooper lying on his back quite dead, his Scull being cleft asunder with a Hatchet that lay by him. At the sight of this I called for the Linguist, and bid him ask the Negroes between Decks, "Who had killed the white Man?" They answered, "They knew nothing of the matter; for there had been no design of mutinying among them." Which upon Examination we found true; for above one hundred of the Negroes then on board, being bought to the Windward, did not understand a word of the Gold-Coast Language, and so had not been in the Plot. But this Mutiny was contrived by a few Cormantee-Negroes, who had been purchased about two or three days before. At last, one of the two Men-Negroes we had taken up along the Ship side, impeached his Companion, and he readily confessed he had kill'd the Cooper, with no other View, but that he and his Countrymen might escape undiscovered by swimming on Shore. For on their coming upon Deck, they observed, that all the white Men set to watch were asleep; and having found the Cook's Hatchet by the Fire-place, he took it up, not designing then to do any Mischief with it; but passing by the Cooper, who was sentry, and he beginning to awake, the Negroe rashly struck him on the head with it, and then jump'd over-board. Upon this frank Confession, the white Men would have cut him to Pieces; but I prevented it, and carried him to my own Ship. Early the next morning, I went on board the *Elizabeth* with my Boats, and sent away all the Negroes then in her, into my own Ship: not one of the other Ship's Company offering to oppose it. Two of them, the Carpenter and Steward, desired to go with me, which I readily granted; and by way of Security for the future success of the Voyage, I put my chief Mate, and four of my under Officers (with their own Consent,) on board the *Elizabeth*; and they arrived, about five Months after this, at Jamaica, having disposed of most part of the Cargoe.

After having sent the Slaves out of the *Elizabeth*, as I have just now mentioned, I went on board my own Ship; and there being then in the Road of Anamaboe, eight sail of Ships besides us, I sent an Officer in my Boat to the Commanders of them, "To desire their Company on board my Ship, because I had an Affair of great Consequence to communicate to them." Soon after, most of them were pleased to come; and I having acquainted them with the whole Matter, and they having also heard the Negroe's Confession, "That he had killed the white Man." They unanimously advised me to put him to death; arguing, "That Blood required Blood, by all Laws both divine and human; especially as there was in this Case the clearest Proof, namely the Murderer's Confession: Moreover this would in all probability prevent future Mischiefs; for by publickly executing this Person at the Ship's Foreyard Arm, the Negroes on board their Ships would see it; and as they were very much disposed to mutiny, it might prevent them from attempting it." These Reasons, with my being in the same Circumstances, made me comply.

Accordingly we acquainted the Negroe, that he was to die in an hour's time for murdering the white Man. He answered, "He must confess it was a rash Action in him to kill him; but he desired me to consider, that if I put him to death, I should lose all the Money I had paid for him." To this I bid the Interpreter reply, "That tho' I knew it was customary in his Country to commute for Murder by a Sum of Money, yet it was not so with us; and he should find that I had no regard to my Profit in this respect: For as soon as an Hour-Glass, just then turned, was run out, he should be put to death;" At which I observed he shewed no Concern.

Hereupon the other Commanders went on board their respective Ships, in order to have all their Negroes upon Deck at the time of Execution, and to inform them of the occasion of it. The Hour-Glass being run out, the Murderer was carried on the Ship's Forecastle, where he had a Rope fastened under his Arms, in order to be hoisted up to the Fore-yard Arm, to be shot to death. This some of his Countrymen observing, told him, (as the Linguist informed me afterwards) "That they would not have him to be frightened; for it was plain I did not design to put him to death, otherwise the Rope would have been put about his neck, to hang him." For it seems they had no thought of his being shot; judging he was only to be hoisted up to the Yard-arm, in order to scare him: But they immediately saw the contrary; for as soon as he was hoisted up, ten white Men who were placed behind the Barricado on the Quarter-deck fired their Musquets, and instantly killed him. This struck a sudden Damp upon our Negroe-Men, who thought, that, on account of my Profit, I would not have executed him.

The Body being cut down upon the Deck, the Head was cut off, and thrown overboard. This last part was done, to let our Negroes see, that all who offended thus, should be served in the same manner. For many of the Blacks believe, that if they are put to death and not dismembred, they shall return again to their own Country, after they are thrown overboard. But neither the Person that was executed, nor his Countrymen of Cormantee (as I understood afterwards,) were so weak as to believe any such thing; tho' many I had on board from other Countries had that Opinion.

When the Execution was over, I ordered the Linguist to acquaint the Men-Negroes, "That now they might judge, no one that killed a white Man should be spared:" And I thought proper now to acquaint them once for all, "That if they attempted to mutiny again, I should be obliged to punish the Ringleaders with death, in order to prevent further Mischief." Upon this they all promised to be obedient, and I assured them they should be kindly used, if they kept their Promise: which they faithfully did. For we sailed, two days after, from Anamaboe for Jamaica; and tho' they were on board near four Months, from our going off the Coast, till they were sold at that Island, they never gave us the least reason to be jealous of them; which doubtless was owing to the execution of the white Man's Murderer.

After the Captain [Messervy, of *Ferrers* galley] had told me this story, he desired me to spare him some Rice, having heard, I had purchased a great many Tuns to the Windward; where he had bought little, not expecting to meet with so many Slaves. This request I could not comply with, having provided no more than was necessary for my self, and for another of my Owner's Ships, which I quickly expected. And understanding from him, that he had never been on the Coast of Guinea before, I took the liberty to observe to him, "That as he had on board so many Negroes of one Town and Language, it required the utmost Care and Management to keep them from mutinying; and that I was sorry he had so little Rice for them: For I had experienced that the Windward Slaves are always very fond of it, it being their usual Food in their own Country; and he might certainly expect dissatisfactions and Uneasiness amongst them for want of a sufficient quantity."

This he took kindly, and having asked my Advice about other Matters, took his leave, inviting me to come next day to see him. I went accordingly on board his Ship, about three a clock in the afternoon. At four a clock the Negroes went to Supper, and Captain Messervy desired me to excuse him for a quarter of an hour, whilst he went forward to see the Men-Negroes served with Victuals. I observed from the Quarter-Deck, that he himself put Pepper and Palm Oyl amongst the Rice they were going to eat. When he came back to me, I could not forbear observing to him, "How imprudent it was in him to do so: For tho' it was proper for a Commander sometimes to go forward, and observe how things were managed; yet he ought to take a proper time, and have a good many of his white People in Arms when he went; or else the having him so much in their Power, might incourage the Slaves to mutiny: For he might depend upon it, they always aim at the chief Person in the Ship, whom they soon distinguish by the respect shown him by the rest of the People."

He thanked me for this Advice, but did not seem to relish it; saying, "He thought the old Proverb good, that "The Master's Eye makes the Horse fat." We then fell into other Discourse, and among other things he told me, "He designed to go away in a few days:" Accordingly he sailed three days after for Jamaica. Some Months after I went for that place, where at my arrival I found his Ship, and had the following melancholy account of his Death, which happened about ten days after he left the Coast of Guinea in this manner.

Being on the Forecastle of the Ship, amongst the Men-Negroes, when they were eating their Victuals, they laid hold on him, and beat out his Brains with the little Tubs, out of which they eat their boiled Rice. This Mutiny having been plotted amongst all the grown Negroes on board, they run to the forepart of the Ship in a body, and endeavoured to force the Barricado on the Quarter-Deck, not regarding the Musquets or Half Pikes, that were presented to their Breasts by the white Men, through the Loop-holes. So that at last the chief Mate was obliged to order one of the Quarter-deck Guns laden with Partridge-Shot, to be fired amongst them; which occasioned a terrible Destruction: For there were near eighty Negroes kill'd and drowned, many jumping overboard when the Gun was fired. This indeed put an end to the Mutiny, but most of the Slaves that remained alive grew so sullen, that several of them were starved to death, obstinately refusing to take any Sustenance: And after the Ship was arrived at Jamaica, they attempted twice to mutiny, before the Sale of them began. This with their former Misbehaviour coming to be publickly known, none of the Planters cared to buy them, tho' offered at a low Price. So that this proved a very unsuccessful Voyage, for the Ship was detained many Months at Jamaica on that account, and at last was lost there in a Hurricane. . . .

27. MERCATOR HONESTUS

A DEFENSE OF THE AFRICAN SLAVE TRADE. 1740.

In July 1740, Mercator Honestus (a pseudonym) had "A Letter to the Gentlemen Merchants in the Guinea Trade, Particularly Addressed to the Merchants in Bristol and Liverpool" published in the Gentleman's Magazine (vol. X, p. 341). This letter argued against slavery and the slave trade and concluded with a request that some of the gentlemen who engaged in the trade should justify their participation. The following letter written in reply to that challenge, presents the most common argument in defense of the slave trade—that life in Africa was so unbearable that Africans were better off removed from it, even if by bondage and servitude.

Sir, The Guinea Trade, by the Mistake of some, or Misrepresentation of others, hath been charged with Inhumanity, and a Contradiction to good Morals. Such a Charge at a Time when private and publick Morals are laugh'd at, as the highest Folly, by a powerful Faction; and Self-interest set up as the only Criterion of true Wisdom, is certainly very uncourtly: But yet as I have a profound Regard for those superannuated Virtues; you will give me Leave to justify the African Slave Trade, upon those Stale Principles, from the Imputations of "Mercator Honestus"; and shew him that there are People in some boasted Regions of Liberty, under a more wretched Slavery, than the Africans transplanted to our American colonies.

The Inhabitants of Guinea are indeed in a most deplorable State of Slavery, under the arbitrary Powers of their Princes both as to Life and Property. In the several Subordinations to them, every great Man is absolute lord of his immediate Dependents. And lower still; every Master of a Family is Proprietor of his Wives, Children, and Servants; and may at his Pleasure consign them to Death, or a better Market. No doubt such a State is contrary to Nature and Reason, since every human Creature hath an absolute Right to Liberty. But are not all arbitrary Governments, as well in Europe, as Africa, equally repugnant to that great Law of Nature? And yet

From "Defense of the African Slave Trade, 1740," *London Magazine*, vol. IX, pp. 493–494, 1740, in Elizabeth Donnan, *Documents Illustrative of the History of the Slave Trade to America* (Washington, D. C.: Carnegie Institution, 1930, vol. II, pp. 469–470. Reprinted by permission.

it is not in our Power to cure the universal Evil, and set all the Kingdoms of the Earth free from the Domination of Tyrants, whose long Possession, supported by standing Armies, and flagitious Ministers, renders the Thraldom without Remedy, while the People under it are by Custom satisfied with, or at least quiet under Bondage.

All that can be done in such a Case is, to communicate as much Liberty, and Happiness, as such circumstances will admit, and the People will consent to: And this is certainly by the Guinea Trade. For, by purchasing, or rather ransoming the Negroes from their national Tyrants, and transplanting them under the benign Influences of the Law, and Gospel, they are advanced to much greater Degrees of Felicity, tho'not to absolute Liberty.

That this is truly the Case cannot be doubted by any one acquainted with the Constitution of our Colonies, where the Negroes are governed by Laws, and suffer much less Punishment in Proportion to their Crimes, than the People in other Countries more refined in the Arts of Wickedness; and where Capital Punishment is inflicted only by the Civil Magistrates. . . .

Perhaps my Antagonist calls the Negroes Allowance of a Pint of Corn and an Herring, penurious, in Comparison of the full Meals of Gluttony: But if not let him compare that Allowance, to what the poor Labourer can purchase for Tenpence per Day to subsist himself and Family, and he will easily determine the American's Advantage. . . .

Nevertheless, Mercator will say, the Negroes are Slaves to their Proprietors: How Slaves? Nominally: Not really so much Slaves, as the Peasantry of all Nations is to Necessity; not so much as those of Corruption, or Party Zeal; not in any Sense, such abject Slaves, as every vicious Man is to his own Appetites. Indeed there is this Difference between Britons, and the Slaves of all other Nations; that the latter are so by Birth, or tyrannical Necessity; the former can never be so, but by a wicked Choice, or execrable Venality....[1]

---

1. In December the *Gentleman's Magazine* (vol. XI, pp. 145–146, 186–188) contained a second article, brought forth by the letter of "Mercator Honestus," from inhabitants of the Leeward Islands. This refers to a controversy over the morality of the trade in which a negro, Moses Bon Saam, had taken part. The article distributed responsibility for the trade, first, on the African chiefs; secondly, on the English traders who bought in Africa; thirdly, on the people who protected the trade because of the gain in it or in the sugar trade which rested on it; lastly, on the planters, who would prefer white labor but could not get it. From this time forward the adherents of the trade were more and more frequently placed upon the defensive, being forced to consider not so much the economic contribution made to the nation by the slave trade as its ethical aspects. Their defense is in reality usually directed, as it is here, not to the trade but to the institution of slavery.

28. JAMES BRUCE

SHEIK ADLAN AND THE BLACK HORSE CAVALRY OF SENNAR. 1772

James Bruce of Kinnaird (1730–1794) spent the early part of his life in study and travel. He was appointed British Consul in Algiers, but determined to seek the source of the Nile, which had baffled men for centuries, he visited Ethiopia in 1769. Here he found the origins of the Blue Nile at the Sacred Springs of Safala below Mt. Gish. Although Pedro Paez had arrived at the same source over 150 years before in 1618 and although that source was but the beginning of one branch of the Nile River, Bruce's Travels to Discover the Source of the Nile, 1768–73, stimulated others to seek the origins of the Nile. Moreover, the narrative of his travels remains one of the few eighteenth-century descriptions of Ethiopia and the Funj kingdom of Sennar in the Sudan. The Funj were a mysterious people whose origins are unknown but who suddenly appeared on the Blue Nile in 1504 and established their capital at Sennar. Having been converted to Islam, the Funj asserted their hegemony over the middle Nile and reached the height of their power in the seventeenth century. At the time Bruce visited Sennar in 1772. the Funj kingdom was in decline, yet the Black Horse Cavalry of Sheik Adlan appeared to the traveler as impressive as its reputation.

It was not till the 8th of May I had my audience of Shekh Adelan at Aira, which is three miles and a half from Sennaar; we walked out early in the morning, for the greatest part of the way along the side of the Nile, which had no beauty, being totally divested of trees, the bottom foul and muddy, and the edges of the water, white with small concretions of calcareous earth, which, with the bright sun upon them, dazzled and affected our eyes very much.

We then struck across a large sandy plain, without trees or bushes, and came to Adelan's habitation; two or three very considerable houses, of one storey, occupied the middle of a large square, each of whose sides was at least half of an English mile. Instead of a wall to inclose this square, was a high fence or impalement of strong reeds, canes, or stalks of dora (I do not know which), in fascines strongly joined together by stakes and cords. On the outside of the gate, on each hand, were six houses of a slighter construction than the rest; close upon the fence were sheds where the soldiers lay, the horses picqueted before them with their heads turned towards the sheds, and their food laid before them on the ground; above each soldier's sleeping-place, covered only on the top and open in the sides, were hung a lance, a small oval shield, and a large broad-sword. These, I understood, were chiefly quarters for couriers, who, being Arabs, were not taken into the court or square, but shut out at night.

Within the gate was a number of horses, with the soldiers barracks behind them;

From James Bruce, *Travels to Discover the Source of the Nile, 1768–73* (Edinburgh: Archibald Constable and Co., and Manners and Miller, 1813), vol. VI, pp. 359–365.

they were all picqueted in ranks, their faces to their masters barracks. It was one of the finest sights I ever saw of the kind. They were all above sixteen hands high, of the breed of the old Saracen horses, all finely made, and as strong as our coach horses, but exceedingly nimble in their motion; rather thick and short in the forehand, but with the most beautiful eyes, ears, and heads in the world; they were mostly black, some of them black and white, some of them milk-white, foaled so, not white by age, with white eyes and white hoofs, not perhaps a great recommendation.

A steel shirt of mail hung upon each man's quarters, opposite to his horse, and by it an antelope's skin, made soft like shamoy, with which it was covered from the dew of the night. A head-piece of copper, without crest or plumage, was suspended by a lace above the shirt of mail, and was the most picturesque part of the trophy. To these was added an enormous broad-sword, in a red leather scabbard; and upon the pummel hung two thick gloves, not divided into fingers as ours, but like hedgers gloves, their fingers in one poke. They told me that, within that inclosure at Aira, there were 400 horses, which, with the riders, and armour complete for each of them, were all the property of Shekh Adelan, every horseman being his slave, and bought with his money. There were five or six (I know not which) of these squares or inclosures, none of them half a mile from the other, which contained the king's horses, slaves, and servants. Whether they were all in as good order as Adelan's I cannot say, for I did not go further; but no body of horse could ever be more magnificently disposed unde the direction of any Christian power.

Adelan was then sitting upon a piece of the trunk of a palm-tree, in the front of one of these divisions of his horses, which he seemed to be contemplating with pleasure; a number of black people, his own servants and friends, were standing around him. He had on a long drab-coloured camlet gown, lined with yellow sattin, and a camlet cap like a head-piece, with two short points that covered his cars. This, it seems, was his dress when he rose early in the morning to visit his horses, which he never neglected. The Shekh was a man above six feet high, and rather corpulent, had a heavy walk, seemingly more from affectation of grandeur, than want of agility. He was about sixty, of the colour and features of an Arab, and not of a Negro, but had rather more beard than falls to the lot of people in this country; large piercing eyes, and a determined, though, at the same time, a very pleasing countenance. Upon my coming near, him, he got up; "You that are a horseman," says he without any salutation, "what would your king of Habesh give for these horses?" "What king," answered I, in the same tone, "would not give any price for such horses, if he knew their value?" "Well," replies he, in a lower voice, to the people about him, "if we are forced to go to Habesh, as Baady was, we will carry our horses along with us." I understood by this he alluded to the issue of his approaching quarrel with the king.

We then went into a large saloon, hung round with mirrors and scarlet damask; in one of the longest sides, were two large sofas covered with crimson and yellow damask, and large cushions of cloth of gold, like to the king's. He now pulled off his camlet gown and cap, and remained in a crimson sattin coat reaching down below his knees, which lapped over at the breast, and was girt round his waist with a scarf or sash, in which he had stuck a short dagger in an ivory sheath, mounted with gold; and one of the largest and most beautiful amethysts upon his finger that ever I saw, mounted plain, without any diamonds, and a small gold ear-ring in one of his ears.

"Why have you come hither," says he to me, "without arms and on foot, and without attendants?" *Yagoube* [Bruce]. "I was told that horses were not kept at Sennaar, and brought none with me." *Adelan.* "You suppose you have come through great dangers, and so you have. But what do you think of me, who am day and night out in the fields, surrounded by hundreds and thousands of Arabs, all of whom would eat me alive if they dared?" I answered, "A brave man, used to command as you are, does not look to the number of his enemies, but to their abilities; a wolf does not fear ten thousand sheep more than he does one." *Ad.* [Adelan]. "True; look out at the door; these are their chiefs whom I am now taxing, and I have brought them hither that they may judge from what they see whether I am ready for them or not." *Yag.* "You could not do more properly; but, as to my own affairs, I wait upon you from the king of Abyssinia, desiring safe conduct through your country into Egypt, with his royal promise, that he is ready to do the like for you again, or any other favour you may call upon him for." He took the letter and read it. *Ad.* "The king of Abyssinia may be assured I am always ready to do more for him than this. It is true, since the mad attempt upon Sennaar, and the next still madder, to replace old Baady upon the throne, we have had no formal peace, but neither are we at war. We understand one another as good neighbours ought to do; and what else is peace?" *Yag.* "You know I am a stranger and traveller seeking my way home. I have nothing to do with peace or war between nations. All I beg is a safe conduct through your kingdom, and the rights of hospitality bestowed in such case on every common stranger; and one of the favours I beg is, your acceptance of a small present. I bring it not from home; I have been long absent from thence, or it would have been better." *Ad.* "I'll not refuse it, but it is quite unnecessary. I have faults like other men, but to hurt, or ransack strangers, was never one of them. Mahomet Abou Kalec, my brother, is, however, a much better man to strangers than I am; you will be lucky if you meet him here; if not, I will do for you what I can, when once the confusion of these Arabs is over."

I gave him the Sherriffe's letter, which he opened, looked at it, and laid by without reading, saying only, "Aye, Metical is a good man, he sometimes takes care of our people going to Mecca; for my part, I never was there, and probably never shall." I then presented my letter from Ali Bey [Mamluk ruler of Egypt] to him. He placed it upon his knee, and gave a slap upon it with his open hand. *Ad.* "What! do you not know, have you not heard, Mahomet Abou Dahab, his Hasnadar, has rebelled against him, banished him out of Cairo, and now sits in his place? But, don't be disconcerted at that; I know you to be a man of honour and prudence; if Mahomet, my brother, does not come, as soon as I can get leisure I will dispatch you." The servant that had conducted me to Sennaar, and was then with us, went forward close to him, and said, in a kind of whisper, "Should he go often to the king?" "When he pleases; he may go to see the town, and take a walk, but never alone, and also to the palace, that, when he returns to his own country, he may report he saw a king at Sennaar, that neither knows how to govern, nor will suffer others to teach him; who knows not how to make war, and yet will not sit in peace." I then took my leave of him; but there was a plentiful breakfast in the other room, to which he sent us, and which went far to comfort Hagi Ismael for the misfortune of his patron, Ali Bey. At going out, I took my leave by kissing his hand, which he submitted to without reluctance.

"Shekh," said I, "when I pass these Arabs in the square, I hope it will not disoblige you if I converse with some of them out of curiosity?" *Ad.* "By no means, as much as you please; but don't let them know where they can find you at Sennaar, or they will be in your house from morning till night, will eat up all your victuals, and then, in return, will cut your throat, if they can meet you upon your journey."

I returned home to Sennaar, very well pleased with my reception at Aira. I had not seen, since I left Gondar, a man so open and frank in his manners, and who spoke, without disguise, what apparently he had in his heart; but he was exceedingly engaged in business, and it was of such extent that it seemed to me impossible to be brought to an end in a much longer time than I proposed staying at Sennaar. The distance, too, between Aira and that town was a very great discouragement to me. The whole way was covered with insolent, brutish people; so that every man we met between Sennaar and Aira produced some altercation, some demand of presents, gold, cloth, tobacco, and a variety of other disagreeable circumstances, which had always the appearance of ending in something serious.

29. ANDREW SPARRMAN

THE BOERS. 1776

Andrew Sparrman was a Swede who studied medicine at the University of Uppsala and subsequently accompanied Captain James Cook to the Antarctic as assistant naturalist. Between 1772 and 1776 he traveled in the Cape Colony, and although he was primarily concerned with its fauna, he provided the first complete description of the character, manners, and attitude of the Boer settlers at the frontier. The following selection was written in January 1776.

All the colonists who follow the grazing business, and particularly those at *Agter Bruntjes-boogte* lead an easy and pleasant life. One of these boors usually puts to his plough eight or ten of his fat, or rather pampered oxen; and it is hardly to be conceived, with what little trouble he gets into order a field of a moderate size; and in consequence of his feeding so great a number of cattle, how easily he can render it in the highest degree fertile. So that, always sure of a rich harvest from a soil not yet worn out, and ever grateful to the culture bestowed upon it, he may be almost said merely to amuse himself with the cultivation of it, for the bread he wants for himself and his family; while many other husbandmen must sweat and toil themselves

From Andrew Sparrman, *A Voyage to The Cape of Good Hope from 1772 to 1776* (2nd ed.; London: Robinson, 1786), pp. 164–169.

almost to death, both for what they use themselves, and for that which is consumed by others, who frequently live in ease and indolence. By his extensive pastures, and by throwing a sufficient quantity of land into tillage, he rears a considerable number of horses, which frequently are used only a few days in a year, for the purpose of treading out and threshing his corn. With pleasure, but without the least trouble to himself, he sees the herds and flocks, which constitute his riches, daily and considerably increasing. These are driven to pasture and home again by a few Hottentots or slaves, who likewise make the butter; so that it is almost only with the milking, that the farmer, together with his wife and children, concern themselves at all. To do this business, however, he has no occasion to rise before seven or eight o'clock in the morning; and notwithstanding his having enjoyed his bed so long in the morning, he can afford, without neglecting any thing of consequence, to allow himself an afternoon's nap, which the heat of the climate renders more agreeable than it is in our northern regions.

That they might not put their arms and bodies out of the easy and commodious posture in which they had laid them on the couch, they have been known to receive travellers lying quite still and motionless, excepting that they have very civilly pointed out the road, by moving their foot to the right or left. Professor THUNBERG, who has had greater opportunities than I had of exploring the warmer *Carrow* districts, where the inhabitants were still more indolent, has given me an account much to the same purpose.

The leaning of their arms on the table at meal times, is a custom very common with the colonists, and considered by them as a very laudable one, and in this particularly I followed my host's example; but I could not sufficiently admire the inventive spirit of idleness, exhibited in the voluptuous posture in which they universally indulge themselves when they smoke their pipes. Sitting on a bench or a chair without elbows, with their backs moderately bent, they lay their left leg over their right knee, and upon the left knee again thus raised, they rest their left elbow, while with the hand on the same side they support their chin, or one of their cheeks, at the same time holding their pipes in their mouths. Their right hand is then at liberty to grasp the small of their left leg with, or else to convey now and then to their mouth a cooling draught of tea. Let the reader represent to himself several people sitting together in this posture, and he will readily conceive what an elegant figure they would make in a group. I never saw any of the fair sex, however, in a posture of this kind. Among a set of beings so entirely devoted to their ease, one might naturally expect to meet with a variety of the most commodious easy chairs and sofas; but the truth is, that they find it much more commodious to avoid the trouble of inventing and making them.

I remarked as a very singular circumstance, that a wealthy farmer at *Agter Bruntjes-boogte*, who had plenty of timber to sell, had nevertheless only a rickety elbow-chair in his house, and a few scanty stools of the most simple construction, made of a single board, with four rough-hewn ill-shapen legs. What, however, was still more singular was, that notwithstanding that one of these stools had lost a leg, yet it was frequently made use of to the endangering of the person's limbs who sat upon it, without either the master of the house or any of his three sons, who were otherwise all alert enough at the chase, having ever once thought of mending it. Nor did the inhabitants of this place exhibit much less simplicity and moderation, or to speak more properly, slovenliness and penury in their dress than in their furniture; neither of which, therefore, were in any wise correspondent to the large flocks and herds possessed by these graziers, and the plentiful tables they could afford to keep in consequence of these possessions. The distance at which they are from the Cape, may, indeed, be some excuse for their having no other earthenware or china in their houses, but what was cracked or broken; but this, methinks, should not prevent them from being in possession of more than one or two old pewter pots, and some few plates of the same metal; so that two people are frequently obliged to eat out of one dish, using it besides for every different article of food that comes upon table.

Each guest must bring his knife with him, and they frequently make use of their fingers instead of forks. The most wealthy farmer here is considered as being well dressed in a jacket of home-made cloth, or something of the kind made of any other coarse cloth, breeches of undressed leather, woollen stockings, a striped waistcoat, a cotton handkerchief about his neck, a coarse calico shirt, Hottentot field-shoes, or else leathern-shoes, with brass buckles, and a coarse hat. Indeed it is not in dress, but in the number and thriving condition of their cattle, and chiefly in the stoutness of their draught oxen, that these peasants vie with each other. It is likewise by activity and manly actions, and by other qualities, that render a man fit for the married state. and the rearing of a family, that the youth chiefly obtain the esteem of the fair sex; none of whom likewise were ever known, for the sake of vying with each other in point of dress, to have endangered either their husband's property or their own virtue. A plain close cap, and a coarse cotton gown, virtue and good housewifery, are looked upon by the fair sex as sufficient ornaments for their persons; a flirting disposition, coquetry and paint, would have very little effect in making conquests of young men, brought up in so hardy a manner, and who have had so homely and artless an education, as the youth in this place. In short, one may here, if any where in the world, lead an innocent, virtuous, and happy life.

When in company with these plain artless husbandmen, I used frequently to start such questions and subjects of conversation, as tended to give them a proper sense of the happiness of their situation, and make them set a higher value upon it, than they perhaps had done before. Indeed, I thought I could not more properly or more agreeably employ the little Dutch I had learned, than in persuading the good people among whom I sojourned, to be content with their lot, and consequently to be happy. One day, when I was urging this point, I received the following pertinent, but kind reply, from a discreet sensible woman, who was daughter to an inferior magistrate at Zwellendam, and was married to a yeoman in this place.

"My good friend," said she, "you talk like a prudent sensible man; I am quite of you opinion, and wish you every happiness that can attend you: why need you wander any longer up and down the world in quest of happiness? You find it here, and are welcome to enjoy it among us. You have already a waggon, oxen, and saddle horses; these are the chief things requisite in order to set up a farmer; there are yet uncultivated places enough in this neigbourhood, proper either for pasturage tillage, so that you may choose out of an extensive tract of land the spot that pleases you best. Here are people enough, who will send you that part of their cattle to keep which they cannot conveniently look after themselves, on conditions that you shall have the young ones produced by them for your trouble. In this way, many young beginners have acquired a competency in a few years. With your knowledge of disorders and plants, you may render yourself serviceable to your neighbours, and now and then get a heifer or a calf. In short, I will venture to prophesy, that you will soon have cows and sheep in abundance. Yet there is still somewhat wanting, which is most essential to your happiness; this is, a prudent and discreet wife: take my advice and look about you, and I will take upon me to assure you, that you will not long be without one in this country."

This advice, so consonant to the voice of nature, and coming with such kind intention from the fair sex, could not but greatly affect me: it is remarkable, however, that the poor woman who gave it me, had herself a bad husband.

30. ARCHIBALD DALZEL
DAHOMEY AND ITS NEIGHBORS. 1793.

During the latter part of the eighteenth century, the trader Archibald Dalzel spent nearly thirty years on the Guinea Coast, during four of which he was governor of Ouidah. Although his purpose in writing his well-known The History of Dahomey, an Inland Kingdom of Africa *was to demonstrate how savage the country was (thereby justifying the slave trade), he related the traditions or origins of Dahomey (located in present-day Benin) and described the rival neighboring kingdoms over which Dahomey was to establish its supremacy.*

The Dahomans were formerly called Foys, and inhabited a small territory, on the north-east part of their present kingdom, whose capital, *Dawhee*, lay between the towns of Calmina and Abomey, at about 90 miles from the sea-coast.

Early in the last century, Tacoodonou, chief of the Foys, having, at the time of his festivals, murdered a neighbouring prince, who was with him on a friendly visit, seized on his chief town, Calmina, and soon after made himself master of his kingdom.

Thus strengthened, he dared to wage war against a more powerful state, to the northward of Foy, and laid siege to Abomey, its capital; but meeting here with more resistance than he expected, he made a vow, if he should prove successful, that he would sacrifice Da, its prince, to the Fetische, or deity, whose succour he then implored.

At length, having reduced the town, and captured the unfortunate prince, he built a large palace at Abomey, in memory of his victory. And now it was that he fulfilled

From Archibald Dalzel, *The History of Dahomey, an Inland Kingdom of Africa* (London: T. Spilsbury and Son, Snowhill, 1973), pp. 1–7, 12–15.

his vow, by ripping open the belly of his royal captive: after which he displayed the body on the foundation of the palace he was building; and carrying on the wall over it, he named the structure, when finished, Da-homy, or the house in Da's belly.

The conquest of Abomey happened about the year 1625; after which, Tacoodonou fixed his residence in that town, assuming the title of King of Dahomy. His subjects changed the name of Foys for that of Dahomans; and at the present hour, their former appellation, except amongst a few of the inland people, seems quite forgot.

Nothing further is related of Tacoodonou; nor, indeed, of his two immediate successors, Adahoonzou, and Weebaigah, except that the former ascended the throne about the year 1650, and the latter thirty years after.

It is not till the reign of Guadja Trudo, who succeeded Weebaigah in 1708, that any thing is precisely known about this extraordinary people. All before this time stands on the ground of tradition, which is ever more or less precarious, in proportion to the number of relators, and the frequency of the narration. Among the Dahomans, for reasons assigned in the Introduction, subjects of this nature are little known, and less discussed.

But when the active spirit of Trudo began to threaten the maritime states, his neighbours, it quickly attracted the attention of the Europeans, whom commerce had brought and settled amongst them. It was then that, by the assistance of writing, each transient fact was fixed, and scattered information collected into a body; it was then that tradition gave place to record, and legend to history.

Before we enter upon the memoirs of this enterprising and warlike Prince, it will not be improper to take a slight political view of the states around him, as they stood about the beginning of his reign, the better to form a judgment of the several transactions that are to pass in review before us.

In doing this, let us begin on the coast, with Coto or Quitta, to the west; which is a small kingdom, whose prince, about Bosman's time [late seventeenth century], resided at the village of Quitta, called also Coto and Verbun, and was at continual war with its neighbours, the Popoes, with various success.

Little Popo joins Quitta to the eastward. This is a small but very warlike kingdom, the remains of the Acras, who were driven out of their own territories on the Gold Coast, by the Aquamboes, in 1680. They were in alliance, at times, with Ardra, and fought her battles against Offra, and even Whydah itself. They were at continual war with the Quittas, which was fomented by the King of Aquamboe, for the purpose of directing the attention of both from his gold mines; and he managed this contention so cunningly, that he suffered neither nation to prevail too much over the other. Indeed, during the dissensions at Aquamboe, in 1700, Popo prevailed, and drove the Quittas out of their country; but they were, somehow, reinstated not long after.

Both these countries are flat, the soil poor and sandy, with few trees, except palms and wild cocoas. They have, indeed, some cattle and fish, but most at Quitta;[1] so that this and Great Popo were then frequently obliged to the Whydahs for sub-

---

1. At present, provision is more plentiful; they bring a number of fine cattle from the inland parts of Quitta.

sistence; from whom, though their enemies, they always found means to smuggle as much as they were in need of.

Great Popo joins to Little Popo. The country is more fertile; and the city, which is very large, is situated in a marshy lake at the mouth of the river Toree. This city is, from its situation, very strong; as a proof of which, when besieged by the Ardras, assisted by the French shipping, it was able to repulse them both with great loss. In 1682, this people was at war with both Quitta and Whydah; but, from prudential motives, they made a temporary peace with the latter, and obtained its assistance against the former. Some writers consider Quitta, Popo, and Whydah, as dismemberments of Ardra, with which kingdom, however, they are not more often at war, than they are with one another.

Whydah and Ardra were the two greatest maritime states in the neighbourhood of Dahomy;[2] rivals in trade, and consequently ever jealous of each other. The people of Whydah, at that time, are described as the most polite and civilized of any on the whole coast; those of Ardra being much more insolent and mercenary.

The country of Whydah is the very reverse of those already mentioned, being, for beauty and fertility, almost beyond description; and, before the invasion of the Dahomans, was so populous, that one village contained as many inhabitants as a whole kingdom on the Gold Coast. It was reputed, that the Whydahs were able to bring into the field, two hundred thousand effective men.

The country of Ardra is no less beautiful than that of its neighbour; but this abounds with hill and dale, whereas the former is one uniform surface, one great park. Nor was this kingdom less formidable than Whydah, before the incursions of the Eyeos in the year 1698. Even at the time in question her power was very considerable; for we find, when invaded by Dahomy, her army consisted of more than fifty thousand men. Yet both these nations are branded by Bosman with pusillanimity, who tells us, they employed mercenary soldiers, such as the Aquamboes, or other Gold Coast negroes, to fight their battles: which we shall find to be true.

The capital of Whydah was then Xavier or Sabee, seven or eight miles from the beach; that of Ardra was a town of the same name, about twenty miles from the sea. This must be distinguished from another Ardra, or Alladah, which is also a great town on the road from Whydah to Calmina. As both these countries are particularly described in other parts of this work, it will be unnecessary to enlarge on the subject here. And with respect to the several small and independent states, interspersed amongst those we have already mentioned, such as Toree, Weemey, Offra, or Little Ardra, &c. it will be sufficient, in this place, to refer our readers to the map, for their respective situations; reserving their political connexions till they become of sufficient consequence to be taken notice of in our history.

Of the inland kingdoms, that to the west of Dahomy is called Mahee; that to the north-east, Eyeo. Snelgrave calls the former of these Yahoo; but as there was little of either of these known before the reign of Trudo, their description properly

---

2. The trade here was very considerable, this being the principal part of all the Guinea Coast for slaves. In its flourishing state, there was above 20,000 negroes yearly exported, from this and the neighbouring places, to the several European plantations.

belongs to the History. The Tappahs, to the north-east of Eyeo, were unknown in his time; and indeed till very lately, when they made themselves as formidable to the Eyeos, as these to all the southern nations.

Such were the states around Dahomy, and such their jarring and divided interests, about the time of the accession of Trudo; where a new scene opens, that displays to wiser nations, how soon a small state may become too formidable, and how necessary to their own preservation are those alliances, that maintain in equilibrio the balance of power.

The kingdom of Eyeo[3] lies many days journey to the north-east of Abomey, beyond a great and famous lake, the fountain of several large rivers that empty themselves into the Bay of Guinea. The people are numerous and warlike, and, what is here singular, their armies totally consist of cavalry; and as every savage nation has some cruel method of rendering themselves dreadful to their enemies, this people were said to have a custom of cutting of the privities of those they have slain in battle; and that no one dared, on pain of death, to take an enemy prisoner, that was not furnished with a hundred of these trophies.

The Eyeos are governed by a king, no less absolute than the King of Dahomy, yet subject to a regulation of state, at once humiliating and extraordinary. When the people have conceived an opinion of his ill government, which is sometimes insidiously infused into them, by the artifice of his discontented ministers, they send a deputation to him, with a present of parrots eggs, as a mark of its authenticity, to represent to him that the burden of government must have so far fatigued him, that they consider it full time for him to repose from his cares, and indulge himself with a little sleep. He thanks his subjects for their attention to his ease; retires to his apartment, as if to sleep; and there gives directions to his women to strangle him. This is immediately executed; and his son quietly ascends the throne, upon the usual terms, of holding the reins of government no longer than whilst he merits the approbation of the people.

This seems to have been the first inland nation in this part of Africa, of which the Europeans had any intimation. Bosman speaks of an invasion of Ardra, in 1698, by a potent inland people, which could, from his description, be no other than the Eyeos. From him we learn, that some of the Ardras, who had been ill treated by their king, or his caboceers, flying to this inland prince for redress, he sent an ambassador to remonstrate with the King of Ardra on the subject, and to inform him, if his viceroys and other deputies did not govern the people more justly and tenderly, he should be obliged, however unwilling, to interfere. Ardra treated the monition with contempt, and put the ambassador to death; but the King of Eyeo took a dreadful revenge: his troops poured like a torrent[4] into Ardra; destroyed almost half the king-

3. Called Oyeo, Okyou. Probably this may be the kingdom of Gago, which lies to the northward of Dahomy, eight or ten days journey. The Moorish aspirated sound of G being nearly like a hard H, as in the word George, spelt Jorje by the Spaniards, and pronounced Horké, or Horché; whence Gago may have been sounded Haho, Haiho, or Haiko.

4. The Whydahs, say the Eyeos, invaded Ardra with ten hundred thousand horse; from which, without taking it literally, we may suppose the number must have been immense. We shall see, further on, the idea of the Dahomans about the number of an Eyeo army.

dom; and, what marks at once his severity and his justice, notwithstanding his general had obtained so signal a victory, he caused him to be hanged, on his return, because he had not brought with him the King of Ardra, who was the author of all this evil.

It was this nation that, shortly after the conquest of Ardra, made war on Trudo, at the instigation of several fugitive princes, whose fathers had been conquered and slain by the Dahomans. They entered Dahomy with an immense body of horse, amounting to many thousands. Trudo immediately left Ardra; and, though he had none but infantry,[5] yet, these having fire-arms, as well as swords, he had some hopes that he might at least make a stand against them. He knew, however, that they were well mounted, and armed with bows, javelins, and cutting swords; that they were, besides, courageous, and had spread terror through the adjacent countries; he also knew, that he had to contest in an open country, where horse would have every advantage; yet all this could not damp his daring spirit. He marched boldly to face the enemy; and, on meeting them, supported such a fire from his musquetry as effectually affrighted the horses, so that their riders could never make a regular charge on the Dahomans. Notwithstanding this, their numbers were so great, and the dispute so obstinate, that, after fighting for four days, the troops of Dahomy were greatly fatigued, and all was in danger of being lost: at this critical moment a stratagem entered the mind of the king, worthy of the most enlightened general, and which has been several times practised, with equal success, in times both ancient and modern.

Trudo had in his camp great quantities of brandy, at that time one of the principal articles of the French trade to Guinea. This, with many valuable goods, he contrived to leave in a town, adjacent to his camp, and under favour of the night withdrew to a convenient distance. In the morning the Eyeos, seeing the enemy fled, secure of victory, began to burn and plunder the town, and to indulge themselves very freely with the treacherous liquor: this soon intoxicated, and spread the ground with the major part of their army. At this juncture, the Dahomans, who had timely intimation of the enemy's disorder, fell upon them with redoubled fury, destroyed a great number, completely routed the rest; and those that escaped, owed their safety to their horses.[6]

In this manner did Trudo happily clear his country of a very formidable enemy; but however he might consider himself victorious in the present instance, he knew there was every thing to be feared from the inroads of such a numerous nation, and that too a nation of horsemen. He, therefore, with a foresight that did him much honour, sent ambassadors many presents to the King of Eyeo, to avert his further anger; but, without depending too much on their success, he laid his plans, in case of anoth-

---

5. There are few or no horses in Dahomy. Such as they have are very small; which indeed was the case with the inland countries, in Leo's time (about 1492). when good horses, from the north of Africa, were bought up at Gago, at a high price; perhaps with intention to improve the breed, and establish a numerous cavalry.

6. The Dahomans pretend, that in their flight, the terror and precipitation of the Eyeos was so violent, that great numbers tumbled into, and filled up part with of the deep moat which surrounds Abomey, the rest making themselves a bridge of their bodies, to effect their escape.

er invasion. He knew that the Fetische of the Eyeos was the sea; and that themselves, and their king, were threatened with death, by the priests, if they ever dared to look on it: he therefore resolved, in case he should be defeated by them in a future battle, to repair with his people to the sea-coast for security, and leave the upland towns and country to their disposal; in which he knew they could not remain after they had destroyed the forage; and that all the damage they might otherwise do, to thatched houses and mud walls, would easily be repaired.

31. MUNGO PARK

THE NIGER AT SEGU. 1796.

Before the nineteenth century, Europe's knowledge of the interior of West Africa was confused and fragmentary. The Europeans had learned from the Arabs that great cities existed in the western Sudan whose reputations for wealth seemed confirmed by the profits and goods of the trans-Saharan trade. The city of Timbuktu became synonymous with the mystery of unknown Africa in an age of Romanticism in Europe—a mystery that was deepened by Arab reports of a great river comparable with the Nile, on which were located several bustling and prosperous commercial centers. Yet no European had seen this river, its source, or its outlet. A few thought the river to be the source of the Nile. A more common assumption was that this river, the Niger, rose in the east and flowed westward, where its branches formed the Senegal, Gambia, and Jeba Rivers. No one connected the Oil Rivers, which entered the Bight of Biafra, with the delta of the Niger. The mystery of the Niger stimulated not only scientific inquiry but also the idea that perhaps the river would turn out to be a highway into the commercial centers of the interior. Under the auspices of the African Association, a group of wealthy London men interested in geography and commerce, three expeditions were sent inland between 1788 and 1793. All three failed. A fourth was undertaken by a young Scottish doctor, Mungo Park, who marched into the interior from the Gambia River at the end of 1795. On July 20, 1796, he reached the Niger at Segu and described in his journal that dramatic moment when he saw the Niger flowing to the east. Park had opened the way to the western Sudan. He was one of the first to seek to exploit his discovery. In 1805 he returned to the Niger to follow the river to its mouth but was tragically drowned in the Bussa Rapids.

Departing from thence, we passed several large villages, where I was constantly taken for a Moor, and became the subject of much merriment to the Bambarrans; who, seeing me drive my horse before me, laughed heartily at my appearance.—He has been at Mecca, says one; you may see that by his clothes: another asked me if my horse was sick; a third wished to purchase it, &c.; so that I believe the very

From Mungo Park, *Travels in the Interior Districts of Africa: Performed under the Direction and Patronage or the African Association in the Years 1795, 1796, and 1797* (London, 1799), pp. 193–198.

slaves were ashamed to be seen in my company. Just before it was dark, we took up our lodging for the night at a small village, where I procured some victuals for myself, and some corn for my horse, at the moderate price of a button; and was told that I should see the Niger (which the Negroes call Joliba, or *the great water*), early the next day. The lions are here very numerous: the gates are shut a little after sun-set, and nobody allowed to go out. The thoughts of seeing the Niger in the morning, and the troublesome buzzing of musketoes, prevented me from shutting my eyes during the night; and I had saddled my horse, and was in readiness before daylight; but, on account of the wild beasts, we were obliged to wait until the people were stirring, and the gates opened. This happened to be a market day at Sego, and the roads were every where filled with people, carrying different articles to sell. We passed four large villages, and at eight o'clock saw the smoke over Sego.

As we approached the town, I was fortunate enough to overtake the fugitive Kaartans, to whose kindness I had been so much indebted in my journey through Bambarra. They readily agreed to introduce me to the king; and we rode together through some marshy ground, where, as I was anxiously looking around for the river, one of them called out, *geo affilli* (see the water); and looking forwards, I saw with infinite pleasure the great object of my mission; the long sought for, majestic Niger, glittering to the morning sun, as broad as the Thames at Westminster, and flowing slowly to the eastward. I hastened to the brink, and, having drank of the water, lifted up my fervent thanks in prayer, to the Great Ruler of all things, for having thus far crowned my endeavours with success.

The circumstance of the Niger's flowing towards the east, and its collateral points, did not, however, excite my surprise; for although I had left Europe in great hesitation on this subject, and rather believed that it ran in the contrary direction, I had made such frequent inquiries during my progress, concerning this river; and received from Negroes of different nations, such clear and decisive assurances that its general course was towards the rising sun, as scarce left any doubt on my mind; and more especially as I knew that Major Houghton [who traveled inland from the Gambia between 1790 and 1791 to die near Nioro in the Republic of Mali] had col-lected similar information, in the same manner.

Sego, the capital of Bambarra, at which I had now arrived, consists, properly speaking, of four distinct towns; two on the northern bank of the Niger, called Sego Korro, and Sego Boo; and two on the southern bank, called Sego Soo Korro, and Sego See Korro. They are all surrounded with high mud-walls; the houses are built of clay, of a square form, with flat roofs; some of them have two stories, and many of them are whitewashed. Besides these buildings, Moorish mosques are seen in every quarter; and the streets, though narrow, are broad enough for every useful pur-pose, in a country where wheel carriages are entirely unknown. From the best inquiries I could make, I have reason to believe that Sego contains altogether about thirty thousand inhabitants. The King of Bambarra constantly resides at Sego See Korro; he employs a great many slaves in conveying people over the river, and the money they receive (though the fare is only ten Kowrie shells for each individual) furnishes a considerable revenue to the king, in the course of a year. The canoes are of a singular construction, each of them being formed of the trunks of two large trees, rendered concave, and joined together, not side by side, but end ways; the junction being exactly across the middle of the canoe; they are therefore very long and disproportionably narrow, and have neither decks nor masts; they are, however, very roomy; for I observed in one of them four horses, and several people. crossing over the river. When we arrived at this ferry, we found a great number waiting for a passage; they looked at me with silent wonder, and I distinguished, with concern, many Moors among them. There were three different places of embarkation, and the ferrymen were very diligent and expeditious; but, from the crowd of people, I could not immediately obtain a passage; and sat down upon the bank of the river, to wait for a more favorable opportunity. The view of this extensive city; the numerous canoes upon the river; the crowded population, and the cultivated state of the surrounding country, formed altogether a prospect of civilization and magnificence, which I little expected to find in the bosom of Africa.

I waited more than two hours, without having an opportunity of crossing the river; during which time the people who had crossed, carried information to Mansong the King, that a white man was waiting for a passage, and was coming to see him. He immediately sent over one of his chief men, who informed me that the king could not possibly see me, until he knew what had brought me into his country; and that I must not presume to cross the river without the king's permission. He therefore advised me to lodge at a distant village, to which he pointed, for the night; and said that in the morning he would give me further instructions how to conduct myself. This was very discouraging. However, as there was no remedy, I set off for the village; where I found, to my great mortification, that no person would admit me into his house. I was regarded with astonishment and fear, and was obliged to sit all day without victuals, in the shade of a tree; and the night threatened to be very uncomfortable, for the wind rose, and there was great appearance of a heavy rain; and the wild beasts are so very numerous in the neighbourhood, that I should have been under the necessity of climbing up the tree, and resting amongst the branches. About sunset, however, as I was preparing to pass the night in this manner, and had turned my horse loose, that he might graze at liberty, a woman, returning from the labours of the field, stopped to observe me, and perceiving that I was weary and dejected, inquired into my situation, which I briefly explained to her; whereupon, with looks of great compassion, she took up my saddle and bridle, and told me to follow her. Having conducted me into her hut, she lighted up a lamp, spread a mat on the floor, and told me I might remain there for the night. Finding that I was very hungry, she said she would procure me something to eat. She accordingly went out, and returned in a short time with a very fine fish; which, having caused to be half broiled upon some embers, she gave me for supper. The rites of hospitality being thus performed towards a stranger in distress; my worthy benefactress (pointing to the mat, and telling me I might sleep there without apprehension) called to the female part of her family, who had stood gazing on me all the while in fixed astonishment, to resume their task of spinning cotton; in which they continued to employ themselves great part of the night. They lightened their labour by songs, one of which was composed extempore; for I was myself the subject of it. It was sung by one of the young women, the rest joining in a sort of chorus. The air was sweet and plaintive, and the words, literally translated, were these. "The winds roared, and the rains fell. The poor white man, faint and weary, came and sat under our tree. He has no mother to bring him milk; no wife to grind his corn. *Chorus*. Let us pity the white man; no mother has he, &c. &c." Trifling as this recital may appear to the reader, to a person in my situation, the circumstance was affecting in the highest degree. I was oppressed by such unexpected kindness; and sleep fled from my eyes. In the morning I presented my compassionate landlady with two of the four brass buttons which remained on my waistcoat; the only recompence I could make her.

32. FATHER PINTO
THE KINGDOM OF THE KAZEMBE. 1799.

Francisco José Maria de Lacerda e Almeida (d. 1798) was Governor of Sena (on the Zambezi River) when he was ordered to open a transcontinental route from Mozambique to Angola. His expedition reached the Kazembe capital, where Lacerda died. A record of the expedition had been kept by its chaplain. Father Pinto. The kingdom of the Kazembe originated in the early eighteenth century when the Lunda adventurer Nganda Bilonda was invested with the title of kazembe and organized a state on the upper Lualaba. His successors expanded eastward, and under Kazembe III, or Lukwesa (c. 1760–1850), the kingdom reached its height, becoming the strongest of all Lunda states and embracing southern Katanga and parts of northeastern Zambia. Kazembe III had established trade relations with the Portuguese settlers around Tete. Although he refused to permit Lacerda's expedition to proceed westward, trade developed with the coast, and the Kazembe capital became a major terminus for routes to Kilwa and Tete.

February 17, 1799—At 8 A.M. the Sana Muroptle returned to my house, and, in presence of all the whites, delivered a message from the Cazembe that, as there was no more talk of Angola, he wanted the now superfluous presents intended for the Muropúe and the Mueneputo.[1] I put it to the vote of all: they were in a panic lest I should refuse: knowing the demand would be made, they augured the worst, some, for fear of being plundered and stripped, could not sleep at night. Lieut. Colonel Pedro Velasco (sic pro Noiasco) Vieira d'Araujo, the chief sergeant Pedro Xavier Velasco, and Antonio José da Cruz, were the only officers who did not show fear.

All being of one opinion, namely, that refusal would be dangerous, I was oblig-

From *Lacerda's Journey to Cazembe in 1798*, trans. and edited by Captain R. F. Burton. and *Journey of the Pombeiras R. J. Baptista and Amara José Across Africa from Angola to Tette on the Zambeze*, trans. by B. A. Beadle (London: Royal Geographical Society, 1873), pp. 124–136.

1. This was one of the strongest reasons for the transit not being allowed. The message was delivered by the apparent friend of the party, the Sana Muropúe, after the bully Fumo Anceva had been allowed to frighten them. All was perfectly en *règle*.

ed to consent; but before doing so, I inquired of the Sana Muropúe what the Cazembe meant by such a claim, he replied it was all done in good friendship. I added that the presents should be put into his hands, not into those of the Fumo Anceva, as the latter had received a considerable gift in the name of our sovereign, and we did not know whether it had reached its destination. Moreover, that besides plundering what was given to his master, he robbed what the Cazembe sent to his friends and relatives (buenozes). But I insisted that in presence of the king the first present should be referred to. The Fumo Anceva changed colour, now denying that he had received the gift, then affirming that he had given up all to his master. The Sana Muropúe confirmed this last assertion, and relieved the Caffre whose guilt was evident; either to please the Cazembe who much affected his minister, or to draw him from a confusion which also fell upon all the nation (Murundas). Yet I persisted that the present gift should be reported before delivery, and to that purpose I sent the lieutenant, Antonio José da Cruz, who could not, however, find the Cazembe at home. The poor king has the *naïveté* to believe that over-zeal for his interests makes the Furno Anceva, who is the greatest thief in his dominions, suffer from our false charges. I was therefore obliged to deliver the present without further ado, and without verifying the delivery of the former gift, a fact committed to paper and signed by all the party.[2] In the evening I began to inquire into the misdemeanour of Pedro Xavier Velásco.

18*th*–21*st*—There was drumming and dancing (tombocacao), which other Caffres of these parts call "Pemberaçao,"[3] between Prince Muenebuto and his brother-in-law Chibuery, already alluded to on January 20th. The Cazembe was present with his usual dignity, but guarded by armed Caffres, as the prince danced with his large knife drawn in order to touch with it that of his father, a sign of honour and respect. The Cazembe, however, thus favoured only his son. The ceremony took place in the open space before the principal gate of the palace, a great crowd of people having instruments collected, and there also were our troops, for whom the Cazembe sent, and whose discharge of musketry he himself directed. It was said that this fête was to celebrate his having closed once for all the Angola road, so as to increase his connection with Tete, whence their best things came. This was not confirmed, as they do not wish to break off with Angola.

I will now describe Muenebuto the prince, and his Murundas. Muenebuto is tall, good-looking, and well proportioned; his expression is pleasing, nay, almost always cheerful and smiling; he cares only for amusement, and his age—twenty years— permits nothing else. On the contrary, the Cazembe shows gravity and inspires respect; he also is tall, and well built, and his age may be about fifty. As he has many wives—the greatest sign of Caffre dignity—he becomes every year the father of two, three, or four children. He is very generous at times in giving slaves and pieces of cloth to his vassals, as well as to strangers and whites, when he is not set against

2. Those who have not travelled in Africa often wonder at all the importance attached to these trifling presents. But the fact is that without supplies the journey is brought to a dead stop, not taking into account the hardships and suffering of return. The explorer, therefore, must fight for every cubit of cloth, and this is, perhaps, the severest part of his task.

3. Native festivities, including drinking and cancan.

them; and every day he sent the Muzungos money and different presents of provisions, captives, ivory or copper bars, in proportion to their offerings of cloth and beads, and according to his regard for them.

He is severe; death, or at least amputation of the hand, being the usual punishment. He is barbarous; every new moon he causes a Caffre to be killed by his medicine-man, and with the victim's blood, heart, and part of the entrails, they make up his medicine, always mixing it with oil. When these charms are prepared, they are inserted into the horns of various animals, and even into scrivellos, which are closed with stoppers of wood or cloth. These fetishes are distributed about his palace and courts; they are hung to the doors, and for fear of sorcery the king never speaks to any one without some of these horns lying at his feet.[4]

He holds assemblies of his chiefs, who are invited to drink pombe, or millet-beer, which is mixed with other pulse or not, as each man's taste is. These drinkings begin with the full moon, and continue to the end; they commence daily at or before 1 P.M., and they last two hours. All those present drink as much as they please, but should any one vomit in the assembly, the wretch is instantly put to death. Though superstition -ridden, like all these people, the Cazembe is not so much so as are others. He visits no one in person, and never leaves his palace to walk; he has the name of being proud, but his people make him inconsistent.

The subjects (Murundas), who say that sixty years ago they came from the Western regions and established themselves in the lands of the conquered Vaciras (Messiras), are of the same nation as the Cazembe, whose rites and customs they follow.

Usually the men are tall, dark, well made, and good-looking; they tattoo (incise), but do not paint their bodies, nor do they jag their teeth. Their dress is a cloth extending from the waist to the knees, which are exposed by the garment being raised in front; it is girt by a leathern belt, 4 to 10 fingers broad. Their gala-dress is called "Muconzo;" it is of woollen or cotton, but it must be black. To make it they cut a piece 5.5 fathoms, or a little less in length, and if it be too short they add a bit of the same quality; the breadth is 2.5 hands, and if wider it is reduced to that size. It must be finished with a full edging, which increases it in all parts; this border is made of three strips of a different cloth, each 4 fingers broad. When the colour is red, for instance, the middle is white; it is yellow if the middle be red or white. Finally, they diversify these strips as they please, always taking care that the colour differs from the body or the principal part of the cloth. When putting on the "Muconzo," they cover the waist and legs, finishing at the front of the person with a great band of artificial pleats; and the larger it is. the grander is the garb. For arm-ornaments they use strings of fine beads like bracelets; their feet are covered with strung cowries, large opaque stoneware beads (pedras de côres), and white or red porcelains (velorios). Over their combed head-dresses, which are of many braids, large and small, they wear a cap (carapuqa), covered with exquisite birds'-plumes; the locks are also striped (barradellas) with a certain clay, which, when dry, resem-

---

4. Small horns of goats and antelopes are thus used in Unyamwezi. stuffed with thin iron wire; in Congo with strips of cloth.

bles the levigated sandalwood used by the Moors and Gentoos (Hindus); the stripes, however, are only on the crown and temples (molleira). Others rub their bodies upon the waist and upwards to the hair with a certain vermilion (vermelhao),[5] here common.

Such is the gala dress. Their every-day clothing is a little cloth, 1.5 to 2 fathoms long, with or without a border of a single strip; others wear bark cloth, like the Muizas, or edgeless cotton; and finally, coarse native cotton (maxilas de Gondo),[6] as each one has or can afford.

As usual the women dress better than the men, as to the kind of cloth, which is of wool (collomanha) or similar stuff. They also use, like the males, strings of many sorts of beads, to cover their ankles, but they are not so fond of cowries or porcelain (velorio). Their coiffure is unlike that of the men; they cut off all the hair, leaving a little lock in the middle, which in time, growing long, serves to support a kind of diadem [ornamental headband]; the rest of the hair, when it grows, forming sundry lines of short braid. Their ordinary dress is extremely poor, consisting of one very small cloth. These women, who also can be sold by their husbands, lead the lives of slaves, doing all the labour of domestic slavery.

The Murundas,[7] like other peoples of this country, have no (practical) religion. They recognize the existence of a sovereign creator of the world, and call him "Reza," but they consider him a tyrant that permits his creatures' death. They have great veneration for their Azimos (murimos), or dead, whom they consult on all occasions of war or good fortune. The Caffre servants of any Moçaza,[8] or place in which a king is buried, have many privileges. The Azimos require offerings of provisions, as dough (massa), a food made of manioc flour, to stew with the porridge, which in the Brazil is called Angú; of quiriaqa (any mess of meat, fish, or herbs), and of pombe, the millet-beer before described. They greatly respect what the oracle says to them. Their sons are circumcised between the ages of fourteen and eighteen,[9] and they affect polygamy, which they regard as their greatness, much wondering at the one-wife marriage of the whites.

Their unions are effected without ceremony: the would-be husband goes to the father or guardian of the girl, who may be quite a child, and with him arranges the dowry in cloths, which, if great, may reach a dozen. After this arrangement, called betrothal (roboracção), the payment being left to the bridegroom's convenience, they arrange a day for leading home the bride, who, until of nubile years, remains with her parents. Consummation is done thus: carried by the horse of some Caffre, and accompanied by her female relations and friends, beating drums, the bride is escorted to near the bridegroom's house, and when close to it they send him word

5. It has previously been described as being woodpowder.
6. The expression is fully explained in the diary of June 20–23. Dr. Kirk says that a "Maxila de garda" is a hammock of native cloth. "Maxila de Gondo" is a stuff so coarse that hammocks can be made of it. Hence Monteiro and Gamitto call the coarse cotton cloth made by the Marave "Manxila."
7. In the original misprinted "Mosundas."
8. Mussassa is a camp: here it must be the burial place before called Miximo.
9. In Dahomey this rite is deferred often till the twentieth year, and then it becomes dangerous. I have repeatedly recorded my opinion that it is of African origin, borrowed by the Jews from the negroid race.

that they bring his wife. This done, they drum and dance till some velorio beads are sent to them, after which they advance two paces or so, and stop till they get more. Thus, on his marriage-day, the poor Caffre must not only strip himself, but also go out borrowing, to show that he has given all his own. Seeing nothing more come, they inspect the sum offered them, then they advance nearer, and at length they hand over the bride to the chief wife and her companions, and retire to their homes, leaving her in tears. As the Caffres may buy an unlimited number of spouses, even their slaves being wives to them, they choose one, and call her the great woman, and she is the most respected. Her peculiar duties are to preserve the husband's wardrobe and medicines, and to apply the latter when required; without using them no one goes to war, to hunt, or to travel, or, indeed, on any important business.

The funerals of these people are proportioned to the means of the deceased. Their pomp consists in the great cortége by which the body is borne to the grave, and in the quantity of food and drink expended upon the crowd of people, who sing and dance to the sound of drums. If the deceased be a king, he must carry with him all that he possesses, with slaves to serve him and women for his pleasures. Throughout his dominions robberies and disorder (cleirero) are allowed for ten or fifteen days, or even more. Their deadliest crimes are witchcraft, adultery, and theft. The first, and the most enormous, is always punished capitally; the second sometimes, but more often by mutilation of the hands, the ears, and the offending member. They are less severe with the women, as a rule, but some plaintiffs are not satisfied except by death. Although they cut off the their hands and ears, many wretches have exposed themselves to such mutilation.

The soil of this land is fertile, and would produce all that the people want; there are many kinds of food, but the principal is manioc. They eat it in dough, toasted and boiled and even raw, and they drink it in pombe with a little mixture of millet. Manioc flour for dough is easily made in the following way: after gathering the root, they peel it, and soak it in a stream, for three days; on the fourth, when it is almost rotten, they dry it in the summer sun, or in winter over a fire which they light under the cots used for this purpose; and, finally, they pound it in a treetrunk mortar. We may say that they are collecting and sowing this root all the year round, but the harvest is when provision is wholly wanting. At such times they dig up a small quantity to last for a few days, and in its stead they bury a few bits of stalk which act as seed. The rains are abundant and regular. Fruits are few, except bananas of many kinds: of live stock, poultry is the most plentiful and goats are rare. Game and fish suffice, but they cannot salt their provision, so to keep it they dry it with fire and smoke, making it unfit for us to eat. The black cattle is well flavoured, but only the king keeps them in certain places, to show his greatness: he does not eat their flesh, saying that they are Fumos [black in color], like himself, also he does not milk them, not knowing how, so the cows are almost wild. Here we find traces of the Metempsychosis theory.[10] With this idea the king sends his cattle as gifts to his

10. Superficial observers often confound the highly philosophical and complicated theory of metempsychosis with the vulgar metamorphosis of the savage African. [Metempsychosis is the passing of the soul at death into another body either animal or human.]

guests, and when they die or are killed for injuring millet fields-these animals pasture by night and sleep by day he divides the meat amongst his people, who, not considering them, like their king, great Fumos, eat them unscrupulously. Cow leather makes their girdles, that of other horned cattle their dress, and cows' blood enters into their medicines. Therefore they sent us only dead and skinned animals.

There may be many articles of trade, but it is now confined to two-ivory and slaves. A tusk of 32 lbs. to 48 lbs. costs 2 to 3 pieces of cloth, the piece being 1.5 to 2 fathoms long, and ten couros.[11] The tusk of 80 lbs. to 96 lbs. is worth 5 to 6 pieces, with a little couro or velorio. There are copper bars sold for four common cloths, or pagnes (pannos de fato), or 40 to 50 couros; the small bars cost as a rule one cloth's worth of missanga. Uncut greenstone (malachite)[12] of different sizes is sold cheap, but the two latter articles are not indigenous.

22nd—The Sana Muropúe took away, in presence of all the whites, the gifts destined for the Muropúe and the Mueneputo, as was promised at our assembly on the 17th instant.

23rd—Having ordered Lieutenant Antonio José da Cruz, commandant of the troops, to chastise a soldier with forty blows, he not only disobeyed me, but he also falsely reported having carried out my orders.

February 24*th* to March 1*st*—The men, instigated by their officers, demanded an advance of three months' pay, which I sent to them without receiving any reply.

2nd–4th—I gave Pedro Xavier Velasco leave to go back to Tete, not only at his request, but because I wished to avoid the disgust shown by all the Expedition to the Cazembe, with whom, it is said, this arrangement of return had been made in anticipation of my desires. José Rodrigues Caleja, hearing this, wished to interfere and exceeding his duties as guide and Receiver of the Treasury, he addressed me a note in which, after a fashion, he made himself accessory to the command. As I took no notice of his false reasonings, he began to show me aversion and to seek his revenge.

5th—The manioc grown in the land which the Cazembe had offered to the whites (muzungos) on the 27th January was divided, but their carelessness prevented them sending their slaves (checundas) to receive the portion appertaining to them.

6th–9th—Loud murmurs arose about the Expedition arriving at the Cazembe's city—which it could not at once leave during the early month of January, when the evils caused by the wet season and the country rendered a long rest necessary. As José Rodrigues Caleja, by declaring me to be the cause of the delay and of their consequent sufferings, showed signs of stirring up against me even the most indifferent, I assembled all the whites. They knew what were my reasons for wintering here, so I resolved that each should separately declare his opinion touching our inaction, whether it could have been avoided or not and how. I told the writer, or notary, to take the paper in which all had recorded their opinions, to draw it up in legal form, and to get their signatures. It was late when we separated, and the scribe was not

---

11. From the context it would appear that these couros are some kind of bead.

12. Monteiro and Gamitto mention malachite "malaquites," which the Cazembes call "chifuvia." I have seen fine copper from the Cazembe's country.

skilled enough to draft the deed without the aid of others. He went to José Rodrigues Caleja, being of that party, and with him falsified not only Caleja's vote but also that of Vasco Joaquim Pires, as is proved in the forged paper. I was disregarded by Captain João da Cunha Pereira, and when I wished to punish him there and then he would not be arrested, nay, with threats he declared that His Excellency, the Captain-General of Mozambique, should not deprive him of his receivership, as had been done to Lieut. Manoel dos Santos Silva.

As I had little power, nothing was effected. I asked Gonçalo Caetano Pereira, the first guide, how to ascertain from Chinhimba and Mossindassaro the deficiency of the loads entrusted to them for carriage to the Cazembe's court. He replied, in the presence of many, that this must be done with the beneplacet of the king, whose vassals they were. Finding the answer reasonable, I entrusted to him the business, which he undertook promptly and with good will.

10th—Lieutenant Antonio José da Cruz, when ordered to attest in writing the refusal of Captain João da Cunha Pereira to submit to arrest yesterday, gave in his attestation which denied all that had happened.

11th–14th—Gonçalo Caetano Pereira, whom I had resolved to send on the 8th instant to the Cazembe in the matter of Mossindassaro and Chinhimba, when asked by José Rodrigues Caleja not to delay, excused himself by means of his Caffre Inharugue [interpreter] saying that the latter did not wish to bear any message to the Cazembe. The most embarrassing thing is, that they try to lay the blame upon me, when at the same time they bar my road to the king, and they prevent the two Caffres obeying all my summons. At last I tried every effort to send some other person on this errand to the king, who deferred it till the morrow.

15th—Sending back to the Cazembe the messenger who had returned yesterday, I heard to-day that the king was pleased with my calling up and examining the two Caffres before mentioned. When they declined to obey my summons I reported the fact to the king, begging that his messenger would conduct them into my presence. He promised but he never performed, which I attributed to the intrigues of Caleja. This man, under colour of benefiting D. Francisca Josefa of Tete, whose niece he had married, declared that the late Governor de Lacerda, who had taken charge of that lady's venture, and whose death had caused the goods to be confused, had concealed by means of the Mossindassaro, six bales (moteros)[13] of cloth, and had changed the mark or mixed the articles, removing 150 pannos and two bags (guissapos)[14] of velorio beads. These he had wished to make over to D. Francisco's slave, Candeone, in order to exchange for ivory. And this was done with the knowledge of the governor's managing man, whose duty it was to take charge of those articles, pretexting the report spread by José Rodrigues Caleja that the manager had wished to appropriate the said spoils. This trick of José Rodrigues Caleja's was very ingenious, for not only was that Caffre encouraged to conceal 912 more cloths (pagnes) of royal property, but Chinhimba, the other Caffre messenger, also took heart suc-

13.This is afterwards explained to be one-third of 456 cloths, that is to say, each 152 cloths.
14. The word "guissapo" means a bag of bamboo rind or grass cloth. Monteiro and Gamitto speak of "um Quissipo, sacco feito de palma."

cessfully to embezzle from the Crown 456 cloths, three bags (guissapos) of velorio, two ditto of (red) beads, and one of cowries.

16th–28th—José Rodrigues Caleja was always imposing upon them the necessity of giving the Cazembe time to prepare for our departure. The others being sick, I directed him to go with a "mouth" or parcel of cloth and to make preparations, at the same time reviving the matter of the two Caffres. The Cazembe received him well, and said that he knew—the winter now being over—that the Expedition would wish to return to Tete. As regards the defaulting Caffre, he said that the whites had allowed a long time to pass in silence, and had finally received everything. The first part of this reply could not have come from a Caffre, who all hold that the palaver (milando) never dies, nor wastes, but is kept up till "settled" from generation to generation. So I resolved either that the king had not said it, or had been taught to say it by José Rodrigues Caleja. The affair was not pushed further, because it was not advisable to call Chinimba to account until the appearance of Mossindassaro, who would hear of it from the Cazembe and conceal himself.

29th–30th—I gave the said Caffires some small quantity of clothing for which they asked, thus hoping to assemble them and to elicit something about the hidden goods.

31st—The Cazembe sent me the chair enclosed in his present (mirambo), begging me to have it lined with "cherves," which was done at once.

April 1st–7th—By an accidental fire eight of my slaves were burned in their own huts; many of the Expedition rejoiced thereat, and a certain José Thomaz Gomes da Silveira, openly wished that the accident had taken place in my house. I report this and other things, which do not exactly relate to the service of the Crown, both to carry out my instructions and to show the character of my subordinates.

8th–9th—The Cazembe forbade the whites, who had begun their cabals greatly to his disgust, all intercourse with him, thus avoiding their impertinences, and he wondered at our disunion.

10th—José Rodrigues Caleja, an old enemy of Lieutenant Manoel dos Santos e Silva, with whom he appeared friendly only when wishing to insult me, after visiting him in his sickness, declared to me that he wished for death, and that if he knew of anything to end his life he would take it.

11th–12th—I had some inklings that the crime charged upon Pedro Xavier Velasco, was a mere imputation, and Lieutenant José Vicente Pereira Salema confessed that he had been intimidated to give false witness by José Rodrigues Caleja. I also learned that Captain João da Cunha Pereira, after his deposition, went to Pedro Xavier Velasco's quarters, and told him that I wanted to drink his blood, which was my reason for drawing up papers against him, but that no depositions made by himself or his colleagues would do him any injury.

13th—José Rodrigues Caleja convoked, in the house of Gonçalo Caetano Pereira, to debate over the affair of the 9th of March, all those of his party, viz., Captain João da Cunha Pereira, Lieutenant Manoel dos Santos e Silva, Captain José da Cruz, José Thomaz Gomes da Silva, Lieutenant José Vicente Pereira Salema, and Ensign José Joaquim Pires; they agreed to outrage me in that business, first by word and then by deed. The Lieut. Colonel Pedro Nolasco Vieira de Araujo and the chief sergeant Pedro Xavier Velasco were sick, and not of the league. I had no testimony whereby to convict them, thus they could insult me with impunity. The former of these two, however, came unexpectedly upon them, and the project fell to the ground. All this was told to me by Lieutenant José Vicente Pereira Salema, whom as the most timorous they sent to me with a paper of their requisitions.

14th–15th—José Rodrigues Caleja, who was in the habit of troubling me morning and evening, came early to report that messengers were expected from Tete to recall the troops, as there was great alarm of the French.

16th—José Rodrigues Caleja required me to assemble the members in order to determine how to sell the Crown stores remaining in the receiver's hands. My reply was that I had reasons for not convening any more of such assemblies. He went at once and wrote me a letter representing the loss that would result from taking the goods back to Tete. In view of all this trouble I at once ordered the stores to be valued.

17th—The effects were valued by the arbitrators at only double their cost-price at Tete, and the receiver, with sundry impertinences, demanded permission to sell them. I ordered them to be sold for the sums offered, finding that nothing more advantageous could be obtained.

18th–19th—I sent to compliment the Cazembe, who was then a great friend of mine; he sent back that he wanted to see me.

20th—I returned an answer to the Cazembe's message, declaring that I would call upon him personally.

21st—José Rodrigues Caleja, angry because, without consulting him, I had allowed Pedro Xavier Velasco to return to Tete, and because I would not be made the tool of his private enmities, did all he could to annoy me. He teazed me with requests to smuggle out the cloth required for our return march, as the Cazembe would never allow it, after once entering, to leave the country. Fearing his malice, I appointed him and the guide, Gonçalo Caetano Pereira, to fix upon the quantity and the place. The former was settled, the latter they refused to tell me, pleading that, as we had travelled together, I—a chaplain—must know as much as they (the guides) did.

22nd–23rd—I again ordered the two aforesaid guides to tell me the "cache," and they refused.

24th—The Cazembe consented to receive me on the morrow, and to send a household officer to conduct me, as the Fumo Anceva wished all the whites to be purely dependent upon himself. José Rodrigues Caleja happened to be present, and, dissimulating his jealousy of my getting an audience when he had failed, begged me to forward the departure of the Expedition, which, depending upon the Cazembe, would easily be forgotten unless often brought to mind.

25th—After a short delay I was admitted to the Cazembe, who received my compliments kindly, responding briefly after the country fashion. This over, I earnestly prayed him to forward the time of our return; to which he also replied favourably. I then submitted to him that on reaching Tete there would be a difficulty in explaining to my superiors the prohibition of passing over to Angola; he bade me leave two members of the party to proceed there after our departure. The Fumo Anceva wrested this into a demand that each of the whites should leave behind one or two Cheundas.[15] Knowing that the slaves would be pawns for our future communication, and that the Caffres being scarce, and many of them sickly, the whites would not consent to the measure. I replied that when Catira, and Chinimba had come with friendly messages to Tete, we had at once set out without hostages. Hearing me speak to the soldier-linguist in the Sena dialect, the Cazembe at once explained that he did not want hostages, but two persons to go to Angola. I could not reply to so sudden and unexpected a permission, so I told the king that the presents destined for the Muropúe and the Muenebuto having been given away, and the treasury being exhausted, my confusion prevented my returning an answer. The Cazembe at once said that he would manage about the presents, and that all I had to do was to look after the subsistence and the means of travel. I finally answered that the matter should be thought over. He then spoke of the opaque stoneware beads (pedras de côres) which he wanted from the whites, who still, he knew, had good things. I contented him as well as possible, and left deeply preoccupied about Angola. After my return, José Rodrigues Caleja, on hearing the affair, malignantly remarked, that if I had proposed Pedro Xavier Velasco as envoy to the Cazembe, he would soon close the road with a new prohibition; and much of the same kind to throw obstacles in my way.[16]

26th—José Rodrigues Caleja came, and insultingly showed me a paper in which the lieutenant-colonel Pedro Nolasco Vieira de Araujo and Pedro Xavier Velasco had complained of him, and charged him with being their informant. As if a secret between nine persons could be kept, especially when of the many councillors are Captain João da Cunha Pereira and Lieutenant José Vicente Pereira Salema, who do nothing but tittle-tattle. I tried to avoid a scandalous rupture, but from that day forward he did nothing but oppose me, wishing to commit all the goods to the Cazembe, and thus to frustrate the transit to Angola.

27th—The Fumo Anceva came from the Cazembe, refusing passage to Tete for Lieut.-Colonel Pedro Nolasco Vicira de Araujo, who wished to leave these bad men. I answered that he was not going, because I had not given him leave. This reply closed the Caffre's mouth. He doubtless had been taught to oppose this departure, though not by his friendship for the departer. It was José Rodrigues Caleja's plan, in opposing the going of the two Pedros, Nolasco and Velasco, to forewarn all those who might be useful to him at Tete, adding as many lies as possible, and well knowing that the thing first heard, though false, is generally credited in preference to truth.

Not satisfied by this mischief, that perverse man went with Lieutenant Antonio José da Cruz to the Cazembe, designing to traduce me and Pedro Nolasco, but the Cazembe, who hated his mutinous disposition, refused him access. He must indeed

15. This, I presume, is "checunda"—a slave.
16. This permission for two of the party to proceed to Angola was a sham, to see if any presents had been withheld, and to try the perseverance of the whites. The Cazembe must have thought unfavourably of the leader when he hesitated at once to reply—a thing ever to be avoided in Africa. The two soldiers were eventually left behind as was proposed, but they never, it need hardly be said, reached Angola. In 1806 the Angolan Pombeiros found one man still waiting for permission.

be a bad white man who is hated by Caffres. He reported to the Fumo Anceva that the Lieut.-Colonel Pedro Nolasco and the other whites had so well hidden many fine cloths and coloured stoneware beads (pedras pintadas), that these could be discovered only by opening their boxes. The Cazembe, despite his generosity, was persuaded to give this order, or the Fumo Anceva fabricated it. I sent for the lieutenant-colonel, Pedro Nolasco, to hear the message: he excused himself, but he could not prevent the search. I positively refused to sanction it in the case of other whites, knowing that the Fumo Anceva wanted only to enter the receiver's house and to carry off everything for his king.[17]

17. There is a Furno Anceva at every African court, who thinks only of recommending himself to the king by giving any amount of trouble to Strangers. Of course it is a shallow, short-sighted policy, but nothing better can come from the negro's brain. It is, however, dangerous, and must be carefully watched, as it is calculated to cause disagreeables between the members of an expedition, and then everything goes to ruin.

33. CAPTAIN HUGH CROW

BONNY. 1880.

Hugh Crow (1765–1829) was an English sea captain and merchant who had long been engaged in the African slave trade. The following extract from his memoirs describes the kingdom of Bonny, which, at the end of the eighteenth century, was an important slave trading center in the eastern Niger River delta, a region known as the Oil Rivers. Bonny continued to trade in slaves during the nineteenth century but turned increasingly to the sale of palm oil.

The inhabitants of Bonny, when our author last visited that port, amounted to about 3,000. They are chiefly a mixture of the Eboe, or Heebo, and the Brass tribes; the latter deriving their name from the importation into their country, which lies to the northward and westward of Bonny, of a kind of European-made brass pans, known in the trade by the name of neptunes, and used for the making of palm oil and salt, with which last the countries in the interior have been supplied by the coast from the earliest times on record. The article is now largely imported from Liverpool, both to Bonny and Calabar. The Eboes, who are also from a neighbouring country, have already been spoken of as a superior race, and the inhabitants, generally, are a fair dealing people, and much inclined to a friendly traffic with Europeans, who humour their peculiarities. Their general honesty, when the loose nature of their laws, as respects Europeans, and the almost entire absence of the moral influence of religion amongst them, are considered, affords a favourable

From Hugh Crow, *The Memoirs of the Late Captain Hugh Crow of Liverpool* (London: Longman, Rees, Orme, Brown, and Green, 1830), pp. 197–201, 215–219, 227–228.

prognostic of what the negro character would be if placed under the restraints and precepts of an enlightened system of jurisdiction.

It is probable (and this opinion is entertained by Captain Adams and others) that Bonny, and the towns on the low line of the coast on either side of it were original-ly peopled from the Eboe country, and that before the commencement of the slave trade, if it then existed; the inhabitants employed themselves in the making of salt, by evaporation from sea water. The country, says Adams, for many miles into the interior is "a vast morass, heavily timbered, and unfit, without excessive labour, to produce sufficient food for a very scanty population; and as the trade in slaves increased, these towns, particularly Bonny, grew into importance. The king of New Calabar, in the neighbourhood, and Pepple, king of Bonny, were both of Eboe descent, of which also are the mass of the natives; and the number of the slaves from the Eboe country, which, throughout the existence of the British trade were taken from Bonny, amounted to perhaps three-fourths of the whole export. It is calculat-ed that no fewer than 16,000 of these people alone were annually exported from Bonny within the twenty years ending in 1820; so that, including 50,000 taken with-in the same period from New and Old Calabar, the aggregate export of Eboes alone was not short of 370,000."

The Eboes, tho' not generally a robust, are a well-formed people, of the middle stature: many of their women are of remarkably symmetrical shape, and if white, would in Europe be deemed beautiful. This race is, as has been already remarked, of a more mild and engaging disposition than the other tribes, particularly the Quaws, and though less suited for the severe manual labour of the field, they are preferred in the West India colonies for their fidelity and utility, as domestic ser-vants, particularly if taken there when young, as they then become the most indus-trious of any of the tribes taken to the colonies. Their skin is generally of a yellow-ish tinge, but varying to a jet black. Of the same tribe, and speaking the same lan-guage, are the Brechés, so called from the word Breché, signifying gentleman, or, like Hidalgo in Spanish, son of a gentleman. As these had seen better days, and were more liable than their countrymen, who are inclined to despond when sent on board ship, to take some desperate means of relieving themselves, and encouraging others to shake off their bondage, the masters of the slave ships were generally averse to purchasing them. The Brechés informed us, that in their country every seventh child of their class, when about six or seven years of age, undergoes the operation, to dis-tinguish its rank, of having the skin of the forehead brought down from the hair, so as to form a ridge or line from temple to temple.

This disfigurement gives them a very disagreeable appearance, and the custom is chiefly confined to the sons of great men, and our author never saw but one female so marked. But the Eboes and Brechés are tatooed with their country and family marks. The national tatoo of the commonalty consists of small thickly placed per-pendicular incisions, or cuts on each temple, as if done with a cupping apparatus. These people are kind and inoffensive in their manners, but so fearful of the whites when first brought amongst them, that they imagine they are to be eaten by them; and while under this impression they would sometimes attempt to jump overboard, or destroy themselves in some other way, so that it was necessary to watch them narrowly. Their apprehensions, however, were to be overcome by mild treatment, and they soon became reconciled to their lot. Their mutual affection is unbounded, and, says our author, I have seen them, when their allowance happened to be short, divide the last morsel of meat amongst each other thread by thread.

Besides the Eboes and Brechés, we received at Bonny negroes of several other nations, named Quaws, Appas, Ottams, and Brasses. The Quaws, (or Moscoes of the West Indies) are an ill-disposed people, whom the Eboes regard with great aversion, as they consider them cannibals in their own country; an assumption which their desperate and ferocious looks would seem to warrant. Their skins are blacker than those of the Eboes, and their teeth are sharpened with files, so as to resemble those of a saw. These men were ever the foremost in any mischief or insurrection amongst the slaves, and from time to time many whites fell victims to their fury at Bonny. They are mortal enemies to the Eboes, of whom, such is their masculine superiority, and desperate courage, they would beat three times their own number. The slave ships were always obliged to provide separate rooms for these men between decks, and the captains were careful to have as few of them as possible amongst their cargoes. The females of this tribe are fully as ferocious and vindictive as the men.

The Appas are a race of people so slothfully inclined, that they trust for a subsistence to the spontaneous productions of the earth, and rather than betake themselves to cultivation, will even eat grass and soil. The few of them whom our author knew were extremely indolent in their habits; and probably owing to this, and the coarseness of their usual food, their flesh was loose and soft, and their bodies feeble. They are however of a harmless disposition, and the Eboes take a great delight in tantalizing them.

The Ottam tribe are stout and robust, and of a deeper black than any of the other tribes at Bonny. Their bodies and, faces are carved and tatooed in a frightful manner; they seem nevertheless to be a well-disposed good-tempered race, and are much liked by the Eboes. Besides these we sometimes got a few natives of Benin, which is about 160 or 170 miles from Bonny. These resemble the Eboes, and it is probable were partly of the same nation. They are the most orderly and well-behaved of all the blacks. In their own country they are famous for the manufacture of a beautiful sort of tablecloth.

The kings of Bonny (there were two during our author's intercourse with the natives) although in many respects they appeared to exercise an absolute power, unrestrained by any fixed principles, may be properly termed the heads of an aristocratic government. This is evinced by their having a grand Palaver-house, in which they themselves presided, but the members of which, composed of the chiefs or great men, were convened and consulted on all matters of state emergency, and sometimes (as appears in the case of the illness of king Holiday's wife) in matters relating to the domestic affairs of the kings themselves. The government, indeed, may be said to combine three estates, the kings, the great men, and the feticheros, or priests; the last being probably considered as instruments of popular subjection, whose influence over the people the two first consider it politic to tolerate, if not to encourage. In some of the great kingdoms of the interior, as Ashantee, Aquainbo, and Dahomy, the kings are absolute; but at Bonny, and many other parts of the coast, the monarchs appear to hold a very mild and popular sway over their subjects; and whatever we find of apparent cruelty or barbarity in their conduct, or that of their head men, is attributable not to any wanton or uncontrolled indulgence in a savage disposition, but to an accordance with those superstitious customs and ceremonies, sometimes ridiculous, and often horrible in the eyes of Europeans, which they have been taught, in common with their countrymen, to consider as fit and necessary either for the purposes of justice, or the conciliation of their gods.

The revenues of the kings are derived from the duties on shipping and trade, contributions drawn from their subjects of all necessaries for their houshold, fines adjudged in criminal and civil cases, presents from Europeans, and from other less honorable sources. When paying for the negroes (says our author) the kings are sure to have two men on board to take the customs from the traders, which amounts to the tenth part, or "bar," as they call it. Besides the usual payment for firewood, water, yams, palm oil, and even for burying ground, whether we made use of it or not, we were obliged to pay customs' duties on all these. With respect to the slaves, we had to pay for them a second time, for after the payment of the first purchase-money, we were called upon to pay what were called "work bars," a few days before the vessel sailed.

The body dress of the kings consists of shirts and trowsers, and like all the kings on the coast, they generally wear goldlaced hats. They are attended, when they board a ship, by a large retinue of servants, one of whom carries a gold-headed cane, which, when sent off to a vessel by the king, serves as a note, or authority, when he is in want of any thing. "It is rather singular," says our author, "that although the two chiefs, Pepple and Holiday, were relations and copartners in the throne, they could never agree: and I do not recollect having ever seen them together on board of any ship. Pepple was the superior, and maintained the ascendant over Holiday in a high degree." Their houses were only distinguished from those of their subjects by their being somewhat larger, detached, and more numerous, and being furnished in a superior manner, as many articles are imported for them from Europe. Bonny has long been celebrated for the size and construction of her canoes; and those of the king deserve notice. They are formed out of a single log of the capot, a species of cotton tree, which attains so enormous a size, that it is said that one was seen at Akim, which ten men could scarcely grasp. The canoes in general use, have about fifteen paddles on a side; but those of the king, which are superior vessels of the sort, carry, besides the rowers, as many as a hundred and fifty warriors, well furnished with small arms. They have also a long nine-pounder at each end of the canoe; and when they are equipped for war, with drums beating, horns blowing, and colours flying, they make a very dashing and formidable appearance. The kings often take excursions in their canoes, attended by about thirty stout men paddling, and a steersman. Several others are employed in playing some musical instrument, while others dance in the middle of the canoe. The rowers keep admirable time with their paddles, so that they drive through the water at a rapid rate, and appear to great advantage. Whenever king Pepple came off in his state canoe to the ship, all the traders, rich and poor, precipitately betook themselves to their canoes; and, on his coming on board, we always manned the side, and hoisted the colours.

Our author was not perhaps aware that Bonny owes its sovereignty to Benin, otherwise he would naturally have attributed the visit, which he records in the following passage, to that circumstance. "While I lay," he remarks, "at Bonny, on my last voyage, two large canoes arrived from Benin, full of presents, consisting of the manufactures and produce of the country, and with these came two remarkably fine looking men of from thirty to forty years of age, well formed, and about six feet high. Their look and manner were of a superior order, and they walked in a majestic style, followed by a retinue of servants. They were robed in a loose flowing dress; I found they spoke pretty good English, and I conversed with them on several occasions, particularly on the subject of the slave trade. They expressed their conviction that so long as there were lands to cultivate, and seas for ships to sail on, slavery would continue to exist. These men were near relations of King Pepple, and had been sent to Bonny, as ambassadors by the king of Benin. They remained about a month feasting in their way, and then returned with their large canoes laden with presents. I never met with any black princes so sensible and well informed as these men, or who had so noble and commanding an appearance."

The principal trade of Bonny, in our author's time, was in slaves; but since its abolition amongst the British they have happily turned their attention to procuring and exporting palm oil. Ivory is rarely offered for sale, and only in small quantities and at dear rates, the elephants being probably fewer in the neighbourhood than on other parts of the coast. The slaves are procured from the interior, and much bustle takes place when the inhabitants are preparing their canoes for the trade. These vessels, which are large of the kind, are stored for the voyage with merchandise and provisions. "Evening," says Adams, "is the period chosen for the time of departure, when they proceed in a body accompanied by the noise of drums, horns, and gongs. At the expiration of the sixth day they generally return, bringing with them 1500 or 2000 slaves, who are sold to Europeans the evening after their arrival, and taken on board the ships." The Africans become domestic slaves, or are sold to Europeans, by losing their liberty in war, resigning it in famine, or forfeiting it by insolvency, or the crimes of murder, adultery, or sorcery. It may be inferred, too, without libelling the character of the Africans, that European cupidity has often led them to hunt their unoffending fellow-beings for the sole purpose of enriching themselves by the sale of their bodies! "The traders," our author further remarks, "have, in general, good memories, and some of them can reckon their accounts with as much expedition as most Europeans can with the aid of pen and ink. If they know the captain with whom they are dealing to be particular, they will generally calculate with accuracy; but, like many amongst ourselves, they will frequently overreach if they can, and although I have had occasion to remark upon their honesty, I must say, that many of them were in general restrained only by the dread of detection. Most of them, I must in strict justice add, are addicted to lying, and whatever be their probity amongst themselves, they do not make it a matter of conscience to take an advantage of strangers.

34. ABD ALLAH IBN MUHAMMAD

THE HIJRA AND HOLY WAR OF
SHEIK UTHMAN DAN FODIO. 1804.

Abd Allah ibn Muhammad (c. 1766–1828) was the younger brother of Sheik Uthman dan Fodia. A man of great learning, he served as his brother's wazir after the declaration of holy war against Yunfa, the Sarki of Gobir. Uthman had begun his preaching against religious corruption and paganism in 1786, but not until Yunfa succeeded his father as Sarki of Gobir in 1802 did hostilities erupt. Yunfa marched against Uthman in February 1804, at which time Uthman made his hijra, or flight of the faithful, and from that time he regarded himself as God's chosen instrument to defeat the unbelievers and establish the pure religion throughout Hausaland. Uthman gathered his followers, mostly Fulani, at Gudu, and sent them, under the leadership of Abd Allah, against Yunfa and the army of Gobir. Yunfa was defeated, and thereafter the jihad was carried throughout the Hausa states until the Fulani acquired control over them. Overwhelmed by his success and unable to assert complete authority over his subordinates, Uthman retired from public life and appointed his son, Muhammad Bello, ruler of the eastern region, the capital of which was Sokoto. Uthman gave the western region to Abd Allah. The capital of this region was Gwandu, in Kebbi. Abd Allah recorded the hijra and the jihad in prose and verse in his Tazyin al-Waraqat.

SECTION CONCERNING THE CAUSES OF OUR HIJRA, AND OUR HOLY WAR 1804

Now when the kings and their helpers saw the *Shaikh*'s community making ready their weapons, they feared that. Moreover, before that the numerousness of the community, and its cutting itself off from their jurisdiction had enraged them. They made their enmity known with their tongues, threatening the community with *razzias* [raids] and extermination, and what their breasts hid was worse than that. They began to forbid what they heard concerning the dress of the community, such as the turbans, and the order that the women should veil. Some of the community feared their threats, namely the people of our brother Abd al-Salam, and they emigrated before us to a place in Kebbi called Ghimbana.¹ Then the Sultan of Ghubir [Gobir] sent word to them, that they should return, and they refused. Then that Sultan sent word to the shaikh, that he should travel to him, and we set out to (visit?) him. His intention was to destroy us, but God did not give him power over us, and when we went into his presence in his castle, he came towards us, we being three,

From Abd Allah ibn Muhammad, *Tazyin al-Waraqat*, trans. from the Arabic and edited by M. Hiskett (Ibadan: Ibadan University Press, 1963), pp. 107–109, 114–115. I have retained the original number of the footnotes in the text by M. Hiskett. Reprinted by permission.

1. Gimbama.

the *shaikh*, myself, and Umar al-Kammawi,[2] the *shaikh*'s friend. He fired his naph-tha[3] in order to burn us with its fire, but the fire turned back on him, and nearly burnt him while we were watching him; and not one of us moved, but he retreated hasti-ly. Then he turned back to us after a while, and sat near to us. We approached him, and spoke to him. He said to us: "Know that I have no enemy on the earth like you," and he made clear to us his enmity, and we made clear to him that we did not fear him, for God had not given him power over us. Then he said concerning that which God had ordained him to say, such as I am not now able to relate. God kept him back from us, and we went away from him to our house, and none knew anything of that (affair) other than we ourselves. And the *shaikh* said to us, "Both of you con-ceal this, and pray God Most High on our behalf that we may never again meet with this unbeliever." He prayed for that, and we said "Amen" to it.

Then we returned to our country, and (the Sultan of Ghubir) dispatched an army after that against the community of Abd al-Salam, and it attacked them, and some of the Muslims were killed, and some were taken prisoner, and the rest of them scat-tered in the country of Kebbi. Now this increased him in pride and arrogance, and he, and those who followed him from among the people of his country, unbelievers and evil-doers, began to threaten us with the like of that until the Sultan sent word to the *shaikh* that he should go away from his community and leave them for a far place, he together with his family, alone. The *shaikh* sent word to him (saying) "I will not forsake my community, but I will leave your country, for God's earth is wide!" Then we made ready to emigrate, and he sent word to the *shaikh* that he should not leave his place. The *shaikh* refused, and we emigrated to a place on the far borders of his lands, in the desert places, called Qudu,[4] (with *damma* on the *qaf* and *dal*). Then (the Sultan) ordered the governors of his towns to take captive all who travelled to the *shaikh*, and they began to persecute the Muslims, killing them and confiscating their property. Then the affair came to the point where they were sending armies against us, and we gathered together when that became serious, and appointed the *shaikh*, who had previously been our *imam* and our *amir*, as our com-mander, in order that he might put our affairs in order, and I, praise be to God, was the first who pledged obedience to him, in accordance with the Book[5] and the sunna. Then we built[6] a fortress there; after that we began to revenge ourselves upon those who raided us, and we raided them, and conquered the fortress[7] of Matankari[8] then the fortress of the Sultan of Kunni.[9] Then the Sultan of Ghubir, Yunfa, came against us, having collected armies of Nubians and Touareg, and the Fulani who followed

2. "The Kammaite"; there is a Kamma in Bornu.

3. Professor David Ayalon has shown that the term *naft* in the Arabic sources came to mean "gun-powder" or "firearm" not "naphtha" as early as the fourteenth century, and continued to be used in this sense until the Ottoman conquest....

4. The description "in the desert places" would fit with a place in the area of Barikin Daji.

5. A reference to *Quran*, vi, 62.

6. *Hafarna—lit.* "we dug": the reference is to the digging of earth to build the mud walls with which Sudanese towns are fortified.

7. The word *hisn* as used by Abd allah probably means simply "walled town."

8. There are seven places called Matankiri in the Sokoto area!

9. Birni Koni (?), in present French territory.

him such as none knows except God. The Commander of the Believers dispatched for us an army against him, and appointed me to command it. We met (Yunfa) in a place called Qurdam near to a stretch of water here called Kutu (spelt with *kaf* and *ta* taking the *damma* which gives one vowel the scent of another). God routed his armies by His favour and grace, and to Him be the praise, and the thanks. We took booty from their property, and we killed them, and drove them away. Then we returned to the *shaikh* safely, and I composed verses concerning this.

Now when God had driven away the Sultan of Ghubir and his army, we began to raid them, while they did not raid us. This angered all the kings in Hausa, and humiliated them. Then they began to persecute the Muslims who were in their midst so that the Muslims fled to a far place. Then they fought them, and God gave us victory over the Country of the Amir of Kabi, and we moved to (Kabi) about a month after the defeat of Yunfa. We then returned after about two months to the country of Ghubir, and we conquered certain towns in it which will be mentioned, if God wills, in the *qasida*, "The Army of the Conquests." Then the Commander of the Believers fitted out an army and gave me command over it against the fortress of the Amir of Ghubir, al-Qadawa.[10] We arrived there, and attacked them fiercely three times from all sides of the fortress. God did not enable us to conquer them at this time. We returned to the *shaikh* when we heard that the Touareg were raiding our families. Now I had been struck in my leg by an arrow at the time of the first battle, and God had made the matter easy for me to bear. When we reached the *shaikh*, he set out with all the community and the families until we arrived at a place called Thunthuwa.[11] The armies of Ghubir gathered together with their Touareg, and made them attack us by surprise. We did not hear them until they were upon us among our families. The community met them and suffered defeat, and more than can be numbered of its noble men suffered martyrdom, among them the standard bearer on that day, our brother Muhammad Sad b. al-Hasan, famous by the nickname of Sadar, and the Imam Muhammad Thanbu b. Abd al-Rahman, and Zayd b. Muhammad Sad, and others. Now on that day I was not able to rise up on account of the arrow wound in my leg, but when defeat came to us, I rose up lame and confronted the fugitives, chiding them. Some of them followed me until we came upon the first of the enemy, who were killing and taking booty. I formed those who were with me into ranks, and we fired one volley at them. They turned back towards their main body, and not one stood his ground. God by His power drove them off, and we followed them. News of this defeat reached the shaikh, and he mounted and followed us. He arrived, but God had driven off the enemy.

Then after that we set out until we came near to the fortress of al-Qadawa, and we besieged them for about a month. Then when hunger bore heavily upon the community we set out for the country of Zanfara,[12] and God enabled us to take it with-

10. Alkalawa. Oral tradition places this on the River Rima, near to the present Sabon Birni.
11. Tsuntsuwa. Arnett places it S. of Alkalawa.
12. The former state of Zanfara, lying S.E. of Gobir: roughly the area of present eastern Sokoto and western Katsina.

out fighting, and we reached it at the end of the (first) year of our *hijra*[13] in the month of Dhu al-Qada. When we had celebrated the Id al-Adha we made ready to escort the Amir of Kabi who had accepted Islam, he and those with him, and he followed our community until we returned with him to that place in which we had encamped, namely Sabun Ghari,[14] in order that I should bring him back to his place, and that we should then wage Holy War against the town of the Sultan of Kabi who had refused to follow. I prepared an army for this—the "Army of the Conquests." We set out with those who followed us, and the people of the country of the Sultan of Qumi[15] met us in battle, from their fortress called Kunda[16] towards the further side of his territories. And we left no fortress of his which we did not conquer. Then the Sultan of Qumi sought a truce from us. We granted him a truce in his fortress only, on condition that I, when I returned from raiding, should travel with him to the Commander of Believers.

Thus it happened, and God conquered for us more than twenty fortresses, among them the fortress of the Sultan of Kabi.[17] They will be enumerated in the poem. We returned in safety with booty, with praise to God.

13. The hijra commenced on 10 Dhu al-Qada 1218/21 February 1804, *InfM*. Abdullah therefore reached Zanfara at some time in February 1805.
14. Sabon Gari. Brass sites this S. of Sherabi on the Gulbin Ka. The present Sabon Gari is on the W. bank of the Niger.
15. Gumi.
16. Brass locates this north of the River Jega (i.e. Zanfara).
17. Namely, Birnin Kebbi.

35. P. J. BAPTISTA

THE KAZEMBE. 1806.

In 1806 two pombeiros (African traders), P. J. Baptista and Anastasio Josi, arrived at the capital of Kazembe and there met Lukwesa's successor, his son Kibangu Keleka, or Kazembe IV. After a prolonged residence at the capital, Kazembe IV permitted the pombeiros to complete their trans-African journey in 1810. The following excerpts are from Baptista's diary.

[74th.] *Saturday*, 20*th*—Halted in the Cazembe's sister's farm, by her own order. At two in the morning, she sent for us, and we went inside her walls. She asked whence we came. We replied, from Angola and the court of Muropue, who had given us the guide. That we had come to speak with her brother King Cazembe, to get permission to go on to the town of Tette. She replied it was very good on the

From *Lacerda's Journey to Cazembe in 1798*, trans. and edited by Captain R. F. Burton, and *Journey of the Pombeiros F J Baptista and Amaro José, Across Africa from Angola to Tette on the Zambeze*, trans. by B. A. Beadle (London: Royal Geographical Society, 1873), pp. 186–188.

part of Muropue to send white people to speak with her brother; that none of Muropue's predecessors had done so; that it was a very great fortune for her brother Cazembe's heir to the State. She offered us a large she-goat, forty fresh fish, two bottles of a drink called "pombe," and six quicapos of dry mandioca flour. We presented her with thirty-two xuabos, a blue glass, and a "mozenzo" of a hundred white stones. She said she was much pleased with our gifts. We waited there that she might send notice of our arrival to her brother, King Cazembe, as it is obligatory on her part when travellers come to report them to her brother. With this end we waited six days at her farm, when the carriers came in search of us.

[75th.] *Saturday, 27th*—Got up and left the farm of Cazembe's sister at 7 A.M. Had no rain. We followed down the course of the Luapula. Passed a river of two fathoms' width, name unknown, which runs into the Luapula. During the journey we came to the farm of a black named Murumbo: we reached it at midday. We met no one, and marched with the sun on our right. We lodged in the houses of the farm, and saw nothing rare or important.

[76th.] *Sunday, 28th*—We got up at 2 A.M., and started from the farm of Murumbo. We marched down with the above-named river on our left. We passed two rivers, Lufubo and Capueje, which run into the above-named river. During the journey we came to the farm of a black named Gando, near a river called Gona, here we gave no presents. We reached it at six in the afternoon. We marched with the sun as before.

[77th.] *Monday, 29th*—At 5 A.M. we got up and started from the farm of Gando, near the river Gona. We passed two rivers, one called Belenje, the other's name not known; during the march we came to the place of a black named Canpungue. We reached this place at three in the afternoon, and met a good number of King Cazembe's people carrying firewood. We presented this black, Canpungue, with a chuabo of "Zuarte" or Indian cloth; he told us to continue our journey, as the Cazembe was expecting us.

[78th.] *Tuesday, 30th*—At seven A.M. we started from the place of the black, Canpungue—had no rain; we passed no river, and during the journey came to the place of a black named Luiagamára, of the Cazembe. Reaching this place at four in the afternoon, we lodged in the houses near a river called Canengua, narrow, and running into the river called Mouva, near which Cazembe's city is situated. We gave no present to the owner of this place; we halted there, and sent forward a day's notice of our arrival; we waited a little time, when the King Cazembe's messenger arrived, bringing us, as guest-gift, four murondos of a drink called "pombe," one hundred pieces of fresh meat, with some manioc flour for our consumption, and also a message from King Cazembe, asking us to remain at present where we were, that he would send for us later. Day breaking directly, and it being two o'clock in the morning, he sent for us by his chief, with orders that on our arrival near the walls of his chiefs (ancestors?), we should fire off all our guns, as a signal that we had arrived at his capital. He ordered us to lodge with one of his gatekeepers, named Furno Aquibery. We did nothing respecting our journey on this day: he sent us for our people, however, some provisions, manioc flour, fish, fresh meat, and "pombe," she-goats, and meats already prepared; he said he would see us with great pleasure.

When morning broke, he sent word for us to come and tell him what brought us there. We found him seated in the public highway, where he was accustomed to deliver his judgments to his people, surrounded by all the great potentates of his councils. He was robed in his silks and velvets, and had beads of various kinds on his arms and legs; his people surrounded him, and he had all his instruments of barbarous grandeur round about him. He sent to say that the guide who had come with us from his Muropue should speak. The guide said, "I bring you some white men here from the king they call Muenuputo; they come to communicate with you, King Cazembe; treat them well, without malice, and execute the wishes entrusted to them: grant them, King Cazembe, permission, together with some guide, who you may see able to conduct them, to go to the town of Tette, to deliver a letter to the Most Illustrious Governor of that town, they being entrusted with this mission in Angola, whence they came. Muropue also strongly recommends you will do all necessary to despatch the travellers where they wish to go, and afterwards send them back to Muropue, in order that he may return them whence they came." The King Cazembe said that he esteemed it much, and not a little, his Muropue's having sent travellers from afar; that for a long time past he had entertained the idea of opening the road to Senna; that he was very pleased to see travellers from Muropue, none of whose predecessors had similarly acted before; that he would do all in his power- not only provide a guide, but go with us himself as far as the Warcamp, to fight the highwaymen and robbers who meet with and intercept people on the road coming to communicate with him, King Cazembe. We had gone with King Cazembe as far as a farm of his people, about half a league from Cazembe, with numerous troops to escort us on the road; after this, a perturbation spread among his people, who did not wish to fight, so the attempt was frustrated; we returned to the farm with him against his wish. He began to cast out his chiefs; he cut the ears of some, others he mulcted in slaves and manilhas (bracelets); and on the second month he handed us over to his chief named Muenepanda to accompany us with more people. On our reaching a desert-lodging called Quipire, he turned back, saying that the town of Tette was a long way off, that the force he (Muenepanda) had to oppose to the potentates he might meet on the road was very small; that he did not wish to run any risk. We returned with him, and after waiting another half month, the black, named Nharugue, belonging to Gonçalo Caetano Pereira arrived, and we started and marched in his company till we reached this town of Tette.

King Cazembe is very black, a fine, stout young man, with small beard, and red eyes; he is very well accustomed to white traders, who come to his court to buy and sell such articles as seed, manioc flour, maize, millet, haricot beans, a good many "canas" (sugar-cane?), and fish which the people catch in the river near there called Mouva. Ivory comes from the other side the river Luapula, and is brought as tribute by the people; green stones (malachite) are found in the ground, called "catanga"; traders from the Muizas people come and buy ivory, in exchange for tissues and merchandise; another nation, named Tungalágazas, brings slaves and brass bracelets, cowries, palm-oil, and some goods which King Cazembe has, come from the Cola (Angola?), a land of Muropue, also fine large beads. There is a good deal of salt in that part, which they get from the ground; there is also another kind of rock-salt which is brought as tribute from the salt district, on the road to Muropue's territory, called Luigila, where he has a chief and a relation, named Quibery, who takes account of the Salina, and sends tributes of salt to his Muropue, besides buying it of the travellers who come from Muropue. I have made no entry of the rainy days we stopped, or of those when we were detained by sickness. I saw nothing more at the Court of King Cazembe which I have forgotten to write; I saw nothing but that already stated.

36. AL-KANAMI

THE CASE AGAINST THE JIHAD. 1813.

In the late eighteenth century a Muslim cleric, Uthman dan Fodio, began to preach in the Hausa state of Gobir against religious corruption and pagan practices. Although the Sarki (King) of Gobir sought to counter the teachings of Uthman dan Fodio, he only provoked him to declare a jihad or holy war against the unbelievers in 1802. Thereafter, Uthman's Fulani followers defeated the Hausa armies, captured the Hausa city-states, and replaced the Hausa rulers. In 1805 Uthman's lieutenants carried the jihad into the Muslim state of Bornu, defeated the armies of the mai, or king, and convinced his councillors to request assistance from Muhammad al-Amin ibn Muhammad Ninga, more commonly known as Shaykh al-Kanami. Al-Kanami was born in the Fezzan and studied in Cairo and Medina; upon his return to Kanem, he won a great following as a result of his piety, scholarship, and charisma. Rallying his army, he marched into Bornu, drove out the Fulani and recaptured Ngazargamu, the capital. During the war he wrote a series of letters to Muhammad Bello, successor to Uthman dan Fodio, in an attempt to understand why the Fulani should attack fellow Muslims. Shaykh al-Kanami continued to govern Bornu until his death in 1835.

Praise be to God, Opener of the doors of guidance, Giver of the means of happiness. Prayer and peace be on him who was sent with the liberal religion, and on his people who prepared the way for the observance of His law, and interpreted it.[1]

From him who is filthy with the dust of sin, wrapped in the cloak of shame, base and contemptible, Muhammad al-Amin ibn Muhammad al-Kanami to the Fulani "*ulama*" and their chiefs. Peace be on him who follows His guidance.

The reason for writing this letter is that when fate brought me to this country, I found the fire which was blazing between you and the people of the land. I asked the reason, and it was given as injustice by some and as religion by others. So according to our decision in the matter I wrote to those of your brothers who live near to us asking them the reason and instigation of their transgression, and they returned me a weak answer, not such as comes from an intelligent man, much less

From Thomas Hodgkin, *Nigerian Perspectives* (London: Oxford University Press, 1960), pp. 198–201. Reprinted by permission.

from a learned person, let alone a reformer. They listed the names of books, and we examined some of them, but we do not understand from them the things which they apparently understood. Then, while we were still perplexed, some of them attacked our capital, and the neighbouring Fulani came and camped near us. So we wrote to them a second time beseeching them in the name of God and Islam to desist from their evil doing. But they refused and attacked us. So, when our land was thus confined and we found no place even to dwell in, we rose in defence of ourselves, praying God to deliver us from the evil of their deeds; and we did what we did. Then when we found some respite, we desisted, and for the future God is all-knowing.

We believe in writing; even if it makes no impression on you, it is better than silence. Know that if an intelligent man accepts some question in order to understand it, he will give a straightforward answer to it.

Tell us therefore why you are fighting us and enslaving our free people. If you say that you have done this to us because of our paganism, then I say that we are innocent of paganism, and it is far from our compound. If praying and the giving of alms, knowledge of God, fasting in Ramadan and the building of mosques is paganism, what is Islam? These buildings in which you have been standing of a Friday, are they churches or synagogues or fire temples? If they were other than Muslim places of worship, then you would not pray in them when you capture them. Is this not a contradiction?

Among the biggest of your arguments for the paganism of the believers generally is the practice of the amirs of riding to certain places for the purpose of making alms-giving sacrifices there; the uncovering of the heads of free women; the taking

---

1. Further extracts from Muhammad Bello, *Infaq al-maysur*, Whitting edition, London, 1951, pp. 124–7, 142–4, 150, and 157, translated by Mr. Charles Smith. I am much indebted to Mr. Smith, not only for his translation, but also for advice about the historical significance of the whole lengthy al-Kanami-Bello correspondence, from which these brief extracts are taken. The interest of this correspondence ties in the light it throws on the relations between the rulers of Sokoto and Bornu after the Fulani *jihad*: on the methods of diplomacy of the period; and on the political standpoints and characters of the two principals. Copies of nine letters were published by Muhammad Bello in *Infaq al-maysur*, one from al-Kanami to Bello, five from Bello to al-Kanami, two from Uthman dan Fodio to al-Kanami, and one from al-Kanami to Uthman. Not all of Bello's letters appear to have been delivered. All belong to the period before 1813. The first of the extracts translated here is taken from letter No. 1 in *Infaq.*, an early letter of al-Kanami, written after the sack of Ngazargamu, the Bornu capital, by the Fulani under Gwani Mukhtar and their subsequent expulsion by al-Kanami. The second extract comes from letter No. 5 in *Infaq.*, an apparently much later letter from Bello, which counters arguments put forward by al-Kanami in No. 1. Mr. Smith describes this letter as "a remarkable testimony to the literary leanings of Bello," and containing "evidence of his wide reading of the Islamic classics."

The correspondence ranges over the main questions in dispute between Bello and al-Kanami, i.e. between Sokoto and Bornu. Was the Fulani jihad justifiable on accepted Muslim principles? That is to say, was it conducted against states which were in the strict sense "pagan" (kafir), and therefore *dar al-harb*, not *dar al-Islam*? Was Bornu in fact such a state? Were there appropriate precedents for such a *Jihad*? (Muhammad Bello argued at length that the actions of another reforming ruler, Muhammad Askia of Gao, three centuries previously, were in fact a precedent.) Was its real purpose the spreading of the frontiers of Islam, not of Fulani imperial power? Had the *jihad* been conducted according to the strict rules which ought to be applied in such cases, or had there been excesses? Had the Fulani been the aggressors, or had Bornu, by allying itself with supposedly pagan Hausa governments, been responsible for provoking the conflict? In the extracts quoted here the main issue under discussion is whether Bornu at the time of the *jihad* could properly be described as a land of paganism (*dar kufrn*).

of bribes; embezzlement of the property of orphans; oppression in the courts. But these five charges do not require you to do the things you are doing. As for this practice of the amirs, it is a disgraceful heresy and certainly blameworthy. It must be forbidden and disapproval of its perpetrators must be shown. But those who are guilty of it do not thereby become pagans; since not one of them claims that it is particularly efficacious, or intends by it to associate anything with God. On the contrary, the extent of their pretence is their ignorant idea that alms given in this way are better than otherwise. He who is versed in the books of *fiqh* [Muslim theology], and has paid attention to the talk of the imams in their disputation, when deviation from the right road in matters of burial and slaughter are spoken of will know the test of what we have said. Consider Damietta, a great Islamic city between Egypt and Syria, a place of learning and Islam: in it there is a tree, and the common people do to this tree as did the non-Arabs. But not one of the "*ulama*" rises to fight them or has spoken of their paganism.

As for uncovering the head in free women, this is also *haram* [forbidden], and the *Quran* has prohibited it. But she who does it does not thereby become a pagan. It is denial which leads to paganism. Failing to do something while believing in it is rather to be described as disobedience requiring immediate repentance. If a free woman has prayed with the head uncovered, and the time passes, but she does not repeat the prayer in accordance with what we know they say in the books of *fiqh*, surely you do not believe that her prayer is not proper because she has thereby become a pagan?

The taking of bribes, embezzlement of the property of orphans and injustice in the courts are all major sins which God has forbidden. But sin does not make anyone a pagan when he has confessed his faith. And if you had ordered the right and forbidden the wrong, and retired when the people did not desist, it would have been better than these present doings. If ordering and forbidding are confined within their proper limits, they do not lead to anything more serious. But your forbidding has involved you in sin, and brought evil on you and the Muslims in this world and the next. . . .

Since acts of immorality and disobedience without number have long been committed in all countries, then Egypt is like Bornu, only worse. So also is Syria and all the cities of Islam. There has been corruption, embezzlement of the property of orphans, oppression and heresy in these places from the time of the Bani Umayya [the Umayyad dynasty] right down to our own day. No age and no country is free from its share of heresy and sin. If, thereby, they all become pagan, then surely their books are useless. So how can you construct arguments based on what they say who are infidel according to you? Refuge from violence and discord in religion is with God. . . .

We have indeed heard of things in the character of the Shaikh Uthman ibn Fudi, and seen things in his writings which are contrary to what you have done. If this business does originate from him, then I say that there is no power nor might save through God, the most high, the most glorious. Indeed we thought well of him. But now, as the saying is, we love the Shaikh and the truth when they agree. But if they disagree it is the truth which comes first. We pray God to preserve us from being those of whom he said:

Say: "Shall we tell you who will be the greatest losers in their works? Those whose striving goes astray in the present life, while they think that they are working good deeds."[2]

And from being those of whom he also said:

"But they split in their affair between them into sects, each party rejoicing in what is with them."[3]

Peace.

2. Quran, Sura 18, verses 103–4. This and the three following quotations from the Quran are taken from the English renderings of A. J. Arberry, in *The Koran Interpreted*, London: Macmillan, 1955.

3. Quran. Sura 23, verse 55.

37. JOHN LEWIS BURCKHARDT

SHENDI. 1814.

John Lewis Burckhardt (1784–1817) was born in Lausanne and was educated at several European universities, As an employee of the Association for Promoting the Discovery of the Interior Parts of Africa, he traveled in Asia Minor, Egypt, and the Sudan. At the end of 1813 Burckhardt crossed the Nubian Desert and arrived in 1814 at Shendi, the important caravan center and market town on the Middle Nile. He continued his journey eastward from Shendi to Sawakin on the Red Sea. Burckhardt died from dysentery in Cairo in October 1817 at the age of thirty-three.

Shendi in 1814 was ruled by Nimr Muhammad Nimr (1785–1846) of the Jaaliyin Arabs. Nimr spent his youth in exile among the Batahin and then returned to Shendi, where he was declared mek, or king, in 1802. He ruled Shendi until 1822, when he opposed the invasion of the forces of Muhammad Ali of Egypt by assassinating the viceroy's son and commander of the invading army, Ismail. Punitive expeditions from Egypt forced Mek Nimr to flee from Shendi; he took up exile on the Ethiopian frontier where he became a redoubtable warlord until his death in 1846. His descendants were granted amnesty in 1865 and subsequently returned to Shendi.

Next to Sennaar, and Kobbe (in Darfour), Shendy is the largest town in eastern Soudan, and larger, according to the report of the merchants, than the capitals of Dongola and Kordofan. It consists of several quarters, divided from each other by public places, or markets, and it contains altogether from eight hundred to a thousand houses. It is built upon the sandy plain, at about half an hour's walk from the river; its houses are similar to those of Berber; but it contains a greater number of large buildings, and fewer ruins. The houses seldom form any regular street, but are

From John Lewis Burckhardt, *Travels in Nubia* (London: J. Murray, 1822), pp. 247–256, 263–266.

spread over the plain in great disorder. I nowhere saw any walls of burnt bricks. The houses of the chief, and those of his relatives, contain courtyards twenty feet square, inclosed by high walls, and this is the general description of the habitations of Shendy. The government is in the hands of the Mek; the name of the present chief is Nimr, i.e. Tiger [Leopard]. The reigning family is of the same tribe as that which now occupies the throne of Sennaar, namely, the Wold Adjib, which, as far as I could understand, is a branch of the Funnye. The father of Nimr was an Arab of the tribe of Djaalein [Jaaliyin] but his mother was of the royal blood of Wold Adjib; and thus it appears that women have a right to the succession. This agrees with the narrative of Bruce, who found at Shendy a woman upon the throne, whom he calls Sittina (an Arabic word, meaning our Lady). The Mek of Shendy, like the Mek of Berber, is subject to Sennaar; but, excepting the purchase money paid for his government, on his accession, and occasional presents to the king and vizier[1] of Sennaar, he is entirely independent, and governs his district, which extends about two days journey farther to the south, quite at his own pleasure.

Before the arrival of the Marmelouks in Dongola, Mek Nimr had been for many years in continual warfare with the Arabs Sheygya [Shayqiyya] who had killed several of his relatives in battle, and, by making inroads into his dominions with large parties of horsemen, had repeatedly laid waste the whole western bank of the river. The Sheygya made peace with him, in order more effectually to oppose the Mamelouks, when his own brother, to whom the command of the western bank had been entrusted, declared against him, and they have now carried on war for several years, with little success or loss on either side, as they are separated from each other by the river, and can never pass it but in small parties.

The government of Shendy is much to be preferred to that of Berber: the full authority of the Mek is not thwarted by the influence of powerful families, which in these countries tends only to insecurity, nor has he adopted that system of rapacity which makes Berber so justly dreaded by strangers. His absolute power is owing to the diversity of Arab tribes inhabiting Shendy, none of which is strong enough to cope with his own family and its numerous branches. The largest of these tribes are the Nimrab, Nayfab, and Djaalein, the greater part of whom still lead the Bedouin life. The most respectable class of the inhabitants of Shendy are the merchants, amongst whom are great numbers of foreign settlers from Sennaar, Kordofan, Darfour, and Dongola: the last are the most numerous, and they occupy an entire quarter of the town, but their nation is less esteemed than any other. They are reproached with inhospitality, and their avarice has become proverbial; the broker business, which is almost exclusively in their hands, has added to the odium of their name, so that an Arab of Shendy considers it as an insult to be called a Dongolawy, a name here considered as equivalent to that of Jew in Europe.

Commerce flourishes at Shendy, because the Mek does not extort any taxes from the merchants, which many people assured me he dared not do from his fear of the vizier of Sennaar. I am not able to judge how far this may be true; but the fact is,

1.The vizier of Sennaar, of the Adelan family, is said to be the real master there, while the king has a mere shadow of authority.

that caravans pay nothing whatever by way of duty; they generally make up a small present to the Mek, in order to enjoy his particular protection, and add something further for one of his brothers, who is a principal man in the place. Our party of Ababdes [Abdallab]sent him a small parcel of soap and sugar, of which my quota amounted to half a dollar. I did not hear of any subordinate offices in the government of Shendy, and the Mek seems to unite all the branches of authority in his own person. His relatives are the governors of villages; and his court consists of half a dozen police officers, a writer, an Imam, a treasurer, and a body-guard, formed principally of slaves. The character of the people is much the same as that of the inhabitants of Berber. They are kept in some order, it is true, by the Mek; but wickedness and injustice govern all their conduct, for they know that the law can do little more than endeavour to prevent crimes, and that it very seldom punishes them. Nightly robbers, drunken people who have assaulted strangers, thieves detected in the market, &c. &c. are often carried before the Mek, but he is generally satisfied with imprisoning them for two or three days; and I did not hear a single instance of his having ordered any person to be put to death, or even flogged, although such crimes as I have mentioned were committed daily during my stay at Shendy. The delinquents were permitted to return quietly to their homes, on paying a small fine to the Mek and his people. I was told that at Kordofan thieves are always punished with death.

Debauchery and drunkenness are as fashionable here as at Berber; the latter, I think, is even more common. No night passed without my hearing the loud songs of some Bouza meeting, though our quarter, that of the Dongolawy, who are too avaricious to be addicted to these vices, was one of the quietest. At Berber public women were constantly seen in the street; at Shendy I very seldom met any of them, though within the inclosures of the houses they are almost as numerous as at Berber.

The dress, habits, and manners of the inhabitants of Shendy are the same as those of the places last described, and appear to prevail as far as Darfour, and Sennaar. I observed more well-dressed people at Shendy than at Berber, and clean linen was much oftener seen. Gold being a very current article in the Shendy market, the women have more frequently golden rings at their noses and ears than those of Berber; the people also possess more wealth. It is not uncommon to see a family possessed of a dozen slaves, acting as servants in the house, and labourers in the field.

The people of Shendy, like those of Berber, are shepherds, traders, and husbandmen. Agriculture, however, seems to be little thought of by the inhabitants themselves, being chiefly left to the Arab peasants of the vicinity; the cultivable soil in the neighbourhood of the city is narrow; but to the north and south of it are some fine arable plains. Water-wheels are common; they are erected generally on those parts of the high banks, which the most copious inundations of the river cannot overflow; by means of them the cultivators raise one winter-crop; but they are too lazy to bestow the labour necessary for watering the soil a second or third time, as is done in the most elevated parts of Upper Egypt, where also the river very seldom rises high enough to overflow the banks. Dhourra [dura, i.e.,sorghum] is the chief produce; Dokhen [millet] and wheat are sown in small quantities, the former for the consumption of the western traders who visit Shendy, the latter almost exclusively for the families of the great. Large quantities of onions, some red pepper (brought from Kordofan), Bamyes, chick-peas, Meloukhye, and Tormos,[2] are always found in the market either green or dried. During the inundation some water-melons and cucumbers are sown, but for the use only of the Harem of the Mek.

The cattle are very fine; and the inhabitants say that their size and quality continue to increase, in proportion as you ascend the river. I saw no domestic animals that are not common in Egypt. Elephants are first met with at Abou Heraze, two or three days to the north of Sennaar; and they have never been known to pass to the northward of that district, which is bounded by a chain of mountains six or eight hours in breadth, reaching close to the river. I was told that tigers are frequently seen in the Wadys east of Shendy. In the mountains of Dender, a district towards the Atbara, and six or eight journies south-east of Shendy, the giraffa is found. It is hunted by the Arabs Shukorein [Shukriyya] and Kowahel, and is highly prized for its skin, of which the strongest bucklers are made. I frequently saw mountaingoats of the largest size brought to the market of Shendy; they have long horns bending to the middle of the back; their flesh is esteemed a great dainty. They call them Areal, a name given in Syria to the red deer. In Upper Egypt they are called Teytal and in Syria Beden. They are caught by the Djaalein Bedouins in nooses, in the same manner as they catch ostriches, which are also very common in this neighbourhood. The ostrich-feathers however are inferior to those of the western deserts. Those most esteemed in Egypt are from Kordofan and Darfour, which the caravans from the latter place bring to Siout. The Djaalein peasants bring the feathers to the market in bundles, good and bad together, and exchange them for Dhourra. Their price, when I was at Shendy, was about one tenth of what they would bring at Cairo, where the best kinds, in 1812, sold at two hundred and eighty piastres per pound. The Pasha of Egypt has lately included them among the articles monopolized by him.[3]

The hippopotamus is not common at Shendy, though it occasionally makes its appearance there; during my stay there was one in the river in the vicinity of Boeydha [Bayuda],which made great ravages in the fields. It never rose above water in the day-time, but came on shore in the night, and destroyed as much by the treading of its enormous feet, as it did by its voracity; the people have no means of killing them. At Sennaar, where hippopotami are numerous, they are caught in trenches, slightly covered with reeds, into which they fall during their nightly excursions. It is generally said that no musketball can bring them to the ground, unless they are hit in the vulnerable spot, which is over the car. The whips called Korbadj, which are

2. In Egypt, the meal of the Tormos is used as a substitute for soap in washing the head and body.

3. The trade in ostrich-feathers is one of the most complicated in the markets of Africa: at Cairo the feathers are assorted into several different qualities, and parcels are made up by the Jews (who alone understand the trade well) containing portions of every kind. Each parcel of ten pounds weight must contain one pound of the finest and whitest sort, one pound of the second quality, also white, but of a smaller size, and eight pounds of the sorts called Jemina. Bajoca, Coda, and Spadone, the last of which is black, and of little value. The market-price of white sorted feathers is at present (1816) two hundred and eighty piastres per rotolo, or pound, or two thousand eight hundred piastres, each parcel of ten pounds.

formed of their skins, are made at Sennaar, and on the Nile, above that place; the skin, immediately after being taken off, is cut into narrow strips, about five or six feet in length, gradually tapering to a point: each strip is then rolled up, so that the edges unite, and form a pipe, in which state it is tied fast and left to dry in the sun. In order to render these whips pliable, they must be rubbed with butter or grease. At Shendy they are sold at the rate of twelve or sixteen for a Spanish dollar; in Egypt, where they are in general use, and the dread of every servant and peasant, they are worth from half a dollar, to a dollar each. In colder climates, even in Syria, they become brittle, crack, and lose their elasticity.

Crocodiles are very numerous about Shendy. I have generally remarked that these animals inhabit particular parts of the Nile, from whence they seldom appear to move; thus, in Lower Egypt, they have entirely disappeared, although no reasonable cause can be assigned for their not descending the river. In Upper Egypt, the neighbourhood of Akhmim, Dendera, Orment, and Edfou, are at present the favourite haunts of the crocodile, while few are ever seen in the intermediate parts of the river. The same is the case in different parts of Nubia towards Dongola. At Berber nobody is afraid of encountering crocodiles in the river, and we bathed there very often, swimming out into the midst of the stream. At Shendy, on the contrary, they are greatly dreaded; the Arabs and the slaves and females, who repair to the shore of the river near the town every morning and evening to wash their linen, and fill their waterskins for the supply of the town, are obliged to be continually on the alert, and such as bathe take care not to proceed to any great distance into the river. I was several times present when a crocodile made its appearance, and witnessed the terror it inspired; the crowd all quickly retiring up the beach. During my stay at Shendy, a man who had been advised to bathe in the river, after having escaped the small-pox, was seized and killed by one of these animals. At Sennaar crocodiles are often brought to market, and their flesh is publicly sold there. I once tasted some of the meat at Esne, in Upper Egypt; it is of a dirty white colour, not unlike young veal, with a slight fishy smell; the animal had been caught by some fishermen in a strong net, and was about twelve feet in length. The Governor of Esne ordered it to be brought into his court-yard, where more than an hundred balls were fired against it without effect, till it was thrown upon its back, and the contents of a small swivel discharged at its belly, the skin of which is much softer than that of the back. Fish are very seldom caught by the Arabs at Shendy. Nets appear to be unknown, but children often amuse themselves in angling with hooked nails.

The produce of the fields of Shendy and its neighbourhood is not sufficient for the supply of the population, the wants of which are much increased by the continual arrival of caravans. Dhourra is imported principally from Abou Heraze, in the route to Sennaar. A caravan of more than three hundred camels arrived from thence with Dhourra during my stay at Shendy, and the price, which, on our arrival, was at the rate of one dollar for twelve measures, fell to twenty measures per dollar. The price of grain varies almost daily, the market being affected by the arrival of every caravan of traders, who always buy up a considerable quantity for the food of the slaves and camels. The Mek also monopolizes the corn-trade as much as he can. At Abou Heraze and Sennaar, Dhourra is said to be in great plenty: forty measures being sold for a dollar. This grain is of the same shape and size as that of Shendy and Upper Egypt; but it is of an ash gray colour; it is said to be less nourishing, and of course is less esteemed than the other.

Horses are more numerous here than at Berber. The Mek, it is said, can raise within Shendy itself from two to three hundred horsemen. According to the custom of the Eastern Arabs, the Djaalein Bedouins ride mares in preference to stallions; but the latter are preferred by the inhabitants of the town. The Mek's brother, Ras Saad ed Dyn, had a horse for which he had given in the southern districts thirteen slaves; it surpassed in beauty any other horse I ever remember to have seen. At a public festival on the occasion of the circumcision of one of Mek Nimr's sons, all the horsemen of Shendy met, and accompanied the family of the chief through the town, their horses prancing about. They appeared to me but very indifferent horsemen; none attempted any of the manoeuvres for which the Mamelouks are so famous; they contented themselves with galloping backwards and forwards, nor did I see one bold rider amongst them. It is in this cavalry, however, that the Mek places his chief strength, and it decides the fate of all the battles he is obliged to fight with his enemies. The saddles, and bridles, as well as the stirrups, in which they place the great toe only, are the same as those used at Berber and by the Arabs Sheygya, who appear to be as celebrated for their horsemanship in this country as the Mamelouks once were in Turkey. Mek Nimr has about twenty firelocks, which he has either bought or taken from Egyptian traders; with these he arms his favourite slaves, but few of them have courage sufficient to fire them off, and there are none who dare take an aim by placing the gun against the shoulder. The sight of it alone generally frightens the enemy, and so far it fully answers their purpose, for it is always the wish of both parties to finish the battle with as little bloodshed as possible, because the law of retaliation is in full force amongst these Arabs. Several of Mek Nimr's musquets are either broken, or so much rusted, as to make them unserviceable, and nobody could be found to clean and mend them. Having been seen one day cleaning my gun, I was supposed to be skilful in this art, and serious proposals were made to me, to enter into the Mek's service as gunsmith. He offered me one male and two female slaves, and as much Dhourra as I might want for their maintenance; and it was with difficulty that I could persuade the slaves who made me the proposal in the name of their master, that I knew nothing of the business of a gunsmith. Travellers in these countries ought to avoid showing their capacity in the most trifling things that may be of use or afford pleasure to the chiefs, who will endeavour to force them into their service. Not having succeeded in prevailing upon me to remain, the Mek wished at least to have my gun. He sent for it, and kept it for several days; and upon my urgent entreaties to have it returned to me, he sent me four Spanish dollars, ordering his slaves at the same time to carry me several dishes of bread and meat from his own kitchen. Upon complaining to some of the inhabitants of this treatment, they replied, that having now eaten of the Mek's food I had become his friend, and that it would therefore be a disgrace to me to make any difficulty in parting with my gun. I was very sorry to lose it, especially when I considered in what countries I still intended to travel; but in my present circumstances four dollars were not be despised. Seeing no chance therefore of either getting back my gun, or obtaining a higher price for it, I accepted the Mek's four dollars with many professions of thanks.

It will appear very singular that firearms are not more frequently met with here, as they may so easily be imported. But the fact is, that traders are afraid to carry them, lest they should excite the cupidity of some or other of the chiefs; and it is not to be supposed, that until they are more numerous, they can be taken to market like other goods, or be paid for at a regular price. To the country people, who seldom visit the towns where traders make any stay, a musquet is an object of the greatest terror, and will frighten away dozens of them. A Djaalein Arab, who had some ostrich-feathers to sell, came one day to the house where I lodged, to barter with my companions for his feathers. The moment he espied my gun standing in the corner of the room, he got up, and desired it might be removed, for that he did not like to remain near so deadly an instrument.

On the great market days, which are every Friday and Saturday, several thousands of people resort to Shendy from the distance of three or four days; the greater part of whom bring cattle for sale. Judging from the individuals I saw in the market, all these Arabs appear to be entirely of the same race, excepting only that the true Djaalein Bedouins [Beja] who come from the eastern desert are much fairer-skinned than the inhabitants of the banks of the Nile, which arises probably from their taking greater care not to mix in concubinage with the Negro race. I was much struck with the physiognomy of many of these Djaaleins, who had exactly the countenance and expression of features of the Bedouins of eastern Arabia; their beards are even shorter, and thinner. Some individuals of a tribe of Djaalein who border, to the south, upon the Shukorye, appeared at the market with hats on their heads, made of reeds; they were high and pointed, with broad brims, and were tied under the chin with a leather thong. They are worn both by men and women.

About four or five hundred camels, as many cows, a hundred asses, and twenty or thirty horses, were on sale on the great market-days. Every merchant then takes his stand in one of the open shops, or in the open market, and exposes part of his merchandize; for even the richest traders are not ashamed of trafficking in the minutest detail. The Egyptian, Souakin, Sennaar, and Kordofan merchants form separate corps, in the midst of which is a great circle of slaves, thus exposed for sale. The country people bring to market mats, baskets, ox hides, and other skins, coarse pottery, camel saddles, wooden dishes, and other articles of their own manufacture, &c. About a dozen shoemakers, or rather sandal-makers, from the country, work for these two days in the market, and will make a pair of sandals at an hour's notice. The works in leather are very prettily done. The leather is tanned with the Garadh or pulse of the acacia; the Bedouins about Sennaar are said to be the most skilful in its preparation. Leather sacks are likewise sold here; they serve for the transport of every kind of baggage and merchandize, excepting Dhourra, gum arabic, and salt, which are carried in baskets. Many blacksmiths repair to Shendy from the country; they make and sell the small knives generally worn among these people. The knives are about eight inches long, and are worn in a leather scabbard tied over the left elbow: they are two-edged, like those worn by the Berabera.

The market is so crowded, and the dust and heat are so great, during the mid-day hours, which is the favourite time for transacting business, that I was unable to remain in the market-place many hours together, and always left one of my companions in charge of the little I had to sell. In different parts of the place are stationed peasants with jars of water, which they sell to the thirsty, at the rate of a handful of Dhourra for as much water as two persons can drink. Several of the Fakys [*faqi*, holyman] have water-cisterns in the courtyards of their houses, which are always kept full, and at which every one may drink gratis. Many of them have likewise small chapels annexed to their dwellings. There is no mosque in the whole place.

The only artizans I saw at Shendy were blacksmiths, silversmiths, who work very coarse ornaments for the women, tanners, potters, and carpenters. If a house is to be built, the owner, his relatives, and slaves, with a few labourers, execute the masonry, and the carpenter is only called in to lay the roof and make the doors. Like the Bedouins of the desert, these Arabs are their own artizans upon all ordinary occasions.

There are no weavers at Shendy, but all the women and grown up children, and many of the men, are seen with a distaff constantly in their hands, spinning cotton yarn, which they sell to the people of Berber. The distaff, Mugzil, resembles that used in Egypt and Syria. Cotton is cultivated in this neighbourhood, and is a general produce of all the countries on the banks of the Nile, although nowhere in any great quantity, except at Damer and about Sennaar.

The wholesale trade at Shendy is principally conducted through the agency of brokers. Most of these are Dongolawy, who seem, in general, to be the most acute and intelligent traders of this part of the country. A caravan no sooner arrives, than every merchant's house is crowded with brokers; but the avidity and parsimony of all parties are too great to allow them to bring their transactions to a speedy conclusion. Even after the bargain is made, each party endeavours to cheat the other before the goods are delivered and the money paid. In addition to this, every attempt to enter into an engagement of any importance becomes known all over the place, and the jealousy of the traders often prevents its taking place. No merchandize has its fixed price; there is no such thing as a price current; every one sells according to the prospect he has of cheating the buyer and bribing the broker. The purchase money, or, in cases of barter, its equivalent in merchandize, is almost always immediately paid down; the longest credit I have witnessed is a couple of days; and it is evident, on the termination of every commercial transaction, that the buyer and seller reciprocally entertain suspicions of each other's honesty. To oblige a debtor to settle his accounts, recourse is generally had to the slaves of Mek, who act as police officers; but man who is unprotected, and without friends is sure to lose the greater part of his goods if he allows them to go out of his hands without immediate payment.

38. THOMAS PRINGLE

BOER MEETS BANTU. 1820.

Thomas Pringle (1789–1834) was born in Scotland. Associated with various literary reviews as poet and editor, he emigrated from his homeland to South Africa in 1820 withthe wave of British settlers after the Napoleonic wars and established his home in the Albany district of the Eastern Province. Finding the frontier too dull, he moved in 1822 to Cape Town, where he became well known as the co-founder, with John Fairbairn, of the South African Commercial Advertiser, as well as for the controversy surrounding the subsequent suppression of the publication for his outspoken comments on the autocratic actions of the governor, Lord Charles Somerset. Pringle returned to Britain in 1826 and a year later became Secretary of the Anti-Slavery Society. He published two volumes of poetry, the second of which included a description of his experiences in South Africa and some aspects of South African history. The following selection is taken from a republication of the prose section of this volume, entitled Narrative of a Residence in South Africa, *in which Pringle provides his interpretation of the first contacts between the southern Nguni and the whites.*

The term *Caffer*, like that of *Hottentot*, is entirely unknown in the language of the people to whom it is applied. It was originally a term of contumely (being the Arabic word *Cafir* or *Kafir*, signifying *Infidel*) employed, by the Moorish or Arabian inhabitants of the north-eastern coast, to designate the nations of Southeastern Africa who had not embraced the Mohammedan faith; and from them the term was adopted by the early European navigators. The appellation, though sometimes still applied in a more extensive sense, is generally used, in the Cape Colony, to denote the three contiguous tribes of Amakosa, Amatembu, and Amaponda; of whom the last may be considered identical with the Mambo, or what used to be called the Mambookie, nation. These three tribes, though governed by several independent chiefs, are decidedly one people; their language, manners, customs, and polity being essentially the same. The Amakosa, whose territory borders with the colony from the Winterberg to the coast, is the tribe with whom our intercourse, both in peace and war, has been far the most frequent.

The Caffers are a tall, athletic, and handsome race of men, with features often approaching to the European or Asiatic model; and, excepting their woolly hair, exhibiting few of the Peculiarities of the negro race. Their colour is a clear dark brown. Their address is frank, cheerful, and manly. Their government is patriarchal; and the privileges of rank are carefully maintained by the chieftains. Their principal wealth and means of subsistence consist in their numerous herds of cattle. The females also cultivate pretty extensively maize, millet, water-melons, and a few other esculents; but they are decidedly a nation of *herdsmen*—war, hunting, barter, and agriculture, being only occasional occupations.

From Thomas Pringle, *Narrative of a Residence in South Africa* (London: E. Moxon, 1840), pp. 92–95.

In their customs and traditions, there seem to be indications of their having sprung, at some remote period, from a people of much higher civilisation than is now exhibited by any of the tribes of Southern Africa; whilst the rite of circumcision, universally practised among them, without any vestige of Islamism, and several other traditionary customs greatly resembling the Levitical rules of purification, would seem to indicate some former connexion with a people of Arabian, Hebrew, or, perhaps, Abyssinian lineage. Nothing like a regular system of idolatry exists among them; but we find some traces of belief in a Supreme Being, as well as in inferior spirits, and sundry superstitious usages that look like the shattered wrecks of ancient religious institutions. Of their superstitions, the belief in sorcery is far the most mischievous, leading, in the same way as among the negroes on the west coast, to many acts of revolting oppression and cruelty.

The clothing of both sexes consists entirely of the skins of animals, rendered soft and pliable by a sort of currying. Their arms are the assagai or javelin, a short club, and a large shield of bullock's or buffalo's hide. The wars between contiguous tribes above-mentioned, or several clans with each other, are seld very bloody, generally arising from quarrels relating to their respective pasture grounds or the stealing of cattle, and being little resemblance to the ferocious mode of warfare recently pursued with such destructive effect by the Zoola [Zulu] nations. The females are seldom slain in their internal wars; and in the conflicts with the colonists, there many well-known examples of the humanity towards females who had fallen into their hands. They are *barbarians*, not *savages*, in the strict and proper sense of the term.

It is a curious and characteristic circumstance that the earliest notice or record of intercourse between the Cape colonists and the Caffers, is an account of a marauding expedition by a party of former against the latter. In 1701, a band of Cape-Dutch freebooters, under name of traders or barterers, marched eastward, and after an absence of seven months returned with a large quantity of cattle and sheep, which they I obtained by plundering a nation called Cabuquas, or Great Caffers, (probably Tambuquas, *i.e. Amatembu*,) together with two kraals of Hottentots. In the attacks made upon these then remote tribes numbers of the natives had been slaughtered. The facts are stated in a despatch sent to Holland in 1702 by the Governor and Council of the Cape of Good Hope, who, while they deplore "the intolerable and continued excesses of some of the inhabitants, in committing acts of violence, with robberies and murders, and these abominable means depriving the poor people of their subsistence," declared at the same time their inability to punish the delinquents.

The impunity thus enjoyed by colonial freebooters (who consisted the most part of the very refuse of Europe, disbanded soldiers from mercenary regiments in the Dutch service, and the like), led, as was to be expected, to the frequent renewal of similar marauding excursions. By this means, and by the gradual occupation of all the best parts of the country, the Hottentot race were, as we have seen, at length either extirpated, reduced to thraldom, or driven to the northern deserts. The Caffers, a more numerous and warlike people, and acting together in large masses, were not so easily overwhelmed. They appear to have successfully resisted on many occasions the attacks of the colonists; but, having only their slender missiles to oppose to the musket, they also often suffered dreadfully from their aggressions.

The Caffers had been for several generations gradually pressing upon the Hottentot race from the eastward. This is not only known from traditionary memorials, but is manifest from most of the names of the rivers west of the Kei being of Hottentot etymology. The Hottentot hordes do not appear to have been extirpated by them, but to have been partly pushed farther westward, and partly incorporated with their frontier clans. The Ghonaqua tribe, once numerous and powerful, consisted of a people of mixed Caffer and Hottentot lineage; and the dialect now spoken by the frontier Caffers partakes to a certain extent of the Hottentot *cluck* [the distinctive click of Khoisan languages], a peculiarity not to be found among the tribes farther back.

The country between the Camtoos and Great Fish rivers was, up to 1778, partly occupied by the Ghonaqua tribes and other hordes of Hottentots still enjoying a precarious independence, partly by Caffer clans, intermingled with the Ghonaquas, and partly by European colonists, who, in defiance of the colonial regulations, had taken possession of the choicest spots they could find beyond the nominal boundary— then Camtoos River. In 1778, the Governor, Van Plattenberg, having, in the course of an extensive tour which he made into the interior, visited Bruintjes-hoogtè, and finding a considerable number of colonists occupying tracts beyond the frontier, instead of recalling them within the legal limits, he extended the boundary (according to the ordinary practice of Cape Governors, before and since), adding, by a stroke of his pen, about 30,000 square miles to the colonial territory. It was at this period that the Great Fish River was first declared to be the colonial boundary on the east. The rights of the Ghonaquas and other independent Hottentot tribes within the extensive region thus acquired, do not appear to have occupied a single thought; the Boors were left to deal with them as they had dealt with their brethren already extinct: but with the more formidable Caffers the form of an agreement was observed. Colonel Collins relates that Colonel Gordon was sent in search of Caffers as far as the Keiskamma, and that he conducted "a few" to the Governor, who obtained their consent that the Great Fish River should thenceforth be considered the boundary between the two countries.

Who were "the few" that concurred in this agreement, it would be vain to inquire; but it is certain that the principal Caffer chiefs who had an interest in the affair refused to recognize it. Jalumba, then chief of the Amandanka clan of the Amakosa, endeavoured to maintain his ground in Bruintjes-hoogtè. "The *inhabitants*," says Col. Collins, "reminded Jalumba (in 1781) of the recent treaty, and required his immediate departure. Their remonstrance having been disregarded, a commando assembled, by which the intruders were expelled with the loss of Jalumba and a great number of his followers. His son Dlodlo perished two years afterwards, in a similar attempt." Such is the colonial account of the affair; but Col. Collins, who derived his information entirely from the Boors and local functionaries, has not mentioned that on this occasion the expedition (of which Adrian Van Jaarsveld was the leader) plundered the Caffers of 5,200 head of cattle, which he divided "after consultation with the Veld-wagtmeester and corporals, amongst the commando." Nor was this the worst. We have got from Mr. Brownlee the Caffer account of the transaction, which is at least as much deserving of credit as the reports of the colonists who had enriched themselves with the spoils of the slaughtered Caffers; and from this it appears, that Jalumba and his clan were destroyed by a most infamous act of treachery and murder. The details may be found in the works both of Thompson and Kay. Vaillant, who spent a considerable time in this part of the country in the following year (1782), gives an account of the spirit of the frontier Boors, and of the oppressions perpetrated upon the Caffers, that but too well accords with the story told by Mr. Brownlee, from Caffer tradition, of the massacre of the Amandanka. "A mulatto colonist," he says, "informed me that the report of this nation being barbarous and bloody was industriously circulated by the colonists, in order to justify the atrocious thefts they were daily guilty of towards them, and which they wished to have passed for reprisals. That they often formed pretences of losing cattle, purposely to make inroads into the Caffers' settlements, exterminating whole hordes without distinction of age or sex, carrying away their herds, and laying waste the country; this means of procuring cattle appearing much easier than the slow method of breeding them. In this manner, Hans assured me, twenty thousand head had been obtained the last year." After giving some details of particular atrocities reported to him, and making some very pertinent remarks upon the flagitious impunity enjoyed by these barbarous backsettlers, Vaillant states that when he expressed to one of them his surprise that the governor did not send down a troop of soldiers to arrest those who committed such acts in defiance of all authority, the Boor replied, that if such a thing were attempted, they would kill half the soldiers, and send them back salted by those that were spared, as an earnest of what they would do to any authority that should dare to interfere with them! Such were the men who rose in arms in 1796, and again in 1815, against the British Government, in order to vindicate their right to rob and murder the natives without control!

Nearly about the same period, Zaka, the head of the Gunuquebi clan, with some other bands of the Amakosa, had obtained possession of the Zureveld, by purchasing with a large number of cattle permission to settle there from Kohla (called by the colonists Ruiter), who was then chief of the Ghonaqua Hottentots, the original possessors of the country. The colonists at the same time advanced into the Zureveld from the west. For a number of years the Boors and the Caffiers occupied that district together, with their habitations and herds amicably intermingled; until, in 1786, some differences arising between them, the colonists called in the chief Islambi, the enemy of Zaka, to their assistance. The latter chief, being attacked simultaneously by the Boors on one side and by Islambi with 3000 warriors on the other, was defeated and slain; and his tribe (the Gunuquebi) were plundered by the confederates of almost the whole of their cattle, and driven by necessity to plunder the colonists for means of subsistence. The Boors, however, did not by this means accomplish their object. Kongo, the son of Zaka, having been soon afterwards joined by Maloo, Toli, Etoni, and several other chiefs at enmity with Islambi and Gaika, and by the remnant of the Amandanka under Olila the brother of Jalumba, the Gunuquebi, with their allies, re-established themselves in the Zureveld, in spite of the colonists, and plundered them in their turn of many cattle; and it is from the period of this struggle, and from the destruction of the Amandanka in Bruintjes-hoogtè, that the bitter animosity of the border tribes, formerly friendly, and their extensive depredations against the colonists, are to be dated.

In consequence of the representations of the colonists, a large commando of Burgher militia was collected in 1793, to chastise the Caffers. This force, under the command of Mr. Maynier, landdrost of Graaff-Reinét, marched through the Zureveld, and penetrated into the Amakosa country, four days' journey beyond the Great Fish River, driving the natives everywhere before them into the woods, and capturing some herds of cattle; but without obtaining any decided advantage over the enemy, who, as soon as the commando retreated, returned to their former position. A treaty was at length concluded, leaving things precisely as they were, and in which, as Colonel Collins remarks, nothing was mentioned about the retreat of the Caffers from the disputed territory. In a report made to Government by the land-drost, Maynier, respecting the causes of this war, he observes, "that the excursions of the Boors into Cafferland for the purpose of hunting, the trade carried on between them and the Caffers, and the improper treatment which the latter had experienced from the former when in their service, were the principal occasions of the rupture."

In 1795, the colony was captured by the British arms; and the Boors of the Graaff-Reinét district having in the following year driven away their new magistrate, Mr. Bresler, the whole of the eastern province was thrown into a state of the utmost anarchy. Some of the Caffer chiefs were instigated by the colonists to attack the British troops who had been sent down by Sir James Craig to maintain order. Many of the Hottentots, as has been already noticed, availing themselves of the crisis, rose against their masters, and prevailed on the Caffer clans of the Zureveld to join them in plundering and driving out the frontier Boors, who were thus caught in the net of mischief they had themselves spread; and devastation and bloodshed continued to prevail for several years, during which much misery and many barbarities were reciprocally inflicted by both parties.

Such was the state of affairs on the eastern frontier in 1797, when Earl Macartney assumed the government, and Mr. Barrow was sent on a mission to Cafferland, of which he has given so interesting an account in his able work on the colony. The policy of the British government towards the native tribes at this period was unquestionably characterised by a spirit of justice and benevolence. The firm repression by Sir James Craig of an audacious attempt by the Boors of Bruintjes-hoogtè to obtain permanent possession of the country on the Kat and Koonap rivers; the testimony of Mr. Barrow on that subject; and the tone of Lord Macartney's proclamation of July 14, 1798, in establishing a fixed boundary for the colony, afford satisfactory evidence of the enlightened sentiments by which those Governors were actuated. But some great and lamentable mistakes were also then committed. The unjust and mischievous policy was adopted of treating with *one* Caffer chief instead of those who were far more directly interested in the question of boundaries; and this, notwithstanding that Gaika, while he stated truly enough that he was the chief first in rank on the frontier (for he was secondary to Hinza in the Amakosa tribe), carefully informed Mr. Barrow at the same time that those who held possession of tracts of country west of the Great Fish River, "were chiefs as well as himself, and entirely independent of him." No consideration was had to the claims of the Caffer chiefs in the Zureveld, who absolutely refused to accede to the treaty with Gaika or to leave the country, which they considered, and not without good reason, as their own both by purchase and conquest. Still less consideration appears to have been given to the yet more indisputable rights of the aborigines of the soil, the Ghonaquas, and other Hottentot hordes, to whom had originally belonged the large tract of country usurped so unscrupulously by Governor Plettenberg in 1778. The limits then assigned to the colony were now reclaimed without qualification, by the proclamation of Earl Macartney.

For the details of the policy pursued towards the Caffers for the twelve years at war which followed Mr. Barrow's embassy to Gaika, I must refer to the works of that Zureveld writer and of Lichtenstein, and to the more recent publications of Thompson, Bannister, and Kay. The Gunuquebi clan, under Kongo, kept possession of the fastnesses of the Zureberg and the adjacent country, to the mouths of the Bushman and Sunday rivers. Islambi, who was at war with Gaika, had also crossed the Great Fish River, and fixed himself in the Zureveld. Their alliance with the insurgent Hottentots had been already mentioned. With the Boors they were sometimes at war, and sometimes living in precarious truce.

39. MAJOR DIXON DENHAM

BORNU AND SHAYKH AL-KANAMI. 1823.

Although Mungo Park had shown the way to the Niger, he drowned in the rapids near Bussa before completing his journey to the river's mouth. The next attempt to reach the Niger was undertaken by an expedition consisting of Dr. Walter Oudney, Major Dixon Denham, and Lieutenant Hugh Clapperton, R.N., who were authorized by the British government in 1822 to reach the Niger by crossing the Sahara along the well-established trade routes. Denham explored the country around Lake Chad, particularly the kingdom of Bornu, where he met Shaykh al-Kanami. Oudney and Clapperton continued southwest toward the Niger. Oudney died, but Clapperton reached Kano and Sokoto. Here Sultan Muhammad Bello, successor to Uthman don Fodio, refused to permit Clapperton to proceed to the river. Clapperton made his way back to Bornu and, accompanied by Denham, returned to England in 1825.

From *Missions to the Niger*, edited by E. W. Bovill (New York: Cambridge University Press, 1966), vol. II, pp. 243–250, 289–291; vol. III, pp. 429–430. Reprinted by permission of Cambridge University Press on behalf of The Hakluyt Society.

Feb. 16—Halted. Our visitors here were not very numerous, although we were not above one hour's journey from the sheikh's residence, Kouka.[1] Various were the reports as to the opinion the sheikh formed of the force which accompanied Boo-Khaloom: all agreed, however, that we were to be received at some distance from the town, by a considerable body of troops; both as a compliment to the Bashaw, and to show his representative how well prepared he was against any attempt of those who chose to be his enemies.

One of the Arabs brought to me this day a Balearic crane; it measured thirteen feet from wing to wing.

Feb. 17—This was to us a momentous day, and it seemed to be equally so to our conductors. Notwithstanding all the difficulties that had presented themselves at the various stages of our journey, we were at last within a few short miles of our destination; were about to become acquainted with a people who had never seen, or scarcely heard of, a European;[2] and to tread on ground, the knowledge and true situation of which had hitherto been wholly unknown. These ideas of course excited no common sensations; and could scarcely be unaccompanied by strong hopes of our labours being beneficial to the race amongst whom we were shortly to mix; of our laying the first stone of a work which might lead to their civilization, if not their emancipation from all their prejudices and ignorance, and probably, at the same time, open a field of commerce to our own country, which might increase its wealth and prosperity. Our accounts had been so contradictory of the state of this country, that no opinion could be formed as to the real condition or the numbers of its inhabitants. We had been told that the sheikh's soldiers were a few ragged negroes armed with spears, who lived upon the plunder of the Black Kaffir countries, by which he was surrounded, and which he was enabled to subdue by the assistance of a few Arabs who were in his service; and, again, we had been assured that his forces were not only numerous, but to a certain degree well trained. The degree of credit which might be attached to these reports was nearly balanced in the scales of probability; and we advanced towards the town of Kouka in a most interesting state of uncertainty, whether we should find its chief at the head of thousands, or be received by him under a tree, surrounded by a few naked slaves.

These doubts, however, were quickly removed. I had ridden on a short distance in front of Boo-Khaloom, with his train of Arabs, all mounted, and dressed out in their best apparel; and, from the thickness of the trees, soon lost sight of them, fancying that the road could not be mistaken. I rode still onwards, and on approaching a spot less thickly planted, was not a little surprised to see in front of me a body of several thousand cavalry drawn up and extending right and left quite as far as I

---

1. In the Kanuri language, as in Hausa, *kuka* means the baobab or monkey bread tree, *Adansonia digitata*. Barth, in whose time the town of Kuka had come to be called Kukawa, comments as follows: "Though the town of Kukawa has received its name from the circumstance that a young tree of this species was found on the spot where the sheikh Mohammed el Kanemi . . . laid the first foundation of the present town, nevertheless scarcely any kuka is seen for several miles round Kukawa."

2. Nevertheless, many of them might have seen Hornemann [who reached the Niger in 1800 but later died], and, as we have seen, there were a good many renegades wandering about northern Africa at this time.

could see and, checking my horse, I awaited the arrival of my party, under the shade of a widespreading acacia. The Bornou troops remained quite steady, without noise or confusion; and a few horsemen, who were moving about in front giving directions, were the only persons out of the ranks. On the Arabs appearing in sight, a shout, or yell, was given by the sheikh's people, which rent the air: a blast was blown from their rude instruments of music equally loud, and they moved on to meet Boo-Khaloom and his Arabs. There was an appearance of tact and management in their movements which astonished me: three separate small bodies, from the centre and each flank, kept charging rapidly towards us, to within a few feet of our horses' heads, without checking the speed of their own until the moment of their halt, while the whole body moved onwards. These parties were mounted on small but very perfect horses, who stopped, and wheeled from their utmost speed with great precision and expertness, shaking their spears over their heads, exclaiming, "*Barca! barca! Alla hiakkum cha, alla cheraga!* —Blessing! blessing! Sons of your country! Sons of your country!" and returning quickly to the front of the body, in order to repeat the charge. While all this was going on, they closed in their right and left flanks, and surrounded the little body of Arab warriors so completely, as to give the compliment of welcoming them very much the appearance of a declaration of their contempt for their weakness. I am quite sure this was premeditated; we were all so closely pressed as to be nearly smothered, and in some danger from the crowding of the horses and clashing of the spears.[3] Moving on was impossible; and we therefore came to a full stop: our chief was much enraged, but it was all to no purpose, he was only answered by shrieks of "Welcome!" and spears most unpleasantly rattled over our heads expressive of the same feeling. This annoyance was not however of long duration; Barca Gana, the sheikh's first general, a negro of a noble aspect, clothed in a figured silk tobe, and mounted on a beautiful Mandara horse, made his appearance; and, after a little delay, the rear was cleared of those who had pressed in upon us, and we moved on, although but very slowly, from the frequent impediment thrown in our way by these wild equestrians.

The sheikh's negroes, as they were called, meaning the black chiefs and favourites, all raised to that rank by some deed of bravery, were habited in coats of mail composed of iron chain, which covered them from the throat to the knees, dividing behind, and coming on each side of the horse:[4] some of them had helmets, or rather skull-caps, of the same metal, with chin-pieces, all sufficiently strong to ward off the shock of a spear. Their horses' heads were also defended by plates of

3. The manner of el Kanemi's welcome to the Mission, especially its display of armed strength, may have been partly due to the trouble there had been over the detention of his children in Murzuk. But it was chiefly due to the Europeans having arrived with an escort of foreign troops, who were unwelcome and of whom El Kanemi intended to rid himself as soon as possible.

4. Suits of mail are still sometimes worn by the retainers of important Western Sudan chiefs. Their striking resemblance to the mail worn by the Crusaders led to the popular belief that these suits had survived from the Middle Ages. They are in fact modern and of African manufacture. In the thirties of the present century mail made from wire rings pinched together was being manufactured in Omdurman, and being sold to local notables at about £25 a suit. But the mail the Mission saw in Kuka had been made in Hausa, probably in Kano. "Some of the Kanem Negroes called the sheikh's Guard," wrote Denham, "were habited in Coats of Mail composed of Iron Chain work from sudan."

iron, brass, and silver, just leaving sufficient room for the eyes of the animal.

At length, on arriving at the gate of the town, ourselves, Boo-Khaloom, and about a dozen of his followers, were alone allowed to enter the gates; and we proceeded along a wide street completely lined with spearmen on foot, with cavalry in front of them, to the door of the sheikh's residence. Here the horsemen were formed up three deep, and we came to a stand: some of the chief attendants came out, and after a great many "Barca's! Barca's!" retired, when others performed the same ceremony. We were now again left sitting on our horses in the sun: Boo-Khaloom began to lose all patience, and swore by the Bashaw's head, that he would return to the tents if he was not immediately admitted: he got, however, no satisfaction but a motion of the hand from one of the chiefs, meaning "wait patiently"; and I whispered to him the necessity of obeying, as we were hemmed in on all sides, and to retire without permission would have been as difficult as to advance. Barca Gana now appeared, and made a sign that Boo-Khaloom should dismount: we were about to follow his example, when an intimation that Boo-Khaloom was alone to be admitted again fixed us to our saddles. Another half hour at least passed without any news from the interior of the building; when the gates opened, and the four Englishmen only were called for, and we advanced to the skiffa (entrance). Here we were stopped most unceremoniously by the black guards in waiting, and were allowed, one by one only, to ascend a staircase; at the top of which we were again brought to a stand by crossed spears, and the open flat hand of a negro laid upon our breast. Boo-Khaloom came from the inner chamber, and asked "If we were prepared to salute the sheikh as we did the Bashaw?" We replied "Certainly": which was merely an inclination of the head, and laying the right hand on the heart. He advised our laying our hands also on our heads, but we replied, "the thing was impossible! we had but one manner of salutation for any body, except our own sovereign."

Another parley now took place, but in a minute or two he returned, and we were ushered into the presence of this Sheikh of Spears.[5] We found him in a small dark room, sitting on a carpet, plainly dressed in a blue lobe of Soudan and a shawl turban. Two negroes were on each side of him, armed with pistols, and on his carpet lay a brace of these instruments. Firearms were hanging in different parts of the room, presents from the Bashaw and Mustapha L'Achmar, the sultan of Fezzan, which are here considered as invaluable. His personal appearance was prepossessing, apparently not more than forty-five or forty-six, with an expressive countenance, and a benevolent smile. We delivered our letter from the Bashaw; and after he had read it, he inquired "what was our object in coming?" We answered: to see the country merely, and to give an account of its inhabitants, produce, and appearance; as our sultan was desirous of knowing every part of the globe. His reply was, "that we were welcome! and whatever he could show us would give him pleasure: that he had ordered huts to be built for us in the town; and that we might then go, accompanied by one of his people, to see them; and that when we were recovered from the fatigue of our long journey, he would be happy to see us." With this we

5. "Among the Kanui," wrote Sir Richmond Palmer, "a spear surmounted by a trident was the symbol of office of the principal chiefs."

took our leave.

Our huts were immediately so crowded with visitors, that we had not a moment's peace, and the heat was insufferable. Boo-Khaloom had delivered his presents from the Bashaw, and brought us a message of compliment, together with an intimation that our own would be received on the following day. About noon we received a summons to attend the sheikh; and we proceeded to the palace, preceded by our negroes, bearing the articles destined for the sheikh by our government; consisting of a double-barrelled gun, by Wilkinson, with a box, and all the apparatus complete, a pair of excellent pistols in a case, two pieces of superfine broad cloth, red and blue, to which we added a set of china, and two bundles of spices.

The ceremony of getting into the presence was ridiculous enough, although nothing could be more plain and devoid of pretension than the appearance of the sheikh himself. We passed through passages lined with attendants, the front men sitting on their hams; and when we advanced too quickly, we were suddenly arrested by these fellows, who caught forcibly hold of us by the legs, and had not the crowd prevented our falling, we should most infallibly have become prostrate before arriving in the presence. Previous to entering into the open court, in which we were received, our papouches, or slippers, were whipped off by those active though sedentary gentlemen of the chamber; and we were seated on some clean sand on each side of a raised bench of earth, covered with a carpet, on which the sheikh was reclining. We laid the gun and the pistols together before him, and explained to him the locks, turnscrews, and steel shot-cases holding two charges each, with all of which he seemed exceedingly well pleased: the powder-flask, and the manner in which the charge is divided from the body of powder, did not escape his observation; the other articles were taken off by the slaves, almost as soon as they were laid before him. Again we were questioned as to the object of our visit. The sheikh, however, showed evident satisfaction at our assurance that the king of England had heard of Bornou and himself; and, immediately turning to his kaganawha (counsellor), said, "This is in consequence of our defeating the Begharmis [people of Bagirmi]." Upon which, the chief who had most distinguished himself in these memorable battles, Bagah Furby (the gatherer of horses), seating himself in front of us, demanded, "Did he ever hear of me?" The immediate reply of "*Certainly*" did wonders for our cause. Exclamations were general; and, "Ah! then, your king must be a great man!" was re-echoed from every side. We had nothing offered us by way of refreshment, and took our leave.

I may here observe, that besides occasional presents of bullocks, camel-loads of wheat and rice, leather skins of butter, jars of honey, and honey in the comb, five or six wooden bowls were sent us, morning and evening, containing rice, with meat, paste made of barley flour, savoury but very greasy; and on our first arrival, as many had been sent of sweets, mostly composed of curd and honey.

In England a brace of trout might be considered as a handsome present to a traveller sojourning in the neighbourhood of a stream, but at Bornou things are done differently. A camel-load of bream, and a sort of mullet, was thrown before our huts on the second morning after our arrival; and for fear that should not be sufficient, in the evening another was sent.

We had a fsug, or market, in front of one of the principal gates of the town. Slaves, sheep, and bullocks, the latter in great numbers, were the principal live stock for sale. There were at least fifteen thousand persons gathered together, some of them coming from places two and three days distant. Wheat, rice, and gussub [sorghum], were abundant: tamarinds in the pod, ground nuts, ban beans, ochroes, and indigo; the latter is very good, and in great use amongst the natives to dye their lobes (shirts) and linen, stripes of deep indigo colour, or stripes of it alternately with white, being highly esteemed by most of the Bornou women: the leaves are moistened, and pounded up altogether when they are formed into lumps, and so brought to market. Of vegetables there was a great scarcity—onions, bastard tomatoes, alone were offered for sale; and of fruits not any: a few limes, which the sheikh had sent us from his garden, being the only fruit we had seen in Bornou. Leather was in great quantities; and the skins of the large snake, and pieces of the skin of the crocodile, used as an ornament for the scabbards of their daggers, were also brought to me for sale; and butter, leban (sour milk), honey, and wooden bowls, from Soudan. The costumes of the women, who for the most part were the vendors, were various: those of Kanem and Bornou were most numerous, and the former was as becoming as the latter had a contrary appearance. The variety in costume amongst the ladies consists entirely in the head ornaments; the only difference, in the scanty covering which is bestowed on the other parts of the person, lies in the choice of the wearer, who either ties the piece of linen, blue or white, under the arms, and across the breasts, or fastens it rather fantastically on one shoulder, leaving one breast naked. The Kanemboo women have small plaits of hair hanging down all around the head, quite to the poll of the neck, with a roll of leather or string of little brass beads in front, hanging down from the centre on each side of the face, which has by no means an unbecoming appearance: they have sometimes strings of silver rings instead of the brass, and a large round silver ornament in front of their foreheads. The female slaves from Musgow,[6] a large kingdom to the south-east of Mandara, are particularly disagreeable in their appearance, although considered as very trustworthy, and capable of great labour: their hair is rolled up in three large plaits, which extend from the forehead to the back of the neck, like the Bornowy; one larger in the centre, and two smaller on each side: they have silver studs in their nose, and one large one just under the lower lip of the size of a shilling, which goes quite through into the mouth; to make room for this ornament, a tooth or two is sometimes displaced.

The principal slaves are generally intrusted with the sale of such produce as the owner of them may have to dispose of, and if they come from any distance, the whole is brought on bullocks, which are harnessed after the fashion of the country, by a string or iron run through the cartilage of the nose, and a saddle of nut. The masters not unfrequently attend the fsug with their spears, and loiter about without interfering: purchases are mostly made by exchange of one commodity for another, or paid for by small beads, pieces of coral and amber, or the coarse linen manufac-

6. The Musgu, a pagan people of the Logone basin, who were much preyed on by powerful neighbours. They owed their survival to the impassable nature of their country which is much intersected by swampy waterways.

tured by all the people, and sold at forty gubka[7] for a dollar. . . .

Bornou March 12 1823

EXTRACT

On Monday the 17th Febry we made our entry into Kouka the present Capital of Bornou, altho' not the largest or most populous Town, but still it is the Capital. It has not been built above 8 years and is the work of an Usurper, if he may be so called, named Lameen el Kalmi [Al-Kanami], who built it after conquering the Country and driving out the Fellatas a Tribe who had some Years before overthrown the ancient Sultans and then reigned in their place. El Kalmi an Arab of strong natural understanding & courage, had long resided in Kanem as a Fighi [*faqi*, holyman] or writer of Charms & much respected for his abilities and Charity, he had sufficient address to raise an Army in Kanem to drive the Fellata [Fulani] from all the Bornou Country and when his Victorious Army whom the Natives of Bornou dared not oppose would have proclaimed him Sultan. He had magnanimity enough to refuse the Crown and not only place it on the Head of the remaining branch of the Ancient Sultans [Saifwa Dynasty], but first doing homage himself he insisted on all his followers doing likewise—there was quite as much policy as magnanimity in this act of Kalmi's as by that means he gained the hearts of all the Bornou people, who were too numerous for him to have set at defiance, for several years he lived at Angornou, the largest and most populous of any in the Country, having at least 50,000 Inhabitants, while he established the Sultan at Birnie, a Town about 3 miles distant; 12 years ago he however determined on building Kouka [Kakwa] which is about 18 miles N.W. of Angornou—His Kanem followers have here colonized and he is daily reconciling by the force of his Arms & otherwise the Shouans [Shuwa] or Arabs which are in his neighbourhood and already many of them have become Citizens of Kouka. These Shouans are of a fine dark copper colour with oval faces & acquiline noses; they seldom intermarry with the Negroes for each has an aversion to the color of the other—They were however always amongst Kalmi's bravest and most determined Enemies and the Measures he has taken to conciliate them will tend to give him more power than he ever possessed before—He can now bring 50,000 Men into the Field most of them mounted, and if they are any thing like the 4000 that met us on our approaching the Town on the 17th they are a very formidable force for a Barbarian Ruler. His Court is simplicity itself, as well as his manners, the dark avenues of his Mud Palace leading to his Apartment are lined with his Kanem Guards all plainly dressed in a Blue Tobe, or large Shirt, uncovered shaved heads with spears in their hands, round his person sit one or two of his principal Chiefs who on great occasions are clothed in the presents which the Bashaw may from time to time have sent him, two Negroe Slaves lay close behind him on a small Carpet with loaded pistols and a few fire arms, the only ones in his Country and of which he is uncommonly proud, are hung round the Walls—his dress is generally a Tobe of Soudan [?] or of Blue Linen with a Cashimere Turban—some of his horses are

---

7. Gubka; about a yard English.

beautiful, and he has a body guard of Kanem Negroes all habited in Coats of Iron Chain with skull caps of Iron on their heads, who really ride beautifully and have a very warlike appearance . . . Kalmi has been most successful in overcoming all the neighbouring Negro States, several[8] Kerdi Kafir Nations have by his means embraced Mohomatanism. By plundering them first, and demanding Tributes after, he has increased the consequence of the Bornou Sultan greatly. Beghermi has been a constant resource for him for the last 5 or 6 years as he has nearby annually made a most profitable expedition into that Country. By these means he has been enabled to indulge the Sultan's natural propensity who with his Court revel in all the folly and Bigotry of their Ancestors—this has had the effect of alienating the affections of the mass of the people greatly from the reigning Family and fixing them on himself, who with the half only his successes bring him, which he retains the other half going to the Sultan, he builds Towns and distributes alms to 1000s of the Inhabitants—Kalmi has I am convinced at any time the power of overthrowing the Ancient Government by a wave of his hand, but he is quite keen enough to know when that step should be taken, so as best to answer his Views.

Miram (princess in the Bornou language), now the divorced wife of the sheikh El Kanemy [Al-Kanami], was residing at Angala, and I requested permission to visit her. Her father had built for her a house, in which she constantly resided; and her establishment exceeded sixty persons. She was a very handsome, beautifully formed negress, of about thirty-five, and had imbibed much of that softness of manner which is so extremely prepossessing in the sheikh. Seated on an earthen throne, covered with a turkey carpet, and surrounded by twenty of her favourite slaves, all dressed alike, in fine white shirts, which reached to their feet, their necks, ears, and noses thickly ornamented with coral, she held her audience with very considerable grace, while four eunuchs guarded the entrance; and a negro dwarf, who measured three feet all but an inch, the keeper of her keys, sat before her with the insignia of office on his shoulder, and richly dressed in Soudan tobes. This little person afforded us a subject of conversation, and much laughter. Miram inquired whether we had such little fellows in my country, and when I answered in the affirmative, she said "*Ah gieb*! what are they good for? do they ever have children?" I answered, "Yes; that we had instances of their being fathers to tall and proper men." "Oh, wonderful!" she replied: "I thought so; they must be better then than this dog of mine; for I have given him eight of my handsomest and youngest slaves, but it is all to no purpose. I would give a hundred bullocks, and twenty slaves, to the woman who would bear this wretch a child." The wretch, and an ugly wretch he was, shook his large head, grinned, and slobbered copiously from his extensive mouth, at this flattering proof of his mistress's partiality. . . .

---

8. These two terms are synonimous & mean unbelievers.

40. RENÉ CAILLIÉ

THE TRANS-SAHARAN CARAVAN. 1828.

The French explorer René Caillié (1799–1838) was the first European to visit Timbuktu and return alive. Disguised as an Arab returning to Egypt. he made his way from the Rio Nunez to Djenné, whence he traveled by canoe down the Niger to Timbuktu. He found the mysterious city in 1828 to be a rather squalid, middle-sized Sudanic town with no sign of the great splendors described by Leo Africanus. Leaving Timbuktu, Caillié crossed the desert from Arawan and Taghaza with a caravan of 1,400 camels taking slaves, gold, ivory, gum, and ostrich feathers to Morocco. After many harrowing adventures he reached Fez and then France, where his description shattered, but did not completely destroy, Europe's romantic image of Timbuktu as a magnificent and glamorous city.

The caravan destined for el-Arawan, with which I had resolved to travel, was to set out on the 4th of May, at sun-rise. My host was up so early that morning as to allow me time, before my departure, to breakfast with him on tea, new bread, and butter. That nothing might diminish the agreeable impression which my stay at Timbuctoo had made upon me, I met, on departing, the host of Major Laing, who made me accept some new clothing for my journey.

Sidi-Abdallahi accompanied me to some distance from his house, and, at parting with me, he affectionately pressed my hand and wished me a good journey. This farewell detained me almost too long. To rejoin the caravan, which had already proceeded to a considerable distance, I was obliged, as well as three slaves who had also remained behind, to run a whole mile through the sand. This effort fatigued me so much, that, on reaching the caravan, I fell down in a state of insensibility; I was lifted up and placed on a loaded camel, where I sat among the packages, and though dreadfully shaken I was too glad at being relieved from the labour of walking to complain of my beast.

On the 4th of May, 1828, at eight in the morning, we directed our route to the north over a sandy soil, almost moving, quite level, and completely barren. However, at the distance of two miles from the town, we met with a few shrubs resembling junipers, and some rather tall clusters of *mimosa ferruginea* which yield a gum of inferior quality. The inhabitants of Timbuctoo send their slaves hither for fire-wood. The heat was most oppressive, and the progress of the camels was extremely slow; for, as they moved along, they browsed on the thistles and withered herbs, which they found scattered here and there on these plains. During this first day the slaves were allowed to drink at discretion, as I was. This conduct was doubtless very humane; nevertheless, I was soon shocked by an act of barbarity, which I had the misfortune to see too often repeated. A poor Bambara slave of twenty-five

From René Caillié, *Travels through Central Africa to Timbuctoo, and Across the Great Desert to Morocco*, Performed in the Years 1824–28 (London: H. Colburn and R. Bentley, 1830), vol. II, pp. 88–97.

was cruelly treated by some Moors, who compelled him to walk, without allowing him to halt for a moment, or to quench his burning thirst. The complaints of this unfortunate creature, who had never been accustomed to endure such extraordinary privations, might have moved the hardest heart. Sometimes he would beg to rest himself against the crupper [hindquarters] of a camel, and at others he threw himself down on the sand in despair. In vain did he implore, with uplifted hands, a drop of water; his cruel masters answered his prayers and his tears only with stripes.

At Timbuctoo the merchants give the slaves shirts, such as are worn in the country, that they may be decently covered; but on the route the Moors of the caravans, who are the most barbarous men I ever knew, take the good shirts from them and give them others all in rags.

At five in the evening the caravan, the camels of which amounted to nearly six hundred, halted in a ravine of yellow sand, which was, however, pretty solid. Here these animals found some herbage, and the spot appeared to me delightful. A slave, who was barely allowed time to take a drink of water, was ordered to look after our camels, and we thought of nothing but how to pass the night quietly; but before we laid ourselves down to sleep, we made our supper on a calabash of water, some dokhnou [dukhn: millet], and the bread which I had received from Sidi-Abdallahi; the bread being hard we soaked it in the water, into which we put a little butter and honey. This mixture was to us a delicious beverage. The slaves had for their supper some sangleh seasoned with butter and salt. These good-natured creatures were so kind as to offer me some of their meal.

On the 5th of May, at sun-rise, we resumed our journey. We still proceeded towards the north, upon ground similar to that over which we passed on the preceding day. A few stunted bushes were descried here and there, and also some salvadoras, which the camels devoured.

Towards noon we approached a less level region, where the ground was raised into slightly elevated mounds, all inclining in the direction from east to west. The heat was suffocating, on account of the east wind, which raised great clouds of sand: our lips were covered with it; our thirst became insupportable; and our sufferings increased in proportion as we advanced further in the desert. We fell in with two Tooariks [Tuaregs], who were going to el-Arawan, and whom we took to be the scouts of a troop of these marauders. Fortunately they were alone. They were both mounted on one camel. On the left arm they had a leather buckler; by the side, a poniard; and in the right hand, a pike. Knowing that they should meet us in their route, they had brought no provisions with them, and trusted to the caravan for a supply. These robbers, who would have trembled at the slightest menace, if seriously made, took advantage of the terror which their name and the crimes of their tribe every where spread, and obtained whatever they demanded: in a word, the best of every thing was presented to them. On the one hand, there was a sort of rivalship in offering them whatever they chose to eat; on the other, to give them water, though it would be six days before we should come to any. At last, after they had staid with us three days, we had the satisfaction to see them depart, and to be delivered from their troublesome company.

At four in the evening we encamped to pass the night, during which we were oppressed by excessive heat, caused by a dead calm. The sky was heavy and covered with clouds which seemed immoveable in the immensity of space. Still the heat continued intense.

Before proceeding farther, I ought to inform the reader how I continued to make an estimate of the route. We travelled, at an average, about two miles an hour. At night we proceeded almost constantly in a northerly direction. Being afraid that my pocket compass would be noticed if I took it out to consult it, I judged of our course during the day by the sun; in the night, by the pole-star.

It is by this star that the Arabs are guided in all their excursions through the desert. The oldest caravan conductors go first, to lead the way. A sand-hill, a rock, a difference of colour in the sand, a few tufts of herbage, are infallible marks, which enable them to recognize their situation. Though without a compass, or any instrument for observation, they possess so completely the habit of noticing the most minute things, that they never go astray, though they have no path traced out for them, and though the wind in an instant completely covers with sand and obliterates the track of the camels.

The desert, however, does not always present the same aspect, or, consequently the same difficulties. In some parts I found it covered with rocks and gravel, which bore the traces of caravans that had passed long before. Besides, though the desert is a plain of sand and rock, the Arab commits few errors in crossing it, and is seldom wrong to the extent of half an hour in fixing the time of arrival at the wells. I ought not to omit to mention, that these wells are almost constantly found covered over, and that the first thing done on the arrival of a caravan is to clear away the sand.

On the 6th of May we resumed our march, at three in the morning, and continued our route to the north. Still the same soil, the same aridity, and the same uniformity, as on the preceding days.

The atmosphere was very heavy all day, and the heat excessive. It seemed as if we should have rain. The sun, concealed by clouds, appeared only at long intervals. But our prayers did not obtain from Heaven a drop of rain. In spite of all the prognostics no shower fell. The further northward we proceeded the more barren the country became. We no longer saw either thistles or salvadoras: sad consolations, where all nature wears so frightful an aspect! The plain had here the precise appearance of the ocean; perhaps such as the bed of a sea would have, if left by the water. In fact, the winds form in the sand undulating furrows, like the waves of the sea when a breeze slightly ruffles its surface. At the sight of this dismal spectacle, of this awful abandonment and nakedness, I forgot for a moment my hardships, to reflect on the violent convulsions which thus appeared to have dried up part of the ocean, and of the sudden catastrophes which have changed the face of our globe.

At eleven in the morning we halted. The heat was insupportable, and we seated ourselves beside some unhealthy looking mimosas, over which we extended our wrappers, for these shrubs being destitute of leaves afforded no shade of themselves. Under our tents thus formed, we had distributed to us a calabash of water, which was rendered tepid by the east wind. According to our custom, we threw into the water some handfuls of dokhnou. Finally, to relieve ourselves from every immediate care, we sent a slave to watch our camels, which were endeavouring to refresh themselves by browsing on some withered herbage. We then lay down to sleep on the sand, which at this place was covered with small stones. This was not done from indolence, but from consideration; for it was proper to wait for night to take advantage of the coolness, when we might travel more at our ease than during the day, in which the calms were sometimes more insupportable than the burning sun. During these calms I could not close my eyes, while the Moors slept soundly. The same kind of calm often prevails during the night, but then there is some compensation in the absence of the sun. In the inhabited countries, the night, or rather the latter part of the night, is always the most agreeable portion of the twenty-four hours. It is at day-break that the flowers exhale all their perfumes: the air is then gently agitated, and the birds commence their songs. Recollections, at once pleasing and painful, turned my thoughts to the south. In the midst of this frightful desert could I fail to regret the land which nature has embellished?

The caravans which traverse the desert are under no absolute commander; every one manages his camels as he pleases, whether he has many or few; some have fifteen, others six or ten; and there are individuals who possess not more than three; I have even seen some with only two, but these were very poor. Such persons join richer travellers and take care of their camels; in return, they are supplied with provisions and water during the journey.

The Moors always lay out the profits of their journeys in the purchase of camels, and none of them travel to Timbuctoo without possessing at least one. The camels do not advance in files, as they would do in our roads lined by hedges and cultivated lands. On the contrary they move in all directions, in groupes, or single, but in this journey their route is always between N.N.E. and N.N.W. Those which belong to one master keep together, and do not mix with strange camels; and I have seen as many as fifty grouped together in this way. A camel's load is five hundred pounds, and the carriage from Timbuctoo to Tafilet costs ten or twelve gold mitkhals,[1] which are paid in advance.

The camels which convey merchandise of light weight, such as ostrich feathers, clothes, and stuffs in the piece, have their loads made up with slaves, water, and rice; for, the load being paid for according to its weight, the proprietors of the camels, if that weight were not completed, would gain nothing by the carriage of merchandise more cumbersome than heavy. When the caravan stops, the groupes of camels are kept at the distance of two hundred paces from each other, to obviate the confusion which would arise if they were suffered to mix together.

When the Moors return to their country, they do not carry back merely ostrich feathers and ivory; but they take also gold, some more, and some less. I saw some who had as much as the value of a hundred mitkhals. This gold is generally sent to the merchants of Tafilet by their correspondents at Timbuctoo, in return for the merchandise sent by the former, and sold on their account by the latter. During our halts in the deserts, I often saw the Moors weighing their gold in little scales similar to ours, which are made in Morocco. The gold which is conveyed by these travelling

1. The value of the gold mitkhal is about twelve francs, and the silver mitkhal about four.

clerks of the desert is carefully rolled up in pieces of cloth, with a label, on which are written the weight of the metal and the name of the individual to whom it belongs.

When night set in, we took our usual supper, consisting of water, bread, butter, and honey. Several Moors, with whom we were not acquainted, came and asked us for a supper; they then invited the two Moors who were of our party to share their mess of baked rice and butter. Though they knew that they had partaken of my provisions, yet they did not think proper to invite me, a proof, that notwithstanding all my efforts, there existed a feeling of distrust towards me. At sun-set a north breeze arose, which, though not very cool, was nevertheless very reviving, and enabled me to enjoy a little sleep.

About eleven at night we set out, still proceeding northward, and directing our course by the pole-star. The camels are so well acquainted with the desert that, as soon as they are loaded, they take, as if by instinct, the northern course. It would seem that they are guided by the recollection of the springs of water which are found in that direction. I really believe that a traveller, though alone, might safely trust himself to the guidance of his camel.

The night was hot and calm, and the clear sky was studded with stars. We had before us the great and the little wain which appeared very near the horizon. As I could not sleep, I amused myself by observing the courses of the stars; I saw in the east the remarkable groupe called the constellation of Orion; I watched it during nearly half its course, almost to our zenith. On the approach of day, the stars disappeared and seemed to sink into an ocean of sand.

The camels never accelerate their pace, which is naturally somewhat tardy. When they are in haste, they thrust forward their necks, the motion of which corresponds with that of their legs. They are led by men on foot, whose labour is so fatiguing, that it is necessary to relieve them every two hours.

The ground over which we travelled during the night appeared to me to be even more barren than that which we had passed on the preceding days. For whole hours in succession we did not see a single blade of grass.

At eleven in the morning the heat became excessive, and we halted at a place where we found a few little banks of sand. A slave was sent to seek out a few bushes that might afford us shade, but no such thing was to be discovered. The reflection of the rays of the sun on the sand augmented the heat. It was impossible to stand barefoot on the sand without experiencing intolerable pain. The desert is here and there interspersed with a few hills, and we found at very distant intervals a little grass for the camels.

We had been the whole of the morning without drink, and as soon as our tents were pitched we slaked our thirst. Our water began to diminish in proportion as our thirst increased, therefore we did not cook any thing for supper, but merely drank a little dokhnou. About eleven at night we broke up our camp and proceeded northward: at seven in the morning we turned N.N.W.

At eleven o'clock on the 8th of May, the insupportable heat obliged us to halt on a spot as flat and barren as that at which we had stopped on the preceding day. We pitched our tents, and assembled beneath them. Some drink was distributed to us;

and, as we had tasted none since five o'clock on the preceding evening, our thirst was very great. Though the water had received a bad taste from the leathern bag, it was nevertheless exceedingly grateful. I observed some ravens and vultures, the only inhabitants of these deserts. They subsist on the carcases of the camels that die and are left behind on the road. At half past six in the evening, after having refreshed ourselves with a glass of water and dokhnou, we proceeded on our journey. We travelled all night in a northerly direction. The camels, finding no pasture, went on without stopping.

About 8 o'clock on the morning of the 9th of May, we halted in a sandy plain, where we found a little grass for our poor camels. There we perceived at a distance the camels of el-Arawan.

In the morning, little before sun-rise, the Moors who accompanied me shewed me the spot where Major Laing was murdered [in 1826]. I there observed the site of a camp. I averted my eyes from this scene of horror, and secretly dropped a tear — the only tribute of regret I could render to the ill-fated traveller, to whose memory no monument will ever be reared on the spot where he perished.

Several Moors of our caravan, who had witnessed the fatal event, told me that the major had but little property with him when he was stopped by the chief of the Zawâts, and that he had offered five hundred piastres to a Moor to conduct him to Souyerah (Mogador). This the Moor refused to do, for what reason I was not informed, and I dared not inquire. They also spoke of the sextant, which I have mentioned above.

Having pitched our tents near some water, we could drink as much as we pleased. Rice was boiled for our dinner and we were somewhat indemnified for the privations we had undergone in the preceding days. At six in the evening we proceeded northwards over a very level sandy soil, on which were scattered a few solitary patches of vegetation. Though the sand has a tolerable consistency, yet not a tree was to be seen. Towards nine in the evening, we arrived at El-Arawan, another commercial entrepot. We encamped outside the city, and in the neighbourhood I observed several tents and camels, which I was told belonged to the caravan, waiting for the signal for departure. Our arrival was greeted by the howling of dogs, a circumstance which reminded me that I had seen none of those animals at Timbuctoo.

Being unaccustomed to riding on camels, I found myself extremely fatigued by the journey. The moment we stopped, I spread my wrapper upon the sand, and fell into a profound sleep. I did not find the heat so oppressive as it had been on the preceding days. I was roused to partake of an excellent couscous brought from the city.

41. HENRY FRANCIS FYNN

SHAKA. 1830.

Henry Francis Fynn arrived in South Africa in 1818, and six years later went to Port Natal as leader of an expedition of the Farewell Trading Company that was sent to open up the eastern coast. Soon after his arrival he visited Shaka, ruler of the Zulu state. Fynn's accounts of the events of this time and of Nguni history are the earliest and most reliable surviving record. Fynn remained at Port Natal and traded with Shaka and his successor, Dingane, until 1834, after which time he became an interpreter to Governor Benjamin D'Urban and British Resident for various southern Nguni chiefdoms. In 1852 he returned to the British colony of Natal, where he served as a magistrate and was regarded as an expert on native affairs. He never published the book based on his experience because he lost the original of his journal, but his writings have been preserved in the works of other travelers and annalists and in government reports. Fynn died in Natal in 1861.

I may at once state that the distance from the port to Shaka's residence was 200 miles. Our progress was exceedingly slow, each day's journey being arranged by Mbikwana [Shaka's uncle]. We afterwards found out that he had not taken us by a direct route, but to kraals of minor chiefs and some of the barracks of Shaka's regiments. Cattle-slaughtering occurred sometimes twice and thrice a day. Numbers of Zulus joined our column in order to relieve Mbikwana's people of their burdens. We were struck with astonishment at the order and discipline maintained in the country through which we travelled. The regimental kraals, especially the upper parts thereof, also the kraals of chiefs, showed that cleanliness was a prevailing custom and this not only inside their huts, but outside, for there were considerable spaces where neither dirt nor ashes were to be seen.[1]

Frequently on the journey we saw large parties seated with grotesquely dressed men apparently lecturing in their midst, and on several occasions saw individuals seized and carried off and instantly put to death. The grotesque characters we learned were "witch finders" whilst those singled out and put to death were said to be "evil doers."[2]

From Henry Francis Fynn, *Diaries*, edited by James Stuart and Daniel McKinnon Malcolm (Pietermaritzburg, South Africa: Shuter & Shooter [Pty.] Ltd., 1950). pp. 70–80. Reprinted by permission.

1. One afternoon seeing a flock of vultures near us, I shot one and on going to pick it up found they were devouring dead bodies, of which there were five. They appeared to have been killed the day before. Author's MS.

2. One day we arrived at a large kraal containing 190 huts, the barracks of one of Shaka's regiments. We had not been there many minutes before our attention was drawn to a party of 150 natives sitting in a circle with a man opposite them, apparently interrogating them. In reply, they each beat the ground with a stick and said, He-sa-gee! [*Yizwa Zhil Editor.*] After they had been answering with the same word about an hour, three of them were pointed out and killed on the spot. This man, whom they called an inyanga, or as we should say a necromancer, was dressed in an ape skin cap; a number of pieces of different roots were tied round his neck; and a small shield and assegai were in one hand, and the tail of cow in the other. He was an interpreter of dreams and thought capable of telling what has happened in any other part of the country, also if one has injured another by poison or otherwise. His decision is fatal to the unfortunate individuals pointed out by him. Author's MS.

Messengers passed three or four times a day between Shaka and Mbikwana, the former enquiring about our progress and doubtless directing how we should proceed so as to fall in with his own preparations for our reception. We had thus dallied 13 days on the road in travelling 200 miles, when the locality of Shaka's residence was pointed out to us about 15 miles off. While encamped that night we saw much commotion going on in our neighbourhood. Troops of cattle were being driven in advance; regiments were passing near by and on distant hills, interspersed with regiments of girls, decorated in beads and brass with regimental uniformity, carrying on their heads large pitchers of native beer, milk, and cooked food. The approaching scene we anticipated witnessing cheered us considerably that evening. Farewell and Petersen expressed extreme affection and attachment for one another, with mutual apologies for past small differences.

It was not until ten o'clock the following morning that a proposal was made about advancing. In about two hours we arrived at a ridge from which we beheld an extensive and very picturesque basin before us, with a river running through it, called the Umfolozi.[3]

We were requested to make a stand under a large euphorbia tree, from whence, about a mile before us, we saw the residence of Shaka, viz: a native kraal nearly two miles in circumference.

While in this position, messengers went backwards and forwards between Mbikwana and Shaka. At length one came and desired Mr. Farewell and myself to advance, leaving Mr. Petersen and our servants and native followers, who were carrying Shaka's present, at the euphorbia tree. Mbikwana and about 20 of his followers accompanied us.

On entering the great cattle kraal we found drawn up within it about 80,000 natives in their war attire.[4] Mbikwana requested me to gallop within the circle, and immediately on my starting to do so one general shout broke forth from the whole mass, all pointing at me with their sticks. I was asked to gallop round the circle two or three times in the midst of tremendous shouting of the words, "*UJojo wokhalo!*" (the sharp or active finch of the ridge).[5] Mr. Farewell and I were then led by

3. Evidently the Umhlathuze is meant, for the Umfoloxi cannot be seen from the position the travellers had now got to. *Editor*.

4. "On entering its gates we perceived about 12,000 men in their war attire, drawn up in a circle to receive us." The author here refers to warriors only, whereas in the text he includes regiments of girls, women, servants, etc., as well. *Editor*.

5. Literally the words mean: Long tailed Finch of the Ridge, which implies that the person to whom the words are applied is quick and brave in attacking and overcoming his enemy. *Editor*. It is customary for the principal warriors of each regiment, in their war dances, to dance forwards [i.e. each dances a passeul by rushing forwards, gesticulating as he does so with shield and weapons he is carrying.—*Editor*.], when they are applauded by their own heroic names. They, therefore, on the occasion in question, considered I was adopting their own practice, hence cheered me by a phrase or name commonly found among their own heroes. On entering the kraal's gates . . . we were desired to gallop two or three times round. then twice more; then to return and bring the remainder of the party with us. We were desired to gallop four times more round the kraal and then stand all together about 20 yards from a large tree at the head of the kraal. Author's note.

The probabilities are that Fynn began galloping alone, hence he was acclaimed, his prowess as a pioneer doctor having already become known, as stated in the text, and that in the succeeding gallops he was accompanied by Farewell. *Editor*.

Mbikwana to the head of the kraal, where the masses of the people were considerably denser than elsewhere. The whole force remained stationary, as, indeed, it had been since the commencement of the reception.

Mbikwana, standing in our midst, addressed some unseen individual in a long speech, in the course of which we were frequently called upon by him to answer "*Yebo*," that is to affirm as being true all he was saying, though perfectly ignorant of what was being said.[6]

While the speech was being made I caught sight of an individual in the background whom I concluded to be Shaka, and, turning to Farewell, pointed out and said: "Farewell, there is Shaka." This was sufficiently audible for him to hear and perceive that I had recognised him. He immediately held up his hand, shaking his finger at me approvingly. Farewell, being near-sighted and using an eye-glass, could not distinguish him.[7]

Elephant tusks were then brought forward. One was laid before Farewell and another before me.[8] Shaka then raised the stick in his hand and after striking with it right and left,[9] the whole mass broke from their position and formed up into regiments. Portions of each of these rushed to the river and the surrounding hills, while the remainder, forming themselves into a circle, commenced dancing with Shaka in their midst.[10]

It was a most exciting scene, surprising to us, who could not have imagined that a nation termed "savages" could be so disciplined and kept in order.

Regiments of girls, headed by officers of their own sex, then entered the centre of the arena to the number of 8,000–10,000, each holding a slight staff in her hand. They joined in the dance, which continued for about two hours.

Shaka now came towards us, evidently to seek our applause. [The following from Bird's *Annals of Natal*, contributed by the author, describes the scene.] "The King came up to us and told us not to be afraid of his people, who were now coming up to us in small divisions, each division driving cattle before it. The men were singing and dancing and whilst so doing advancing and receding even as one sees the surf do on a seashore. The whole country, as far as our sight could reach, was covered with numbers of people and droves of cattle. The cattle had been assorted

6. Evidently the King, but Shaka was so surrounded by his chiefs that we could not see him. Author's note.

7. A speech in answer to Mbikwana's was then made by a chief opposite. Author's note.

8. Mbikwana now made another speech. Author's MS.

9. "and springing out from amidst the chiefs." Author's MS.

10. In another MS. Fynn has: The whole body then ran to the lower end of the kraal, leaving us alone, with the exception of one man who had been hidden in the crowd. This man proved to be a native of the Cape Frontier, who had been taken prisoner in a war between the Colonists and Kaffirs and sent to Robben Island. Captain Owen of the Leven had taken him as an interpreter to attend him during his survey of the Eastern coast. Afterwards the interpreter had been given over to Farewell on his voyage to St. Lucia Bay. There he ran off and sought protection with Shaka, who gave him the name of Hlambamanzi, denoting one who had crossed (swum) the water. Among the colonists he had been known by the name of Jacob Sumbiti. He spoke good Dutch.

Further particulars about this man will be found in Isaacs, *Travels and Adventures in Eastern Africa*, II, 251–58, 264–69; Owen, *Narratives of Voyages to Explore Shores of Africa, Arabia and Madagascar*, I, 59, II, 222. *Editor.*

according to their colour. . . . After exhibiting their cattle for two hours, they drew together in a circle, and sang and danced to their war song. Then the people returned to the cattle, again exhibiting them as before, and, at intervals, dancing and singing. The women now entered the kraal, each having a long thin stick in the right hand, and moving it in time to the song. They had not been dancing many minutes, when they had to make way for the ladies of the seraglio [harem], besides about 150 others, who were called sisters. These danced in parties of eight, arranged in fours, each party wearing different coloured beads, which were crossed from the shoulders to the knees. Each wore a head-dress of black feathers, and four brass collars, fitting closely to the neck. When the King joined in the dance, he was accompanied by the men. This dance lasted half an hour. The order observed and the precision of every movement was interpreted to us by his interpreter, Hlambamanzi. He desired to know from us if ever we had seen such order in any other state, assured us that he was the greatest king in existence, that his people were as numerous as the stars, and that his cattle were innumerable. The people now dispersed, and he directed a chief to lead us to a kraal where we could pitch our tents. He sent us a sheep, a basket of corn, an ox, and a pot of beer, about three gallons. At seven o'clock, we sent up four rockets and fired off eight guns. He sent people to look at these, but from fear did not show himself out of his hut. The following morning we were requested to mount our horses and proceed to the King's quarters. We found him sitting under a tree at the upper end of the kraal decorating himself and surrounded by about 200 people. A servant was kneeling by his side holding a shield above him to keep off the glare of the sun. Round his forehead he wore a turban[11] of otter skin with a feather of a crane erect in front, fully two feet long, and a wreath of scarlet feathers, formerly worn, only, by men of high rank. Ear ornaments made from dried sugar cane, carved round the edge, with white ends, and an inch in diameter, were let into the lobes of the ears, which had been cut to admit them. From shoulder to shoulder, he wore bunches, five inches in length, of the skins of monkeys and genets, twisted like the tails of these animals. These hung half down the body. Round the ring on the head,[12] were a dozen tastefully arranged bunches of the loury feathers, neatly tied to thorns which were stuck into the hair. Round his arms were white ox-tail tufts, cut down the middle so as to allow the hair to hang about the arm, to the number of four for each arm. Round the waist, there was a kilt or petticoat, made of skins of monkeys and genets, and twisted as before described, having small tassels round the top. The kilt reached to the knees, below which were white ox-tails fitted to the legs so as to hang down to the ankles. He had a white shield with a single black spot,[13] and one

11. This word, often applied to Zulu head-dresses and especially Shaka's, seems to us inaccurate. Zulus do not wear turbans. They wear headbands or circlets cut out or made of various skins or other substances. *Editor.*

12. This clearly proves that Shaka wore a head-ring (*isicoco*). We have sometimes heard doubts expressed on this point by Europeans. Well-informed natives, however, believe the King to have worn a ring, without, in these latter days, being able to prove it. The only portrait of Shaka we know of which can claim to be authentic (that in Isaacs' *Travels and Adventures in Eastern Africa*, I, 58) leaves one in doubt, for the band there shown round the head may well be the circlet or headband known as *umqhele.* *Editor.*

13. Somewhat oval in shape (seven inches by five inches) about the size of a man's open hand, it was midway down the shield and on the right-hand edge thereof. *Editor.*

assegai. When thus equipped he certainly presented a fine and most martial appearance.

While he was dressing himself, his people proceeded, as on the day before, to show droves of cattle, which were still flocking in, repeatedly varying the scene with singing and dancing. In the meantime, we observed Shaka gave orders for a man standing close to us to be killed, for what crime we could not learn, but we soon found this to be a very common occurrence.[14]

Mr. Petersen, unfortunately, at this moment placed a musical box on the ground, and, striking it with a switch, moved the stop. Shaka heard the music. It seemed to produce in him a superstitious feeling. He turned away with evident displeasure and went back immediately to the dance.

Those portions of regiments which had separated prior to the dance now returned from the river and from behind the adjoining hills, driving before them immense herds of cattle. A grand cattle show was now being arranged. Each regiment drove towards us thousands of cattle that had been allotted to their respective barracks, the colour of each regiment's cattle corresponding with that of the shield the men carried, which, in turn, served to distinguish one regiment from another. No cattle of differing colour from those allotted to a given regiment were allowed to intermix. There were many droves without horns, others with pendulous projections, four or six inches long, which covered a considerable portion of the animal. The cattle of the other droves had four, six, and eight horns apiece. This show of cattle continued till sunset, with dancing at intervals, when we proposed to pitch the tents we had brought with us. A man was ordered to point out a spot for the purpose. Greatly to Farewell's astonishment, this man proved to be Jacob, his interpreter, who had landed at St. Lucia the year previous when he, Farewell, lost his boats and the sailors therein were drowned. Jacob had been taken to Shaka, who immediately appointed him one of the sentries for guarding his establishment.

Two oxen were slaughtered for us. After dinner we prepared to retire, but messengers from Shaka requested us to go to him, with Jacob the interpreter.[15] I was then led into the seraglio, where I found him seated in a carved wooden chair and surrounded by about 400 girls, two or three chiefs and two servants in attendance.

My name Fynn had been converted into Sofili by the people in general: by this, after desiring me to sit in front of him, he several times accosted me in the course

14. Bird, *Annals of Natal*, I, 77.

15. The first meeting of Shaka with Farewell, Fynn, and the rest of the party was manifestly a unique and memorable occasion. Instead of the formal, stiff and constrained ceremonial customary at such a moment, Shaka, whose heart had been mysteriously touched by the advent of British settlers to his shores converted the occasion into a grand and dramatically planned festival. We cannot but think these warm-hearted exhibitions of regard should be attributed in the main to two influences seemingly trivial in themselves: (a) Jacob's previous lengthy contact with worthy officers of the Royal British Navy; (b) Fynn's discreet, courageous and humane bearing during the weeks he was striving to open up communication with Shaka. His spontaneous humanity straightway disarmed all suspicion and even caused him to be taken as typical of the race he belonged to. Thus, through the agency of Fynn and Jacob, the British people henceforth began to stand in a favourable light. Shaka, despot though he was, one of the greatest the world has ever known, took them to his heart and, as will he seen, never failed to treat them as friends. More than this, the conviction then arrived at as to their friendliness has, after many sad and trying vicissitudes of later years, been honoured down to the present time. *Editor.*

of the following dialogue:

"I hear you have come from umGeorge, is it so? Is he as great a king as I am?"

Fynn: "Yes; King George is one of the greatest kings in the world."

Shaka: "I am very angry with you," said while putting on a severe countenance. "I shall send a messenger to umGeorge and request him to kill you. He sent you to me not to give medicine to my dogs." All present immediately applauded what Shaka had said. "Why did you give my dogs medicine?" (in allusion to the woman I was said to have brought back to life after death).

Fynn: "It is a practice of our country to help those who are in need, if able to do so."

Shaka: "Are you then the doctor of dogs? You were sent here to be my doctor."

Fynn: "I am not a doctor and not considered by my countrymen to be one."

Shaka: "Have you medicine by you?"

Fynn: "Yes."

Shaka: "Then cure me, or I will have you sent to umGeorge to have you killed."

Fynn: "What is the matter with you?"

Shaka: "That is your business to find out."

Fynn: "Stand up and let me see your person."

Shaka: "Why should I stand up?"

Fynn: "That I may see if I can find out what ails you."

Shaka stood up but evidently disliked my approaching him closely. A number of girls held up lighted torches. I looked about his person and, after reflecting on the great activity he had shown during the day, was satisfied he had not much the matter with him. I, however, observed numerous black marks on his loins where native doctors had scarified him, and at once said he had pains in his loins. He held his hand before his mouth in astonishment, upon which my wisdom was applauded by all present. Shaka then strictly charged me not to give medicine to his dogs, and, after a few commonplace questions in which he showed good humour, I was permitted to retire for the night.[16]

Very few, if any, of the Zulu army had any sleep that night. Cattle were slaughtered in great numbers, and all the country round about was illuminated by the fires, around which the people sat in groups.

The following day had been appointed by Shaka for receiving our present, which, fortunately, had been well chosen by Farewell for presentation to so superior a chief as Shaka. It consisted of every description of beads at that time procurable in Cape Town, and far superior to those Shaka had previously obtained from the Portuguese at Delagoa. There was a great variety of woollen blankets, a large quantity of brass bars, turned and lacquered, and sheets of copper, also pigeons, a pig, cats, and dogs. There was, moreover, a full-dress military coat, with epaulettes covered with gold lace. Though Shaka showed no open gratitude, we saw clearly that he was satisfied. He was very interested in the live animals, especially the pig, until it got into his milk stores where it committed great havoc, and set all the

16. I remained till ten o'clock when I left him with a promise that, agreeable to his request, I would remain with him a month after the departure of Messrs. Farewell and Petersen. Author's MS.

women in the seraglio screaming for assistance. All this ended in the pig being killed.[17]

The showing of cattle and dancing continued during the day, whilst other regiments, which had come from a great distance, arrived and took part in the festivities. Among the articles we had brought were some Congreve rockets. These we kept back. On returning to our camp, as the evening was dark, we fired them off, having first informed Shaka, and asked him to order his people to look upwards. Their surprise was great; I, however, question if the showing of such wonders to ignorant natives is advisable after so short an acquaintance between white and black as ours had been. In conversation on our object in coming to Natal, this part of South Africa, Shaka showed great desire that we should live at the port. Each evening he sent for me and conversed with me through the Kaffir Jacob, the interpreter, for three or four hours.

On the first day of our visit we had seen no less than ten men carried off to death. On a mere sign by Shaka, viz: the pointing of his finger, the victim would be seized by his nearest neighbours; his neck would be twisted, and his head and body beaten with sticks, the nobs of some of these being as large as a man's fist. On each succeeding day, too, numbers of others were killed; their bodies would then be carried to an adjoining hill and there impaled. We visited this spot on the fourth day. It was truly a Golgotha, swarming with hundreds of vultures. The effects of this together with the scenes of death made Mr. Petersen decide at once to dissolve the partnership and leave for the Cape.

In the afternoon of the fifth day Shaka sent for me and requested me to proceed with some of his servants to a distant kraal where the chief Mupangazitha was very ill. I went and found him in high fever. I bled him, gave him medicine, and caused him to be brought to a full perspiration. At midday on the following day he was able to report himself comparatively well.[18] As this captain was a great favourite with Shaka, my success gave him much pleasure.

On taking leave of the King on the following morning, Shaka presented Farewell and myself with five elephant tusks each and 40 head of cattle, and promised he would send out his soldiers to kill elephants for us. I accompanied Messrs. Farewell and Petersen a few miles, returned to Shaka by sunset, and sat with him two or three hours in the evening.

---

17. The bringing of the live animals to Shaka was due to a suggestion by Shaka's uncle Mbikwana, who had returned with me to Natal to accompany us all to Shaka's residence. He asked us not to omit to take one of each species of domestic animals we had brought with us, among which was a pig. All were taken to the *isigodlo*, a seraglio, for the amusement of the women. Author's MS.

18. Five days afterwards I heard of his final recovery. Author's note.

42. A. C. P. GAMITTO

THE MARAVI. 1831.

A. C. P. Gamitto (1806–1866) was second in command of the Monteiro expedition that set out to open a transcontinental route from Mozambique to Angola between 1831 and 1832—an abortive mission that Lacerda similarly had failed to accomplish a generation before. The Maravi described by Gamitto are one of the principal groups in the modern state of Malawi, which takes its name from the former chiefdoms of the Maravi west of Lake Malawi. The Maravi claim to have originated in Lubaland, and although the Portuguese believed that the Maravi built a great empire, the probability is that no one chief became paramount, as was the case in the kingdom of the Kazembe.

The territory occupied by these people is one of the largest in this part of Africa. Its inhabitants, who are in continual warfare among themselves, are the subjects of a great number of small chiefs or princes who are forever trying to destroy one another; this is one reason for the poor opinion that foreigners hold of this country in spite of its size and population. The land, properly known today by the name of Marave, is bounded in the west by the Shombwe stream, which divides it from the Cheva; and in the east by the Mukakamwe torrent, which separates it from the Portuguese dominions of Tete district which extend on the left bank of the Zambezi as far as the Lupata. In the north, the boundary is with the Bororo and the Maganja; and in the south the boundary is the Zambezi, which divides it from the Munhaes of Monomotapa and the Portuguese territory of the district mentioned.

The part which we traversed, which is not its widest part, would be about 59 leagues. Its length from north to south comprises a very great extent, but not knowing how much I am unable to calculate the total area. In the east, north, and south these people border Portuguese lands.

Formerly this region was divided into two dominions, Munhaes and Maraves; and today these people have taken various names. Those referred to above are propely the Marave; Bororos are those who dwell on the left bank of the Zambezi and are bordered by the territory of Quelimane and on the west by the Shire. Between these and the Lupata are the Maganjas. And from the north to the coast at Cape Delgado are the Makwa. West of the Marave, as far as the river Luangwa, live the Cheva, and to the east of these and near the mouth of that river are the Senga and between these and the Portuguese territories of the left bank of the Zambezi are the Mogoa. East of the Makwa, and on the shores of the river or lake Nyanja, are the Yao or Nguru. All these people today are totally independent of each other, and each is known by its own name. Nevertheless it is beyond dispute that all are of the same Marave race, having the same habits, customs, language, etc.

From A. C. P. Gamitto, *King Kazembe and the Marave, Cheva, Biso, Bemba, Lunda, and Other Peoples of Southern Africa, Being the Diary of the Portuguese Expedition to that Potentate in the Years 1831 and 1832*, trans. by Ian Cunnison (Lisbon: Junta de Investigações do Ultramar, 1960), vol. I, pp. 63–73. Reprinted by permission.

This country is of very vast extent, and according to my information there are many impassable regions in it, because of the bad treatment received from the savage inhabitants, and the thick forests covering it. The Nguru are of ferocious appearance, and do not agree to penetration by strangers into their land beyond the western margin of the aforesaid lake or river. It is only there that commerce with them takes place.

II

It is still not known whether the Lake Marave of the geographers, called Nyania-Mukulu (Rio Grande) by the Blacks, and Rio Nyanja by the Portuguese, has communication with the sea. it seems certain however that it forms a mighty river which has its mouth on the Zanzibar coast, being perhaps the Koavo, which debouches opposite Kilwa. It seems it was visited by the early Portuguese,[1] but I have no information that it has been visited by any European traveller, but only by Moors and Blacks who have gone there from Mozambique to trade, and Bisa who are today the merchants of those regions. From all of these I have received the following unanimous information.

The river Nyanja-Mukulu, or great Nyanja, has an extraordinary breadth. Embarking in canoes to cross it, it is necessary to sleep two nights on islands, with which it is sprinkled, before arriving on the third day in the afternoon on the opposite shore: a distance which, according to my calculation, must be about nine leagues. It has a strong easterly current. The many islands it contains, some of which are very large, are for the most part inhabited, those on the west by the Marave, and those on the east by the Yao or Nguru. This is the story that merchants who have been there generally give.

There is another river called by the Africans Nyanja-Panono, or little river, and, which the Portuguese call Nyanja-Pequefio. I cannot say if it comes out of the Rio Grande, from which at some places it is several days away.

On this point, and on the matter of its shores being inhabited by Marave and Yao, I can affirm nothing positively, because these were not things I observed.

To this information on the two Nyanjas we may add what is read in the diary of the march made to Kazembe in 1798 by Dr. Lacerda, "On September 21st he found

---

1. Father Manoel Godinho, in his *Voyage from India to Portugal by Land* in 1663, says as follows: "The road from Angola to India by land is not yet discovered; but it certainly will be, and the passage will be easy, because from Angola to Lake Zachaf (which is in the middle of Ethiopia and is fifteen leagues broad, although its length is not yet known) is less than 250 leagues. Cosmographers put this lake at 15° 50', and according to a map I have seen, made by a Portuguese who went many years to the kings of Monomotapa, Manica, Butua and others of Kaffraria, this lake is not far from the Zimbawe, or court, of Mesura or Marabia. There issues from it the river Aruvi which flows into the Zambezi above our fort of Tete. And also the river Chire which, cutting through many lands, and latterly through those of the Rondo, joins the river Cuama below Sena. This assured I now say: he who would make this journey from Angola to India by way of Mozambique, crossing the interior of Kaffraria, should ask for the said Lake Zachaf, and on finding it, descend by the rivers to our forts of Tete and Sena and from there to the Quelimane delta; from Quelimane by land and sea to Mozambique, and from Mozambique to Goa in a month. That there is such a lake is stated not only by the Kaffirs, but also by Portuguese who already went there, navigating up the rivers and who, for lack of funds, have not yet discovered this route."

himself in the village of the Fumo Mouro-Achinto, situated 10° 20' 35" lat. S., and 39° 10' 0" long. E. of Lisbon according to observations made on the sun and two eclipses of Jupiter's satellites: and he mentions that he was told there that to the north, between the Sukuma nation which reaches the banks of the Shire or Nyanja, and the Bisa, lay the Bemba nation: and that the lands to the south were peopled by the Lamba and Ambo, and that these two nations do commerce with the Africans in the neighbourhood of Zumbo."

I have said already that the Bisa today have no land of their own, it having been conquered by the Muembas, who are probably the Bemba (Uemba) mentioned above. As to the Shire being the same as the Nyanja, we add nothing to what is already stated.

It would not be difficult to confirm the truth about the Nyanja Grande if a small expedition left the Sena Rivers, another left Mozambique and another left the isles of Cape Delgado, without military equipment but with all possible trade goods, each taking a man capable of making an exact description to satisfy the aims of the exploration. It would be best to leave from these three points, making arrangements to communicate and inform each other of discoveries made, because in this way, if one or two of them miscarried through various obstacles (of which the main is the desertion of Kaffirs who have to be taken as carriers), one of them would probably arrive at its destination and this would be enough. All should be ordered to make for the River, and there buy canoes in sufficient number to provide transport for all, or a part, and navigate downstream to its mouth. A craft appropriate to the task would have to be sent from Mozambique to where its mouth is supposed to be, in order to bring them back. This should be easy and would involve little expense.

I calculate the width of the great Nyanja at nine leagues because, according to my information, it has a strong current; therefore the canoes have to go obliquely and so they have to spend three days on a journey which, with a slow current, they could do in half the time. The same width in slightly different circumstances takes longer.

The best season for such an exploration would be spring, and it should not begin before the end of April or even May.

The Portuguese rule in Cape Delgado by right, but by the neglect which this territory has suffered it has been left to the Arabs of the Imam of Muscat to profit by all its commerce; this they do mainly through contraband, without the Portuguese government of the district having the power to embarrass them; and so they monopolise the trade and take all the profits. As this is another subject I shall keep what I have to say for another memorandum on Portuguese East Africa; but just now I felt it was necessary to explain about these explorations.

III

In the middle of Marave land is a small area occupied also by some Marave who are known as Chupeta; and their district has the same name. Although they have the same habits, etc., they live quite independently. Each village has a supreme chief, who belongs to the family composing it, and who recognises no political superior:

it is better to let oneself be annihilated or destroyed completely, than to give obedience to another. In case of a dispute or outbreak of war between two chiefs, which is very frequent, the members of the two villages fight one another but it never finishes with the first fight. He who weakens retreats and gets another one to help him, and thus the two factions grow incessantly to the point where often all the chiefs are eventually involved in the contest. On each occasion, the quarrel is brought to an end by the appointment of arbitrators to judge the matter, which may be nothing more than the purloining of a millet stalk. Often enough war breaks out again if the guilty party does not agree to pay an indemnity which appears too exorbitant, or if the innocent party is not satisfied with it. In such cases when fighting has been heavy, the quarrel is brought to an end and the condemned party pays war damages to the satisfaction of all the chiefs who helped the winning side, who assess all the damage since the start of the fighting. It usually happens that the lives of all those who died are indemnified if there are deaths on only one side; but if both sides lost lives, then deaths on the losing side are discounted. These payments go to the profit of the chiefs of both sides and are usually made in livestock, i.e. cattle, sheep, and goats, or in slaves.

These people are much more warlike and industrious than other Marave, but are also bigger liars and thieves. The land of the Chupeta is flat, with few trees, and those that exist are very small. Hence they lack firewood, and use instead millet stalks, dry shrubs, and particularly cattle dung which they are careful to keep dry. They have peat, but do not know its use. They keep many cattle, sheep, and goats, and in other respects they are like the Marave.

IV

The climate in summer—i.e. May to September—is agreeable, being mild rather than hot. In the rains the sun is burning.

In general, Marave country is much cut about with rivers and has plenty of water; and there are many mountain ranges and hilly districts which the people prefer for their dwellings: in the valleys, they have few villages, and these they use as keeps or outposts. Generally the gardens are on the hills and slopes, and as I mentioned they inhabit one of the hilliest regions of East Africa. I saw no navigable rivers on my march.

V

The population of this country is enormous, although the populated districts are smaller than the deserted ones. If the chiefs were united they would constitute a respectable nation. The Marave busy themselves for the most part with agriculture, from which they gain their livelihood. Weavers, smiths, and basket makers, and those that practise other trades, do so mostly for amusement rather than as a way of life. They have also a large number of lazy people and highway robbers.

VI

Government is despotic and hereditary succession going to sister's son, and never to brother's son; if there is none, then the dead man's brother succeeds. A Fumo or Mambo is rarely recognised before months, or even years, have elapsed in civil war, brothers and kinsmen fighting one another until one side is triumphant and, having the advantage, supplants all the others. It is from these continual wars and expulsions that the sale and killing of prisoners and outlaws, who are all themselves Marave, result. The chief of the nation has the title Unde; his orders are executed without question or delay in all the dominions in which he is obeyed; but no important matter is decided without being heard by a council composed of elders, or of those in whom he has equal trust. On rare occasions this council meets in secret session; it gathers usually under a great tree in the Muzinda (the name of the village in which the Mambo or Fumo resides), against whose trunk Unde sits back with the council about him; round the council are seated the people who want to listen to the case. The spectators who do not belong to the council often speak and are heard as if they belonged to it. When the subject has been talked over, Unde declares that he agrees with the council's deliberations, or amends them, as he thinks fit. The councillors always follow Unde's opinion if they know it beforehand; and if any speak against it, it is because they do not know it; for as soon as it is known, everyone assents. But Unde usually opens the council. The village in which he lives is called Muzinda-a-Unde.

The whole of Marave country is divided into territories or provinces governed by Mambos, and these are subdivided into districts whose chiefs are the Fumos. Both are hereditary and succession takes place in the same way as for Unde. Neither he nor the Mambos and Fumos wear insignia of any kind to mark them off from other Marave; they usually go dressed in a skin or a Nyanda, a kind of cloth, not woven but made from the inner bark of certain trees. The form and process of government is the same throughout the Marave. Alliances are of short duration, and often broken; any new interest may persuade Mambos and Fumos to change their allies, or become neutral or hostile. These changes often occur when they are in the process of negotiating with their allies. The wars, in which they are at most times involved, often start from bagatelles. All affairs can be judged by arbitrators, but if they are not satisfied, they litigate before the authorities, appealing from one Fumo to another, and then to the Mambo; but at times, if they are not satisfied with the judgment of the Mambo in council, they have resort to arms, and this gives rise to a small war which may spread. This happens sometimes, but not very often. When the Fumos are at war, the Mambos to whom they are subordinate do not interfere, and at the end receive the tribute due to them. If one of the Fumos is killed, his place is usurped by his enemy, who pays the Mambo and receives recognition and rules in peace as if he were the legal heir. This happens in all ranks. The Marave authorities are Unde, the paramount chief of the nation; and the Fumos and Mambos in their districts and provinces, who all exercise in them the same arbitrary power. All legislation is traditional. In judgments and sentences they look to sentences already given in similar cases, which custom has made law: all the same, some judgments are invariable and do not change, as those relating to sorcery, adultery, theft, and homicide, the most important being directed against sorcerers and adulterers. They have no statute law.

VII

The strength of these people consists in their great number. They know no elements of attack or defence apart from courage. Although continually engaged in small civil wars, the result in no way alters the general state of the nation because the victor is always a Marave and is subject to the same laws and customs. When Unde is attacked, a rare enough eventuality, the whole nation takes up arms without regard to age, as many as can manage; those unable to fight take to the hills and forests with everything they possess. The number of fighting men is great, but there is no discipline or military plan. In time of peace there are no standing armies, but when war breaks out, people gather in groups, called Mangas, of which the Mambos or Fumos of the districts they belong to are the leaders. If they are large, each one acts on its own; if they are small, two or more may join together. The word Manga, though used by the Portuguese in this part of Africa, is certainly African, and has no other meaning than a column or group of armed men. Perhaps the Portuguese adopted it from them.

As Unde is nearly always in a safe place with a large population, he is seldom subject to a close attack: but he engages in frequent distant wars, and only gets notice of them when they are over or nearly so.

As they have no formal military organisation into armies, so they have no recruitment: but in each Muzinda there is a big drum called Ngoma which can be heard a great way off, and which is used as a call to arms when the enemy is expected or imminent or when the spies or Sopozos, who are distributed around the roads to get news from travellers, come and give information that armed men are near. At the sound of the alarm, there come armed as many as belong to the district under the Muzinda; and in the next district also the alarm is sounded, and people gather, and so on successively until all are up in arms. Warriors arm themselves and maintain themselves at their own cost during a war, and this they do mainly by pillage.

There is no other way of calling up, and no way of finding out if anyone capable of fighting is missing, even if he is one of those obliged to turn out. But it is only those who are totally incapable of fighting who fail to present themselves, because the hope of plunder moves them all.

VIII

Their legs are their only defensive weapons and they put them to good use. Offensive arms are bows, poisoned arrows, spears, axes, and knives. The bow is carried in the left hand with the spear, the arrows being in a leather quiver called Mutumba. The bow is Uta, the spear Dipa, the arrow Miseve, the axe Bazo and the knife Shisu. Axe and knife are worn in the belt, one on each side. The arrows have very small heads, but are entirely barbed; they are inserted into canes which they use for shafts in such a way that when an arrow hits its mark the head enters the body and the shaft falls, and within two hours the poison has taken effect and has killed. But if a certain kind of oil, called by the Portuguese "Frei Pedro" and by the Africans Mafuta, is used upon it, no harm results. I do not know the composition of this antidote—it was not divulged.

Africans come with it for sale, but much of it is not genuine, and the only way to be sure is to see the effect it produces. This syrup was discovered by a Portuguese friar of that name in Zumbo [a town 600 miles up the Zambezi River], who found it to be a swift and efficacious anti-toxin. It is from Zumbo that this discovery has spread to all parts.

They say that among other things the poison contains certain substances considered essential—crocodile gall, hippopotamus brain, a kind of kapok, and the sap of some grasses. The effect produced is to stop the circulation of the blood, making it coagulate immediately.

The Marave are completely ignorant of any military operational planning, and of the division of armies into corps, and the formation of lines for defense and attack. On the contrary, the crowds march against the enemy as a body and as soon as they see him they become completely disorganized, utter the Tunguro cries and start letting off their arrows at random, without revealing themselves or leaving the shelter of the trees which defend them. There is no command, every warrior fights as he likes and because it appears the safest thing for him to do he attends mainly to his self-preservation. They use the spear only to finish off the wounded, and the axe and knife only to cut heads off the dead bodies. As superstition is at the base of all their beliefs, the Mambos and Fumos propagate the notion that the safety and prosperity of their lands depend upon their being sorcerers, and so they are all thought to be; they are feared and respected by their people and by strangers alike. The higher they stand in the hierarchy, the more they seek to inculcate the superiority of their medicines, of which they boast. The most important thing is to have in one's dominions under one's protection the most renowned magicians, to whom the public attributes supernatural powers by means of their Mankwaras, or magic. Nothing is done which has not the approval of the magic.

The Ganga or Surjao is the one who divines and makes the supposed magic or divination. The latter term may be a corruption of the Portuguese word Cirurgião.[2]

In times of war it is the Gangas who go in front of the Mangas, much attired with feathers, bones, tails of various animals, horns, etc. etc. They make long speeches in which they exhort the warriors to trust their medicines, because they are efficacious and infallible, and assert that they alone will be able to conquer the enemy.

The Marave place complete faith in these charlatans. If the outcome is fortunate, the Gangas attribute it entirely to themselves; and if it is adverse they blame someone for the breach of the elaborate taboos they impose, which consist usually in abstinence from certain foods, from cohabitation with someone of the other sex, etc. When they fight the Portuguese, these try first to procure the death of the Ganga who is reckoned infallible. This obtained, victory is not far ahead, because resistance then is weak, since they think that the Europeans have better magic than they. which it would be useless to resist. But in an internecine war this does not happen; all avoid shooting at the Ganga for fear that if they killed or wounded him they would be lost for his blood would fall upon the man who spilt it and the Muzimos would thus have to take vengeance.

2. Surgeon. (Trans.).

IX

The Mambos or Fumos, according to their rank, receive Chipatas, or presents for safe conduct, from all traders passing through their lands; fees, or costs, for hearing and judging cases; Mouths (Muromos) and tribute from the land, etc. The only way they spend this is by sharing it out among the people about them, and the more liberal they are, the greater the number of followers, the larger the Muzindas, the stronger their cause and the greater their power. They spend it also in making new houses for their wives, and in paying the debts they contract; these are all personal expenses. But apart from them the Fumos pay tribute to the Mambos to whom they are subordinate, and the Mambos pay to Unde.

The Chipata, or safe-conduct, is a tribute which has to be paid in merchandise to the Mambos and Fumos through whose country one passes. Its size should correspond to the category of chief to whom it is made and to the wealth of the person making the payment. The safe-conduct gives right of transit and obliges the authorities on the land to guarantee the life and property of the merchants. There is no sure rule about the value of this tribute; the traveller can only learn from practice. Nearly always the chiefs ask for more, however much is given, and it is always necessary to take this into account when the Chipata is made up.

The Muromo, a word signifying mouth, is the fee for asking to speak to an African authority, and this cannot be done without first presenting something, this being the "morsel for the mouth," whose value should be relative to the nature of the business or discussion desired. There is no set price.

43. ANNA ELIZABETH STEENKAMP

THE GREAT TREK. 1835.

Anna Elizabeth Steenkamp was a member of the famous Retief family. Pieter Retief was the foremost of the Voortrekkers—those Boers who moved from the Cape Colony inland to the high veld of the Transvaal and the plains of Natal in the decade after 1835. This article written by Anna Steenkamp first appeared in the Cape Monthly Magazine in September 1876 and has since become one of the best-known manifestos of the Great Trek. The reader should remember however that this account was written some forty years after the events.

This record is written for the sake of my relations, children and grandchildren, now still residing in the interior, in order that they may know for what reason their parents and grandparents have forsaken their mother country, and what anxiety and anguish, grief and pain, destitution and distress, by reason both of foes and fire,

Anna Steenkamp, "Record or Journal of Our Migration from Our Mother Country to Port Natal," *Cape Monthly Magazine*, September 1876. Reprinted in John Bird, *Annals of Natal* (Pietermaritzburg: P. Davis and Sons, 1888), vol. I, pp. 459–468.

have befallen us, and have been the cause of many a sad sigh and bitter tear; whilst, nevertheless, amidst these trying

circumstances, we were being guided and guarded by our faithful God, our Father.

The reasons for which we abandoned our lands and homesteads, our country and kindred, were the following:

1. The continual depredations and robberies of the Kafirs [black South Africans], and their arrogance and overbearing conduct: and the fact that, in spite of the fine promises made to us by our Government, we nevertheless received no compensation for the property of which we were despoiled.

2. The shameful and unjust proceedings with reference to the freedom of our slaves: and yet it is not so much their freedom that drove us to such lengths, as their being placed on an equal footing with Christians, contrary to the laws of God and the natural distinction of race and religion, so that it was intolerable for any decent Christian to bow down beneath such a yoke; wherefore we rather withdrew in order thus to preserve our doctrines in purity.

3. But it is unnecessary to mention anything further just now about these questions, as I am aware that you are acquainted with these matters; but I shall rather relate to you what occurred to us on our expedition. Two bodies of people had left before us. The foremost were the Taljaards and Liebenbergs, among whom the first sad massacre was perpetrated by the great Kafir king (Masilikatzi).[1] At this battle, Potgieter with forty men defeated fully a thousand Kafirs, but we were ourselves not in that band. The rumours of this massacre, however, were the cause of our leaving the colony all the sooner, in order to hasten to the assistance of our brethren. The massacre committed by Masilikatzi took place on 2nd September, 1836. Another troop under the leadership of G. Maritz, as well as my aged father, François Retief, departed from the colony on 15th November, 1836, and I and my family had to stay behind, as my husband was very ill; but on 5th May, 1837, we also left the colony, alone with our children, servants, four wagons, and cattle. Our departure from Zeekoe River was accompanied with many troubles; for I had a sick husband and a sick child to attend to, and was myself suffering from a bad cold. The most difficult part of all still was, that we had to bury our lead and gunpowder under ground every day, and to send for them by night with a wagon. The reason of this was that we had a great deal of ammunition, and there was a prohibition against leaving with it. At length with great danger and much trouble we crossed the Orange River, and there I offered my thanks to God, because thus far He had helped us. Then to our misfortune we arrived among the Bastards [people of mixed blood—white Europeans and black Africans—later known as Griquas], who received us very brutally, saying they had the right and orders to rob and despoil us of everything: for this tribe has since long ago been known to be the greatest thieves and robbers in the world. Our servants deserted us, and the girls, although weak and delicate, were obliged to lead and drive the wagons, nay even to drive the cattle on through all these ungovernable tribes. Our company was not increased: we were only with four wagons. Never-

1. Umsilikazi [Mzilikazi].

theless we were cheerful, cherishing the hope of better days, consoling our hearts and longing for gladder times. We had, however, still to travel through two kinds of Bastards, the Korannas and Boschjesmans, with the loss of a number of our cattle and horses. With joy and gladness we reached the Riet River, and there we found a multitude of people, who were the first Christians whom we had seen on our long journey. Here we delayed twenty days on account of my husband being too ill to proceed further on the journey; but scarcely was he better than we set out with our four wagons. We then came into a desolate country, without any wood or manure (for fuel), where the grass was so high that we could hardly find the children and the cattle. Here also we had bitterly cold weather, and heavy rains.

At last we reached King Maroko, and the Kafirs came to meet us by hundreds, surrounding our four wagons like two walls. At the mission-house we delayed a little, and the great King Moshesh, with his servant and the clerk of Maroko, came to look if we had any slaves or apprentices by us, in order to take them away from us. After we left Maroko we had to experience severe trials, as we could find no road, and for that reason we had to wander hither and thither, and could find no one to show us the right way and give us instructions; but we saw abandoned kraals and encampments, and our cattle died in great numbers; and above all we were in a country destitute of wood, but full of deserted kraals, and here and there heaps of bones of tribes murdered and destroyed by Masilikatzi. Here there was an abundance of game of all kinds.

At length after four months' travelling we reached Sand River; but as we were quite on the wrong road, my son rode forward on horseback to see whether he could find anybody to show us the way, and to our great joy he succeeded on 24th August, 1838, to meet people; and on 25th I was delivered of my youngest child. Herein I perceived the truth of the word of the Lord, that when our needs are sorest He is nearest. Nevertheless we had not yet found the formed company of which Maritz was the leader, nor my father; but three days after the birth of my child, 28th August, Commandant Potgieter proceeded on his journey with all his company, and then we all came together.

It was, however, still too troublesome for us to travel forward with so many people, and for that reason we were compelled to pass through a burning country, where we were in great anxiety lest our children should be burned. A number of our cattle, and of others whole herds, were burned. In the course of our journey we travelled through the country of two kinds of Bastards, Korannas and Bushmen (Maroko and Moshesh). Now we had to go through the country of the great Masilikatzi, but as his power had been broken by Mr. Maritz we had nothing to fear from him.

When we had left the Sikonyela behind us, we met Mr. Piet Retief in the neighbourhood of Drakensberg with the first emigrants, as well as my aged father, François Retief, and the Rev. Mr. Smit. This caused us great joy, as we had in the first some one to execute our existing laws, and in the last-mentioned a minister to give instruction in God's word, to administer baptism and the holy sacrament, so that our religious service flourished. Every Sunday and every evening there were public services, and this made our journey through the wilderness pleasant, seeing that the Lord had not forsaken us.

Mr. Maritz had gone on with a part of the emigrants; but we soon after left, under the command of Mr. Retief, as far as the great Drakensberg; and from there Mr. Retief departed, with five men, for King Dingaan [Shaka's successor], to get the land from him, by purchase or by exchange, and in this he succeeded.

I must now relate to you something about Sikonyela. Whilst we remained on the Drakensberg, Sikonyela was found guilty of theft and robbery; for he had sent his people, on horseback, with guns and clothed, to Dingaan to steal cattle. We were not aware of this; but when Mr. Retief came to the king, the latter asking him whether he was not afraid to visit himself, as he had stolen his (the king's) cattle, Mr. Retief replied, "No; I have not done so." "Then," said the king, "you have fired on my people; they tell me it is the Malungus (white people) who have done so." After Mr. Retief had cleared himself of guilt, Dingaan entertained him in a friendly manner. This was mere hypocrisy, as you will see from the sequel.

Mr. Retief then started for the Bay. When he left King Dingaan, the latter gave him two chieftains and some of his people to see if any of his cattle were with Sikonyela. Mr. Retief then rode with the Kafirs and a portion of his men to Sikonyela, and found the cattle with him, and delivered them to the two chieftains to hand them over to the king.

With great difficulty we passed over the Drakensberg, and we encamped before the Great Tugela, when the emigrants under Mr. Maritz had collected together. Then the council resolved that Mr. Retief, after having convinced the king of the above-mentioned robberies, should go to acquire the land from him, which was done. He left us, accompanied by sixty-three men and three children, besides the "after-riders."

When Mr. Retief came to the king, the latter willingly gave him, as he had found the cattle at Sikonyela's, the country from the Tugela to the Umzimvubu as a present, according to the contract which was afterwards found with the persons who were murdered. Nevertheless, all the friendliness of Dingaan proves that he intended carrying out a cruel and fearful murderous design, which he actually accomplished on 11th February, by the tyrannical murder of Mr. Retief and sixty-six other men; and on 17th February, the Kafirs attacked us also. Oh! dreadful, dreadful night! wherein so much martyred blood was shed; and two hundred innocent children, ninety-five women, and thirty-three men were slain, and hurled into an awful eternity by the assagais of those bloodthirsty heathens. Excluding the servants, the number was over four hundred souls. Oh! it was unbearable for flesh and blood to behold the frightful spectacle the following morning. In one wagon were found fifty dead, and blood flowed from the seam of the tent-sail down to the lowest. Ah! how awful it was to look upon all those dead and wounded. The following day we fled altogether to another encampment at Doornkop, between the Tugela and the Bushman's River. The massacre was perpetrated between Blaauwkrantz and Bushman's River. Mr. Maritz was at Doornkop with the first emigrants. The Kafirs came in in force in the daytime, but were gallantly repulsed and driven off by Mr. Maritz; and as the river was full, and the Kafirs had to go across, a large number was killed, so that the river ran as red as blood.

I must also tell you, my dear children, how it was that the Kafirs could so easily perpetrate the massacre that night. It was on account of disobedience and imprudence: the greater portion of the people were on the mission, and others engaged in buffalo-hunting; others, moreover, were on the road to the Drakensberg to assist their families in coming down: so that the Kafirs found the women and children quite alone, and sleeping peacefully. Mr. Retief had cautioned us at Doomkop to remain by each other till he came back, as he was ill at ease. He also wrote to us afterwards that we should not separate from each other; but the trouble we had with the cattle obliged many to proceed down the river with their families in small troops. We were alone, feeling secure and contented. Mr. Retief left his wife at Doornkop with Mr. Smit, and the Kafirs did not come there.

The day after our arrival there, the wounded (the women and children who were left) came; some on foot, some on horseback, and a portion in wagons. Our field-commandant, Mr. Piet Greyling, carefully provisioned and strengthened our encampment. He also took back our cattle from the Kafirs; that is to say, our sheep, as the oxen were across the river, which was full.

The commandant had the dead buried and the wounded attended to. On all sides one saw tears flowing, and heard people weeping by the plundered wagons, painted with blood; tents and beds torn to shreds; pregnant women and little children had to walk for hours together, bearing the signs of their hasty flight. Oh! how weary and fatigued were those women and children, and how terrible it was to see unborn children rent asunder by the murderous Kafirs. When the women came up to us, they fell upon their knees and thanked God for their deliverance out of the hands of the cruel tyrant. In our encampment there was nothing but lamentation and weeping. Every day we had to bury the dead bodies of the wounded. This spectacle, and the terrible circumstances, cannot be described by my pen.

In April our encampment was at Blaauwkrantz. There Field-commandant Piet Uys arrived. He went out with a commando, and perished with ten other men on the 10th May, 1838. The men who betrayed us, Stubbs and Blanckenberg, also went out on a marauding expedition to the Bay at the same time that our commando left; but the Kafirs flew round and murdered seventeen Englishmen, a number of Natal Kafirs, and also Stubbs; so that our betrayers fell into their own toils.

Thereafter, our whole force was assembled at the Blaauwkrantz River. Oh! my children, to live in so large a "laager" [enclosed encampment] of a thousand wagons is hard, and it is also injurious to cattle. In July our laager went as far as Bushman's River. Listen now, my children, to my sad misfortunes.

On 2nd February your beloved younger sister died. On the 11th February the commission was murdered, amongst whom were my uncle Retief, his two sons, and other relations. On the 17th February the great massacre occurred. On the 10th May Piet Uys, with ten of his men, perished. On 23rd July your dear father died, and many other of our nearest relations and acquaintances. The last cases of death were probably caused by the dampness of our encampment, for nearly every day we had rain, and we could wear no shoes on account of the mud.

On the 10th August we were again attacked by the Kafirs at Bushman's River. Their bands were stretched out by thousands as far as the eye could see. It was a terrible sight to witness. I cannot describe their number, for one would have thought that entire heathendom had gathered together to destroy us. But thanks and praise are due to the Lord, who so wonderfully has rescued us out of the hands of our numberless and bloodthirsty foes, and granted us the victory. Their foremost band wore clothes and had the guns of the killed, and swarmed down upon us, whilst the others surrounded us. Our number of fighting men was considerably diminished, for a portion was with Maritz at Tugela, and another portion had gone ahead to Port Natal, so that our strength consisted of only two field-commandants and two field-comets, with their men. The names of the field-commandants and field-cornets were Joachim Prinsloo, Jacobus Potgieter, Johannes du Plessis, and Johannes de Lange. Thirty of Plessis' men and also a portion of Prinsloo's were with our cattle at the Drakensberg, so that we had only a few men capable of bearing arms at our laager, and the heathen had entirely overwhelmed us had God suffered them to do so. Now you may imagine, my dear children, in what a state of anxiety we women were when we beheld the onslaught of the enemy. The majority of the women consisted of widows and orphans. For we could not imagine that so few people would gain the victory; but the Lord strengthened us and weakened our enemy. They rushed down on us in a circle till almost within range of our guns. Then they attacked us at different points, so that our men were obliged to walk one behind the other to shoot down the enemy, now at one and then at another corner of the encampment. We had arranged our cannon so that they could not break into it. The Kafirs kept us busy for two days and two nights, and constantly fired at us, but not one of our men received any injury from their bullets, and seeing that a multitude of theirs were killed in that conflict, and that they were severely defeated, they left us with a war-song, and fired charges as far as we could hear them. The second day our men went in pursuit of them with the view of recovering our cattle, but the horses were too few and almost too famished in the encampment, so that they were obliged to return, and the enemy retained our cattle; but we thanked God for the preservation of our lives, with the exception of the loss of one man, who was murdered whilst with his sheep, and my faithful female slave who had fled from the encampment. After this occurrence we departed for Tugela, as Maritz wished his men to get out of the mountain. We remained together, however, for six months. In the meanwhile your brother, François Marthinus Hattingh, had left for the interior in order to collect a commando, and also to get horses in order to take away our cattle from the enemy, for there was famine among those who had been ruined by the enemy; but we assisted each other until we were entirely deprived of means of subsistence.

I was also married a second time to a stranger, a widower, named Thomas Engenaar Steenekamp. Mr. Maritz died; Mr. Retief had been murdered; Mr. Uys had been slain. All our leaders had been killed, and we were as sheep without a shepherd. On 10th November my son arrived with his uncle, Andries W. J. Pretorius, who was then by the general vote appointed head-commandant. He thereupon collected a commando, and had a fight with the Kafirs. Through God's blessing the Kafirs sustained a defeat, whilst a large number of them perished, and five of our men were killed. After the battle we left the Tugela in January, 1839, and arrived here at Pietermaritzburg. I must tell you what occurred to me on this last journey.

We left on the 20th January, and on the 23rd of the same month, my son, François Marthinus Hattingh, was killed by lightning during a violent thunderstorm, while he was with his cattle, at the age of twenty-eight years, and left a widow and two children behind to deplore his loss. Oh! what a blow it was for me and his whole family when he was snatched away by death. He was a peaceful man, respected and esteemed by everyone, and deplored by all. But the hand of the Lord doth what He willeth, and with death there is no respect of persons.

Since our arrival here we lived a whole year in laagers, and in the last of them a sad misfortune occurred to us. On the 28th August, 1839, at nine o'clock in the evening, our encampment caught fire through a little servant girl lighting a candle; and some had already gone to bed when the fire broke out, but we were still busy, teaching the children. Suddenly a cry was raised of "Kafirs" and we did not think otherwise than that our enemies had put the encampment on fire. As soon as the first house stood in flames, all the rest caught fire. The laagers were plentifully supplied with lead and gunpowder; for our father, Steenekamp, alone had a barrel containing six hundred pounds of powder, and the other houses were full of the same article, so that it was very dangerous to remain within the encampment. I fled with my twelve children out of the gate, as I was afraid of the fire and of the reported Kafirs, and went as far as the first hollow; further I could not go. Afterwards the other women followed me, and there we remained until the fire was burned out. Then I received information who the persons were that had perished in the fire; and people also told me that my husband was amongst the number: but this message gave me no anxiety, as I thought that it was impossible that the whole of us should have our lives spared. That night I had still more terrible thoughts: it was, in short, like unto the Day of Judgment; and the words of St. Peter occurred to my mind, when he says: "The day of the Lord shall come as a thief in the night: in which the heavens and earth shall pass away with loud noises, and the elements shall burn and be destroyed; and the earth and the works which are within it shall be burnt." The most terrible part still of that night was to see when the gunpowder caught fire, and the pieces of the wagons around us flew about in all directions. As soon as the danger was passed, we betook ourselves again to the laager to assist the injured and bury the dead. When the first house caught fire, there were ten men to quench the flames, and when the gunpowder ignited three of them were killed, and the others severely injured. A trading wagon containing a large quantity of powder also caught fire. Two men attempted to save it, whereby one was so severely injured that he died immediately afterwards, and the other lived a short time. The gunpowder wagon was in the middle of the encampment. Two white children and two little Kafirs were burned to death in the house. The following day we found nine dead and twelve wounded, lying in the ashes. The heat was so intense that we could not take out the dead that night. Everything belonging to us was roasted and broiled: four wagons, nine "salted" fat oxen, as also fat, soap, salt, sugar, &c., were consumed, for we were wealthy, and provided with everything. Thirteen houses also were burned down. We had to sit by the fire the whole night, without clothing or bedding. Some of the wives and mothers were weeping, for they had seen their husbands and sons perishing in the fire. We, poor women and little children, had to struggle through many serious trials on account of the cold and the enemy, as we lay by night beside the houses; but to remain by so great a fire, wherein so many people were burned, was a still greater hardship; and the night was bitterly cold. In the morning of the following day, we bound the bones in a counterpane and buried them in a hole. There were three Steenekamps, two Polgieters, one Deventer, two children, and two Kafirs burned: and two Steenekamps severely injured, of whom my husband was one, but by God's goodness he recovered.

Here now, my dear children and friends, you may see with what sad misfortunes I had to struggle in my journey of twenty months before we had a home or a shelter. Shortly after the fire we were visited by measles, through which a great many deaths occurred. My old husband and myself had alone to provide for twenty-three children and grandchildren who were laid up, and who had to be attended by us, without house or tent, in only a wagon. Several days I was so weak through these exertions that I could hardly endure it; but God be praised, who has strengthened me in body, so as to bear the burdens which He has laid upon us; so then I was able to perform my duties.

For about two years after this we lived quietly, securely, and at peace with all the surrounding tribes, so that every one was again beginning to acquire the means of subsistence; for the country is very fertile, so that one could very well make a living, if not visited by wars or other misfortunes. But to our grief and sorrow the peace was again disturbed, and all our dreams of prosperity and happiness vanished; for on 6th May, 1842, Captain Smith [the commander of British forces] arrived in the bay of Port Natal, and on the 25th of that month he attacked us. He came along the shore of the sea with pieces of cable twisted round the axles of his guncarriages. Here, also, my darlings, I wish you to see how the Lord has visibly assisted our men; for in spite of all the treachery displayed in this war, and all the heavy ordnance brought to bear against us, five men only were killed, whilst two were murdered by the Kafirs. Women and children were stripped of their clothes, and had to fly naked. Farms and lands were laid waste by the heathens, and again much cattle was taken from us by the Kafirs, so that we, through the unceasing thefts of the Kafirs, again fell into poverty. On 15th July, the first Cloete [British commissioner] arrived at Pietermaritzburg, and made peace with eleven persons, and fixed that day to be celebrated as a festival of happiness for us and for our children. On 9th May, 1843, the second Cloete arrived here, and we were fated to be deprived of the land which we had earned and bought: that was the satisfaction promised us.

But, my dear friends and children, I may finally mention, that if everything remains in the same unfortunate position as it is already, we shall be completely ruined; and it is possible that, after a few months, you will meet with very few of your kindred at Port Natal, for we are entirely impoverished, and wish to travel inland, if God grants us health and His blessing.

Your affectionate Mother and
Grandmother,
(Signed) ANNA ELIZABETH
STEENKAMP
(née RETIEF)

44. ROBERT MOFFAT

MZILIKAZI. 1840.

Chief of the Khumalo Nguni and one of Shaka's most trusted generals, Mzilikazi defied Shaka's authority about 1821 and marched up to the high veld of the Transvaal, where he settled with his followers. None of the tribes of the Transvaal could stand against Mzilikazi's regiments, and between 1825 and 1834 prisoners from defeated Sotho-speaking tribes swelled the ranks of Mzilikazi's people, evolving into the Ndebele [Matable] nation. The Ndebele nation crystallized along the lines of a typical Nguni military state but soon found itself under assault from half-caste Korana and Griqua peoples from the south who were equipped with firearms. Mzilikazi was able to defeat them, but in 1837 Boer commandos defeated the Ndebele and convinced Mzilikazi to take his people north to safety across the Limpopo River in the upland pastures of Zimbabwe. The Ndebele rapidly recovered in their new home, and their state developed under their king until his death in 1868.

A pioneer missionary and the father-in-law of David Livingstone, Robert Moffat (1795–1883) went to South Africa on behalf of the London Missionary Society in 1817. In 1825 he settled at Kuruman, where he lived and worked for nearly half a century. He first visited Mzilikazi in 1829 and established a profound influence over the Ndebele monarch. Mzilikazi probably found in the stern, uncompromising missionary the qualities of a father figure that he had not experienced in his youth since the execution of his own father, Mashobane, by the Khumalo overlord, Zwide. Mzilikazi's devotion to Moffat was repaid, and the two shared a deep, lifelong friendship.

. . . Umbate and two of his relations, whom he wished to introduce to my notice, remained behind till a late hour. One of these appeared to be a man of superior intellect, and put rather striking questions on the subjects which I had brought before the attention of the great man. The stillness of a serene night, far from the dance and war song, which echoed from the neighbouring hills, inspired confidence in these chieftains, who spoke in whispers, as if afraid that their king should hear their liberty of speech. Umbate repeated to his friend much that he had heard from me on the road about divine things. Though extremely cautious in their remarks, it was evident that they were not insensible of the rigours of the despotism under which they lived. I had been struck with the fine, open countenances of many of the warriors, who, though living amid the bewildering mazes of ignorance and superstition, debased, dejected, and oppressed under the iron sceptre of a monarch addicted to shedding blood, possessed noble minds; but, alas! whose only source of joy was to conquer or die in the ranks of their sovereign. The following morning was marked by a melancholy display of that so-called heroism which prefers death to dishonour. A feast had been proclaimed, cattle had been slaughtered, and many hearts beat high in anticipation of wallowing in all the excesses of savage delight; eating, drinking,

From Robert Moffat, *Missionary Labours and Scenes in Southern Africa* (London: J. Snow, 1842), pp. 539–546.

dancing, and singing the victors' song over the slain, whose bones lay bleached on the neighbouring plains. Every heart appeared elate but one. He was a man of rank, and what was called an Entuna, (an officer,) who wore on his head the usual badge of dignity. He was brought to head-quarters. His arm bore no shield, nor his hand a spear; he had been divested of these, which had been his glory. He was brought into the presence of the king, and his chief council, charged with a crime, for which it was in vain to expect pardon, even at the hands of a more humane government. He bowed his fine elastic figure, and kneeled before the judge. The case was investigated silently, which gave solemnity to the scene. Not a whisper was heard among the listening audience, and the voices of the council were only audible to each other, and the nearest spectators. The prisoner, though on his knees, had something dignified and noble in his mien. Not a muscle of his countenance moved, but his bright black eyes indicated a feeling of intense interest, which the moving balance between life and death only could produce. The case required little investigation; the charges were clearly substantiated, and the culprit pleaded guilty. But, alas! he knew it was at a bar where none ever heard the heart-reviving sound of pardon, even for offences small compared with his. A pause ensued, during which the silence of death pervaded the assembly. At length the monarch spoke, and, addressing the prisoner, said, "You are a dead man, but I shall do to-day what I never did before; I spare your life for the sake of my friend and father"—pointing to the spot where I [Moffat] stood. "I know his heart weeps at the shedding of blood; for his sake I spare your life; he has travelled from a far country to see me, and he has made my heart white, but he tells me that to take away life is an awful thing, and never can be undone again. He has pleaded with me not to go to war, nor destroy life. I wish him, when he returns to his own home again, to return with a heart as white as he has made mine. I spare you for his sake, for I love him, and he has saved the lives of my people. But," continued the king, "you must be degraded for life; you must no more associate with the nobles of the land, nor enter the towns of the princes of the people; nor ever again mingle in the dance of the mighty. Go to the poor of the field, and let your companions be the inhabitants of the desert." The sentence passed, the pardoned man was expected to bow in grateful adoration to him whom he was wont to look upon and exalt in songs applicable only to One to whom belongs universal sway and the destinies of man. But, no! holding his hands clasped on his bosom, he replied, "O king, afflict not my heart! I have merited thy displeasure; let me be slain like the warrior; I cannot live with the poor." And, raising his hand to the ring he wore on his brow, he continued, "How can I live among the dogs of the king, and disgrace these badges of honour which I won among the spears and shields of the mighty? No, I cannot live! Let me die, O Pezoolu!" His request was granted, and his hands tied erect over his head. Now my exertions to save his life were vain. He disdained the boon on the conditions offered, preferring to die with the honours he had won at the point of the spear—honours which even the act that condemned him did not tarnish—to exile and poverty among the children of the desert. He was led forth, a man walking on each side. My eye followed him till he reached the top of a precipice, over which he was precipitated into the deep pool of the river beneath, where the crocodiles, accustomed to such meals, were yawning to devour him ere he could reach the bottom! This was a sabbath morning scene such as heathenism exhibits to the view of the Christian philanthropist, and such as is calculated to excite in his bosom feelings of the deepest sympathy. This magnanimous heathen knew of no hereafter. He was without God and without hope. But, however deplorable the state of such a person may be, he will not be condemned as equally guilty with those who, in the midst of light and knowledge, self separated from the body, recklessly rush into the presence of their Maker and their Judge. We have often read of the patriotism of the Greeks and Romans, and heard that magnanimity of soul extolled which could sacrifice honour, property, and life itself, for the public good, rather than become the vassals of a foe, and live divested of the poor trappings of human glory; if this be virtue, there are, even among Africa's sons, men not inferior to the most illustrious of the Romans. The very monarch who was thus influenced by the presence of the Christian missionary, needed only to ask his warriors, "Who among you will become a sacrifice for the safety of the state, and the country's good?" and his choicest men would have run upon the thick bosses of the enemy's buckler.

Moselekatse's [Mzilikazi] conduct in this affair produced a strange impression among his people, some of whom regarded me as an extraordinary being, who could thus influence one more terrible to them than the fiercest lion of the forest. His government, so far as I could discover, was the very essence of despotism. The persons of the people, as well as their possessions, were the property of their monarch. His word was law, and he had only to lift his finger or give a frown, and his greatest nobles trembled in his presence. No one appeared to have a judgment of his own; none dared negative an opinion breathed by his sovereign. When any were permitted to approach his person, they crouched softly, muttering his great names. Messengers from the distant out-stations of his dominions were constantly arriving. These laid down their shields and spears at a distance, approached, and then kneeled about thirty yards from his royal person; and when it was his pleasure to receive the communication, it was conveyed by one of his chiefs in waiting. Some of these brought the news of the attacks of lions on some parts of his distant herds, but no one presumed to be the reporter without bringing the head and paws of the animal which had dared to assail the possessions of its mighty namesake.

Although his tyranny was such, that one would have supposed his subjects would execrate his name, they were the most servile devotees of their master. Wherever he was seated, or wherever he slept, a number of sycophants, fantastically dressed, attended him, whose business was to march, jump, and dance about, sometimes standing adoring his person, then manoeuvring with a stick, and vociferating the mighty deeds of valour performed by himself and Machobane. The same things are repeated again and again, often with a rapidity of articulation which baffles the understanding of their own countrymen. After listening many times, I was able, with the assistance of one of these parasites, to pick up the following expressions: "O Pezoolu, the king of kings, king of the heavens, who would not fear before the son of Machobane, mighty in battle! Where are the mighty before the presence of our great king? Where is the strength of the forest before the great Elephant? The proboscis is breaking the branches of the forest! It is the sound of the shields of the son of Machobane. He breathes upon their faces; it is the fire among the dry grass! His enemies are consumed before him, king of kings! Father of fire, he ascends to the blue heavens; he sends his lightnings into the clouds, and makes the rain to descend! Ye mountains, woods, and grassy plains, hearken to the voice of the son of Machobane, king of heaven!" This is a specimen of the sounding titles which incessantly meet the ear of this proud mortal, and are sufficient to make the haughty monarch believe that he is what the terror of the name of Dingaan convinced him he was not; for, notwithstanding all his vain boasts, he could not conceal his fears of the successor of the bloody Chaka [Shaka], against whose iron sway he had rebelled.

It may be necessary to notice here, very briefly, the origin of this great man. When a youth his father was the chief of an independent tribe. His people were attacked by one more powerful, and routed. He took refuge under the sceptre of Chaka, who was then rendering his name terrible by deeds of crime. Moselekatse, from his intrepid character, was placed at the head of a marauding expedition, which made dreadful havoc among the northern tribes; but, instead of giving up the whole of the spoils, he made a reserve for himself. This reaching the ears of Chaka, revenge instantly burned in the tyrant's bosom, who resolved to annihilate so daring an aggressor. Moselekatse was half prepared to take flight, and descend on the thickly peopled regions of the north, like a sweeping pestilence. He escaped, after a desperate conflict with the warriors of Chaka, who killed nearly all the old men, and many of the women. His destructive career among the Bakone tribes has been noticed; but dire as that was, it must have been only a faint transcript of the terror, desolation, and death, which extended to the utmost limits of Chaka's conquests. Though but a follower in the footsteps of Chaka, the career of Moselekatse, from the period of his revolt till the time I saw him, and long after, formed an interminable catalogue of crimes. Scarcely a mountain, over extensive regions, but bore the marks of his deadly ire. His experience and native cunning enabled him to triumph over the minds of his men, and made his trembling captives soon adore him as an invincible sovereign. Those who resisted, and would not stoop to be his dogs, he butchered. He trained the captured youth in his own tactics, so that the majority of his army were foreigners; but his chiefs and nobles gloried in their descent from the Zoolu [Zulu] dynasty. He had carried his arms far into the tropics, where, however, he had more than once met with his equal; and on one occasion, of six hundred warriors only a handful returned, who were doomed to be sacrificed, merely because they had not conquered, or fallen with their companions. Abject representatives came, while I was with him, from the subjugated tribes of the Bamanguato, to solicit his aid against a more distant tribe, which had taken their cattle. By means like these, it may be said, "He dipped his sword in blood, and wrote his name on lands and cities desolate." In his person he was below the middle stature, rather corpulent, with a short neck, and in his manner could be exceedingly affable and cheerful. His voice, soft and effeminate, did not indicate that his disposition was passionate; and, happily for his people, it was not so, or many would have been butchered in the ebullitions of his anger.

The above is but a faint description of this Napoleon of the desert,—a man with whom I often conversed, and who was not wanting in consideration and kindness, as well as gratitude. But to sympathy and compassion his heart appeared a stranger.

---

45. THOMAS FOWELL BUXTON

THE PRINCIPLES OF ABOLITION. 1840.

Thomas Fowell Buxton (1786–1845) was one of England's leading nineteenth-century philanthropists. At the request of the great abolitionist William Wilberforce, Buxton assumed the leadership of the antislavery party in the House of Commons in May 1824. Buxton previously had been a champion of prison reform, and in March 1823 when the Antislavery Society was formed, he was a charter member. Taking up the cause of abolition, Buxton concerned himself with the statistics of slavery operations. He prepared documents containing irrefutable facts to present in the House of Commons and framed positive principles on which to base his attack on the slave trade and slavery in Africa. These principles were included in his famous book, The African Slave Trade.

It appears to me a matter of such peculiar moment that we should distinctly settle and declare the PRINCIPLES on which our whole intercourse with Africa, whether economic or benevolent, whether directed exclusively to her benefit, or mingled (as I think it may most fairly be) with a view to our own, shall be founded, and by which it shall be regulated, that I venture, though at the risk of being tedious, to devote a separate chapter to the consideration of them. The principles, then, which I trust to see adopted by our country, are these—

Free Trade.

Free Labor.

FREE TRADE

Nothing, I apprehend, could be more unfortunate to the continent we wish to befriend, or more discreditable to ourselves, than that Great Britain should give any color to the suspicion of being actuated by mercenary motives; an apology would thus be afforded to every other nation for any attempt it might make to thwart our purpose. We know, from the Duke of Wellington's dispatches, that the powers on the continent were absolutely incredulous as to the purity of the motives which prompted us, at the congress of Aix la Chapelle, to urge, beyond everything else, the extinction of the Slave Trade.[1]

In a letter to Mr. Wilberforce, dated Paris, 15th Sept., 1814, the Duke of Wellington says, "It is not believed that we are in earnest about it, or have abolished the trade on the score of its inhumanity. It is thought to have been a commercial

From Thomas Fowell Buxton, *The African Slave Trade* (New York: S. W. Benedict, 1840), vol. II, pp. 154–159, 163–168.

speculation; and that, having abolished the trade ourselves, with a view to prevent the undue increase of colonial produce in our stores, of which we could not dispose, we now want to prevent other nations from cultivating their colonies to the utmost of their power."

And again, in another letter to the Right Honorable J. C. Villiers

Paris, 31st August, 1814.

"The efforts of Great Britain to put an end to it (the Slave Trade) are not attributed to good motives, but to commercial jealousy, and a desire to keep the monopoly of colonial produce in our own hands."

The grant of twenty millions may have done something to quench these narrow jealousies, but still, the nations of the continent will be slow to believe that we are entirely disinterested. It should, then, be made manifest to the world, by some signal act, that the moving spring is humanity; that if England makes settlements on the African coast, it is only for the more effectual attainment of her great object; and that she is not allured by the hopes either of gain or conquest, or by the advantages, national or individual, political or commercial, which may, and I doubt not, will follow the undertaking. Such a demonstration would be given, if, with the declaration, that it is resolved to abolish the Slave Trade, and, that in this cause we are ready, if requisite, to exert all our powers, Great Britain, should couple an official pledge that she will not claim for herself a single benefit, which shall not be shared by every nation uniting with her in the extinction of the Slave Trade; and especially

First—That no exclusive privilege in favor of British subjects shall ever be allowed to exist.

Secondly—That no *custom-house* shall ever be established at Fernando Po [in the Gulf of Guinea].

Thirdly—That no distinction shall be made there, *whether in peace or in war*, between our own subjects and those of any such foreign power, as to the rights they shall possess, or the terms on which they shall enjoy them. In short, that we purchase Fernando Po, and will hold it for no other purpose than the benefit of Africa. I am well aware that these may appear startling propositions. I am, however, supported in them by high authorities; the suggestion as to the custom-house was made to me by Mr. Porter, of the Board of Trade; and that respecting neutrality in peace or in war, originated with the learned Judge of the British Vice Admiralty Courts. Supported by his authority, I may venture to say that, though a novel, it would be a noble characteristic of our colony. As it is intended for different ends, so it would be ruled by different principles, from any colony which has ever been undertaken: it would have the distinction of being the neutral ground of the world, elevated above the mutual injuries of war; where, for the prosecution of a good and a vast object, the subjects and the fleets of all nations may meet in amity, and where there shall reign a perpetual truce.

Let us look to the tendency of the proposition, that no custom-house shall be established at Fernando Po, or at the post to be formed at the junction of the Niger and the Tchadda: we might then hope that the history of these stations would be a counterpart to that of Singapore, which is described as having been, in 1819, "an insignificant fishing-village, and a haunt of pirates," but now stands as an eloquent eulogy on the views of its founder, Sir Stamford Raffles, proving what may be effected, and in how short a time, for our own profit and for the improvement of the uncivilized world, "by the union of native industry and British enterprise," when uncurbed by restrictions on trade.

FREE LABOR

I now turn to the second great principle, viz.—Free Labor.

It may be thought by some almost superfluous that this should be urged, considering that there is an Act of Parliament, which declares that "Slavery shall be, and is hereby utterly and for ever abolished in all the colonies, possessions, and plantations of Great Britain." But if ever there were a case in which this great law should be strictly and strenuously enforced, and in which it is at the same time peculiarly liable to be neglected or evaded, it is in the case of any possessions we may obtain in Africa. It is necessary to be wise in time, and never to suffer this baneful weed to take root there. Let us remember what it has cost us to extirpate it from our old colonies. It is remarkable that among the whole phalanx of antagonists to the abolition of West India Slavery, there was never one who was not, by his own account, an ardent lover of freedom. Slavery, in the abstract, was universally acknowledged to be detestable; and they were in the habit of pathetically deploring their cruel fate, and of upbraiding the mother-country, which had originally planted this curse among them; but property had entwined itself around the disastrous institution, and we had to contend with a fearful array of securities, marriage settlements, and vested interests of all kinds. Again, bondage, it was said, had seared the intellect, and withered all that was noble in the bosoms of its victims. To have begun such an unrighteous system was an error, only less than that of suddenly eradicating it, and of clothing with the attributes of freemen, those whose very nature had been changed and defiled by servitude.

I firmly believe that much of all this was uttered in perfect sincerity; and yet, I feel the most serious apprehensions lest these wholesome convictions should evaporate before the temptations of a country, where land of the richest fertility is to be had for 1d. [pence] per acre, and laborers are to be purchased for 41d. per head. We know, not only that the Portuguese are turning their attention to plantations in the neighborhood of Loango, but that they have been bold enough to ask us to guarantee to them their property, that is their slaves, in these parts. This, together with certain ominous expressions which I have heard, convinces me that my apprehensions are not altogether chimerical; and I am not sure that we shall not once more hear the antique argument, that Negroes, "from the brutishness of their nature," are incapable of being induced to work by any stimulus but the lash: at all events, we shall be assured, that if we attempt to establish Free Labor, we shall assail the prejudices of the African chiefs in the tenderest points. If we do not take care, at the outset, to render the holding of slaves by British subjects in Africa highly penal, and perilous in the last degree, we shall see British capital again embarked, and vested interest acquired in human flesh. We shall, in spite of the warning we have had, commit a second time, the monstrous error, to say nothing of the crime, of tolerating slavery. A second time the slave-master will accuse us of being at least accomplices in his guilt; and once more we shall have to buy off opposition by an extravagant grant of money.

The suggestion, then, that I make is, that we shall lay it down, as a primary and sacred principle, that any man who enters any territory that we may acquire in Africa, is from that moment "Free, and discharged of all manner of slavery," and that Great Britain pledges herself to defend him from all, civilized or savage, who may attempt to recapture him. That one resolution will do much to give us laborers—to obtain for us the affections of the population—to induce them to imitate and adopt our customs—and to settle down to the pursuits of peaceful industry and productive agriculture.

I will subjoin in the Appendix further proof on the authority of General Turner, Colonel Denham, and Major Ricketts, who also spoke from what they saw at Sierra Leone, as to the disposition of Africans to work for wages.

The Rev. W. Fox, missionary at McCarthy's Island [off the Gambia] whom I have already quoted, says, "The Eastern Negroes . . . come here and hire themselves as laborers for several months, and, with the articles they receive in payment, barter them again on their way home for more than their actual value on this island." In the journal of the same gentleman, just received, under date of April, 1838, he writes thus: "I have to-day paid off all the laborers who had been employed on the mission ground, and have hired about eighty more, with three overseers; *many others applied for work*, and I should have felt a pleasure in engaging them, but that I wished to keep the expenses within moderate bounds."

It thus appears that free labor is to be obtained in Africa, even under present circumstances, if we will but pay the price for it, and that there is no necessity at all for that system of coerced labor, which no necessity could justify. I am aware that I have trespassed on the patience of many of my readers, who require no arguments against slavery; but I have already expressed, and continue to feel, if there be danger anywhere in the plan for the cultivation of Africa, it lies in this point. And I wish the question of slavery to be definitively settled, and our principles to be resolved on, in such a way as shall render it impossible for us to retract them, before a single step is taken, or a shilling of property invested in the attempt to grow sugar and cotton in Africa.

I shall here introduce the consideration of two other points, which though they cannot precisely be classed as principles, yet are nearly akin to them, and deserve our very serious attention.

The proposal of a settlement in Africa, necessarily recalls to mind our vast empire in India: and, surely, no soberminded statesman would desire to see renewed, in another quarter of the globe, the career we have run in the East.

I entirely disclaim any disposition to erect a new empire in Africa. Remembering what has now been disclosed, of the affliction of that quarter of the globe, and of the horrors and abominations which every spot exhibits, and every hour produces, it would be the extreme of selfish cruelty to let a question so momentous be decided with an eye to our own petty interests; but there is another view of the case—it would also be the most extreme folly to allow ourselves to swerve one iota from its right decision, by any such indirect and short-sighted considerations.

What is the value to Great Britain of the sovereignty of a few hundred square miles in Benin, or Eboe, as compared with that of bringing forward into the market of the world millions of customers, who may be taught to grow the raw material which we require, and who require the manufactured commodities which we produce? The one is a trivial and insignificant matter; the other is a subject worthy the most anxious solicitude of the most accomplished statesmen.

It appears to me, however, that the danger of our indulging any thirst for dominion is rather plausible than real. In the first place, the climate there forbids the employment of European armies, if armies indeed formed any part of my plan, which they do not. I look forward to the employment, almost exclusively, of the African race. A few Europeans may be required in some leading departments; but the great body of our agents must have African blood in their veins, and of course to the entire exclusion of our troops.

2dly. In Asia, there was accumulated treasure to tempt our cupidity: in Africa, there is none. Asia was left to the government of a company: the African establishments will, of course, be regularly subjected to parliamentary supervision. Our encroachments upon Asia were made at a time, when little general attention was bestowed, or sympathy felt, for the sufferings and wrongs of a remote people. Now, attention is awake on such topics. India stands as a beacon to warn us against extended dominion; and if there were not, as I believe there are, better principles among our statesmen, there would be a check to rapacity, and a shield for the weak, in the wakeful commiseration of the public.

I may add, that, were the danger as great as some imagine, it would have disclosed itself ere this. The French have had for some time a settlement on the Senegal; the Danes on the Rio Volta; the Dutch on the Gold Coast; the Portuguese at Loango; the Americans at Cape Mesurado; and the English at Sierra Leone, in the Gambia, and on the Gold Coast; and I know not that there has been upon the part of these a desire manifested to raise an empire in Central Africa. Certainly, there has been none on the part of the British: on the contrary, I think there is some reason to complain that our government has been too slow, at least for the welfare of Africa, in accepting territory which has been voluntarily offered to us, and in confirming the treaties which have been made by our officers. We have been in possession of Sierra Leone not very far short of half a century; and I am not aware that it can be alleged that any injury has been thereby inflicted upon the natives.

Lastly. There is this consideration, and to me it seems conclusive—Granting that the danger to African liberty is as imminent as I consider it to be slight, still the state of the country is such, that, change as it may, it cannot change for the worse.

The other point to which I would call attention is, the encouragement which may be afforded to the infant cultivation of Africa, by promoting the admission and use of its productions. I shall not advert to the assistance which we may fairly expect from the Legislature in this respect, when the subject is brought under its consideration in all its important bearings; with the example of France and the United States before them, I cannot doubt that Government will introduce such measures as a liberal and enlightened policy will dictate. But individuals have it in their power to contribute largely to the encouragement of African produce, by a preference that will cost them little. Let them recollect that for centuries we were mainly instrumental in checking cultivation in Africa: we ransacked the whole continent in order to procure laborers for the West Indies. Is it, then, too much to ask, now when we are endeavoring to raise her from the gulf of wretchedness into which we have contributed to plunge her, that while she is struggling with enormous difficulties, we should force her industry and excite her to unfold her capabilities by anxiously encouraging the consumption of her produce?

46. THEODORE CANOT

SLAVING IN LIBERIA. 1850.

Like many nineteenth-century slavers, Theodore Canot was a soldier of fortune and served under many flags. Although he had been brought up in Florence, Italy, he was educated by the captain of an American vessel. Canot had no religion, many vices, and few weaknesses.

By this time the sub-factory of New Sestros was somewhat renowned in Cuba and Porto Rico. Our dealings with commanders, the character of my cargoes, and the rapidity with which I despatched a customer and his craft, were proverbial in the islands. Indeed, the third year of my lodgment had not rolled over before the slave-demand was so great that, in spite of rum, cottons, muskets, powder, kidnapping, and Prince Freeman's wars, the country could not supply our demand.

To aid New Sestros, I had established several *nurseries*, or junior factories, at points a few miles from the limits of Liberia. These "chapels of ease" furnished my parent barraccons [slave stockades] with young and small negroes, mostly kidnapped, I suppose, in the neighbourhood of the beach.

When I was perfectly cured of the injury I sustained in my first philanthropic fight, I loaded my spacious cutter with a choice collection of trade-goods, and set sail one fine morning for the outpost at Digby. I designed also, if advisable, to erect another receiving barracoon under the lee of Cape Mount.

But my call at Digby was unsatisfactory. The pens were vacant, and our merchandise squandered *on credit*. This put me in a very uncomfortable passion, which would have rendered an interview between "Mr. Powder" and his agent anything

From Theodore Canot, *Adventures of an African Slaver: Being a True Account of the Life of Captain Theodore Canot, Trader in Gold, Ivory, and Slaves on the Coast of Guinea* (Garden City, NY: Garden City Publishing Co., 1928), pp. 330–334. Reprinted by permission of Albert & Charles Boni, Inc.

but pleasant or profitable, had he been at his post. ortunately for both of us he was abroad carousing with a king; so that I refused landing a single yard of merchandise and hoisted sail for the next village.

There I transacted business in regular ship-shape. Our rum was plenteously distributed and established an *entente cordiale* which would have charmed a diplomatist at his first dinner in a new capital. The naked blackguards flocked around me like crows. I clothed their loins in partu-colored calicoes that enriched them with a plumage worthy of parrots. In five days nineteen newly "conveyed" darkies were exchanged for London muskets, Yankee grog, and Manchester cottons.

My cutter, though but twenty-seven feet long, was large enough to stow my gang, considering that the voyage was short, and the slaves but boys and girls; so I turned my prow homeward with contented spirit and promising skies. Yet before night, all was changed. Wind and sea rose together. The sun sank in a low streak of blood. After a while, it rained in terrible squalls; till finally darkness caught me in a perfect gale. So high was the surf and so shelterless the coast, that it became utterly impossible to make a less of any headland where we might ride out the storm in safety. Our best hope was in the cutter's ability to keep the open sea without swamping; and accordingly, under the merest patch of sail, I coasted the perilous breakers, guided by their roar, till day dawn. But, when the sun lifted over the horizon—peering for an instant through a rent in the storm-cloud, and then disappearing behind the grey vapour—I saw at once that the coast offered no chance of landing our blacks at some friendly town. Everywhere the bellowing shore was lashed by surf, impracticable even for the boats and skill of the Kroomen. On I dashed, driving and almost burying the cutter, with loosened reef, till we came opposite Monrovia; where, safe in the absence of cruiser, I crept at dark under the less of the cape, veiling my cargo with our useless sails.

Sunset killed the wind, enabling us to be off again at dawn; yet hardly were we clear of the cape when both gale and current freshened from the old quarter, holding us completely in check. Nevertheless, I kept at sea till evening, and then sneaked back to my protecting anchorage.

By this time, my people and slaves were well-nigh famished, for their sole food had been a scant allowance of raw cassava. Anxiety, toil, rain, and drenching spray, broke their spirits. The blacks, from the hot interior, and now for the first time off their mother earth, suffered not only form the inclement weather, but groaned with the terrible pangs of sea-sickness. I resolved, if possible, to refresh the drooping gang by a hot meal; and beneath the shelter of the tarpaulin, contrived to cook a mess of rice. Warm food comforted us astonishingly; but alas! The next day was a picture of the past. A slave—cramped and smothered amid the crowd that soaked so long in the salt water at our boat's bottom—died during the darkness. Next morning, the same low, leaden coffin-lid sky, hung like a pall over sea and shore. Wind in terrific blasts, and rain in deluging squalls, howled and beat on us. Come what might, I resolved not to stir. All day I kept the people beneath the sails, with orders to move their limbs as much as possible, in order to overcome the benumbing effect of moisture and packed confinement. The incessant drenching from sea and sky to which they had been so long subjected, chilled their slackened circulation to such a degree that death from torpor seemed rapidly supervening. Motion, motion, motion was my constant command; but I hoarded my alcohol as a last resource.

I saw that no time was to be lost, and that nothing but a bold encounter of hazard would save either lives or property. Before dark my mind was made up as to the enterprise. I would land in the neighbourhood of the colony, and cross its territory during the shadow of night.

I do not suppose that the process by which I threw my stiffened crew on the beach, and revived them with copious draughts of brandy, would interest the reader; but midnight did not strike before my cargo, under the escort of Kroo guides, was boldly marching through the colonial town, and safe on its way to New Sestros! Fortunately for my daredevil adventure, the tropical rain poured down in ceaseless torrents, compelling the unsuspicious colonists to keep beneath their roofs. Indeed, no one dreamed of a forced march by human beings on that dreadful night of tempest, else it might have gone hard had I been detected in the desecration of colonial soil. Still, I was prepared for all emergencies. I never went abroad without the two great keys of Africa—gold and firearms; and had it been my lot to encounter a colonist, he would either have learned the value of silence, or have been carried along, under the muzzle of a pistol, till the gang was in safety.

While it was still dark, I left the caravan advancing by an interior path to Little Bassa, where one of my branches could furnish it with necessaries to cross the other colony of Bassa San Juan, so as to reach my homestead in the course of three days. Meanwhile I retraced my way to Monrovia, and reaching it by sunrise, satisfied the amiable colonists that I had just taken shelter in their harbour, and was fresh from my dripping cutter. It is very likely that no one in the colony to the present day knows the true story of this adventure, or would believe it unless confessed by me.

---

47. HEINRICH BARTH

AL-HAJJ BASHIR, KUKAWA, AND TIMBUKTU. 1852.

Heinrich Barth (1821–1865) was one of the greatest and most intelligent of the nineteenth-century African explorers. A German, he left Tripoli and crossed the Sahara in 1850 as a member of an English expedition to the Sudan. The commander, James Richardson, died, but Barth and another German, Adolf Overweg, visited Katsina and Kano, traveled to Bornu and its capital, Kukawa, explored Lake Chad, and reached the Benue River. Overweg died in 1852, and Barth continued alone to Sokoto and Timbuktu. He then returned to Bornu, crossed the Sahara, and reached England near the end of 1855. His journal contains immense information on the Western Sudan that was collected from his precise and penetrating observations. Kukawa was built as the capital of Bornu in 1814 by Shaykh al-Kanami but

From Heinrich Barth, *Travels and Discoveries in North and Central Africa from the Journal of an Expedition Undertaken under the Auspices of H.B.M.'s Government in the Years 1849–1855* (Philadelphia: J. W. Bradley, 1859), pp. 181–189, 447–450.

*was destroyed in 1846 by the Sultan of Wadai in support of the titular mai of Bornu.
The Wadai forces were driven back by al-Kanami's son and successor, Umar
(1835–1880), who rebuilt Kukawa as a twin town, the eastern part (billa gediba) of
which was the seat of the ruler and was separated by an open space from the western part (billa futela). Umar confined himself to his palace and devoted himself to
religious studies, leaving control in the hands of such wazirs as al-Hajj Bashir.
Leaving Kukawa, Barth eventually made his way west to Timbuktu. Probably founded sometime in the eleventh century, Timbuktu seems to have remained only an
insignificant settlement until the thirteenth century, when it became an emporium
for trans-Saharan trade. Unlike Djenné, however, Timbuktu never became a real
city-state, and its heterogeneous population never achieved the unity of other
Sudanic cities. Timbuktu was always dominated by outsiders—Mali, Songhay,
Tuareg, Moors, Fulani. Nevertheless, its Sankore quarter was an important center
of African Islamic learning. Timbuktu's reputation for scholarship lasted well into
the nineteenth century and fired the imagination of Alfred, Lord Tennyson (who won
the poetry prize at Cambridge for his poem "Timbuctoo") and other romantics long
after the city's greatness had passed.*

I have peculiar reason to thank Providence for having averted the storm which
was gathering over his head during my stay in Bornu, for my intimacy with him [al-
Hajj Bashir] might very easily have involved me also in the calamities which befell
him. However, I repeat that altogether, he was a most excellent, kind, liberal, and
just man, and might have done much good to the country if he had been less selfish
and more active. He was incapable, indeed, of executing by himself any act of
severity, such as in the unsettled state of a semi-barbarous kingdom may at times be
necessary; and, being conscious of his own mildness, he left all those matters to a
man named Lamino, to whom I gave the title of "the shameless left hand of the
vizier," and whom I shall have frequent occasion to mention.

I pressed upon the vizier the necessity of defending the northern frontier of
Bornu against the Tawarek [Tuareg] by more effectual measures than had been then
adopted, and thus retrieving, for cultivation and the peaceable abode of his fellow
subjects, the fine borders of the Komidugu, and restoring security to the road to
Fezzan. Just about this time the Tawarek had made another expedition into the border districts on a large scale, so that Kashella Belal, the first of the warchiefs, was
obliged to march against them; and the road to Kano, which I, with my usual good
luck, had passed unmolested, had become so unsafe that a numerous caravan was
plundered, and a well-known Arab merchant, the Sherif el Ghali, killed.

I remonstrated with him on the shamefully-neglected state of the shores of the
lake, which contained the finest pasturegrounds, and might yield an immense quantity of rice and cotton. He entered with spirit into all my proposals, but in a short
time all was forgotten. He listened with delight to what little historical knowledge I
had of these countries, and inquired particularly whether Kanem had really been in
former times a mighty kingdom, or whether it would be worth retaking. It was in
consequence of these conversations that he began to take an interest in the former
history of the country, and that the historical records of Edris Alawoma [Idris
Alawma] came to light; but he would not allow me to take them into my hands, and

I could only read over his shoulders. He was a very religious man; and though he admired Europeans very much on account of their greater accomplishments, he was shocked to think that they drank intoxicating liquors. However, I tried to console him by telling him that, although the Europeans were also very partial to the fair sex, yet they did not indulge in this luxury on so large a scale as he did, and that therefore he ought to allow them some other little pleasure.

He was very well aware of the misery connected with the slave-trade; for, on his pilgrimage to Mekka, in the mountainous region between Fezzan and Ben-Ghazi, he had lost, in one night, forty of his slaves by the extreme cold, and he swore that he would never take slaves for sale if he were to travel again. But it was more difficult to make him sensible of the horrors of slave-hunting, although, when accompanying him on the expedition to Musgu, I and Mr. Overweg urged this subject with more success, as the further progress of my narrative will show. He was very desirous to open a commerce with the English, although he looked with extreme suspicion upon the form of articles in which the treaty was proposed to be drawn up; but he wished to forbid to Christians the sale of two things, viz., spirituous liquors and Bibles. He did not object to Bibles being brought into the country, and even given as presents, but he would not allow of their being sold.

Having now a horse whereon to mount, I rode every day, either into the eastern town to pay a visit to the sheikh or to the vizier, or roving around the whole circuit of the capital, and peeping into the varied scenes which the life of the people exhibited. The precincts of the town, with its suburbs, are just as interesting, as its neighborhood (especially during the months that precede the rainy season) is monotonous and tiresome in the extreme. Certainly the arrangement of the capital contributes a great deal to the variety of the picture which it forms, laid out as it is, in two distinct towns, each surrounded with its wall, the one occupied chiefly by the rich and wealthy, containing very large establishments, while the other, with the exception of the principal thoroughfare, which traverses the town from west to east, consists of rather crowded dwellings, with narrow, winding lanes. These two distinct towns are separated by a space about half a mile broad, itself thickly inhabited on both sides of a wide, open road, which forms the connection between them, but laid out less regularly, and presenting to the eye a most interesting medley of large clay buildings and small thatched huts, of massive clay walls surrounding immense yards, and light fences of reeds in a more or less advanced state of decay, and with a variety of color, according to their age, from the brightest yellow down to the deepest black. All around these two towns there are small villages or clusters of huts, and large detached farms surrounded with clay walls, low enough to allow a glimpse from horseback over the thatched huts which they inclose.

In this labyrinth of dwellings a man, interested in the many forms which human life presents, may rove about at any time of the day with the certainty of never-failing amusement, although the life of the Kanuri people passes rather monotonously along, with the exception of some occasional feasting. During the hot hours, indeed, the town and its precincts become torpid, except on market-days, when the market-place itself, at least, and the road leading to it from the western gate, are most animated just at that time. For, singular, as it is, in Kukawa, as well as almost all over this part of Negroland, the great markets do not begin to be well attended till the heat of the day grows intense; and it is curious to observe what a difference prevails in this, as well as in other respects, between these countries and Yoruba, where almost all the markets are held in the cool of the evening.

The daily little markets, or durriya, even in Kukawa, are held in the afternoon. The most important of these durriyas is that held inside the west gate of the billa futebe, and here even camels, horses, and oxen are sold in considerable numbers; but they are much inferior to the large fair, or great market, which is held every Monday on the open ground beyond the two villages which lie at a short distance from the western gate.

I visited the great fair, "kasuku leteninbe," every Monday immediately after my arrival, and found it very interesting, as it calls together the inhabitants of all the eastern parts of Bornu, the Shuwa and the Koyam, with their corn and butter; the former, though of Arab origin, and still preserving in purity his ancient character, always carrying his merchandise on the back of oxen, the women mounted upon the top of it, while the African Koyam employs the camel; the Kanembu with their butter and dried fish, the inhabitants of Makari with their tobes; even Budduma, or rather Yedina, are very often seen in the market, selling whips made from the skin of the hippopotamus, or sometimes even hippopotamus meat, or dried fish, and attract the attention of the speculator by their slender figures, their small, handsome features, unimpaired by any incisions, the men generally wearing a short black shirt and a small straw hat, "suni ngawa," their neck adorned with several strings of kungona or shells, while the women are profusely ornamented with strings of glass beads, and wear their hair in a very remarkable way, though not in so awkward a fashion as Mr. Overweg afterward observed in the island Belarigo.

On reaching the market-place from the town, the visitor first comes to that part where the various materials for constructing the light dwellings of the country are sold, such as mats; poles and stakes; the framework for the thatched roofs of huts, and the ridge-beam; then oxen for slaughter, or for carrying burdens; farther on, long rows of leathern bags filled with corn, ranging far along on the south side of the market-place. These long rows are animated not only by the groups of the sellers and buyers, with their weatherworn figures and torn dresses, but also by the beasts of burden, mostly oxen, which have brought the loads, and which are to carry back their masters to their distant dwelling-places; then follow the camels for sale, often as many as a hundred or more, and numbers of horses, but generally not first-rate ones, which are mostly sold in private. All this sale of horses, camels, &c., with the exception of the oxen, passes through the hands of the broker, who, according to the mode of announcement, takes his percentage from the buyer or the seller.

The fatigue which people have to undergo in purchasing their week's necessaries in the market is all the more harassing, as there is not at present any standard money for buying and selling; for the ancient standard of the country, viz., the pound of copper, has long since fallen into disuse, though the name, "rotl," still remains. The "gabaga," or cotton strips, which then became usual, have lately begun to be supplanted by the cowries or "kungona," which have been introduced, as it seems, rather by a speculation of the ruling people than by a natural want of the inhabitants, though nobody can deny that they are very useful for buying small articles, and infinitely more convenient than cotton strips. Eight cowries or kungona are reckoned equal to one gabaga, and four gabaga, or two-and-thirty kungona, to one rod. Then, for buying larger objects, there are shirts of all kinds and sizes, from the "dora," the coarsest and smallest one, quite unfit for use, and worth six rotls, up to the large ones, worth fifty or sixty rotls. But, while this is a standard value, the relation of the rotl and the Austrian dollar, which is pretty well current in Bornu, is subject to extreme fluctuation, due, I must confess, at least partly, to the speculations of the ruling men, and principally to that of my friend the Haj Beshir. Indeed, I cannot defend him against the reproach of having speculated to the great detriment of the public; so that when he had collected a great amount of kungona, and wished to give it currency, the dollar would suddenly fall as low as to five-and-forty or fifty rotls, while at other times it would fetch as much as one hundred rotls, or three thousand two hundred shells, that is, seven hundred shells more than in Kano. The great advantage of the market in Kano is that there is one standard coin, which, if too large amount of dollars be not on a sudden set in circulation, will always preserve the same value.

But to return to the picture of life which the town of Kukawa presents. With the exception of Mondays, when just during the hottest hours of the day there is much crowd and bustle in the market-place, it is very dull from about noon till three o'clock in the afternoon; and even during the rest of the day those scenes of industry which in the varied panorama of Kano meet the eye are here sought for in vain. Instead of those numerous dyeing-yards or marina, full of life and bustle, though certainly also productive of much filth and foul odors, which spread over the town of Kano, there is only a single and a very poor marina in Kukawa; no beating of lobes is heard, nor the sound of any other handicraft.

There is a great difference of character between these two towns; and the Bornu people are by temperament far more phlegmatic than those of Kano. The women in general are much more ugly, with square, short figures, large heads, and broad noses with immense nostrils, disfigured still more by the enormity of a red bead or coral worn in the nostrils. Nevertheless, they are certainly quite as coquettish, and, as far as I had occasion to observe, at least as wanton also as the more cheerful and sprightly Hausa women. I have never seen a Hausa woman strolling about the streets with her gown trailing after her on the ground, the fashion of the women of Kukawa, and wearing on her shoulders some Manchester print of a showy pattern, keeping the ends of it in her hands, while she throws her arms about in a coquettish manner. In a word, their dress, as well as their demeanor, is far more decent and agreeable. The best part in the dress or ornaments of the Bornu women is the silver ornament which they wear on the back of the head, and which in taller figures, when the hair is plaited in the form of a helmet, is very becoming; but it is not every woman who can afford such an ornament, and many a one sacrifices her better interests for this decoration.

The most animated quarter of the two towns is the great thoroughfare, which, proceeding by the southern side of the palace in the western town, traverses it from west to east, and leads straight to the sheikh's residence in the eastern town. This is the "dendal" or promenade, a locality which has its imitation, on a less or greater scale, in every town of the country. This road, during the whole day, is crowded by numbers of people on horseback and on foot; free men and slaves, foreigners as well as natives, every one in his best attire, to pay his respects to the sheikh or his vizier, to deliver an errand, or to sue for justice or employment, or a present. I myself very often went along this well-trodden path—this high road of ambition; but I generally went at an unusual hour, either at sunrise in the morning, or while the heat of the midday, not yet abated, detained the people in their cool haunts, or late at night, when the people were already retiring to rest, or, sitting before their houses, beguiling their leisure hours with amusing tales or with petty scandal. At such hours I was sure to find the vizier or the sheikh alone; but sometimes they wished me also to visit and sit with them, when they were accessible to all the people; and on these occasions the vizier took pride and delight in conversing with me about matters of science, such as the motion of the earth, or the planetary system, or subjects of that kind.

The city of Timbuktu, according to Dr. Peterman's laying down of it from my materials, lies in 17° 37' N. and 3° 5' W. of Greenwich. Situated only a few feet above the average level of the river, and at a distance of six miles from the principal branch, it at present forms a sort of triangle, the base of which points toward the river, while the projecting angle is directed toward the north, having for its centre the mosque of Sankore. But, during the zenith of its power, the town extended a thousand yards further north, and included the tomb of the Faki Mahmud, which, according to some of my informants, was then situated in the midst of the town.

The circumference of the city at the present time I reckon at a little more than two miles and a half; but it may approach closely to three miles, taking into account some of the projecting angles. Although of only small size, Timbuktu may well be called a city—medina—in comparison with the frail dwelling-places all over Negroland. At present it is not walled. Its former wall, which seems never to have been of great magnitude, and was rather more of the nature of a rampart, was destroyed by the Fulbe [Fulani] on their first entering the place in the beginning of the year 1826. The town is laid out partly in rectangular, partly in winding streets, or, as they are called here "tijeraten," which are not paved, but for the greater part consist of hard sand and gravel, and some of them have a sort of gutter in the middle. Besides the large and the small market there are few open areas, except a small square in front of the mosque of Yahia, called Tumbutu-bottema.

Small as it is, the city is tolerably well inhabited, and almost all the houses are in good repair. There are about 980 clay houses, and a couple of hundred conical huts of matting, the latter, with a few exceptions, constituting the outskirts of the town on the north and northeast sides, where a great deal of rubbish, which has been accumulating in the course of several centuries, is formed into conspicuous mounds. The clay houses are all of them built on the same principle as my own residence, which I have described, with the exception that the houses of the poorer people have only one court-yard, and have no upper room on the terrace.

The only remarkable public buildings in the town are the three large mosques: the Jingere-ber, built by Mansa Musa; the mosque of Sankore, built at an early period at the expense of a wealthy woman; and the mosque Sidi Yahia, built at the expense of a kadhi [qadi] of the town. There were three other mosques: that of Sidi Haj Mohammed, Msid Belal, and that of Sidi el Bami. These mosques, and perhaps some little msid, or place of prayer, Caillié must have included when he speaks of seven mosques. Besides these mosques there are at present no distinguished public buildings in the town; and of the royal palace, or Ma-dugu, wherein the kings of Songhay used to reside occasionally, as well as the Kasbah, which was built in later times, in the southeastern quarter, or the "Sane-gungu," which already at that time was inhabited by the merchants from Ghadames, not a trace is to be seen. Besides this quarter, which is the wealthiest, and contains the best houses, there are six other quarters, viz., Yubu, the quarter comprising the great market-place (yubu) and the mosque of Sidi Yahia, to the west of Sane-gungu; and west of the former, forming the southwestern angle of the town, and called, from the great mosque, Jingere-ber or Zangere-ber. This latter quarter, from the most ancient times, seems to have been inhabited especially by Mohammedans, and not unlikely may have formed a distinct quarter, separated from the rest of the town by a wall of its own. Toward the north, the quarter Sanegungu is bordered by the one called Sarakaina, meaning literally the "little town," and containing the residence of the sheikh, and the house where I myself was lodged. Attached to Sara-kaina, toward the north, is Yubu-kaina, the quarter containing the "little market," which is especially used as a butcher's market. Bordering both on Jingere-ber and Yubukaina is the quarter Bagindi, occupying the lowest situation in the town, and stated by the inhabitants to have been flooded entirely in the great inundation which took place in 1640. From this depression in the ground, the quarter of Sankore, which forms the northernmost angle of the city, rises to a considerable elevation, in such a manner that the mosque of Sankore, which seems to occupy its ancient site and level, is at present situated in a deep hollow—an appearance which seems to prove that this elevation of the ground is caused by the accumulation of rubbish, in consequence of the repeated ruin which seems to have befallen this quarter pre-eminently, as being the chief stronghold of the native Songhay. The slope which this quarter forms toward the northeastern end in some spots exceeds eighty feet.

The whole number of the settled inhabitants of the town amounts to about 13,000, while the floating population during the months of the greatest traffic and intercourse, especially from November to January, may amount on an average to 5,000, and under favorable circumstances to as many as 10,000.

[Dr. Barth made an excursion with the sheikh to Kabara, the harbor of Timbuktu, and they took up their residence at the desert camp already described.]

Notwithstanding trifling incidents which tended occasionally to alleviate the tediousness of our stay, I was deeply afflicted by the immense delay and loss of time, and did not allow an opportunity to pass by of urging my protector to hasten our departure; and he promised me that, as I was not looking for property, he should not keep me long. But, nevertheless, his slow and deliberate character could not be overcome, and it was not until the arrival of another messenger from Hamda-Allahi, with a fresh order from the sheikh to deliver me into his hands, that he was induced to return into the town.

My situation in this turbulent place now approached a serious crisis; but, through the care which my friends took of me, I was not allowed to become fully aware of the danger I was in [because of being a Christian]. The sheikh himself was greatly excited, but came to no decision with regard to the measures to be taken; and at times he did not see any safety for me except by my taking refuge with the Tawarek [Tuareg], and placing myself entirely under their protection. But as for myself I remained quiet, although my spirits were far from being buoyant; especially as, during this time, I suffered severely from rheumatism; and I had become so tired of this stay outside in the tents, where I was not able to write, that, when the sheikh went out again in the evening of the 16th, I begged him to let me remain where I was. Being anxious about my safety, he returned the following evening. However, on the 22d, I was obliged to accompany him on another visit to the tents, which had now been pitched in a different place, on a bleak sandy eminence, about five miles east from the town, but this time he kept his promise of not staying more than twenty-four hours. It was at this encampment that I saw again the last four of my camels, which at length, after innumerable delays, and with immense expense, had been brought from beyond the river, but they were in a miserable condition, and furnished another excuse to my friends for putting off my departure, the animals being scarcely fit to undertake a journey.

48. PAUL DU CHAILLU

TRADE IN GABON. 1859.

Paul Belloni du Chaillu (1831–1903) spent eight years in Africa—four as a trader and four as a naturalist and explorer. During his travels between 1856 and 1859, he explored Gabon, Congo (Brazzaville), and areas that were the Spanish colony of Rio Muni, hitherto unknown to Europeans. As a trader he well knew the methods of commerce then in use in equatorial Africa, as well as the role of the African trader in the systems of controlled barter and exchange with European traders along the coast and in the interior.

. . . Each of these tribes assumes to itself the privilege of acting as go-between or middle-man to those next to it, and charges a heavy percentage for this office; and no infraction of this rule is permitted under penalty of war. Thus a piece of ivory or ebony may belong originally to a negro in the far interior, and if he wants to barter it for "white man's trade," he dares not take it to a market himself. If he should be rash enough to attempt such a piece of enterprise his goods would be confiscated,

From Paul Belloni du Chaillu, *Explorations and Adventures in Equatorial Africa* (London: J. Murray, 1861), pp. 10–16.

and he, if caught, fined by those whose monopoly he sought to break down, or most likely sold into slavery.

He is obliged by the laws of trade to intrust it to some fellow in the next tribe nearer to the coast. He, in turn, disposes of it to the next chief or friend, and so ivory, or ebony, or bar-wood, passes through probably a dozen hands ere it reaches the factory of the trader on the coast.

This would seem to work against the white trader by increasing the price of products. But this is only half the evil. Although the producer sold his ivory, and though it was resold a dozen times, all this trade was only a *commission* business with no advances. In fact, the first holder has *trusted* each successive dispenser with his property without any equivalent or "collateral" security. Now, when the last black fellow disposes of this piece of ebony or ivory to the white merchant or captain, he retains, in the first place, a very liberal percentage of the returns for his valuable services, and turns the remainder over to his next neighbour above. *He*, in turn, takes out a commission for *his* trouble and passes on what is left; and so, finally, a very small remainder—too often nothing at all—is handed over to the poor fellow who has inaugurated the speculation or sent the tusk.

Anyone can see the iniquity of this system, and the fatal clog it throws on all attempts at the building up of a legitimate commerce in a country so rich in many products now almost indispensable to civilized nations. The poor interior tribes are kept by their neighbours in the profoundest ignorance of what is done on the coast. They are made to believe the most absurd and horrid stories as to the ferocity, the duplicity, and the cunning of the white traders. They are persuaded that the rascally middle-men are not only in constant danger of their lives by their intercourse with the whites, but that they do not make any profit on the goods which they goodnaturedly pass on to a market; so that I have known one of these scoundrels, after having appropriated a large share of the poor remainder of returns for a venture of ivory, actually, by a pitiful story, beg a portion of what he had handed over to his unsuspicious client. Each tribe cheats its next neighbour above, and maligns its next neighbour below. A talent for slandering is, of course, a first-rate business talent; and the harder stories one can tell of his neighbours below the greater profit he will make on his neighbour above.

The consequence is that the interior tribes—who own the most productive country—have little or no incentive to trade, or to gather together the stores of ivory, bar-wood [mahogany], ebony, &c., for which they get such small prices, and these at no certain intervals, but often after long periods, even years elapsing sometimes before a final settlement is found convenient. Thus they are discouraged, and perforce remain in their original barbarism and inactivity.

The trade in slaves is carried on in exactly the same way, except that sometimes an infraction of trade-laws, or some disturbance on account of witchcraft, causes a war between two tribes in the commission business, when, of course, each side takes all it can of the opposite and ships them direct to the coast—to the barracoons or slave-depôts, of which I shall have something more detailed to say farther on.

There are, however, other obstacles to the prosecution of a regular commercial enterprise even by the shrewder among the negroes. It is not permitted that any member of a tribe shall get into his hands more than his share of the trade. It occurred some years ago to a shrewd Mpongwe fellow that in trade transactions honesty might be the best policy, and he followed the suggestion so well that presently both the whites and the interior natives threw a very considerable trade into his honest hands. But no sooner was this observed than he was threatened with poisoning, accused of witchcraft, and such a hullaballoo raised about his ears that he was forced to refuse the trade offered him, and, in a measure, retire from business to save his life.

More recently still, there were three or four men in the river who had obtained by long good conduct quite a character for honesty, and also, in consequence, got a good deal of business. At last a captain came for a load of bar-wood, and declared that he would trust only the three or four men in question, to the bitter disappointment of other traders. The vessel was quickly filled and departed; and there arose a great "palaver"—the Mpongwe cant for a quarrel—in which the kings and chiefs and all the disappointed trading fellows met together at Glass Town—the residence of my honest friends—to advise about such an outrage. The men were called up for trial. They had been educated at the American mission, and knew how to write; and the charge made against them now was that they had written to the white man's country to say that there were no good men in Gaboon but themselves.

To this the accused shrewdly replied that the white men would not believe men who should thus praise themselves.

But reply was useless. They were threatened that if they took the next ship that came, the malcontents would "make a boondgi," or work a spell of witchcraft upon them, and kill them. Fortunately, in this case, the honest fellows had learned at the mission not to fear such threats; and the French commander for once stepped in and protected them against their envious fellows, so that for this time, on the West Coast of Africa, honesty seems likely to get its reward.

Again, through the anxiety of white traders to secure "trade," there has sprung up along the coast an injurious system of "trust." A merchant, to secure to himself certain quantities of produce yet to come down from the interior, gives to such black fellows as he thinks he can depend upon advances of trade goods, often to very considerable amounts. In this way, on the Gaboon and on the coast, often many thousand dollars' worth of goods are in the hands of natives, for which no consideration has been received by the white trader, who meantime waits, and is put to trouble and expense, and thinks himself lucky if he does not eventually lose a part of his investment.

This system of "trust," as it is called, does great injury to the natives, for it tempts them to practise all sorts of cheats, for which they are sharp enough-indeed, much too shrewd often for the white man. Of course, *his* only dependence lies in the knowledge of his black debtor that if he cheats too badly his future supplies will be stopped entirely. But the practice develops all kinds of overtrading as well as rascality—negroes seldom hesitating to contract to supply much greater quantities of produce than they can hope to procure during a season.

Even the slave-trade, I found, on my visit to Cape Lopez, is burdened with this evil of "trust," and some of the Portuguese slavers, I was told, get preciously cheated in their advances on shipments of slaves sold "to arrive," but which do not come to hand.

I have heard the negroes called stupid, but my experience shows them to be anything but that. They are very shrewd traders indeed; and no captain or merchant who is a new hand on the coast will escape being victimized by their cunning in driving a bargain.

Say that to-day the good ship *Jenny* has arrived in the river. Immediately every black fellow is full of trade. The ship is boarded by a crowd of fellows, each jabbering away, apparently at random, but all telling the same story.

Never was there such dearth of ivory, or whatever the captain may want!

Never were the interior tribes so obstinate in demanding a high price!

Never was the whole coast so bare!

Never were difficulties so great!

There have been fights, captain!

And fever, captain!

And floods, captain!

And no trade at all, captain!

Not a tooth!

This point settled, they produce their "good books," which are certificates of character, in which some captain or other white trader who is known on the coast vouches for the honesty—the great honesty and entire trustworthiness—of the bearer. It is not worth while for a fellow to present himself without a certificate, and the papers are all *good*, because when "the bearer" has cheated he does not apply for a "character." Now these certificates help him to cheat. When he finds the need of a new set of papers, he conducts himself with scrupulous honesty towards two or three captains. These, of course, "certify" him, and then he goes into the wildest and most reckless speculations, upheld by the "good books," which he shows to every captain that comes.

Now, while they are pretending that nothing is to be bought, that there is no ivory on the coast, all this time the lying rascals have their hands full, and are eager to sell. They know the captain is in a hurry. The coast is sickly. The weather is hot. He fears his crew may fall sick or die, and he be left with a broken voyage. Every day is therefore precious to him; but to the black fellows all days are alike. They have no storage, no interest account, no fever to fear, and, accordingly, they can tire the captain out. This they do. In fact often, if they have an obstinate customer to deal with, they even combine and send all the trade a day's journey up river, and thus produce a fair show of commercial scarcity. At last, when high prices have been established, when the inroads of fever on his crew or the advance of the season have made the poor captain desperately willing to pay anything, the ivory comes aboard, and the cunning black fellows chuckle.

Even then, however, there are tedious hours of chaffering. A negro has perhaps only one tooth to sell, and he is willing—as he must live on this sale for a long period of idleness—to give much time to its proper disposal. He makes up his mind beforehand how much more he will ask than he will eventually take. He brings his tooth alongside; spends the afternoon in bargaining, and probably takes it back ashore at dusk, to try again the next day; till at last, when he sees he cannot possibly get more, he strikes the trade. I have known several days to be spent in the selling of a single tooth or a single cask of palm-oil.

Of course the captain protests that he is not in a hurry—that he can wait—that they shan't tire him out. But the negroes know better; they know the fatal advantage their climate gives them.

When it is supposed that a captain or trader will return to the coast no more after his present voyage, then he is properly victimized, as then the native has no fear of future vengeance before him; and I have known many individuals who, by the system of "trust," were all but ruined—getting scarce any return at all.

It is much to be wished that white traders would combine to put down at least this abuse. But until the spread of commerce shall break down the scoundrelly system of middle-men in this land, there will be no really prosperous trade there. And this will not happen till the merchants themselves visit the headquarters whence the produce is brought, and until the rude tribes shall be somewhat civilized by lengthened contact with the whites. At present things are in a state of utter disorganization, and the "trust" abuse seems a real necessity. For so hardly and often have the interior tribes been cheated of all returns for their wares, that now they have come to demand at least part payment in advance; and, of course, this advance is exacted of the white trader on the coast, to lure whom great rumours are spread through the tribes of teeth of a marvellous size lying ready for purchase, &c. Too often, when an advance has been made for a specific purchase—of a tooth, say—it is, after all, seized for some intermediate party's debt on its way down, and thus the poor trader is again victimized.

So eager are the Mpongwe for trade that they have even set up a regular coasting business. Every considerable negro trader owns several canoes; but his great ambition is to buy or build a larger vessel, in which he may sail along the coast, and, getting goods on trust from white merchants, make his regular voyage, or establish his little factory on some out-of-the-way point on the shore. The splendid harbour of the Gaboon has made them tolerably fearless on the water, and their rage for trade leads them to all manner of adventures.

Their coasting-vessels are only large boats, but I have seen some of so, considerable size as to hold conveniently eight to ten tons. To make one of these they cut down an immense tree, sharpen it at the ends, then burn out the interior, guiding the fire so as to burn the heart of the tree and leave them the shell they need. For this hull, which is then scraped smooth, and otherwise finished and strengthened, they next make masts and sails, the latter being of matting, and then they are ready for sea. These cockle-shells stand the wind and sea remarkably well, as is evident when the squally and blustery weather of this country is considered, and when we know that they make voyages from the Gaboon as far as Cape St. Catherine's south, and as far as Banoko and Cameroon north.

The start for one of these voyages is a great occasion. Guns are fired, and the people shout and wish a pleasant voyage; and the lucky vessel is received at her port of destination with similar ceremonies.

The great aim of a Mpongwe trader, however, is to get "trust" from a white man, with authority to go off up or down the coast and establish a factory. Then there is double rejoicing. But the poor white trader is generally sadly victimized; for his agent goes to some spot where he thinks he can get ivory and other trade and settles down. Then, first, he mostly picks out the best and most valuable of the goods with which he has been intrusted, and secretes these for his own use. His next step is to buy himself some slaves and to marry several wives; all which being accomplished, it is at last time to think of the interests of his principal. Thus, after many months, perhaps he makes returns on his sales, or perhaps he fails altogether to make returns, if he thinks he can cheat so far with impunity.

These fellows understand all the dialects spoken on the coast, as well as English, French, Spanish, and Portuguese. On their voyages, as they go poorly provisioned, and depend more on luck than real skill, they often suffer extreme hardships, but they are seldom drowned.

The chief product of the Gaboon country is its ivory. This is said to be the finest on the western coast. It produces also bar-wood, a dye-wood, from which is obtained a dark red dye, and ebony, the last taken from the great forests of this wood which abound near the head-waters of the Gaboon River. I have seen very large sticks brought thence, but the supply is not yet large. The bar-wood tree is found in great plenty along the shores of the river and its numerous tributary creeks. It is also found on the Moondah and Danger rivers. Copal is another product of this country, but it is of inferior quality, and is not sought.[1]

Ivory comes down the river from the interior by inland journeys in great quantities. Upwards of 80,000 pounds are taken from the Gaboon River yearly when home prices are good; for the ruling prices here are so high that traders cannot buy to advantage unless the home demand is very brisk. I suppose that the country from Banoko to Loango furnishes in brisk years at least 150,000 pounds of ivory.

But however important may be these commercial resources of the Gaboon country, I am convinced that the people will never prosper till they turn their attention more to agricultural operations, for elephants must finally disappear. This, indeed, is the great evil of all the nations of Western Africa. The men despise labour, and force their women and slaves to till the fields; and this tillage never assumes the important proportions it deserves, so that the supply of food is never abundant; the tribes, almost without exception, live from hand to mouth, and, with a fertile soil, are half the time in a state of semi-starvation.

1. Copal is a resinous substance exuded from various tropical trees that is used in making varnishes and lacquers (ed.).

49. CHARLES LIVINGSTONE

THE PRAZEROS. 1859.

David Livingstone (1813–1873) was the greatest Christian missionary-explorer of the nineteenth century. Between 1853 and 1856 he traveled overland from Kuruman, the mission station of his father-in-law, Robert Moffat, to the Victoria Falls, which he was the first white man to see, and thence to Luanda and back across Africa to the mouth of the Zambezi River. His Missionary Travels and Researches aroused great enthusiasm in Victorian England for the opening of the interior of Central Africa to Christianity and commerce. With the support of the Royal Geographical Society and the assistance of the British government, Livingstone returned to Portuguese East Africa in 1859 with a large expedition that included his brother, Charles, and that aimed to establish the Zambezi as a highway into the interior. The Zambezi proved unnavigable beyond Tete, but Livingstone's descriptions of the slave trade and the Prazeros of Zambezia continued to excite humanitarian and commercial interests in England

By the eighteenth century, a group of half-caste Portuguese had carved out for themselves great feudal estates in Zambezia. These Prazeros were warlords beyond the reach of any authority, African or European, and dominated vast areas. From the profits of their plantations and the slave trade they equipped large private armies that terrorized the countryside. The Portuguese were unable to root out the Prazo system until the 1890s. A typical Prazero was Antonio Vincente da Cruz, commonly known as Bonga. Like his brother, Mariano, he was an illiterate, thieving, cruel, barbarous drunkard.

On reaching Mazaro, the mouth of a narrow creek which in floods communicates with the Quillimane River, we found that the Portuguese were at war with a half-caste named Mariano, *alias* Matakenya, from whom they had generally fled, and who, having built a stockade near the mouth of the Shire, owned all the country between that river and Mazaro. Mariano was best known by his native name Matakenya, which in their tongue means "trembling," or quivering as trees do in a storm. He was a keen slave-hunter, and kept a large number of men, well armed with muskets. It is an entire mistake to suppose that the slave-trade is one of buying and selling alone, or that engagements can be made with laborers in Africa as they are in India; Mariano, like other Portuguese, had no labor to spare. He had been in the habit of sending out armed parties on slave hunting-forays among the helpless tribes to the northeast, and carrying down the kidnapped victims in chains to Quillimane, where they were sold by his brother-in-law Cruz Coimbra, and shipped as "Free emigrants" to the French island of Bourbon. So long as his robberies and murders were restricted to the natives at a distance, the authorities did not interfere; but his men, trained to deeds of violence and bloodshed in their slave forays, natu-

From David and Charles Livingstone, *Narrative of an Expedition to the Zambesi and its Tributaries; and of the Discovery of the Lakes Shirwa and Nyassa, 1858–1864* (New York: Harper and Brothers, 1866), pp. 26–30, 38–43.

rally began to practice on the people nearer at hand, though belonging to the Portuguese, and even in the village of Senna, under the guns of the fort. A gentleman of the highest standing told us that, while at dinner with his family, it was no uncommon event for a slave to rush into the room pursued by one of Mariano's men with spear in hand to murder him.

The atrocities of this villain, aptly termed by the late governor of Quillimane a "notorious robber and murderer," became at length intolerable. All the Portuguese spoke of him as a rare monster of inhumanity. It is unaccountable why half-castes, such as he, are so much more cruel than the Portuguese, but such is undoubtedly the case.

It was asserted that one of his favorite modes of creating an impression in the country, and making his name dreaded, was to spear his captives with his own hands. On one occasion he is reported to have thus killed forty poor wretches placed in a row before him. We did not at first credit these statements, and thought that they were merely exaggerations of the incensed Portuguese, who naturally enough were exasperated with him for stopping their trade and harboring their runaway slaves; but we learned afterward from the natives that the accounts given us by the Portuguese had not exceeded the truth, and that Mariano was quite as great a ruffian as they had described him. One expects slave-owners to treat their human chattels as well as men do other animals of value, but the slave trade seems always to engender an unreasoning ferocity, if not bloodthirstiness.

War was declared against Mariano, and a force sent to take him; he resisted for a time, but, seeing that he was likely to get the worst of it, and knowing that the Portuguese governors have small salaries, and are therefore "disposed to be reasonable," he went down to Quillimane to "arrange" with the governor, as it is termed here; but Colonel da Silva put him in prison, and then sent him for trial to Mozambique. When we came into the country his people were fighting under his brother Bonga. The war had lasted six months, and stopped all trade on the river during that period. On the 15th of June we first came into contact with the "rebels." They appeared as a crowd of well-armed and fantastically-dressed people under the trees at Mazaro. On explaining that we were English, some at once came on board and called to those on shore to lay aside their arms. On landing among them we saw that many had the branded marks of slaves on their chests, but they warmly approved our objects, and knew well the distinctive character of our nation on the slave question.[1] The shout at our departure contrasted strongly with the suspicious questioning on our approach. Henceforth we were recognized as friends by both parties.

At a later period we were taking in wood within a mile of the scene of action, but

1. Toward the close of the eighteenth century, a small group of high-principled Englishmen organized a campaign against slavery and the slave trade. Outraged by the horror and injustice of the trade, the abolitionists were convinced of its moral wrongness, and through their influence slavery was declared illegal in England in 1772. In 1807 an act of Parliament prohibited British subjects from engaging in the African slave trade, and finally in 1833 another act abolished slavery throughout the British Empire. Thereafter Britain used its diplomatic and military power to persuade other nations to abandon the trade (ed.).

a dense fog prevented our hearing the noise of a battle at Mazaro; and on arriving there immediately after, many natives and Portuguese appeared on the bank.

Dr. Livingstone, landing to salute some of his old friends among the latter, found himself in the sickening smell and among the mutilated bodies of the slain; he was requested to take the governor, who was very ill of fever, across to Shupanga, and just as he gave his assent, the rebels renewed the fight, and the balls began to whistle about in all directions. After trying in vain to get some one to assist the governor down to the steamer, and unwilling to leave him in such danger, as the officer sent to bring our Kroomen did not appear, he went into the hut, and dragged along his excellency to the ship. He was a very tall man, and as he swayed hither and thither from weakness, weighing down Dr. Livingstone, it must have appeared like one drunken man helping another. Some of the Portuguese white soldiers stood fighting with great bravery against the enemy in front, while a few were coolly shooting at their own slaves for fleeing into the river behind. The rebels soon retired, and the Portuguese escaped to a sand-bank in the Zambesi, and thence to an island opposite Shupanga, where they lay for some weeks, looking at the rebels on the main land opposite. This state of inactivity on the part of the Portuguese could not well be helped, as they had expended all their ammunition and were waiting anxiously for supplies; hoping, no doubt, sincerely that the enemy might not hear that their powder had failed. Luckily, their hopes were not disappointed; the rebels waited until a supply came, and were then repulsed after a three and a half hours' hard fighting. Two months afterward Mariano's stockade was burned, the garrison having fled in a panic; and as Bonga declared that he did not wish to fight with this governor, with whom he had no quarrel, the war soon came to an end. His excellency meanwhile, being a disciple of Raspail, had taken nothing for the fever but a little camphor, and after he was taken to Shupanga became comatose.[2] More potent remedies were administered to him, to his intense disgust, and he soon recovered. The colonel in attendance, whom he never afterward forgave, encouraged the treatment. "Give what is right; never mind him; he is very (*muito*) impertinent;" and all night long, with every draught of water, the colonel gave a quantity of quinine: the consequence was, next morning the patient was cinchonized and better.

Bonga, the brother of the rebel Mariano, and now at the head of the revolted natives, with some of his principal men, came to see us, and were perfectly friendly, though told of our having carried the sick governor across to Shupanga, and of our having cured him of fever. On our acquainting Bonga with the object of the expedition, he remarked that we should suffer no hinderance from his people in our good work. He sent us a present of rice, two sheep, and a quantity of fire wood. He never tried to make any use of us in the strife: the other side showed less confidence by carefully cross-questioning our pilot whether we had sold any powder to the enemy. We managed, however, to keep on good terms with both rebels and Portuguese.

Being unable to take the steamer up the shoal channel along which Senna stands

---

2. François Vincent Raspail (1794–1878), French chemist and revolutionary (ed.).

we anchored at Nyaruka, a small hamlet of blacks, six miles below, and walked up to Senna next morning. The narrow winding footpath, along which we had to march in Indian file, lay through gardens and patches of wood, the loftiest trees being thorny acacias. The sky was cloudy, the air cool and pleasant, and the little birds, in the gladness of their heart poured forth sweet strange songs, which though equal to those of the singing birds at home on a spring morning, yet seemed somehow, as if in a foreign tongue. We met many natives on the road. Most of the men were armed with spears, bows and arrows, or old Tower muskets; the women had short-handled iron hoes, and were going to work in the gardens; they stepped aside to let us pass, and saluted us politely, the men bowing and scraping and the women, even with heavy loads their heads, courtesying—a courtesy from bare legs is startling!

Senna is built on a low plain, on the right bank of the Zambesi, with some pretty detached hills in the background; it is surrounded by a stockade of living trees to protect its inhabitants from their troublesome and rebellious neighbors. It contains a few large houses, some ruins of others, and a weatherbeaten cross, where once stood a church; a mound shows the site of an ancient monastery, and a mud fort by the river is so dilapidated that cows were grazing peacefully over its prostrate walls. This grieves not the villagers, for its black garrison was wont to keep within doors when the foe came near, leaving the merchants to settle the strife as best they could; and they therefore consider that the decay of the fort has not caused them to be any more helpless than they were before.

The few Senna merchants, having little or no trade in the village, send parties of trusted slaves into the interior to hunt for and purchase ivory. It is a dull place, and very conducive to sleep. One is sure to take fever in Senna on the second day, if by chance one escapes it on the first day of a sojourn there; but no place is entirely bad. Senna has one redeeming feature: it is the native village of the large-hearted and hospitable Senhor H. A. Ferrão. The benevolence of this gentleman is unbounded. The poor black stranger passing through the town goes to him almost as a matter of course for food, and is never sent away hungry. In times of famine the starving natives are fed by his generosity; hundreds of his own people he never sees except on these occasions; and the only benefit derived from being their master is, that they lean on him as a patriarchal chief, and he has the satisfaction of settling their differences, and of saving their lives in seasons of drought and scarcity. His father, a man of superior attainments, was formerly the Portuguese governor of Senna, and acquired a vast tract of rich country to the southward, called Chiringoma, in a most honorable manner; but the government ordered it to be split up, and reserved two leagues only for the heir, apportioning the rest in free grants to emigrants; the reason assigned for the robbery was that "it would never do for a subject to possess more land than the crown of Portugal." The Landeens soon followed, took possession of the whole, and spoiled the spoilers.

Senhor Ferrão received us with his usual kindness, and gave us a bountiful breakfast. During the day the principal men of the place called, and were unanimously of opinion that the free natives would willingly cultivate large quantities of cotton, could they find purchasers. They had in former times exported largely both cotton and cloth to Manica and even to Brazil. "On their own soil," they declared, "the natives are willing to labor and trade, provided only they can do so to advantage: when it is for their interest, blacks work very hard." We often remarked subsequently that this was the opinion of men of energy; and that all settlers of activity, enterprise, and sober habits had become rich, while those who were much addicted to lying on their backs smoking invariably complained of the laziness of the negroes, and were poor, proud, and despicable. We dined with another very honorable Portuguese, Major Tito A. D'A. Sicard, who quoted the common remark that Dr. Livingstone's discovery of the Kongone Bar had ruined Quillimane; for the government had proposed to abandon that fever-haunted locality, and to found a new town at the mouth of the Kongone. It was not then known that householders in the old village preferred to resign all offices rather than remove. The major had a great desire to assist Dr. Livingstone in his enterprise; and said that when the war was past he would at once take up his goods to Tette, in canoes; and this he afterward most generously did. While returning to Nyaruka, we heard a bird like a nightingale pouring forth its sweet melody in the stillness of the evening.

50. JOHN HANNING SPEKE

UNYAMWEZI AND BUGANDA. 1862.

John Hanning Speke (1827–1864) arrived in Zanzibar with Richard Burton in 1856 for the purpose of finding the inland sea of Ujiji in East Africa. During the expedition the two explorers reached Lake Tanganyika, and while Burton was recovering from an illness at Tabora, Speke wandered off to the north, where he saw the waters of Lake Victoria. Speke jumped to the conclusion that he had discovered the source of the Nile. To prove his assumption, he returned to East Africa in 1860 and, accompanied by J. A Grant, traversed the Unyamwezi country of what is now western Tanzania and visited Uganda on the west and the northern shore of Lake Victoria. He was the first European to visit the powerful interlacustrine kingdom of Buganda, and his reports of the richness of the country and the prospects for "Christianity, Commerce, and Civilization" encouraged others to follow. Speke and Grant reached Gondokoro on the Upper Nile in 1863. They had contributed much to Europe's geographical knowledge of the interior of eastern Africa but had failed to resolve completely the question of the Nile source.

U-n-ya-muezi—Country of Moon—must have been one of the largest kingdoms in Africa. It is little inferior in size to England, and of much the same shape, though now, instead of being united, it is cut up into petty states. In its northern extremities it is known by the appellation U-sukuma—country north; and in the southern, U-takama—country south. There are no [written] historical traditions known to the people; neither was anything ever written concerning their country, as far as we

From John Hanning Speke, *Journal of the Discovery of the Source of the Nile* (Edinburgh and London: William Blackwood and Sons, 1863), pp. 84–88, 273–279.

know, until the Hindus, who traded with the east coast of Africa, opened commercial dealings with its people in slaves and ivory, possibly some time prior to the birth of our Saviour, when, associated with their name, Men of the Moon, sprang into existence the Mountains of the Moon. These Men of the Moon are hereditarily the greatest traders in Africa, and are the only people who, for love of barter and change, will leave their own country as porters and go to the coast, and they do so with as much zest as our country-folk go to a fair. As far back as we can trace they have done this, and they still do it as heretofore. The whole of their country ranges from 3000 to 4000 feet above the sea-level—a high plateau, studded with little outcropping hills of granite, between which, in the valleys, there are numerous fertilising springs of fresh water, and rich iron ore is found in sandstone. Generally industrious—much more so than most other negroes—they cultivate extensively, make cloths of cotton in their own looms, smelt iron and work it up very expertly, build tembes to live in over a large portion of their country, but otherwise live in grass huts, and keep flocks and herds of considerable extent.

The Wanyamuezi, however, are not a very well-favoured people in physical appearance, and are much darker than either the Wazaranio or the Wagogo, though many of their men are handsome and their women pretty; neither are they well dressed or well armed, being wanting in pluck and gallantry. Their women, generally, are better dressed than the men. Cloths fastened round under the arms are their national costume, along with a necklace of beads, large brass or copper wire armlets, and a profusion of thin circles, called sambo, made of the giraffe's tailhairs bound round by the thinnest iron or copper wire; whilst the men at home wear loincloths, but in the field, or whilst travelling, simply hang a goat-skin over their shoulders, exposing at least three-fourths of their body in a rather indecorous manner. In all other respects they ornament themselves like the women, only, instead of a long coil of wire wound up the arm, they content themselves with having massive rings of copper or brass on the wrist; and they carry for arms a spear and bow and arrows. All extract more or less their lower incisors, and cut a ʌ between their two upper incisors. The whole tribe are desperate smokers, and greatly given to drink.

On the 24th, we all, as many as were left of us, marched into the merchants' depot, S. lat. 5° 0' 52", and E. long. 33° 1' 34", escorted by Musa, who advanced to meet us, and guided us into his tembe, where he begged we would reside with him until we could find men to carry our property on to Karague. He added that he would accompany us; for he was on the point of going there when my first instalment of property arrived, but deferred his intention out of respect to myself. He had been detained at Kaze ever since I last left it in consequence of the Arabs having provoked a war with Manua Sera, to which he was adverse. For a long time also he had been a chained prisoner; as the Arabs, jealous of the favour Manua Sera had shown to him in preference to themselves, basely accused him of supplying Manua Sera with gunpowder, and bound him hand and foot "like a slave." It was delightful to see old Musa's face again, and the supremely hospitable, kind, and courteous manner in which he looked after us, constantly bringing in all kind of small delicacies, and seeing that nothing was wanting to make us happy. All the property I had sent on in advance he had stored away; or rather, I should say, as much as had reached him, for the road expenses had eaten a great hole in it.

Once settled down into position, Sheikh Snay and the whole conclave of Arab merchants came to call on me. They said they had an army of four hundred slaves armed with muskets ready to take the field at once to hunt down Manua Sera, who was cutting their caravan road to pieces, and had just seized, by their latest reports, a whole convoy of their ammunition. I begged them strongly to listen to reason, and accept my advice as an old soldier, not to carry on their guerilla warfare in such a headlong hurry, else they would be led a dance by Manua Sera, as we had been by Tantia Topee in India. I advised them to allow me to mediate between them, after telling them what a favourable interview I had had with Manua Sera and Maula, whose son was at that moment concealed in Musa's tembe. My advice, however, was not wanted. Snay knew better than any one how to deal with savages, and determined on setting out as soon as his army had "eaten their beef-feast of war."

On my questioning him about the Nile, Snay still thought the Nyanza was the source of the Jub river,[1] as he did in our former journey, but gave way when I told him that vessels frequented the Nile, as this also coincided with his knowledge of navigators in vessels appearing on some waters to the northward of Unyoro. In a great hurry he then bade me good-bye; when, as he thought it would be final, I gave him, in consideration for his former good services to the last expedition, one of the gold watches given me by the Indian Government. I saw him no more, though he and all the other Arabs sent me presents of cows, goats, and rice, with a notice that they should have gone on their war-path before, only, hearing of my arrival, out of due respect to my greatness, they waited to welcome me in. Further, after doing for Manua Sera, they were determined to go on to Ugogo to assist Salem bin Saif and the other merchants on, during which, at the same time, they would fight all the Wagogo who persisted in taking taxes and in harassing their caravans. At the advice of Musa, I sent Maula's son off at night to tell the old chief how sorry I was to find the Arabs so hotheaded I could not even effect an arrangement with them. It was a great pity; for Manua Sera was so much liked by the Wanyamuezi, they would, had they been able, have done anything to restore him.

Next day, after crossing more of those abominable rush-drains, whilst in sight of the Victoria Nyanza, we ascended the most beautiful hills, covered with verdure of all descriptions. At Meruka, where I put up, there resided some grandees, the chief of whom was the king's aunt. She sent me a goat, a hen, a basket of eggs, and some plantains, in return for which I sent her a wire and some beads. I felt inclined to stop here a month, everything was so very pleasant. The temperature was perfect. The roads, as indeed they were everywhere, were as broad as our coachroads, cut through the long grasses, straight over the hills and down through the woods in the dells—a strange contrast to the wretched tracks in all the adjacent countries. The huts were kept so clean and so neat, not a fault could be found with them—the gardens the same. Wherever I strolled I saw nothing but richness, and what ought to be wealth. The whole land was a picture of quiescent beauty, with a boundless sea in the background. Looking over the hills, it struck the fancy at once that at one period the whole land must have been at a uniform level with their present tops, but that, by the constant denudation it was subjected to by frequent rains, it had been cut down and sloped into those beautiful hills and dales which now so much pleased the eye; for there were none of those quartz dykes I had seen protruding through the same kind of aqueous formations in Usui and Karague; nor were there any other sorts of volcanic disturbance to distort the calm quiet aspect of the scene.

From this, the country being all hill and dale, with miry rush-drains in the bottoms, I walked, carrying my shoes and stockings in my hands, nearly all the way. Rozaro's "children" became more and more troublesome, stealing everything they could lay their hands upon out of the village huts we passed on the way. On arrival at Sangua, I found many of them had been seized by some men who, bolder than the rest, had overtaken them whilst gutting their huts, and made them prisoners, demanding of me two slaves and one load of beads for their restitution. I sent my men back to see what had happened, and ordered them to bring all the men on to me, that I might see fair play. They, however, took the law into their own hands, drove off the Waganda villagers by firing their muskets, and relieved the thieves. A complaint was then laid against Nyamgundu by the chief officer of the village, and I was requested to halt. That I would not do, leaving the matter in the hands of the governor-general, Mr. Pokino, whom I heard we should find at the next station, Masaka.

On arrival there at the government establishment—a large collection of grass huts, separated one from the other within large enclosures, which overspread the whole top of a low hill—I was requested to withdraw and put up in some huts a short distance off, and wait until his excellency, who was from home, could come and see me; which the next day he did, coming in state with a large number of officers, who brought with them a cow, sundry pots of pombe [beer], enormous sticks of sugar-cane, and a large bundle of country coffee. This grows in great profusion all over this land in large bushy trees, the berries sticking on the branches like clusters of holly-berries.

I was then introduced, and told that his excellency was the appointed governor of all the land lying between the Katonga and the Kitangule rivers. After the first formalities were over, the complaint about the officers at Sangus was preferred for decision, on which Pokino at once gave it against the villagers, as they had no right, by the laws of the land, to lay hands on a king's guest. Just then Maula arrived, and began to abuse Nyamgundu. Of course I would not stand this; and, after telling all the facts of the case, I begged Pokino to send Maula away out of my camp. Pokino said he could not do this, as it was by the king's order he was appointed; but he put Maula in the background, laughing at the way he had "let the bird fly out of his hands," and settled that Nyamgundu should be my guide. I then gave him a wire, and he gave me three large sheets of mbugu, which he said I should require, as there were so many watercourses to cross on the road I was going. A second day's halt was necessitated by many of my men catching fever, probably owing to the constant crossing of those abominable rush-drains. There was no want of food here, for I never saw such a profusion of plantains anywhere. They were literally lying in heaps on the ground, though the people were brewing pombe all day, and cooking them for dinner every evening.

After crossing many more hills and miry bottoms, constantly coming in. view of the lake, we reached Ugonzi, and after another march of the same description, came to Kituntu, the last officer's residence in Uddu [a province of Buganda]. Formerly it was the property of a Beluch named Eseau, who came to this country with merchandise, trading on account of Said Said, late Sultan of Zanzibar; but having lost it all on his way here, paying mahongo, or taxes, and so forth, he feared returning, and instead made great friends with the late king Sunna, who took an especial fancy to him because he had a very large beard, and raised him to the rank of Mkungu. A few years ago, however, Eseau died, and left all his family and property to a slave named Uledi, who now, in consequence, is the border officer.

I became now quite puzzled whilst thinking which was the finest spot I had seen in Uddu, so many were exceedingly beautiful; but I think I gave the preference to this, both for its own immediate neighbourhood and the long range view it afforded of Uganda [Buganda] proper, the lake, and the large island, or group of islands, called Sese, where the king of Uganda keeps one of his fleets of boats.

Some little boys came here who had all their hair shaved off excepting two round tufts on either side of the head. They were the king's pages; and, producing three sticks, said they had brought them to me from their king, who wanted three charms or medicines. Then placing one stick on the ground before me, they said, "This one is a head which, being affected by dreams of a deceased relative, requires relief;" the second symbolised the king's desire for the accomplishment of a phenomenon to which the old phalic worship was devoted; "and this third one," they said, "is a sign that the king wants a charm to keep all his subjects in awe of him." I then promised I would do what I could when I reached the palace, but feared to do anything in the distance. I wished to go on with the march, but was dissuaded by Nyamgundu, who said he had received orders to find me some cows here, as his king was most anxious I should be well fed. Next day, however, we descended into the Katonga valley, where, instead of finding a magnificent broad sheet of water, as I had been led to expect by the Arabs' account of it, I found I had to wade through a succession of rush-drains divided one from the other by islands. It took me two hours, with my clothes tucked up under my arms, to get through them all; and many of them were so matted with weeds, that my feet sank down as though I trod in a bog.

The Waganda all said that at certain times in the year no one could ford these drains, as they all flooded; but, strangely enough, they were always lowest when most rain fell in Uganda. No one, however, could account for this singular fact. No one knew of a lake to supply the waters, nor where they came from. That they flowed into the lake there was no doubt—as I could see by the trickling waters in some few places—and they lay exactly on the equator. Rising out of the valley, I found all the country just as hilly as before, but many of the rush-drains going to northward; and in the dells were such magnificent trees, they quite took me by surprise. Clean-trunked, they towered up just as so many great pillars, and then spread out their high branches like a canopy over us. I thought of the blue gums of Australia, and believed these would beat them. At the village of Mbule we were gracefully received by the local officer, who brought a small present, and assured me that the king was in a nervous state of excitement, always asking after me. Whilst speaking he trembled, and he was so restless he could never sit still.

Up and down we went on again through this wonderful country, surprisingly rich in grass, cultivation, and trees. Watercourses were as frequent as ever, though not quite so troublesome to the traveller, as they were more frequently bridged with poles or palm-tree trunks.

This, the next place we arrived at, was Nyamgundu's own residence, where I stopped a day to try and shoot buffaloes. Maula here had the coolness to tell me he must inspect all the things I had brought for presentation to the king, as he said it was the custom; after which he would hurry on and inform his majesty. Of course I refused, saying it was uncourteous to both the king and myself. Still he persisted, until, finding it hopeless, he spitefully told Nyamgundu to keep me here at least two days. Nyamgundu, however, very prudently told him he should obey his orders, which were to take me on as fast as he could. I then gave Nyamgundu wires and beads for himself and all his family round, which made Maula slink farther away from me than ever.

The buffaloes were very numerous in the tall grasses that lined the sides and bottoms of the hills; but although I saw some, I could not get a shot, for the grasses being double the height of myself, afforded them means of dashing out of view as soon as seen, and the rustling noise made whilst I followed them kept them on the alert. At night a hyena came into my hut, and carried off one of my goats that was tied to a log between two of my sleeping men.

During the next march, after passing some of the most beautifully-wooded dells, in which lay small rush-lakes on the right of the road, draining. as I fancied, into the Victoria Lake, I met with a party of the king's gamekeepers, staking their nets all along the side of a hill, hoping to catch antelopes by driving the covers with dogs and men. Farther on, also, I came on a party driving one hundred cows, as a present from Mtesa to Rumanika, which the officers in charge said was their king's return for the favour Rumanika had done him in sending me on to him. It was in this way that great kings sent "letters" to one another.

51. GEORG SCHWEINFURTH

KING MUNZA. 1871.

During his second sojourn in Africa, the botanist and traveler Georg Schweinfurth (1836–1925) spent three years (1868–1871) in the Upper Nile hinterland. His travels and work were a major contribution to European knowledge of the southern Sudan and the northeast Congo. He describes his visit to the powerful Munza, king of the Mangbettu people who inhabited the valley of the upper Uele River in the eastern reaches of the Congo basin.

From Dr. Georg Schweinfurth, *The Heart of Africa*, trans. by Ellen E. Frewer (New York: Sampson Low, Marston, Searle, and Rivington, 1874), vol. II, pp. 40–52.

As we approached the huts, the drums and trumpets were sounded to their fullest powers, and the crowds of people pressing forward on either hand left but a narrow passage for our procession. We bent our steps to one of the largest huts, which formed a kind of palatial hall open like a shed at both ends. Waiting my arrival here was one of the officers of state, who, I presume, was the master of the ceremonies, as I afterwards observed him presiding over the general festivities. This official took me by the right hand, and without a word conducted me to the interior of the hall. Here, like the audience at a concert, were arranged according to their rank hundreds of nobles and courtiers, each occupying his own ornamental bench and decked out with all his war equipments. At the other end of the building a space was left for the royal throne, which differed in no respect from the other benches, except that it stood upon an outspread mat; behind this bench was placed a large support of singular construction, resting as it seemed upon three legs, and furnished with projections that served as props for the back and arms of the sitter: this support was thickly studded with copper rings and nails. I requested that my own chair might be placed at a few paces from the royal bench, and there I took up my position with my people standing or squatting behind me, and the Nubian soldiers forming a guard around. The greater number of the soldiers had their guns, but my black squires, who had never before been brought face to face with so mighty a potentate, subsequently confessed to me that their hearts beat fast, and that they could not help trembling to think how a sign from Munza could have brought all our limbs to the spit.

For a considerable time I had to sit waiting in expectation before the empty throne. My servants informed me that Munza had attended the market in his ordinary costume, but that he had been seen to hasten home to his private apartments, where he was now undergoing a process of anointing, frizzling, and bedizening at the hands of his wives, in order that he should appear before me in the imposing splendour of his state attire. I had thus no other alternative than patiently to abide my time; for what could be more flattering to a foreign guest than for a king to receive him in his costliest toilet?

In the interval of waiting there seemed a continuous uproar. The fitful beating of kettle-drums and the perpetual braying of horns resounded through the airy building until it shook again, and mingling with the boisterous strains rose the voices of the assembled courtiers as they whiled away the time in loud and eager conversation. There was no doubt that I was myself the main cause of their excitement; for although I sat with my back to the majority, I could not be otherwise than quite aware that all eyes were intently fixed upon me. All, however, kept their seats at a respectful distance, so that I could calmly look about me and note down my observations of what I saw.

The hall itself was the chief object that attracted my attention. It was at least a hundred feet in length, forty feet high, and fifty broad. It had been quite recently completed, and the fresh bright look of the materials gave it an enlivening aspect, the natural brown polish of the woodwork looking as though it were gleaming with the lustre of new varnish. Close by was a second and more spacious hall, which in height was only surpassed by the loftiest of the surrounding oil-palms; but this, although it had only been erected five years previously, had already begun to show symptoms of decay, and being enclosed on all sides was dark, and therefore less adapted for the gathering at a public spectacle. Considering the part of Africa in which these halls were found, one might truly be justified in calling them wonders of the world; I hardly know with all our building resources what material we could have employed, except it were whalebone, of sufficient lightness and durability to erect structures like these royal halls of Munza, capable of withstanding the tropical storms and hurricanes. The bold arch of the vaulted roof was supported on three long rows of pillars formed from perfectly straight tree-stems; the countless spars and rafters as well as the other parts of the building being composed entirely of the leaf-stalks of the wine-palm (*Raphia vinifera*).[1] The floor was covered with a dark red clay plaster, as firm and smooth as asphalt. The sides were enclosed by a low breastwork, and the space between this and the arching roof which at the sides sloped nearly to ground, allowed light and air to pass into the building. Outside against the breastwork stood crowds of natives, probably the "great unwashed" of the Monbuttoo, who were unable to obtain places within, and contented themselves with eagerly gazing through this opening at the proceedings. Officials with long sticks went their rounds and kept order among the mob, making free use of their sticks whenever it was necessary; all boys who ventured uninvited into the hall being vigorously beaten back as trespassers.

I had probably been left for an hour, and was getting lost in the contemplation of all the wonders, when a louder sound of voices and an increasing clang of horns and kettle-drums led me to suppose that there was an announcement of the approach of the king; but, no, this was only a prelude. The sovereign was still being painted and beautified by the hands of his fair ones. There was, however, a fresh and increasing commotion near the entrance of the hall, where a number of ornamental weapons was being arranged. Posts were driven into the ground, and long poles were fastened horizontally across them; then against this extemporized scaffolding were laid, or supported crosswise, hundreds of ornamental lances and spears, all of pure copper, and of every variety of form and shape. The gleam of the red metal caught the rays of the tropical noontide sun, and in the symmetry of their arrangement the rows of dazzling lance-heads shone with the glow of flaming torches, making a background to the royal throne that was really magnificent. The display of wealth, which according to Central African tradition was incalculable, was truly regal, and surpassed anything of the kind that I had conceived possible.

A little longer and the weapons are all arranged. The expected king has left his home. There is a running to and fro of heralds, marshals, and police. The thronging masses flock towards the entrance, and silence is proclaimed. The king is close at hand. Then come the trumpeters flourishing away on their huge ivory horns; then the ringers swinging their cumbrous iron bells; and now, with a long firm stride, looking neither to the right nor to the left, wild, romantic, picturesque alike in mien and in attire, comes the tawny Caesar himself! He was followed by a number of his

---

1. This palm is found in every bank-forest in the Monbutto country, and its leaves vary from 25 to 35 feet in length: the midrib of the leaf (rhachis) is of a bright brown colour, and furnishes the most popular building material throughout Central Africa.

favoured wives. Without vouchsafing me a glance, he flung himself upon his unpretending chair of state, and sat with his eyes fixed upon his feet. Mohammed had joined the retinue of his royal friend, and took up his position opposite me on the other side of the king on a stool that was brought for his accommodation. He also had arrayed himself in a suitable dress in honour of the occasion, and now sat in the imposing uniform of a commander of Arnauts.

I could now feast my eyes upon the fantastic figure of the ruler. I was intensely interested in gazing at the strange weird-looking sovereign, of whom it was commonly reported that his daily food was human flesh. With arms and legs, neck and breast, all bedizened with copper rings, chains, and other strange devices, and with a great copper crescent at the top of his head, the potentate gleamed with a shimmer that was to our ideas unworthy of royalty, but savoured far too much of the magazines of civic opulence, reminding one almost unavoidably of a well-kept kitchen! His appearance, however, was decidedly marked with his nationality, for every adornment that he had about him belonged exclusively to Central Africa, as none but the fabrications of his native land are deemed worthy of adorning the person of a king of the Monbuttoo.

Agreeably to the national fashion a plumed hat rested on the top of his chignon, and soared a foot and a half above his head; this hat was a narrow cylinder of closely-plaited reeds; it was ornamented with three layers of red parrots' feathers, and crowned with a plume of the same; there was no brim, but the copper crescent projected from the front like the vizor of a Norman helmet. The muscles of Munza's ears were pierced, and copper bars as thick as the finger inserted in the cavities. The entire body was smeared with the native unguent of powdered camwood, which converted the original bright brown tint of his skin into the colour that is so conspicuous in ancient Pompeian halls. With the exception of being of an unusually fine texture, his single garment differed in no respect from what was worn throughout the country; it consisted of a large piece of fig bark impregnated with the same dye that served as his cosmetic, and this, falling in graceful folds about his body, formed breeches and waistcoat all in one. Round thongs of buffalo-hide, with heavy copper balls attached to the ends, were fastened round the waist in a huge knot, and like a girdle held the coat, which was neatly hemmed. The material of the coat was so carefully manipulated that it had quite the appearance of a rich *moiri antique*. Around the king's neck hung a copper ornament made in little points which radiated like beams all over his chest; on his bare arms were strange-looking pendants which in shape could only be compared to drumsticks with rings at the end. Halfway up the lower part of the arms and just below the knee were three bright, horny-looking circlets cut out of hippopotamus-hide, likewise tipped with copper. As a symbol of his dignity Munza wielded in his right hand the sickle-shaped Monbuttoo scimitar, in this case only an ornamental weapon, and made of pure copper.

As soon as the king had taken his seat, two little tables, beautifully carved, were placed on either side of his throne, and on these stood the dainties of which he continually partook, but which were carefully concealed by napkins of fig bark; in addition to these tables, some really artistic flasks of porous clay were brought in, full of drinking water.

Such was Munza, the autocrat of the Monbuttoo, with whom I was now brought face to face. He appeared as the type of those half-mythical potentates, a species of Mwata Yanvo or Great Makoko, whose names alone have penetrated to Europe, a truly savage monarch, without a trace of anything European or Oriental in his attire, and with nothing fictitious or borrowed to be attributed to him.

He was a man of about forty years of age, of a fair height, of a slim but power-ful build, and, like the rest of his countrymen, stiff and erect in figure. Although belonging to a type by no means uncomely, his features were far from prepossess-ing, but had a Nero-like expression that told of *ennui* and satiety. He had small whiskers and a tolerably thick beard; his profile was almost orthognatic, but the per-fectly Caucasian nose offered a remarkable contrast to the thick and protruding negro lips. In his eyes gleamed the wild light of animal sensuality, and around his mouth lurked an expression that I never saw in any other Monbuttoo, a combination of avarice, violence, and love of cruelty that could with the extremest difficulty relax into a smile. No spark of love or affection could beam forth from such features as his.

A considerable time elapsed before the king looked directly at the pale-faced man with the long hair and the tight black clothes who now for the first time appeared before him. I held my hat in my hand, but no greeting had as yet taken place, for, observing that everyone kept his seat when the king entered the hall, I had done the same, and now waited for him to address me. The wild uproar of the cannibals still continued, and Munza, sitting in a careless attitude, only raised his eyes now and then from their fixed stare upon the ground as though to scan the whole assemblage, but in reality to take stray glances at my person, and in this way, little by little, he satisfied his curiosity. I could not help marvelling at the compo-sure of this wild African, and wondering where in the world he could have learnt his dignity and self-possession.

At length the monarch began to ask me questions. They were fluently translated into the Zandey [Zande, Azande] dialect by the chief interpreter, who always played a principal part in our intercourse with the natives. The Niam-niam [Azande] in their turn rendered the sense to me in Arabic. The conversation, however, was of the most commonplace character, and referred neither to the purpose of my coming nor to the country from which I came. Munza's interrogations brought to my mind the rough reception afforded to Reinhold Forster, the companion of the renowned Captain Cook, by Frederick the Great, who bluntly asked him if he had ever seen a king? "Yes, your Majesty," was the answer, "several; two tame and three savage." Munza appeared extremely anxious to keep up to an Oriental measure the principle of *nil admirari*; nothing could disturb his composure, and even at my subsequent visits, where there was no state ceremonial, he maintained a taciturnity nearly as resolute.

My servants now brought forth the presents I had brought and spread them at the king's feet. These consisted, in the first place, of a piece of black cloth, a telescope, a silver platter, and a porcelain vase; the silver was taken for white iron, and the porcelain for carved ivory. The next gift was real piece of carved ivory, brought as a specimen to show the way in which the material is employed; there was a book with gilt edges, a gift which could not fail to recall to my mind the scene in which

Speke describes Kamrasi's first lesson in the Bible; then came a double mirror, that both magnified and reduced what it reflected; and last, though by no means least, was a large assortment of beads of Venetian glass, including thirty necklaces, composed of thirty distinct pieces, so that Munza was in possession of more than a thousand separate beads. The universal principle followed by the Nubians forbade that any presents of firearms should be made to native rulers. Munza regarded all these offerings with great attention, but without committing himself to any audible expression of approval. Not so his fifty wives, who were seated on stools arranged behind his throne; they gave frequent half-suppressed utterances of surprise, and the double mirror was passed admiringly from hand to hand, its contortions eliciting shouts of delight.

There were fifty of these ladies present: they were only the most intimate, or wives of the first rank, the entire number of court ladies being far larger. Except in the greater elegance of their attire, they departed in no way from the fashion of the country, the description of which must be deferred for the present.

After a time Munza turned his attention to his refreshments. As far as I could distinguish them, they consisted of lumps of plantain-meal and tapioca piled on leaves, of dried plantains, and of a fruit which to my surprise I immediately recognised as the cola-nut of the west. From this rosy-shelled kernel the king cut a few slices, and chewed them in the intervals of smoking his tobacco. His pipe, in the shape of an iron stem six feet long, was handed to him by a chibbukchak, who was in attendance for that purpose. Very remarkable was the way in which Munza smoked. To bring himself into the correct position he threw himself far back in his seat, supported his right elbow on the arm-rest, put one leg across the other, and with his left hand received the pipe-stem. In this attitude he gravely took one long inhalation, then, with a haughty gesture, resigned his pipe to the hands of his attendant and allowed the smoke slowly to reissue from his mouth. It is a habit among Turks of rank to smoke thus by taking only two or three inhalations from a pipe handed to them by their servants; but where, again, may I ask, could this cannibal prince have learnt such a custom?

To my request for a cola-nut the king responded by graciously passing me a specimen with his own hand. Turning to Mohammed, I expressed my surprise at beholding this fruit of the far west amongst the Monbuttoo; I told him of its high value as a spice in Bornoo, where it is worth its weight in silver, and I went on to say that it confirmed my impression that the Welle was identical with the river of Baghirmy, called the Shary [Shari], and that this nut accordingly came to me like a key to a problem that I was seeking to solve. Then again addressing Munza, I made him understand that I knew the fruit, and pointing in the direction of Lake Tsad [Chad], I told him that there it was eaten by the great people of the country. I hoped in this way to induce him to give me some information on the subject; but he had made up his mind to be astonished at nothing, nor could I ever even on future occasions draw him into a geographical discussion. All that I could learn was that the cola-nut grew wild in the country, and that it was called "nangweh" by the natives, who were accustomed to chew it in the intervals of their smoking.

The performances that had been prepared for our entertainment now commenced. First of all a couple of hornblowers stepped forward, and proceeded to execute solos upon their instruments. These men were advanced proficients in their art, and brought forth sounds of such power, compass, and flexibility that they could be modulated from sounds like the roar of a hungry lion, or the trumpeting of an infuriated elephant, down to tones which might be compared to the sighing of the breeze or to a lover's whisper. One of them, whose ivory horn was so huge that he could scarcely hold it in a horizontal position, executed rapid passages and shakes with as much neatness and decision as though he were performing on a flute.

Next appeared a number of professional singers and jesters, and amongst them a little plump fellow, who acted the part of a pantomime clown, and jumped about and turned somersaults till his limbs looked like the arms of a windmill; he was covered from head to foot with bushy tufts and pigtails, and altogether his appearance was so excessively ludicrous that, to the inward delight of the king, I burst into a hearty fit of laughter. I called him a court fool, and in many respects he fully deserved the title. I hardly know why the Nubians should have drawn my attention, as though to something quite new, to the wooden Monbuttoo scimitar that he wore in his girdle. His jokes and pranks seemed never ending, and he was permitted to take liberties with every one, not excepting even Munza himself, and amongst other tricks he would approach the king with his right hand extended, and just as Munza had got hold of it, would start backwards and make off with a bound. A short time before he appeared, some freshly baked ears of maize, the first of the season, had been laid before me; of this delicacy the fool, with the most comical gestures, made me comprehend that he wished to partake; I therefore took up some detached grains, and threw them, one by one, into his open mouth; he caught them with a snap, and devoured them with such comical grimaces, that the performance called forth a roar of applause from the whole assembly.

The next episode consisted of the performances of a eunuch, who formed a butt for the wit of the spectators. How Munza had come into possession of this creature, no one seemed to know, and I could only learn that he was employed in the inner parts of the palace. He was a fat grotesque-looking figure, and when he sang looked exactly like a grunting baboon; to add to the oddity of his appearance, Munza, as though in mockery of his Nubian guests, had had him arrayed in a red fez, and thus he was the only one in all the immense concourse of natives who had anything foreign in his attire.

But the most important part of the programme was reserved for the end: Munza was to make in oration. Whilst all the audience remained quietly seated on their stools and benches, up jumped the king, his coat, cleared his throat, and commenced his harangue. Of course I could not understand a single word, and double interpretation would have been worse than useless: but, from what I could see and hear, it was evident that Munza endeavoured to be choice and emphatic in his language, as not only did he often correct himself, but he made pauses after the sentences that he intended to be impressive, to allow for the applause of his auditors. Then the shout of "Ee, ee, tchupy, tchupy, ee, Munza, ee," resounded from every throat, and the musical instruments caught up the strain, until the uproar was truly demoniacal. Several times after this chorus, and as if to stimulate the tumult, Munza uttered a stentorian "brrr—" [2] with a voice so sonorous that the very roof vibrated, and the swallows fled in terror from their nests in the eaves.

The kettle-drums and horns now struck up a livelier and more rhythmical strain, and Munza assumed a new character and proceeded to beat time with all the solemnity of a conductor. His *bâton* was something like a baby's rattle, and consisted of a hollow sphere of basket-work filled with pebbles and shells, and attached to a stick.[3]

The discourse lasted full half an hour, during which time I took the portrait of the king. . . . Hunger at length compelled me to take my leave of the sovereign and retrace my steps to the camp. At parting Munza said to me, "I do not know what to give you in return for all your presents; I am sorry I am so poor and have nothing to offer you." Fascinated by his modesty and indulging the idea that it was only a preface to a munificent gift worthy of royalty, I replied, "Don't mention that: I did not come for what I could get; we buy ivory from the Turks, and pay them with yellow lead and white iron, and we make white stuffs and powder and guns for ourselves. I only ask for two things: a pig (*Potamochoerus*) and a chimpanzee."

"You shall certainly have them," said Munza; but I was thoroughly deceived, and, in spite of my repeated reminders, neither pig nor chimpanzee ever appeared.

As I left the hall the king commenced a new oration. As for myself, I was so thoroughly fatigued with the noise and tumult, that I was glad to spend the remainder of this memorable day quietly in my tent.

2. It may interest the reader to learn that in the Shamane prayers "brrr—" is synonymous with "hail," and I have little doubt that it here meant some sort of applause, as it was always the signal for the repetition of the hymn in celebration of the glories of Munza.

3. A similar contrivance is used on the river Gabon on the West Coast.

52. JOHN MACKENZIE

BUSHMAN LAND. 1873.

The eastern Tswana states—the Ngwato, Kwena, and Ngwaketse—were scattered over the Kalahari Desert, a wilderness of scrub and thorns broken only by a few seasonal waterholes. The Kalahari was inhabited only by the Sarwa, a people of Bushman extraction, and the Kgalagadi, probably descendants of the earliest Sotho migrants to southern Africa. The following selection describes the relationship between the Tswana and the inhabitants of the desert.

The Reverend John Mackenzie (1835–1899) spent most of his life as a missionary among the Tswana. Ordained in 1858, he left for South Africa later in that year and, after a time of uncertainty as to where he would take up mission work settled at Shoshong, capital of the Ngwato state, in 1864. Between 1870 and 1871 he made

From John Mackenzie, *Ten Years North of the Orange River: A Story of Everyday Life and Work Among the South African Tribes* (Edinburgh: Edmonston and Douglas, 1871), pp. 128–139.

a trip to Britain, where he wrote Ten Years North of the Orange River. During a second term at Shoshong (1871–1876) and Kuruman (1876–1882) he became increasingly involved in the political aspects of British-South African-Tswana relationships. In 1883 and 1884 he returned to Britain to campaign for the annexation of Bechuanaland. In subsequent years he served briefly as the British deputy commissioner in southern Bechuanaland and as a political adviser and propagandist. In 1891 he retired from his position as pastor to a mission station for Negroes on the eastern Cape, where he died.

. . . There are two distinct races held in subjection in this country, and we now met with specimens of both at every fountain. Those called Bakalahari are Bechuanas, whose tribes have been worsted in former contests, and who, not able to preserve their own independence, "khetha" or pay tribute to a powerful neighbouring chief [the state of the Bamangwato or Ngwato, a Tswana (Bechuana) people]. Like their rulers, these vassal Bechuanas are not all of one tribe, nor do they all speak the same dialect of Sechuana. Within the memory of those now living, tribes once independent have been reduced to the condition of Bakalahari; while others who had been long Bakalahari, have been called, through the grace of their chief, to the privileges of citizenship, and appointed a place in the town of the tribe. The other subject race is that of the Bushmen, called Barwa by the Bechuanas in the south, and Masarwa by those in the north of the country. The relationship between the Bakalahari and their masters is much more friendly than that between the same masters and their Bushmen. The helplessness of the Bakalahari excites the contempt of their owners, and they are usually spoken of with the diminutive form of the word—Bakhalahatsane; but otherwise they are regarded as "bathu hela"—"like other people." The master therefore, knowing that he can trust to instincts and traditions similar to his own in the mind of the Bakalahari, sends his flocks and sometimes his herds to be taken care of by his vassals. The children of the Bakalahari luxuriate in goats' milk, while their father imagines himself considerably elevated in society as he gazes night and morning on the cattle as they enter and leave their pen. When the owner of the stock now and then makes his appearance at the post, he speaks of the cattle as if they belonged to the Bakalahari; and when it is his intention to sell or to slaughter a certain animal he usually announces it, and sometimes even goes through the form of asking permission to do so, although all the cattle belong to himself. The pastoral instincts of the Bakalahari thus find full occupation, to the satisfaction of their lord, and to the advantage of the vassals. Then the master provides dogs for hunting—the ivory and ostrich feathers, the furs and skins, to be his, the meat to belong to the Bakalahari. And when he visits the little settlement, it is usually with a little present of some tobacco or wild hemp for smoking, or a clasp-knife or a few beads, which he has purchased from a trader. He now receives the "tribute" of his vassals, staying with them a longer or shorter time according to his taste. As among Europeans, there are some Bechuanas who are happiest when "out of town" and in the huntingfield with their vassals. It is only at the positive command of the chief in time of disturbance that such Nimrods reluctantly return to their houses in the town.

But the Bushmen seldom secure much liking or consideration from their Bechuana masters. "Masarwa a bolotsana thata"—"Bushmen are great rascals," "Masarwa ki linoga hela"—"Bushmen are perfect snakes," are remarks often heard among the Bechuanas. The fact is, there is less in common between the two. Their allegiance is never so genuine, and while they yield tribute they hardly conceal their contempt for their masters. The Bushman is of use only in hunting. When his Bechuana master arrives he takes possession of the little huts, and receives all skins, etc., which the family have collected. And now they hunt every day in company, the Bushmen with their spears, bows and arrows, and dogs—their master with his spears, or, in recent years, with his gun. Woe betide the Bushmen should it be found out that they have hidden away part of the produce, or that, instead of keeping the skins for his master, the Bushman has ventured to make with some of them a mantle for himself or his wife! Thus Bushmen are continually on the alert for the arrival of their masters in the country; and should they cross the path and see his foot-mark on it, they are able to recognise it at once, and if possible will hasten home before him to hide that which must not meet the eye of their lord.

Looked at in this connection, it is not difficult to account for the well-known reluctance of Bechuana chiefs to allow traders and travellers to pass through their country. . . . While the Bamangwato, in whose country I was travelling, participate in the advantages of the trade recently begun with Europeans, they have lost property to the value of many hundreds of pounds through the opening up of the waggon roads to the Lake and to the Zambese. Both roads lead through districts occupied by their vassals, and it is well known that the latter do not hesitate to keep back part of the produce from their masters, and barter with it themselves as soon as a European waggon makes its appearance. . . . It has been found impossible by the Bamangwato to stop this "contraband" trade. They began with severity, and put some of their vassals to death for daring to sell what belonged to their masters. But they found that severity did not answer their purpose, and so the masters now are in point of fact competitors with the European hunters and traders for the purchase of ivory and feathers from their own vassals. Of course they do not acknowledge that they occupy such a position, but the "presents" which they now give their vassals are every year more handsome, and the whole transaction assumes more the appearance of barter than the levying of tribute. In a few instances masters have intrusted their Bakalahari and Bushmen with guns. The latter take to this weapon at once. What with their skill in stalking, and their steady aim, they soon excel their master in its use. Public opinion is against putting such dangerous weapons into the hands of the "lower classes," as an unsafe proceeding. But as it is to the decided advantage of the masters it is increasingly practised.

It is very interesting to observe how this vassalage becomes all but impracticable, and melts away before the teachings of Christianity and the increasing intercourse which now obtains among tribes that were formerly isolated. The missionaries in the southern district of Bechuanaland did not preach directly against this system; but they taught that the love and mercy of God were toward all, and that God was no respecter of persons. It was the custom even in the olden time, and is still in heathen towns, that if a slave regarded himself as ill-used by his master, or thought that his life was in danger, he might flee to the chief, and cast himself upon his protection. If the master complained of was a favourite with the chief, he would formally reprove him, and persuade the slave to return to his service. But if a charge of cruelty was proved against a master with whom the chief had a quarrel, he would at once release the slave from his obligations to him, and provide for him another master. It can readily be seen that Christianity, finding the slave enjoying such an amount of liberty, would speedily secure for him more. Thus in the southern district, and especially where Christian churches exist, this vassalage exists in many cases more in name than in reality. In most cases, as long as the vassals remain with their masters they receive some kind of payment for their service; and when they go away, there does not seem to be any power which is able and ready to bring them back. It is one of the faults which the heathen prefer against the partially Christianized district in the south, that there the "batianka" or slaves are no longer under their masters' control, as in the times of undisturbed heathenism. Christianity thus quietly lets the oppressed go free, and breaks every yoke.

But while under this system of appeal to the chief, the lot of these vassals is just bearable in time of peace, it is beyond conception wretched in time of war. I do not mean war among themselves in the country; they are too poor to quarrel seriously, or for a long time: but they are deeply interested in all the political questions of the town, being part of the property of the head men—a quarrel among whom is often followed up in the country in a way which astonishes as it shocks the Christian man. The contest for the possession of certain villages of Bakalahari or Bushmen, is a fruitful source of strife in Bechuana towns. The vassals with all their belongings are the subject of litigation and endless jealousies; and it needs all the skill of a chief to settle these matters between greedy and plausible rivals. When a decision is come to, the poor people in the country are hastily "lifted" by the successful litigant, to be brought back again should he afterwards lose his case. When rival chiefs fight for supremacy in the same tribe, the condition of the harmless vassals is wretched in the extreme. They are then scattered and peeled, driven hither and thither, and mercilessly killed, as the jealousy, caprice, or revenge of their masters may dictate. It is quite fair in such a struggle to kill all the vassals, as it would be to lift the cattle, of him who cannot be displaced from his chieftainship. And so with the varying fortunes of a "civil war," the vassals might be attacked by both parties in turn.

Again, when one Bechuana tribe attacks another, the Bushmen and Bakalahari belonging to both are placed in the same category with cattle and sheep—they are to be "lifted" or killed as opportunity offers. In such cases, therefore, all Bakalahari and Bushmen flee into wastes and inaccessible forests, and hide themselves until the commotion is past.

We found an illustration of the terror and mistrust in which these people live, when we reached the fountain of Lotlakane. A "civil war" was still going on, in an intermittent fashion, between Macheng and Sekhome, for the chieftainship of the Bamangwato tribe. It mattered little to these serfs who the chief was to be; with them the important question was, to escape both parties while the strife was going on. And so for the first night we saw nobody at Lotlakane; but in the morning my men told me that there were footmarks of Bushmen all round our camp. They had come in the night to satisfy themselves that there were no Bamangwate in my party, before they ventured to come amongst us. How they distinguished as the men lay asleep between the two Bakwena whom I had hired from Sechele and Bamangwato, I know not; but their midnight inspection was held to be satisfactory, and next day several made their appearance at our waggon. It was affecting to witness the earnestness with which they asked if the Bamangwato were still fighting among themselves.

On all subjects lying within the range of the Bushman's observation you will meet with extreme shrewdness and intelligence. The Bushman has the most extensive knowledge of the *materia medica* of the country. If my own medicines were not available, I would trust myself sooner to the care of a Bushman than to any other native doctor. Nothing can exceed the skill and intelligence of the Bushman as a hunter, and an observer of the habits of the wild animals. And as to religion, if I am not greatly mistaken, the Bushmen are the most "superstitious" race in Southern Africa. The fact that they are so peculiarly dependent for subsistence upon what is beyond their control will perhaps account for this. With other natives the chief season of praying and necromancing begins when they have sown their corn, and stand in need of rain. But all seasons are the same to the Bushman. Therefore whilst he is most accomplished in everything belonging to his own way of life, and by general consent the guide and leader of every hunting party of which he is a member, he constantly seeks by charms and by spells to supply his own deficiencies. Whether the European has bent his knee in prayer or not before he springs to the saddle in the morning of a hunt, the Bushman has not failed to consult his "oracles." Approaching with mysterious and confident mien, he announces to the hunters that if they will only proceed in a given direction they will find the game they seek. In short, he has assumed the office of "seer" for the party. He has been inquiring of his dice or charms, and announces to you their verdict with confidence. If you still hesitate, he explains to you that Morimo [God] has told him where the game is, and at the same time shakes the dice which he carries round his neck. If you smile, and say that these are merely bits of ivory or bone, he assents at once, and would readily dispose of them to you for a few beads. But then at the earliest opportunity he would repair the deficiency, and replace them by another set. The bits of bone are nothing, he will admit, but through them he "makes inquiry" of the ex-human if not super-human. No party of Bushmen would consent to take the field without these charms. Whoever fancies he is self-contained, and able in himself, without prayer, or without divining, to cope with the difficulties of human existence, the Bushman in Bechuana-land is not. I believe life to a Bushman without this professed addressing something out of and beyond himself would be complete misery.

The relics of a tribal rite are also to be found among these Bushmen. If you point to the pierced cartilage of the nose, he will explain to you that that was done when he was introduced to Bushman manhood. He here uses the word "rupa," which in Sechuana means the introductory ceremony of circumcision. This, then, is to him what circumcision is to the Bechuanas. You point to certain marks on his face, or bits of wood on his hair, or tied round his neck. These are medicines or charms to be taken in sickness, or proximity to lions, or in other circumstances of danger. This is the fetichism which is common throughout Africa at the present time, as it was in Europe in past ages, and which is not unknown in our own day in rural districts of England and Scotland. If you point to the dice, the Bushman will say that they are "Lilo tsa Morimo oa me,"—"Things of my God." lie will add, "Lia impuléléla mahuku,"—"They tell me news." If he does not know much Sechuana, he will point to them and say, "Se se Morimo, se,"—"This is God." As in the other cases, this explanation is to be regarded in its connection with such views of Morimo as are known to these Bushmen. The Bushman means to say that what Morimo is to the Bechuanas and to you his dice and charms are to him. To affirm from such data that the Bushmen have a definite notion of Morimo (God) would be to say too much; to say that their God is a bit of ivory or bone would be equally incorrect; while to affirm that they have no religion or superstition to distinguish them from the brutes that perish is entirely false. . . .

In sleeping at the same fire with Bushmen or Bakalahari you are sure to be roused twice in the course of the night, or oftener, by the rising of one after the other of your companions. Their first stretchings, yawnings, and gruntings over, they assume a sitting position in a row round the fire, which they replenish with fresh logs. Sometimes they fall asleep in this position, and you see them nodding over the flames. When they lie down again you take notice that it is always in the opposite position with reference to the fire from that which they last occupied. Thus if they had their backs to the fire before they got up, they now turn their faces to it. Having no blanket or covering whatever, except a little skin mantle, which just covers their shoulders, it is only by repeated "turnings" that they are able to keep up heat in their bodies during the cold winter nights. Thus their bodies are always scorched and scarred, and generally "over-done" on both sides, by the fire at night. Before the day is fairly broken you again hear the yawning and other demonstrations—now in a louder tone. As the light increases the restless eye of the Bushman scans the heavens with a close scrutiny. On the ground also, as far as the eye can reach, he seems to notice every living thing. The process of roasting meat on the live coals now commences; and as this early breakfast goes on each one parenthetically mentions what he observes. At length one starts to his feet. What has he descried? After great effort you can just see "manong" or vultures in the distance sweeping over a certain spot. Seizing their weapons two or three men start at once in that direction; they hope to get there before the lion has finished the antelope or zebra which has been his midnight meal. If they find the killer of the prey still at his repast, with a jackal venturing to approach the opposite end, while hyenas or younger lions bide their time at a distance—the Bushmen, who have been talking loudly as they approached, to give due notice of their arrival, now shout at the top of their voice, rattle their spears, break off decayed branches from trees, or shake their mantles, to frighten the lion and his courtiers, who retire into the adjoining thicket. Everything is now collected which is at all edible, and carried to the encampment. Should their visit be too late, and they find only bits of bone and hide and hoofs to reward them for their trouble, all these are collected and brought away; the vulture and the hyena or jackal finding little to pick up after the visit of the Bushman. Thus although Bakalahari object to lions in their vicinity, on account of the live stock which they are rearing for themselves and their masters, the Bushmen do not at all object to this proximity, for they have a good deal to gain from it, and if they only keep up a good fire at night in self-preservation they have nothing whatever to lose.

53. ERNEST LINANT DE BELLEFONDS

KABAKA MUTESA I. 1875.

Ernest Linant de Bellefonds was the son of his more famous father, Louis-Maurice-Adolphe Linant de Bellefonds (1800–1883), by his Abyssinian mother. He joined C. G. ("Chinese") Gordon as an administrator in Equatoria in 1874 after the death of his brother Auguste-Édouard, from malaria. After the failure of a mission by the American Charles Chaillé-Long to bring Buganda within the sphere of the Egyptian government, Gordon sent Linant to Buganda to negotiate an agreement whereby the Kabaka Mutesa I (b. Mukabaya, 1838–1884) would recognize Egyptian sovereignty. He arrived at Rubaga with a small force of Egyptian troops in April 1875, only to discover that the American explorer Henry Morton Stanley had preceded him by five days. Impressed by Stanley's large and well-equipped expedition, Mutesa ignored Linant's proposal to place Buganda under Egyptian suzerainty. He sent Linant back to Gordon bearing Stanley's famous letter, in which Mutesa appealed to the British public for Christian missionaries to be sent to Buganda. During his return to Gondokoro, Linant and his detachment of some forty troops of the Egyptian army were annihilated on August 4, 1875, by the Moogie clan of the Bari people.

21, 22, 23 April—I have had many different discussions with M'Tesa during the last three days. Our conversation had dwelled on all the different powerful forces of the world in turn: America, England, France, Germany, Russia, the Ottoman Empire, constitutions, government, military might, production, industry and religion.

The King's sister was present at these sessions. The daughters and sisters of the King never go on foot; they are always carried by their slaves.

25th April—M'Tesa summoned me at eleven o'clock at the same time as the Fakir of the Xodcria. Our talk therefore was exclusively about the Koran. The poor Fakir was at a loss as to how to answer all the King's questions. I had to give him some help.

I informed the King of the system of trade by means of money. The value of all goods is based on the tallari. This system makes trade and transactions easier.

From E. Linant de Bellefonds, "Itinéraire et Notes. Voyage de service fait entre le poste militaire de Fatiko et la capitale de M'Tesa, roi d'Uganda. Fevrier–Juin 1875." *Bulletin Trimestriel de la Socété Khédiviate de Geographie du Caire*, ser. I, 1876–77, pp. 58–52, 73, 81–82. D. A. Low, *The Mind of Buganda* (Berkeley and Los Angeles: University of California Press, 1971), pp. 2–4. Reprinted by permission of the University of California Press.

27th April—In answer to all M'Tesa's questions concerning the earth, the sun, the moon, the stars and the sky and in order to make him understand the movements of the heavenly bodies. I had to make shapes on a board, the heavenly bodies being represented by little glass balls. The lecture took place today. The gathering was not very large. The two viziers Katikiro* and Chambarango,* four leading officers, the two scribes and a few favourites. The four cardinal points, the rotation of the earth, its movement round the sun, night and day, the seasons, the movement of the moon round the earth and its phases (which I did by means of a mirror) and the general movement of our system in space.

M'Tesa grasped everything perfectly. We were seated on the ground in a circle and there was a very friendly atmosphere. I have never seen M'Tesa so happy. It was the first time that we had spoken to each other directly without using interpreters, and this is against all the laws of etiquette. M'Tesa himself explained afterwards to the wonder-struck gathering. What was so surprising was that M'Tesa was able to inspire in his associates and in many of his people this quest for understanding, for self-instruction and for knowledge. There is great rivalry among them and they are very eager to improve. They are an inquiring, observant, intelligent people with minds longing for the learning of white people whose superiority they recognize; and with the help of a mission having farmers, carpenters and smiths amongst them, these Gandas will soon become an industrial people. This being so, Ganda would be the centre of civilization of all this part of Africa. . . .

I left the King at two o'clock after we had arranged to meet again at four. The same people were there as in the morning. The talk was of Genesis, M'Tesa had the story of Genesis from the Creation to the Flood taken down on a writing-tablet. We parted at nightfall. M'Tesa is spellbound and I shall be able to obtain all I want from him. . . .

17th May—Yesterday and today we had long discussions with M'Tesa concerning the duties of man towards himself and towards his neighbour. I gave him various precepts, a mixture of Socrates' philosophy and Christian morality. What troubled the King most is knowing what paradise, hell and the angels are composed of. Where are they set and what sort of joy and punishment await us after death? Is it true that the body lives again after death? If this is so and given that the body is matter, should not God then have a body? . . .

26 May— . . . In as much as M'Tesa believes himself to be of divine essence, so he is led by pride and vanity to continually brag and boast, and this makes him look ridiculous and sets people against him. In spite of his faults, he is certainly the most intelligent African living between Sobat* and Lake Ukerewe.* He learns about the customs, habits and governments of every country and all this not merely out of idle curiosity, but with the idea of becoming better informed and of bringing about some useful reforms in his own country.

Katikiro: chief minister.
Chambarango: Kyambalango, a county chief.
Sobat: the river Sobat now in the Sudan.
Ukerewe: an island at the south end of Lake Victoria.

Thanks to him, the people of Uganda are today as much above the other tribes I have visited, as civilized Europe is above the Bedouin Arabs, those primitive nomads of the desert.

The self-esteem of M'Tesa is extreme. He is very concerned about what the civilized world thinks of him and his greatest ambition, and very laudable it is, is that his name should go down in posterity. He wants history to think of him as the founder of the human race.

"I am called M'Tesa," he said one day, "which means in Ganda language, *reformer, benefactor*. I want history to say of me one day that if I had not been given that name at my birth, posterity would give it to me at my death."

54. EDGAR CANISIUS

RUBBER COLLECTING IN THE CONGO. 1885.

In 1885 King Leopold II of Belgium became sovereign of the Congo Free State and set out to establish the state's authority throughout the Congo basin and beyond. The task soon absorbed the king's private resources, and despite loans from Belgium, by the early 1890s the Congo Free State was on the verge of bankruptcy. It was saved from financial collapse by the rubber industry. King Leopold leased vast territories of the Congo to concessionaire companies while exploiting the royal domain with his own agents. Soon rubber was exported from the Congo in ever increasing quantities, to the profit of the companies and the king. Unhappily, rubber could be collected only by employing brutal and repressive methods against the Africans who derived no profit from tapping the vines and collecting the sap and consequently had no wish to work. The atrocities that were perpetrated to force Africans into the forest to tap the vines soon caused an international scandal and ultimately resulted in the transfer of the Congo Free State to Belgium. Edgar Canisius was a young American who joined the service of the Congo Free State in 1896 and was stationed in the Province Orientale. After completing his tour of duty, he joined the Société Anversoise du Commerce au Congo and as an agent of that concessionaire company, he was able to describe at first hand the methods employed to collect rubber.

There are, or were, in the immediate vicinity, of N'Dobo about a dozen villages, the people of which were obliged to bring in rubber every fifteen days. On these occasions the natives crowded into the post, each village in charge of a "capita," or headman, whose most important duty it was to ensure that the demanded amount of rubber was collected. These capitas usually belonged to tribes settled in other districts of the State, and were as a general rule, armed with muskets of the gas-pipe variety, although some had breech-loaders. They were paid by the company, but the

From Edgar Canisius, "A Campaign Amongst Cannibals," in Captain Guy Burrows, *The Curse of Central Africa* (London: R. A. Everett & Co., 1903), pp. 74–80.

villagers were expected to supply them with food, and this Mr. "Capita" was never remiss in deciding should be of the best and of sufficient quantity.

The natives carried to the muster small baskets supplied by the post, and supposed to be full of rubber. When all had arrived, the people were ranged by the capitas according to their villages. The agent, who had their names inscribed in a book kept for the purpose, then called the people forward, first by villages, then individually. As each man stepped up I noticed that he carried, attached to his neck by a cord, a small disc of metal evidently cut from the zinc lining of a packing-case, and that each disc bore a number corresponding with that entered in the book opposite the man's name. The soldiers having ranged the people in lines, each man with his basket before him, the agent proceeded to verify the individual numbers—not without some difficulty, however, for the natives by some means or other frequently get their "tags" mixed, and much time and a fearful amount of shouting and gesticulation are required, on the part of both natives and white man, to set matters right.

As each man or boy presented his basket, the agent carefully inspected the quantity of rubber it contained, and paid the bearer accordingly in *mitakos*—pieces of brass wire about six inches long, the estimated value of which at N'Dobo was about a half-penny. I calculated that the rubber was paid for at the rate of rather less than one penny per pound, which certainly could not be considered excessive in view of the fact that at that time the product in Europe was fetching from two to three shillings a pound. Those natives who had brought in quantities which the agent deemed insufficient were ordered to one side, and as soon as the entire village had been thus inspected and paid, these delinquents were seized by some of the "soldiers" attached to the post, thrown upon the ground, and soundly flogged. Some received twenty-five lashes, others fifty, but I have occasionally seen even 100 lashes administered, the instrument used being the "chicotte," a heavy whip of hippopotamus hide. This proceeding—inspection and eventual punishment—was repeated until all the villages had been dealt with. Then the natives started off for their jungle homes, usually at a sharp trot, apparently only too glad to escape with life from a place which no doubt they looked upon much as the Belgians' forefathers regarded the torture-chambers to which they were oftimes led by their Spanish masters. They, of course, carried with them their baskets and their *mitakos*, which they did not want but were forced to accept. The manager of the post had accumulated perhaps no less than a thousand pounds of rubber at the cost of about £4 sterling, including presents to the chiefs and capitas, Thus was rubber "gathered" twice each month at N'Dobo.

I found that it was usual to "tag" not all, but only three-fourths or so of the male villagers. Those "tagged" at once became mere slaves to the company, for rubber-making occupied all their time, the victim having to search far and wide for the giant vines from which the sap is extracted. They were not even fed by their taskmasters, their only remuneration being merchandise or *mitakos* distributed in ridiculously small quantities, as already described.

The cruel flogging of so many men and boys would probably have had a peculiar effect upon a new-comer, but I was in a measure case-hardened. My experience in the State service during three years had made me familiar with many such, and worse incidents of Congolese life. For instance, at the Government post where I was for a long time stationed, a man had died as the result of an exceptionally severe castigation at the hands of a white official, and elsewhere I had seen blood drawn from the backs of women.

At N'Dobo I found many brick houses and magazines in course of construction under the direction of an ex-architect and builder. At that time, it was evident, the company's officials at Mobeka entertained keen hopes that the fierce and hitherto intractable Budjas of the interior were about to tumble over each other in their eagerness to bring in rubber—an idea which proved very erroneous, as will later be seen.

The Brazilian rubber-gatherer has no reason to envy the people engaged in a similar occupation in the wilds of Africa, for his work in comparison is a mere picnic. The great rubber-trees of the Amazonian forest yield to him their precious sap after but a few blows of the axe, and fill the bucket of the collector without entailing upon the latter any necessity of raising himself above the ground. Nor does the extraction of a few quarts of sap deprive him of another supply from the same source later on.

Not so, however, with the Congolese rubber-gatherer. In the African jungle the sap is drawn from a giant creeper (often six inches in diameter at the base), which, shooting upward towards the lifegiving light of heaven, twists about the surrounding vegetation—its rivals in the struggle for existence. After reaching the crown of the highest monarch of the forest (often a hundred feet above the ground), the vine rises still further until it is bent back by its own weight to the topmost branches of its original support. Then it climbs along these branches, and those probably of half-a-dozen other great trees, until the machete of the rubber-gatherer cuts short its career.

The Congo native, when about to gather rubber, generally goes with his fellow-villagers far into the jungle. Then, having formed a rough, shelterless camp, he begins his search for the creepers. Having found one of sufficient size, he cuts with his knife a number of incisions in the bark, and, hanging a small earthenware pot below the vine, allows the sap to slowly trickle into it. Should the creeper have been already tapped, the man must climb into the supporting tree at more or less personal risk and make an incision in the vine high above the ground where the sap has not been exhausted; and here he will remain, perhaps the whole of the day, until the flow has ceased. Not unfrequently the natives slumber on their lofty perches, and, falling to the ground, become victims to the white man's greed. Few Africans will imperil their lives in rubber-gathering unless under compulsion. The natives, if pressed for time, as they usually are in the Congo in consequence of the threats of the white man and the fear of the Albinis [rifles] of the soldiers and the muskets of the capitas, cut down long lengths of the giant creepers and then subdivide them to make the sap ooze out more quickly.

Of late, the people have been compelled to so frequently tap the vines that the latter soon dry up and die. Each tribe has only a limited extent of forest which it can call its exclusive domain, and it consequently very frequently happens, when their own "bush" is worked out, that natives from one village penetrate the territory of the other in defiance of tribal usage. Such an invasion is naturally resented by their neighbours, who, equally pressed no doubt by circumstances and the white man, are themselves experiencing difficulty in making up the quota of rubber definitely fixed for each village, and a deficient production of which may entail dire punishment and even death. In consequence, disputes arise between villages which heretofore, perhaps for quite a long period, have been at peace; and then come wars, involving more or less loss of life, destruction and cannibalism. Natives, I may add, have often come to me with bitter laments over the disappearance of their brothers after accidents when rubber-gathering, or the attacks of leopards or hostile tribesmen.

The coagulation of the sap is effected in a variety of ways. In some regions, the natives smear the latex over their chests, and with their hands rub it until a small ball is formed. This process is repeated until the ball is the size of a small walnut. These balls have often a reddish hue, the result of the powdered camwood with which the natives usually smear their bodies. In other parts, the juice is poured into a pot in which is boiling water, and is then allowed to boil until all the water has evaporated and the rubber forms a kind of cake over the bottom of the pot. This product, when brought to the stations, is cut into fine strips and hung upon battens in a drying-shed for several months. In the Province Orientale the natives generally pour the sap into an oblong form of box, made of flat-sided sticks laid upon the ground. The heat of the sun is utilized to coagulate the sap, a thin layer of latex being poured on the top from time to time until the whole forms a solid mass of rubber some fifteen to twenty inches long, eight inches wide, two or three inches thick, and weighing from eight to ten pounds. After reaching the stations, these slabs are cut into small strips or *vidoles* (fingers), and then placed in sheds to dry upon shelves made of poles.

I have seen it stated in official documents, and in books written by persons represented to have travelled through the African forests, that there are regions where the jungle is literally a tangled mass of rubber-vines. Such stories are ridiculous, for nowhere does the creeper exist in such luxuriance; like all tropical jungle vegetation, it is scattered over large areas with many other similar plants, which may belong to the same genus but are not the true rubber-vine. On an acre of jungle one rarely finds two trees of a kind, and the same may be said of the large creepers, or lianas, with which the tropical bush abounds.

That the stock of rubber-vines in those parts of the Congo which have been worked for any length of time is being rapidly exhausted is evidenced by the ever-increasing difficulty experienced in inducing the natives to exploit it. Wherever I have been in this vast territory, always excepting, of course, the Budja country, which has never been much worked, the natives bitterly bemoaned the scarcity of the rubber-producing lianas, and piteously begged to be allowed to perform other service than rubber-gathering. In some places they brought in large quantities of "false rubber," a resinous matter much resembling caoutchouc, from which, indeed, when freshly-made, it cannot be easily distinguished. In the course of drying, however, the false rubber assumes a glossy appearance, unlike that of the genuine article.

55. THE KANO CHRONICLE

KINGS OF KANO. 1892.

The history of the Hausa is dominated by the growth of their city-states, which were formed in the eleventh and twelfth centuries as a result of an intermingling of the diverse peoples that wandered across the plains of northern Nigeria. The political unit of the Hausa was the birni, or walled village, which became a city-state when one birni secured control over a wider circle of villages. At this point the village headman was made the city chief, the sarki, and was surrounded by an elaborate court and ritual. The birni of Kano remained a small settlement from the time that it was established in about 1000 A.D. until about the fourteenth century, when it became a city-state and acquired a reputation as a manufacturing center. Nevertheless, Kano remained of little importance compared with the larger city-state of Katsina. The two city-states carried on an eighty-year war from 1570 to 1650, when both were attacked by the Jukun (or Kwararafa) from the south. Kano apparently strengthened its position in the eighteenth century and, despite the Fulani conquest in 1809, continued to be a manufacturing and commercial center throughout the nineteenth century.

XIII. KANAJEJI, SON OF YAJI
(A.H. 792–812. A.D. 1390–1410)

The thirteenth Sarki was Kanajeji. His father's name was Yaji. His mother's name Aunaka. He was a Sarki who engaged in many wars. He hardly lived in Kano at all, but scoured the country round and conquered the towns. He lived for some time near the rock of Gija. He sent to the Kwararafa and asked why they did not pay him tribute. They gave him two hundred slaves. Then he returned to

Kano and kept sending the Kwararafa horses while they continued to send him slaves. Kanajeji was the first Hausa Sarki to introduce "Lifidi" [quilted armor] and iron helmets and coats of mail for battle. They were introduced because in the war at Umbatu the losses had been so heavy. He visited Kano and returned to Umbatu the next year, but he had no success in the war. He returned a second time to Kano, and again went out the following year. He again failed, but said, "I will not return home, if Allah wills, until I conquer the enemy." He remained at Betu two years. The inhabitants, unable to till their fields, were at length starved out, and had to give in to him. They gave him a thousand male, and a thousand female slaves, their own children. They also gave him another two thousand slaves. Then peace was made. The Sarkin Kano said: "No one shall again conquer Umbatu as I have conquered it, though he may gain spoil." In the following year the Sarki made war on Zukzuk and sat down in Turunku. The men of Zukzuk came out and defeated the Kano host, saying, "What is Kano! Kano is 'bush'" [primitive]. The Sarkin Kano went back to

From "The Kano Chronicle," in H. R. Palmer, *Sudanese Memoirs* (Lagos, 1928), vol. III, pp. 107–109, 127–132.

Kano in a rage and said: "What shall I do to conquer these men of Zukzuk?" The Sarkin Tchibiri said: "Re-establish the god that your father and grandfather destroyed." The Sarki said: "True, but tell me what I am to do with it." The Sarkin Tchibiri said: "Cut a branch from this tree." The Sarki cut off a branch. When it was cut, the Sarki found a red snake in the branch. He killed the snake, and made two *huffi* [slippers] with its skin. He then made four *dundufu* and eight *kuntakuru* [drums] from the branch. These objects he took to Dankwoi and threw them into the water and went home. After waiting forty days he came back to the water, and removed the objects to the house of Sarkin Tchibiri. Sarkin Tchibiri sewed the rest of the snake's skin round the drums and said to Kanajeji, "Whatever you wish for in this world, do as our forefathers did of old." Kanajeji said: "Show me, and I will do even as they did." The Sarkin Tchibiri took off his robe and put it on the *huffi* of snake's skin and walked round the tree forty times, singing the song of Barbushe. Kanajeji did as Sarkin Tchibiri did, and walked round the tree forty times. The next year he set out to war with Zukzuk. He encamped at Gadaz. The Sarkin Zukzuk came out and they fought; the men of Kano killed the Sarkin Zukzuk. The Zukzuk men fled, scattered in ones and twos, and the chiefs of Zukzuk were killed. The Sarkin Kano entered Zukzuk and lived there close to the Shika eight months. The people gave him a vast amount of tribute. Because of this feat the song of Kanajeji was sung, which runs: "Son of Kano, hurler of the *kere*, Kanajeji, drinker of the water of Shika, preventer of washing in the Kubanni, Lord of the town, Lord of the land." Kanajeji returned to Kano. Among his great men of war were Berdi Gutu, Jarumai Sabbo, Maidawaki Babaki, Makama Toro, Dan Burram Jatau, Jakafada Idiri, Jambori Sarkin Zaura Bugau, Lifidi Buzuzu and Dan Akassan Goderi. He reigned twenty years.

XIV. UMARU, SON OF KANAJEJI
(A.H. 812–824. A.D. 1410–1421)

The fourteenth Sarki was Umarti. His mother's name was Yatara. He was a mallam, earnest in prayer. He was a pupil of Dan Gurdamus Ibrahimu and a friend of Abubakra. When he became Sarkin Kano his friend upbraided and left him and went to Bornu, where he remained eleven years. On his return to Kano finding Umaru still Sarkin Kano, he said to him: "O Umaru, you still like the fickle dame who has played you false, with whom better reflection refuses to be troubled. In time you will be disgusted, and get over your liking for her. Then regret will be futile even if you do regret." He preached to him about the next world and its pains and punishments, He reviled this world and everything in it. Umaru said, "I accept your admonition." He called together all the Kanawa, and said to them: "This high estate is a trap for the erring: I wash my hands of it." Then he resigned, and went away with his friend. He spent the rest of his life in regret for his actions while he had been Sarki. Hence he was called "Dan Terko." He ruled twelve years. In his time there was no war and no robbery. The affairs of Kano were put into the hands of the Galadima [Governor of the western provinces]. For this reason it was said of the Galadima Dana that he was the "Trusted guardian of the city, the dust-heap of disputes."

XLIII. MOHAMMA ALWALI, SON OF YAJI
(A.H. 1195–1222. A.D. 1781–1807)

The forty-third Sarki was Mohamma Alwali, son of Yaji. His mother's name was Baiwa. As soon as he became Sarki he collected stores of "Gero" [millet] and "Dawa" [guinea corn] in case of war and famine. Nevertheless famine overtook him. His chiefs said to him, "Sarkin Kano, why do you refuse to give cattle to Dirki?" The Sarki said, "I cannot give you forty cattle for Dirki." They said, "What prevents you? If any Sarkin Kano does not allow us cattle for Dirki, we fear that he will come to some ill." Alwali was very angry and sent young men to beat "Dirki" with axes until that which was inside the skins came out. They found a beautiful Koran inside Dirki. Aiwali said, "Is this Dirki?" They said, "Who does not know Dirki? Behold here is Dirki." Dirki is nothing but the Koran. In Alwali's time the Fulani conquered the seven Hausa States on the plea of reviving the Muhammadan religion. The Fulani attacked Alwali and drove him from Kano, whence he fled to Zaria. The men of Zaria said, "Why have you left Kano?" He said, "The same cause which drove me out of Kano will probably drive you out of Zaria." He said, "I saw the truth with my eyes, I left because I was afraid of my life, not to save my wives and property." The men of Zaria drove him out with curses. So he fled to Rano, but the Fulani followed him to Burum-Burum and killed him there. He ruled Kano twenty-seven years, three of which were spent in fighting the Fulani.

XLIV. SULIMANU, SON OF ABAHAMA
(A.H. 1222–1235. A.D. 1807–1819)

The forty-fourth Sarki was Sulimanu, son of Abahama, a Fulani. His mother's name was Adama Modi. When he became Sarkin Kano, the Fulani prevented him from entering the palace. He went into the house of Sarkin Dawaki's mother. One of the remaining Kanawa said to Sulimanu, "If you do not enter the Giddan Rimfa, you will not really be the Sarki of city and country." When Sulimanu heard this he called the chief Fulani, but they refused to answer his summons, and said, "We will not come to you. You must come to us, though you be the Sarki. If you will come to Mallam Jibbrim's house we will assemble there." Sulimanu went to Jibbrim's house and called them there. When they had assembled, he asked them and said, "Why do you prevent me entering the Giddan Rimfa?" Mallatin Jibbrim said, "If we enter the Habe's houses and we beget children, they will be like these Habes, and do like them." Sulimanu said nothing but set off to Shehu-Osuman Dan Hodio [Uthman Dan Fodio] asking to be allowed to enter the Giddan Rimfa. Shehu Dan Hodio gave him a sword and a knife[1] and gave him leave to enter the Giddan Rimfa, telling him to kill all who opposed him. He entered the house, and lived there. All the Kano towns submitted to him, except Faggam, which he attacked. He took many spoils there. On his way back to Kano the chiefs of the Fulani said to him, "If you leave Faggam alone, it will revolt." So he divided it into two, and returned home. In his time Dabo Dan Bazzo raised a revolt. He dared to look for a wife in Sokoto and

---

1. A flag was also given him as well as a knife and sword. He did not go to Sokoto, but sent a message. Had he gone himself, he would never have regained his position.

was given one. Sarkin Kano said, "What do you mean by looking for a wife at Sokoto?" So Dabo was caught and bound. His relations, the Danbazzawa, however, came by night and cut his bonds, and set him free. He ran to Sokoto with Sulimanu following him. At Sokoto they both went before Dan Hodio. Dabo Dan Bazzo said, "I do not wish to marry your daughters, but I wish for a reconciliation between myself and your Sarki Sulimanu." So a reconciliation was made and they returned to Kano. Sulimanu sent the Galadima Ibrahima to Zaria to make war. Ibrahima conquered Zaria and took many spoils. He returned to Kano. Sulimanu was angry because of the Galadima's success, and had sinister designs against him when he died himself without having an opportunity of carrying them out. He ruled thirteen years.

XLV. IBRAHIM DABO, SON OF MOHAMMADU (A.H. 1235–1262. A.D. 1819–1846)

The forty-fifth Sarki was the pious and learned Ibrahim Dabo, son of Mohammadu, protector of the orphan and the poor, a mighty conqueror—a Fulani. His mother's name was Halimatu. When he became Sarki he entered the Giddan Rimfa. Dabo made Sani Galadima. He, however, immediately tried to raise a revolt and incite all the towns to disaffection. The country Sarkis assembled and became "Tawayi" [rebellious] from Ngogu to Damberta, from Jirima to Sankara, and from Dussi to Birnin Kudu and Karayi. Dabo said, "I will conquer them, if Allah wills." He entered his house and remained there forty days praying to Allah for victory. Allah heard his prayers. He went out to hasten his preparations for war, and made a camp on Dalla Hill. Because of this he got the name of "The man who encamped on Dalla." He spent many days on Dalla,[2] and then returned home. He sent Sarkin Dawaki Manu Maituta to fight with Karayi. When the Sarkin Dawaki reached Karayi he sacked the town and returned to Dabo. Dabo said, "Praise be to God," and prepared himself to go out to war. He went to Jirima and sacked that town and afterwards sacked Gasokoli and Jijita. Hence he was known as "Dabo, the sacker of towns." After he returned home he kept on sending out men to raid towns. He went in person to attack Dan Tunku and found him at Yan Yahiya. They fought. The Yerimawa ran away, and deserted Dan Tunku, who fled to Damberta, and thence, with Dabo following him, to Kazauri. When the Sarki reached the Koremma in pursuit he stopped, turned round again, and went back to Damberta, where he wrecked Dan Tunku's house. Dabo then returned home. Dabo was celebrated in the song:

The sacker of towns has come: Kano is your land, Bull Elephant, Dabo, sacker of towns When he went to war the trumpets played: The sacker of towns is mounting.

He made war on Birnin Sankara and Bimin Rano, took the town of Rano, and lived in the house of Sarkin Rano. After this exploit he shaved his head. He never shaved his head except when he sacked a town. When the Kano towns saw that Dabo would not leave any town unconquered, they all submitted to him, and his power exceeded all other Sarkis. He had a friend whose name was Ango. When the

2. Perhaps forty, I am not sure.

Galadima Sini died, he made Ango Galadima, and as Galadima the latter reached great power through his pleasant manner and his persuasiveness. In Dabo's time there was no foreign war and people had food in plenty. Dabo conquered and spoiled Yasko. He had many war captains, a few among whom may be mentioned as: Berde, Kano Buggali, Sarkin Dawaki Manu, Sarkin Jarumai Dumma, Sulimanu Gerkwarn Karifi (he it was who killed Tunari, the son of Sarkin Sankara), Juli Kuda, Lifidi, Maidawaki Gawo and many others. These warriors of Dabo's time had no fear in war. When Dabo mounted to go to war no such dust was ever seen, so many were his horses. The dust was like the Harmattan. Dabo was called "Majeka Hazo." His was a wonderful and brilliant reign, but we will not say any more for fear of "Balazi." He ruled Kano twenty-seven years and three months and nine days, his reign ending on the ninth of Safar.

XLVI. OSUMANU, SON OF DABO
(A.H. 1262–1272. A.D. 1846–1855)

The forty-sixth Sarki was Osumanu, son of Dabo. His mother was Shelkara. The first act of his reign was to build a house for Shekara at Tafassa with a big room the like of which was never seen before. Shekara was called "the mistress of the big room." Osumanu was a learned and good man and generous. He was called "The skin of cold water." The Galadima Abdulahi obtained in his time almost as much power as the Sarki, while Osumanu was like his Waziri. There was no war in his time except with Hadeijia. He built a house at Gogel and had a farm there. In his time mallams [learned holy men] obtained great honour—among them Mallam Ba-Abseni, and others. In Osumanu's time Sarkin Dussi Bello revolted, but the Sarki enticed him to Kano and deposed him. Highway robbers were very numerous because Osumanu was so good-tempered and merciful. He could not bring himself to cut a man's hand off nor, because he was so pitiful, could he cut a robber's throat. He was called "Jatau rabba kaya." There was no Sarki like him for generosity. He ruled Kano nine years and ten months.

XLVII. ABDULAHI, SON OF DABO
(A.H. 1272–1300. A.D. 1855–1883)

The forty-seventh Sarki was Abdulahi, son of Dabo. His mother's name was Shekara. When he became Sarki he set to work to kill all the robbers and cut off the hands of the thieves. He was called "Abdu Sarkin Yenka" because he was a strong-minded Sarki, ruthless, and victorious. He was quick to depose chiefs, but kept his word to his friends. He never stayed long in one place but went from town to town. In his time there was a very great famine, and the quarrel with Urnbata grew big from small beginnings. The Sarkin Kano was eager to make war upon Umbatu. His first move was to attack Kuluki. Dan Iya Lowal of Kano died at Kuluki, whereupon the Sarki returned home himself, but sent Abdulahi Sarkin Dawaki Dan Ladan and his son Tafida to war in Zaria country. They went to Zaria together. This was in the time of Sarkin Zaria Abdulahi Dan Hamada. When they returned from Zaria it was not long before Dan Boskori made a descent upon Gworzo. The Sarkin Kano sent

Sarkin Dawaki on ahead and followed himself personally to meet Dan Boskori Sarkin Maradi, west of Gworzo. A battle took place. The Kanawa ran away, deserting the Sarkin Dawaki Dan Ladan. Dan Boskori killed him. The Kanawa returned home in ones and twos. The Sarkin Kano was very angry. He gave orders that a house was to be built at Nassarawa for him to live in during the hot season; he also built a house at Tarkai for the war with Umbatu. He had a house at Keffin Bako where he lived almost two years because of Dan Maji the neighbour of Umbatu. He fought with Warji after the war with Kuluki, and took enormous spoil. No one knows the amount of the spoil that was taken at a town called Sir. The corpses of Warjawa, slaughtered round their camp, were about four hundred. The Sarki returned home. After a short time, the Sarki attacked Warji again, and once more took many spoils. Kano was filled with slaves. Abdulahi went to Sokoto, leaving his son Yusufu at Tarkai. While he was there Dan Maji came to attack Yusufu. A battle was fought at Dubaiya. The Kanawa fled and deserted Yusufa. Many men were slain and captured. After this Yusufu was made Galadima Kano, and hence acquired much power. Abdulahi sent him to Dal from Tarkai to capture Haruna, the son of Dan Maji. Yusufu met Haruna at Jambo, and a battle took place. The Urnbatawa ran away, deserting Haruna. Yusufu killed and took many men. It is said that about seven hundred were killed. Afterwards Yusufu tried to stir up rebellion and was deprived of his office and had to remain in chagrin and poverty till he was penniless. Abdulahi turned the Sarkin Dawaki Abdu out of his office and with him Makama Gadodamasu, Chiroma Diko, Dan Iya Alabirra, Galadima Abdul-Kadiri, and Galadima Yusufiu. Abdulahi killed the Alkali Kano Ahmedu Rufaiyi, and degraded Maäiji Sulimanu, Maji Gajere, and San Kurmi Musa. He deprived Mallam Dogo of his office of Waziri. The number of people that he turned out of office was countless. Hence the song

Son of Ibrahim, a pick-axe to physic hard ground.

He sacked many towns. He made a new gate, the Kofan Fada. In his father's time it had been built up. He rebuilt the mosque and house of the Turaki Mainya early in his reign. They had been in ruins for many years. In his time Soron Giwa was built. At Woso he met Dan Maji in war. It was towards evening when the battle was fought. Dan Maji retreated. If it had not been that the light failed he would have been killed. Abdulahi attacked Betu, but failed. Abdulahi used to have guns fired off when he mounted his horse, till it became a custom. His chief men were: Sarkin Yaki, called Mallam Dogo, Mallam Isiaka, Mallam Garuba, Sarkin Gaiya, Mallam Abdu Ba-Danneji, Alhaji Nufu, his friend Mallam Masu, Tefida his son, Shamaki Naamu, Manassara, Jekada of Gerko, and Dan Tabshi. Mallam Ibrahim was his scribe, and was made a Galadima. This man was afterwards turned out of office in the time of Mohammed Belo. Others were the Alkali Zengi and Alkali Sulimanu. Abdulahi went to Zaria and sat down at Afira, and then at Zungonaiya. The Madawaki Ali of Zaria was in revolt against Sarkin Zaria. The Sarkin Kano made peace between them and returned home. In Abdulahi's time Salemma Berka became great. In the time of Mohammed Belo this man revolted and was degraded. In Abdulahi's time, too, the palace slaves became so great that they were like free men. They all rebelled in Mohammed Belo's time, but Allah helped Mohammed

Belo to quell the rebellion. There were many great captains of war in Abdulahi's time, men without fear—so many of them that they could not be enumerated, but a few may be mentioned: Sarkin Yaki, Mallam Dogo and his son Duti, Jarumai Musa, Sarkin Bebeji Abubakr, Sarkin Rano Ali, Sarkin Gesu Osuman, Sarkin Ajura Jibbr. In this reign Sarkin Damagaram Babba came as far as Jirima and sacked Garun Allah. Sarkin Gummel Abdu Jatau came to Pogolawa to attack it. Sarkin Maradi Dan Boskori came to Katsina. Abdulahi went to meet him. They met at Kusada, but did not fight. For this reason the meeting was called "Algish Bigish Zuru Yakin Zuru," for they looked at each other and went back. There was also a fight between Barafia Sarkin Maridi and Sarkin Kano at Bichi. Barafia ran away and Abdulahi took all the spoils. It is not known how many men were killed and slain. We do not know much of what Abdulahi did in the early part of his reign. He ruled Kano twenty-seven years and eight days, and died at Karofi on his way to Sokoto.

XLVIII. MOHAMMED BELO, SON OF IBRAHIM DABO (A.H. 1300–1310. A.D. 1883–1892)

The forty-eighth Sarki was Mohammed Belo, son of Ibrahim Dabo. His mother was Shekara. He was a very generous Sarki. He said to his friend Sarkin Fada Dan Gatuma, "You are Waziri Kano; I place in your hands the management of Kano." The Sarkin Fada was unrivalled as a settler of disputes. Belo was like his Wazir, and Sarkin Fada was like Sarki. When Sarkin Fada died Mohammed Belo stretched out his legs because he saw that now he must become Sarki in earnest. He expelled the Galadima Ibrahim from his office and banished him to Funkui in Zaria, whence his name, "Galadima na Funkui." Belo gave the post of Galadima to his son Tukr, and his son Zakari was made San Turaki. Another son, Abubakr, he made Chiroma in place of Chiroma Musa.

56. NDANSI KUMALO

THE NDEBELE REBELLION. 1896.

Defeated and bitterly discontented over the loss of land and cattle to settlers in Zimbabwe, the Ndebele rebelled in March 1896, when the military resources of the British South Africa Company were preoccupied in the Jameson Raid in the Transvaal. Over a hundred Europeans were killed in the revolt, and the remainder were besieged until a relief force under Major Plumer reached Bulawayo. The Ndebele rebels were then defeated by the superior firepower of Maxim guns and driven into the Matopo Hills, where Cecil Rhodes personally arranged the surrender of the principal Ndebele Ndunas (chieftains) and their followers.

From Margery Perham, *Ten Africans* (London: Faber and Faber Ltd., 1963), pp. 72–75. Reprinted by permission of Northwestern University Press and Faber and Faber Ltd.

So we surrendered to the white people and were told to go back to our homes and live our usual lives and attend to our crops. But the white men sent native police who did abominable things; they were cruel and assaulted a lot of our people and helped themselves to our cattle and goats. These policemen were not our own people; anybody was made a policeman. We were treated like slaves. They came and were overbearing and we were ordered to carry their clothes and bundles. They interfered with our wives and our daughters and molested them. In fact, the treatment we received was intolerable. We thought it best to fight and die rather than bear it. How the rebellion started I do not know; there was no organization, it was like a fire that suddenly flames up. We had been flogged by native police and then they rubbed salt water in the wounds. There was much bitterness because so many of our cattle were branded and taken away from us; we had no property, nothing we could call our own. We said, "It is no good living under such conditions; death would be better—let us fight." Our King gone, we had submitted to the white people and they ill-treated us until we became desperate and tried to make an end of it all. We knew that we had very little chance because their weapons were so much superior to ours. But we meant to fight to the last, feeling that even if we could not beat them we might at least kill a few of them and so have some sort of revenge.

I fought in the rebellion. We used to look out for valleys where the white men were likely to approach. We took cover behind rocks and trees and tried to ambush them. We were forced by the nature of our weapons not to expose ourselves. I had a gun, a breech-loader. They—the white men—fought us with big guns and Maxims and rifles.

I remember a fight in the Matoppos when we charged the white men. There were some hundreds of us; the white men also were many. We charged them at close quarters: we thought we had a good chance to kill them but the Maxims were too much for us. We drove them off at the first charge, but they returned and formed up again. We made a second charge, but they were too strong for us. I cannot say how many white people were killed, but we think it was quite a lot. I do not know if I killed any of them, but I know I killed one of their horses. I remember how, when one of their scouts fell wounded, two of his companions raced out and took him away. Many of our people were killed in this fight: I saw four of my cousins shot. One was shot in the jaw and the whole of his face was blown away—like this—and he died. One was hit between the eyes; another here, in the shoulder; another had part of his ear shot off. We made many charges but each time we were beaten off, until at last the white men packed up and retreated. But for the Maxims, it would have been different. The place where we have been making the film is the very place where my cousins were killed.

We were still fighting when we heard that Mr. Rhodes was coming and wanted to make peace with us. It was best to come to terms he said, and not go shedding blood like this on both sides. The older people went to meet him. Mr. Rhodes came and they had a discussion and our leaders came back and discussed amongst themselves and the people. Then Mr. Rhodes came again and we agreed at last to terms of peace.

So peace was made. Many of our people had been killed, and now we began to die of starvation; and then came the rinderpest and the cattle that were still left to us perished. We could not help thinking that all these dreadful things were brought by the white people. We struggled, and the Government helped us with grain; and by degrees we managed to get crops and pulled through. Our cattle were practically wiped out, but a few were left and from them we slowly bred up our herds again. We were offered work in the mines and farms to earn money and so were able to buy back some cattle. At first, of course, we were not used to going out to work, but advice was given that the chief should advise the young people to go out to work, and gradually they went. At first we received a good price for our cattle and sheep and goats. Then the tax came. It was 10s. a year. Soon the Government said, "That is too little, you must contribute more; you must pay £1." We did so. Then those who took more than one wife were taxed; 10s. for each additional wife. The tax is heavy, but that is not all. We are also taxed for our dogs; 5s. for a dog. Then we were told we were living on private land; the owners wanted rent in addition to the Government tax; some 10s., some £1, some £2 a year. After that we were told we had to dip our cattle and pay 1s. per head per annum.

Would I like to have the old days back? Well, the white men have brought some good things. For a start, they brought us European implements—ploughs; we can buy European clothes, which are an advance. The Government have arranged for education and through that, when our children grow up, they may rise in status. We want them to be educated and civilized and make better citizens. Even in our own time there were troubles, there was much fighting and many innocent people were killed. It is infinitely better to have peace instead of war, and our treatment generally by the officials is better than it was at first. But, under the white people, we still have our troubles. Economic conditions are telling on us very severely. We are on land where the rainfall is scanty, and things will not grow well. In our own time we could pick our own country, but now all the best land has been taken by the white people. We get hardly any price for our cattle; we find it hard to meet our money obligations. If we have crops to spare we get very little for them; we find it difficult to make ends meet and wages are very low. When I view the position, I see that our rainfall has diminished, we have suffered drought and have poor crops and we do not see any hope of improvement, but all the same our taxes do not diminish. We see no prosperous days ahead of us. There is one thing we think an injustice. When we have plenty of grain the prices are very low, but the moment we are short of grain and we have to buy from Europeans at once the price is high. If when we have hard times and find it difficult to meet our obligations some of these burdens were taken off us it would gladden our hearts. As it is, if we do raise anything, it is never our own: all, or most of it, goes back in taxation. We can never save any money. If we could, we could help ourselves: we could build ourselves better houses; we could buy modern means of travelling about, a cart, or donkeys or mules.

57. MARY KINGSLEY

THE CROWN COLONY SYSTEM IN WEST AFRICA. 1897.

Mary Kingsley (1862–1900) was one of the most remarkable women travelers of Victorian times. A niece of the famous novelist Charles Kingsley, she first visited the West African coast in 1893, when she developed her method of traveling like an African trader, subsisting on local food and living among the people of the regions through which she passed. She traveled in Angola, the Belgian Congo, and the French Congo. She returned to West Africa in 1895, intending to travel up the Niger and Benue Rivers. However, she changed her plans and proceeded up the Ogoué River in Gabon, after which she visited German Kamerun. Her Travels in West Africa was first published in 1897 and widely read. Both this book and her second book, West African Studies, were influential in changing the attitudes of European administrators toward their African subjects and laying the foundation for today's scientific anthropological study of Africa. Her sympathy, understanding, and enthusiasm for Africa and its inhabitants did much to make Europeans approach Africans with a willingness to understand them rather than simply dismiss them as inferior savages.

Wherein is set down briefly in what manner of ways the Crown Colony system works evil in Western Africa.

I have attempted to state that the Crown Colony system is unsuited for governing Western Africa, and have attributed its malign influence to its being a system which primarily expresses the opinions of well-intentioned but ill-informed officials at home, instead of being, according to the usual English type of institution, representative of the interests of the people who are governed, and of those who have the largest stake in the countries controlled by it—the merchants and manufacturing classes of England. It remains to point out how it acts adversely to the prosperity of all concerned; for be it clearly understood there is no corruption in it whatsoever: there is waste of men's lives, moneys, and careers, but nothing more at present. By and by it will add to its other charms and functions that of being, in the early future, a sort of patent and successful incubator for hatching a fine lively brood of little Englanders, who will cry out, "What is the good of West Africa?" and so forth; and they will seem sweetly reasonable, because by then West Africa will be down on the English rates, a pauper.

It may seem inconceivable, however, that the present governing body of West Africa, the home officials, and the English public as represented in Parliament, can be ill-informed. West Africa has not been just shot up out of the ocean by a submarine volcanic explosion nor are we landing on it out of Noah's ark, for the thing has been in touch with Europe since the fifteenth century; yet, inconceivable as it may seem that there is not by now formulated and in working order a method of governing it suitable for its nature, the fact that this is so remains, and providentially for

From Mary H. Kingsley, *West African Studies* (New York, 1899), pp. 267–275.

us it is quite easy of explanation without abusing any one; though no humane person, like myself for example, can avoid sincerely hoping that Mr. Kipling is wrong when he sings

> *Deep in all dishonour have we stained our*
> *garments' hem.*
> *Yet be ye not dismayed, we have stumbled and*
> *have strayed.*
> *Our leaders went from righteousness, the Lord*
> *will deal with them.*

For although it is true that we have made a mess of this great feeding ground for England's manufacturing millions; yet there are no leaders on whom blame alone can fall, whom we can make scapegoats out of, who can be driven away into the wilderness carrying the sins of the people. The blame lies among all those classes of people who have had personally to deal with West Africa and the present system; and the Crown Colony system and the resolution of '65 are merely the necessary fungi of rotten stuff, for they have arisen from the information that has been, and has not been, placed at the disposal of our Government in England by the Government officials of West Africa, the Missionaries, and the Traders.[1]

We will take the traders' blame first—their contribution to the evil dates from about 1827, and consists in omission—frankly, I think that they, in their generation, were justified in not telling all they could tell about the Coast. They found they could get on with it, keep it quiet and manage the natives fairly well under the system of Courts of Equity in the Rivers, and the Committee of merchants with a Governor approved of by the Home Government, which was working on the Gold Coast up to 1843. In 1841 there arose the affair of Governor Maclean, and the inauguration of the line of policy which resulted in the resolution of 1865. The governmental officials having cut themselves off from the traders and taken over West Africa, failed to manage West Africa, and so resolved that West Africa was not worth managing—a thing they are bound to do again.

The abuse showered on the merchants, and the terrific snubs with which the Government peppered them, did not make the traders blossom and expand, and shower information on those who criticised them—there are some natures that are not sweetened by Adversity. Moreover, the Government, when affairs had been taken over by the Offices in London, took the abhorrent form of Customs, and displayed a lively love of the missionary made African, as he was then—you can read about him in Burton—and for the rest got up rows with the traders' best customer, the untutored African; rows, as the traders held, unnecessary in their beginning and

---

1. In 1865 a Select Committee of the House of Commons considering British policy toward the coast of Guinea felt that Britain had acquired greater obligations than could be justified by her interests. The committee recommended that the administration of the Gold Coast, Lagos, and Gambia be united under the governor of Sierra Leone; that Britain decline to extend its rule or protection over African territories; and that Britain should urge Africans under British protection to prepare for self-government. The recommendations were adopted by the British government (ed.).

feeble-handed in their termination. The whole of this sort of thing made the trader section keep all the valuable information to itself, and spend its energies in eluding the Customs, and talking what Burton terms "Commercial English."

Then we come to the contribution made by the Government officials to the formation of an erroneous opinion concerning the state of affairs in West Africa. This arose from the conditions that surrounded them there, and the way in which they were unable, even if they desired, to expand their influence, distrusted naturally enough by the trading community since 1865, held in continuously by their home instructions, and unprovided with a sufficient supply of men or money on shore to go in for empire making, and also villainously badly quartered—as you can see by reading Ellis's *West African Sketches*. It is small wonder and small blame to them that their account of West Africa has been a gloomy one, and such it must remain until these men are under a different system: for all the reasons that during the past have caused them to paint the Coast as a place of no value to England, remain still in full force—as you can see by studying the disadvantages that service in a West African Crown Colony presents to-day to a civilian official.

Firstly, the climate is unhealthy, so that the usual make of Englishman does not like to take his wife out to the Coast with him. This means keeping two homes, which is expensive, and it gives a man no chance of saving money on an income say of E600 a year, for the official's life in West Africa is necessarily, let him be as economical as he may, an expensive one; and, moreover, things are not made more cheerful for him by his knowing that if he dies there will be no pension for his wife.

Secondly, there being no regular West African Service, there is no security for promotion; owing to the unhealthiness of the climate it is very properly ordained that each officer shall serve a year on the Coast, and then go home on a six months' furlough. It is a fairly common thing for a man to die before his twelve months' term is up, and a still more common one for him to have to go on sick leave. Of course, the moment he is off, some junior official has to take his place and do his work. But in the event of the man whose work he does dying, gaining a position in another region, or promotion, the man who has been doing the work has no reason to hope he will step into the full emoluments and honours of the appointment, although experience will thus have given him an insight into the work. On the contrary, it too often happens that some new man, either fresh from London or who has already held a Government appointment in some totally different region to the West African, is placed in the appointment. If this new man is fresh to such work as he has to do, the displaced man has to teach him; if he is from a different region, he usually won't be taught, and he does not help to develop a spirit of general brotherly love and affection in the local governmental circles by the frank statement that he considers West African officials "jugginses" or "muffs," although he freely offers to "alter this and show them how things ought to be done."

Then again the civilian official frequently complains that he has no such recognition given him for his services as is given to the military men in West Africa. I have so often heard the complaint, "Oh, if a man comes here and bums half a dozen villages he gets honours; while I, who keep the villages from wanting burning, get nothing;" and, mind you, this is true. Like the rest of my sex I suffer from a chronic form of scarlet fever, and, from a knowledge of the country there, I hold it rubbish to talk of the brutality of mowing down savages with a Maxim gun when it comes to talking of West African bush fighting; for your West African is not an unarmed savage, he does not assemble in the manner of Dr. Watts's ants, but wisely ensconces himself in the pleached arbours of his native land, and lets fly at you with a horrid scatter gun. This is bound to hit, and when it hits makes wounds worse than those made by a Maxim; in fact he quite turns bush fighting into a legitimate sport, let alone the service done him by his great ally, the climate. Still, it is hard on the civilian, and bad for English interests in West Africa that the man who by his judgment, sympathy, and care, keeps a district at peace, should have less recognition than one who, acting under orders, doing his duty gallantly, and all that, goes and breaks up all native prosperity and white trade.

All these things acting together produce on the local Government official a fervid desire to get home to England, or obtain an appointment in some other region than the West Coast. I feel sure I am well within the mark when I say that two-thirds of the present Government officials in the West African English Crown Colonies have their names down on the transfer list, or are trying to get them there; and this sort of thing simply cannot give them an enthusiasm for their work sufficient to ensure its success, and of course leads to their painting a dismal picture of West Africa itself.

I am perfectly well aware that the conditions of life of officials in West Africa are better than those described by Ellis. Nevertheless, they are not yet what they should be: a corrugated iron house may cost a heap of money and yet not be a Paradise. I am also aware that the houses and general supplies given to our officials are immensely more luxurious than those given to German or French officials; but this does not compensate for the horrors of boredom suffused with irritation to which the English official is subjected. More than half the quarrelling and discontent for which English officials are celebrated, and which are attributed to drink and the climate, simply arise from the domestic arrangements enforced on them in Coast towns, whereby they see far too much of each other. If you take any set of men and make them live together, day out and day in, without sufficient exercise, without interest in outside affairs, without dividing them up into regular grades of rank, as men are on board ship or in barracks, you are simply bound to have them dividing up into cliques that quarrel; the things they quarrel over may seem to an outsider miserably petty, but these quarrels are the characteristic eruption of the fever discontent. And may I ask you if the opinion of men in such a state is an opinion on which a sound policy wherewith to deal with so complex a region can be formed? I think not, yet these men and the next class alone are the makers of our present policy—the instructors of home official opinion.

The next class is the philanthropic party. It is commonly confused with the missionary, but there is this fundamental difference between them. The missionary, pure and simple, is a man who loves God more than he loves himself, or any man. His service (I am speaking on fundamental lines, as far as I can see) is to place in God's charge, for the glory of God, souls that, according to his belief, would otherwise go elsewhere. The philanthropist is a person who loves man; but he or she is frequently no better than people who kill lapdogs by over-feeding, or who shut up skylarks in cages; while it is quite conceivable to me, for example, that a missionary could kill a man to save his soul, a philanthropist kills his soul to save his life, and there is in this a difference. I have never been able to get up any respectful enthusiasm for the so-called philanthropist, so that I have to speak of him with calm care; not as I have spoken of the missionary, feeling he was a person I could not really harm by criticising his methods.

It is, however, nowadays hopeless to attempt to separate these two species, distinct as I believe them to be; and they together undoubtedly constitute what is called the Mission party not only in England but in Germany. I believe this alliance has done immense harm to the true missionary, for to it I trace that tendency to harp upon horrors and general sensationalism which so sharply differentiates the modern from the classic missionary reports. Take up that noble story of Dennis de Carli and Michael Angelo of Gattinal and read it through, and then turn on to wise, clear-headed Merolla da Sorrento, and read him; you find there no sensationalism. Now and again, when deeply tried, they will say, "These people live after a beastly manner, and converse freely with the Devil," but you soon find them saying, "Among these people there are some excellent customs," and they give you full details of them, with evident satisfaction. You see it did not fundamentally matter to these early missionaries whether their prospective converts "had excellent customs" or "lived after a beastly manner," from a religious standpoint. Not one atom—they were the sort of men who would have gone for Plato, Socrates, and all the Classics gaily, holding that they were not Christians as they ought to be; but this never caused them to paint a distorted portrait of the African. This thing, I believe, the modem philanthropist has induced the modern missionary only too frequently to do, and the other regrettable element which has induced him to do it has been the apathy of the English public, a public which unless it were stirred up by horrors would not subscribe. Again the blame is with England at home, but the harm done is paid for in West Africa. The portrait painted of the African by the majority, not all, but the majority of West African mission reports, has been that of a child, naturally innocent, led away and cheated by white traders and grievously oppressed by his own rulers. I grant you, the African taken as a whole is the gentlest kind of real human being that is made. I do not however class him with races who carry gentleness to a morbid extent, and for governmental purposes you must not with any race rely on their main characteristic alone; for example, Englishmen are honest, yet still we require the police force.

The evil worked by what we must call the missionary party is almost incalculable; from it has arisen the estrangement of English interests, as represented by our reason for adding West Africa to our Empire at all—the trader—and the English Government as represented by the Crown Colony system; and it has also led to our present policy of destroying powerful native States and the power of the African ruling classes at large. Secondarily it is the cause of our wars in West Africa. That this has not been and is not the desire of the Mission party it is needless to say; that the blame is directly due to the Crown Colony system it is as needless to remark; for any reasonable system of its age would long ere now have known the African at first hand, not as it knows him, and knows him only, at its headquarters, London, from second-hand vitiated reports. It has, nowadays, at its service the common sense and humane opinions of the English trade lords as represented by the Chambers of Commerce of Liverpool and Manchester; but though just at present it listens to what they say—thanks to Mr. Chamberlain—yet it cannot act on their statements, but only querulously says, "Your information does not agree with our information." Allah forbid that the information of the party with whom I have had the honour to be classed should agree with that sort of information from other sources; and I would naturally desire the rulers of West Africa to recognise the benefit they now enjoy of having information of a brand that has not led to such a thing as the Sierra Leone outbreak for example, and to remember in this instance that six months before the hut tax there was put on, the Chambers had strongly advised the Government against it, and had received in reply the answer that "The Secretary of State sees no reason to suppose that the hut tax will be oppressive, or that it will be less easy to collect in Sierra Leone than in Gambia." Why, you could not get a prophetic almanac into a second issue if it were not based on truer knowledge than that which made it possible for such a thing to be said. Nevertheless, no doubt this remarkable sentence was written believing the same to be true, and confiding in the information in the hands of the Colonial Office from the official and philanthropic sources in which the Office believes.

58. LORD LUGARD

INDIRECT RULE IN TROPICAL AFRICA. 1900.

Frederick Dealtry Lugard (1858–1945) served in the Indian Army before arriving in East Africa in 1888. Thereafter, he was instrumental in establishing the British presence in Nyasaland, Uganda, and Nigeria. In 1900 he was appointed high commissioner in Northern Nigeria. As governor of Northern and Southern Nigeria (1912–1913), he united the two provinces in 1914, and he served as the governor general of Nigeria from 1914 to 1919. He was later appointed to several international commissions with interests in Africa, but he is best known for the development and implementation of the administrative policy known as "indirect rule." Not only did indirect rule become identified with British colonial rule throughout Africa, but it became widely accepted by British colonial officials both in London and overseas "first as a useful administrative device, then that of a political doctrine, and finally that of a religious dogma."[1] The fundamentals of indirect rule as a

From Frederick Dealtry Lugard, *The Dual Mandate in British Tropical Africa* (London: William Blackwood and Sons Ltd., 1926), pp. 200–207, 209–218. Reprinted by permission.

1. Lord Hailey, "Some Problems Dealt with in *An African Survey*," *International Affairs*, vol. 18, no. 2, pp. 179–210, March/April 1939.

method for ruling subject peoples were presented by Lord Lugard in his discussion
of the relations between native rulers and the British staff.

The system adopted in Nigeria is therefore only a particular method of the application of these principles—more especially as regards "advanced communities," and since I am familiar with it I will use it as illustrative of the methods which in my opinion should characterise the dealings of the controlling power with subject races.

The object in view is to make each "Emir" or paramount chief, assisted by his judicial Council, an effective ruler over his own people. He presides over a "Native Administration" organised throughout as a unit of local government. The area over which he exercises jurisdiction is divided into districts under the control of "Headmen," who collect the taxes in the name of the ruler, and pay them into the "Native Treasury," conducted by a native treasurer and staff under the supervision of the chief at his capital. Here, too, is the prison for native court prisoners, and probably the school. . . . Large cities are divided into wards for purposes of control and taxation.

The district headman, usually a territorial magnate with local connections, is the chief executive officer in the area under his charge. He controls the village headmen, and is responsible for the assessment of the tax, which he collects through their agency. He must reside in his district and not at the capital. He is not allowed to pose as a chief with a retinue of his own and duplicate officials, and is summoned from time to time to report to his chief. If, as is the case with some of the ancient Emirates, the community is a small one but independent of any other native rule, the chief may be his own district headman.

A province under a Resident may contain several separate "Native Administrations," whether they be Moslem Emirates or pagan communities. A "division" under a British District Officer may include one or more headmen's districts, or more than one small Emirate or independent ("independent" in this connection is meant "independent of other native control") pagan tribe, but as a rule no Emirate is partly in one division and partly in another. The Resident acts as sympathetic adviser and counsellor to the native chief. being careful not to interfere so as to lower his prestige, or cause him to lose interest in his work. His advice on matters of general policy must be followed, but the native ruler issues his own instructions to his subordinate chiefs and district heads—not as the orders of the Resident but as his own—and he is encouraged to work through them, instead of centralising everything in himself—a system which in the past had produced such great abuses. The British District Officers supervise and assist the native district headmen, through whom they convey any instructions to village heads, and make any arrangements necessary for carrying on the work of the Government departments, but all important orders emanate from the Emir, whose messenger usually accompanies and acts as mouthpiece of a District Officer.

The tax—which supersedes all former "tribute," irregular imposts, and forced labour—is, in a sense, the basis of the whole system, since it supplies the means to pay the Emir and all his officials. The district and village heads are effectively supervised and assisted in its assessment by the British staff. The native treasury retains the proportion assigned to it (in advanced communities a half), and pays the remainder into Colonial Revenue. . . .

In these advanced communities the judges of the native courts administer native law and custom, and exercise their jurisdiction independently of the native executive, but under the supervision of the British staff, and subject to the general control of the Emir, whose "Judicial Council" consists of his principal officers of State, and is vested with executive as well as judicial powers. No punishment may be inflicted by a native authority, except through a regular tribunal. The ordinances of government are operative everywhere, but the native authority may make by-laws in modification of native custom—e.g., on matters of sanitation, &c.—and these, when approved by the Governor, are enforced by the native courts.

The authority of the Emir over his own people is absolute, and the profession of an alien creed does not absolve a native from the obligation to obey his lawful orders; but aliens—other than natives domiciled in the Emirate and accepting the jurisdiction of the native authority and courts—are under the direct control of the British staff. Townships are excluded from the native jurisdiction.

The village is the administrative unit. It is not always easy to define, since the security to life and property which has followed the British administration has caused an exodus from the cities and large villages, and the creation of innumerable hamlets, sometimes only of one or two huts, on the agricultural lands. The peasantry of the advanced communities, though ignorant, yet differs from that of the backward tribes in that they recognise the authority of the Emir, and are more ready to listen to the village head and the Council of Elders, on which the Nigerian system is based.

Subject, therefore, to the limitations which I shall presently discuss, the native authority is thus defacto and dejure ruler over his own people. He appoints and dismisses his subordinate chiefs and officials. He exercises the power of allocation of lands, and with the aid of the native courts, of adjudication in land disputes and expropriation for offences against the community; these are the essential functions upon which, in the opinion of the West African Lands Committee, the prestige of the native authority depends. The lawful orders which he may give are carefully defined by ordinance, and in the last resort are enforced by Government.

Since native authority, especially if exercised by alien conquerors, is inevitably weakened by the first impact of civilised rule, it is made clear to the elements of disorder, who regard force as conferring the only right to demand obedience, that government, by the use of force if necessary, intends to support the native chief. To enable him to maintain order he employs a body of unarmed police, and if the occasion demands the display of superior force he looks to the Government—as, for instance, if a community combines to break the law or shield criminals from justice—a rare event in the advanced communities.

The native ruler derives his power from the Suzerain, and is responsible that it is not misused. He is equally with British officers amenable to the law, but his authority does not depend on the caprice of an executive officer. To intrigue against him is an offence punishable, if necessary, in a Provincial Court. Thus both British and native courts are invoked to uphold his authority.

The essential feature of the system (as I wrote at the time of its inauguration) is that the native chiefs are constituted "as an integral part of the machinery of the administration. There are not two sets of rulers—British and native—working either separately or in co-operation, but a single Government in which the native chiefs have well-defined duties and an acknowledged status equally with British officials. Their duties should never conflict, and should overlap as little as possible. They should be complementary to each other, and the chief himself must understand that he has no right to place and power unless he renders his proper services to the State." . . .

Comparatively little difficulty, it may be said, would be experienced in the application of such a system to Moslem States, for even if their rulers had deteriorated, they still profess the standards of Islam, with its system of taxation, and they possess a literate class capable of discharging the duties I have described. No doubt the alien immigrants in the northern tropical belt afford better material for social organisation, both racially and through the influence of their creed, than the advanced communities of negro stock which owe nothing to Islam, such as the Baganda, the Ashantis, the Yorubas, the Benis, and others. But the self-evolved progress in social organisation of these latter communities is in itself evidence that they possessed exceptional intelligence, probably more widely diffused among the peasantry than would be found among those over whom an alien race had acquired domination. They too had evolved systems of taxation and of land tenure, and had learnt to delegate authority. The teaching of missions through many decades had in most cases produced a class who, if their energies were rightly directed to the service of their communities instead of seeking foreign outlets, would form a very valuable aid in the building up of a "Native Administration." That these communities are fully capable of adopting such a system has been proved in recent years in South Nigeria.

They have not produced so definite a code of law, or such advanced methods of dispensing justice, as the Koran has introduced, and they lack the indigenous educational advantages which the use of Arabic and the religious schools have conferred on the Moslem. On the other hand, many—especially the Baganda—have benefited greatly by the Christian schools, and a wider range of knowledge, including English. Some of their chiefs—notably Khama of Bechuana, and several of those in Uganda—have been remarkable men. Among many of these communities the chiefs exercise an influence different in its nature from that accorded to an alien ruler, and based on superstitious veneration.

The limitations to independence which are frankly inherent in this conception of native rule—not as temporary restraints to be removed as soon as may be, but as powers which rightly belong to the controlling Power as trustee for the welfare of the masses, and as being responsible for the defence of the country and the cost of its central administration—are such as do not involve interference with the authority of the chiefs or the social organisation of the people. They have been accepted by the Fulani Emirs as natural and proper to the controlling power, and their reservation in the hands of the Governor has never interfered with the loyalty of the ruling chiefs, or, so far as I am aware, been resented by them. The limitations are as follows:

1. Native rulers are not permitted to raise and control armed forces, or to grant permission to carry arms. . . .

2. The sole right to impose taxation in any form is reserved to the Suzerain power. . . .

3. The right to legislate is reserved. That this should remain in the hands of the Central Government—itself limited by the control of the Colonial Office, as I have described—cannot be questioned. . . .

4. The right to appropriate land on equitable terms for public purposes and for commercial requirements is vested in the Governor. . . . If the pressure of population in one community makes it necessary to assign to it a portion of the land belonging to a neighbour with a small and decreasing population, the Governor (to whom appeal may be made) would decide the matter. . . .

5. In order to maintain intact the control of the Central Government over all aliens, and to avoid friction and difficulties, it has been the recognised rule that the employees of the native administration should consist entirely of natives subject to the native authority. . . .

6. Finally, in the interests of good government, the right of confirming or otherwise the choice of the people of the successor to a chiefship, and of deposing any ruler for misrule or other adequate cause, is reserved to the Governor.

The habits of a people are not changed in a decade, and when powerful despots are deprived of the pastime of war and slave-raiding, and when even the weak begin to forget their former sufferings, to grow weary of a life without excitement, and to resent the petty restrictions which have replaced the cruelties of the old despotism, it must be the aim of Government to provide new interests and rivalries in civilised progress, in education, in material prosperity and trade, and even in sport. . . .

On the other hand, the personal interests of the rulers must rapidly become identified with those of the controlling Power. The forces of disorder do not distinguish between them, and the rulers soon recognise that any upheaval against the British would equally make an end of them. Once this community of interest is established, the Central Government cannot be taken by surprise, for it is impossible that the native rulers should not be aware of any disaffection.

This identification of the ruling class with the Government accentuates the corresponding obligation to check malpractices on their part. The task of educating them in the duties of a ruler becomes more than ever insistent; of inculcating a sense of responsibility; of convincing their intelligence of the advantages which accrue from the material prosperity of the peasantry, from free labour and initiative; of the necessity of delegating powers to trusted subordinates; of the evils of favouritism and bribery; of the importance of education, especially for the ruling class, and for the filling of lucrative posts under Government; of the benefits of sanitation, vaccination, and isolation of infection in checking mortality; and finally, of impressing upon them how greatly they may benefit their country by personal interest in such matters, and by the application of labour-saving devices and of scientific methods in agriculture. . . .

I have throughout these pages continually emphasised the necessity of recognising, as a cardinal principle of British policy in dealing with native races, that institutions and methods, in order to command success and promote the happiness and welfare of the people, must be deep-rooted in their traditions and prejudices. Obviously in no sphere of administration is this more essential than in that under discussion, and a slavish adherence to any particular type, however successful it may have proved elsewhere, may, if unadapted to the local environment, be as ill-suited and as foreign to its conceptions as direct British rule would be.

The type suited to a community which has long grown accustomed to the social organisation of the Moslem State may or may not be suitable to advanced pagan communities, which have evolved a social system of their own, such as the Yorubas, the Benis, the Egbas, or the Ashantis in the West, or the Waganda, the Wanyoro, the Watoro, and others in the East. The history, the traditions, the idiosyncracies, and the prejudices of each must be studied by the Resident and his staff, in order that the form adopted shall accord with natural evolution, and shall ensure the ready co-operation of the chiefs and people. . . .

Native etiquette and ceremonial must be carefully studied and observed in order that unintentional offence may be avoided. Great importance is attached to them, and a like observance in accordance with native custom is demanded towards British officers. Chiefs are treated with respect and courtesy. Native races alike in India and Africa are quick to discriminate between natural dignity and assumed superiority. Vulgar familiarity is no more a passport to their friendship than an assumption of self-importance is to their respect. The English gentleman needs no prompting in such a matter—his instinct is never wrong. Native titles of rank are adopted, and only native dress is worn, whether by chiefs or by schoolboys. Principal chiefs accused of serious crimes are tried by a British court, and are not imprisoned before trial, unless in very exceptional circumstances. Minor chiefs and native officials appointed by an Emir may be tried by his Judicial Council. If the offence does not involve deprivation of office, the offender may be fined without public trial, if he prefers it, in order to avoid humiliation and loss of influence.

Succession is governed by native law and custom, subject in the case of important chiefs to the approval of the Governor, in order that the most capable claimant may be chosen. It is important to ascertain the customary law and to follow it when possible, for the appointment of a chief who is not the recognised heir, or who is disliked by the people, may give rise to trouble, and in any case the new chief would have much difficulty in asserting his authority, and would fear to check abuses lest he should alienate his supporters. In Moslem countries the law is fairly clearly defined, being a useful combination of the hereditary principle, tempered by selection, and in many cases in Nigeria the ingenious device is maintained of having two rival dynasties, from each of which the successor is selected alternately.

In pagan communities the method varies; but there is no rigid rule, and a margin for selection is allowed. The formal approval of the Governor after a short period of probation is a useful precaution, so that if the designated chief proves himself unsuitable, the selection may be revised without difficulty. . . .

There are some who consider that however desirable it may be to rule through the native chiefs of advanced communities, such a policy is misplaced, if not impossible, among the backward tribes. Here, they would say, the Resident and his staff must necessarily be the direct rulers, since among the most primitive peoples there are no recognised chiefs capable of exercising rule. The imposition of a tax is in their view premature, since (they say) the natives derive no corresponding benefit, and learn to regard the District Officer merely as a tax-collector. Moreover, refusal to pay necessitates coercive expeditions—scarcely distinguishable from the raids of old times. To attempt to adapt such methods—however suitable to the Moslem communities—to the conditions of primitive tribes, would be to foist upon them a system foreign to their conceptions. In the criticisms I have read no via media is indicated between those who are accounted to rank as advanced communities, entitled before long to independence, and direct rule by the British staff.

Let us realise that the advanced communities form a very minute proportion of the population of British Tropical Africa. The vast majority are in the primitive or early tribal stages of development. To abandon the policy of ruling them through their own chiefs, and to substitute the direct rule of the British officer, is to forgo the high ideal of leading the backward races, by their own efforts, in their own way, to raise themselves to a higher plane of social organisation, and tends to perpetuate and stereotype existing conditions.

We must realise also two other important facts. First, that the British staff, exercising direct rule, cannot be otherwise than very small in comparison to the area and population of which they are in charge. That rule cannot generally mean the benevolent autocracy of a particular District Officer, well versed in the language and customs of the people, but rule by a series of different white men, conveying their orders by police and couriers and alien native subordinates, and the quartering of police detachments in native villages. Experience has shown the difficulty in such conditions of detecting and checking cases of abuse of office, and of acquisition of land by alien and absentee native landlords. There is a marked tendency to litigation, and the entire decay of such tribal authority as may previously have existed.

The changed conditions of African life is the second important fact for consideration. The advent of Europeans cannot fail to have a disintegrating effect on tribal authority and institutions, and on the conditions of native life. This is due in part to the unavoidable restrictions imposed on the exercise of their power by the native chiefs. They may no longer inflict barbarous and inhuman punishments on the individual, or take reprisals by force of arms on aggressive neighbours or a disobedient section of the community. The concentration of force in the hands of the Suzerain Power, and the amenability of the chiefs to that Power for acts of oppression and misrule, are evidence to primitive folk that the power of the chiefs has gone. This decay of tribal authority has unfortunately too often been accentuated by the tendency of British officers to deal direct with petty chiefs, and to ignore, and allow their subordinates to ignore, the principal chief. It has been increased in many cases by the influx of alien natives, who, when it suited them, set at naught the native authority, and refused to pay the tribute which the chiefs were given no means of enforcing, or acquired lands which they held in defiance of native customary tenure.

But the main cause of the great change which is taking place in the social conditions of African life is to be found in the changed outlook of the African himself. There is, as a writer in "New Europe" says, "something fantastically inconceivable about the policy of keeping the forces and ideas of the modern world out of Africa," and it is the negation of progress "to fasten down upon the African his own past. . . . Over most of tropical Africa the old order of tribal society is dead, dying, or doomed." He is apparently speaking of East Africa. His views were strongly endorsed by the Governor, Sir P. Girouard—than whom few have shown a greater insight into problems of native administration. In his report on East Africa for 1909–10, Sir P. Girouard enumerates the various agencies which are "breaking down the tribal systems, denationalising the native, and emancipating him from the rule of his chief." "There are not lacking," he writes, "those who favour direct British rule; but if we allow the tribal authority to be ignored or broken, it will mean that we, who numerically form a small minority in the country, shall be obliged to deal with a rabble, with thousands of persons in a savage or semi-savage state, all acting on their own impulses, and making themselves a danger to society generally. There could only be one end to such a policy, and that would be eventual conflict with the rabble. . . ."

The smattering of knowledge and caricature of the white man's ways acquired by these children react on their village, and upset tribal customs and authority. A few years ago one would find communities in which no individual had ever been twenty miles from his home. To-day the young men migrate in hundreds to offer their labour at the mines or elsewhere, and return with strange ideas. Some perhaps have even been overseas from West to East Africa during the war.

The produce of the village loom, or dye-pit, or smithy, is discounted by cheap imported goods, and the craftsman's calling is not what it was. Traders, white and black, circulate under the pax Britannica among tribes but recently addicted to head-hunting, and bring to them new and strange conceptions. The primitive African is called upon to cope with ideas a thousand years in advance of his mental and social equipment. He cannot proceed leisurely along the road to progress. He must be hurried along it, or the free and independent savage will sink to the level of the helot and the slave.

Here, then, in my view, lies our present task in Africa. It becomes impossible to maintain the old order—the urgent need is for adaptation to the new—to build up a tribal authority with a recognised and legal standing, which may avert social chaos. It cannot be accomplished by superseding—by the direct rule of the white man—such ideas of discipline and organisation as exist, nor yet by "stereotyping customs and institutions among backward races which are not consistent with progress."[2]

The first step is to hasten the transition from the patriarchal to the tribal stage, and induce those who acknowledge no other authority than the head of the family to recognise a common chief. Where this stage has already been reached, the object is to group together small tribes, or sections of a tribe, so as to form a single administrative unit, whose chiefs severally, or in Council as a "Native Court," may be constituted a "Native Authority," with defined powers.

2. Debate on Colonial Office vote 26th April 1920.

59. LORD DELAMERE

WHITE MAN'S COUNTRY. 1903.

Hugh Cholmondeley (1870–1931), Lord Delamere, was born in Cheshire, England, educated at Eton, and first visited the Kenya highlands in 1897 while on a hunting trip. Captivated by the region, he returned and settled in Kenya in 1903. As the leading pioneer of white settlement in East Africa, Lord Delamere devoted the remainder of his life to making the Kenya highlands a while man's country. In the two letters that follow, he discusses two principal interests of the European settler in East Africa: land and the Indian immigrants, both of which became a persistent source of tension between the Africans and the Europeans. The Europeans contested African claims that the land occupied by while settlers rightfully belonged to the Africans but at the same time feared economic competition from Indian traders.

September 2nd, 1903

NAIROBI

At the present time, for an agricultural farmer with a small capital, the staple product is potatoes. They grow extremely well here for several years without manure. The crop varies between two to ten tons to the acre. Through freights from Nairobi to the South African ports run three pounds a ton. Prices there vary from £8:10:0 to £3:10:0 a ton.

This harvest some settlers are sending potatoes direct through to Johannesburg and expect good results. Last season (there are two in a year) all the crop practically was sent to the South African ports and to Zanzibar, Mozambique, &c., and realised good prices. The only difficulty is getting the potatoes to market.

All the men worth their salt at present in the country are writing home to their relations and friends to join them. There are four settlers within short distance of Nairobi who have lately got out their brothers. Now these are men practically without capital and they evidently think it good enough. There are three dairy farmers not far from Nairobi who are doing well chiefly with native cows, although there are now two or three bulls in the country.

A man called Sandbach Baker who was formerly a Manchester cotton merchant and went broke gambling on cotton is one of the dairy farmers. His wife told Lady Delarnere the other day that if she had sufficient cows she could sell 1000 lbs. of butter a month in Nairobi and Mombasa. Of course that is only a small thing, but it is an opening for one or two at the present time. As soon as we can get a refrigerating plant going, which I think will be very shortly, there should be as good a sale for butter and cheese as from New Zealand. The drawback to cattle is the danger of occasional outbreaks of rinderpest.

Another opening in a small way at present, and later for export, is fruit. There is only one man in the country at present who grows fruit to any extent, because set-

From Elspeth Huxley, *White Man's Country: Lord Delamere and the Making of Kenya* (London, 1935), pp. 1, 108–110, 206–208. By permission of author: Chatto & Windus, and Frederick A. Praeger.

tlers go in for potatoes which bring a quick return. He grows excellent apples, plums, greengages, Japanese plums, strawberries, &c., and gets rid of the small amount he can grow in the country without trouble, and there is a demand for considerably more. Fruit at present of course fetches more or less fancy prices, but that would hardly continue when any amount was grown.

With potatoes to keep a man going, coffee promises a certain high return with the cheap land and labour procurable. Several settlers are at present growing it as fast as they can. It grows *extraordinarily* well and badly cleaned coffee in the parchment has been valued at 70 to 80 shillings a hundredweight. I am sure that there is a fortune in coffee for a man who is willing to lay out a little money or who chooses to start small and work hard himself. Coffee at its high price is not touched by freight, and for good class coffee which we can certainly grow here there is an unlimited market in London. I have gone carefully into coffee estimates with settlers here and I am sure it is a first rate speculation, absurdly easy to grow, grows here like a weed.

I believe myself that money is to be made out of sheep. Grazing land, which is said by New Zealanders and others to be first class, can be hired on a 99 years' lease (which will almost certainly be convertible some day into freehold) up to 10,000 acres at a ha'penny an acre per annum. I intended to write a pamphlet for publication but my eyes have been giving me a lot of trouble lately and I have been unable to do more than begin it.

I have got my 100,000 acres of land but not at the place I originally intended, but I think at a better, though a little further from the coast. I have been unable to get a freehold but have got a 99 years' lease at 1/2 d. [pence] an acre per annum. My own opinion is that land will carry four or five sheep to the acre, but one cannot tell till one tries.

Besides coffee, tobacco and cotton appear to offer a good return.

Cotton has been produced (only in experimental plots) which has been valued by the Oldham Chamber of Commerce at 6d. a pound, or a penny more than middling American on the same day. With land and labour as cheap as they are, this should give a good return.

At present there is *no* one in the country with *any* capital except myself and some of the coast merchants, so none of these things are being developed except on a small scale, but it must be remembered that directly money is made land is sure to go up largely in value. At the present time the land here seems to me absurdly cheap. A South African who has had much experience was here the other day and said he wouldn't take 20 acres in South Africa for one here. My own opinion is that there is a fortune for any of the early-comers that are worth anything. Of course, if markets and so on were all fixed, land could not be got at the price or anything like it.

August, 1907

Personally I can imagine no argument [he wrote] which is capable of justifying unchecked immigration of Asiatics into a country which we all of us hope may some day be part of a United South Africa, a great white colony stretching from the Cape to the Zambesi and governed for His Majesty by a true Afrikander bond.

Supposing that Indian immigration is allowed into South Africa it must carry with it that freedom which is one of the boasts of the British Empire. Indian colonists must be allowed to enter freely into competition in all trades and to hold land there. There is therefore only one choice before the Imperial Government. To choose whether South Africa is to be a colony of men of our own race holding the same ideals of civilisation and religion as ourselves, or whether it is to become an Asiatic colony peopled by a race whose civilisation is decadent and at its best stopped short of European civilisation, whose ideals and religion are totally different from our own and above all a people who undoubtedly, and I think naturally, look forward to a day when they can throw off the yoke of their white conquerors. . . .

In all new countries the backbone of the country is the small man, the white colonist with small means, but there is no place for him in a country when once the Asiatic is there. I have some years' experience myself of the newest of the colonies of the Crown in Africa and I know from personal observation and knowledge that every two or three Indians in the country mean the loss of a white colonist. There is no place for the small white man arriving in the country. All the vegetable growing for the towns is done by Indians, all the butchers with one or two exceptions are Indians, all the small country stores are kept by Indians and most of the town shops, all the lower grade clerks are Indians, nearly all the carpentry and building is done by Indians. They thus fill all the occupations and trades which would give employment to the poorer white colonists, especially those arriving new in the country.

That is what Indian immigration means in the early days of a very new country in Africa. It means that if open competition is allowed the small white colonist must go to the wall.

What is the next stage in the history of a country which has once allowed Asiatic immigration to get a foothold? The small man having been pretty well squeezed out, planters and farmers employ Indian labour, and then comes the stage that Natal has reached to-day when the Asiatics are as numerous as the white colonists and when they own large areas of land and businesses all over the country. White colonists will not go to a country which is filled with Asiatics, and the Asiatics go on increasing.

This shows again that it lies with the Imperial Government to-day to say whether Africa is to become a white daughter colony or an Asiatic granddaughter colony, to use an expression of Mr. Winston Churchill's.

And what does Indian immigration mean to the native? Because surely in Africa, in his own country, his rights both at the present time and in the future should be safeguarded. Admitting that at present he is lazy and relatively so well off that work has no particular attraction for him, will it always be so? Increasing as they do owing to cessation of wars and other benefits of civilisation, will they not be forced by circumstances into the life of the country and have to work for a living like European or Asiatic? And is his birthright, the right to work for a living in his own land, to be taken away from him? Is it only Europeans who are affected by Asiatic competition? I should say that the Indian took the place of the African quite as much as that of the European.

And later on will it not be worse, when the African has been brought by education and training to a point where he will be able to take positions of trust and responsibility? Are these all to be taken away beforehand and given to the Asiatic? And to put the matter on a higher plane. Should not the African be protected from the decadent civilisation of India and from the influence of its Hindu religion? Is it desirable that such religions should be introduced among the African natives who are like children and capable of easily absorbing impressions?

Is the introduction of Hindu rites and practices among the natives of Africa to be calmly viewed by all the great missions which have hundreds of earnest men teaching the ideals of our own religion to the natives all over Africa?

I am fain to admit that all civilisation has a deteriorating effect on a certain proportion of natives, but in the case of the evils caused by contact with Europeans, wise laws can be enacted to prevent such evils. I submit that no government of Europeans can make laws to check the evils arising from the mixture of African and Asiatic, because the average European is incapable of understanding the mind of the Asiatic, nor can laws be enforced except by public opinion.

This I consider one of the greatest evils of Asiatic immigration into a country governed by Europeans—that owing to a lack of understanding of the Asiatic and the impossibility of getting European police capable of dealing with Asiatic crime, Asiatic police have to be employed, and only those who have seen the methods of bribery and corruption of Indian police, even when dealing with their own people, the harm done by allowing Indians to have control over natives.

Time after time I have heard a native; they have been stopped by an Indian policeman and when I asked them how got away they always said, "Oh, I gave him something."

I earnestly hope that the very powerful missionary organisations in Africa will take this matter up. It is a thing to be remembered that public opinion sooner or later asserts itself among our own people to do the right thing by the people of the country.

60. MOHAMMED ABDILLE HASAN
THE SAYYID'S REPLY. 1904.

Between 1895 and 1899, Sayyid Mohammed Abdille Hasan, commonly known as the Mad Mullah, urged the Muslim Somali of Berbera to reform. In 1899 he and his followers retreated inland from Berbera, where Sayyid Mohammed forced his reforming tenets on the Somali and declared a jihad, or holy war, against the infidels or those who refused to accept his teachings. Between 1901 and 1904, British

From Mohammed Abdille Hasan, "The Sayyid's Reply," in B. W. Andrzejewski and I. M. Lewis, *Somali Poetry and an Introduction* (Oxford: Clarendon Press, 1964), pp. 74, 76, 78, 80, 82. Reprinted by permission of the Clarendon Press, Oxford.

and Ethiopian expeditions failed to curtail his operations. He moved for a time into Italian Somaliland, but in 1909 he was back in British territory and remained in virtual control of the hinterland until sufficient British forces were released by the conclusion of World War I to crush him. Throughout his long struggle against the British, Sayyid Mohammed employed poetry as an effective instrument to counter British charges against him. As a master of invective, ridicule, and scorn, he defended himself in poems such as the one that follows.

1. Concerning your plea "Do not incite the Ogaadeen against us" I also have a complaint.

2. The people of the Ethiopian region[1] look for nothing from you,

3. So do not press my claim against them.

4. Do not claim on my behalf the blood money which they owe me.

5. I will myself seek to recover the property and the loot which they have seized.

6. Were I to leave a single penny with them my pledge would be perverted.

7. What I claim from you is only what you yourself owe me;

8. Since you are the government the responsibility is yours,

9. Can you disclaim those whom you tricked into attacking me?

10. Do they not swim in the prosperity which they have gained from what they devoured of mine?

11. Do they not drive their livestock from the valley of 'Aado to the west?

12. What did they seek from the lands between Burao and your stations?

13. Had you a pact with them by God and by consent?

14. Or did thirst drive them mad? Fools easily lose their way.

15. And afterwards was it not into your pockets that you poured the wealth?

16. Did you not enter the amounts of the booty in your printed books and cash ledgers?

17. And have you not openly admitted this in the full light of day?

18. Are not these spoils laden upon you as upon a burden-donkey?

19. That is my statement: if you are honest with me what can you answer?

20. What profit will you gain by denial? I have clearly established my case.

21. Concerning your plea: "Do not incite the Ogaadeen against us." I also have a complaint.

22. As to your statement "We have not seen the sailing ship"[2] I also have a complaint.

23. Why are you tiring yourself out,[3] working your wiles?

24. Do you not get weary with pointless talk?

25. Who rules the sea and controls the sails and holds of ships?

26. The Italians are your followers, the foundlings whom you drive with you;

27. Had they not been led by you they would not have come to Dannood,

28. They would not have sent an expedition to Doollo and 'Iid;

---

1. Mainly of the Ogaadeen clan.
2. Here the Sayyid refers to his claim that one of his dhows had been intercepted by the British.
3. Lit. "Why are you dying, running fast with deceit?"

29. They would not have sent their armies against me.

30. They would not have harassed me with assaults at daybreak.

31. I had no issue with the Italians until you summoned them to your aid.

32. It was you who intrigued and plotted with them;

33. It was you who said "Join us in the war against the Dervishes;"

34. And they did not say "Leave us, and stop conspiring with us;"

35. Did you never tire of these evil machinations?

36. Was it not through these schemes that the landings at Obbia took place?

37. Did they not greatly aid you with their arms and supplies?

38. You fools, those who attacked yesterday on your side

39. Will they not strike at me from the back if we fight tomorrow?40. Will they be prevented from attacking me, by disclaiming their bond with you?[4]

41. It is you who lead to pasture these weaker infidels;

42. Can I distinguish between you and your livestock?

43. As to your statement "We have not seen the sailing ship," I also have a complaint.

44. As to the raiders of whom you talk, I also have a complaint.

45. It is you who have oppressed them and seized their beasts,

46. It is you who took for yourselves their houses and property,

47. It is you who spoilt their settlements and defiled them with ordure,

48. It is you who reduced them to eating the tortoise and beast of prey;

49. This degradation you brought upon them.

50. If they (in turn) become beasts of prey and loot you

51. And steal small things from the clearings between your huts,

52. Then they were driven to this by hunger and famine;

53. Do not complain to me and I will not complain to you.

54. If you do not accept my statement,

55. And unless your servants confuse you with lies,

56. That I harboured them, or that I sent them against you,

57. Bring me clear evidence; otherwise it is you who are guilty of the sin.

58. As to the raiders of whom you talk, I also have a complaint.

59. Concerning your demand "Turn aside from the Warsangeli," I have a complaint.

60. If they prefer you, then they and I shall be at variance:

61. It is not in my nature to accept people who cringe to you.

62. But if they are Dervishes, how can I turn aside from them?

63. Do you also share their ancestry from Daarood Ismaaiil?[5]

64. Are you trying to steal towards me through my ancestor's genealogy?

4. Lit. "Will they become fenced off by (the words) '(You) are not my company (or allies)?'"

5. Daarood Ismaaiil, the eponymous ancestor of the Daarood clan to which the Sayyid belongs and which include the Warsangeli. The Sayyid refers to the fact that while the Warsangeli are of one blood with him, the British have no connexion with them, and therefore in Somali values, no claims upon their loyalty.

65. Of late have you not turned them into gazelles,[6] (fugitive and homeless)?

66. Have you not seen how they loathe you?

67. For have you not seized their shops and stored their goods in your houses?

68. Have you not set fire to their ships so that smoke rose from them?

69. You, with your filthy genitals, have you not hanged their men?

70. They soon found out that you would have no mercy on them.

71. You are against both worship and the Divine Law.

72. You are building a mat partition between them and the streams of Paradise and Heaven.

73. You are casting them into the raging fury and fumes of Hell.

74. Do they not see how deceitful You are?

75. Or are they well pleased with your prevarication?

76. Will they be divorced from their womenfolk and wives?[7]

77. Concerning your demand "Return the camels," I have a complaint.[8]

78. I also have suffered damage and loss;

79. You threw me on the ground and skinned my knee,

80. It was you who snatched the camels as they grazed,

81. It was you who scattered the white-turbanned army,

82. It was I who was first hammered at Gallaadi and experienced your bitterness;

83. A fool understands nothing, but the warning did not elude me.

84. The tethering rope with which you bound Iise[9] was meant for me.

---

6. Lit. "Did you not turn them into Speke's gazelles (*deero*) and Soemering's gazelles (*'awl*)." In our interpretation gazelles symbolize here living in deserted places, away from human habitations, in constant fear and always on the move. We have also heard of another possible interpretation of this line: the Sayyid apparently refers to the internal split which occurred among the Warsangeli, when those who sided with him would no longer associate with those who opposed him. The two different species of gazelle mentioned in this line live in separate herds.

7. This passage is very obscure. Literally it means: "Are they divorcing their womenfolk, they have divorced their wives?" Most probably this amounts to a rhetorical question "Are they becoming apostates from Islam?" According to oral traditions the Sayyid declared that marriages of those men who refused to follow him became void on the legal grounds of apostasy from Islam. Their wives were therefore automatically divorced and were bound to leave them.

8. The reference here is to livestock seized from the clans friendly to the British by the Sayyid's forces.

9. Iise was the captain of the dhow referred to in line 22 and allegedly captured by the British.

61. RECORDS OF MAJI MAJI

THE MAJI MAJI REBELLION. 1905–1907.

On a fateful morning in July 1905 the men of Matumbi in southeast Tanganyika rebelled against the German administration of German East Africa. They had been forced by Arab government agents, akidas, to cultivate cotton for negligible wages, to the neglect of their own subsistence cultivations. A stateless society, the Matumbi resented the authoritarian imposition of colonial rule, which sought to draft them into the colonial rule that sought to draft them into the colonial economic order. Without a traditional structure of centralized leadership the Matumbi resistance rallied around the prophet Kinjikitile Ngwale who, possessed by the spirit of Hongo, a subordinate to Bokero, the principal of the stateless peoples of southern Tanganyika, became the locus of grievances whose loyalty he insured by distributing sacred water, maji, accompanied by a ritual whose origins appear to have come from the Southern Sudan, and which would guarantee the insurgents protection against the bullets from European rifles. Under the leadership of Kinjikitile, who took the title of Bokero, the cult, known in history as Maji Maji, swept through southern Tanganyika mobilizing the disparate clans against the German administration until they were ruthlessly suppressed in 1907. The saga of this African resistance is recorded in the writings and memories of the participants.

Our news is this, that the Germans treat us badly and oppress us much, because it is their will.

So wrote an eighteen-year-old schoolgirl from Chiwata in southern Tanzania in 1898. Thirteen years before, German adventurers had claimed a protectorate in East Africa. They had fought their way in/and along the caravan routes, establishing garrisons of askari *at key points, recognising or deposing tribal leaders, and creating an administration of subordinate staff called* akidas *and* jumbes. *By the late 1890s Tanzania was an occupied country:*

Here at Chiwata there is a court every Wednesday, and many people are beaten and some are imprisoned by order of the German Government. But we, who have for so long been used to govern ourselves, find the laws of these Germans very hard, especially the taxes, because we black people have no money, our wealth consists of millet, maize, oil, and groundnuts, etc. Here at Chiwata two houses have been built, one for the court and one for the prison. . . .

The Germans began to seek profit from south-eastern Tanzania by forcing the people to grow cash crops for export to Europe. A few German settlers established cotton plantations in Matumbi, while smaller plots were laid out by the jumbes *and* akidas. *The Matumbi were forced to work in the fields, and their hatred grew:*

The cultivation of cotton was done by turns. Every village was allotted days on

From *Records of the Maji Maji Rising*, ed. G. C. K. Gwassa and John Iliffe (Nairobi: East African Publishing House, 1967), Historical Association of Tanzania, Paper No. 4, pp. 3–30. *Records of the Maji Maji Rising* has been elucidated by the editors, so rather than delete their editorial comments, I have retained them in italics to make the records themselves more meaningful. Robert O. Collins, ed.

which to cultivate at Samanga Ndumbo and at the Jumbe's plantation. One person came from each homestead, unless there were very many people. Thus you in might be told to work for five or ten days at Samanga. So a person would go. Then after half the number of days another man came from home to relieve him. If the new man did not feel pity for him, the same person would stay on until he finished. . . . Then after arriving there you all suffered very greatly. Your back and your buttocks were whipped, and there was no rising up once you stooped to dig. The good thing about the Germans was that all people were the same before the whip. If a jumbe or akida made a mistake he received the whip as well. Thus there were people whose job was to clear the land of trees and undergrowth; others tilled the land, others would smooth the field and plant; another group would do the weeding and yet another the picking; and lastly others carried the bales of cotton to the coast beyond Kikanda for shipping. . . . The work was astonishingly hard and full of grave suffering, but its wages were the whip on one's back and buttocks. And yet he [the German] still wanted us to pay him tax. . . . Thus they hated the rule which was too cruel. It was not because of agriculture not at all. If it had been good agriculture which had meaning and profit, who would have given himself tip to die. . . ?

There were European planters in Matumbi, but elsewhere along the southern coast cash crops were grown on communal plots supervised by akidas and headmen. These plots were established between 1902 and 1905 by European-controlled district development committees called "Communes." Two officials of the Dar es Salaam Commune described how the plots were organised in Uzaramo:

When and how were the village plots organised?

Village plots were set up in each akida's and headman's area early in 1902 (September–October). Bushland was mainly chosen. The people were consulted in choosing the post. Each headman made a plot for his area in the neighbourhood of his headquarters. The principle was that every 30–50 men were to cultivate 2.5 acres. . . . Where possible the advice of the natives was obtained as to the crop to be grown. So far as possible, one crop was to be grown on each plot, according to the type of soil. Some 2,000 acres were cleared and cultivated. The size varied from 2.5 to 35 acres; the average was about 12.5 acres.

In 1903–04 it was ordered that each village plot should be extended by at least a quarter. The total area in that year came to 3,215 acres. Maize, millet, sini. sim, groundnuts, rice, chiroko, and coconut palms were grown during 1902–03. Cotton was added in 1903–04.

No extension took place in 1904–05, but the cultivation of other crops was abandoned in favour of cotton.

What was the labour situation and the supervision?

. . . According to returns by the headmen, the number of able-bodied men amounted to:

1902–03 c. 25,00 men
1903–04 c. 26,000 men
1904–05 c. 25,000 men

During the last year, women and children had to be brought in to help, since the men frequently refused to work.

In Herr von Geibler's opinion, two days' work a week, as proposed by the District Office order, was insufficient from the start: 50–100 per cent more had to be worked from the first. When cotton became a main crop, continuous work was sometimes necessary. . . .

Were refractory workers punished, and by whom?

Last year (1904–05), following reports from the akidas and from Sergeant Holzhausen, who was sent to inspect the headmen, numerous headmen were punished by the District Office with imprisonment in chains or solitary confinement for totally neglecting their village plots as a result of the natives' refusal to work. The last, in June, was headman Kibasila, who got one month in chains. . . .

Forced cultivation of unprofitable cash crops was a widespread grievance in southern Tanzania, but it was not the only one. Each area had its own sufferings. The Matumbi, for example, hated the Arab akidas and the askari whom the Germans set over them:

Another reason again had its origin in ruling, that was the second reason: the rule of Arabs which arose from the German Government when it ruled this country and brought Arab akidas. Since the days of old, Warriatumbi had refused to be ruled. Those Arabs had failed in the past to penetrate into this country, because they had been completely barred from coming to capture people to enslave them. But when they got work as akidas they began to seize people and reduce them to slavery: in fact they practised complete fraud and extortion and tortured them unjustly. . . .

Behind all these particular grievances lay the fact of alien rule:

All these are words that buzz like bees. If you had experienced it, you would have known how grave it was. To be chained, to be shot with bullets in the crown of one's head and in one's chest, while in addition you carried loads as the great eye of heaven rose up! Alas, such was life, and those iron chains were many—he made them in his own country. Better remove such suffering; fight him off so that the loads are carried by the askari themselves. . . .

The people waited and suffered, conscious of their disunity and the military strength of their rulers. Then, in the year 1904, a prophet arose. His name was Kinjikitile. Near his home at Ngarambe there was a pool in a tributary of the River Rufiji. Kinjikitile was possessed by the spirit Hongo who dwelt in the pool:

He was taken by an evil spirit one day in the morning at about nine o'clock. Everyone saw it, and his children and wives as well. . . . Then he disappeared in the pool of water. He slept in there and his relatives slept by the pool overnight waiting for him. Those who knew how to swim dived down into the pool but they did not see anything. Then they said, "If he is dead we will see his body; if he has been taken by a beast or by a spirit of the waters we shall see him returned dead or alive." So they waited, and the following morning, at about nine o'clock again, he emerged unhurt with his clothes dry and as he had tucked them the previous day. After returning from there he began talking of prophetic matters. He said, "All dead ancestors will come back, they are at Bokero's in Rufiji Ruhingo. No lion or leopard will eat men. We are all the Sayyid Said's, the Sayyid's alone. . . ."

Pilgrims began to flock to Ngarambe early in 1905. A German officer later described these pilgrimages. He was probably wrong to think they were engineered by a conspiracy of chiefs:

The chiefs of the Matumbi and Kichi Hills spread it among their people that a spirit, living in the form of a snake in the Pangani Rapids on the River Rufiji, had given a magic medicine to a medicine man living in Ngarambe who had assumed the title Bokero (intermediary between men and the spirit). The medicine would free those who possessed it from all agricultural cares. Further, it would confer prosperity and health, would protect them from famine and sickness, and would especially protect the fields against devastation by wild pigs. It guaranteed a good harvest, so that in future people would no more need to perform wage labour for foreigners in order to obtain accustomed luxuries (cloth, beads, etc.). Finally—and here mention was made only of the warfare customary between natives—the medicine would also give invulnerability, acting in such a way that enemy bullets would fall from their targets like raindrops from a greased body. . . . The medicine consisted of water, maize, and sorghum grains. The water was applied at Ngarambe by pouring it over the head and by drinking. It was also handed out in small bamboo stems, to be hung round the neck. . . .

Kinjikitile prepared the people for war He promised them protection against European weapons. He offered them leadership, organisation, unity. But he told them not to fight until he gave the order. By July 1905 no order had come, and the Matumhi were impatient:

At Ngarambe he told them, "The Germans will leave. War will start from up-country towards the coast and from the coast into the hinterland. There will definitely be war. But for the time being go and work for him. If he orders you to cultivate cotton or to dig his road or to carry his load, do as he requires. Go and remain quiet. When I am ready I will declare the war." Those elders returned home and kept quiet. They waited for a long time. Then the elders wondered. "This mganga said he would declare war against the Germans. Why then is he delaying? When will the Europeans go? After all, we have already received the medicine and we are brave men. Why should we wait?" Then the Africans asked themselves, "How do we start the war? How do we make the Germans angry? Let us go and uproot their cotton so the war may rise. . . ."

They heard that cotton had been uprooted in Wolo [Nandete]. The Arab at Kibata told Jumbe Kapungu to send his wife to investigate the reports of cotton uprooting. Jurmbe Kapungu refused, saying, "If you have heard they have uprooted cotton you must realise that this is the beginning of war. . . ."

The movement had begun in a religious message of a prophet. The power of *the maji—power over European weapons—depended on religious faith. And as the movement expanded away from the Riufiji Valley during August and September it was again carried by prophets. These men called themselves hongo, messengers. They carried maji which they administered to the people. They promised unity and invulnerability. They called on all black men to rise against European rule. Theirs was a revolutionary, or more accurately, a millennial, message, a promise to rid the world of the evils witchcraft and European rule. It is likely that the people of southern Tanzania had heard such millennial teachings before, but only as attacks on witchcraft. Now this religious tradition was mobilised against the Germans. It was a revolutionary message because established leaders who opposed it often found themselves swept aside by the force of popular belief. The following account of a hongo comes from a remote area, Uvidunda. It is unsympathetic, but it shows very clearly the millennial character of the movement:*

In that year there arrived in the country a certain man, a great deceiver, called Hongo. . . . Hongo asked the people, whether they were prepared to sit down under the European order to pay the tax, of three rupees every year and they answered that they could not help themselves, for how could they fight the Europeans with their guns when they themselves had only spears. Hongo then explained his troublesome teaching to them. He said that he was a son of God and that with his help they would be able to defeat the Europeans for he had a medicine which resisted the penetration of their bullets, and in fact they would not be able to fire at all as their bullets would turn into water. . . .Then Hongo gave orders that every man must anoint himself with his Using a medicine: anyone who refused was to be caught and killed. People began to fear that they would be called witches and all the people of Kidodi and the people of Jumbe Kulumzima went to Hongo to receive his medicine. When they had been anointed with it, he lay in the road and ordered that everyone should jump over him without touching him and if anyone touched him he should be killed. . . .When Hongo saw that his strength was increasing and that many people were following him, he gathered them together to go and take Kilosa. . . .

August 1905 was the month of victories. By its end, German forces existed only on the coast and in the four powerful military stations at Mahenge, Kilosa, Iringa, and Songea. If they were to win, the Maji Maji fighters had to capture these stations. On 30 August, the Mbunga and Pogoro peoples tried to take Mahenge. A missionary described this greatest single action of the rising. In Mahenge boma [fort], the day had begun with executions:

Scarcely were the five condemned men hanging on the trees when a messenger rushed in with the news that the enemy was approaching. Everyone made for the post allotted to him and peered out in the direction of Isongo, from which they were supposed to be coming. We did not have to wait long before catching sight of the first groups. These groups halted in sight of the boma, probably waiting for each other. Shortly after seven o'clock they advance on the boma in close columns. There must have over a thousand men. Since they came to make an end of all of us, we had to defend ourselves and take part in the firing, which opened on the attackers at about a thousand metres. Two machine-guns, Europeans, and soldiers rained death and destruction among the ranks of the advancing enemy. Although we saw the ranks thin, the survivors maintained order for about a quarter of an hour, marching closer amidst a hail of bullets. But then the ranks broke apart and took cover behind the numerous small rocks. Now and again a group rushed out on the road, lifted one of the fallen and quickly fled again behind the rocks. Scurrying from rock to rock, they made their retreat. Then suddenly the cry rang out: "New enemy on the Gambria side!" Everyone looked in that direction, and there thick clouds of smoke were rising from our three schools and a second column of at least 1,200 men was advancing towards us. Fire was opened upon them immediately. The enemy sought to reach Mahenge village at the double. There they were hidden by the houses and stormed up the road towards the boma. As soon as they reappeared within range they were met by deafening fire. The first attackers were only three paces from the firing line when they sank to the ground, struck by deadly bullets. Those behind them lost courage, turned, and scattered. Fortunately, the attack had been beaten off. When no more enemy could be seen, the Station Commander climbed down from the top of the boma tower, from which he "had commanded the defence" and distributed champagne. . . .

By October 1905, three months after the rising had started, German forces were gaining the initiative. Now the Maji Maji fighters had to defend themselves by guerilla action. The terms of surrender were harsh:

The following terms of submission, either for individuals or for whole areas, are to be imposed according to circumstances:

1. The surrender of ringleaders and witch-doctors.

2. The surrender of all firearms, bows, arrows. And spears. If necessary pressure may be exerted on the people by arresting the headmen until the required weapons have been surrendered. . . .

3. Besides the tax which he normally pays, every man who submits is to pay a fine of three rupees. In cases where this is not available, the man is to be required to perform paid labour for a productive enterprise of a public corporation, in order to earn the fine. . . .The requirement of fines does not prejudice the right of military commandeers to require especially refractory tribes to perform compulsory labour, e.g. to construct fortifications. . . .

4. Major sultans and other influential tribal leaders who declare the submission of the native communities they rule are to be required to provide contingents of several hundred men for punitive and compulsory labour for the government on the coast. The punitive labour will last three to six months for every contingent. . . .

The great men of Ungoni were dead, but other men were fighting for their lives in guerilla warfare throughout the south:

The war is going on just the same: the Wamakonde are to the north of Chitangali river; they have rebelled again in these days, and the fighting is there. I think it will be many days before the fighting ceases, for the rebels on every side would rather die than be under the Germans, and many of them have died and their wives and children have been take for spoil, but they will not leave off fighting.

German forces had no military answer to guerilla warfare. Instead, they used famine. One commander had recommended this as early as October 1905:

In my view only hunger and want can bring about a final submission. Military actions alone will remain more or less a drop in the ocean. The people will be compelled to abandon their resistance completely only when the food supplies now available have been consumed, their houses have been destroyed by constant raids, and they have been deprived of the opportunity to cultivate new fields.

Some officers saw famine as the final solution to the threat of revolt. Captain Richter in Songea believed this:

When Fr. Johannes drew the District Officer's attention to the possibly imminent famine, he replied, "That's right, the fellows can just starve. We shall be sure to get food for ourselves. If I could, I would even prevent them from planting anything.

This is the only way that we can make the fellows sick of war."

Nine years before, a schoolgirl in Chiwata had expressed her bitterness at German rule. Now, a married woman, she recorded the horror of starvation:

We and all the people in our village are in the same condition, we are suffering from famine. Since my birth I have never seen such scarcity. I have seen famine but not one causing people to die. But in this famine many are dying, some are unable to do any work at all, they have no strength, their food consists of insects from the woods which they dig up and cook and eat. Some they eat without cooking. Many have died through eating these things from the woods and wild fruits. Some do not die at once but when they taste good food like millet, maize, or beans, etc., which is their usual food, at once their bodies swell and they feel ill and die, but some recover.

For many people, as for the Matumbi, the famine marked the end of a way of life:

There came three years of famine. Those who survived did so by Providence. . . . It was extremely fierce famine and people denied their children and wives. It was only those who really loved each other who remained together. And even these cooked their food under strict regulations, like this: Down in the cooking pot was the child's food over which were laid pieces of wood. Above these sticks was put the wife's food and more sticks were placed. The food of the husband came on top. During eating they followed a similar procedure. The husband started first. When he reached the sticks he knew his wife's food lay immediately below the sticks and that his share stopped above them. In the same way, when the wife reached the sticks she knew that only the child's share remained. On the other hand, if they did not love each other everyone went his way struggling to survive. That is why some men had to marry the same woman twice, for they had deserted them during the famine. When he searched for his former wife her parents asked him, "Where did you leave her?" So he had to pay dowry again. This famine was called Fugufugu. There has never been the like either before or after Maji Maji. Other famines are merely babes before the famine after Maji Maji. People died in multitudes and bodies were left to rot as there was nobody able to bury them. People slept in the open for there were no houses, and lions ate one after the other. There was no seed to plant. During famine we ate insects. . . . Before the war the population was very dense and it was very difficult to find a piece of land on which to grow food. If you got a small piece of land you thanked God—there were too many people. Now alas you only see much bush everywhere.

62. SIR APOLO KAGWA

COURT LIFE IN BUGANDA. 1910.

In an attempt to improve on the description of the Baganda by a missionary, the Reverend John Roscoe [The Baganda, *London: Macmillan, 1911], Sir Apolo Kagwa (d. 1927), regent and prime minister of Buganda, wrote* The Customs of the Baganda *in Luganda in 1918 during the early part of the reign of Kabaka Daudi Chwa. In this work Kagwa recalls the enthronement of Kimera in 1910 and the pomp and ceremony of the courts of the kabakas (kings) of Buganda.*

The next morning Kibale, Mpewo clan, and Nakatanza, Lugave clan, came to the palace and knocked at the door of the king's house. At eight o'clock a council was held by the provincial chiefs to lay plans for the enthronement. Mugema, who tied the knot in the king's barkcloth on the right shoulder, demanded the right to tie the one on the left shoulder. This caused a disagreement in the council. It was finally settled against Mugema by the men of the royal family. Then the chiefs went to the royal palace.

Kabumba, of the Lugave clan, brought the carpet and Kiini, of the Mamba clan, the tanner, brought the skins of lions, leopards, hyenas, and cows. Apolo Kagwa escorted the king and his sister, Djuma Katebe. He headed the procession, carrying the king's spears and shields. He marched at the right of the king because he is next to the king and insures his peace. At the palace gate Mugema led the king to the throne and placed him on it. He then placed the barkcloth on the king and knotted it on the right shoulder, as an indication that the king was the owner of the country. He laid a calfskin over the barkcloth because Kimera wore a calfskin. Then he said, "You will perform all the acts and duties befitting a king."

The Kasudju knotted a barkcloth on the king's left shoulder which meant, "You are His Majesty who rules over all other officials and men." On top of this he put a leopard skin meaning, "A king is the leopard; the common people are squirrels." Then he too said, "You will perform all the acts and duties befitting a king."

Kakinda, of the Kobe clan, brought a differently decorated barkcloth and this was placed over all the other ceremonial robes. This was several yards long and was wrapped from the right shoulder around the body and back again.

Then the Mukwenda, Sabagabo, brought a shield and two spears and handed them to the king. This meant that the king would overthrow his enemies. Kadjubi tied a string of sparkling beads about the king's left arm as a memorial to Wanyana, saying, "You are Kimera." Segulu, of the Lugave clan, put a bracelet on the king's right hand to show that he among the princes was the king elect. Narnutwe, assistant Sekibobo, handed a bow and arrow to the king to assure him of his jurisdiction over the subjugated Basagala. Those who remember Greek history know that there

From Sir Apolo Kagwa, *The Customs of the Baganda*, trans. by Ernest B. Kalibala and edited by May Mandelbaum Edel (New York: Columbia University Press, 1934), pp. 63–67, 170–173. Reprinted by permission.

was a king who had a slave remind him about his victory over the Athenians at all his meals (sic!).

Kaima by virtue of his office of chief in charge of the weapons brought a bow and arrow to the king. Then Masembe came and stood before the king with a milk jar. Mugema introduced him, saying, "This is your head herdsman who takes care of Namala's cow from which your great-great-grandfather, Kimera, drank his milk." Then the king touched the jar and Masembe took it away. Sebalidja, the head shepherd, brought a brass milk jar, and handed it to Mpinga, who had been Kimera's shepherd. Mpinga introduced him to the king, saying, "When milking my cow Mbulide, given me by Kimera, I use this jar."

Luboyera, of the Butiko clan, brought a beer jar known as Mwendanvuma, saying, "This is the jar in which I make your beer." Kalinda presented the type of jar in which the king's drinking water is kept, saying, "This is your water jar."

Sernwanga and Kabogoza, Nonge clan, the barkcloth makers, brought a mallet, saying, "This is the mallet upon which your barkcloths are made." Segirinya, Ngo clan, brought the iron tool used in engraving the crown and royal stick. He presented this to the king, saying, "This is omuindu.[1] I use it to adorn your crown and to fashion your walking sticks." Walukaga, of the Kasimba clan, a blacksmith, brought a hammer, saying, "With this I make the spear with which you conquer." Mutalaga, of the Nvuma clan, another blacksmith, brought a dagger. He gave it to Kasudju, who gave it to the king saying, "Whoever rebels against you, you will destroy with this dagger."

Then Mugema introduced the chief royal drums, known as Mudjaguzo. Kaula, of the Lugave clan, brought the drumsticks and Kasudju gave them to the king. The king beat the drum. Kimomera, of the Butiko clan, the assistant drummer, gave the king another pair of drumsticks and the king beat on another drum known as Namanyonyi.

Muyandia, of the Nyonyi clan, brought axe and said, "This is your axe Nankunga that builds your boats." Omusoloza,[2] of the Nyonyi clan, presented the king with two pieces of firewood and said, "These two pieces of wood keep the fire in Gombolola, whence you obtain the ashes to smear yourself for war."

This ended the introductory ceremony. Several others followed.

Sekaiba, of the Mbogo clan, came covered with a barkcloth known as "Throne" and carried the king on his shoulders for about twenty feet, while the princesses the huge crowd that had assembled homage to the enthroned king. They shouted and gave the yells of their clans. Then the prime minister with a shield and spears escorted the king to his dwelling house. Here the relatives of the king offered him gifts. They came in order, his grandfather, then his aunts, his sisters, brothers and the other princes. They were required to stand at the end of the carpet and introduce themselves formally.

After that another group of kinsmen came. This comprised the children of the princesses. They adorned their heads in proper fashion and came singing beautiful

1. A stick with branches.
2. Tax-collector.

melodies. The king gave them bull and bade them farewell. His mother's relatives also offered gifts, and introduced themselves. Before the conclusion of the ceremony his grandfathers the Nonge clan, the grandfathers of Tcwa I of the Ngeye clan, and those of Kimera of the Nsenene clan, in the order named, introduced themselves.

The men who served the various chiefs on their estates were mostly young men. It was they who were the most energetic and successful in the looting campaigns the king ordered from time to time against the neighbors. When the booty was brought home the chief selected that which pleased him most from among the loot of his subordinates, and so became a rich man. The king might show favoritism and assign his favorite chiefs to frequent and lucrative campaigns.

This custom may have had something to do with the Baganda ignorance of trading. They were used to use force to get anything they desired, or else to receive it from the king as a gift. Those who were appointed to the various estates cultivated them by means of the peasants, who moved wherever they pleased. They very commonly went to the estate of a newly appointed chief who they thought might be honored with presents and booty. This meant that there was very great instability, the great mass of the peasantry shifting about and chiefs long established being left alone with their wealth.

The following account gives an idea of the pomp of the King of Buganda and of his power in governing. When the king was about to appear, that is, to open the parliament [the Buganda parliament or lukiko], there was an overwhelming display. All people who were in their houses remained indoors; those in the street kneeled down; and all the drums, trumpets, and every sounding instrument was used to proclaim his majesty's approach. There was a band of executioners who walked near his majesty, ready to imprison and if necessary to kill any person who was found guilty of any sort [of] offense. When a verdict was passed in the parliament, the guilty person was quickly enveloped in a multitude of ropes; even if he tried to plead for mercy, it was impossible that his majesty should hear him because he was almost choked to death.

There were many who, in order to gain recognition, told lies about other chiefs, so that they might lose their offices. It was not until Mutesa [1856–1884] that that kind of system was done away with. When one person accused another, the king sent for the accused person and told him that such and such a thing had been said about him. Mutesa was against people who told him untruths. He demanded the truth of the accused. If the man was guilty and told the truth, he was soon acquitted. If he lied and witnesses were produced who certified as to his guilt, he was finally killed.

When the king walked for exercise, there were many people about him. If he came to a place where there was no road, the people soon made one for him. During his journeys, all doorkeepers were required to carry their doors with them. When the king rested, they enclosed him with the doors and guarded him. To understand the kingly power it should be said that he was a law unto himself, an absolute monarch.

The following were the king's palace officers.

Kauta	Chef
Seruti	Butler
Kaula	Drummer
Nsandja	King's priest, who guarded all horns
Banda	Potter
Omukweya	King's spear carrier during the journeys
Omusoloza	Man in charge of the firewood</UNL>

There was also the executioner's division. All these and many other petty divisions made up the king's household and contributed to his pomp. Sabakaki was the title of a person who was the head of the king's palace, including the division of the king's pages. He was promptly obeyed in everything he said. In the division of the king's pages there were about one thousand young men appointed by various chiefs to serve his majesty in the palace. They were under a chief named Sabawali.

Next to the king came his prime minister. He too was honored. When his drums sounded, all chiefs hurried to his palace to go with him to the king's court. The prime minister walked very slowly to give the people a chance to join him. When he reached the court he sat down to render judgment. When the king appeared to open the court, the prime minister presented the cases. Those who appealed to his majesty were given a chance to present their own cases. The prime minister had two assistants to help him dispose of the cases. One assistant was in Masengere and the other in Gombolola in the outer royal court. The communication between his majesty and the prime minister was carried on by means of constant messengers, a man and a woman from the prime minister and a messenger from the king. The prime minister's messengers kept the king acquainted with what was going on in the country at large and the king's messenger kept the prime minister informed of the latest decisions or suggestions or new decrees issued by the king. Oftentimes there was concerted action, for they respected each other. If the king wished to do anything or to order something from his estates, the word went through the prime minister. The prime minister's messenger working with the king's messenger were certain to bring anything from any part of the country, but one without the other could do nothing.

All chiefs, high or low, when they visited the capital, brought news, or something to give to the king. First they reported to the prime minister and got his assent. All secrets to be told the king went through the prime minister, and vice versa. When the king decided to appoint another prime minister, he stopped the prime minister's reception of all important and secret messages. Instead he designated Kimbugwe, the king's twin guard, to receive information concerning state affairs pending the appointment of the new prime minister. When the new prime minister was to be charged with state affairs . . . the king stood outside the parliament house with his scepter; a group of chiefs selected as candidates faced him. Then the king gave his scepter to the man he designated as prime minister saying, "Go and judge my Buganda country." The newly appointed chief repeated the oath of allegiance, saying, "I shall render justice." After which he left and entered his official residence and the king returned to his palace. The prime minister never gave thanks or knelt down as did other chiefs.

All Saza [county] chiefs were equally powerful in their respective counties. No messenger of whatever nature could travel in a county without a Saza chief's messenger to accompany him. If the king's and the prime minister's messengers were sent to Muwemba to assist Mukwenda in buying cows for the king, they couldn't bring anything unless they had with them a Saza chief's messenger. They were regarded as thieves. This is one point to show how well Buganda was governed. The Baganda, as far back as can be remembered, have been an obedient and well-governed people, respecting their king, chiefs, and country. This may account for the respect and encouragement with which the British Government has consented to regard the native system of government.

63. THE DEVONSHIRE WHITE PAPER

THE INDIANS IN KENYA. 1923.

In Kenya, as in South Africa, Indian immigrants were regarded with suspicion and even hostility by the European community. After World War I, Indians in Kenya began to demand equal representation with the Europeans on the Legislative Council, the end of segregation, and the right to acquire land in the highlands. Both the Indians and the European settlers sent delegations to London to plead their respective causes. In presenting their case to the colonial secretary, the Duke of Devonshire, both sides stressed their desire to maintain native interests. In this way both sides, but particularly the European deputation led by Lord Delamere, who emphasized the virtues of British as against Indian traditions in guiding the Africans, overplayed their hand by providing a welcome way of escape for the British government, which in 1923, in a White Paper issued by the Duke of Devonshire, promptly proclaimed that the interests of the Africans were paramount in Kenya. Kenya was not in the future to become another Rhodesia.

GENERAL STATEMENT OF POLICY

The general policy underlying any decision that may be taken on the questions at issue must first be determined. It is a matter for satisfaction that, however irreconcilable the views of the European and Indian communities in Kenya on many points may be, there is one point on which both are agreed, namely, the importance of safeguarding the interests of the African natives. The African population of Kenya is estimated at more than 2.5 millions; and according to the census of 1921, the total numbers of Europeans, Indians and Arabs in Kenya (including officials) were 9,651, 22,822 and 10,102 respectively.

From *Indians in Kenya Memorandum* (London: Her Majesty's Stationery Office, 1923), pp. 9–12. Reprinted by permission.

Primarily, Kenya is an African territory, and His Majesty's Government think it necessary definitely to record their considered opinion that the interests of the African natives must be paramount, and that if, and when, those interests and the interests of the immigrant races should conflict, the former should prevail. Obviously the interests of the other communities, European, Indian or Arab, must severally be safeguarded. Whatever the circumstances in which members of these communities have entered Kenya, there will be no drastic action or reversal of measures already introduced, such as may have been contemplated in some quarters, the result of which might be to destroy or impair the existing interests of those who have already settled in Kenya. But in the administration of Kenya His Majesty's Government regard themselves as exercising a trust on behalf of the African population, and they are unable to delegate or share this trust, the object of which may be defined as the protection and advancement of the native races. It is not necessary to attempt to elaborate this position; the lines of development are as yet in certain directions undetermined, and many difficult problems arise which require time for their solution. But there can be no room for doubt that it is the mission of Great Britain to work continuously for the training and education of the Africans towards a higher intellectual moral and economic level than that which they had reached when the Crown assumed the responsibility for the administration of this territory. At present special consideration is being given to economic development in the native reserves, and within the limits imposed by the finances of the Colony all that is possible for the advancement and development of the Africans, both inside and outside the native reserves, will be done.

His Majesty's Government desire also to record that in their opinion the annexation of the East Africa Protectorate, which, with the exception of the mainland dominions of the Sultan of Zanzibar, has thus become a Colony, known as Kenya Colony, in no way derogates from this fundamental conception of the duty of the Government to the native races. As in the Uganda Protectorate, so in the Kenya Colony, the principle of trusteeship for the natives, no less than in the mandated territory of Tanganyika, is unassailable. This paramount duty of trusteeship win continue, as in the past, to be carried out under the Secretary of State for the Colonies by the agents of the Imperial Government, and by them alone.

FUTURE CONSTITUTIONAL EVOLUTION

Before dealing with the practical points at issue directly connected with the claims of Indians, it is necessary, in view of the declaration of policy enunciated above, to refer to the question of the future constitutional evolution of Kenya.

It has been suggested that it might be possible for Kenya to advance in the near future on the lines of responsible self-government, subject to the reservation of native affairs. There are, however, in the opinion of His Majesty's Government, objections to the adoption in Kenya at this stage of such an arrangement, whether it take the form of removing all matters affecting Africans from consideration in the Council, or the appointment of the Governor as High Commissioner for Native Affairs, or provision for a special veto by the Crown on local legislation which touches native interests; and they are convinced that the existing system of government is in present circumstances best calculated to achieve the aims which they have in view, namely, the unfettered exercise of their trusteeship for the native races and the satisfaction of the legitimate aspirations of other communities resident in the Colony.

His Majesty's Government cannot but regard the grant of responsible self-government as out of the question within any period of time which need now to be taken into consideration. Nor, indeed, would they contemplate yet the possibility of substituting an unofficial majority in the Council for the Government official majority. Hasty action is to be strongly deprecated, and it will be necessary to see how matters develop, especially in regard to African representation, before proposals for so fundamental a change in the Constitution of the Colony can be entertained. Meanwhile, the administration of the Colony will follow the British traditions and principles which have been successful in other Colonies, and progress towards self-government must be left to the lines which the passage of time the growth of experience may indias being best for the country.

PRACTICAL POINTS AT ISSUE

Turning now to the practical points at arising directly out of the claims of Indians domiciled in Kenya, these may be considered under the following heads—

Representation on the Legislative Council
Representation on the Executive Council
Representation on Municipal Councils
Segregation
Reservation of the Highlands for Europeans
Immigration

REPRESENTATION ON THE LEGISLATIVE COUNCIL

(a) *Elective System*—In no responsible quarter is it suggested that the Indians in Kenya should not have elective representation upon the Legislative Council of the Colony. The point at issue is the method whereby such elective representation should be secured. There are two alternative methods—

(i) A common electoral roll
(ii) Communal franchise

Under the former system, Kenya would divided up into a given number of constituencies, in each of which European and Indian voters on the roll would vote together at an election for candidates of either race, and the qualifications for admission to the voters' roll would be the same for Europeans and for Indians. Under the latter system, European and Indian constituencies would be demarcated independently, not necessarily coinciding in number or boundaries; the qualifications for admission to the voters' roll would not necessarily be the same for the two communities; and while Europeans would vote in the European constituencies for European candidates, Indians would vote in the Indian constituencies for Indian candidates.

As a variant of the former system, there is the common electoral roll with reservation of seats. This arrangement would involve the setting apart of a certain number of seats in a given constituency for candidates of a certain race; for example, in a constituency returning three members, with two seats reserved for Europeans and one for Indians, the two European candidates and the one Indian candidate highest in the poll would be elected, irrespective of the position in the poll of other candidates of either race.

The common electoral roll for all British subjects and British protected persons, with reservation of seats, was proposed in the Wood-Winterton report, and it was further suggested that the qualifications for voters should be such as to admit, if possible, ten per cent of the domiciled Indians to the register.

For the common electoral roll it is claimed that it would bridge the gap between the Europeans and Indians by giving a candidate of one race an incentive to study the needs and aspirations of the other race. Further, Indian sentiment, both in India and Kenya, strongly favours the common electoral roll, even though a communal franchise exists in India itself.

A communal franchise secures that every elector shall have the opportunity of being represented by a member with sympathies similar to his own, a consideration which in other Colonies has led the domiciled Indians to press for its adoption; it is well adapted to the needs of a country such as Kenya; no justification is seen for the suggestion that it is derogatory to any of the communities so represented, and it is believed that, so far from having a disruptive tendency, it would contract rather than widen the division between races in Kenya.

So far as Africans are concerned, a communal franchise provides a framework into which native representation can be fitted in due season.

From the point of view of the Indian residents themselves, this system permits of a far wider franchise being given than would be the case if a common electoral roll were introduced, and this alone should render it acceptable to all supporters of the Indian claims who have at heart the political development of the Indian people.

Finally, it allows of the immediate grant of electoral representation with a wide franchise to the other community in Kenya which is ripe for such institutions, the Arabs of the Coast.

These considerations were weighed before the Wood-Winterton report was drawn up; the recommendation then made turned largely on the desire to meet Indian feelings so far as conditions in Kenya would admit. The result of the reference to opinion in Kenya of the recommendation that a common electoral roll should be adopted, even though combined with a reservation of seats, was to show that the advantages claimed for the common electoral roll would in practice have been illusory. In the special conditions existing in Kenya it is clear that no candidate, European or Indian, could stand as an advocate of the interests of the other race without sacrificing the support of his own. If elections were to be fought on racial lines, as they undoubtedly would have been in Kenya, the main advantage claimed for the common electoral roll, namely, the bringing of the races nearer together, would be lost.

Having regard to all the circumstances, His Majesty's Government have decided that the interests of all concerned in Kenya will be best served by the adoption of a communal system of representation.

64. HAILE SELASSIE

AT THE LEAGUE OF NATIONS. June 30, 1936.

Italy invaded Ethiopia in October 1935, and, despite heroic resistance by the Ethiopians, Italian troops marched relentlessly behind clouds of poison gas and an intense air bombardment to capture Addis Ababa, the capital, on May 5, 1936. The Emperor Haile Selassie (b. Tafari Wakonnen, 1891–1975) fled into exile to plead for the collective security that was the cornerstone of the League of Nations—the very principle upon which the League had been founded—and to request that the members come to the aid of his beleaguered country. Although the League had voted overwhelmingly in October 1935 to condemn the Italian invasion, and even voted for limited sanctions against Italy, both Britain and France, in an humiliating effort to appease Benito Mussolini, lifted even these innocuous sanctions in July 1936. Undaunted by this impending capitulation to Italy, Haile Selassie was determined to argue the case for Ethiopia before the assembled members of the League in Geneva. As this diminutive man cloaked in black took the rostrum, from his seat in the fifth row of the Assembly Hall, he was greeted by obscenities shouted from the gallery by the Italian press corps. Unperturbed, he proceeded with calm determination before the embarrassed and humbled members to deliver the funeral oration of the League of Nations. He failed to move the League to act collectively as they had pledged to do upon signing the Covenant of the League, but he became overnight the conscience of a world over which the shadows of Nazi Germany and Fascist Italy were lengthening. His speech remains not only one of the most important political acts of the twentieth century, but a monument for all time.

I Haile Selassie, emperor of Ethiopia, am here today to claim that justice which is due to my people, and the assistance promised to it eight months ago, when fifty nations asserted that aggression had been committed in violation of international treaties.

There is no precedent for a head of state himself speaking in this Assembly. But there is also no precedent for a people being victim of such injustice, and being at present threatened by abandonment to its aggressor. Also, there has never before been an example by any government proceeding to the systematic extermination of a nation by barbarous means in violation of the most solemn promises made by the nations of the earth that there should not be used against innocent human beings the terrible poison of harmful gases. It is to defend a people struggling for its age-old independence that the head of the Ethiopian empire has come to Geneva to fulfill this supreme duty, after having himself fought at the head of his armies.

I pray to Almighty God that He may spare nations the terrible sufferings that have just been inflicted on my people and of which the chiefs who accompany me here have been the horrified witnesses. It is my duty to inform the governments assembled in Geneva, responsible as they are for the lives of millions of men,

From *Selected Speeches of His Imperial Majesty Haile Selassie I: 1918–1967* (Addis Ababa: Ministry of Information, 1967), pp. 304–316.

women, and children, of the deadly peril which threatens them, by describing to them the fate which has been suffered by Ethiopia.

It is not only upon warriors that the Italian government has made war. It has above all attacked populations far removed from hostilities, in order to terrorize and exterminate them.

At the beginning, towards the end of 1935, Italian aircraft hurled upon my armies bombs of tear-gas. Their effects were but slight. The soldiers learned to scatter, waiting until the wind had rapidly dispersed the poisonous gases. The Italian aircraft then resorted to mustard gas. Barrels of liquid were hurled upon armed groups. But this means also was not effective. The liquid affected only a few soldiers and barrels upon the ground were themselves a warning to troops and to the population of the danger.

It was at the time when the operations for the encircling of Makalle [in northern Ethiopia] were taking place that the Italian command fearing a rout, followed the procedure which it is now my duty to denounce to the world. Special sprayers were installed on board aircraft so that they could vaporize, over vast areas of territory, a fine, death-dealing rain. Groups of 9, 15, 18 aircraft followed one another so that the fog issuing from them formed a continuous sheet. It was thus that, as from the end of January 1936, soldiers, women, children, cattle, rivers, lakes and pastures were drenched continually with this deadly rain. In order to kill off systematically all living creatures, in order the more surely to poison waters and pastures, the Italian command made its aircraft pass over and over again. That was its chief method of warfare.

The very refinement of barbarism consisted in carrying ravage and terror into the most densely populated parts of the territory, the points farthest removed from the scene of hostilities. The object was to scatter fear and death over a great part of the Ethiopian territory.

These fearful tactics succeeded. Men and animals succumbed. The deadly rain that fell from the aircraft made all those whom it touched fly shrieking with pain. All those who drank the poisoned water or ate the infected food also succumbed in dreadful suffering. In tens of thousands, the victims of the Italian mustard gas fell. It is in order to denounce to the civilized world the tortures inflicted upon the Ethiopian people that I resolved to come to Geneva.

None other than myself and my brave companions in arms could bring the League of Nations the undeniable proof. The appeals of my delegates addressed to the League of Nations had remained without any answer; my delegates had not been witnesses. That is why I decided to come myself to bear witness against the crime perpetrated against my people and give Europe a warning of the doom that awaits it, if it should bow before the accomplished fact.

Is it necessary to remind the Assembly of the various stages of the Ethiopian drama? For 20 years past either as heir apparent, regent of the empire, or as emperor, I have never ceased to use all my efforts to bring my country the benefits of civilization, and in particular to establish relations of good neighborliness with adjacent powers. In particular I succeeded in concluding with Italy the Treaty of Friendship of 1928, which absolutely prohibited the resort, under any pretext whatsoever, to force of arms, substituting for force and pressure the conciliation and arbitration on which civilized nations have based international order.

In its report of October 5, 1935, the Committee of 13 [of the League] recognized my effort and the results that I achieved. The governments thought that the entry of Ethiopia into the League, whilst giving that country a new guarantee for the maintenance of her territorial integrity and independence, would help her to reach a higher level of civilization. It does not seem that in Ethiopia today there is more disorder and insecurity than in 1923. On the contrary, the country is more united and the central power is better obeyed.

I should have procured still greater results for my people if obstacles of every kind had not been put in the way by the Italian government, the government which stirred up revolt and armed the rebels. Indeed the Rome government, as it has today openly proclaimed, has never ceased to prepare for the conquest of Ethiopia. The treaties of friendship it signed with me were not sincere; their only object was to hide its real intention from me. The Italian government asserts that for fourteen years it has been preparing for its present conquest. It therefore recognizes today that when it supported the admission of Ethiopia to the League of Nations in 1923, when it concluded the Treaty of Friendship in 1928, when it signed the pact of Paris outlawing war, it was deceiving the whole world.

The Ethiopian government was, in these solemn treaties, given additional guarantees of security which would enable it to achieve further progress along the pacific path of reform on which it had set its feet and to which it was devoting all its strength and all its heart.

The Walwal incident, in December 1934, came as a thunderbolt to me. The Italian provocation was obvious, and I did not hesitate to appeal to the League of Nations. I invoked the provisions of the treaty of 1928, the principles of the covenant [of the League]; I urged the procedure of conciliation and arbitration.

Unhappily for Ethiopia, this was the time when a certain government considered that the European situation made it imperative at all costs to obtain the friendship of Italy. The price paid was the abandonment of Ethiopian independence to the greed of the Italian government. This secret agreement [of January 1935], between Britain and Italy, recognizing Italian influence over Ethiopia, contrary to the obligations of the covenant, has exerted a great influence over the course of events. Ethiopia and the whole world have suffered and are still suffering today its disastrous consequences.

This first violation of the covenant was followed by many others. Feeling itself encouraged in its policy against Ethiopia, the Rome government feverishly made war preparations thinking that the concerted pressure which was beginning to be exerted on the Ethiopian government might perhaps not overcome the resistance of my people to Italian domination.

The time had to come, thus all sorts of difficulties were placed in the way with a view to breaking up the procedure of conciliation and arbitration. All kinds of obstacles were placed in the way of that procedure. Governments tried to prevent the Ethiopian government from finding arbitrators amongst their nationals: when once the arbitral tribunal was set up, pressure was exercised so that an award favorable to Italy should be given. All this was in vain: the arbitrators—two of whom were Italian officials—were forced to recognize unanimously that in the Walwal incident, as in the subsequent incidents, no international responsibility was to be attributed to Ethiopia.

Following on this award, the Ethiopian government sincerely thought that an era of friendly relations might be opened with Italy. I loyally offered my hand to the Rome government.

The Assembly was informed by the report of the Committee of Thirteen, dated October 5, 1935, of the details of the events which occurred after the month of December 1934 and up to October 3, 1935. It will be sufficient if I quote a few of the conclusions of that report (Nos. 24, 25, and 26): The Italian memorandum (containing the complaints made by Italy) was laid on the Council table on September 4, 1935, whereas Ethiopia's first appeal to the Council had been made on December 14, 1934. In the interval between these two dates, the Italian government opposed the consideration of the question by the Council on the ground that the only appropriate procedure was that provided for in the Italo-Ethiopian Treaty of 1928. Throughout the whole of that period, moreover, the dispatch of Italian troops to East Africa was proceeding. These shipments of troops were represented to the Council by the Italian government as necessary for the defense of its colonies menaced by Ethiopia's preparations. Ethiopia, on the contrary, drew attention to the official pronouncements made in Italy which, in its opinion, left no doubt "as to the hostile intentions of the Italian government."

From the outset of the dispute, the Ethiopian government has sought a settlement by peaceful means. It has appealed to the procedures of the covenant. The Italian government desiring to keep strictly to the procedures of the Italo-Ethiopian Treaty of 1928, the Ethiopian government assented. It invariably stated that it would faithfully carry out the arbitral award even if the decision went against it. It agreed that the question of the ownership of Walwal should not be dealt with by the arbitrators, because the Italian government would not agree to such a course. It asked the Council to dispatch neutral observers and offered to lend itself to any inquiries upon which the Council might decide.

Once the Walwal dispute had been settled by arbitration, however, the Italian government submitted its detailed memorandum to the Council in support of its claim to liberty of action. It asserted that a case like that of Ethiopia cannot be settled by the means provided by the covenant. It stated that, "since this question affects vital interests and is of primary importance to Italian security and civilization," it "would be failing in its most elementary duty, did it not cease once and for all to place any confidence in Ethiopia reserving full liberty to adopt any measures that may become necessary to ensure the safety of its colonies and to safeguard its own interests."

Those are the terms of the report of the Committee of Thirteen. The Council and the Assembly unanimously adopted the conclusion that the Italian government had violated the covenant and was in a state of aggression.

I did not hesitate to declare that I did not wish for war, that it was imposed upon me, and I should struggle solely for the independence and integrity of my people, and that in that struggle I was the defender of the cause of all small states exposed to the greed of a powerful neighbor.

In October 1935, the fifty-two nations who are listening to me today gave me an assurance that the aggressor would not triumph, that the resources of the covenant would be employed in order to ensure the reign of right and the failure of violence. I ask the fifty-two nations not to forget today the policy upon which they embarked eight months ago, and on faith of which I directed the resistance of my people against the aggressor whom they had denounced to the world. Despite the inferiority of my weapons, the complete lack of aircraft, artillery, munitions, hospital services, my confidence in the League was absolute. I thought it to be impossible that fifty-two nations, including the most powerful in the world, should be successfully opposed by a single aggressor. Counting on the faith due to treaties, I had made no preparation for war, and that is the case with certain small countries in Europe.

When the danger became more urgent, being aware of my responsibilities towards my people, during the first six months of 1935 1 tried to acquire armaments. Many governments proclaimed an embargo to prevent my doing so, whereas the Italian government, through the Suez Canal, was given all facilities for transporting, without cessation and without protest, troops, arms and munitions.

On October 3, 1935, the Italian troops invaded my territory. A few hours later only I decreed general mobilization. In my desire to maintain peace I had, following the example of a great country in Europe on the eve of the Great War, caused my troops to withdraw 30 kilometers so as to remove any pretext of provocation.

War then took place in the atrocious conditions which I have laid before the Assembly. In that unequal struggle between a government commanding more than 42 million inhabitants, having at its disposal financial, industrial and technical means which enabled it to create unlimited quantities of the most death dealing weapons, and, on the other hand, a small people of 12 million inhabitants, without arms, without resources, having on its side only the justice of its own cause and the promise of the League of Nations, what real assistance was given to Ethiopia by the fifty-two nations who have declared the Rome government guilty of a breach of the covenant and had undertaken to prevent the triumph of the aggressor? Has each of the states members, as it was its duty to do in virtue of its signature appended to Article 15 of the covenant, considered the aggressor as having committed an act of war personally directed against itself? I had placed all my hopes in the execution of these undertakings. My confidence had been confirmed by the repeated declarations made in Council to the effect that aggression must not be rewarded, and that force would end by being compelled to bow before right.

In December 1935 the Council made it quite clear that its feelings were in harmony with those of hundreds of millions of people who, in all parts of the world, had protested against the proposals to dismember Ethiopia. It was constantly repeated that there was not merely a conflict between the Italian government and the League of Nations, and that is why I personally refused all proposals to my personal advantage made to me by the Italian government, if only I would betray my people and the covenant of the League of Nations. I was defending the cause of all small peoples who are threatened with aggression.

What have become of the promises made to me as long ago as October 1935? I noted with grief, but without surprise, that three powers considered their undertakings under the covenant as absolutely of no value. Their connections with Italy impelled them to refuse to take any measures whatsoever in order to stop Italian aggression. On the contrary, it was a profound disappointment to me to learn the attitude of a certain government which, whilst ever protesting its scrupulous attachment to the covenant, has tirelessly used all its efforts to prevent its observance. As soon as any measure which was likely to be rapidly effective was proposed, various pretexts were devised in order to postpone even consideration of the measure. Did the secret agreements of January 1935 provide for this tireless obstruction?

The Ethiopian government never expected other governments to shed their soldiers' blood to defend the covenant when their own immediately personal interests were not at stake. Ethiopian warriors asked only for means to defend themselves. On many occasions I have asked for financial assistance for the purchase of arms. That assistance has been constantly refused me. What, then, in practice, is the meaning of Article 16 of the covenant and of collective security?

The Ethiopian government's use of the railway from Djibouti to Addis Ababa was in practice hampered as regards transport of arms intended for the Ethiopian forces. At the present moment this is the chief, if not the only, means of supply of the Italian armies of occupation. The rules of neutrality should have prohibited transports intended for Italian forces, but there is not even neutrality since Article 16 lays upon every state member of the League the duty not to remain a neutral but to come to the aid not of the aggressor but of the victim of aggression. Has the covenant been respected? Is it today being respected?

Finally a statement has just been made in their parliaments by the governments of certain powers, amongst them the most influential members of the League of Nations, that since the aggressor has succeeded in occupying a large part of Ethiopian territory, they propose not to continue the application of any economic and financial measures that may have been decided upon against the Italian government.

These are the circumstances in which, at the request of the Argentine government, the Assembly of the League of Nations meets to consider the situation created by Italian aggression.

I assert that the problem submitted to the Assembly today is a much wider one. It is not merely a question of the settlement of Italian aggression. It is collective security: it is the very existence of the League of Nations. It is the confidence that each state is to place in international treaties. It is the value of promises made to small states that their integrity and their independence shall be respected and ensured. It is the principle of the equality of states on the one hand, or otherwise the obligation laid upon small powers to accept the bonds of vassalship. In a word, it is international morality that is at stake. Have the signatures appended to a treaty value only in so far as the signatory powers have a personal, direct and immediate interest involved?

No subtlety can change the problem or shift the grounds of the discussion. It is in all sincerity that I submit these considerations to the Assembly. At a time when my people are threatened with extermination, when the support of the League may ward off the final blow, may I be allowed to speak with complete frankness, without reticence, in all directness such as is demanded by the rule of equality as between all states members of the League?

Apart from the Kingdom of the Lord, there is not on this earth any nation that is superior to any other. Should it happen that a strong government finds it may with impunity destroy a weak people, then the hour strikes for that weak people to appeal to the League of Nations to give its judgment in all freedom. God and history will remember your judgment.

I have heard it asserted that the inadequate sanctions already applied have not achieved their object. At no time, and under no circumstances, could sanctions that were intentionally inadequate, intentionally badly applied, stop an aggressor. This is not a case of the impossibility of stopping an aggressor, but of the refusal to stop an aggressor. When Ethiopia requested and requests that she should be given financial assistance, was that a measure which it was impossible to apply whereas financial assistance of the League has been granted, even in times of peace, to two countries and exactly to two countries who have refused to apply sanctions against the aggressor?

Faced by numerous violations by the Italian government of all international treaties that prohibit resort to arms and the use of barbarous methods of warfare, it is my painful duty to note that the initiative has today been taken with a view to raising sanctions. Does this initiative not mean in practice the abandonment of Ethiopia to the aggressor? On the very eve of the day when I was about to attempt a supreme effort in the defense of my people before this Assembly, does not this initiative deprive Ethiopia of one of her last chances to succeed in obtaining the support and guarantee of states members? Is that the guidance the League of Nations and each of the states members are entitled to expect from the great powers when they assert their right and their duty to guide the action of the League?

Placed by the aggressor face to face with the accomplished fact are states going to set up the terrible precedent of bowing before force?

Your Assembly will doubtless have laid before it proposals for the reform of the covenant and for rendering more effective the guarantee of collective security. Is it the covenant that needs reform? What undertakings can have any value if the will to keep them is lacking? Is it international morality which is at stake and not the articles of the covenant?

On behalf of the Ethiopian people, a member of the League of Nations, I request the Assembly to take all measures proper to ensure respect for the covenant. I renew my protest against the violations of treaties of which the Ethiopian people has been the victim. I declare in the face of the whole world that the emperor, the government, and the people of Ethiopia will not bow before force; that they maintain their claims that they will use all means in their power to ensure the triumph of right and the respect of the covenant.

I ask the fifty-two nations, who have given the Ethiopian people a promise to help them in their resistance to the aggressor, what arc they willing to do for Ethiopia? And the great powers who have promised the guarantee of collective security to small states on whom weighs the threat that they may one day suffer the fate of Ethiopia, I ask what measures do you intend to take?

Representatives of the world, I have come to Geneva to discharge in your midst the most painful of the duties of the head of a State. What reply shall I have to take back to my people?

65. FÉLIX EBOUÉ

NATIVE POLICY AND POLITICAL INSTITUTIONS IN FRENCH EQUATORIAL AFRICA. 1941.

Félix Eboué (1884–1944) became governor general of French Equatorial Africa in 1940. Originally from French Guiana, he was one of the most famous colonial administrators in the French Empire and a leading figure at the French African Conference at Brazzaville in 1944. He was best known for his policies of decentralization and his rejection of the strict assimilationist policy in colonial administration. The eloquent definition of his policies that follows was made in November 1941.

French Equatorial Africa has reached a decisive moment in its existence. It is useless to look back on the errors of the past. We will do better to criticize and be sorry. The balance sheet of our good and bad points and the relative merits of the colonization plan that was imposed upon us have been made clear by long experience and by the lessons of the war, so that we can say in certainty what we should do and how it should be done.

Unfortunately, the implementation of progress cannot be as prompt as we would like. Although financial means are sufficient, at least, to make a start, personnel and material are lacking, and money does not always inspire their acquisition. The men have been mobilized, and we can buy only the surplus—the fools—left over by the devouring industries of war. This does not mean that all we can do is sit back and fold our arms; on the contrary, no opportunity to create will be neglected, and there is always opportunity for whoever is patient and decided. But lacking immediate manpower, we can act by taking advantage of the delay to find the best position from which to begin. Together we will set ourselves to this task. Together we will make sure that Equatorial Africa, instead of being served by France, as has too often been the case, will be prepared to serve France tomorrow.

As a first condition for this indispensable success, we must have at our disposal a native population that will not only be healthy, stable, and peaceful but that will increase in number and will progress materially, intellectually, and morally so that

From Jean de la Roche and Jean Gottmann, *La Fédération Française* (Montreal: Editions de l'Arbre, 1945), pp. 583–589. Trans. from the French by Nell Elizabeth Painter and Robert O. Collins. Reprinted by permission.

we will have the collaboration of leadership that is the contribution of the masses and without which development would never be more than just a word. If we do not obtain this cooperation, our only choice will be between absolute impotence (that is to say, ruin) or the settling in the colony of a foreign race that would take the place of the indigenous tribes. Pride forbids us the first choice; conscience and elementary interest forbid the second.

Here then is the basic and urgent need dictated to us: to establish native society on bases that will push the colony forward on the road to prosperity. But this is not the need of the administration alone. If it is to be brought to a good end, all the leadership of the colony must participate. The whole of Equatorial Africa will have its own native policy; this policy, the expression of the will of all—industrialists, colonists, missionaries, traders, and civil servants—will survive any reign. When its results are measured in ten or twenty years, it will be recognized that it was not born of individual caprice but of the unanimous resolve of a team that, having drawn itself up to redeem and liberate France, decided to save French Equatorial Africa as well.

I use the word "save" advisedly. The colony is in danger, threatened in the interior, like a granary emptying itself out. Whether the cause is sought in the prolonged system of large concessions, in disorderly economic exploitation, in sometimes tactless proselytising, in the disregard of learning, or finally and especially in the neglect, or one could say the distrust, of native political and social leaders; the consequences are there, and we can put our finger on them: a population that, in one place, does not increase, and in another shrinks; a land incapable of furnishing the auxiliary and directive personnel that are absolutely indispensable to commerce, public works, and the administration; a mass, disintegrating and dispersing; voluntary abortion and syphilis spreading throughout a nascent proletariat; these are the evils inflicted all at once upon the colony by an absurd individualism.

I know very well that a more comprehensive and better executed system of medical and hygienic training, plus a more intensive system of general and moral education, would correct some of these vices. But the basic cause of the evil will remain untouched so long as a policy for the population is not defined and implemented once and for all. We will share the results of this policy together.

To attempt to make or remake a society (if not in our image, then at least according to our mental habits) is to court certain disaster. The native has behavior, laws, and motherland, which are not ours. We will not be the source of his happiness by following the principles of the French Revolution, which is our revolution, or by enforcing the Napoleonic Code, which is our code, or by substituting our civil servants for his chiefs, for our civil servants think for him, not as he does.

On the contrary, we insure his equilibrium, by treating him as a person on his own—that is to say, not as an isolated and interchangeable individual, but as a human personage permeated by traditions, the member of a family, of a village and of a tribe, capable of progress within his milieu and probably lost if he is taken from it. We apply ourselves to the development of his sense of dignity and responsibility and his moral progress, and to his enrichment and his material progress; but we will do so within the framework of his natural institutions. If these institutions have been altered through our contact, we will reorganize them, of necessity in new forms, yet close enough to him to retain his interest in his country and his desire to prove himself before moving on. In a word, we will give back to the native what no man can relinquish without damage to himself; we will not give him an illusory gift, we will, at the same time, reconstitute his profound sense of life and his desire to perpetuate it.

OF POLITICAL INSTITUTIONS

Here Lyautey[1] shows us the way. Let him cite Lanessan[2] his first master in colonization: "In all countries there is leadership. For the European people who come there as conquerors, the great error is in destroying this leadership. Then the country, deprived of its framework, falls into anarchy. It is necessary to govern with the mandarin, not against the mandarin. Not being numerous enough, the European cannot act as his substitute, but control him." And Lyautey himself adds: "Therefore break no traditions, change no customs. In every society there is a leading class, born to lead, without which nothing is done. It must be in our interests."

Starting from such a principle, we must first confirm or reconfirm their recognition, and in all cases, promote native political institutions. Let one [principle] be well understood: there is no question of considering political custom as something set or immutable as museum objects, it is very clear that custom changes and will change, and that we are not here to sterilize it by fixing it. But we must understand its profound meaning and consider it as essential as the tradition that shaped it and feelings that gave birth to it. This tradition is that of the motherland. To strip the native of these two motors of human life is to rob him without retribution. it would be about as insane as taking his land, vineyard, cattle, and soup pot from the French peasant in order to make an ordinary factory worker, charged with handling the products of an industrialized countryside.

Furthermore, if we do not reconfirm the bases of native political institutions, these bases will themselves disappear and will give way to an uncontrollable individualism. And how will we be able to act on this collection of individuals? When I see impatient administrators seize, unmake, condemn, and remake chiefs and thus sap the strength of a traditional institution, I think that they do not reflect on what will happen when that institution, due to their faults, loses its efficiency along with its vital character. I could tell them this: the only means remaining to ward off the breakdown of natural command will be administration by native civil servants. Because the chief of a subdivision cannot directly watch each person he administers, he will have to use civil servants as intermediaries instead of the chiefs he will have lost. I leave it to each person to judge the best solution from his own experience. If an ambitious administrator pretends to do without chiefs and civil servants, at least to reduce them to the state of simple instruments in his hands—precise and

1. Marshall Louis H. G. Lyautey (1854–1934) sought to establish French authority and introduce European economic development in colonial areas while respecting indigenous rights and customs (ed).

2. Jean-Louis de Lanessan was a governor-general of Indochina who was best known for his book *Principes de Colonisation* (ed).

punctual instruments—I am sure that he is fooling himself, but in any case, I am convinced that his successor would not have the same good fortune. The continuity of effort, whose prerequisite is the decisive superiority of a single administrator, would be compromised from the moment of his departure. He would have built his cathedrals on the sand.

I have just been speaking of chiefs. In truth, although native institutions are often monarchical, they are not always. The opposite is true. The nomadic tribes of the North, which live under a regime of organized anarchy, could be cited as an example. And even within a monarchical state, the chief does not represent the only political institution. His power is amended, attenuated, and shared by more than one principle and more than one institution. Nothing must be forgotten or rejected of all this. No constituted council will be omitted, no guardian ousted, and no religious taboo neglected on the pretext that it would be ridiculous, bothersome, or immoral. There is no question of denying or condemning what exists and what counts, but to lead it along the way to progress.

The institution of the chief, however, is most important, and we will take the most care with his person. A preliminary question is posed here: Who should be chief? I will not answer as I did in Athens: "The Best One." There is no best chief, there is a chief, and we have no choice. I have already spoken of the frequent mutations of the chiefs; they are deplorable and no less absurd. There is a chief designated by custom; the point is to *recognize him.* I use the term in the diplomatic sense. If we arbitrarily replace him, we divide the command into two parts, the official and the real; no one is fooled except us, and if we flatter ourselves for getting better results from *our chief* we overlook, most of the time, that he himself obeys the *real chief* and that we are dealing with dupes.

Chiefs are not interchangeable. When we depose them, public opinion does not; the chief preexists. This preexistence often remains unknown to us, and the most difficult thing for us is to discover the real chief. I want the governors and administrators henceforth to adhere to this tenet. Not only do I mean that power will no longer be given to a parvenu whose services must be repaid (are there not a hundred other ways to repay them?), but I want the legitimate chiefs to be searched out where our ignorance has let them hide and reestablished in their outward dignity. I know what will be said: that all that has disappeared, that it is too late, that poor incorrigibles will be found from whom nothing is to be had. I believe that this is not true; occult power subsists because it is traditional power. May it be discovered and brought out into the light of day, may it be honored and educated. Results are certain to be forthcoming.

66. JOMO KENYATTA

MEETING AT NYERI. July 26, 1952.

The Second World War was a great watershed in the evolution of Kenya. The many Africans (75,000) who had served in the British forces returned from overseas with a worldly outlook, imbued with universal ideas acquired through their association with many peoples from far-off lands. Within the colony, there were long-standing grievances about the alienation of land and the requirements of the settlers for African labor; the overseas experience of Kenyan soldiers gave them a new and more militant perspective on these questions. The discontent manifested itself in two forms: a revival of oathing among the Kikuyu; and the founding of the Kenya African Union (KAU) as a more demanding political party to replace the rather benign Kikuyu Central Association (KCA). Oathing ceremonies had been practiced by the Kikuyu for centuries, with different oaths for different needs; the practice was deeply embedded in Kikuyu culture and generally regarded by the colonial authorities as relatively harmless. The young militants of KAU perceived in the custom of oathing a means to mobilize the Kikuyu against the European presence, whether colonial or settler. The grievance over the alienation of land reached its most serious proportions at the meeting in Olenguruone between some 12,000 displaced Kikuyu from the highlands, who had settled in Masailand on the edge of the Mau plateau, and the colonial administration that refused to recognize their rights to the land upon which they had been squatters since the 1920s. Here in Olenguruone the oathing tradition of the Kikuyu was employed to ensure the unity of the Kikuyu people in their claims to the land of the Masai. The colonial administration ultimately prevailed and the "squatters" were evicted. However, the unity of the Kikuyu of Olenguruone cemented through oathing, and it took on a new dimension that was hostile, not only to the British administration, but to the European settler community. The settlers, by the displacement of the Kikuyu, had precipitated the Olenguruone dispute over Kenya's most precious commodity—land.

In the midst of this confrontation in September 1946, Jomo Kenyatta (1889–1978) returned from his long absence in England. He had been born an orphan in Mitumi, Kenya, and was educated at a Scottish mission school before becoming a herd boy. He joined the Kikuyu Central Association in 1922 and became its president. In 1929, during his term in this office, he made his first visit to Great Britain. He returned to England in 1931 as the representative of the KCA, and studied for a year at London University under the distinguished anthropologist Professor B. Malinowski. During this period he wrote his well-known book, Facing Mount Kenya (1938), visited the Soviet Union on three separate occasions, and, on May 11, 1942, married an Englishwoman, Edna Grace Clarke. Upon returning to Kenya in 1946, he immediately involved himself in the Kenya African Union (KAU), which had been established on October 1, 1944, to represent African interests, following the

From "Kenya African Union Meeting At Nyeri: Report on Mass Meeting Held Between 11 a.m. and 3 p.m. on 26th July 1952 by Assistant Superintendent of Police, Nyeri," in *Historical Survey of the Origins and Growth of Mau Mau* (Her Majesty's Stationery Office [Cmnd. 1030], May 1960), App. F, pp. 301–308. This report in which this document is included in the appendices is frequently referred to as the "Corfield Report," after its principal author, F. D. Corfield.

*suppression of the KCA. Always an enigma, or at least an ambiguous and equivo-
cal figure, Kenyatta—who was elected president of the KAU on June 1, 1947—was
increasingly caught up in the militancy of the younger members of the KAU, without, however, losing supreme control of the party. His relationship to the Mau Mau
movement still remains a subject of controversy; in 1952 the colonial authorities
tried and sentenced him to seven years' hard labor for his presumed leadership of
the terrorist Mau Mau movement. Although the Mau Mau were ultimately defeated,
there no longer remained any doubt about the ultimate control of Kenya by the
Africans; Kenyatta was released in 1958. Elected president of the Kenya African
National Union, the successor of the KAU, in 1961, he became prime minister in
1963, and president of Kenya in December 1964. He remained in these offices until
his death as a revered figure, the Mwalimu (teacher) of his people.*

*One of the crucial turning points in Kenyatta's career was the climatic meeting
at Nyeri on July 26, 1952. Since April, Kenyatta had been making speeches throughout Kenya seeking to disassociate the KAU from the Mau Mau, while advocating the
achievement of independence by peaceful means and hard work and the safeguarding of the integrity of the non-African peoples of Kenya. Over 25,000 people came
to Nyeri, charged with fervor and emotion that Kenyatta found difficult to control,
but from the Nyeri meeting there was no turning back on the road to independence.*

At 11 a.m. there were in the vicinity 20,000 Africans at the meeting. By 1 p.m.
the attendance was estimated at 25,000. The meeting was held on an open flat, three
miles out of Nyeri, bordering the Kikuyu Reserve and was an authorized meeting.
Terence Patrick O'Brien, the suspect European Communist, was present and took
photographs of the assembly.

Prominent African politicians present included Jomo Kenyatta, Ochieng Oneko,
Anderson Wamuthenya, Morris Mwai, Samuel Kagotho, Henry Muoria, Henry
Wambugu, Willy George and many others prominent in African politics and Trade
Unionists from Nairobi and various K.A.U. branches in the country. The Transport
and Allied Workers' Union, various sections of the old Labour Trade Union of East
Africa and most African trading societies and organizations were represented. Jesse
Kariuki interpreted from Kikuyu into Swahili.

First Speaker—Jomo Kenyatta

"I am very pleased to come to Nyeri and see so many of you here at this meeting of K.A.U., but before we open the meeting, I appeal to you to sit down and keep
quiet so that you can hear what we are going to say. (Considerable shouting and ill-
behavior on the part of the crowd at this moment.) I want to explain to you that if
you want self-Government you must first sit down and keep quiet. (Points to various groups who are standing and making a noise and admonishes them.) Our time
at this meeting is limited and we office-bearers have travelled a long way to address
you, and if you are going to waste the time of the meeting our purpose will be
spoiled. Those who are continuing to make a noise must be removed from this meeting. I do not want any interruptions. Quiet. Quiet. I am the leader of Mumbi and I
ask you yet again to keep quiet. (Tremendous applause and the crowd becomes
more orderly.) If one is born of Mumbi, sit down on this earth of ours and keep

quiet, otherwise leave. Those of you who are near the main road will be covered in dust unless you sit down. (Applause, and the crowd is more or less quiet now.) What God has told me to say to you today I will now say, although our loudspeaker has nor yet arrived from Nairobi. You are the earth and the earth is ours, so listen to me and do not interrupt any more. We will start this meeting with prayers. Our brother Wachira will say these prayers to you. I have asked him to make our prayers very short as our time is restricted by Government." (Jeers.)

Second Speaker—The Rev. Wachira

"Those who are despised are those who fight for freedom. God said that one man cannot knock down a wall and continue to freedom, but if people unite and push together they could break the wall and pass over the ground towards independence. May God be with us on this day. We are here to follow the principles of justice. May God lead us on to out goal. Jomo is a disciple of God who will lead you along the righteous path. In the name of Jesus Christ and the people of Mumbi, I give you my blessing." (Crowd hums three times the religious answer to such prayers, according to Kikuyu tradition.)

Jomo Kenyatta Again

(He begins with his usual "eeeeee" which is characteristic of all his speeches, and this is given vociferous applause.)

"Time is limited and I am now starting. I want you to know the purpose of K.A.U. It is the biggest purpose the African has. It involves every African in Kenya and it is their mouthpiece which asks for freedom. (Applause.) K.A.U. is you and you are the K.A.U. If we unite now, each and every one of us, and each tribe to another, we will cause the implementation in this country of that which the European calls democracy. True democracy has no colour distinction. It does not choose between black and white. We are here in this tremendous gathering under the K.A.U. flag to find which road leads us from darkness into democracy. In order to find it we Africans must first achieve the right to elect our own representatives. That is surely the first principle of democracy. We are the only race in Kenya which does not elect its own representatives in the Legislature and we are going to set about to rectify this situation. (Applause.) We feel we are dominated by a handful of others who refuse to be just. (Applause. Jesse Kariuki is working the crowd up by translating Kenyatta's speech in such a way that he is conveying to the people an inference which Jomo Kenyatta does not convey.) God said this is our land. Land which we are to flourish as a people. We are not worried that other races are here with us in our country, but we insist that we are the leaders here, and what want we insist we get. We want our cattle to get fat on our land so that our children grow up in prosperity; we do not want that fat removed to feed others. (Applause.) He who has ears should now hear that K.A.U. claims this land as its own gift from God and I wish those who are black, white or brown at this meeting to know this. K.A.U. speaks in daylight. He who calls us the *Mau Mau* is not truthful. We do not know this thing *Mau Mau*. (Jeers and applause.) We want to prosper as a nation, and as a nation we demand equality, that is equal pay for equal work. Whether it is a chief, headman or labourer he needs in these days increased salary. He needs a salary that compares with a salary of a European who does equal work. We will never get our freedom unless we succeed in this issue. We do not want equal pay for equal work tomorrow—we want it right now. Those who profess to be just must realize that this is the foundation of justice. It has never been known in history that a country prospers without equality. We despise bribery and corruption, those two words that the European repeatedly refers to. Bribery and corruption is prevalent in this country, but I am not surprised. As long as a people are held down, corruption is sure to rise and the only answer to this is a policy of equality. If we work together as one, we must succeed.

Our country today is in a bad state for its land is full of fools—and fools in a country delay the independence of its people. K.A.U. seeks to remedy this situation and I tell you now it despises thieving, robbery and murder for these practices ruin our country. I say this because if one man steals, or two men steal, there are people sitting close by lapping up information, who say the whole tribe is bad because a theft has been committed. Those people are wrecking our chances of advancement. They will prevent us getting freedom. If I have my own way, let me tell you I would butcher the criminal, and there are more criminals than one in more senses than one. The policeman must arrest an offender, a man who is purely an offender, but he must not go about picking up people with a small horn of liquor in their hands and march them in procession with his fellow policemen to Government and say he has got a Mau Mau amongst the Kikuyu people. (Applause.) The plain clothes man who hides in the hedges must, I demand, get the truth of our words before he flies to Government to present them with false information. I ask this of them who are in the meeting to take heed of my words and do their work properly and justly. (Applause.) We are black people and when we achieve our freedom. we will also have police and plain clothes men.

Amongst you people before me are those future policemen and plain clothes men and informers whom I mention. I want, therefore, to teach you now that our Government will demand nothing short of fact and we will never have fitina-merchants. (Tremendous applause. This is obviously a crack against informers and I know the few African policemen here are feeling a little bit disturbed and uncomfortable.) We K.A.U. do not have divisions amongst our ranks. Each one of you may join. The only division and condition is that we refuse completely to enlist those who are not truthful. (The loud speaker arrives at this stage and is erected with considerable difficulty amongst the teeming masses.) I do not want you to associate yourselves with the present campaign of *fitina*—it is a salty campaign and it is harming us. (Applause.) Europeans are said to be the cleverest—they must therefore sift the information they get. (At this stage the crowd begins to get restless and there is a distinct change of attitude in Jomo Kenyatta. He appeals repeatedly to the masses to quieten down and Mr. Henderson sends him a message and tells him that unless he first brings his meeting to order he will not be permitted to make any more racial remarks.) Jomo Kenyatta agrees and takes considerable pains to quieten the masses. He leaves his platform and personally wanders about shaking his hand at the worst sections of the crowd. (After 15 minutes the crowd is pacified and Jomo returns to his platform.) Our friend Ochieng is here. Peter Mbiu is still in the United Kingdom. They went away because of our land hunger. I ask you to note that our land discussions are held in daylight. We want a commission in this country, a Royal Commission to enquire into the land problem. Anyone here who wants more land is to raise their right hand. (The whole meeting raises their hands, each individual raises both.) Now, who does nor want more land and who is not supporting us over this land problem? (Nobody moves.) I think the Europeans here realize in their heart of hearts that our grievance is true. (Shouts of "What are they going to do about it?") Who of you are going to support K.A.U.? (All raise their hands and there is tremendous applause.) Is it your heart that supports the K.A.U., or is it merely your mouth? (Answer, "Our hearts" and the whole meeting rises and many start waving their arms about. Another seven minutes is taken to restore the crowd to order.) Then join us today in this union of ours. Do not be scared of the few policemen under those trees who are holding their rifles high in the air for you to see. Their job is to seize criminals, and we shall save them a duty today. I will never ask you to be subversive (uses the English word which the meeting does not understand), but I ask you to be united, for the day of Independence is the day of complete unity and if we unite completely tomorrow, our independence will come tomorrow. This is the day for you to work hard for your country (applause), it is not words but deeds that count and the deeds I ask for come from your pockets. The biggest subscribers to K.A.U. are in this order. First, Thomson's Fall branch, second, Elburgon branch and third Gatundu branch. Do you, in Nyeri branch, want to beat them; (Answer, "Yes".) Then let us see your deeds come forth." (Applause. Samuel Kagotho now goes on to the platform and appeals to people to join the Union. Jomo tells the meeting that the most important points are to follow—this is calculated to hold the crowd, many of whom do not like subscribing—Samuel Kagotho tells the meeting where the different tables and K.A.U. clerks are to be found for those who wish to subscribe.). . . .

Next Speaker, Ebrahim, the African District Officer at Nyeri

"Ladies and gentlemen. I cannot say much, except that this is the biggest meeting I have seen in this District. I want to ask Mr. Kenyatta what he is going to do to stop *Mau Mau*." (This causes such a state of affairs that I cannot hear anything else Ebrahim says. He leaves the platform a minute or two later and Jomo Kenyatta replaces him.)

Jomo Kenyatta Again

"Eeeeeeee" (applause). "Quiet, because if you do not take my last warning we will never be permitted to hold another K.A.U. meeting in this District. Regarding Mr. Ebrahmi's speech. I do not want you to think he is wrong, for if there are two different types amongst a single people, we separate unity. K.A.U. is a good union and we do not want divided people. I think, *Mau Mau* is a new word. Elders do not know it. K.A.U. is not a fighting union that uses fists and weapons. If any of you here think that force is good, I do not agree with you: remember the old saying that he who is hit with a *rungu* returns, but he who is hit with justice never comes back. I do nor want people to accuse us falsely—that we steal and that we are *Mau Mau*." (Tremendous applause.) "I pray to you that we join hands for freedom and freedom means abolishing criminality. Beer harms us and those who drink it do us harm and they may be the so-called *Mau Mau*." (Tremendous applause. It is obvious that Jomo is side-stepping denouncing *Mau Mau*.) "Whatever grievances we have, let us air them here in the open. The criminal does not want freedom and land—he wants to line his own pocket. Let us therefore demand our rights justly. The British Government has discussed the land problem in Kenya and we hope to have a Royal Commission to this country to look into the land problem very shortly. When this Royal Commission comes, let us show it that we are a good peaceful people and not thieves and robbers. . . ."

Ochieng Oneko[1]

"I am very pleased to be here to talk to you. I would be more pleased if every one kept quiet. It is always said that there is noise and disturbance at African meetings, and I want to demonstrate that this theory is false. I have only a few minutes and can therefore only say a few words. Some laws of Kenya are bad and we want Government to know that we do not like them." (Crowd surges and speaker and Jesse Kariuki try to stop them. Jomo himself again goes into the crowd to try and pacify them.) "We do not want this meeting to turn into a riot. Sit down and keep quiet, I ask you, or we will not be permitted to hold another meeting." ("That does not matter" from the crowd. Mr. Henderson calls over Ochieng and tells him that the police are not very impressed with the conduct of the crowd and that unless order is restored he will not be permitted to speak. Eventually order is restored. Ochieng returns to the platform with a grin.) "You selected us to go as your representatives to the United Kingdom and U.N.O. When the Europeans came to this country we were a peaceful people—tribal wars were merely minor disputes. The Europeans came here as our guests." (Terrific applause.) "This invitation has turned out to be false. They went for land and have established themselves in Kenya in such numbers that we suffered; this is why we went to the U.K. We do not want to be led. We want our own African Government and we will get it soon. We want the country to begin with peace between us, the Government and the European, but that peace can only come if we get justice. Before the European came, every African had sufficient land—that is not the case today. If we were to get education and advancement by losing land, then I wish we never get advancement. I wish to thank many of the British people in the United Kingdom who support us. Some ridicule Fenner Brockway, but I know he is our friend. We discussed in the U.K. the land problem with the Colonial Secretary and he promised he would send a Commission to this

---

1. Ochieng Oneko, a Luo militant, was removed from the executive committee of the KAU by the British authorities after the Emergency Proclamation of October 20, 1952, and arrested. Although his case was dismissed by the Supreme Court of Kenya, he was held in detention until after the Lancaster House Constitutional Conference conferred self-government on Kenya in 1963.

Country. We demand that the Commission not only looks into African land but compares African land to the White Highlands. We know a report on land is to come out from the Colonial Office and we must remain peaceful until we see how things go. We have had a measure of success. We are also completely against the system of appointment to Legislative Council. We must elect our own representatives for some of our members in Legislative Council are good, but due to the fact that they were nominated by Government, the time may come when others turn half-Government to major issues. We are also against some controls, particularly regarding the difference in price between European and African grown maize. When in the United Kingdom, we asked that such controls and laws be revoked. We have seen for too long that the European gets first place." (This speaker is stirring up the meeting and is obviously most dangerous.) "Regarding Trade Unionism this is vital, for when the cost of living rises we must ensure that we are assisted in the same way as Europeans and that means equal pay for equal work. Then look at D.C.s' Offices. You see that an African is an "aaaaaaO". We only want an "O" and we refuse to listen to excuses from Government that the reason for these "a's" is that the African is not sufficiently responsible or suitable. Those Africans holding the titles "aaaaa" are doing the same work as D.C.s [District Commissioner] and P.C.s [Provincial Commissioner] and should therefore be given this office. We told the Secretary of State this quite clearly. We want mass-education. A man without education is only half a man but we want the chance to learn properly. The Indians have most schools because they breed like locusts. We want co-operation and friendship between races but we do not want that friendship that resembles the friendship of the crocodile and the fish. We are a peaceful people and we will not chase the European away, but I assure you we will watch him most closely. Europeans are visitors and they know it, and those who are here know it—here at this meeting, but they will not admit it. They have to give us permission before we can go to the lavatory. If we want freedom we must hit back. I know we will get it. We will get it in the same way as the people in the Gold Coast and Nigeria. There is no doubt that we will get it. You and I will achieve it—the K.A.U. —a body for all Africans in Kenya. We must not discard our traditions for they are us. I do not want to hear a person calling himself Peter Johnston William Tableson for those are European names and every time we ask something or do something people overseas will say we are Europeans. If your name is Njeroge, we know you are a Kikuyu and you should be proud of it. If your name is Omolo you are a Luo, or Patel an Indian, or George a European. (Laughter at "George".) Then stick to your names and languages. We learnt 'Yes, yes' and 'What there' which is English, only because we wanted to get trade, for in the trade world English is spoken. We do not copy our visitors. Regarding religion. We do not know God. What we know is *Ngai*. We believe in *Ngai* whether the missionaries say we are pagans or not. Are we not led by the God of Africa? We will wait in peace now for the developments regarding the Commission and I will then come back to tell you the news. I want you to love all Africans and I want tribes to get together. I said in Kiambu that I would marry a Kikuyu girl to show good relationship amongst tribes." (Three years ago this would have been taken by the Kikuyu as an insult for an uncircumcised Luo was the most despised thing imaginable to the

Kikuyu. Today it is applauded.) "Freedom cannot come without suffering and unity. If you do not unite. you will be the person who is kicked in the backside and called 'Boy'. Laws were made for all Africans and if you bring tribal difficulties into the picture you will delay advancement. Europeans have complete unity and when I was in the United Kingdom I saw that. The European once ruled the European but then they got together. They will leave this country in time. Legislation will eventually cause that. Those who came to this country to eke out a living when they were kicked out of India will repeat the performance of evacuation in time. For the present I want no trouble, let us only trouble ourselves to get together. That is all I have to say." (This man, Ochieng, is obviously fanatically anti-British and speeches of this nature made to primitive masses are extremely harmful. The meeting is more or less an uproar now.)

Jomo Kenyatta

(He returns to the platform to restore the masses to order.)

"You have, until now, done me a great favour in remaining quiet. Do not let people say we left this meeting like hungry hyenas. (After another 15 minutes the crowd was quiet.) Now, I will tell you about our flag. It has three colours as you see — black at the top, red in the middle and green at the bottom. Black is to show that this is for black people. Red is to show that the blood of an African is the same colour as the blood of a European and green is to show that when we were given this country by God it was green, fertile and good, but now you see the green is below the red and is suppressed. (Tremendous applause.) You also see on the flag a shield, a spear and an arrow. This means that we should remember our forefathers who used these weapons to guard this land for us. K.A.U. is marked on the flag. The 'U' is placed over the shield and indicates that the shield will guard the Union against all evils. The weapons do not mean that we should fight like our fathers. What could a spear do against an atom bomb. The weapon with which we will fight is justice and brains. The silver on the spear is the same colour as the silver on the shilling. That means our land was prosperous in the bygone days. Now do you approve of our flag? (Answer "Yes" amidst tremendous applause.) Does anyone not approve of it? If he does he is to stand up. (One poor misfortunate individual who misunderstood the question stands and is carried by the crowd over their heads to the perimeter and told to become a European.) God who gave us this land will see that this flag leads us throughout this land. (Applause.) We are to stop soon for these days everything depends on a permit. Nevertheless if we are given a permit whilst we are to be governed let us comply with it. Remember though that when we get our own Government there will not be permits. (Applause.) Those police armed in the trees came here to control Kenyatta's flock. Let us relieve them of a job today and disperse peacefully from this meeting. If you do not disperse peacefully and go back to your homes and shops in an orderly manner, you will do us a great disservice, for you will prevent the K.A.U. holding another meeting. Remember that he who hates another takes the snuff out of the other's nose. (This is a proverb which means that if one is permitted to do something and does not do it properly he will suffer by his actions.). . . ." The meeting dispersed without incident.

67. M. D. C. DE WET NEL

THE PRINCIPLES OF APARTHEID. 1959.

The Honorable W. D. C. de Wet Nel (1901–) was formerly Bantu commissioner general for the ethnic units of Venda and Tsonga (in the upper Transvaal). He was formerly minister for Bantu Administration and Development in the South African government, and a principal Cabinet spokesman for the ideal form of apartheid— separate development of black and white South Africans, including segregation of the Bantu peoples into their own states, called Bantustans, where they might run their own affairs and preserve their own culture. Wet Nel had a degree of Doctor of Philosophy from Pretoria University, and was secretary of the Nationalist party between 1939 and 1948. The following selection is an extract from his speech in the House of Assembly on May 18, 1959, explaining Nationalist party policy during the debate on the second reading of the bill promoting Bantu self-government.

I want to say that it is my deep and honest conviction that we have reached the stage where serious attention should be devoted to actually giving the Bantu the opportunity to manage their own affairs, because that is one of the elementary and the most moral rights to which every person is entitled. It is the legacy demanded by every nation in the world, and the Bantu eagerly demands it just like the White man and every other nation. Every nation in the world finds its highest expression and fulfilment in managing its own affairs and in the creation of a material and spiritual heritage for its successive generations. We want to give the Bantu that right also. The demand for self-determination on the part of the non-White nations is one of the outstanding features of the past decade. Outside Africa more than a dozen non-White nations have already obtained their freedom. In Africa it is the greatest phenomenon of the time. There are a number of people in Africa who have already received their freedom, and others are on the way to receiving it. This desire to manage their own affairs exists in the hearts of the Bantu population, just as it exists in the hearts of all other nations in the world. It is therefore our duty to approach these matters soberly and realistically. It is no use putting our heads in the sand and pretending to see nothing. We have to face the real facts. These matters lie near to the soul of the nation, and no safety valve in the world can smother them forever. The late Dr. Malan described it very pithily in this House once when he said that one might just as well try to stop the Southeaster with a sieve as to suppress the national sentiments of a nation. That applies to the Bantu also.

I say we must approach these matters soberly and with clear minds. If we close our eyes to them we are heading for self-destruction and death. People who are reckless in that regard are committing treason to their own people and digging the grave of the nation. We hear so many provocative remarks about Bantu nationalism and Black nationalism, but it is my conviction that there is nothing of the kind. If it

From *Debates of the House of Assembly* (Hansard). Union of South Africa (Cape Town: Hansard, 1959), CI. cols. 6006–6011, 6018–6024.

exists, then there is also something like White nationalism. But what does exist in fact is hatred on the part of the Black man for the White man. That is the monster which may still perhaps destroy all the best things in Africa. But I want to ask whether this monster not to a large extent been created by White man himself? The fact that he ignored the existence of national entities, that he has ignored their own form of government and that he has ignored their own cultural assets, has led to growth of this monster, and that is the reason why we plead that this monster must not rear its head in South Africa. That is why we want to give them these opportunities.

Mr. Speaker, I want to say frankly that I believe in the existence of nationalism on the part of the Bantu population groups. We cannot deny it; it is there. Amongst the Zulus there is a feeling nationalism which can serve as an example to more than one of us, but it is a Bantu nationalism; it is their own racial nationalism, just as it exists amongst White people of South Africa and of world. I grant them that nationalism. If the White man is entitled to it, I ask what right we have to say that those people should not be entitled to it also? Let us be honest and fair. Moreover, nationalism is one of the forces which puts into motion the best things in the spirit of human being. Nationalism is one of forces which has led to the most beau deeds of idealism and sacrifice and in ration. Should the Bantu not have it? It is the Nationalist who has learned to appreciate the cultural assets of other nations, and as someone once put it strikingly, a Nationalist is the best citizen of the world. That is my belief in regard to this matter. For that reason I want to say this. It will always be my task to respect these things of the Bantu, but to assist them to develop it as something beautiful and something which is in the interest of South Africa. It is our task to provide the opportunities for developing these matters, so that we may have cooperation instead of racial clashes. To think that we can solve this problem by lumping together in one community everything which is Bantu is nothing less than a crime towards the Bantu. One of the good things contained in this Bill is that it formally recognises these national units among the Bantu, and to give them the right and to encourage them to continue along this road of national development.

The question may be put in all fairness: Will it not be better, in the interest of South Africa, rather to continue building on the pattern we have now? I want to deal with a few considerations only.

In the first place, I stated the proposition that the overwhelming majority of the national groups in South Africa, including the Bantu, have rejected the ideal of a multi-racial community and have chosen separate development on their own. If we continued to build further on the present pattern, it would be nothing else but a negation of the will and the desires of the overwhelming majority of the population groups in South Africa, White as well as Bantu. In the second place we must be fair and honest and admit that the present state of affairs is very unsatisfactory to the Bantu and very uncertain for the Whites. If we continue building on the present pattern the position of the Whites will be very uncertain and the Bantu will not be satisfied. Let us remember that in this House there are three representatives who represent only the Bantu population of the Cape Province. The rest of the Bantu in South Africa are not represented in this House. Do hon. members want to tell me that the Bantu population takes no notice of that and that they are satisfied with it? It is an injustice which rankles in the minds of the Bantu in the other parts of the country. That is one of the main factors which engenders a spirit of suspicion and doubt regarding the honesty and the fairness and the justice of the White man. It is a political state of affairs which can no longer be tolerated. If hon. members want to be fair and logical, they should ask that at least the rest of the Bantu population in South Africa should be represented in this House on an equal footing with those in the Cape Province, and if they do that, I ask: Where will it end? We would then be setting in progress the same process which is being experienced in Kenya, Nyasaland, and Northern Rhodesia today. We just cannot foresee the results of it.

In the third place, it is my honest conviction that these Bantu population groups can best be guided on the road to progress if their whole development is Bantu orientated, which means that all the administrative bodies from the highest to the lowest should be linked up and the whole of the Bantu population should be concerned in them. It must form part of the whole structure. The present pattern was White orientated, because it was coupled to the White man. The result was that there was a flight from the Bantu community. The developed Native no longer sought the satisfaction of his ambition to develop amongst his own people, but in the White areas. Surely that is a very sad state of affairs. There was a migration going on, not only of migrant labourers from the Bantu areas, but also of educated people from the Bantu areas, that most essential material for building up of a community. In my opinion every nation in the world is entitled to benefit from the efforts of its best sons and daughters and a policy which is calculated to deprive them of it is immoral; it is human erosion. A policy like that cannot be tolerated. Such a policy is one of the chief causes of racial hatred.

In the fourth place, I am convinced in my mind that the expansion of the present system will have the result that the White population of South Africa will be dominated by the political power of the Bantu population. If this pattern is extended logically in the future, I say that the White people will be dominated by the political power of the Bantu. Surely it must be a very stupid politician who cannot appreciate the logical consequences of this.

The present system of Bantu representation has really made no contribution in any way towards creating sound racial relations in South Africa. I challenge any person to deny that. All it has done is to increase racial tension. That is the only result which can today stand as a monument for those people, with few exceptions. If we extended the present system, what would the result be? It would create a racial hatred which South Africa simply cannot afford, because, in the course of years, we would then have a bitter struggle on the part of the White man to ensure that he is not ploughed under politically by the non-White groups of the population, but, at the same time, it must be remembered that if we accepted that principle today, then the Bantu would have to accept this Parliament as his Parliament, and he would then become involved in a struggle in which he would demand representation in this House on at least the same basis as the White man. That is the trouble which awaits South Africa, and I say that anybody who does not realise that, must be stupid. Mr. Speaker, if there are people who say that the Bantu will always be satisfied to be represented in Parliament by a few people, I say to them that they are living in a fool's paradise. No nation in the world would agree to it, and still much less the proud Bantu. . . .

One of the fine things that we are doing in this Bill is to give formal recognition to the various Bantu population groups. That is a desire that we find on the part of all the groups of the population. In the short time during which I have had some dealings with them, one of the questions which has been put to me everywhere is this: "Can't you give us recognition; why are you tearing us asunder?" In this Bill formal recognition is being given to the existence of those population groups, but particularly to the process of national development by and in the population groups themselves. I think by this time hon. members will concede that you cannot start a process of development by simply linking it up with the White man's way of life. That would be nonsensical. No process in which the Bantu's dignity is not acknowledged can form the basis on which development can take place, and in refusing to appreciate his own system of government and his own rights we slight the dignity of the Bantu himself. But hon. members will also concede a second thing, Mr. Speaker, and that is that that process cannot be started by creating an artificial unit, in other words, by bundling all the Bantu together in one common society, as many hon. members on the other side want to do, because there are only two bonds which bind them together: The first is their colour and the other is their hatred of the White man. But there is something greater than that, something higher than that which binds people together, and that is their spiritual treasures, the cultural treasures of a people. It is these fine things which have united other nations in the world. That is why we say that the basis of our approach is that the Bantu too will be linked together by traditional and emotional bonds, by their own language, their own culture, their national possessions. I am convinced that for this measure I shall receive the gratitude of the Bantu throughout South Africa.

This Bill also gives the various population groups their own territorial authorities. That is very important. Where there are no territorial authorities as yet, a Territorial Council will be established in the meantime, but I am convinced that within a year or two all these matters will be disposed of.

But the most important consideration is that this Bill makes it possible for the Governor-General to transfer his legislative powers systematically to those Territorial Authorities. Because of the nature of our national structure it is not possible today to see this in clear perspective, but I am convinced that once these Territorial Authorities have all been established, and these powers have been systematically transferred to them, we are going to achieve excellent results. This is an act of faith in the Bantu such as we have never had before in South Africa, and it is something which is going to satisfy him and for which he is already very grateful today. I readily concede that many of these things will take a little time before they can all be arranged and before all these powers can be granted, but once all the Territorial Authorities are in operation, it is my intention to review this whole matter and to see how we can best shape it in the interests of every population group and in the interests of the whole of South Africa. But the Bantu himself will have to help in extending this system. He will be called upon to extend it, and that is one of the fine principles contained in this Bill, because now it will no longer be the White man who will be doing these things; it will be the Bantu himself.

In the second place I want to mention another important aspect, and that is that we envisage that the Bantu will develop his own courts. Let me put it this way: The Bantu has developed a very fine legal system which ensures a high degree of justice. That is why it has also been recognised by the authorities, but the mistake that was made was that no attention was given to the question of allowing the courts to develop together with the development of the community. It was looked down upon and jeered at. After all, according to the United Party it was just a court conducted by barbarians. Mr. Speaker, that is not fair towards the Bantu; it is not reconcilable with the general development of the Bantu. That is why this Bill provides for special attention to be given to this matter so that it will become possible for them to administer their own system of justice. They will be assisted actively to extend their own courts, and I anticipate that the time will come when they themselves will have their own supreme court in their own territories with their own judges on the Bench. I propose to give very serious attention to this matter.

But this Bill goes further. It holds out this prospect that the Territorial Authorities are going to look after their own education. I just want to announce that the Department of Bantu Education is ready, as soon as the Bantu Territorial Authorities are in operation, to place a large portion of the education in the areas concerned directly under the Territorial Authorities. That will mean that the Territorial Authority will exercise authority and control over all the school boards and committees in this area. In exercising that control it will have in its hands the most important means of building up its community culturally and economically. Just think what it will mean to the Bantu if he himself exercises control over his education. Welfare work and social services will also be placed under them in due course. We shall see to it that it takes place on a sound basis.

Then I want to mention another important matter and that is that in due course the Native Trust Lands will be transferred to the Territorial Authorities, a very important decision. It must not be forgotten that the land which has been set aside for them—7,250,000 morgen—falls under the Native Trust. The Native Trust is responsible for the development of that land, etc. We now envisage transferring this land in due course to the Territorial Authorities. They will then be responsible for the proper conservation of the soil and its development, etc. I need only say this, Mr. Speaker, that when we look at the results which are being achieved at the present time, there can be no doubt that it would be in the interests of the Bantu and of South Africa as a whole to entrust that task to the Natives. It is a question of faith. They would be responsible for the allocation of that land and all that type of thing. Let me just say this: There are very few things which have caused so much dissatisfaction amongst the Bantu as the fact that the land which was purchased at the time—I refer to the land which was promised to them at the time by General Hertzog and of which a portion was bought—was placed under the Native Trust and not directly under the chiefs. Throughout the whole of South Africa I have heard this reproach. Under the system which is now being introduced it will fall under the Territorial Authority, which is a responsible body. This is an important step forward.

Then I want to mention another important principle which is contained in this Bill. Formerly the Governor-General could appoint or dismiss any chief at will. He will now be obliged to consult the Territorial Authority. I admit that in the past the Governor-General has always consulted the tribe, but the responsibility is now going to rest with the Territorial Authority. In this way it is being given status, it is being given the status in its own territory which our Government has in the territory of the White man. That is the basic approach in connection with this matter.

But there is another important principle embodied in this legislation, and that is that for the first time official links are being instituted between the Bantu territories and the Natives in the cities. For the first time! I admit at once that here we are facing a very great problem. I readily admit that there are many Bantu in the White areas. But I also want to make this further submission that very large numbers of those Bantu were not born in South Africa. There are many of them whose home is Basutoland. Do you know, sir, that there are approximately 1,000,000 Sothos in South Africa? Large numbers of them were born in the Protectorate of Bechuanaland, and Swaziland is the home of a large section. Do not let us overlook that factor. That is a factor which will have to be faced squarely sooner or later. But that does not detract from the fact that there are also large numbers of our own Natives in the cities, and that is a very important problem. The question which is frequently asked is this: What is to be their future?

Let me first say this—and in this regard I want to be explicit and clear. It must be quite clearly understood by the United Party and by the whole world that those Natives will never become part of the White community; we are not going to follow a policy which is going to lead to a common society in South Africa. Let us be perfectly clear and explicit on that point. But in the second place, I want to make this statement that the vast majority of those people have never lost their links with their own territories. I personally made some pilot surveys and the Tomlinson Commission made a large number of pilot surveys over the whole country, and it was found that easily 80 per cent, if not more, of those Bantu had always retained some link or other with the Bantu areas. We are not faced here with a problem of displaced persons. Our practical experience has been that although a Bantu has been in the city for years, for perhaps two or three generations, he still knows where his tribe is, and you will be surprised to know, sir, how readily he is absorbed again into his tribe. Why do hon. members come along and make a mountain out of a mole-hill? The fact of the matter is that links will now be created between the Bantu areas and those people in the cities. I have no doubt that it will have a very salutary effect. It will also have a salutary effect on the moral standards of those people. It must not be forgotten that as far as customs, etc. are concerned, the Bantu in the cities constitute rather a loose population, and in those places where the different ethnic groups are already separately housed and where we have given them non-official recognition, it has already been shown that a new ideal has been created for these people, where they have their own links and their own mother-tongue and when we restore to them these emotional links which are of so much value to every nation in the world, I have no doubt that in this way we are going to create a very fine link as far as the whole Native population is concerned.

Then I just want to say that in this process we should at least concede to the Bantu what the English people did not begrudge themselves. Let me just remind the House that the whole democratic system of the British nation was developed around the Royal house and the nobility. Let them deny it. It took years, but that is the position. Today every Englishman is proud of that democratic system. But it must not be forgotten that it is only since 1832 that that system has actually taken definite shape. Why then do we begrudge this same process to the Bantu? Here we have the same process. What is contained in this Bill is something that Bantu understands, something that is integrated into his life.

But hon. members may ask perhaps why we do not carry on with this matter and leave alone the question of Native representation; why we do not allow Native representatives to remain in this House; why we do not first complete the whole pattern and then consider thereafter whether we want to abolish the Native representation in this House. I just want to say that that is an attitude which can only be adopted by a person who has no knowledge of the Native. Any person who has taken the slightest trouble to make a study of the approach of the Bantu population to these matters, could never adopt such an attitude. Because in connection with this political issue, they have an axiom which runs as follows, that the idea of two bulls in one kraal never works. The Native does not want it; to him it is unthinkable. To have two political processes which are diametrically opposed to each other and which try to destroy each other, is something which the Native simply cannot understand, and he would regard that as the greatest dishonesty on the part of the White man. Sir, there are Natives who have asked me to abolish the Native representation immediately. If we want to be honest, then we must take into account the approach of the Bantu himself, and then we cannot start such a process; we must adopt the course that is acceptable and understandable and honest towards the Bantu population, a course which in their eyes is not a conflicting policy but which they regard as an honest policy.

The question may be put to me: What does the Native population think about this matter? How do they feel? I just want to say that after the introduction of this Bill I made it my business to make its contents known to all the Bantu population groups throughout South Africa. More than 3,000 copies of the Bill and of the White Paper were distributed amongst them. The full contents were also published in the journal *Bantu*, more than 30,000 copies of which were distributed. What was the reaction? The reaction was this, that I have here a large number of telegrams from all parts of South Africa, from all the important Bantu population groups, from Cyprian, from Victor Poto, from Botha Sigcau, from the Venda chiefs, from the Ciskei, etc. I have had telegrams from the responsible groups in every territory conveying their gratitude and congratulations and telling me to go ahead with this. And do you know, Sir, that I did not have a single letter or telegram of protest? Do you know where I came across a protest? A moment ago at the entrance to Parliament, where there is a placard bearing the words "no taxation without representation." The Black Sash!

MRS. BALLINGER: Hear, hear!

MR. DE WET NEL: I agree, but that is one of the great principles embodied in this Bill, because here it is envisaged that in the future they will impose their own taxes, and the time will come when all taxes in the Bantu areas will be imposed by the Bantu themselves. That is the only protest that I received. Everywhere the Bantu have acclaimed this as a new day and a new era which has dawned for the Bantu in South Africa. That is their approach to this matter.

The aims of this Bill could be briefly summarised as follows:

1. It gives expression to the racial pattern and the philosophy of life of the people of South Africa in respect to the colour question. It is the product of a deep and honest conviction which flows from historical experience and which is based on the Christian principles underlying the approach of our people, because we do not begrudge those people what we claim for ourselves.

2. It rests on the conviction that it will ward off those factors which may possibly plough the White man under, but at the same time it also creates the possibility for the Bantu to bring to the fullest fruition his personal and national ideas within his own population group. What we demand for ourselves, we do not begrudge the Bantu. Our approach is not simply negative but also positive.

3. It converts the Bantu development which was formerly instituted under the direction of the White man, into a development which will be anchored in the Bantu community itself, a development in terms of which all the factors of nation and community building will be actively placed in the service of each group of the Bantu population, on the same lines as in the case of the White man. In this way the material and spiritual growth of the Bantu population groups will be set in motion, so that they will also be able to make a contribution to the eternal and lasting values of South Africa and of the world as a whole.

4. It lays the foundation of a form of government in which all population groups, on a basis of honour and mutual respect, can be informed and consulted about the great problems of South Africa and where everyone's efforts can be harnessed in a spirit of mutual trust for the welfare of South Africa.

5. It creates, I am convinced, a future of hope and expectation for all population groups in South Africa, a future of peace and security, not only for the White population of South Africa, but also for the Bantu population groups. Now every group will know in which direction it is moving. It removes the mists of doubt and uncertainty, which are the greatest cause of mistrust of the White man. Those mists of doubt and uncertainty have now disappeared. Everybody will know in which direction he is heading and it is that certainty which gives man the greatest satisfaction.

6. I am deeply convinced that this is the only basis on which a great and happy South Africa can be built for all population groups.

68. NELSON ROLIHLAHLE MANDELA

VERWOERD'S TRIBALISM. 1959.

Nelson Rolihlahle Mandela (1918–) is one of South Africa's foremost African nationalist leaders. He had been serving a sentence of life imprisonment on Robben Island when, in February 1990, he was released by the government of South Africa and resumed the leadership of the African National Congress. The son of a Tembu chief, Mandela left the University of Fort Hare in 1940 and went to Johannesburg, where he became involved in the formation of the Youth League of the African National Congress (ANC), a radical "ginger-group" within South Africa's oldest African nationalist organization. When the ANC launched its passive resistance campaign in defiance of apartheid legislation, Mandela was volunteer-in-chief and was later elected to the National Executive of the ANC. Restrictions were subsequently placed on him by the government, and in 1956 he was arrested and was one of the defendants in the abortive treason trial (1956–1961). He rose to prominence in the white community in 1961, when South Africa declared itself a republic. Mandela went underground to organize a stay-at-home campaign and became known as the "Scarlet Pimpernel." While underground he also acted as one of the leaders of a sabotage group known as Umklionto We Sizwe (Spear of the Nation). Many of the leaders of this group were arrested in 1963 at Rivonia, and in 1964 some of them, including Mandela, were sentenced to life imprisonment. During the 1950s, Mandela wrote a number of analytical articles on the South African situation, which were collected into a book entitled No Easy Walk to Freedom, edited by Ruth First.

"South Africa belongs to all who live in it, black and white." —Freedom Charter.

"All the Bantu have their permanent homes in the Reserves and their entry into other areas and into the urban areas is merely of a temporary nature and for economic reasons. In other words, they are admitted as work-seekers, not as settlers." —Dr. W. W. M. Eiselen, Secretary of the Department of Bantu Administration and Development. (Article in *Optima*, March 1959)

The statements quoted above contain diametrically opposite conceptions of this country, its future, and its destiny. Obviously they cannot be reconciled. They have nothing in common, except that both of them look forward to a future of affairs rather than that which prevails at present. At present, South Africa does not "belong"—except in a moral sense—to all. Ninety-seven per cent of the country is legally owned by members (a handful of them at that) of the dominant White minority. And at present by no means "all" Africans have their "permanent homes" in the Reserves. Millions of Africans were born and have their permanent homes in the towns and cities and elsewhere outside the Reserves, have never seen the Reserves, and have no desire to go there.

It is necessary for the people of this country to choose between these two alternative paths. It is assumed that readers of *Liberation* [an anti-apartheid journal] are familiar with the detailed proposals contained in the Charter.

Let us therefore study the policies submitted by the Nationalist Party.

The newspapers have christened the Nationalists' plan as one for "Bantustans." The hybrid word is, in many ways, extremely misleading. It derives from the partitioning of India after the reluctant departure of the British, and as a condition thereof, into two separate states, Hindustan and Pakistan. There is no real parallel with the Nationalists' proposals, for:

(a) India and Pakistan constitute two completely separate and politically independent states.

(b) Muslims enjoy equal rights in India; Hindus enjoy equal rights in Pakistan.

(c) Partition was submitted to and approved by both parties, or at any rate fairly widespread and influential sections of each.

The Government's plans do not envisage the partitioning of this country into separate, self-governing states. They do not envisage equal rights, or any rights at all, for Africans outside the Reserves. Partition has never been approved of by Africans and never will be. For that matter it has never really been submitted to or approved of by the Whites. The term "Bantustan" is therefore a complete misnomer, and merely tends to help the Nationalists perpetrate a fraud.

Let us examine each of these aspects in detail.

It is typical of the Nationalists' propaganda techniques that they describe their measures in misleading titles, which convey the opposite of what the measures contain. Verwoerd called his law greatly extending and intensifying the pass laws the "Abolition of Passes" Act. Similarly, he has introduced into the current parliamentary session a measure called the "Promotion of Bantu Self-Government Bill." It starts off by decreeing the abolition of the tiny token representation of Africans (by Whites) in Parliament and the Cape Provincial Council.

It goes on to provide for the division of the African population into eight "ethnic units" (the so-called Bantustans). They are: North and South Sotho, Swazi, Tsonga, Tswana, Venda, Xhosa, and Zulu. These units are to undergo a "gradual development to self-government."

This measure was described by the Prime Minister, Dr. Verwoerd, as a "supremely positive step" towards placing Africans "on the road to self-government." Mr. De Wet Nel, Minister of Bantu Affairs, said the people in the Reserves "would gradually be given more powers to rule themselves."

The scheme is elaborated in a White Paper, tabled in the House of Assembly, to "explain" the Bill. According to this document, the immediate objects of the Bill are:

(a) The recognition of the so-called Bantu National Units and the appointment of commissioners-general whose task will be to give guidance and advice to the units in order to promote their general development, with special reference to the administrative field.

(b) The linking of Africans working in urban areas with territorial authorities established under the Bantu Authorities Act, by conferring powers on the Bantu

Authorities to nominate persons as their representatives in urban areas.

(c) The transfer to the Bantu territorial authorities, at the appropriate time, of land in their areas at present held by the Native Trust.

(d) The vesting in territorial Bantu authorities of legislative authority and the right to impose taxes, and to undertake works and give guidance to subordinate authorities.

(e) The establishments of territorial boards for the purpose of temporary liaison through commissioners-general if during the transition period the administrative structure in any area has not yet reached the stage where a territorial authority has been established.

(f)The abolition of representation in the highest European governing bodies.

According to the same White Paper, the Bill has the following further objects:

(a) The creation of homogeneous administrative areas for Africans by uniting the members of each so-called national group in the national unit, concentrated in one coherent homeland where possible.

(b) The education of Africans to a sound understanding of the problems of soil conversion and agriculture so that all rights over and responsibilities in respect of soil in African areas may be assigned to them.

This includes the gradual replacement of European agricultural officers of all grades by qualified and competent Africans.

(c) The systematic promotion of a diverse economy in the African areas, acceptable to Africans and to be developed by them.

(d) The education of the African to a sound understanding of the problems and aims of Bantu education so that, by the decentralization of powers, responsibility for the different grades of education may be vested in them.

(e) The training of Africans with a view to effectively extending their own judicial system and their education to a sound understanding of the common law with a view to transferring to them responsibilities for the administration of justice in their areas.

(f) The gradual replacement of European administrative officers by qualified and competent Africans.

(g) The exercise of legislative powers by Africans in respect of their areas, at first at a limited scale, but with every intention of gradually extending this power.

It will be seen that the African people are asked to pay a very high price for this so-called "self-government" in the Reserves. Urban Africans—the workers, businessmen, and professional men and women, who are the pride of our people in the stubborn and victorious march towards modernization and progress—are to be treated as outcasts, not even "settlers" like Dr. Verwoerd. Every vestige of rights and opportunities will be ruthlessly destroyed. Everywhere outside the Reserves an African will be tolerated only on condition that he is for the convenience of the Whites.

There will be forcible uprooting and mass removals of millions of people to "homogeneous administrative areas." The Reserves, already intolerably overcrowded, will be crammed with hundreds of thousands more people evicted by the Government.

In return for all these hardships, in return for Africans abandoning their birthright as citizens, pioneers, and inhabitants of South Africa, the Government promises them "self-government" in the tiny 13 per cent that their greed and miserliness "allocates" to us. But what sort of self-government is this that is promised?

There are two essential elements to self-government, as the term is used and understood all over the modern world. They are:

1. *Democracy.* The organs of government must be representative; that is to say, they must be freely chosen leaders and representatives of the people, whose mandate must be renewed at periodic democratic elections.

2. *Sovereignty.* The government thus chosen must be free to legislate and act as it deems fit on behalf of the people, not subject to any limitations upon its powers by any alien authority.

Neither of these two essentials is present in the Nationalist plan. The "Bantu National Units" will be ruled in effect by the commissioners-general appointed by the Bantu Government, and administered by the Bantu Affairs Department officials under his control. When the Government says it plans gradually increasing self-government, it merely means that more powers in future will be exercised by appointed councils of chiefs and headmen. No provision is made for elections. The Nationalists say that chiefs, not elected legislatures, are "the Bantu tradition."

There was a time when, like all peoples on earth, Africans conducted their simple communities through chiefs, advised by tribal councils and mass meetings of the people. In those times the chiefs were indeed representative governors. Nowhere, however, have such institutions survived the complexities of modern industrial civilization. Moreover, in South Africa we all know full well that no chief can retain his post unless he submits to Verwoerd, and many chiefs who sought the interest of their people before position and self-advancement have, like President Lutuli, been deposed.

Thus, the proposed Bantu authorities will not be, in any sense of the term, representative or democratic.

The point is made with pride by the Bantu Affairs Department itself in an official publication:

"The councillors will perform their task without fear or prejudice, because they are not elected by the majority of votes, and they will be able to lead their people onwards . . . even though . . . it may demand hardships and sacrifices."

A strange paean to autocracy, from a department of a Government which claims to be democratic!

In spite of all their precautions to see that their "territorial authorities" — appointed themselves, subject to dismissal by themselves and under constant control by their commissioners-general and their Bantu Affairs Department—never become authentic voices of the people, the Nationalists are determined to see that even those puppet bodies never enjoy real power of sovereignty.

In his notorious (and thoroughly dishonest) article in *Optima*, Dr. Eiselen draws a far-fetched comparison between the relations between the future "Bantustans" and the Union Government, on the one hand, and those between Britain and the self-governing Dominions on the other. He foresees:

"A cooperative South African system based on the Commonwealth conception, with the Union Government gradually changing its position from guardian and trustee to become instead the senior member of a group of separate communities."

To appreciate the full hypocrisy of this statement, it must be remembered that Dr. Eiselen is an official of a Nationalist Party Government, a member of a party which has built its fortune for the past half century on its cry that it stands for full untrammelled sovereignty within the Commonwealth, that claims credit for Hertzog's achievements in winning the Statute of Westminster, which proclaims such sovereignty, and which even now wants complete independence and a republic outside the Commonwealth.

It cannot be claimed, therefore, that Eiselen and Verwoerd do not understand the nature of a commonwealth, or sovereignty, or federation.

What are we to think, then, in the same article, when Dr. Eiselen comes into the open, and declares:

"The utmost degree of autonomy in administrative matters which the Union Parliament is likely to be prepared to concede to these areas will stop short of actual surrender of sovereignty by the European trustee, and there is therefore no prospect of a federal system with eventual equality among members taking the place of the South African Commonwealth. . . ."

There is no sovereignty then. No autonomy. No democracy. No self-government. Nothing but a crude, empty fraud, to bluff the people at home and abroad, and to serve as a pretext for heaping yet more hardships and injustices upon the African people.

Politically, the talk about self-government for the Reserves is a swindle. Economically, it is an absurdity.

The few scattered African Reserves in various parts of the Union, comprising about 13 per cent of the least desirable land area, represent the last shreds of land ownership left to the African people of their original ancestral home. After the encroachments and depredations of generations of European land-sharks, achieved by force and by cunning, and culminating in the outrageous Land Act from 1913 onwards, had turned the once free and independent Tswana, Sotho, Xhosa, Zulu, and other peasant farmers of this country into a nation of landless outcasts and roving beggars, humble "work-seekers" on the mines and the farms where yesterday they had been masters of the land, the new White masters of the country "generously presented" them the few remaining miserable areas as reservoirs and breeding-grounds for Black labour. These are the Reserves.

It was never claimed or remotely considered by the previous governments of the Union that these Reserves could become economically self-sufficient "national homes" for 9,600,000 African people of this country. The final lunacy was left to Dr. Verwoerd, Dr. Eiselen, and the Nationalist Party.

The facts are—as every reader who remembers Govan Mbeki's brilliant series of articles on the Transkei in *Liberation* will be aware—that the Reserves are congested distressed areas, completely unable to sustain their present populations. The majority of the adult males are always away from home working in the towns, mines, or European-owned farms. The people are on the verge of starvation.

The White Paper speaks of teaching Africans soil conservation and agriculture and replacing European agricultural officers by Africans. This is merely trifling with the problem. The root problem of the Reserves is the intolerable congestion which already exists. No amount of agricultural instruction will ever enable 13 per cent of the land to sustain 66 per cent of the population.

The Government is, of course, fully aware of the fact. They have no intention of creating African areas which are genuinely self-supporting (and which could therefore create a genuine possibility for self-government). If such areas were indeed self-supporting, where would the Chamber of Mines and the Nationalist farmers get their supplies of cheap labour?

In the article to which I have already referred, Dr. Eiselen bluntly admits:

"In fact not much more than a quarter of the community (on the Reserves) can be farmers, the others seeking their livelihood in industrial, commercial, professional, or administrative employment."

Where are they to find such employment? In the Reserves? To anyone who knows these poverty-stricken areas, sadly lacking in modern communications, power resources, and other needed facilities, the idea of industrial development seems far-fetched indeed. The beggarly £500,000 voted to the so-called "Bantu Investment Corporation" by Parliament is mere eyewash: it would not suffice to build a single decent road, railway line, or power station.

The Government has already established a number of "rural locations"—townships in the Reserves. The Eiselen article says a number more are planned: he mentions a total of no less than ninety-six. Since the residents will not farm, how will they manage to keep alive, still less pay rents and taxes and support the traders, professional classes, and civil servants whom the optimistic Eiselen envisages will make a living there?

Fifty-seven towns on the borders of the Reserves have been designated as centres where White capitalists can set up industries. Perhaps some will migrate, and thus "export" their capital resources of cheap labour and land. Certainly, unlike the Reserves (which are a monument to the callous indifference of the Union Parliament to the needs of the non-voting African taxpayers), these towns have power, water, transport, railways, etc. The Nationalist Government, while it remains in office, will probably subsidize capitalists who migrate in this way. It is already doing so in various ways, thus creating unemployment in the cities. But it is unlikely that any large-scale voluntary movement will take place away from the big, established industrial centres, with their well-developed facilities, available materials, and markets.

Even if many industries were forced to move to the border areas around the Reserves it would not make one iota of difference to the economic viability of the Reserves themselves. The fundamental picture of the Union's economy could remain fundamentally the same as at present: a single integrated system based upon the exploitation of African labour by White capitalists.

Economically, the "Bantustan" concept is just as big a swindle as it is politically.

Thus we find, if we really look into it, that this grandiose "partition" scheme, this "supremely positive step" of Dr. Verwoerd, is like all apartheid schemes—high-sounding double-talk to conceal a policy of ruthless oppression of the non-Whites and of buttressing the unwarranted privileges of the White minority, especially the farming, mining, and financial circles.

Even if it were not so, however, even if the scheme envisaged a genuine sharing out of the country on the basis of population figures, and a genuine transfer of power to elected representatives of the people, it would remain fundamentally unjust and dangerously unstable unless it were submitted to, accepted, and endorsed by all parties to the agreement. To think otherwise is to fly in the face of the principle of self-determination, which is upheld by all countries and confirmed in the United Nations Charter, to which this country is pledged.

Now even Dr. Eiselen recognizes this difficulty to some extent. He pays lipservice to the Atlantic Charter and appeals to "Western democracy." He mentions the argument that apartheid would only be acceptable "provided that the parties concerned agreed to this of their own free will." And then he most dishonestly evades the whole issue. "There is no reason for ruling out apartheid on the grounds that the vast majority of the population oppose it," he writes. "The Bantu as a whole do not demand integration, in a single society. This is the idea . . . merely of a small minority."

Even Dr. Eiselen, however, has not the audacity to claim that the African people actually favour apartheid or partition.

Let us state clearly the facts of the matter, with the greatest possible clarity.

NO SERIOUS OR RESPONSIBLE LEADER, GATHERING, OR ORGANIZATION OF THE AFRICAN PEOPLE HAS EVER ACCEPTED SEGREGATION, SEPARATION, OR THE PARTITION OF THIS COUNTRY IN ANY SHAPE OR FORM.

At Bloemfontein in 1956, under the auspices of the United African clergy, perhaps the most widely attended and representative gathering of African representatives, of every shade of political opinion ever held, unanimously and uncompromisingly rejected the Tomlinson Report, on which the Verwoerd plan is based, and voted in favour of a single society.

Even the rural areas, where dwell the "good" (i.e. simple and ignorant) "Bantu" of the imagination of Dr. Verwoerd and Dr. Eiselen, attempts to impose apartheid have met, time after time, with furious, often violent resistance. Chief after chief has been deposed or deported for resisting "Bantu authorities" plans. Those who, out of short-sightedness, cowardice, or corruption, have accepted these plans have earned nothing but the contempt of their own people.

It is a pity that, on such a serious subject, and at such a crucial period, serious misstatements should have been made by some people who purport to speak on behalf of the Africans. For example, Mrs. Margaret Ballinger, the Liberal Party M.P., is reported as saying in the Assembly "no confidence" debate:

"The Africans have given their answer to this apartheid proposition but, of course, no one ever listens to them. They have said: 'If you want separation then let us have it. Give us half of South Africa. Give us the eastern half of South Africa. Give us some of the developed resources because we have helped to develop them.'" (*S.A. Outlook*, March 1959)

It is most regrettable that Mrs. Ballinger should have made such a silly and irresponsible statement towards, one fears, the end of a distinguished parliamentary career. For in this instance she has put herself in the company of those who do not listen to the Africans. No Africans of any standing have ever made the proposals put forward by her.

The leading organization of the African people is the African National Congress. Congress has repeatedly denounced apartheid. It has repeatedly endorsed the Freedom Charter [a manifesto of ideals for future South African society drafted by African nationalists and their associates of other races], which claims South Africa "for all its people." It is true that occasionally individual Africans become so depressed and desperate at Nationalist misrule that they have tended to clutch at any straw to say: give us any little corner where we may be free to run our own affairs. But Congress has always firmly rejected such momentary tendencies and refused to barter our birthright, which is South Africa, for such illusory "Bantustans."

Commenting on a suggestion by Professor du Plessis that a federation of "Bantustans" be established, Mr. Duma Nokwe, secretary-general of the African National Congress, totally rejected such a plan as unacceptable. The correct approach, he said, would be the extension of the franchise rights to Africans. Thereafter a National Convention of all the people of South Africa could be summoned and numerous suggestions of the democratic changes that should be brought about, including the suggestion of Professor du Plessis, could form the subject of the Convention.

Here, indeed, Mr. Nokwe has put his finger on the spot. There is no need for Dr. Eiselen, Mrs. Ballinger, or others to argue about "what the Africans think" about the future of this country. Let the people speak for themselves! Let us have a free vote and a free election of delegates to a national convention, irrespective of colour or nationality. Let the Nationalists submit their plan, and the Congress its Charter. If Verwoerd and Eiselen think the Africans support their schemes they need not fear such a procedure. If they are not prepared to submit to public opinion, then let them stop parading and pretending to the outside world that they are democrats, and talking revolting nonsense about "Bantu self-government."

Dr. Verwoerd may deceive the simpleminded Nationalist voters with his talk of Bantustans, but he will not deceive anyone else, neither the African people, nor the great world beyond the borders of this country. We have heard such talk before, and we know what it means. Like everything else that has come from the Nationalist Government, it spells nothing but fresh hardships and suffering to the masses of the people.

Behind the fine talk of "self-government" is a sinister design.

The abolition of African representation in Parliament and the Cape Provincial Council shows that the real purpose of the scheme is not to concede autonomy to Africans but to deprive them of all say in the government of the country in exchange for a system of local government controlled by a minister who is not responsible to them but to a Parliament in which they have no voice. This is not autonomy but autocracy.

Contact between the minister and the Bantu authorities will be maintained by five commissioners-general. These officials will act as the watchdogs of the minister to ensure that the "authorities" strictly toe the line. Their duty will be to ensure that these authorities should not become the voice of the African people but that of the Nationalist Government.

In terms of the White Paper, steps will be taken to "link" Africans working in urban areas with the territorial authorities established under the Bantu Authorities Act by conferring powers on these authorities to nominate persons as their representatives in urban areas. This means in effect that efforts will be made to place Africans in the cities under the control of their tribal chiefs—a retrograde step.

Nowhere in the Bill or in the various proclamations dealing with the creation of Bantu authorities is there provision for democratic elections by Africans failing within the jurisdiction of the authorities.

In the light of these facts it is sheer nonsense to talk of South Africa as being about to take a "supremely positive step towards placing Africans on the road to self-government," or of having given them more powers to rule themselves. As Dr. Eiselen clearly pointed out in his article in *Optima*, the establishment of Bantustans will not in any way affect White supremacy since even in such areas Whites will stay supreme. The Bantustans are not intended to voice aspirations of the African people; they are instruments for their subjection. Under the pretext of giving them self-government the African people are being split up into tribal units in order to retard their growth and development into full nationhood.

The new Bantu Bill and the policy behind it will bear heavily on the peasants in the Reserves. But it is not they who are the chief target of Verwoerd's new policy.

His new measures are aimed, in the first place, at the millions of Africans in the great cities of this country, the factory workers and intellectuals who have raised the banner of freedom and democracy and human dignity, who have spoken forth boldly the message that is shaking imperialism to its foundations throughout this great continent of Africa.

The Nationalists hate and fear that banner and that message. They will try to destroy them, by striking with all their might at the standard-bearer and vanguard of the people, the working class.

Behind the "self-government" talks lies a grim programme of mass evictions, political persecution, and police terror. It is the last desperate gamble of a hated and doomed fascist autocracy—which, fortunately, is soon due to make its exit from the stage of history.

May 1959

69. STEVE BIKO

BLACK CONSCIOUSNESS AND THE QUEST FOR TRUE HUMANITY. 1977.

Steve Biko was a founder, leader, and major contributor to the ideas of Black Consciousness, a movement initially based among students, which emerged in the late 1960s and was banned in 1977. The movement called for a racially exclusive struggle, emphasizing the need for blacks to reject racial inferiority and submissiveness. Biko died while in prison in 1977. This essay, written for a book on Black Theology, is generally considered to be Biko's best work. "Black Theology" is historically an American product, emerging from the black situation there. Its most articulate exponent in the United States is Dr. James H. Cone, professor of theology at the Union Theological Seminary, New York, author of Black Theology and Black Power *(New York: Seabury, 1969) and* God of the Oppressed *(Seabury, 1975; SPCK, 1977). In the middle of 1970 UCM appointed Sabelo Stanley Ntwasa traveling secretary for 1971 with a special mandate to encourage thinking and writing on Black Theology. The book* Black Theology: the South African Voice, *edited by Basil Moore(London: C. Hurst & Co., 1973) is the result of that year's endeavours, and this paper by Steve Biko is the most eloquent contribution to that book.*

BLACK CONSCIOUSNESS AND THE QUEST FOR A TRUE HUMANITY

It is perhaps fitting to start by examining why it is necessary for us to think collectively about a problem we never created. In doing so, I do not wish to concern myself unnecessarily with the white people of South Africa, but to get to the right answers, we must ask the right questions; we have to find out what went wrong—where and when; and we have to find out whether our position is a deliberate creation of God or an artificial fabrication of the truth by power-hungry people whose motive is authority, security, wealth and comfort. In other words, the "Black Consciousness" approach would be irrelevant in a colourless and non-exploitative egalitarian society. It is relevant here because we believe that an anomalous situation is a deliberate creation of man.

There is no doubt that the colour question in South African politics was originally introduced for economic reasons. The leaders of the white community had to create some kind of barrier between blacks and whites so that the whites could enjoy privileges at the expense of blacks and still feel free to give a moral justification for the obvious exploitation that pricked even the hardest of white consciences. However, tradition has it that whenever a group of people has tasted the lovely fruits of wealth, security and prestige it begins to find it more comfortable to believe in the obvious lie and to accept it as normal that it alone is entitled to privilege. In

From Steve Biko, "Black Consciousness and the Quest for True Humanity" from *I Write What I Like*, edited by Aclred Stubbs(San Francisco: Harper and Row, 1986), pp. 87–98. Reprinted by permission.

order to believe this seriously, it needs to convince itself of all the arguments that support the lie. It is not surprising, therefore, that in South Africa, after generations of exploitation, white people on the whole have come to believe in the inferiority of the black man, so much so that while the race problem started as an offshoot of the economic greed exhibited by white people, it has now become a serious problem on its own. White people now despise black people, not because they need to reinforce their attitude and so justify their position of privilege but simply because they actually believe that black is inferior and bad. This is the basis upon which whites are working in South Africa, and it is what makes South African society racist.

The racism we meet does not only exist on an individual basis; it is also institutionalised to make it look like the South African way of life. Although of late there has been a feeble attempt to gloss over the overt racist elements in the system, it is still true that the system derives its nourishment from the existence of anti-black attitudes in society. To make the lie live even longer, blacks have to be denied any chance of accidentally proving their equality with white men. For this reason there is job reservation, lack of training in skilled work, and a tight orbit around professional possibilities for blacks. Stupidly enough, the system turns back to say that blacks are inferior because they have no economists, no engineers, etc., although it is made impossible for blacks to acquire these skills.

To give authenticity to their lie and to show the righteousness of their claim, whites have further worked out detailed schemes to "solve" the racial situation in this country. Thus, a pseudo-parliament has been created for "Coloureds", and several "Bantu states" are in the process of being set up. So independent and fortunate are they that they do not have to spend a cent on their defence because they have nothing to fear from white South Africa which will always come to their assistance in times of need. One does not, of course, fail to see the arrogance of whites and their contempt for blacks, even in their well-considered modern schemes for subjugation.

The overall success of the white power structure has been in managing to bind the whites together in defence of the *status quo*. By skilfully playing on that imaginary bogey—*swart gevaar*—they have managed to convince even diehard liberals that there is something to fear in the idea of the black man assuming his rightful place at the helm of the South African ship. Thus after years of silence we are able to hear the familiar voice Alan Paton saying, as far away London: "Perhaps apartheid is worth a try." "At whose expense, Dr. Paton asks an intelligent black journalist. Hence whites in general reinforce each other even though they allow some moderate disagreements on the details of subjugation schemes. There is no doubt that they do not question the validity of white values. They see nothing anomalous in the fact that they alone are arguing about the future of 17 million blacks— in a land which is the natural backyard of the black people. Any proposals for change emanating from the black world are viewed with great indignation. Even the so-called Opposition, the United Party, has the nerve to tell the Coloured people that they are asking far too much. A journalist from a liberal newspaper like *The Sunday Times* of Johannesburg describes a black student—who is only telling—as a militant, impatient, young man.

It is not enough for whites to be on the offensive. So immersed are they in prejudice that they do not believe that blacks can formulate their thoughts without white guidance and trusteeship. Thus even those whites who see much wrong with the system make it their business to control the response of the blacks to provocation. No one is suggesting that it is not the business of liberal white oppose what is wrong. However, it appears to us as too much of a coincidence that liberals—few as they are—should not only be determining the *modus operandi* of those blacks who oppose the system, but also leading it, in spite of their involvement in the system. To us it seems that their role spells out the totality of the white power structure—fact that though whites are our problem, it is still other whites who want to tell us how to deal with that problem. They do so by dragging all sorts of red herrings across our paths. They tell us that the situation is a class struggle rather than a racial one. Let them go to van Tonder in the Free State and tell him this. We believe we know what the problem is, and we will stick by our findings.

I want to go a little deeper in this discussion because it is time we killed this false political coalition between blacks and whites as long as it is set up on a wrong analysis of our situation. I want to kill it for another reason—namely that it forms at present the greatest stumbling block to our unity. It dangles before freedom-hungry blacks promises of a great future for which no one in these groups seems to be working particularly hard.

The basic problem in South Africa has been analysed by liberal whites as being apartheid. They argue that in order to oppose it we have to form non-racial groups. Between these two extremes, they claim, lies the land of milk and honey for which we are working. The *thesis*, the *anti-thesis* and the *synthesis* have been mentioned by some great philosophers as the cardinal points around which any social revolution revolves. For the *liberals* the *thesis* is apartheid, the *anti-thesis* is non-racialism, but the *synthesis* is very feebly defined. They want to tell the blacks that they see integration as the ideal solution. Black Consciousness defines the situation differently. The *thesis* is in fact a strong white racism and therefore, the *antithesis* to this must, *ipso facto*, be a strong solidarity amongst the blacks on whom this white racism seeks to prey. Out of these two situations we can therefore hope to reach some kind of balance—a true humanity where power politics will have no place. This analysis spells out the difference between the old and new approaches. The failure of the liberals is in the fact that their *antithesis* is already a watered-down version of the truth whose close proximity to the thesis will nullify the purported balance. This accounts for the failure of the Sprocas commissions [Study Project on Christianity in an Apartheid Society established by the South African Council of Churches and the Christian Institute in 1968] to make any real headway, for they are already looking for an "alternative" acceptable to the white man. Everybody in the commissions knows what is right but all are looking for the most seemly way of dodging the responsibility of saying what is right.

It is much more important for blacks to see this difference than it is for whites. We must learn to accept that no group, however benevolent, can ever hand power to the vanquished on a plate. We must accept that the limits of tyrants are prescribed by the endurance of those whom they oppress. As long as we go to Whitey begging cap in hand for our own emancipation, we are giving him further sanction to continue with his racist and oppressive system. We must realise that our situation is not a mistake on the part of whites but a deliberate act, and that no amount of moral lecturing will persuade the white man to "correct" the situation. The system concedes nothing without demand, for it formulates its very method of operation on the basis that the ignorant will learn to know, the child will grow into an adult and therefore demands will begin to be made. It gears itself to resist demands in whatever way it sees fit. When you refuse to make these demands and choose to come to a round table to beg for your deliverance, you are asking for the contempt of those who have power over you. This is why we must reject the beggar tactics that are being forced on us by those who wish to appease our cruel masters. This is where the SASO message and cry "Black man, You are on your own!" becomes relevant.

The concept of integration, whose virtues are often extolled in white liberal circles, is full of unquestioned assumptions that embrace white values. It is a concept long defined by whites and never examined by blacks. It is based on the assumption that all is well with the system apart from some degree of mismanagement by irrational conservatives at the top. Even the people who argue for integration often forget to veil it in its supposedly beautiful covering. They tell each other that, were it not for job reservation, there would be a beautiful market to exploit. They forget they are talking about people. They see blacks as additional levers to some complicated industrial machines. This is white man's integration—an integration based on exploitative values. It is an integration in which black will compete with black, using each other as rungs up a step ladder leading them to white values. It is an integration in which the black man will have to prove himself in terms of these values before meriting acceptance and ultimate assimilation, and in which the poor will grow poorer and the rich richer in a country where the poor have always been black. We do not want to be reminded that it is we, the indigenous people, who are poor and exploited in the land of our birth. These are concepts which the Black Consciousness approach wishes to eradicate from the black man's mind before our society is driven to chaos by irresponsible people from Coca-cola and hamburger cultural backgrounds.

Black Consciousness is an attitude of mind and a way of life, the most positive call to emanate from the black world for a long time. Its essence is the realisation by the black man of the need to rally together with his brothers around the cause of their oppression—the blackness of their skin—and to operate as a group to rid themselves of the shackles that bind them to perpetual servitude. It is based on a self-examination which has ultimately led them to believe that by seeking to run away from themselves and emulate the white man, they are insulting the intelligence of whoever created them black. The philosophy of Black Consciousness therefore expresses group pride and the determination of the black to rise and attain the envisaged self. Freedom is the ability to define oneself with one's possibilities held back not by the power of other people over one but only by one's relationship to God and to natural surroundings. On his own, therefore, the black man wishes to explore his surroundings and test his possibilities—in other words to make his freedom real by whatever means he deems fit. At the heart of this kind of thinking is the realisation by blacks that the most potent weapon in the hands of the oppressor is the mind of the oppressed. If one is free at heart, no man-made chains can bind one to servitude, but if one's mind is manipulated and controlled by the oppressor as to make the oppressed believe that he is a liability to the white man then there will be nothing the oppressed can do to scare his powerful masters. Hence thinking along lines of Black Consciousness makes the black man see himself as a being complete in himself. It makes him less dependent and more free to express his manhood. At the end of all he cannot tolerate attempts by anybody to dwarf the significance of his manhood.

In order that Black Consciousness can be used to advantage as a philosophy to apply to people in a position like ours, a number of points have to be observed. As people existing in a continuous truggle for truth, we have to examine and question old concepts, values and systems. Having found the right answers we shall then work for consciousness among all people to make it possible for us to proceed towards putting these answers into effect. In this process, we have evolve our own schemes, forms and strategies to suit the need and situation, always keeping in mind our fundamental beliefs and values. . . .

Our culture must be defined in concrete terms. We must relate the past to the present and demonstrate a historical evolution of the modern black man. There is a tendency to think of our culture as a static culture that was arrested in 1652 and has never developed since. The "return to the bush" concept suggests that we have nothing to boast of except lions, sex and drink. We accept that when colonisation sets in it devours the indigenous culture and leaves behind a bastard culture that may thrive at the pace allowed it by the dominant culture. But we also have to realise that the basic tenets of our culture have largely succeeded in withstanding the process of bastardisation and that even at this moment we can still demonstrate that we appreciate a man for himself. Ours is a true man-centred society whose sacred tradition is that of sharing. We must reject, as we have been doing, the individualistic cold approach to life that is the cornerstone of the Anglo-Boer culture. We must seek to restore to the black man the great importance we used to give to human relations, the high regard for people and their property and for life in general; to reduce the triumph of technology over man and the materialistic element that is slowly creeping into our society.

These are essential features of our black culture to which we must cling. Black culture above all implies freedom on our part to innovate without recourse to white values. This innovation is part of the natural development of any culture. A culture is essentially the society's composite answer to the varied problems of life. We are experiencing new problems every day and whatever we do adds to the richness of our cultural heritage as long as it has man as its centre. The adoption of black theatre and drama is one such important innovation which we need to encourage and to develop. We know that our love of music and rhythm has relevance even in this day.

Being part of an exploitative society in which we are often the direct objects of exploitation, we need to evolve a strategy towards our economic situation. We are aware that the blacks are still colonised even within the borders of South Africa.

Their cheap labour has helped to make South Africa what it is today. Our money from the townships takes a oneway journey to white shops and white banks, and all we do in our lives is pay the white man either with labour or in coin. Capitalistic exploitative tendencies, coupled with the overt arrogance of white racism, have conspired against us. Thus in South Africa now it is very expensive to be poor. It is the poor people who stay furthest from town and therefore have to spend more money on transport to come and work for white people; it is the poor people who use uneconomic and inconvenient fuel like paraffin and coal because of the refusal of the white man to install electricity in black areas; it is the poor people who are governed by many ill-defined restrictive laws and therefore have to spend money on fines for "technical" offences; it is the poor people who have no hospitals and are therefore exposed to exorbitant charges by private doctors; it is the poor people who use untarred roads, have to walk long distances, and therefore experience the greatest wear and tear on commodities like shoes; it is the poor people who have to pay for their children's books while whites get them free. It does not need to be said that it is the black people who are poor.

We therefore need to take another look at how best to use our economic power, little as it may seem to be. We must seriously examine the possibilities of establishing business co-operatives whose interests will be ploughed back into community development programmes, We should think along such lines as the "buy black" campaign once suggested in Johannesburg and establish our own banks for the benefit of the community. Organisational development amongst blacks has only been low because we have allowed it to be. Now that we know we are on our own, it is an absolute duty for us to fulfil these needs.

The last step in Black Consciousness is to broaden the base of our operation. One of the basic tenets of Black Consciousness is totality of involvement. This means that all blacks must sit as one big unit, and no fragmentation and distraction from the mainstream of events be allowed. Hence we must resist the attempts by protagonists of the bantustan theory to fragment our approach. We are oppressed not as individuals, not as Zulus, Xhosas, Vendas or Indians. We are oppressed because we are black. We must use that very concept to unite ourselves and to respond as a cohesive group. We must cling to each other with a tenacity that will shock the perpetrators of evil.

Our preparedness to take upon ourselves the cudgels of the struggle will see us through. We must remove from our vocabulary completely the concept of fear. Truth must ultimately triumph over evil, and the white man has always nourished his greed on this basic fear that shows itself in the black community. Special Branch agents will not turn the lie into truth, and one must ignore them. In a true bid for change we have to take off our coats, be prepared to lose our comfort and security, our jobs and positions of prestige, and our families, for just as it is true that "leadership and security are basically incompatible," a struggle without casualties is no struggle. We must realise that prophetic cry of black students: "Black man, you are on your own!"

Some will charge that we are racist but these people are using exactly the values we reject. We do not have the power to subjugate anyone. We are merely responding to provocation in the most realistic possible way. Racism does not only imply exclusion of one race by another it always presupposes that the exclusion is for the purposes of subjugation. Blacks have had enough experience as objects of racism not to wish to turn the tables. While it may be relevant now to talk about black in relation to white, we must not make this our preoccupation, for it can be a negative exercise. As we proceed further towards the achievement of our goals let us talk more about ourselves and our struggle and less about whites.

We have set out on a quest for true humanity, and somewhere on the distant horizon we can see the glittering prize. Let us march forth with courage and determination, drawing strength from our common plight and our brotherhood. In time we shall be in a position to bestow upon South Africa the greatest gift possible—a more human face.

70. JOHN GARANG DE MABIOR

THE GENESIS OF THE SUDAN PEOPLE'S LIBERATION MOVEMENT (SPLM). 1983.

On May 16, 1983, Colonel John Garang led the men of the 116th Battalion of the Sudan Army stationed at Bor into the bush of the Upper Nile Province, Southern Sudan, in rebellion against the government of President Numayri. Born in Wangkulei, north of Bor; on June 23, 1945, Garang received a high school diploma from Magamba Secondary School in Tanzania in 1964, and a B.A. degree from Grinnell College in Iowa in 1969. He returned to the Sudan and served briefly with the Anya-Nya insurgents in the Southern Sudan. After the integration of the Anya-Nya into the Sudan army after the conclusion of peace and the signing of the Addis Ababa Agreement in 1972, Garang was commissioned as a captain. He attended the U.S. Infantry School at Fort Benning, Georgia, and, after a tour of duty in the Sudan, returned to the United States in November 1977 to take up his graduate studies at Iowa State University. from which he graduated with a Ph.D. degree in agricultural economics in December 1981.

Garang had many grievances against Numayri. They were widely shared, not only by his fellow Africans in the Southern Sudan, but by many Arabs in the North. Numayri had personally destroyed the Addis Ababa Agreement of 1972, which had granted regional autonomy to the South, unilaterally intervened to dissolve the Southern Regional government, sought to redefine the boundaries of the Southern provinces to include oil discoveries in the Northern Sudan, ordered the transfer to the North of the Africans in the Sudan army stationed in their Southern homelands, and finally, in September 1983, imposed the Sharia law of Islam upon the Sudan to be binding on all citizens, whether Muslim, Christian, or animist. The last was the final chapter in a liturgy of discontent. In July 1983, Garang officially founded the

From John Garang, *John Garang Speaks*, edited and introduced by Mansour Khalid(London: KPI Ltd., 1987), pp. 19–25. Reprinted by permission.

Sudan People's Liberation Movement (SPLM) and the Sudan People's Liberation Army (SPLA), with the publication of the SPLM Manifesto defining its objectives. Garang's leadership did not go unchallenged, but by March 1984 he had emerged as the uncontested leader of the armed insurgency. This revolt was not simply against the person of President Numayri, who was forced from power in March 1985 by a populist movement in Khartoum, but also against the whole system of government Numayri and his supporters represented, and which the notables of the great sectarian families inherited upon the president's fall from power.

When John Garang accepted the invitation to lead the mutineers, he was not an unknown junior officer but a well-respected colonel attached to the headquarters of the Sudan army in Khartoum. Nor was his disaffection parochial or Southern. From the beginning he espoused a new, democratic, federated government for the whole Sudan, not just the South—a policy that he has consistently maintained to the present day.

Nationalists, Patriots, Comrades, Fellow Countrymen.

The history of the Sudanese people from time immemorial has been the struggle of the masses of the people against internal and external oppression. The oppressor has time and again employed various policies and methods of destroying or weakening the just struggle of our people, including the most notorious policy of "divide and rule." To this end the oppressor has divided the Sudanese people into Northerners and Southerners; Westerners and Easterners, Halfawin and the so-called Awlad el Balad who have hitherto wielded political power in Khartoum; while in the South, people have been politicized along tribal lines resulting in such ridiculous slogans as "Dinka Unity," "Great Equatoria," "Bari Speakers," "Luo Unity" and so forth.

The oppressor has also divided us into Muslims and Christians and into Arabs and Africans. Tomorrow when these divisions become outdated, the oppressor will contrive other ingenious schemes for keeping the Sudanese people and their just struggle divided and weak.

It was therefore natural that secessionist movements and chauvinistic tendencies developed in different periods in different areas of the Sudan thereby jeopardizing the unity of the people and prolonging their suffering and struggle. The Sudan People's Liberation Army (SPLA) has been founded to spearhead armed resistance against Nimeiri's one-man system dictatorship and to organize the whole Sudanese people under the Sudan People's Liberation Movement (SPLM), through revolutionary protracted armed struggle waged by the SPLA and political mass support.

The neo-colonial system that has developed in our country, since 1956 and was represented by Nimeirism since 1969 is a regime in which a few people have amassed great wealth at the expense of the majority. This injustice has resulted in profound crises and distortions in our economy, politics, ethics and even religion which Nimeiri has perverted into an article of trade. A few of the system crisis problems include:

(a) The general fall in production and productivity especially of essential commodities such as dura, wheat and sugar

(b) The mounting rate of unemployment that has resulted in social instability and emigration

(c) Hyper-inflation, currency problems and foreign indebtedness amounting to US1O billion dollars and the consequent entrenchment of dependency relations

(d) An acute inadequacy and deterioration of social services in the whole country and particularly in rural areas

(e) The general social and moral bankruptcy that is reflected in the institutionalisation of corruption and bribery, the daily fear by any Sudanese of being apprehended by agents of the State Security Organization, and the absurd institution of "Kacha."

These crises and many others have plunged the overwhelming majority of the people throughout the country into an abysmal ocean of poverty and suffering from which no land can be sighted unless and until this one-man system of Nimeiri that threatens to drown the nation is destroyed in its entirety.

The general exploitation, oppression and neglect of the Sudanese people by successive Khartoum clique regimes took peculiar forms in the Southern third of our country. Firstly, racial and religious segregation was much more intensely meted out and felt in Southern Sudan than in other parts of the country. Secondly, development plans in the South such as the Melut and Mongalla Sugar industries, Tonj Kengaf, Wau Brewery, Nzara and Mongalla textiles etc. remained on paper as development funds were embezzled in Khartoum while Southern Regional Governments watched on in impotence or participated in the looting. Development Schemes that were implemented in the South were those that did not benefit the local population, such as the extraction of oil from Bentiu via the Chevron projects and extraction of water via the Jonglei Canal. Socio-political neglect, economic backwardness and general underdevelopment therefore became intensified and exacerbated in the South.

The burden and incidence of neglect and oppression by successive Khartoum clique regimes has traditionally fallen more on the South than on other parts of the country. Under these circumstances the marginal cost of rebellion in the South became very small, zero or negative, that is, in the South it pays to rebel. Nevertheless, your mad President Nimeiri and his habitually lying Vice-President Omer Mohammed al Tayeb have openly aggressed and agitated Southern Sudanese into rebellion and civil war. The following provocations precipitated the renewal of civil war in the Sudan:

(a) Nimeiri systematically started to dismantle his Addis Ababa Agreement. He singlehandedly and unconstitutionally dissolved Southern Assemblies and Governments one after the other in 1980, 1981 and 1983.

(b) He signed an unconstitutional Integration Treaty with Egypt to protect himself against insurrection in the South or any other parts of the Sudan.

(c) He unconstitutionally and unsuccessfully tried to change the boundaries of the Southern Region via his 1980 People's Regional Government Act. In this way he wanted to deprive the South of mineral rich or prime agricultural land such as Hofrat el Nahas, Kafia Kingi, Northern Upper Nile, Bentiu etc. *Natural resources, wherever they, are found in the Sudan, belong to the whole Sudanese people.* The location of these resources in the South should not register any negative connotation and suspicions in the mind of a true Sudanese patriot and nationalist. But Nimeiri felt sufficiently agitated to the extent of attempting to legislate the formal exclusion of these areas from the South. Such behaviour can only be explained by Nimeiri's halfhearted belief in Sudan unity, his belief in the hegemony of clique chauvinism and his mistrust of South Sudanese.

(d) Again, when Chevron Company discovered oil in 1978 Nirmeiri started to talk about oil finds 450 miles southwest of Khartoum instead of telling the truth that the oil was in Bentiu in Southern Sudan and that it belongs to the whole Sudanese people. He continued to hatch more transparent tricks when he talked about carving out his so-called "Unity Province" to include Bentiu, Abyei and Kadugli with himself the "Oil Governor." When this failed he came up with another scheme to build the refinery in Kosti instead of Bentiu. Finally, he ended up deciding that all the oil was to be piped out of the country at Port Sudan against the interest of the Sudanese people whether in the South or the North.

(e) Nimeiri completed the abrogation of his Addis Ababa Agreement by agitating for the division of South Sudan into three mini-regions, consistent with his policy of divide and rule. In this way Nimeiri unilaterally proclaimed redivision of the South in June 1983 to the consternation of even his foreign sympathizers.

(f) In all these provocations there was an important catch for Nimeiri. As the old adage says, thieves and rogues end up outwitting themselves. In 1972 Nimeiri agreed to absorb 6000 Anyanya guerillas into his Army, to be stationed in the South. The absorbed Anyanya had opposed Nimeiri's policies since 1972 and they were increasingly becoming an obstacle to his schemes. He therefore decided to crush the absorbed Anyanya forces by summarily transferring them to the North where they would be neutralized. In this Nimeiri was an utter failure. He failed to deceive the South into abandoning armed resistance.

Nimeiri's provocations, recklessness and stupidities in the South resulted in the Akobo mutiny of 1975 which triggered off the Anyanya II Movement; in the Wau mutiny of 1976; in numerous grenade-throwing incidents in which lives were lost; in the Ariath incident of January 1983; the Bor, Pibor and Fashalla clashes of May 1983 in the Malual clash of the same month; the Ayod and Waat clashes of June and July 1983; in the Boma capture of hostages; in the guerilla warfare in Abyei and Bentiu and, finally, in the birth of the Sudan People's Liberation Army and the Sudan People's Liberation Movement as the most advanced forms of armed and political struggle in the Sudan.

From all that I have said, it is clear that a vanguard movement for the liberation of the whole Sudanese people had to have its origins in the South Sudan. Any armed struggle must have as its point of departure the immediate and genuine needs and demands of the masses of the people. This was the case in the South in 1955. At that time the armed struggle was led by reactionaries and it ended in a reactionary revolution in 1972. Again, such was the case in the South in 1975 and again it was led by reactionaries in the form of Anyanya II. Again, such was the case in the South in 1983, but this time the insurrection is led by revolutionaries fighting as the vanguard of the whole Sudanese people. Because of the oneness of the Sudanese people and the unity and integrity of Sudan, the armed struggle in the South must of necessity eventually engulf the whole Sudan.

The anarchy in production, the separacist tendencies in the various regions of our beloved country, the moral decay and all the ills that I have enumerated *can only be solved within the context of a united Sudan under a socialist system that affords democratic and human rights to all nationalities and guarantees freedom to all religions, beliefs and outlooks.* A united and Socialist Sudan can be achieved only through protracted revolutionary armed struggle. Peaceful struggle has always been met with ruthless suppression and callous killing of our beloved people.

In pursuance of protracted revolutionary armed struggle the SPLA has been organised and has already achieved significant victories. In the first offensive after *16 May 1983*, it was the SPLA that captured and destroyed Malual Gahoth on 17 November 1983. At Malual Gahoth the enemy suffered 120 killed, 60 wounded and 1 helicopter shot down, while SPLA forces lost 12 killed and 30 wounded. Omer Mohammed Al Tayeb lied that the SPLA lost 480 killed. Any soldier would know that this could not be true; what, for example, could have been the size of the attacking force? Malual Gahoth is a small garrison where it is not possible to deploy even 200 men in an attack. Our attack force at Malual Gahoth was only 150 men. After Malual Gahoth, beginning from 12 December 1983, SPLA forces occupied for seven days the eastern half of Nasir, capital of the new Sobat Province. In Nasir the enemy suffered 267 killed, 173 wounded, 3 helicopters shot down, 3 river boats destroyed, 1 armoured personnel carrier and the Commander's Land Rover knocked out. The SPLA lost only 4 killed and 9 wounded in Nasir. Nimeiri and Omer hid these facts but they are true. The man in the street in Khartoum believes the SPLA from the funeral ceremonies of officers and soldiers held in the Three Towns [Khartoum, Khartoum North, Omdurman]. As Commander-in-Chief, I commanded. and directed the battles of Malual Gahoth and Nasir. These important and successful battles heralded the victories of the Sudanese people that the SPLA was soon to achieve.

In its second offensive, beginning on 8 February 1984, and ending with the bombardment of Malakal on 22 February 1984, SPLA units under Lt. Col. Kerubino Kuanyin Bol, Lt. Col. William Nyuon Bany and Lt. Col. Kawae Makuei, attacked and overran all of Ayod, CCI Camp at Kilo 215 on the Jonglei Canal, CCI [Compagnie de Construction Internationales—the French company digging the Jonglei Canal] HQ at the Sobat Mouth and a Nile "Busta" Steamer at Wathkei. In its second offensive the SPLA inflicted untold and immeasurable havoc on Nimeiri's regime. In only two weeks Nimeiri's army suffered 1069 killed and 490 wounded to SPLA 30 killed and 59 wounded. The SPLA destroyed 9 T55 tanks, 8 APCs, 8 Magirus army trucks, 1 civilian CCI truck, 2 small Cesna planes, 2 bulldozers, 2 steamers, 2 fuel stations, 1 big winch, a large quantity of medicines and 2 long-range signal sets. The magnitude of these operations and the importance of Nimeiri's army forced CCI to stop digging the Jonglei Canal and Chevron Company to close down all its oil operations in the South. Hereafter, Nimeiri can no longer deceive the Sudanese people that prosperity through exploitation of oil and water, is just around the corner. When the SPLA liberates our country under SPLM government, these two precious liquids shall be developed and used for the benefit of the whole Sudanese people.

The SPLA will continue to destroy Nimeirism or any other minority clique regime in Khartoum until genuine Sudanese unity is achieved and the SPLM transfuses the correct socialist blood into Nimeiri's Sudanese Socialist Union (SSU). Like he does with Islam, Nimeiri has also turned socialism into an article of trade. He correctly sees socialism as the genuine demand of the Sudanese people and uses the SSU to deceive the people that he is implementing socialism while in reality he and his gang pillage and loot the country.

We are aware that by declaring the SPLA/SPLM as a socialist movement, Nimeiri will depict us as Communists. This is only another cheap propaganda Nimeiri will use to beg sympathy, money and material assistance from the Western world. Nimeiri himself says he is a socialist by virtue of his membership and presidency of the Sudanese Socialist Union. Is he therefore a Communist?

The content of our socialism cannot be determined mechanically and equated with Communism as Nimeiri would like the Western world to believe. The conceptualization and particularization of socialism in the Sudan shall unfold as the armed struggle proceeds and as socio-economic development programmes are implemented during and after the war and *according to Sudanese local and objective conditions.*

It is not the first time that Nimeiri and other minority clique regimes in Khartoum have attempted to slander and blackmail a Sudanese movement in South Sudan. In the first civil war, the false propaganda and slander was that the Anyanya Movement was "imperialist inspired" and its leaders stooges of the Western world. This was because at that time Nimeiri's opportunism took him to Moscow. Today the accusation is that the SPLA/SPLM is "Communist inspired" and its leaders stooges of the Eastern world and/or Libya. This is because this time Nimeiri's opportunism has taken him to Washington. But in all this false propaganda, we want to underline the truth that Nimeiri and past clique regimes in Khartoum are directly responsible and accountable for all the civil wars in the Sudan.

We conclude by reiterating that the slogans of the SPLA are "National Unity," "Socialism," *"Autonomy," "where and when necessary,"* and "Religious Freedom." Our belief in and commitment to these slogans are irrevocable. The *SPLA welcomes and embraces all Sudanese nationalists, patriots and socialists*: in short, the movement belongs to the whole Sudanese people and will fight tirelessly for their unity, peace and progress.

71. NELSON MANDELA

ADDRESS TO THE ANC. 1985.

In January 1985, State President P. W. Botha offered to release Nelson Mandela after he had served more than twenty-three years of his life sentence if Mandela would renounce the use of violence. In this speech, read in public in February by Mandela's daughter Zindzi, Mandela rejected the offer. This was the first time since his imprisonment that Mandela was permitted to be quoted directly, addressing his followers. On February 11, 1990, Mandela was released unconditionally from the Victor Verster prison farm outside Cape Town by President F. W. de Klerk, who was convinced that the leader of the ANC was committed to a peaceful resolution of the racial conflict in South Africa. De Klerk succeeded P. W. Botha as president of South Africa in August 1989. In his historic speech on February 27, 1990, he removed crucial restrictions on groups opposed to the South African government.

My father and his comrades wish to make this statement to you, the people, first. They are clear that they are accountable to you and to you alone. And that you should hear their views directly and not through others.

My father speaks not only for himself and for his comrades at Pollsmoor prison but he hopes he also speaks for all those in jail for their opposition to apartheid, for all those who are banished, for all those who are in exile, for all those who suffer under apartheid, for all those who are opponents of apartheid and for all those who are oppressed and exploited.

Throughout our struggle there have been puppets who have claimed to speak for you. They have made this claim, both here and abroad. They are of no consequence. My father and his colleagues will not be like them.

My father says, "I am a member of the African National Congress. I have always been a member of the African National Congress and I will remain a member of the African National Congress until the day I die. Oliver Tambo is much more than a brother to me. He is my greatest friend and comrade for nearly fifty years. If there is any one among you who cherishes my freedom, Oliver Tambo cherishes it more, and I know that he would give his life to see me free. There is no difference between his views and mine."

My father says, "I am surprised at the conditions that the government wants to impose on me. I am not a violent man. My colleagues and I wrote in 1952 to Malan asking for a round table conference to find a solution to the problems of our country but that was ignored. When Strijdom was in power, we made the same offer. Again it was ignored. When Verwoerd was in power we asked for a National Convention for all the people in South Africa to decide on their future. This, too, was in vain. It was only then when all other forms of resistance were no longer open to us that we turned to armed struggle.

From Mary Benson, *Nelson Mandela: The Man and the Movement* (New York: W. W. Norton and Company, 1986), pp. 235–237. Reprinted by permission.

"Let Botha show that he is different to Malan, Strijdom and Verwoerd. Let *him* renounce violence. Let him say that he will dismantle apartheid. Let him unban the people's organization, the African National Congress. Let him free all who have been imprisoned, banished or exiled for their opposition to apartheid. Let him guarantee free political activity so that the people may decide who will govern them.

"I cherish my own freedom dearly but care even more for your freedom. Too many have died since I went to prison. Too many have suffered for the love of freedom. I owe it to their widows, to their orphans, to their mothers and to their fathers who have grieved and wept for them. Not only I have suffered during these long lonely wasted years. I am not less life-loving than you are. But I cannot sell my birthright nor am I prepared to sell the birthright of the people to be free. I am in prison as the representative of the people and of your organization, the African National Congress, which was banned. What freedom am I being offered while the organization of the people remains banned? What freedom am I being offered when I may be arrested on a pass offence? What freedom am I being offered to live my life as a family with my dear wife who remains in banishment in Brandfort? What freedom am I being offered when I must ask for permission to live in an urban area? What freedom am I being offered when I need a stamp in my pass to seek work? What freedom am I being offered when my very South African citizenship is not respected?

"Only free men can negotiate. Prisoners cannot enter into contracts. Herman Toivo Ja Toivo, when freed, never gave any undertaking, nor was he called upon to do so."

My father says, "I cannot and will not give any undertaking at a time when I and you, the people, are not free. Your freedom and mine cannot be separated. I *will* return."